COURTESY FLAGS

NOTE: some of the colonies may have the same flag as the metropolitan power

Paul Duncan Harris

continued on back endpaper

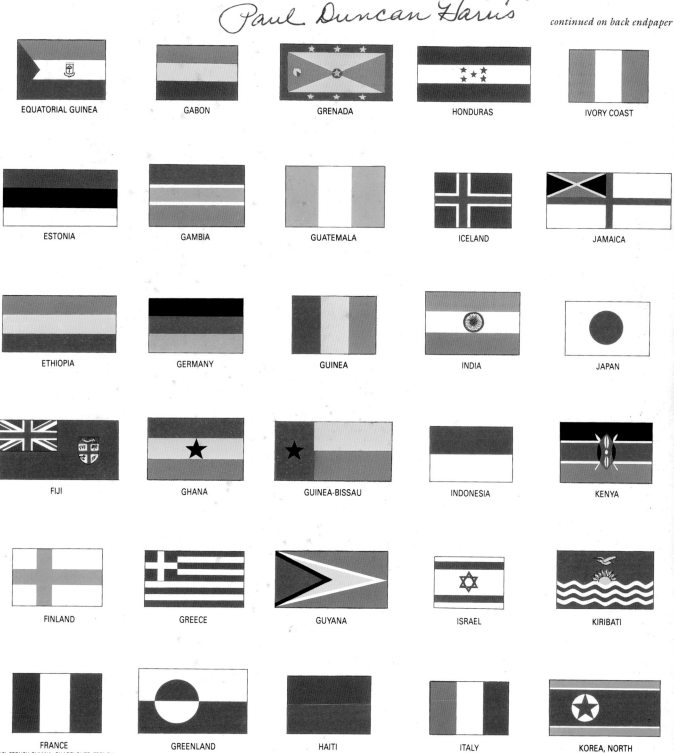

EQUATORIAL GUINEA

GABON

GRENADA

HONDURAS

IVORY COAST

ESTONIA

GAMBIA

GUATEMALA

ICELAND

JAMAICA

ETHIOPIA

GERMANY

GUINEA

INDIA

JAPAN

FIJI

GHANA

GUINEA-BISSAU

INDONESIA

KENYA

FINLAND

GREECE

GUYANA

ISRAEL

KIRIBATI

FRANCE
(INCL FRENCH GUIANA, GUADELOUPE, FRENCH
POLYNESIA, MARTINIQUE, RÉUNION, ST MARTIN,
ST BARTS, WALLIS AND FUTUNA, NEW CALEDONIA,
MAYOTTE)

GREENLAND

HAITI

ITALY

KOREA, NORTH

WORLD CRUISING
HANDBOOK

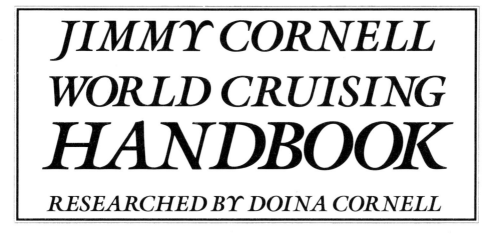

JIMMY CORNELL
WORLD CRUISING
HANDBOOK

RESEARCHED BY DOINA CORNELL

International Marine Publishing

Camden, Maine

Published by International Marine,
Camden, Maine

10   9   8   7   6   5   4   3   2   1

Copyright © Jimmy Cornell 1991
Published by International Marine Publishing, an imprint of
TAB BOOKS. TAB BOOKS is a division of McGraw-Hill, Inc.

TAB BOOKS offers software for sale. For information and a
catalog, please contact TAB Software Department, Blue Ridge
Summit, PA 17294–0850.

Questions regarding the content of this book should be
addressed to:

International Marine Publishing
P.O. Box 220
Camden, ME 04843

First published in Great Britain by Adlard Coles Nautical,
an imprint of A & C Black (Publishers) Ltd, 1991.

Printed and bound in Great Britain.

ISBN 0–87742–297–4

To Mirek Misayat
and
Lucy Hammond
of

Kaprys

for showing how to
enjoy cruising life
to the full.

NEXT EDITION

The information contained in *World Cruising Handbook* has been compiled from a multitude of sources and, because of its nature, the information needs continual updating. A great effort was made to get all facts right, but as the book covers the entire world it is very difficult to keep up with all the changes. Official sources will be used again for future editions, although no one is in a better position to report on the latest requirements in a particular country than those who are actually cruising there. We therefore need your help to keep this book as up to date as possible by providing the latest information for the sailors who will be following in your wake. So please write to us with any relevant details, new requirements and especially with corrections. Every letter will receive a reply and all substantial contributions will be acknowledged in the next edition. Thank you for your help. Letters should be addressed to:

The Editor
Adlard Coles Nautical
A & C Black (Publishers) Ltd
35 Bedford Row
London WC1R 4JH
ENGLAND

Contents

SECTION III

Acknowledgements

Officials do not often receive thanks from sailors and I would like to start by expressing my gratitude to the many customs, immigration and port officials who have taken the time to fill in the detailed questionnaires we sent them. I hope they will be just as helpful with future editions of the book, by which time I may also receive replies from some of the others. Many questionnaires were returned unsigned, so my thanks cannot be addressed to any particular person, but I would like to mention the following officials who often supplied much more information than I had requested: G. K. Harrington, Customs Anguilla; Luis Oscar Zunino, Prefectura Naval Argentina; J. J. Beale, Administrator Ascension Island; R. Viles, Customs Cairns, and Pieter Siep, Customs Darwin, Australia; Geoffrey Butler-Durrant, Customs Bermuda; Vice Admiral Sergio Tavares Doherty, Ministry of Marine, Brazil; Capt. Ned Miller, Cayman Islands Port Authority; Inspector R. J. Wheeler, Christmas Island Police; Harbour Master Djibouti; Matti Autio, Finnish Frontier Guard; Kathrine Everett, Greenland; G. R. Foulon, Customs Guadeloupe; Renan Chéry, Haiti Port Authority; S. C. Leung, Hong Kong Marine Department; Gulshan Rai, Customs Bombay, India; Padraig McMahon, Office of the Revenue Commissioners, Dublin, Ireland; Capt. Edward Myers, Deputy Harbour Master Kingston, Jamaica; Muhammed Razif b. Ahmed, Marine Department, Carol Ann McGuire, Customs, and Dr Muhammed Safaruddin b. Md. Dawan, Veterinary Service, Malaysia; J. G. Gauci, Malta Police, C. P. Portelli, Customs Malta; Hachmi El Affaqui, Port Captain Tangier, Morocco; W. E. Cooper, Customs Norfolk Island; K. Salavau, Customs Papua New Guinea; J. Eberenz and Roy Evans, Panama Canal Commission; G. D. Harraway, Governor's office, Pitcairn Island; Miguel Maldonado, Puerto Rico Port Authority; Ian Brash, Customs, and Gordon Grant, Agriculture Quarantine Service, Whangarei, New Zealand; Eyvind Tybo, Norwegian Customs; V. Kischenin, Customs Réunion; Assistant Harbour Master and J. F. Adrienne, Ministry of Planning and External Relations, Seychelles; R. Kohata, Customs Solomon Islands; H. F. James, Customs Capetown, South Africa; J. Filippi de la Palavesa, Customs Tahiti; Capt. Chris Pearson, Harbour Master, Tanga, and Capt. Peter Best, Dar es Salaam, Tanzania; Lomia Gaualofa, Tokelau; Bernard Pauncefort, Administrator Tristan da Cunha; Capt. Thomas Narruhn, Governor's Office, Truk; J. F. Poncet, Wallis & Futuna; Frederick Figir, Port Director Yap, Federated States of Micronesia.

I have been fortunate in being able to enlist the help of many cruising sailors who have taken the time to send me information on places I have not been able to reach myself. Foremost among them are Phil and Doris Tworoger on *Jolly II Roger*, whom I first met 13 years ago in the Pacific and who are still on their way back to Oregon. Andrew Bishop on *Tamasina* has helped with the latest information on the Windward Islands. I would also like to thank other old sailing friends, Derry and Ian Hancock in Whangarei and Erick Bouteleux in St Raphael.

I am particularly indebted to my fellow commodores in the Seven Seas Cruising Association, as well as both the present editor of its monthly bulletin, Bob Kohlman, and the previous editor Ginny Osterholt, for providing nuggets of information on many of the less-frequented places. I urge any cruising sailor to join this great association, whose valiant members sail far beyond the seven seas of the ancient world.

UTA French Airlines have been particularly helpful in providing flights to some of the destinations on the EUROPA 92 itinerary, where I also gathered material for this book. Grateful thanks are due to Jean Claude Bachelier, Marketing Manager in Paris, and also David Saunders at the London office.

The countries along the EUROPA 92 route have received my close attention recently and I am very grateful for the help given by Micko Sheppard-Capurro, Joe Viale and Ernest Felipes in Gibraltar, Juan Francisco Martin in Gran Canaria, Ted Bull in St Lucia, Michel Alcon, Benoit Soulignac and Jean Patrick Bonnette in Tahiti, Don Mundell, David Hunt, Stuart and Frances Bollam in Tonga, Dick Smith in Fiji, Ross Wilson, Ian and Sue Irving in Vanuatu, Betty Whitten and Ray Thurecht in Port Moresby, Hugh Roberts and David Woodhouse in Darwin, Rick Cameron in Bali and Dop Bär in Jakarta, Martha Comfort and Rod Short in Singapore, Luca Schueli in Phuket, Don Windsor in Sri Lanka, Fathi Soukar and Hassan Luxor in Egypt.

In all my writings I have been able to rely on the prompt assistance of a few people who always find the time to reply to my letters or faxes, and so I would like to thank Chris Bonnett of the Durban Sailing Academy, Angelo Andrade and João Carlos Fraga in Horta, Leo Hageman in Antigua, Bunny Fergusson in Barbados, Robert (Skippy) Lewis in Bermuda, Glafkos Cariolou of Larnaca Marina and Nicolas Terry of Puerto Sherry Marina.

Much practical help for this book has been obtained as a result of my long association with Clive Puttock of Portishead Radio (notably the section on radio communications) and Jesus Vilares of INMARSAT (satellite communications). Maria Reynolds Widdowson of the PPP Medical Centre has been a mine of information on vaccinations and health precautions worldwide. I am also deeply thankful to the Kelvin Hughes staff at the London office in the Minories and particularly to Julian van Hasselt, Brian Walker, Ron Haslett, Eric Thomas, Richard Besse and Lee Palmer.

I have also received considerable help from various tourist offices and I am particularly thankful to Nicholas Thomas of the St Lucia Board of Tourism, Isimeli Bainimara of the Fiji Visitors' Bureau, Arturo Molina and José Ortega of the Patronato de Turismo de Gran Canaria and Semisi Taumoepeau of the Tongan Visitors' Bureau. Both the Malaysian and Indonesian Tourist Offices in London have been extremely helpful. I am grateful for detailed information from: A. Tlili of Sidi-Fredj, Algeria; Samuel Cápiro Hernández of the National Institute of Tourism, Cuba; Jane Camens of the Hong Kong Tourist Association; Yoram Nachsol of the Ministry of Transport, Haifa, Israel; Ellen Ikehara of the Marianas Visitors' Bureau, Saipan; Mrs R. Hauchler of the Mauritius Tourist Office and A. Boolaky of the Mauritius High Commission; Sione Manu of the Tongan Visitors' Bureau in Vava'u and R. Mardassi of the Tunisian National Tourist Office.

In the tradition of helping visiting sailors I have had a great deal of help from yacht clubs and I would like to thank Geoffrey Pidduck, Antigua Yacht Club; Emma Randall, American Samoa; Bill Davis of St George's Dinghy Club, Bermuda and the Secretary, Royal Bermuda Yacht Club; Mette Dankelev, Danish Yachting Association; Robin Storck, Royal Suva Yacht Club, Fiji; Grenada Yacht Club; John Moore, Marianas Yacht Club, Guam; Peter Sharp, Royal Papua Yacht Club and Dorde Pantovic, Adriatic Club Yugoslavia.

We have received a lot of detailed information from the following people, for which I am most grateful: Alex and Dagmar Wopper, Valdivia, Chile; Don Bamford for information on Cuba; Arie Brosh, Miri and Moshe Blander of Tel Aviv, Israel; Philip Mason, Swynford Ltd, Kilifi, Kenya; Susan Kidd, Noumea Yacht Charters, New Caledonia; Vilamoura Marina, Portugal; Lance Ericson, The Moorings, St Lucia; Bodrum and Kusadasi marinas, Turkey; Diana and Francisco Azpurua, Shore Base Yacht Service, Venezuela, Nick and Carolyn Wardle, Nassau, Bahamas; Jon and Maureen Cullen, Keri Keri Marine Radio, New Zealand.

My colleagues at *Cruising World* magazine have always supported my various projects and I am particularly thankful to Betsy Holman, Bernadette Brennan and George Day. On this side of the Atlantic, I am grateful to Dick Johnson of *Yachting World* magazine for his considerable support over the years. In Germany I have been fortunate in being able to draw on the support of *Die Yacht* magazine and particularly the help of Klaus Bartels.

Most of this book was written in the small town of Aups in Provence, where my good friends Stephen and Jean Blake gave me a large table on which to spread all the paperwork. During my retreat into that unlikely ivory tower, Caroline Herring minded the fort at my London office. As in most of my previous writing projects, I have been extremely fortunate in being able to rely on my son Ivan's expertise in computers, and without his help this book would have been written on a stone-age typewriter and would have taken three times as long. However, this book could not have been written at all without the total commitment of my daughter Doina, who has spent one year doing the necessary research work and writing countless letters to officials all over the world. As always, the greatest help and support has come from my wife Gwenda, whose generosity and dedication cannot be matched by my gratitude. Gwenda's determination has helped me see this mammoth project through and my heartfelt thanks go to her for never faltering in her faith that I could do it. I have, but do not deserve, the credit.

Introduction

The planning stage of a cruise is often just as enjoyable as the voyage itself, letting one's imagination loose on all kinds of possibilities. Yet translating dreams into reality means that a lot of practical questions have to be answered. You might have heard about needing a cruising permit for Indonesia, putting up a bond in French Polynesia or the difficulties of changing crew in Turkey, but what about Palau? Tuvalu? Mayotte? The Soviet Union? Do yachts go there? *Can* yachts cruise there? Is it worth going at all? Designed as a companion volume to *World Cruising Routes*, the main objective of this book is to serve as a planner for anyone intending to cruise anywhere in the world. While *World Cruising Routes* helps you plan the best way to get to a place, *World Cruising Handbook* aims to let you know what to expect once you have arrived, and the information it contains is what you should know before arriving.

There is no denying the beauty of the cruising life and cruising sailors are rightly envied for the freedom of their lives and the opportunity they have to live unfettered by the constraints of modern urban existence. As with so many things in life, there is a price to pay for this freedom and the beauty of cruising is often spoilt by bureaucracy, unnecessarily complicated formalities and sometimes difficult, unfriendly and even corrupt officials. As many of the countries visited by yachts are in the developing world and their population, officials included, are poor in comparison with the owner of a yacht, however modest that yacht might be, a yacht is often regarded as a sign of affluence. This might explain the antagonism that is sometimes experienced. The xenophobia and occasionally racism that some officials show towards visiting sailors may well have its roots in the past. Yachtsmen and yachtswomen may be paying the price for the injustices suffered by the local population in the colonial past. Whatever the reason for them, these attitudes can mar the pleasure of visiting a country and ways to avoid this are discussed later in the section 'The Right Attitude'.

While on night watch during a recent Atlantic crossing, I cast my mind back over *Aventura*'s voyage around the world and the many memorable moments spent with my family in some of the most beautiful spots in the world. I tried to recall the few unpleasant incidents and almost without exception they were caused by obnoxious officials. I also added up the time I must have spent clearing in and out of the 60 countries we visited and I was shocked to come up with a total of some 300 hours. This is equivalent to 40 working days, which means that out of six years sailing I had spent eight weeks sitting in or walking between various offices! It was a terrible thought. While not claiming to give tips on how to reduce this waste of time, this book might nevertheless reduce some of the frustrations by preparing the voyager for what to expect in the countries to be visited, what preparations should be made in advance and what formalities complied with once there. It is the kind of book I wish had existed when I set off on my own voyage.

In the research for this handbook, I was greatly assisted by my daughter Doina, who spent one year contacting officials all over the world, gathering material, sorting through letters and reading countless publications for snippets of information. Having spent the best part of her childhood on a cruising yacht, Doina can well remember some of our contacts with local officials, as well as the difficulties encountered in some places. She also remembers vividly the highlights of our life afloat, which have left a lasting impression on her. When she was offered the opportunity to work on this project after finishing her university studies, she embraced it with total enthusiasm. Being a historian, her research into the profile of the countries not surprisingly gave prominence to the history of each place and although we sometimes disagreed on just how much historical fact a book like this should contain, we eventually drew the conclusion that in order to understand a country and its people, one should know something about its history. Equally important is to know something of the economy, the religion of the people and the language or languages they speak. It all helps one to understand, for example, the reasons for the outbreaks of ethnic violence in Sri Lanka, the rift between north and south in Sudan or the undisguised anti-British or anti-American feelings in some parts of the world.

The background information on each country contained in the following pages should answer some of these questions and also prepare you for your dealings with that country. Similarly, the practical information is meant to give an idea of what is available. Although my original intention was to give full details of existing marine facilities, including names and addresses, the sheer mass of material precluded this. From personal experience I know it is relatively easy to find out the name and address of a particular workshop or company in most places. Even if one does not speak the language, the ubiquitous Yellow Pages can usually be understood and local sailing enthusiasts or yacht clubs will often help out. This is why the facilities section includes only general notes, as I felt that what is really important to know, for example, is that there is a 75-ton travelift in Darwin, a sailmaker in Tonga, a

well-stocked chandlery in Papeete and a lot of frozen lobster tails, if not much else, in Tristan da Cunha. It is equally important to know about the places where little or nothing is available, so that when sailing there one can be prepared to be as self-sufficient as possible. The lack of marine supplies in many popular cruising grounds makes it imperative to carry all essential spares on board.

An idea which was pioneered during the EUROPA 92 round the world rally was to compile a catalogue listing the make, serial number, year of manufacture and other relevant details of all the equipment on board, including main engine, outboard engine, generator, instruments, sails, refrigerator, water system, etc. Ideally this list should be left with one's normal chandler or a reliable person who has access to a fax machine. Should anything on the boat break in a place where a replacement is not available, all one has to do is send a simple message requesting, for example, a new fresh water pump for the engine, rather than go into details of part number or year of manufacture.

Originally *World Cruising Handbook* was intended to include only the most important cruising countries on the trade wind route but ended up by embracing

La Aventura at Ilhas Desertas in the Madeira archipelago.

the whole world. Research undertaken for my previous book, *World Cruising Survey*, has shown that cruising yachts sail to more and more out of the way places, and as there is no cruising information available for those less visited places it was decided to include them in this book, even if information was sometimes scanty. After much debate, the line was drawn at 167 countries and only those that are never or very rarely visited by yachts were left out. Autonomous territories and dependencies have usually been treated as separate entries, because the rules applied to cruising yachts often differ from those of the metropolitan power. Thus, some of the regulations applied in Hawaii differ from those in mainland USA, while French territories in the Caribbean, South Pacific or Indian Ocean often apply different rules even towards French sailors. As some of the major sailing countries, such as the United States, United Kingdom or France, are well covered in other books, only essential information which one should know before arrival has been included. Similarly, major cruising destinations which are well covered in cruising guides and pilots, such as the Bahamas, Virgin Islands, Spain or Greece, have been dealt with succinctly by mentioning only the most relevant facts. Each country has been annotated with details of books where further cruising information can be found.

Although I have visited by sea or air most of the countries described in this book, collecting precise data and bringing it up to date had to be done by mail. This was a mammoth task and innumerable letters were written to embassies, tourist offices, yacht clubs, government agencies, customs departments and port authorities of all the countries. Our requirements were clearly explained on detailed questionnaires printed in English, French or Spanish. In every instance, the aims of the book were stressed and also the fact that its main objective was not only to make life easier for visiting sailors, but also for the authorities themselves, as it was in their interest for visiting sailors to know *exactly* what was expected of them. The response from most officials was splendid and due acknowledgement is given to those who took the trouble to fill in the questionnaires and often sent additional material. However, there are still many who have not replied, even after being approached on several occasions and from various directions. They are inevitably some of the countries which cause visiting yachtsmen the most headaches.

An interesting and highly revealing conclusion that I drew from my dealings with officials from so many countries was the confusion that surrounds entry regulations even in the minds of some senior officials. In several instances it was clear that the regulations sent from head office were not understood by the local officials meant to apply them. Sometimes there will be different interpretation of the rules between different ports within the same country and even among persons in the same office. Often local officials take matters into their own hands, which is not always negative, for in many places where yachts are welcome, local officials ignore the rule book and make clearing in as simple and easy as possible. The most revealing confirmation of this confusion came in the candid answer of one customs officer, who wrote on the questionnaire that he could not give exact details of the entry requirements because the exact procedure was not clear even to him!

In the few cases where regulations were unclear or contradictory, I have tried to interpret them and put them in as plain a language as possible. This was not always easy as in some countries the regulations filled a book, while in others the officialese was quite ridiculous. Clarity and conciseness are definitely not attributes of bureaucrats, nor are those who draw up the regulations renowned for their sense of humour, otherwise they might have written differently some of the following gems culled from material sent to us:
'… non-human primates may not be imported except for exhibition purposes …'
'… among articles prohibited are … liquor filled candy, lottery tickets, products made by convicts … and switchblade knives except for use by a one-armed traveller …'
'… also enclosed with my letter is The Panama Canal …'
'… while entering or leaving port … foreign vessels are not allowed to take any other sounding than that taken by means of a hand lead line …'
'… Kung Fu fighting is illegal …'
'… Customs should be notified if there are aliens on board …'

Jimmy Cornell
Aups, Provence
June 1990

SECTION I

1 Formalities

Clearance formalities vary greatly from country to country, being extremely simple in some and ridiculously complicated in others. The complexity of formalities is often a reflection of the nature of the regime in power and totalitarian one-party systems usually operate strict controls and lengthy formalities. But even among western democracies there are some notable exceptions and before anyone complains too vehemently about the cumbersome and time-consuming formalities in the Seychelles, Sudan or Turkey, let me point out that customs formalities in the United States or United Kingdom for foreign yachts can be just as slow, unnecessarily complicated and frustrating. Unfortunately bureaucracy is not the prerogative of developing countries.

Documents

The most common documents that are needed when clearing in are the ship's registration papers, radio licence, passports and vaccination certificates. Clearance papers from the last country to be visited are normally requested. Some countries also want to see the original document of the third-party insurance for the yacht and a certificate of competence for the captain. If firearms are carried, these should be licensed in the country of origin, as this licence will be requested in many places. Similarly pets must have international health certificates and their anti-rabies vaccinations should be kept up to date. Divers who carry scuba diving equipment on board may be asked to show their diving qualification certificates before getting bottles filled. Finally, a prescription or a letter from a doctor specifying the medicine and why it is taken should accompany any medicines containing powerful narcotics or habit-forming drugs, especially those used by a member of the crew on a regular basis, such as heart and blood pressure medication, diuretics, tranquillisers, anti-depressants, stimulants or sleeping tablets.

Several countries require that visiting yachts are properly registered. In the United Kingdom there are two forms of registration. Full British registration is administered by the Registrar of Shipping, who issues a Certificate of British Registry. A simpler alternative is the Small Ship Register, which is administered by the Royal Yachting Association. The International Certificate of Pleasure Navigation is not accepted in some countries, particularly France or Spain, so if planning to cruise further afield, the vessel should have one of the other two types of registration. In the United States yachts can either be registered with the state where the owner lives, or if ownership can be traced to the original owner, the vessel can be documented with the Coast Guard. The latter is generally preferable if cruising abroad.

A certificate of competence can be obtained in the United Kingdom from the Royal Yachting Association, which issues certificates for different degrees of competence, such as Helmsman, Yachtmaster or Oceanmaster. In the United States, sailors may obtain a certificate of competence by enrolling for a course on seamanship or pilotage. The US Coast Guard issues licences for skippers who carry passengers for hire. Such licences are recognised as a mark of competence for operators of commercial craft, including charter yachts carrying six or more persons.

A radio operator's licence, whether for VHF, HF or amateur radio, is required in most countries, although this is rarely checked. Some cruising yachts carry an amateur radio, most of their operators being properly licensed to operate a maritime mobile station. However, in some countries such stations can only be used legally if the operator is in possession of a reciprocal licence issued by the country concerned. In most places this is a simple formality and costs a small fee. In a few countries there are strict restrictions on the use of radio equipment while in port, while in others, such as Thailand and New Zealand, the use of portable VHF radios on land is forbidden.

Although some forms will have to be filled in on the spot, considerable time can be saved by having some papers prepared beforehand. It is always a good idea to have some photocopies of the ship's papers as well as plenty of crew lists, with such details as first name, middle names, surname, date of birth, nationality, passport number and date of expiry of passport. A ship's stamp is greatly appreciated in many countries where, for some strange reason, a rubber stamp has a certain authority.

Visas

One aspect which this book tries to clear up is that of visa requirements. While in some countries these are fairly clear, in others the situation concerning yachts is confusing. Foreign nationals arriving on a yacht can be treated basically in three different ways by the immigration authorities.

1. They are treated the same as ordinary tourists arriving by other means, in which case the usual visa requirements apply.

2. Special visa requirements are applied to those arriving by yacht, which means that in some countries foreign nationals arriving by yacht are treated differently to those visiting the country as ordinary tourists. This may mean that some countries which are happy to grant visas on arrival to tourists arriving by air will insist that anyone arriving on a yacht must have obtained their visa in advance. This is often because tourists arriving by air must have an onward ticket to be given a visa, while possessing a yacht is not always regarded as a guarantee of one's departure.

3. Sailors are sometimes given special treatment by being allowed to enter a country without a visa, which is required from tourists arriving by other means. Sometimes visas are granted on arrival and occasionally are dispensed with altogether. However, in these cases such special concessions are usually only given for a limited time and may be restricted to the duration of the yacht's stay in port or while cruising certain areas. It may be necessary to obtain an ordinary visa to travel to other parts of the country or to leave the country by other means.

There are several suggestions concerning passports and visas which should be followed to avoid some of the problems that are known to have occurred in the past. If at all possible, passports should have a validity well in excess of the intended period of travel. Some countries insist that passports are valid for at least six months beyond the intended stay in their country. Also, if one visits certain sensitive areas or countries, such as South Africa, Cuba, Northern Cyprus, Israel, Libya, etc., the passport should not be stamped in those countries. Preferably, one should try to obtain a second passport if planning to travel to such countries, although this is not always easy and can result in difficulties if the passport is found during a search.

For countries where a visa is required, this should be obtained well in advance, although one should make sure that the visa will still be valid when one arrives in the respective country as some countries stipulate that the entry must take place within three months of the visa being issued. It is also a good idea to obtain visas for difficult countries, even if it is known that visas can be issued on arrival. A visa issued by their diplomatic mission abroad sometimes works wonders with local immigration officers. It is mentioned in the text where this is recommended. Wherever possible one should try to obtain a multiple entry visa, particularly for countries with overseas territories or dependencies, such as France (Martinique, Guadeloupe, French Polynesia, New Caledonia, Mayotte, Réunion), Australia

(Norfolk Island, Christmas Island and Cocos Keeling) or the USA (Virgin Islands, Puerto Rico, American Samoa, Hawaii and Guam).

Something that must be born in mind when cruising is that visa regulations do change and often without warning. One should always try to find out the latest situation before sailing to a certain country. As most countries maintain diplomatic missions in neighbouring countries, these are the best places to ask about changes and to apply for any necessary visas. Occasionally regulations change so quickly that the diplomatic missions do not know about it. While gathering material for this book in Phuket, I happened to be in the immigration office the day the local chief of immigration decided not to extend visas beyond one month for anyone on a yacht visiting Thailand. The decision caused consternation among the sailors who were waiting to have their visas extended, but they were bluntly told that their only solution was to leave the country. It appeared to be a local decision which was probably changed later.

Visa requirements, and the political climate generally, can often change quickly due to the improvement or deterioration of relations between countries. This book was written during a period of profound change on the international political scene and at times it was almost impossible to keep up to date with a rapidly changing world. The process of liberalisation in Eastern Europe has already opened up several countries previously barred to foreign cruising yachts. The changes in South Africa might well alter people's attitude to that country. Just as the book was almost ready to be handed to the publishers, North and South Yemen decided to reunite and a quick rewrite had to be done. The new flag of a united Yemen has been added, and to play it safe, I also decided to add the flags of the three Baltic republics to the courtesy flags on the endpapers, because even if Moscow continues to resist their moves towards independence, a visiting yacht flying the Soviet flag could upset local sensitivities.

Cruising Permits

In some countries, cruising yachts are subjected to special regulations or restrictions concerning their movement. In most places if a cruising permit or transit log is required, it is issued at the first port of entry, so it is not necessary to make any preparations in advance. Any restrictions on the freedom of movement of yachts which do not require a cruising permit to be obtained in advance are discussed in the section on that country. It is most important to know the particulars of those permits which must be applied for before one's arrival, so as to make the correct preparations. The regulations pertaining to at least three such countries, Indonesia, Palau and the Galapagos Islands, have caused great confusion among cruising sailors for years and it is hoped that this book will clear up the situation.

There are various reasons why restrictions on cruising yachts are imposed, the main reasons being the protection of remote communities from intrusion, the preservation of natural parks and reserves, or the wish of authorities to keep foreign sailors away from sensitive military areas or detention centres. Restrictions are also increasingly imposed on genuine cruising yachts because of the fear by local authorities that a boat chartering illegally might slip through their net. In some places, such as Turkey, this fear borders on paranoia and any crew changes are regarded with deep suspicion. In all fairness, it must be said that in many countries charter boats do take advantage of lax laws and operate illegally, pretending to be ordinary cruising boats. The situation has not been helped by some cruising boats doing a bit of chartering on the side without informing the authorities and completing whatever formalities are necessary. After many years of tolerance or ignorance, the authorities in most countries used by charter boats are now aware of what is happening and are trying to get the charter operators to make some contribution to the economy of the country whose beauty they so readily exploit. It is unfortunate that cruising yachts have been caught up in this situation, but sailors should perhaps try to understand that some of these countries have few resources apart from their picturesque scenery, so their attempts to recoup some of the revenue that others are making out of it should not be condemned too harshly. The same line of thought can be applied to the fees sometimes charged for cruising permits and light dues. These fees, which give access to some of the most beautiful and unspoilt areas of the world, are rarely more than one would pay for a few nights in a marina anywhere in Europe or North America.

Flag Etiquette

Although not all countries insist on it, in theory the Q flag should be flown as soon as the yacht has entered territorial waters to signal the intention of requesting pratique. In this way, one cannot be accused of trying to slip in unnoticed and in fact in some countries yachts have got into trouble for not hoisting the Q flag until they were in the harbour. Also to avoid confusion, it is advisable to try to contact the port on VHF radio, especially in those countries which do not readily welcome yachts.

The courtesy flag should also be flown once one enters a nation's territorial waters. The flag should be flown from the starboard spreader in a position above any other flag. The courtesy flag should be in a good state and of reasonable size as some officials take offence at yachts that fly a torn or tiny flag. In some dependencies or autonomous regions, such as the Canaries, Azores, French Polynesia or Corsica, it is appreciated if the regional flag is flown together, but below, that of the metropolitan power. Burgees, house flags and courtesy flags as well as ensigns should be lowered at sunset or 2100, whichever is earlier and hoisted at 0800 in summer and 0900 in winter. It is particularly important to observe this in Scandinavian countries, where people are extremely flag conscious. The courtesy flags of the countries listed in this book are illustrated on the end papers.

The ship should be dressed overall on national days in countries visited. Ships should only be dressed when at anchor or in harbour. Although not essential, and many people are not even aware of it, there is a correct order in which to fly the code signals if the yacht is dressed from bow to stern. This order has been designed to give an interesting variety of both colour and shapes. The correct order, starting from the bow is: E Q p3 G p8 Z p4 W p6 P p1 1 CODE T Y B X 1st H 3rd D F 2nd U A O M R p2 J p0 N p9 K p7 V p5 L C S. If the vessel is two masted, the line between the two masts starts with Y and ends with O.

The Right Attitude

While the actual completion of formalities is usually a matter about which the captain is at the mercy of local officials, unless he is prepared or able to handle formalities through an agent, many unpleasant experiences can be avoided by a right attitude. The first impressions of a visiting sailor's attitude or behaviour can determine how he or she is treated from the start and one should not be surprised if local officials do not treat someone with respect if that person's attitude shows an obvious disrespect for them, their position, customs, language, religion or colour of skin. Often such an attitude is caused by ignorance, and it is hoped that the information contained in this book will help dispel some of this ignorance. However, this attitude is sometimes caused by a feeling of superiority, which people from developed countries, which is where most cruising yachts come from, sometimes display towards people in developing countries. Such a superior attitude is not always put on deliberately – on the contrary, it is often natural and unnoticed by the person, but it can create an immediate antagonism in the local people that person deals with, who are so often so well attuned to this condition that they can pick it up as soon as people step into their office. It pays to try to show a little humility. What one would not do at home, do not do abroad either. Just as one would not behave in a condescending manner to a US or British customs official, why behave differently to a Sri Lankan, Tahitian or Sudanese? I have witnessed many incidents when a small dose of calm and politeness would have resolved matters on the spot without any further aggravation. South Africans arriving without a visa in the Caribbean are often incensed to be dealt with sharply by a black official. Yet with a bit of tact and patience, the situation is usually resolved and the sailor allowed to stay. How different it is in places like London's Heathrow airport, where those arriving without a visa are either repatriated immediately or sent to a detention centre.

An even bigger factor in provoking antagonism is the way some sailors dress, or rather undress, when visiting other countries. It probably does not even occur to them that the way they dress is not only a sign of disrespect for local custom, but can be downright offensive. Particularly when visiting government offices, men should not go barefoot or in rubber thonged sandals, in shorts or singlets. In some countries, such as Brazil, access to government offices is only permitted if properly attired. In many Arab, West Indian, Asian and Latin American countries, shorts are never worn by men in public. Shorts are considered acceptable only for small boys or on a beach. Therefore one should not be offended if officials do not treat someone so dressed with the respect due to the captain of an offshore yacht. Generally a tidy appearance denotes respect for the authorities of one's host country and enables one to be regarded and treated accordingly. The same rules apply when visiting local yacht clubs, where dress rules are often strictly enforced. It is also a good idea to make sure that the boat is tidied up after a long passage, so as to look presentable on arrival, especially in those countries where the yacht is boarded immediately on arrival. Everywhere in the world it is the first impression that counts and it might save one considerable frustration. It might just be the factor that helps the officials decide whether to conduct a search of the yacht or to take your word that you are not carrying anything illegal.

Dress etiquette is a difficult matter as it varies so much from country to country. In some countries, a foreign woman's scanty dress can be interpreted as an indication of her morals, which can lead to sexual harassment and even rape. In most Pacific islands, where bare breasts are considered normal, for a woman to bare her thighs is considered provocative and so very skimpy shorts should be avoided. In Greece women should always cover bare shoulders when entering a church and sometimes their heads too. In Arab countries it is wise for women to wear trousers or long skirts if possible. Footgear should be removed before entering a Buddhist shrine and although it is permissible to photograph Buddha statues, one should not pose beside them. Footwear should be removed when visiting some Asian homes and also when visiting mosques. In strict Muslim countries, access to mosques is forbidden to non-believers. Because the consumption of alcohol is against Muslim belief, one must not be seen consuming alcoholic drinks in public, which may include the cockpit if berthed in a port. Nor should food be consumed in public before sunset during Ramadan. In Muslim countries, dogs are considered unclean and pets are best kept on board. Friday is the day of rest in Muslim countries, when everything is closed. Sunday is observed very religiously in some Pacific countries, particularly Fiji, where sporting events and organised barbecues are among the activities forbidden on Sundays.

An important rule is not to bribe local officials. Although this might ease matters temporarily for one person, it will certainly make life more difficult for all who follow. There are corrupt officials in many countries and often they attempt to procure a bribe, but if this is firmly resisted, or a detailed official receipt is asked for any money demanded, they may give up. When the boat is inspected, if one feels like offering the boarding officers a drink, there is no reason why one should not do so, although it is preferable to stick to non-alcoholic drinks, particularly in Muslim countries. Generally it is not advisable to make gifts, except perhaps the small token gifts some yachts carry with their logo or name on. It can be difficult if an official asks for something or for money, but it should be avoided as politely as possible so as not to set a precedent.

When clearing in, it is extremely foolish to try and hide anything, because the penalties for possessing undeclared firearms, pets or drugs can be severe. If in doubt it is better to declare more than necessary, especially in those countries where moveable items of value such as cameras and radios have to be written on the declaration. Everything should be declared including prescription drugs, such as strong painkillers, and the relevant prescription or doctor's letter may have to be shown. The official attitude towards illegal drugs is becoming stricter and many countries operate zero tolerance, so if any illegal drugs at all are found, one risks paying a heavy fine, going to prison or possibly losing the boat. One should therefore be very careful about crew picked up casually and what they might have in their possession. This subject should be discussed very seriously with all crew members as the boat could be confiscated if drugs are found on board, and ignorance on the part of the owner is not accepted as an excuse. If a yacht is searched, either the captain or a crew member should accompany the searching officer to prevent anything being planted, which is known to have happened in a few cases. If anything is found, it should not be touched, so as not to leave fingerprints. One should also take a photograph of the official holding the incriminating item where it was found. If arrested, one should alert any other yachts in the vicinity immediately, so they can keep an eye on the yacht and also inform one's embassy or consulate. In a few countries people have been wrongly arrested, kept for 24 hours and then released, only to find on their return that their boat has been ransacked and everything of value taken.

Foreign visitors are subject to the laws of the country they are visiting and sailors on yachts are not exempt. The powers of one's ambassador or consul are limited and although they may be able to help those who are faced with an emergency situation, they can rarely help someone who has contravened the laws of the country, except to ensure that they receive fair treatment.

2 Health Precautions Worldwide

It is expected that every cruising boat will carry a comprehensive medical kit to deal with a wide range of accidents and possible illnesses, as help at sea in an emergency is rarely available. Fortunately infectious or contagious diseases are not a risk while at sea, but these become a hazard when ashore in many parts of the world.

The two greatest health hazards are mosquitos and unsafe drinking water or food. These can be guarded against in several ways. Malaria, yellow fever and dengue fever are among the diseases that are mosquito-borne. If cruising for any length of time in the tropics it is wise to have mosquito screens fitted over hatches or mosquito netting that can be rigged over bunks. One should keep as much of the body covered as possible at sunset and use insect repellants, knockdown sprays or burn coils.

Not all vaccinations give total protection against food and waterborne diseases, so one should be scrupulous about checking water supplies, treating the water where necessary or drinking bottled water in dubious areas. Also one should avoid raw vegetables, salads, unpeeled fruit, raw shellfish, ice cream, cream and ice cubes in drinks in risk areas, unless these have been thoroughly washed or prepared by oneself.

It is highly recommended that supplies of sterilised and sealed items such as syringes, needles, sutures, dressings and infusion cannulae are carried. These sterile packs are widely available in kits for travellers and can be given to medical staff if seeking treatment abroad where properly sterilised or disposable equipment is not used or available. This is a precaution to be taken for all countries where there is a risk of Hepatitis B or AIDS from contaminated equipment, blood or blood products. If an accident or emergency needs a blood transfusion in countries where donated blood is not screened or checked properly, it is advisable to contact one's embassy or consulate, as some of them keep a disease-free donor list in certain countries.

Many countries give reciprocal free treatment in an emergency, but this is only on the same terms as that received by nationals of the foreign country concerned. This usually applies to state health-care systems, which leave much to be desired in some countries. For members of the European Community, there is a special form (in the UK Form E111 obtainable from post offices), which entitles the person to emergency medical care throughout the Community. The procedure varies from country to country and details are given on the form. For anyone cruising extensively, it is highly recommended that a worldwide medical insurance is taken out to cover any treatment required, especially if sailing to countries where medical care is expensive, such as the USA, Canada or Australia. This insurance will also often provide for an ill person to be flown home for treatment, which is a wise option to take if the emergency occurs in a country with poor medical facilities.

Sufficient time before departure should be allowed for any vaccinations, as some cannot be given at the same time as others. Details on vaccinations required and precautions against specific diseases are summarised below.

Aids

The Acquired Immune Deficiency Syndrome, commonly called AIDS, is caused by a virus called HIV. It is usually fatal if contracted, but not everyone infected with the HIV virus develops the disease, although they are likely to remain infected and infectious all their lives. There is no way to tell if a person is infected without taking an HIV positive test. A few countries have started asking for an HIV test certificate for visitors coming from certain countries where it is prevalent such as East Africa. If AIDS is not brought under control or a cure found, it may become advisable to carry an HIV test certificate in the future.

The disease is present worldwide. Although found predominantly in the homosexual community, in certain countries such as Haiti and East Africa the disease is endemic in the general population. The two main ways of catching the AIDS virus is by sexual contact or through contaminated blood getting into the body via a transfusion, injection or poorly sterilised medical equipment. The virus cannot be caught by everyday contact, crockery, food, swimming pools or mosquito bites. At present there is no vaccination or cure. The obvious precautions are to avoid casual sexual contacts and to use a condom. One should carry sterile medical supplies for emergencies when one may require an injection. One should also avoid medical or dental treatment involving surgery in countries where there is a risk. In many less developed countries blood for transfusion is not properly screened or treated, but there may be ways of obtaining screened blood if the doctor is asked or diplomatic missions are contacted.

Hepatitis B

This is transmitted in a similar way to AIDS, by sexual contact with an infected person or through infected blood or needles. Hepatitis B is found worldwide. There is a vaccination which gives protection, but the course takes up to six months to come to full protection. The best precautions are as those described above for AIDS.

Hepatitis A

This is sometimes called infectious hepatitis and is caught from contaminated food or water and is prevalent in most parts of the world where there is poor sanitation and hygiene. An injection of gamma globulin will give protection for only about 6 to 8 weeks as it is a blood product containing antibodies. It is essential that this inoculation is made from screened blood. As it protects for such a short time, it is probably only worth taking for cruises to places known for primitive conditions. Otherwise the main precaution is to take scrupulous care over what one eats and drinks as outlined above.

Tetanus

This dangerous disease is found everywhere in the world and results from the tetanus spores entering the body via even a slight scratch or wound. This can easily happen on any dockside, so it is essential that everyone cruising keeps their tetanus vaccination up to date. Fortunately this vaccination is safe and very effective and if one had a full course as a child, as most people have, a booster is only necessary every ten years. If one has failed to keep this up to date and tetanus – commonly called lockjaw – develops, it can be treated if the patient is got to proper medical facilities immediately. These may not be available in more remote areas.

Tuberculosis

This disease is on the increase again in certain areas of Africa, Asia, Central and South America. If one has been vaccinated against tuberculosis in the past, revaccination is not necessary. Vaccination is only necessary if living or working closely with the indigenous population in these areas. It is unlikely that any cruising sailors would need this vaccination.

Smallpox

This disease has been eradicated worldwide and vaccination against it is no longer necessary.

Typhoid

Typhoid is found almost everywhere except Australia, New Zealand, Europe and North America and it is found especially in conditions of poor hygiene and sanitation. It is caught from contaminated food, water or milk. Sensible precautions are to take care over food and drink, but vaccination against typhoid is recommended for all those sailing outside of the above mentioned areas. Vaccination is effective: initially two injections are required 4 to 6 weeks apart, but following that a single revaccination gives protection for three years. After the age of 35, if one has had four regular revaccinations in the past, revaccination is probably unnecessary.

Poliomyelitis

This disease is found everywhere except Australia, New Zealand, Europe and North America. Anyone cruising outside of these areas should ensure that their vaccination against polio is kept up to date. To commence vaccination, a course of three doses of oral vaccine are given, normally when one is a child. Reinforcing doses should be taken every five years to continue protection against polio. Polio is transmitted by direct contact with an infected person and sometimes by contaminated water or food.

Meningococcal Meningitis

This serious disease, which is transmitted by direct contact or droplet infection, has had a rising incidence worldwide. There is a particularly high risk in the meningitis belt, which lies across sub-Saharan Africa and includes Senegal, Gambia and Ivory Coast on the west coast and Sudan, Ethiopia and Kenya on the east coast. There is a season for this disease, from November to May, and pilgrims have taken it to Saudi Arabia during the annual Hadj pilgrimage. Vaccination against meningococcal infection is available for meningitis A and C and this gives protection for three years.

Cholera

Cholera is found in some parts of Africa, Asia and the Middle East and especially in areas of primitive sanitation. The disease is transmitted through contaminated water and food. It is only recommended to be vaccinated if travelling to a country where there is known to be cholera. The cholera vaccine gives some protection for six months, but it is not always effective, so scrupulous care should be taken over food or drink. Usually it is well known where there are cholera outbreaks and these are not usually on the popular cruising tracks. However, in some countries, officials insist on seeing cholera vaccination certificates from people who have passed through a country where there has been cholera, even if not in the part visited. This is not required by International Regulations, but local officials can sometimes be over-zealous and may insist on vaccination being done on arrival, one reason why one should always carry one's own sterile syringes and needles.

Yellow Fever

This disease is only found in some parts of Africa and South America. It is transmitted by the bite of an infected mosquito. Vaccination against yellow fever gives protection for ten years. Vaccination can only be carried out at a designated centre, a list of which can be obtained from health authorities, travel agents or one's own doctor. Although yellow fever is found mainly in tropical forest areas and sailors are unlikely to encounter it, the vaccination is compulsory for travel to some countries, even if only visiting the coast or main ports. A vaccination certificate may be required also in subsequent ports if arriving from countries where yellow fever is present. If not possessing a certificate, one may have to be vaccinated on the spot, another reason for carrying those sterile needles and syringes.

Malaria

This is one of the biggest health risks that may be encountered by cruising sailors and some forms of malaria are particularly virulent and can even be fatal. Malaria is prevalent in many parts of Africa, Asia, Central and South America and the western Pacific. The disease is transmitted by mosquitos, so the first precaution is to avoid getting bitten, as outlined earlier.

Prophylactic treatment is available and anti-malarial tablets should be taken two weeks before entering a malarial area, throughout one's stay and for four weeks after departure. The problem has increased because some strains of malaria have become resistant to the drugs in use and therefore different tablets are recommended for particular areas. Although anti-malarial tablets are available over the counter in pharmacies it is wise to check with a doctor or a centre for tropical

diseases which are the recommended drugs and doses. The tablets are usually taken once a week and it is essential to take them after food. Children take a dose proportionate to their weight.

Areas particularly important for cruising sailors to take precautions in are Vanuatu, the Solomons and Papua New Guinea in the western Pacific, Guyana, French Guiana, Venezuela and Panama in South America, Thailand, Malaysia, Indonesia in South East Asia, and Sri Lanka, Comoros, Maldives, Mauritius and East Africa in the Indian Ocean.

Rabies

Rabies is endemic virtually worldwide and is usually fatal if not treated immediately; many island nations, which are rabies-free, prohibit the entry of animals. The disease can be caught if one is bitten, scratched or even licked by an infected animal such as a dog, cat or monkey. Therefore one should not approach or touch any unknown animal. If one is bitten or scratched by an animal one should wash and disinfect the wound thoroughly and get to medical attention fast. There is a rabies vaccination, which is a course of quite unpleasant injections, which should be started immediately. It is not normally recommended to be vaccinated beforehand against rabies unless one is travelling across country in remote parts where treatment is not available. If bitten, one should try and keep the animal under observation or if it is wild or a stray, note the place, description and date of the attack and inform the local police.

Bilharzia

This is also called schistosomiasis and is a deadly disease caught from parasites which have a secondary host in minute snails found in fresh water. Swimming in fresh water lakes or streams should be avoided in much of South America, Africa, Asia and the Caribbean. Bilharzia cannot be caught from swimming in the sea or salt water estuaries.

Ciguatera

This fish poisoning is caught by eating toxic fish from certain reef areas. Local knowledge should be sought whether fish from a certain coral reef area or island are likely to be affected. Fish caught by trolling in the open ocean are not likely to be toxic. One should avoid large fish such as barracuda caught in reef areas and one should avoid repeated meals from such fish as the toxin is cumulative. Fish should always be gutted very carefully and the head, roe or internal organs never eaten.

Reefwalking and Diving Hazards

Many of these hazards can be avoided by wearing footwear when walking on reefs and by looking carefully before touching anything while diving or reefwalking.

The stone fish is an ugly animal looking just like a stone which gives a poisonous sting if stepped on. If stung, one should keep fairly immobile to delay the spread of poison, flush the puncture with vinegar and put the foot in hot water. Wrap a bandage immediately above the wound and seek medical assistance.

Cone shells have a dart which they launch in defence and in a few species this can be deadly. One should avoid picking up live cone shells, but if one is stung, one should treat it like snake venom and seek medical advice.

If stung by the jellyfish called Portuguese Man-of-War, it is important not to rub the sting, but detoxify it with alcohol of some sort – spirits such as rum will do or even perfume. The sting then should be rinsed gently with warm water.

Jellyfish stings should similarly be bathed with vinegar and hot water. If sea urchin spikes are trod on or got into the flesh, one must try to remove all the spikes, sucking them out if necessary. Again soak in hot water and treat with antibiotic cream or powder. For all coral cuts, bites and rashes obtained from marine life, one should wash well with hot water and disinfect to prevent infection.

The Sun

This is one of the most serious dangers encountered by sailors and the power of the sun should never be underestimated. Sunburn should be avoided by using sun screens on exposed skin, covering the head and body until a tan has been acquired. The eyes are particularly vulnerable and should be protected by good sunglasses. When at anchor it is recommended to rig up some kind of cockpit awning.

Not only can the sun burn one's skin painfully, but it can cause the body to overheat. When sailing in very hot climates, particularly in equatorial regions or in the Red Sea, one should drink plenty of non-alcoholic fluids and also slightly increase one's salt intake to counteract salt loss through sweating.

Heat exhaustion
In very hot temperatures, any fatigue, dizziness, headache or muscle cramps should be taken seriously. The person should be cooled by sponging with tepid water or with a fan and given salt with fruit juice or a sugar solution (1 teaspoonful of salt and 4 of sugar to 1 litre of water).

Heat stroke
This is characterised by a sudden dramatic rise in temperature, lack of sweat and odd behaviour. Plenty of water should be given and the skin cooled with water and fans. Medical help will be needed, especially if the person loses consciousness.

Skin cancer
Whilst the above are immediate problems, one of the most serious problems caused by the sun is long term and that is the danger of skin cancer. This is caused by prolonged exposure to the sun and may not show up for many years, but it has afflicted many cruising sailors. The risk of developing skin cancer increases as people grow older, but it is important to prevent over exposure to the sun in children and young people as this is a cumulative risk.

Chronic exposure to the sun is the main cause of skin cancer and the carcinomas usually appear on exposed parts of the body, such as face, scalp, hands, arms and legs. The people at highest risk are those spending long periods outdoors and particularly those with fair skin, light coloured hair and light coloured eyes, such as blue, green or grey. Also more at risk are those who sunburn easily and tan with difficulty. The geographical location is also a factor and the nearer to the equator, the higher the number of cases reported in fair-skinned people.

Ninety per cent of all skin cancers are curable, especially if detected early. Medical advice should be sought for any unusual or persistent change in the skin, whether a growth or a discolouration, or change in size, colour, shape or thickness of any pre-existing moles. Although the incidence of skin cancer has increased and the death rate in the USA has doubled in the last 35 years, in Queensland in Australia, where a public education programme had been established, the death rate has been decreasing despite an increase in the number of cases reported. The increase in incidence is partly due to people living longer and also pursuing a more active outdoor life into their old age. Prevention is the most important factor and so one should avoid prolonged exposure, use sun screens and cover exposed areas.

Health Protection Checklist

Codes

Hep = Hepatitis, Mal = Malaria, Cho = Cholera, Ty = Typhoid, Pol = Polio, YF = Yellow Fever, r = risk of infection, vaccination recommended.

Cholera

E = vaccination ESSENTIAL for those who have visited or passed through a zone where cholera is present. A vaccination certificate will be demanded.

Yellow fever

★ = vaccination essential if arriving from a country where yellow fever is present. A vaccination certificate will be demanded.
E1 = vaccination ESSENTIAL.
E2 = vaccination essential except for travellers from non-infected areas who are staying less than two weeks.

Malaria

★ = risk absent in some parts at some times
Area A = Proguanil daily PLUS Chloroquine weekly recommended
Area B = Maloprim weekly PLUS Chloroquine weekly recommended
Area C = Proguanil daily OR Chloroquine weekly recommended

1. Mediterranean and Black Sea

	Hep	Mal	Cho	Ty	Pol	YF
Albania	r					★
Algeria	r	C★		r	r	r
Egypt	r	C★		r	r	★
Greece						★
Israel				r	r	
Lebanon	r			r	r	★
Libya	r	C★		r	r	★
Malta						★
Morocco	r	C★		r	r	
Syria	r	C★		r	r	★
Tunisia	r			r	r	★
Turkey	r	C★		r	r	

No vaccinations are needed for Bulgaria, Cyprus, Gibraltar, Italy, Monaco, Romania, Spain, USSR, Yugoslavia.

2. Northern Europe

No vaccinations are needed for Belgium, Denmark, Finland, Germany, Netherlands, Norway, Poland or Sweden.

3. Western Europe and North Atlantic Islands

	Hep	Mal	Cho	Ty	Pol	YF
Azores						★
Cape Verde Islands		A★		r	r	★
Madeira						★

No vaccinations are needed for Bermuda, Canary Islands, Channel Islands, Faeroes, France, Greenland, Iceland, Ireland, Portugal or United Kingdom.

4. West Africa and South Atlantic Islands

	Hep	Mal	Cho	Ty	Pol	YF
Ascension				r	r	★
Falkland Islands				r	r	
Gambia	r	A		r	r	E1
Ivory Coast	r	A	r	r	r	E1
Mauritania	r	A	r	r	r	E2
Namibia	r			r	r	★
St Helena				r	r	
Senegal	r	A	r	r	r	E1
South Africa		A★		r	r	★
Tristan da Cunha				r	r	

5. Caribbean

	Hep	Mal	Cho	Ty	Pol	YF
Anguilla				r	r	★
Antigua/Barbuda				r	r	★
Aruba				r	r	★
Bahamas				r	r	★
Barbados				r	r	★
Bonaire				r	r	★
British Virgin Islands				r	r	
Cayman Islands					r	
Cuba	r			r	r	
Curaçao				r	r	★
Dominica				r	r	★
Dominican Rep.	r	C		r	r	
Grenada				r	r	★
Guadeloupe	r			r	r	★
Haiti	r	C		r	r	★
Jamaica	r			r	r	★
Martinique	r			r	r	★
Montserrat				r	r	★
Puerto Rico	r			r	r	
Saba				r	r	★

	Hep	Mal	Cho	Ty	Pol	YF
St Barts				r	r	★
St Eustatius				r	r	★
St Kitts & Nevis				r	r	★
St Lucia	r			r	r	★
St Martin				r	r	★
St Vincent & Grenadines				r	r	★
Sint Maarten				r	r	★
Trinidad	r			r	r	★
Turks & Caicos				r	r	★
US Virgin Islands				r	r	

	Hep	Mal	Cho	Ty	Pol	YF
Marshall Islands				r	r	
Northern Marianas				r	r	
Palau				r	r	

6. Central and North America

	Hep	Mal	Cho	Ty	Pol	YF
Belize	r	C		r	r	★
Canada						
Costa Rica	r	C★		r	r	
El Salvador	r	C		r	r	★
Guatemala	r	C		r	r	★
Honduras	r	C		r	r	★
Mexico	r	C★		r	r	★
Nicaragua	r	C		r	r	★
Panama	r	A		r	r	E1
USA						

7. South America

	Hep	Mal	Cho	Ty	Pol	YF
Argentina	r	C★		r	r	
Brazil	r	A★		r	r	r
Chile	r			r	r	
Colombia	r	A		r	r	r
Ecuador	r	A		r	r	★
French Guiana	r	A		r	r	E1
Guyana	r	A		r	r	r
Peru	r	C		r	r	r
Surinam	r	A		r	r	★
Uruguay	r			r	r	
Venezuela	r	A★		r	r	

8. North Pacific Islands

	Hep	Mal	Cho	Ty	Pol	YF
Federated States of Micronesia				r	r	★
Guam				r	r	★
Hawaii					r	
Kiribati				r	r	★

9. South Pacific

	Hep	Mal	Cho	Ty	Pol	YF
American Samoa	r			r	r	★
Australia						★
Cook Islands				r	r	
Easter Island				r	r	★
Galapagos Islands				r	r	★
Fiji				r	r	★
French Polynesia				r	r	★
Juan Fernandez Islands				r	r	★
Nauru				r	r	★
New Caledonia				r	r	★
New Zealand						
Niue				r	r	★
Norfolk Island				r	r	★
Papua New Guinea		B		r	r	★
Pitcairn			★	r	r	★
Solomon Islands	r	B		r	r	★
Tokelau				r	r	★
Tonga				r	r	★
Tuvalu				r	r	★
Vanuatu	r	B		r	r	
Wallis & Futuna				r	r	★
Western Samoa	r			r	r	★

10. South East Asia and Far East

	Hep	Mal	Cho	Ty	Pol	YF
Brunei	r			r	r	★
China	r	A★		r	r	★
Hong Kong				r	r	
Indonesia	r	A★		r	r	★
Japan				r	r	
Macao	r			r	r	
Malaysia	r	A★		r	r	
Philippines	r	A★		r	r	★
Singapore				r	r	★
South Korea	r			r	r	
Taiwan	r			r	r	★
Thailand	r	A★		r	r	★

11. North Indian Ocean and Red Sea

	Hep	Mal	Cho	Ty	Pol	YF
Djibouti	r	A		r	r	★
Ethiopia	r	A	r	r	r	r
India	r	A	r	r	r	★
Maldives	r			r	r	★
Oman	r	C		r	r	★
Saudi Arabia	r	C★		r	r	★
Somalia	r	A	rE	r	r	r
Sri Lanka	r	A		r	r	★
Sudan	r	A	rE	r	r	r
Yemen	r	C★		r	r	★

12. South Indian Ocean

	Hep	Mal	Cho	Ty	Pol	YF
Chagos						
Christmas Islands				r	r	
Cocos Keeling				r	r	
Comoros	r	A		r	r	
Kenya	r	A		r	r	r
Madagascar	r	A	r	r	r	★
Mauritius	r	C★		r	r	★
Mayotte	r	A		r	r	
Mozambique	r	A		r	r	★
Réunion				r	r	★
Seychelles	r			r	r	
Tanzania	r	A	r	r	r	r

3 Communications

Radio communications

Very high frequency marine radio

VHF radios are the standard means of coastal and ship-to-ship communications. VHF Channel 16 (156.8 MHz) is the distress, safety and calling frequency and is mandatory in all VHF marine installations. Channel 16 is supposed to be monitored by all commercial vessels while under way. It is also monitored by coastal radio stations as well as by coastguards and similar organisations. Most countries maintain a network of marine radio stations along their coasts and calls through them can be linked into the national or international telephone system. In order to be able to do this, the operator should have a VHF licence and call sign (or marine identification number) and if intending to make calls outside of the country of residence, accounting arrangements should be made before departure so that the calls can be charged to a home account.

High frequency marine radio

An increasing number of cruising yachts are equipped with HF radio transmitters. The main function of these radios is to give the user the possibility to contact coastal radio stations when the vessel is offshore and out of VHF range. Once contacted, a station can place a call in the international telephone system. HF radios also have other uses, such as calling coastal stations or ports on medium frequency (MF), receiving weather facsimile broadcasts, monitoring distress frequencies or being used for ship-to-ship communications.

There are certain rules that must be complied with for the operation of HF marine radio. First of all, the operator of such equipment must have an operator's certificate issued by the licensing authority in the country where the vessel is registered. To obtain a licence usually one has to pass an examination, which comprises questions on the operation of the equipment, the procedure for making calls, dealing with emergencies, as well as the regulations governing radio transmissions at sea. There are courses for radio operators run by colleges and various associations, but it is also possible to pass the examination by studying alone. The actual transceiver must also be licensed and the issuing authority will grant the operator an official call sign. In some countries, both the licence and call sign are also valid for a VHF radio. Before leaving home, it is advisable to open an account with an agency recommended by the national telephone company, so that calls made from abroad can be charged to that account.

Most transceivers on cruising yachts are of relatively low power, usually with a maximum output of 150 W. This is not very powerful as far as marine transmitters go, but coupled with a knowledge of propagation, it should be sufficient for the needs of the average sailor wishing to make telephone calls via commercial radio stations. Particularly for those cruising offshore and at great distances from coastal stations, one of the most important factors to master early on is that of propagation. A basic knowledge of this important subject is essential and some of the best books dealing with this matter are those written by and for amateur radio operators.

Propagation

The distance over which a HF radio signal can travel depends on factors such as transmitter power and antenna gain, but one of the most important aspects is that of radio signal propagation. Radio signals in the ground mode travel along the earth's surface but are rapidly absorbed or masked by other radio frequency emissions. Ground waves are most important on medium frequency transmissions in the 2 MHz band. Although some short-range contacts can be made on HF on the ground wave mode, the propagation mode which is paramount to radiotelephone communications over long distances is sky wave propagation. This phenomenon makes worldwide radio communications possible.

In sky wave propagation, radio signals are refracted, or bent, by electricity-conducting layers in the upper atmosphere called the ionosphere. As a result, the signals are bounced back hundreds or thousands of miles from the point of emission. The area between the point of emission and the point at which the signal returns to earth is called the skip zone. The signal in the skip zone itself, in other words the area which has been skipped over, is either non-existent or negligible.

The distance that a signal can be skipped depends primarily on a process in the ionosphere called ionisation. Ionisation is caused by several factors, the most important being the ultraviolet light from the sun. It is this ionisation which produces the electricity-conducting layers that refract radio waves. As the earth rotates about its axis gradually turning away from the sun, the density of ions over any given point on the ground changes with increases or decreases in the sun's ionising radiations. This is the explanation for the difference in propagation throughout the day/night cycle. Fortunately, the ionosphere affects each frequency in a different manner. This means that if the point with which one wishes to communicate is skipped over by one frequency, all one has to do is choose a lower or higher frequency in order to reach the desired station. With a little practice, one will soon know which frequencies are best suited for which time of day and also are most likely to travel the required distance.

The lowest, least densely ionised layer of the ionosphere, called the 'D' layer, is located between 30 and 50 miles above the earth's surface. While this layer is not effective in refracting radio waves, it does absorb radio signals and is responsible for most of the weakening radio signal strength in the sky wave mode.

The next layer, called the 'E' layer, is located 70 miles above the earth's surface. This layer is slightly more ionised and is capable of bouncing relatively low frequency waves back to earth. It is particularly useful for short distance propagation, between a few hundred and 1500 miles. The next layer, the 'F1' layer, is located about 180 miles above the earth and is more densely ionised than the 'E' layer. The 'F1' layer is capable of bending higher frequency waves and is most useful for distances around 2000 miles. Finally, the highest layer, 'F2', varies from 225 to 270 miles in altitude and has the greatest density of ions. It is capable of refracting higher frequencies than any other layer and is primarily useful for propagation over distances of 2500 miles or more.

During the night, when the sun's radiations are absent, the 'D' and 'E' layers disappear, while the 'F1' and 'F2' layers merge to form a single 'F' layer about 210 miles above the earth. This layer is responsible for night sky wave propagation.

Optimum frequencies

Lower frequencies should be used during periods of low ionisation rather than during periods of high ionisation, in order to communicate over the same distance. It might seem that a frequency which is sufficiently low to be bent back to earth during conditions of low ion density would be suitable for transmission at all times. However, this is not generally the case because absorption of wave energy by the ionosphere increases with increased ionisation and increasing frequency. In other words, during high ionisation periods absorption may so weaken lower frequencies that little or no signal is returned to earth. It is therefore advantageous always to use the highest frequency that will refract down to the area with which one wishes to communicate, since this frequency will be weakened least by absorption.

There are some additional factors which affect radio propagation. Propagation varies not only with the day/night cycle, but also with the summer/winter cycle as well as the phenomenon known as the 11 year sun-spot cycle. Although all this might sound complicated, in practice one quickly learns how to judge the best conditions to make calls ashore. The most important points to remember are the following:

1. Choose the working frequency of the coastal station you wish to contact. If you hear traffic, it is almost certain that you will be able to communicate with that station on that or any other channel in the same frequency band. It is also likely that the next higher or lower bands may also support communications with that station.
2. In order to become familiar with propagation on various bands, it is useful to listen to traffic lists and other broadcasts from a chosen station and to make a note of the bands which are available at all times.
3. Low frequencies are weakened more than high frequencies during high ionisation periods (day time).
4. High frequencies penetrate the ionosphere at night and are lost in space.
5. Low frequencies are not absorbed at night and can be used for relatively long distance communications during periods of darkness.

The simplest rule to remember is: high ionisation, high frequency – low ionisation, low frequency. In other words, low frequencies should be used at night and high frequencies should be used over long distances during daylight hours.

Because of propagation differences between frequencies, proximity to a station is less important than finding a good clear channel on which to transmit. Communication with more distant stations is primarily a matter of selecting the right frequency band. Since all available maritime mobile channels are shared by countries around the world, it is highly likely that at certain times there will be congestion and interference on some frequencies. It is therefore advisable to equip the transceiver with as many channels as possible for each station. Alternatively, one should ensure that additional frequencies can be quickly dialled if one finds that those preselected do not cover optimum bands. This can occur on radios which have all their frequencies preset by the manufacturer and which do not allow the user to add his own frequencies later on. Transceivers with fixed frequencies are therefore best avoided on cruising yachts. By employing favourable propagation conditions and using the best placed coastal stations, one should be able to maintain contact with land most of the time. Details of coastal radio stations worldwide are given in the British Admiralty List of Radio Signals.

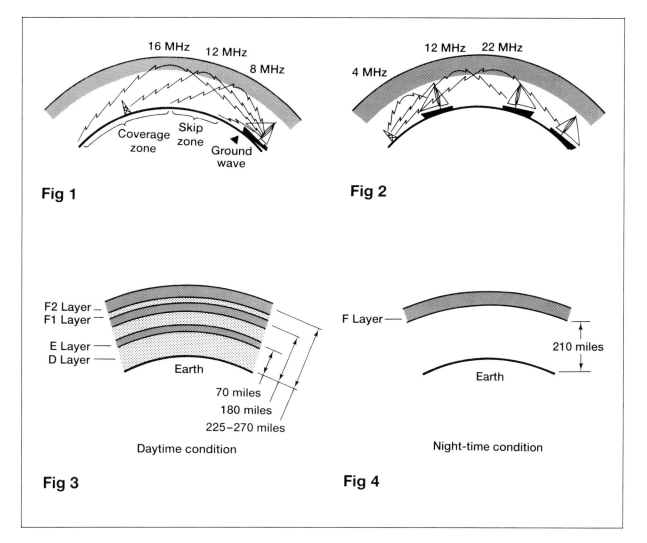

Fig 1

Fig 2

Fig 3

Fig 4

Amateur radio

An alternative preferred by many cruising sailors for long-range communications is amateur radio. The frequency bands allocated to amateur radio operators are interspersed with those used by coastal stations broadcasting on the HF marine radio bands. Not only is the mode of transmission similar but the transceivers are almost identical. A licence is needed to operate an amateur set and operators using their sets on yachts must add the suffix MM (maritime mobile) to their call sign. Among the many attractions of amateur radio are the numerous amateur nets that operate all over the world. Some are extremely informative, giving weather forecasts and other data of interest to cruising sailors, while others are just a means of keeping in touch with other yachts cruising in the same part of the world. Many cruising sailors who are not licensed amateur operators listen in regularly to such nets.

Autolink

A new ship-to-shore service is being introduced in several countries giving vessels with MF and VHF equipment the possibility to dial a number ashore without the need to go through an operator. This facility is made possible by a unit developed by Cimat, an Italian electronics company. The onboard unit, which is connected to the FM/VHF set, allows the pulses to go straight to an exchange installed ashore where they are fed automatically into the telephone network. The onboard unit also allows messages to be scrambled, which is a clear advantage over the existing system which enables anyone to listen to conversations carried out on standard MF and VHF equipment. Scrambled messages are descrambled at the coastal radio station from where normal speech is fed into the telephone network. The system has a range of approximately 200 miles on HF and 40 miles on VHF, which has a significantly greater range than cellular radio systems.

The service will be internationally compatible, so that it will be possible to dial calls anywhere in the world as long as the nearest country has installed the necessary ground equipment. The system is already operational in Italy, Gibraltar and Portugal and will be introduced in the UK by British Telecom from November 1990. Other countries expected to join in the near future are Spain, Ireland, Singapore, Malaysia, South Africa, New Zealand and the Channel Islands.

Cellular telephones

Although originally developed for land use, cellular telephones are found increasingly on yachts. The first comprehensive service was started in the Eastern Caribbean by Boatphone, a subsidiary of the Cable and Wireless Communications Group. The system is extremely simple to use and calls are dialled as on an ordinary telephone. The Caribbean is ideal for this kind of operation as most of the time boats are within range of coastal stations. The system in use is the US system, so that anyone from North America can use their own equipment. On arrival in the Caribbean one only needs to contact the Boatphone operator to be issued with a private number. All subsequent calls are charged directly to one of the major credit cards. Yachts that do not possess a cellular phone, or whose system is incompatible with the US system, can either buy or rent a set.

A similar system operates in the Bahamas and other systems geared primarily to cruise ships and cruising yachts are being developed in other parts of the world, such as the Mediterranean. The major stumbling block which has to be overcome is the incompatibility of the systems used in the various countries bordering on the Mediterranean, but this may be solved either by the introduction of a proposed digital system or by adopting the present US system. For the time being, anyone on a yacht who wishes to use the land based cellular telephone system must first register with the country concerned and be issued with a number by them.

AMVER

The Automated Mutual Assistance Vessel Rescue system (AMVER), operated by the United States Coast Guard, is a maritime mutual assistance organisation which contributes significantly to the co-ordination of search and rescue operations in many areas of the world. Commercial vessels of all nations making offshore voyages are encouraged to send reports on their movements and periodic position updates to the AMVER centre at Coast Guard New York. This is done either via selected coastal radio stations or Inmarsat. Although not available to pleasure craft, cruising yachts should be aware of this system as it has worked very well in search and rescue operations in the past.

The US Coast Guard monitors continuously certain frequencies, but these frequencies are to be used *only* to transmit details of an emergency and otherwise are meant for listening to. The frequencies are also used to transmit information on the location and path of tropical storms.

Ship transmit carrier frequency	Ship receive carrier frequency
4134.3 KHz	4428.7 KHZ
6200.0 KHz	6506.4 KHz
8241.5 KHz	8765.4 KHz
12342.4 KHz	13113.2 KHz
16534.4 KHz	17307.3 KHz

Maritime safety information

This is an international system of radio broadcasts containing information needed for safe navigation. The messages can be received by equipment which automatically monitors MSI frequencies. The information relevant to the individual vessel is then printed out. Messages include navigational and meteorological warnings, forecasts and distress alerts. The main feature of this service is International Navtex, which operates on 518 MHz. Transmissions are coordinated internationally and mutual interference is avoided by limiting the power of transmitters as well as by time-sharing of the frequency. After a successful debut in the Baltic and North Sea, Navtex has been taken up in many parts of the world and will become compulsory on all ships in 1993.

Satellite Communications

Although practically every offshore cruising yacht relies on satellite navigation for its accurate position fixing, satellite communications systems are still a rarity on sailing yachts. However, this will change in the next few years as the existing systems are adapted for small craft use and new systems are developed for cruising yachts.

The inspiration for the maritime satellite communications systems was Intelsat, an organisation which started offering satellite communications in 1965. The system took a big step forward in 1976 with the launch in the USA of the first three maritime satellites in the Marisat programme. In 1979, Inmarsat came into existence to provide satellite communications to civil shipping. By using the existing Marisat system as its core, Inmarsat began commercial services in 1982. Inmarsat is an international organisation comprising about 60 member nations. It is responsible for the operation and maintenance of its satellite system, whereas the ground stations, which provide the connection between the satellites and the world's telecommunications networks, are owned and operated by the countries in which they are located. Maritime satellite communications have seen an explosive development in recent years and although the great majority of users are commercial ships, an increasing number of pleasure yachts use satcoms. Two Inmarsat satcom systems are in use today, Standard-A and Standard-C.

Standard-A

This system is designed primarily for larger vessels or those with sophisticated communications requirements. A Standard-A ship earth station (SES) uses Inmarsat satellites to provide high quality connections into the existing international and national telecommunications networks. Each unit is equipped with an automatic push-button telephone and telex machine. Optional equipment includes such facilities as facsimile, data transfer and television. Making a telephone call via Inmarsat with Standard-A equipment is as simple as dialling a call from home. A two-digit code selects the optimum coast earth station and a single push-button selects a voice call, rather than telex. A suitable circuit is allocated and the subscriber number is dialled preceded by 00 and the country code. Connection is automatic, immediate and the quality is always perfect as the signal is not affected by weather conditions or interference. From most countries it is also possible to call a ship automatically via Inmarsat. Sending or receiving a telex is just as simple.

Another service provided by Standard-A terminals is facsimile, from weather charts to letters, newspapers, drawings or plans. Through Inmarsat satellites it is also possible to exchange huge volumes of data between computers ashore and those on board vessels at sea.

The most noticeable feature of a Standard-A station on a vessel is its radome, which encloses a parabolic dish antenna. The antenna is motorised so that it tracks the satellite precisely, regardless of ship movement. The size of the radome is the main disadvantage for its installation on yachts smaller than 50 feet, although work is already advanced on producing more compact units. Also under development is Standard-B, a digital version of Standard-A. Both systems are primarily suited for merchant ships or larger yachts, but a new system, Standard-M, will become available towards the end of 1992 and will be suitable for use on smaller yachts. Standard-M is a voice and data only system, mainly to be used for telephony, and as it will be very compact it will appeal more to the owners of cruising yachts than the present Standard-A. For the time being, most offshore yachts will probably use the smaller and less expensive satcom version, Standard-C.

Standard-C

For smaller vessels, criteria such as size, weight, power requirements and cost, make the smaller Standard-C system more attractive. The normal Standard-C installation consists of a small omni-directional antenna plus an electronics package not much bigger than the average VHF radio. This is usually connected to a personal computer/printer, teleprinter or keyboard and VDU. The power requirements are very modest ranging from 15 W to 50 W.

Standard-C is a text-only communications system, which can cope with any kind of language and can interconnect with international telex, electronic mail or data networks. It can also handle computer type graphics. Because transmissions to and from the mobile terminal via the satellite are digital, a message can consist of any type of information that can be reproduced on a computer screen or printer. Inmarsat C terminals can be linked or integrated with a wide variety of navigation systems to provide a continuous global position reporting capability. Position reporting from the terrestrial Decca and Loran systems, the satellite based Transit or GPS systems or onboard dead reckoning equipment can be transmitted automatically either on demand or at fixed intervals. Standard-C terminals can be programmed to transmit to a rescue coordination centre a pre-recorded distress message automatically indicating the vessel's latest position.

Every Inmarsat ship station, whether Standard-C or Standard-A, is fitted with a special alert mechanism to cope with emergency situations. Usually this is a single 'Distress' button or a special dialling code. Such a distress signal immediately seizes a telephone, telex or data communications channel and connects it automatically via a coast earth station to a rescue coordination centre (RCC). Distress alerts have top priority and because of the reliability of the satellite system, connection is always made immediately regardless of the location of the emergency or the distance to the coast station. All rescue co-ordination centres are interconnected, often using their own Standard-A equipment, so that a distress call is quickly transmitted to the centre dealing with emergencies.

There are more than twenty coast earth stations operating with the Inmarsat system and several more are under construction. Inmarsat operates eight satellites located in geostationary orbits around the world. Five of these satellites are maintained as operational, but are kept in reserve. The other three are the prime

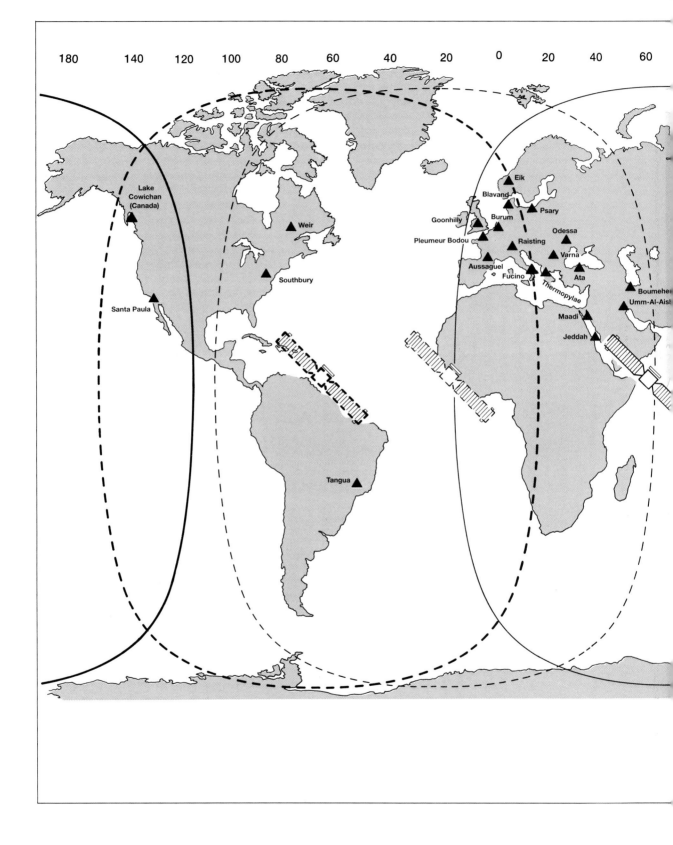

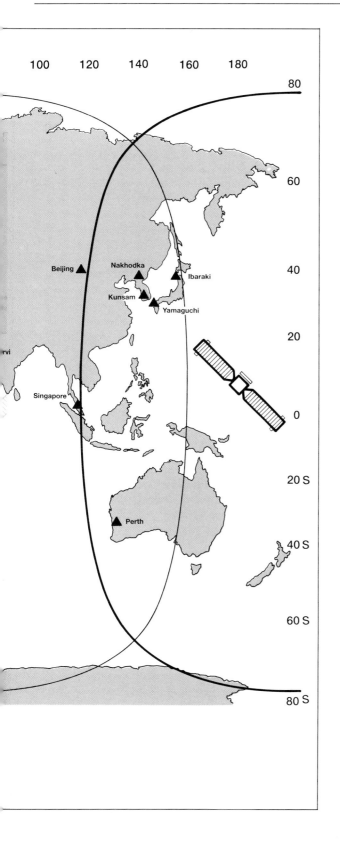

operational satellites and are stationed over the world's three main oceans at 26°W (Atlantic), 180°W (Pacific) and 63°E (Indian). This arrangement gives virtual global coverage except for the extreme polar regions and a narrow gap extending from north to south through the North American landmass into the SE Pacific. Inmarsat has pledged to eliminate this gap as soon as practicable.

Global Maritime Distress and Safety System

Inmarsat has provided a means for the creation of a worldwide emergency communications scheme, rendering obsolete the present radio-based ship-to-ship distress arrangements. The existing radio distress system will be reduced to a subordinate role in the coming satellite-based system. The International Maritime Organisation has combined all requirements in its specification for the Global Maritime Distress and Safety System, due for implementation in 1992. The proposed GMDSS will integrate terrestrial and satellite communications, the satcom element being provided by Inmarsat. The primary aims of GMDSS are to alert search and rescue authorities ashore and to facilitate the coordination of search and rescue operations without delay. Depending on their area of operation, ships will have to carry certain types of communications equipment. Four such areas have been designated:

Area A1: Within range of shore-based VHF coast stations, about 25 miles offshore. Vessels in this area will carry VHF equipment.
Area A2: Within range of shore-based MF coast stations, which is about 100 miles offshore. Vessels in this area will carry VHF and MF equipment.
Area A3: Within the coverage area of Inmarsat satell-

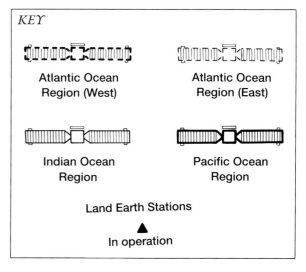

KEY

Atlantic Ocean Region (West)

Atlantic Ocean Region (East)

Indian Ocean Region

Pacific Ocean Region

Land Earth Stations

▲

In operation

ites. Vessels in this area will carry VHF, MF and either HF or satellite equipment.

Area A4: This area is outside of the range of Inmarsat satellites but within the coverage of the polar orbiting Cospas-Sarsat system. Vessels will need VHF, MF and HF equipment.

COSPAS-SARSAT

This international cooperative search and rescue project was set up in the early 1980s to improve the chances of detecting an emergency and to speed up the response by rescue services. In the United States, the National Oceanic and Atmospheric Administration (NOAA) operates geostationary polar orbiting satellites that monitor weather conditions over the entire globe. In addition to weather and environmental sensors, polar orbiting satellites also carry search and rescue satellite aided tracking payloads (SARSAT). These payloads are provided by Canada and France. The Soviet Union operates a similar system, the payload on the Soviet satellites being called COSPAS. The main role of the Soviet system is search and rescue, while the NOAA satellites are primarily used for weather purposes and only have a secondary role within the COSPAS-SARSAT system.

The COSPAS spacecraft follow a path inclined 83° to the equator at an altitude of 621 miles (1000 km) and complete a revolution every 106 minutes, compared to the NOAA satellites which are inclined at 99° at an altitude of 528 miles (850 km) and one revolution every 102 minutes. Together the satellites view the whole surface of the earth in less than three hours. The COSPAS-SARSAT satellites handle signals in a similar way. Those on 121.5 MHz are immediately retransmitted on 1544.5 MHz to any LUT (local user terminal) that is in range, whereas 406 MHz signals are processed to establish the identity of the transmitter and stored in an onboard memory to be retransmitted when a LUT comes into view, so that reception by an earth station is assured.

Apart from the spacecraft and their COSPAS-SARSAT payloads, this system includes the EPIRBs (emergency position indicating radio beacons) on board vessels at sea and ELTs (emergency locator transmitters) on board aircraft, earth receiver stations known as local user terminals (LUT) and mission control centres (MCC). The signal from an EPIRB or ELT triggered by an emergency is received by the satellite, processed and retransmitted to the next LUT to come into view. The LUT uses the data in the signal to calculate the approximate position of the source of the signal. This is transmitted to an MCC, where the most conveniently located rescue coordination centre (RCC) is selected and alerted. Final responsibility for carrying out the search and rescue (SAR) rests with the RCC. Four LUTs are in operation in Canada, four in the USSR, three in the USA and one each in the United Kingdom, France, Brazil, Norway and Chile, with additional ones planned in Australia, India, Japan, Pakistan and Venezuela. Mission control centres have already been established in each of those countries.

EPIRB

These lightweight transmitters radiate on three different frequencies: 121.5 MHz, 243 MHz or 406 MHz. The 243 MHz frequency is monitored only by military aircraft. The 121.5 MHz is used by commercial aircraft and ships and was chosen as the distress frequency before the advent of satellites. The 406 MHz frequency was later chosen to take better advantage of the satellite-based system. The 121.5 MHz frequency will be retained for quite some time as it is carried by ships and aircraft worldwide and it will continue to be monitored by air crews and air traffic control centres. The older frequency has several disadvantages and increasingly vessels are choosing the 406 MHz frequency. The satellite-based 406 MHz offers several improvements, such as more accurate location, at an average of 1–3 miles compared to 5–10 miles for the older system. The signals from the new beacons also give the user's identity and they are processed onboard the satellite before being retransmitted. The data is stored in memory for transmission to the next available LUT. This last feature is very important as the 121.5 MHz signals are simply repeated by the satellite and go unheard if there is no earth station within range, whereas the 406 MHz system's storage capability means that COSPAS-SARSAT gives global coverage.

SECTION II

1 Mediterranean and Black Sea

The Mediterranean's reputation as the cradle of western civilisation is undisputed and the beauty of its scenery as well as the wealth of things to see and do ashore more than make up for the less than exhilarating sailing conditions. From the pyramids of Egypt to the Minoan remains on Crete, from the treasures of Asia Minor to the wonders of Ancient Rome, the elegance of the French Riviera or the biblical heritage of Israel, the shores and islands abound in history and many historical sites are close to the sea. The people of the Mediterranean have always looked to the sea for inspiration and so one never has too far to go to get a taste of the fascinating world that has existed for centuries along these shores.

In most parts of the Mediterranean, the sailing season extends from the end of March until November, but is best enjoyed in the spring and autumn when the ports are not crowded and the weather is also more pleasant than at the height of summer. It is possible to sail even in winter but a careful eye has to be kept on the weather as violent storms can occur with little warning. A complete season is the least anyone should plan on spending in the Mediterranean, as distances are deceptive and it is more than 2000 miles from Gibraltar to the Eastern Mediterranean.

If arriving from the Atlantic, it is best to make the long passages first and head straight for the Aegean, if that is one's prime destination. The strong northerly winds that prevail in the Aegean in summer make it advisable to cruise that area from north to south, although it may be difficult to reach the Northern Aegean before the *meltemi* sets in. If an Atlantic crossing is planned at the end of the season, the Eastern Mediterranean should be left by the end of August at the latest so as to be able to cruise leisurely westward. If arriving from the Atlantic later in the year, one can cruise in the Western Mediterranean and, if time permits, plan to spend the following season in the Aegean by heading that way either in the autumn or early the following spring. The choices are easier if arriving in the Mediterranean from the Red Sea, which normally means a spring arrival, in which case the choice is unlimited. Most ports get very crowded in July and August, so during this time one should try and avoid the most popular areas, such as the French Riviera or Greek Cyclades and other known tourist resorts. An increasingly popular detour is to the Adriatic coast of Yugoslavia, whose hundreds of islands and numerous bays have still a long way to go before they reach saturation.

The Black Sea has a much shorter season and the winters can be extremely cold, so cruises in that area should be confined to April or early May to September. With the profound changes taking place in Eastern Europe and the opening up of the area to cruising, many yachts are sailing to the Soviet Union, some also stopping at its former satellites Romania and Bulgaria. Apart from the interest in visiting these formerly closed countries, the cruising attractions are limited, perhaps with the exception of the Georgian coast of the Soviet Union, where the scenery is more dramatic. A cruise to the Black Sea also has the added reward of a sail through Istanbul, the Bosporus and Dardanelles, an experience which in itself may justify the entire trip.

Yachting facilities are well developed in most parts of the Mediterranean and even countries with no sailing tradition, such as Tunisia, Yugoslavia or Turkey, have developed excellent facilities in recent years. For major repairs, however, it is still better to go to one of the long established centres such as Gibraltar, Palma de Mallorca, Antibes, Porto Cervo, Malta, Athens or Larnaca. There are many other places with good facilities spread all over the Mediterranean, but only those mentioned above offer a fully comprehensive range of services.

The benign Mediterranean winters attract many cruising yachts who spend the off season in one of the many marinas, the most popular wintering spots being Gibraltar, Spain's Costa del Sol, the Balearics, Cyprus (Larnaca), Turkey (Kuşadasi), Malta and Tunisia. Generally, the southern and eastern shores are warmer and have a better winter climate. As most countries have restrictions on the time a foreign vessel can spend in their waters, it is essential to make sure that the maximum period is not exceeded. Although the Mediterranean climate makes it possible to live on a boat and even sail for most of the year, for the more adventuresome there is the alternative of heading south at the end of the summer season. From the

Western Mediterranean the obvious destinations are the Canaries and Madeira, while the Red Sea beckons to those in the Eastern Mediterranean. Both have become increasingly popular winter destinations in recent years.

ALBANIA

Situated on the Adriatic Sea between Greece and Yugoslavia is the Socialist Popular Republic of Albania, known as Shqiperia in Albanian. Since the Second World War Albania has been ruled by a strict Stalinist regime, which has systematically discouraged any contact with the outside world. Relations with western nations have been virtually non-existent and even those with fellow communist countries, including the Soviet Union and China, have been poor. From the outside, Albania has been seen as an enclosed enclave within Europe, its separateness enhanced by being the only Muslim country in Europe. Recent events in Eastern Europe seem to have finally found an echo inside the country, and the Albanian government has been seeking to normalise diplomatic relations with some countries. If this trend continues, it will not be long before Albania opens up to the outside world. Hopefully soon yachts will be allowed to call at Albanian ports, something that should be avoided while the present situation continues.

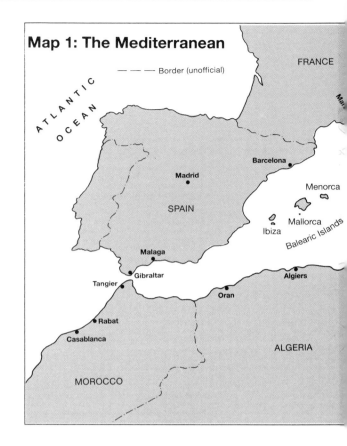

Map 1: The Mediterranean

— — — Border (unofficial)

Country Profile

Albania was under foreign rule for 2000 years as part of the Roman and Byzantine empires, invaded by Goths, then conquered by the Serbs in the north and Bulgars in the south, and it has been successively under Greek, Norman, Serbian and Turkish rule. Part of the Ottoman empire until 1912, Albanian independence was declared after several years of uprisings. The First World War saw the state again under occupation by French, Italian and Serbian troops. In 1917 Italy proclaimed Albania an independent state under Italian

protection, then in 1920 Albania was finally recognised as a sovereign state. From 1922 to 1939 the country was led by Ahmed Zogu, who in 1928 made it a monarchy and became King Zog I. For much of the Second World War Albania was occupied by Italy, then came under German control until liberated by the Allies and Resistance forces. After the war the communists gained power, and in 1946 proclaimed a peoples' republic. Under Enver Hoxha, a strict Stalinist regime was introduced, although links with the Soviet Union were broken. Some links were maintained with China, until the death of Chairman Mao. In 1985 Ramiz Alia replaced Hoxha as leader.

The main elements in the economy are agriculture,

Practical Information

LOCAL TIME: GMT + 1	*ELECTRICITY:* 220 V, 50 Hz	*COMMUNICATIONS*
		There is no direct dialling and any
BUOYAGE: IALA A	*PUBLIC HOLIDAYS*	international calls have to be made
	1 January: New Year's Day	through an operator.
CURRENCY: Lek of 100 quindarka	11 January: Proclamation of the	There are flights from Tirana to various
	Republic	East European capitals, Rome, Vienna,
BUSINESS HOURS	1 May: Labour Day	Athens and Zurich.
Banks: 0700–1400 Monday to Saturday.	28 November: Independence Day	
	29 November: Liberation Day	

mineral extraction (oil and chrome), and livestock raising. Since the war Albania's economy developed considerably, although organised on Stalinist lines, with no private enterprise and an emphasis on heavy industry.

The Albanian-speaking population is 3 million and is mainly Muslim with some Orthodox Christians, although the country is officially atheist and religious practices have been discouraged by the present regime. The capital is Tirana.

The climate is similar to the south of Yugoslavia and on the coast is basically Mediterranean in type, with hot summers and mild winters. The wind in summer is mostly onshore, stronger in the afternoons and dying away at night.

Entry Regulations

Ports of entry
Durres 41°19'N 19°27'E, Vlore 40°29'N 19°29'E, Shengjin 41°49'N 19°36'E, Sarande 39°53'N 20°00'E.

Procedure on arrival
At present yachts who enter Albanian waters are escorted to the nearest port by a patrol boat, and remain there under armed guard until allowed to leave. Those who are forced to call at an Albanian port, because of bad weather or for technical reasons, should make it clear to the authorities that emergency stops are allowed under international maritime law. Those who have no intention of stopping should keep well out of Albanian territorial waters and sail beyond their 12 mile offshore limit.

Immigration
All visitors need visas before arrival. At the time of writing these are not issued to yachts, and the only yachts who have visited Albania have been those who have gone there inadvertently.

Further Reading

Adriatic Pilot

ALGERIA

The Democratic and Popular Republic of Algeria lies on the North African coast between Morocco and Tunisia, and has a mixture of African, Oriental and Mediterranean cultures and traditions. Over 700 miles of coastline fronts the Mediterranean, behind which lie mountains and fertile plains, with the vast Sahara desert to the south. Algeria is a huge country, but much of it is uninhabitable desert and mountains, so most of the population live in cities on the northern coastal strip.

Along its entire length, the Algerian coast has no indentations and all the ports are man-made as there are no natural harbours. With very few exceptions, the ports are crowded and polluted, which is the main reason why cruising yachts very seldom go out of their way to stop in Algeria. The one notable exception is Sidi Fredj, west of the capital Algiers, where a tourist development surrounds the harbour, part of which has been converted into a marina. This is the best place to stop if cruising along the Algerian coast.

Country Profile

Algeria is rare among Mediterranean countries in that the original inhabitants, the Berbers, still make up a sizeable part of the population. The Berbers withdrew to the mountains when invaders came, first the Phoenicians, then the Carthaginians, who controlled the coast around 1100 BC. A thousand years later the area became part of the Roman empire. The Romans were later driven out by the Vandals, followed by the Byzantines and in the seventh century the Arab invasions began. Algeria was ruled by various dynasties as part of the Maghreb together with Morocco and Tunisia. Under Ottoman rule the port of Algiers developed and became a haven for Barbary pirates.

In the nineteenth century France conquered the country and many French settlers immigrated as Algeria was incorporated into France. The Algerians felt alienated, and the 1930s saw the growth of nationalist movements, which became radicalised during the Second World War. In 1954 a rebellion broke out, with Ahmed Ben Bella leading the National Liberation Front (FLN). War with France resulted, and only in 1961 did serious negotiations begin to end this conflict in which over 1 million Algerians lost their lives. A year later Algeria became independent. The first Prime Minister was Ahmed Ben Bella, but although efforts were made to promote economic growth and raise living standards, dissatisfaction continued and in 1965

he was overthrown. A more isolationist foreign policy was followed under Boumediene until his death in 1979. Continuing economic problems have led to civil disturbances in recent years. There is an ongoing conflict with Morocco, as Algeria supports the guerillas fighting Morocco in the Western Sahara.

The discovery of oil and gas has been important to the economy, and there has been some industrialisation, but the majority of the population work in agriculture. Mineral resources are the mainstay of foreign trade and slowly the Sahara is being opened up. Tourism is an expanding industry.

The population is 23 million, being both Arab and Berber, and the majority are Muslim. After independence most settlers of European origin left and many Algerians emigrated to France. Arabic is the official language, but French and Berber dialects are also spoken. Algiers is the capital and has been a port since Roman times, being much feared during the age of Barbary pirates.

The climate is temperate with hot and dry summers. The winters are mild with some rain along the coast. Prevailing summer winds are easterly, while in winter winds are either from the west or north.

Entry Regulations

Ports of entry
Sidi Fredj 36°46′N 2°51′W, Ghazaouet (Ghazawet) 35°06′N 1°52′W, Oran (Wharan) 35°43′N 0°39′W, Mostaganem (Mestghanem) 35°56′N 0°04′E, Ténes 36°31′N 1°19′E, Algiers (Alger/El Djazair) 36°47′N 3°04′E, Tamenfoust 36°49′N 3°14′E, Dellys 36°55′N 3°55′E, Bejaia 36°45′N 5°06′E, Skikda 36°53′N 6°54′E, Annaba 36°54′N 7°45′E, Beni-Saf 35°18′N 1°23′W, Bouharoun 36°38′N 2°40′W, Collo 37°00′N 6°34′E.

Procedure on arrival
Most ports monitor VHF Channels 12 or 14, but apart from Arabic, only French is usually understood. Yachts must clear in and out of each harbour. Sidi Fredj, which has a marina, is the best port of entry as the officials there are used to yachts. One must clear with customs, police and sometimes the military as well.

Customs may search the yacht and will require an inventory. Foreign currency and main dutiable items should be declared. If not the owner of the boat, the captain must have a written authorisation from the owner.

Customs
Firearms need a temporary import licence and deten-

Practical Information

LOCAL TIME: GMT. Summer time GMT + 1 May to October.

BUOYAGE: IALA A

CURRENCY: Algerian dinar (AD) of 100 centimes. A foreign currency declaration form must be completed on arrival and returned on departure. Also on this form one must declare items such as cameras and other equipment. All exchange receipts must be kept. French franc travellers' cheques are the best type to take. One can only import or export AD50 maximum.

BUSINESS HOURS
Friday is the weekly day of rest.
Banks: hours vary, normally 0900–1500 Saturday to Wednesday, 0900–1200 Thursday.
Business: winter 0800–1200/1430–1800 Saturday to Wednesday, 0800–1200

Thursday; summer 0800–1200/1500–1830 Saturday to Wednesday, 0800–1200 Thursday.
Shops: 0800–1200/1430–1800 Saturday to Wednesday.
Government offices: closed Thursday midday to Saturday morning.

ELECTRICITY: 127/220 V, 50 Hz

PUBLIC HOLIDAYS
1 January: New Year's Day
Prophet's birthday*
1 May
Leilat al Meiraj*
19 June: Revival Day
Start of Ramadan*
5 July: Independence Day
Eid al-Fitr*
Eid al-Adhar*
1 November: Anniversary of the Revolution
Hijara*
Al Ashoura*

COMMUNICATIONS
Post office: Algiers, 5 Blvd Mohammed Khemisti for telephones, telegrams, 24-hour telegraph service and telex.
Emergency: dial 14 for police.
There are flights from Algiers to many European and Middle East destinations and some from Oran to European cities.

DIPLOMATIC MISSIONS
In Algiers:
Canada: 27 bis rue d'Anjou, Hydra. ☎ (2) 2606611.
France: rue Larbi Alik, Hydra.
Germany: 165 chemin Findja.
United Kingdom: Residence Cassiopée, Bâtiment B, 7 Chemin des Glycines. ☎ (2) 605601.
United States: 4 chemin Cheich Bachir Brahimi. ☎ (2) 601425.
There is a Cape Verde embassy.

*Variable

tion permit. The firearms are held by police or customs until departure.

Animals must have vaccination certificates.

Immigration

A visa is not required for up to a three-month stay by nationals of: Andorra, Denmark, Egypt, Finland, France, Guinea, Iceland, Iraq, Italy, Ireland, Jordan, Kuwait, Lebanon, Liechtenstein, Mali, Monaco, Norway, San Marino, Spain, Sudan, Sweden, Switzerland, Syria, Tunisia, UK and Yugoslavia. For all other nationalities including Canada, Germany, the Netherlands and USA, a visa is necessary. This should be obtained in advance from Algerian diplomatic missions and consulates abroad. Visas cannot be issued on arrival. There are Algerian consulates in Morocco and Tunisia.

Nationals of Israel, Malawi, South Africa, South Korea and Taiwan are refused entry. Entry is also refused to holders of passports containing an Israeli stamp.

Fees

Overtime fee for customs clearance outside office hours is 1000 DA.

Port charges are free for under 48 hours, after which for an 8 to 10 metre LOA boat, 100 DA per day is charged.

Facilities

Only basic facilities are available in most ports and provisioning in the smaller towns is limited. There are some repair facilities in Sidi Fredj, which has a number of locally owned yachts. There is a 16-ton travelift as well as fuel and water in the marina. In most other ports fuel has to be bought in jerrycans.

Further Reading

Mediterranean Cruising Handbook
Traveller's Guide to North Africa

BULGARIA

In the eastern Balkans, Bulgaria has a coastline on the Black Sea. A small boating community thrives around the port of Varna and in spite of the restrictions imposed by the communist regime in the past, Bulgarian sailors have managed to cruise the Mediterranean, take part in the OSTAR transatlantic single-handed race and one intrepid family have even circumnavigated the globe. There are not many places to cruise to along the coast, but in Varna foreign sailors have always been warmly welcomed and this welcome

Practical Information

LOCAL TIME: GMT + 2. Summer time GMT + 3 April 1 to September 31.

BUOYAGE: IALA A

CURRENCY: Lev (plural: leva), of 100 stotinki (1 stotinka)

BUSINESS HOURS
Shops: 0830–1800; rural areas may close 1200–1500.
Government offices: 0730–1530 Monday to Friday, also alternate Saturdays.

ELECTRICITY: 220 V, 50 Hz

PUBLIC HOLIDAYS
1 January: New Year's Day
3 March: Liberation Day
1–2 May: Labour Days
24 May: Education Day
9–10 September: National Days
7 November: Anniversary of the October Revolution

COMMUNICATIONS
International telephone calls can be made from post offices 0830–1730 Monday to Saturday.
There are international flights from Sofia to most European capitals and charter flights from Varna during summer.

DIPLOMATIC MISSIONS
In Sofia:
United Kingdom: Boulevard Marshal Tolbukhin 65–67. ☎ (2) 885361.
United States: 1A Stamboliiski Boulevard. ☎ (2) 884801.

is certain to continue as restrictions on both local and foreign sailors are considerably eased with the changing political situation.

Country Profile

The Bulgars, of Asiatic origin, crossed the Danube in the seventh century and established the first Bulgarian kingdom, which was later incorporated into the Byzantine Empire. Then the Second Bulgarian Empire was founded by the Asens, until conquered by the Ottoman Turks in 1396. Under Turkish rule some parts of the country were converted to Islam, and Turks settled in the eastern parts.

The Bulgarians rose up against the Turks several times, the most notorious uprising causing the 'Bulgarian atrocities' of 1876 when resistance was brutally crushed. After the Russo–Turkish War of 1877–8, the Congress of Berlin made Bulgaria an autonomous principality under Alexander I, but still dependent on Turkey. Ferdinand of Saxe-Coburg was elected prince in 1889, and became czar when Bulgaria was declared an independent kingdom in 1908.

The First Balkan War of 1912 saw Bulgaria join Serbia, Greece and Montenegro against Turkey, but the issue of the partition of Macedonia led to Bulgaria attacking her allies the following year, only to be defeated and losing both Macedonia and Thrace. An ally of Germany in the First World War, Bulgaria invaded Serbia in 1915. As a defeated power, after the war Bulgaria lost her Aegean coast and most of Macedonia. Boris III ruled the country from 1918 to 1943, with an increasingly reactionary regime. Bulgaria was neutral at the outbreak of the Second World War, then joined the Axis powers. In 1944 the Red Army occupied the country and a pro-Soviet government was formed, which declared war on Germany. A republic was proclaimed in 1946, led by the communists, and a socialist state built along Stalinist lines. Since the war Bulgaria, which traditionally had close links with Russia, has remained in the Soviet camp, one of the last East European countries to respond to the liberalisation occurring in the rest of the communist bloc.

Agriculture remains important. It is mostly collectivised, producing mainly wheat and maize, as well as tobacco, fruit and wine which are the main exports. The iron, steel and chemical industries have developed as well as the traditional textile and food industries.

The population of Bulgaria is 9 million, being mainly Bulgarians, a Slav people, but with Turkish, Macedonian, Armenian, Romanian and gypsy minorities. The Bulgarian language is close to Russian and also uses the Cyrillic alphabet. Turkish and Macedonian are spoken by the respective minorities. Many Bulgarians speak foreign languages, such as French and German but also English. Despite being officially an atheistic state, many Bulgarians are Orthodox Christian and there is also a Muslim minority. The capital is Sofia.

The climate is similar to the Northern Mediterranean, with very hot summers, but colder winters. The prevailing winds of summer are north east, although there is a daily alternation of land and sea breezes.

Entry Regulations

Ports of entry
Burgas 42°30′N 27°29′E, Nessebar 42°40′N 27°44′E, Varna 43°12′N 27°55′E.

Procedure on arrival
One must clear with customs, health and immigration.

The formalities are not complicated, but passports and ship's papers may be retained until departure. There are military ports along the coast and it is wise to check with authorities concerning any sensitive or restricted areas.

Customs
Firearms will be impounded until departure. Animals may be confined on board.

Immigration
It is recommended that visas are obtained in advance. A tourist visa, valid for three months from issue, gives 30 days stay. Extensions are rarely granted.

There is a Bulgarian consulate in Istanbul, where visas are issued in one hour, US$15 per person. Visas can also be obtained on arrival and cost US$24.

Facilities

Only simple repairs are possible and the best workshops are located in Varna, where there is also a slipway. For any repairs it is best to consult the Varna Yacht Club for advice. The club welcomes visitors, particularly at the beginning of July when it holds its annual regatta from Varna to Kavarna. The club charges visiting yachts about US$5 per day for the use of their facilities and a yacht can be left there if travelling inland. Provisioning is rather limited, although there is a reasonable selection of fresh produce. Fuel is available in all ports. The best charts for the Black Sea are Turkish and can be bought in Istanbul.

CYPRUS

A large island tucked into the eastern corner of the Mediterranean, Cyprus has a strategic position, being within close range of Turkey, Syria, Lebanon and Israel. Ironically it is further from Greece, with which it has the closest ties. Cyprus is an attractive island with a pleasant climate, beautiful mountainous landscape and interesting archaeological sites. According to legend, Aphrodite, the Greek goddess of love, emerged from the sea at Paphos. Recent history has been less romantic and since 1974 the island has been divided, with UN troops patrolling the border between the Greek Republic of Cyprus in the south and the northern Turkish Republic of Cyprus.

Southern Cyprus, and Larnaca in particular, has gained great popularity as one of the favourite wintering spots for long-distance cruising yachts. Many of these reach Cyprus after transiting the Suez Canal, while others sail to Cyprus from other parts of the Mediterranean at the end of the cruising season. Lacking natural harbours and anchorages, Cyprus has always been an island to visit from its ports, rather than to cruise around. This has been made even more necessary by the ongoing conflict between south and north which has reduced the few cruising attractions that the island had in the past. However, the reputation of Cyprus as an excellent base for repairs and reprovisioning has ensured its continuing popularity.

Country Profile

The name Kypros comes from Aphrodite's Greek name, Kipris. In ancient times copper deposits brought considerable wealth to the island and many people came to settle, especially Greeks from the mainland. Due to its position Cyprus experienced many invasions and different rulers over the centuries reflecting the history of the region. It was claimed by the Assyrians, Egyptians and Persians, then ruled by Alexander the Great until his death in 323 BC. The Romans were the next to take over and during this time St Paul visited and converted the Roman proconsul in Paphos to Christianity. Later Cyprus became part of the Byzantine Empire until the island was seized by Richard the Lionheart in 1191 during the Crusades. Periods of rule followed by the Franks, Venetians and Ottoman Turks until the late nineteenth century, when the administration was taken over by Britain.

Cyprus was a British colony from 1914 until 1960 when following several years of fighting against the British troops, the independent Republic of Cyprus was established. Later civil war broke out between the Greeks and Turks living on the island and in 1964 the Turkish Cypriots established a Provisional Administration, which was not recognised by the Greek Cypriots. Ten years later a military coup was carried out by Greek officers and following that troops were sent in from Turkey, occupying the northern part of the island, which was declared the North Cyprus Turkish Republic. In 1983 it became the 'Turkish Republic of Cyprus', but has not been recognised by any other countries except Turkey. The Greek Republic of Cyprus, which controls 60 per cent of the island, is internationally recognised as the government of Cyprus. The situation is still far from being resolved.

Cyprus has an agricultural economy with a small manufacturing industry. Tourism is the main industry of the island and most of the commerce is in the southern areas of the Greek Republic.

The population of the island is 640,000 and is

Practical Information

REPUBLIC OF CYPRUS
Information is given for the southern Republic. Information which is different and applies only to the northern Turkish Republic is given separately at the end of the section.

LOCAL TIME: GMT + 3. Summer time GMT + 4 last weekend in March until last weekend in September.

BUOYAGE: IALA A

CURRENCY: Cyprus pound (C£) of 100 cents. No more than C£50 may be exported or imported.

BUSINESS HOURS
Banks: 0800–1200 Monday to Saturday. Main banks open for exchange in afternoons.
Some exchange facilities open 1530–1730 Monday to Friday.
Business and shops: 0800–1300 Monday to Saturday; afternoons, winter 1430–1730, summer 1600–1900, closed Wednesday and Saturday afternoons all year.
Government offices: 0730/0800–1400 Monday to Friday.

ELECTRICITY: 240 V, 50 Hz

PUBLIC HOLIDAYS
1 January: New Year's Day
6 January: Epiphany
Kathara Deftera (Orthodox Shrove Tuesday)*
25 March: Greek Independence Day
1 April: Greek Cypriot National Day
Orthodox Good Friday, Saturday, Monday*
1 May
15 August: Assumption
1 October: Cyprus Independence Day
28 October: Ohi Day
25, 26 December: Christmas
*Variable

EVENTS
Easter is the biggest event in the Orthodox calendar.
Kataklysmos, which means flood and coincides with Pentecost, is a festival unique to Cyprus.

COMMUNICATIONS
Telephones: CITA offices. International operator 192.
Post office: 0730–1330 (1300 in summer) Monday to Saturday, some open in the afternoon. Poste restante and afternoon service: King Paul Square, Larnaca; Eleftheria Square, Nicosia; 1 Gladstone Street, Limassol; Themidos and St Paul Streets, Paphos.

Emergency: dial 199.
There are no postal or telephone communications between the two republics, except by various banks and the British diplomatic missions.
There are international flights from Larnaca to many European and Middle East destinations.

MEDICAL
There is a high standard of medical services.
There are decompression chambers at Nicosia General Hospital and at Akrotiri Hospital near Limassol.

DIPLOMATIC MISSIONS
In Nicosia:
Canada: 13 Themistocles Dervis Street.
☎ (2) 451630.
Egypt: 3 Egypt Avenue (0800–1400 Monday to Friday).
Israel: 4, I. Gryparis Street.
Syria: Corner Androcleous and Thoukidides Street.
United Kingdom: Alexander Pallis Street.
☎ (2) 473131.
United States: Dositheos and Therissos Street. ☎ (2) 65151.

divided on ethnic grounds. The last census in 1960 found 80 per cent Greek Cypriot and 18 per cent Turkish Cypriot. Since the division of the island, Greek Cypriots have left the northern sector for the south and vice versa. There are small minorities of Armenians, Britons and gypsies. Greek is the main language of the island and most Greek Cypriots are Orthodox Christians, although there are some other denominations. Turkish is spoken in the northern sector and most Turkish Cypriots are Muslim. English is widely spoken. Nicosia has been the capital since the tenth century and the old walled city can still be seen within the modern metropolis.

Cyprus has an island climate with daily breezes that can get strong in the afternoons. It is usually calm at night. The summers are very hot and humid with temperatures up to 44°C in July and August. The winters are generally mild and pleasantly sunny, although gales from the south or east do track across the Mediterranean. September to November are usually the best months for cruising.

Entry Regulations

Ports of entry
Larnaca (marina and port) 34°55′N 33°38′E, Limassol 34°40′N 33°03′E, Paphos 34°45′N 32°25′E.

Procedure on arrival
Cyprus Radio maintains continuous watch on VHF Channels 16 and 26. The Cypriot courtesy flag must be flown when entering Greek Cypriot waters. In no circumstances enter any of the above ports flying a Turkish flag as this will cause serious offence. Everyone should remain on board until clearance formalities are completed. Ship's papers will be required by the port authority on arrival. Evidence of insurance may also be requested. A total of five crew lists will be needed.

If a yacht enters Cyprus at a port in the Turkish sector, this is considered by the Greek Republic to be illegal entry and the yacht will not be allowed into the country. The movement of vessels is closely monitored and if a yacht goes directly from the Turkish to the Greek sector, the captain and crew are liable to be arrested. The penalty for illegal entry is up to US$20,000 and/or six months imprisonment.

If a yacht has visited the Turkish sector for any reason, it should then sail to an intermediate port in Turkey, Israel or Syria before returning to clear into Greek Cyprus. Relations with the Turkish sector are very delicate and visitors should avoid getting caught in this war of nerves.

Customs
Firearms must be declared and surrendered to customs on arrival. Sporting guns require a temporary permit which has to be obtained from the Ministry of the Interior.

For animals, an import permit must be obtained in advance from the Director of the Department of Veterinary Services, Nicosia. Animals must remain on board, which is called home quarantine. Dogs and cats have a six-month quarantine period. Parrots and budgerigars are prohibited.

Antiques may not be exported.

Yachts may stay up to one year without paying taxes, as they are considered to be temporarily imported. For an extension a customs authority is needed. This is normally granted up to a total of five years, any number of visits being cumulative and during this time no taxes are paid. During this period foreign yachts can import spare parts duty-free.

Duty-free stores should be declared on entry and may be removed and retained by customs until departure. Duty-free stores are available 24 hours before departure, spirits being limited to one case per person. Duty-free may be obtained in all ports where there are bonded stores.

Immigration
No visas are required by nationals of most countries in Europe, the Americas, Australia, New Zealand and Japan for stays of up to three months. A permit to stay more than three months may be issued by the Chief Immigration officer, Nicosia. Immigration normally retains passports and each person is issued with a landing permit.

Restrictions
There are ill-defined military restricted areas along the coasts and yachts should maintain a distance of 500 metres offshore by day and 1000 metres by night unless approaching a port. Spearfishing is prohibited within bathing areas, which are marked by red buoys. A special licence is required for spearfishing with scuba gear. This is issued only to certified divers and is easily obtained from the District Fisheries Departments, on presentation of a certified diving licence. There is no charge. It is forbidden to take antiquities and sponges from the sea.

Facilities
Every autumn, at the end of the cruising season in the Eastern Mediterranean, scores of cruising yachts congregate in Larnaca preparing for hibernation. Their presence has encouraged the setting up of several workshops, which can deal with a complete range of repairs. Woodwork, carpentry and rigging work is undertaken by a boatyard located in the marina, which also operates a 40-ton travelift. Fuel, LPG and nautical charts are all available and there is also a small chandlery with a limited stock of marine supplies. There are several supermarkets and also a fresh produce market nearby. A marina was opened in Limassol recently, which also has a boatyard and travelift. There is a good selection of marine equipment and the main engine agents are also located in this large commercial harbour.

Further Reading
Mediterranean Cruising Handbook

TURKISH REPUBLIC OF CYPRUS

This is referred to as the 'occupied zone' by Greek Cypriots. With a special pass, visitors who have legally entered Greek Cyprus may cross into the occupied zone and return the same day, through a frontier checkpoint at Ledra Palace Hotel, Nicosia.

Entry Regulations
Ports of entry
Famagusta (Gaze Magosa) 35°07'N 33°56'E, Kyrenia (Girne) 35°20'N 33°19'E.

Procedure on arrival
It is possible to sail from a Greek Cypriot port to a port in the Turkish Republic of Cyprus, so if a yacht does wish to visit the north of the island they should do so after leaving the southern Greek Republic and before proceeding elsewhere.

The Turkish courtesy flag should be flown if approaching Turkish Cyprus. The entry formalities are similar to those in Turkey. The crew passports may be retained in exchange for landing passes.

Practical Information

CURRENCY: Turkish lire are used.

BUSINESS HOURS
Government offices: 0730/0800–1400
Monday to Friday.

PUBLIC HOLIDAYS
1 January: New Year's Day
23 April: Children's Bairam
1 May
19 May: Sports and Youth Bairam
Prophet's birthday*
Sheker Bairam – Ramadan, 2 days*
Qurban Bairam, feast of Sacrifices,
3 days*
30 August

29 October: Turkish Independence Day
15 November

COMMUNICATIONS
All mail directed to 'Cyprus' goes
automatically to the Greek sector. The
correct postal address for any mail to the
Turkish side is 'Mersin 10, Turkey' (Cyprus
must not appear on the envelope).
*Variable

Restrictions

There are ill-defined military zones and it is wise to keep well away from the coast, especially along the north coast and round Cape Andera at the north-eastern end of Karpass Peninsula. In fact because of so many prohibited areas, only the ports of Famagusta and Kyrenia should be approached if sailing to Turkish Cyprus.

Facilities

Facilities in Northern Cyprus are limited, with only simple repairs possible in Kyrenia. There is a small slipway capable of hauling out boats of up to 45 ft. Fuel is available from a station near the port. Provisioning is adequate but prices tend to be higher than in both Turkey and Southern Cyprus.

EGYPT

The Pyramids and the Sphinx at Giza, the temples of Luxor and Karnak, the Valleys of the Kings and Queens are some of the places which make Egypt a major tourist destination and most of the visiting sailors also try to see at least some of these ancient sites. Egypt occupies a large area of northern Africa, but most of it is barren, flat desert. It is only the river Nile which makes Egypt cultivable and most of the population lives in the fertile area around this great river. To the west of the Nile lies the Western desert and Libya, while to the east lies the Red Sea, Suez Canal and the Sinai desert.

Most sailors come to know Egypt through transiting the Suez Canal and very few yachts sail to Egypt solely to visit the country. For those sailing in the Mediterranean, the only alternative to Port Said is the ancient port of Alexandria, a good place to leave the yacht while visiting the interior. Occasionally yachts manage to obtain a permit to sail up the Nile, which is

a fascinating way to see Egypt, although most certainly not the easiest.

Those who approach Egypt from the Red Sea have the opportunity to appreciate the only area of the country which is worth cruising, the reefs and bays that stretch all the way from the Sudanese border to the Gulf of Suez. Day sailing along this coast is the most pleasant way to make progress against the prevailing northerlies. As the Red Sea is increasingly becoming a cruising destination in its own right and yachts sail from the Mediterranean to spend the winter in its more pleasant climate, this coast of Egypt is becoming better known. Whether coming from south or north, the transiting of the Suez Canal is an exciting experience, which can be better appreciated now that the formalities are becoming slightly less complicated.

Country Profile

Egypt has 5000 years of recorded history and one of the earliest civilisations in the world. In 3188 BC Menes united the Upper and Lower Kingdoms with Memphis as the capital, and the pyramids were built during this period. After this came the Middle Kingdom, with its centre at Thebes, which is present day Luxor. The New Kingdom, which was the era of Queen Nefertiti and Tutankhamun, established an empire in the sixteenth to the fourteenth centuries BC. Invasions from Libya, Nubia, Ethiopia and Assyria brought about the empire's decline. The era of the Pharaohs finally ended with the arrival of Alexander the Great in 332 BC. Alexandria became the new capital, a sophisticated city, which was a centre of Greek culture and civilisation. Later it became the cultural centre of the Roman empire. Queen Cleopatra gave the country first to Julius Caesar and then to Mark Antony. After their deaths Rome took over Egypt and the country was the granary of Rome for 650 years.

Arab invasions swept across Egypt from the seventh to the tenth centuries and the capital moved to present-

Practical Information

LOCAL TIME: GMT + 2

BUOYAGE: IALA A

CURRENCY: Egyptian pound (E£) of 100 piastres. No more than E£20 can be taken out of the country, but unused currency can be changed back before departure. A foreign currency declaration must be made on arrival and exchange receipts should be kept. Visitors usually have to change a certain amount per day, although this does not apply to yachts only transiting the Suez Canal and not visiting anywhere else in the country.

BUSINESS HOURS
Friday is the day of rest.
Banks: 0900–1230 Monday to Thursday and Saturday, 1000–1200 Sunday.
Business: summer 0830–1400 Monday to Thursday, winter 0900–1300/1600–1900 except Thursday afternoons and Fridays.
Shops: 0900–1330/1700–2000 Monday to Thursday.
Government offices: summer 0900–1400 Monday to Thursday except holidays; winter 0900–1300/1600–1900 Monday to Wednesday and Thursday mornings.

ELECTRICITY: 110/220 V, 50 Hz

PUBLIC HOLIDAYS
1 January: New Year's Day
22 February: Unity Day
1 May: Labour Day
18 June: Republic Day
1 September: Revolution Day
6 October: Armed Forces Day
24 October: Suez Day
23 December: Victory Day
Variable holidays: Ashoura, Mouloud, Ramadan, Eid el-Fitr, Eid el-Adha, Hijira, 1st Monday after Coptic Easter, Sham el-Nessim (National Spring Festival).
If a holiday falls on a Friday, the following Saturday may also be a holiday.

EVENTS
December Nile festival in Cairo and Luxor.

COMMUNICATIONS
International calls have to be booked in advance and delays are possible.
Post offices open daily Saturday to Thursday.

Mail is slow and not very reliable. There are frequent international flights from Cairo to all major cities in Africa, the Middle East and Europe. There are also internal flights to Luxor and Aswan.

MEDICAL
There are good hospitals in Cairo and Alexandria, but poor facilities elsewhere. Treatment for foreigners can be expensive.

DIPLOMATIC MISSIONS
In Cairo:
Canada: 6 Mohammed Fahmi El Sayed St, Garden City, Kasr el Doubara. ☎ (2) 3543110.
Sudan: 1 Mohammed Fahmi el Sayed St, Garden City. ☎ (2) 25043.
United Kingdom: Ahmed Ragheb St, Garden City, ☎ (2) 3540850.
United States: 5 Sharia Latin America. ☎ (2) 28219, 774666.
In Alexandria:
United States: 110 Avenue Horreya. ☎ (3) 801911.

day Cairo. In the early sixteenth century the Ottoman Turks gained control and Egypt became an unimportant province of their vast empire.

In 1798 Napoleon's expedition to Egypt opened it up to modern European influence. France's subsequent withdrawal created a power struggle, until the Albanian Muhammed Ali became Sultan. Efforts were made to modernise the country and in 1869 the Suez Canal was opened. Britain occupied Egypt 13 years later, but nationalist feelings grew amongst the Egyptians and in 1922 Egypt was recognised as an independent state by Britain, although they occupied the country until 1936 and even after that British troops remained in the Canal area. Amid growing dissatisfaction with Egypt's status and the monarchy, in 1952 a military coup and nationalist revolution led by Gamal Abdel Nasser established a republic. Nasser nationalised the Suez Canal, which provoked the Suez Crisis of 1956, and the military intervention of Israel, France and Britain. Anwar Sadat succeeded Nasser in 1970, establishing better links with the West, and ending the ongoing state of war with Israel in 1979. Sadat was assassinated in 1981, but Egypt still maintains rela-

tions with Israel, despite pressure from other Arab states.

Egypt is agricultural and half the population work in this domain. There is considerable poverty and high unemployment. However, industry is expanding and tourism, the Suez Canal and oil revenues make important contributions to the economy.

The population numbers almost 50 million, comprising Egyptians, Bedouins, Nubians, Arabs and some Italian, Greek and Armenian communities. About 7 million are Copts, who claim to be descendants of the original inhabitants, a Hamitic people who lived along the Nile. Islam is the religion of the majority, although the Copts are Christian, the Coptic church being one of the oldest in existence. There is also a small Jewish community. Arabic is the official language, but some English and French is spoken in the cities. The capital is Cairo, with a population of over 7 million, being the largest city in Africa.

The summers are very hot with extremely high temperatures both inland and in the Red Sea. Winters are mild with little rain. The prevailing winds are northerly. Occasionally the *khamsin*, a hot dry wind, blows off the land laden with dust and sand reducing visibility. The prevailing winds in the Red Sea are northerly, while along the Mediterranean coast there are daily alternating land and sea breezes.

Entry Regulations

Ports of entry
Alexandria 31°11′N 29°52′E, Port Said 31°15′N 32°18′E, Suez 29°58′N 32°33′E, Hurghada 27°15′N 33°49′E, Sharm el Sheik 27°51′N 34°17′E.

Procedure on arrival
The Coast Guard normally maintain a presence in all ports and anchorages, and usually visit the yacht, requesting details of the yacht and its crew. In ports of entry, clearance must be done with customs, health and immigration. Customs make a list of the main dutiable items on board and this is checked again before departure.

Port Said Because of the high density of shipping traffic and the difficult approach to Port Said, the

harbour should not be entered at night. Yachts are normally met by a pilot boat and directed to the Port Fouad Yacht Club on the eastern side of the harbour. If the yacht is transiting the canal and only staying in Port Said as long as it takes to make arrangements for the transit, immigration formalities are simple and no visas will be issued. Those who wish to stay longer and visit other parts of Egypt need to go through the normal entry procedure. See below for further instructions concerning formalities for transiting the Suez Canal.

Suez Yachts are usually met in the approaches by a pilot boat. Otherwise yachts should anchor in the waiting area in Port Ibrahim and contact Port Control on VHF Channel 16 for permission to go to Port Tewfik Yacht Club. Some formalities, such as immigration and health, may have to be completed before proceeding to the yacht club, which is located on the left-hand side of the Canal, just beyond the Canal Authority buildings. Yachts are also met by boats of various agents, who offer their services to deal with all the necessary formalities. If an agent is employed, he will take the passports to immigration and return with the shore passes, which are needed to gain access to the yacht club.

Alexandria Yachts must go to the eastern harbour, and anchor off the Yacht Club of Egypt, who will help with formalities.

Outward clearance
If transiting the Canal and not stopping anywhere else after the transit, the outward clearance can be obtained while doing the transit formalities. Yachts may then proceed to sea as soon as they have dropped the pilot. Once outward clearance is obtained, yachts must leave within 24 hours, or obtain another clearance.

Customs
A list of firearms, with their type and details, must be handed to the authorities on arrival.

There are no restrictions on animals.

Yachts may remain in Egypt for a maximum of six months.

Immigration
Visas are not needed by anyone travelling on a yacht transiting the Suez Canal and remaining in the port area. Shore passes will be issued by immigration on arrival. However, those who intend to visit other places in Egypt must obtain a visa exactly as do other tourists. Nationals of Malta and Arab countries do not require visas. It is advisable to obtain a visa beforehand, although it is usually possible to obtain one on arrival.

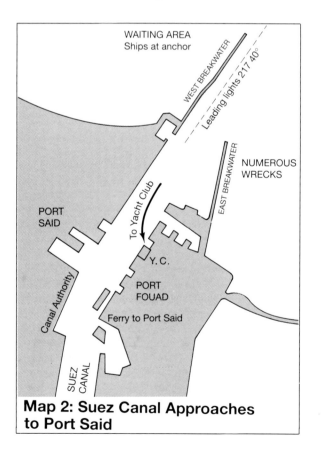

Map 2: Suez Canal Approaches to Port Said

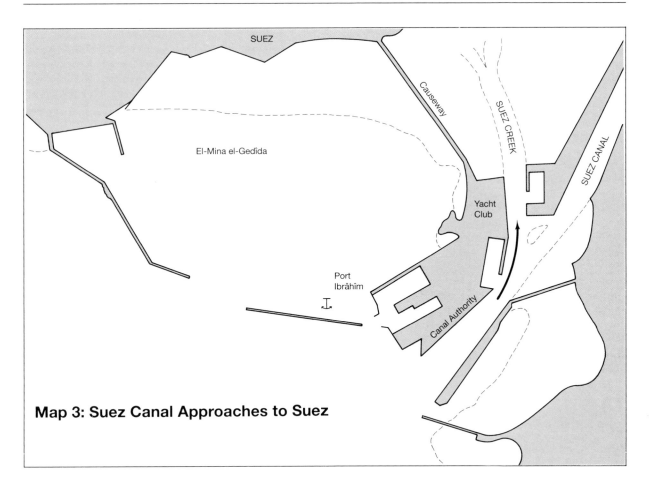

El-Mina el-Gedîda

SUEZ

Causeway

SUEZ CREEK

SUEZ CANAL

Yacht Club

Port Ibrâhîm

Canal Authority

Map 3: Suez Canal Approaches to Suez

Tourist visas are issued for any period up to one month and multiple entry visas can be obtained from Egyptian consulates. All visitors must change US$150 into E£ on arrival. An extension to a visa can be obtained from the police, in which case one has to change another US$150 and show the bank receipt. One may overstay the visa by 15 days, provided one has a good reason, but after this time an extension must be applied for, otherwise one may be fined. Money must be changed each time an extension is obtained. Children under 12 years do not have to change money. Passports must be valid for six months beyond the visa period. Nationals of Taiwan, Yemen and Libya are not allowed entry. Israeli nationals must have a visa obtained in advance from the Egyptian embassy in Israel. South African nationals must also get a visa in advance from an Egyptian consulate abroad. There are Egyptian embassies or consulates in most nearby countries, including Israel (Tel Aviv).

If planning to visit Israel and return to Egypt, it is possible to buy a re-entry permit, which expires one day before the original visa expires, but one does not have to change money on one's return. If visiting Israel from Egypt, even if the Israelis put their stamp on a separate piece of paper, the entry and exit stamps on the Egyptian border will be in the passport. This can be a problem if wanting to visit any other Arab countries, who normally refuse entry to anyone who has visited Israel. In this case it may be necessary to obtain a new passport from one's embassy in Cairo.

Cruising permit

This must be obtained from the Egyptian Coast Guard through one of the yacht clubs. Outside of the official ports of entry, in other ports and anchorages, one may not go ashore except with special permission from the local authorities. Most anchorages have an army post or military station, who usually ask for the yacht's papers. Yachts coming from Sudan and making overnight stops without going ashore do not normally require a cruising permit. If sheltering from strong winds or making an overnight stop, yachts are normally allowed to stay in Egyptian waters before clearing in at an official port of entry. If coming from the Red Sea and intending to stop in Egypt before clearing in, it is advisable to have obtained a visa in advance.

Health
Typhoid, tetanus, polio and hepatitis vaccinations are recommended, as is malaria prophylaxis.

River Nile
A security permit has to be obtained from the Coast Guard as well as permission from the Ministry of Foreign Affairs to navigate the river. The permit is difficult to obtain, although the Yacht Club of Egypt in Alexandria may be able to help. Navigation in the channels is restricted to daytime only. There are several bridges and locks, which open at certain times of the day or on request. Taking photographs of bridges, barrages and dams is strictly forbidden. The maximum draft must not exceed 5 feet (1.5 metres). Navigation is only possible during winter, from October to May, when the level of water is higher. The river depth falls considerably during the summer months.

Fees
Overtime is charged after 1400 Saturday to Thursday and all day Friday.
Customs E£20.
Immigration: visa fee if issued on arrival $US15.
Health E£5.
Departure fees, harbour and light dues.
There are various fees for the Suez Canal. In 1990 the following fees were quoted: insurance E£7.75, Canal transit fee US$20, pilotage fee US$26, US$10 per crew member.

All agent's and Suez Canal fees must be paid in US dollars, therefore some cash should be carried. As a guideline, the Prince of the Red Sea shipping agency in Suez charged in 1990 an all inclusive fee of US$125 for the transit plus US$10 per crew member.

Restrictions
All military zones are prohibited areas.
Spearfishing, the taking of reef fish, collecting of coral, shells and marine animals, are all forbidden in the Red Sea.

Facilities

In both Port Said and Suez, cruising yachts normally berth at the local yacht club, which charges a daily fee. Provisioning is somewhat better in Port Said, which is a duty-free port and stores can be ordered and delivered to the yacht club. There are daily fresh produce markets in both ports. Fuel is sometimes difficult to obtain at the normal pump price, as there is a surcharge for foreign vessels; however, this can be usually avoided. In 1990 each transiting yacht was allowed to buy 200 litres (44 imp. gallons) at the normal pump price, which is extremely cheap. LPG can be found in Suez with the help of the Prince of the Red Sea, a local shipping agent who should be contacted for any kind of help, as he has built up a reputation of being able to fix anything.

The yacht club in Alexandria, located in the eastern harbour, normally allows visitors to use its facilities. Provisioning is good and repair facilities are better than anywhere else in Egypt. There are various workshops known to the yacht club which can undertake engine, electrical and some electronic repairs as well as fibreglass, metal work and carpentry. Nautical charts are also available in Alexandria. There are slipways at Alexandria, Port Said and Suez. Only basic provisions are available at Hurghada, on the Red Sea.

Arrangements can be made at any of the clubs to leave the boat while visiting the interior of Egypt. A local watchman should always be employed in such a case.

Procedure for Transiting the Suez Canal

Port Said Captains of yachts intending to transit the Canal will be informed at the yacht club either by a club official or an official of the Canal Authority on the correct procedure to follow. Although time consuming, taking about 2–3 days, the formalities can be carried out by the captain alone and the service of an agent is not essential. The captain first has to visit the Small Craft Department in the main building of the Canal Authority in Port Said. He will be instructed as to the various formalities to be carried out and also the payments to be made. These payments include the transiting fee, insurance policy, ports and lights fee. The following offices have to be visited:

1. Customs, to obtain a customs clearance certificate.
2. Credit and Commerce Bank to pay the transit fee in foreign currency, and obtain a draft payable to the Suez Canal Authority.
3. Misr Insurance Company, or other insurance company, to obtain an insurance policy for the transit.
4. Ports and Lights Administration, to obtain a harbour clearance permit.
5. Port harbour police station, to obtain a security clearance certificate.

The captain then has to take these five documents back to the Small Craft Department to arrange a technical inspection of the yacht. Following this inspection, a transit permit will be issued and a time arranged for the pilot to come on board. The captain will then have to go with the passports of all on board to the immigration office to have them stamped.

On the day of the transit the pilot will arrive early in the morning to guide the yacht as far as Ismailia in the NW corner of Lake Timsah, where the yacht must spend the night as yachts are not allowed to transit at night. The crew are not allowed to go ashore. Early the following morning, either the same pilot or another one will continue the transit to Suez. Normally yachts stop at the Port Tewfik Yacht Club before continuing into the Red Sea.

Suez After contacting the port authority on VHF Channel 16 and having completed the initial clearance formalities, if permission has been obtained to proceed to Port Tewfik Yacht Club, the yacht should make its way to the club. This is located on the left-hand side of the Canal beyond the Canal Administration building. To transit the Canal, the same formalities have to be gone through as those described for Port Said.

Yachts approaching Suez are usually met by one or more agents who offer to complete transit formalities on their behalf. Although not compulsory, it is advisable to employ the services of an agent in Suez, as it is more difficult to complete the formalities alone than in Port Said. If using an agent, all fees should be agreed in advance and the agent should also be asked to specify exactly which fees and services are included. The agent with the best reputation and who handles most cruising yachts in Suez is Fathi Soukar (Prince of the Red Sea). He normally monitors VHF Channel 16.

The procedure for the transit is identical to the southward passage: the pilot will arrive early in the morning and the night will be spent at Ismailia where the pilot will board the following day and take the vessel to Port Said.

Canal regulations
Yachts must be capable of a consistent speed of 5 knots, which will be checked during the technical inspection. The speed limit in the canal is 9 knots. Yachts normally transit just after the morning convoy.

Further Reading

Yachtsman's Guide to Egypt
Mediterranean Cruising Handbook
Africa on a Shoestring

GIBRALTAR

At the crossroads of two seas and two continents, Gibraltar's unique position as the gateway to the Mediterranean has given it an importance far exceeding its small size and population. Only two and a half miles long, barely a mile wide, the peninsula drops sheerly from a height of 1400 feet down to the sea. The rock is made of limestone and riddled with caves, a feature used by all its inhabitants throughout the ages.

Very few yachts on their way to or from the Mediterranean fail to stop in this historic port, which has become one of the most frequented yachting centres in the world. Over 5000 yachts from all parts of the globe call at Gibraltar every year and the facilities at their disposal are improving all the time. A large new marina is planned for the near future, while the existing marinas are expanding and upgrading their present facilities. Although many yachts spend considerable time in Gibraltar, its main function continues to be that of a transit port, a role which the Rock has fulfilled throughout its colourful and often turbulent history. The movement of yachts is virtually continuous, although there are clearly defined peak periods. Spring and early summer sees boats arriving from across the Atlantic or Northern Europe bound for the Mediterranean. The autumn months see a large movement in the opposite direction as many cruising yachts leave the Mediterranean, usually bound for Madeira and the Canaries en route to the Caribbean. Although a convenient place for repairs and reprovisioning, Gibraltar is also a good place to relax and its cosmopolitan makeup serves this function well.

Country Profile

Prehistoric human remains have been found on the Rock, the early Gibraltarians sheltering in the caves as the Ice Age drew to a close. One of the two Pillars of Hercules, in ancient times Gibraltar marked the limit of the civilised world, beyond which early sailors dared not venture. It was only in the eighth century, with the Moorish expansion into Europe, that people settled. Moorish leader Tarik-ibn-Zeyad conquered most of the Iberian peninsula from this settlement and the Rock was named Tarik's mountain, Gebel Tarik, in his honour, the name evolving eventually into Gibraltar.

The Moors were driven out by the Spanish in 1462 and under Spanish rule Gibraltar assumed its military importance, with the opening up of the New World and the struggles of Spain, France and Britain to gain maritime supremacy in the region. In 1704 an Anglo-Dutch force seized Gibraltar, which Spain agreed to leave in British hands, as the British had backed the successful contender for the Spanish throne, then in dispute. Later Spanish efforts to recapture the Rock failed repeatedly, the most notable being the Great Siege of 1779–82, the successful defence giving rise to the saying 'safe as the rock of Gibraltar'.

Through all the major wars of the last two centuries, Gibraltar played a crucial part for the British Empire. Used as a base during the Battle of Trafalgar in the Napoleonic Wars, it was here that the body of Admiral Nelson was brought by HMS Victory. The Suez Canal further increased the Rock's importance as a provisioning stop. In the two World Wars its position and facilities were greatly appreciated by the Allied navies.

Although still remaining a British colony, since the Second World War Gibraltar has become largely self-governing, with an elected House of Assembly. However, under General Franco, Spain renewed her claim, embarking in the 1960s on the fifteenth siege in

Marina Bay Marina overshadowed by the Rock of Gibraltar

Gibraltar's history. The frontier was closed and other links cut despite the fact that Gibraltarians had voted overwhelmingly in a referendum to remain with Britain. The death of Franco, subsequent liberalisation of Spain and then the Spanish application to join the European Community made the closed frontier absurd, and finally in April 1985 the border was reopened by Spain.

Tourism is Gibraltar's main industry, one in which yachting plays an important role. The opening of the land border with Spain has had an important effect on Gibraltar's economy. Gibraltar is also expanding in the field of international banking and as a tax haven.

The population of Gibraltar is 30,000. Gibraltarians are a mixture of many nationalities, mainly Spanish and British, but also Genoese, Jewish, Menorcan and Maltese settlers, as well as Portuguese and Moroccan immigrants. Although English is the official language, most of the inhabitants usually speak Spanish amongst themselves. Most Gibraltarians are Christian, although there are also Jewish and Muslim communities on the Rock.

The tall rock attracts its own weather, often being

Practical Information

LOCAL TIME: GMT + 1. Summer time GMT + 2 April to September.

BUOYAGE: IALA A

CURRENCY: The Gibraltar pound is equal to the pound sterling, which can also be used. Spanish pesetas are accepted in many shops.

BUSINESS HOURS
Banks: 0930–1530 Monday to Friday.
Shops: 0900–1800.
Government offices: winter: 0845–1315, 1415–1730; Summer; 0800–1430 Monday to Friday.

COMMUNICATIONS
International calls can be dialled direct from public telephones, direct dialling access code 00.
Operator connected international calls can be made on the ground floor of the City Hall in the Piazza.
International telephone calls can also be made from the marinas.
Marina Communications, 2nd floor Neptune House, Marina Bay. Both their telex and fax may be used by clients.
Post office: Main Street, 0900–1300, 1400–1700 Monday to Thursday, 1500–1800 Friday.

Emergency: Police and ambulance 199; fire 190.
There are several daily flights to London with further connections to any part of the world. There are also daily flights to Tangiers.

MEDICAL
British subjects can obtain medical treatment at St Bernards Hospital on the same basis as in Britain. EC nationals can obtain similar treatment on presentation of form E111.

covered by low cloud. Such mist is often a sign that the *Levanter*, a strong easterly wind, is on its way. Usually caused by an approaching Atlantic low, the latter can reach gale force rapidly, lasting for several days. About 80 per cent of the winds blow either from the east or west. *Poniente* is the name of the westerly wind, which is also preceded by low cloud. With the Atlantic Ocean so near, Gibraltar's weather is not entirely Mediterranean. However, it is generally a pleasant climate with warm summers and mild winters.

Entry Regulations

Port of entry
Gibraltar 36°08′N 05°21′W.

Procedure on arrival
The daytime approach to Gibraltar is straightforward. At night, entry into Gibraltar Bay can be more difficult. The easiest way to find the reporting dock is by heading for the airport runway. The main harbour should not be entered at night, as there are several unlit buoys.

Gibraltar Radio monitors VHF Channel 16 permanently, as do the marinas during office hours. The yellow 'Q' flag must be flown by all yachts, who must make their way to the reporting dock, reached by rounding the north end of the north mole. Yachts should come alongside this dock in front of the low white official building next to the fuelling station. In 1990 the various officials were temporarily moved from this building to another building nearby, where yachts can also come alongside the quay. Customs, immigration and port formalities must be completed immediately on arrival and the offices operate 24 hours

a day. After clearance has been completed, one can move to one of the two marinas located nearby, or anchor north of the runway, avoiding the restricted areas shown on the chart. The working channel for Sheppard's Marina is Channel 77 and for Marina Bay Marina Channel 9.

Customs
Firearms must be declared on arrival. Guns are impounded and kept until departure.

Quarantine regulations no longer apply to animals, although they must be declared on arrival.

Any items which yachts wish to import duty free must be reported to customs on arrival.

If sending items out of Gibraltar for repair, customs must inspect them first and be informed of the details. Incoming equipment must be clearly marked 'yacht spares in transit to …'.

Yachts can be temporarily imported into Gibraltar without paying duty by a non-resident for a maximum of 18 months within a three-year period. In excess of this time, the owner becomes a resident, and the yacht becomes eligible for 12 per cent duty. However, yachts can be left unaccompanied in Gibraltar for more than 18 months without paying duty, with the permission of customs, who will place the vessel under bond.

Immigration
As a British colony, holders of EC passports do not require visas when visiting Gibraltar. Generally similar immigration rules apply as for Britain, but nationals of countries normally requiring visas for Britain are usually allowed to stop in Gibraltar if they arrive and leave by yacht.

Immigration should be notified of any crew changes, and any passenger or crew member, who is staying ashore while the yacht is in port, must notify Immigration Control at the Waterport Police Station.

Warning

Tuna nets are a hazard, especially in the spring and summer, as they are laid along the Spanish coast in the approaches to the Straits of Gibraltar, sometimes several miles offshore. Normally the nets have one or more fishing boats in attendance. The vessel on the seaward end of the net should fly a black flag with 'A' on it by day, and two red lights, or red and white lights, on each mast by night. Yachts should pass to seaward of the nets, which often extend 2–3 miles outwards, and float just below the surface. Yachts should not attempt to go between the inner marks and the shore.

Fees

There are no fees for clearance or overtime fees.

Facilities

It was the large charter yachts plying between the Mediterranean and Caribbean each season that stimulated Gibraltar into developing its yachting facilities to such a high standard. Almost everything can be accomplished here in the way of repair or maintenance, with a wide range of boatyards and workshops providing all necessary services. Several companies offer haul-out facilities, either by travelift or slipway, some of the latter being able to cope with vessels of several hundred tons. Most major marine product manufacturers are represented by local agents and there is a very well stocked chandlery at Sheppard's Marina. Whatever is not available locally can be airfreighted from Britain in two days. There is also a British Admiralty chart agent in Gibraltar.

Duty-free stores are also available and the price of spirits is probably the lowest in the Mediterranean. Many shops in town sell goods at duty-free prices but even the local taxes are much lower than in the rest of the European Community as VAT (Value Added Tax) is not charged in Gibraltar. Many foreign yachts based in nearby Spanish ports use Gibraltar for both its good repair facilities, duty-free shopping and the easier importation of vital spare parts as compared to Spain.

Provisioning is very good with several supermarkets, one of them right on the dock in Marina Bay. Most supplies are imported from Britain and prices are reasonable. There is also a good selection of fresh produce, but as virtually all of it is imported either from Spain or Morocco, for a long passage it may be better to shop for fresh produce elsewhere.

Further Reading

Yacht Scene
Centreport Gibraltar
Cruising Association Handbook

GREECE

Spread out in the eastern Mediterranean, Greece consists of the mainland with the capital Athens, the Peloponnese peninsula and a multitude of islands in both the Ionian and Aegean seas, including the large island of Crete to the south.

If one were to grade the top ten cruising destinations in the world according to such criteria as scenic beauty, weather conditions and variety of ports and anchorages, Greece would definitely be among them. If one also takes into account the wealth of things to be seen ashore, as well as that most important ingredient, a pleasant waterfront restaurant or cafe to while away the balmy evening after a hard day's sail, Greece would probably be right at the top of the list.

The Aegean in particular seems to have been tailor-made for cruising and after a relatively slow start in the 1970s, yachting in Greece took off at great speed in the 80s. What will happen in the 90s is already clear as more charter companies are setting up business or opening new bases and some of the more popular spots have already reached saturation point. Yet the situation is not as bad for cruising yachts as it appears from a distance. There are still plenty of less frequented places dotted around the rim of the Aegean and some of the more remote islands rarely see more than a handful of yachts. The crowds are also seasonal and it certainly pays to cruise Greece outside of the peak summer months, ideally around Easter, which is the main holiday in the Greek Orthodox calendar. The autumn months are just as attractive, and in fact both winds and weather are more pleasant than during the *meltemi*-swept months of high summer.

More than the pleasant weather and picturesque ports, what makes Greece such a special place is the profusion of historical sites, most of which are within a short distance of the sea. The Greeks have always had an affinity with the sea and nothing they ever built was far from it. Among the sites that should not be missed are those on the mainland, the Acropolis of Athens and the temple at Delphi. On the northern shore of the Peloponnese is ancient Corinth, while not far inland are the ruins of Sparta, the magnificent stadium at Olympia and the impressive fortifications of Mycenae. The islands also abound in sites, such as those at Delos, the birthplace of Apollo and Artemis, or the palace and

Practical Information

LOCAL TIME: GMT + 2. Summer time GMT + 1 from early April to late September.

BUOYAGE: IALA A

CURRENCY: Drachma (DRA). Notes of greater value than DRA 1000 should not be exported.

BUSINESS HOURS
Banks: 0800–1400 Monday to Friday (some have exchange counters in afternoons and at weekends).
Business: 0800–1330, 1630–1930.
Shops: 0800–1500 Monday, Wednesday, Saturday and 0800–1400/1730–2030 Tuesday, Thursday, Friday.
Government offices: 0730–1430.
Hours may differ in summer.

ELECTRICITY: 220 V, 50 Hz

PUBLIC HOLIDAYS
1 January: New Year's Day
6 January: Epiphany
March Shrove Monday*
25 March: National Holiday
Good Friday, Easter Monday*
Whit Tuesday*
1 May
15 August: Assumption
28 October: Ohi Day
25, 26 December: Christmas
*Variable

EVENTS
The Orthodox Easter is more important than Christmas, and calculated differently to the Catholic and Protestant Easter. Open air festivals of music and drama in summer.

COMMUNICATIONS
International operator 162.
OTE = Telecommunications Organisation, international telephones available in all towns. Metered international calls can also be made from kiosks, tobacconists and shops. ELTA = Post Office.
There are frequent flights from Athens to all parts of the world and also some from Thessalonika. International flights to the islands are mainly charter flights. Frequent ferry services run to all the islands.

DIPLOMATIC MISSIONS
In Athens:
Australia: 37, Dimitriou Soutsou St, Ambelokipi. ☎ (1) 644-7303.
Canada: 4, Ioannou Gennadiou St. ☎ (1) 729511/9.
New Zealand: An. Tsoha 15–17, Ambelokipi. ☎ (1) 641-0311.
United Kingdom: 1, Ploutarchou St. ☎ (1) 723-6211.
United States: 91, Vasilissis Sophias Blvd. ☎ (1) 721-2951.

labyrinth of the legendary King Minos at Knossos on Crete. Closer to modern times are some magnificent churches and monasteries such as those on Patmos, Symi or Chios. Afloat or ashore, Greece undoubtedly caters for all tastes.

Country Profile

Greece is considered the birthplace of Western civilisation, and the oldest state in Europe existed on the island of Crete from about 3000 until 1450 BC. Meanwhile on the mainland Indo-European peoples had moved down from the north and settled, developing other states and kingdoms. The events which Homer wrote about later on were probably based on fact. In this legendary time, Greece was divided into many kingdoms, but these came together under Agamemnon, King of Mycenae, to beseige Troy for nine years. Something of a dark age followed this heroic period until a Renaissance occurred in the ninth century BC based on the city-states of Ionia on the Asia Minor coast. In the fifth century BC Persia, the dominant power of the East, was defeated several times and the city of Athens grew in power and established an empire. After the end of war with Persia and making peace with the bellicose state of Sparta, Athens became the unrivalled cultural centre in the Mediterranean. Alexander of Macedonia established the greatest empire yet seen in Europe and Asia, stretching as far as Persia. Greece's time of greatness came to an end with the rise of Rome and it became a political backwater. Waves of invasions by Macedonians, Franks and Serbs overran the peninsula.

From the fourteenth century the Ottoman empire dominated the Balkans, and the Turks ruled Greece for four centuries. As the Ottoman empire declined, so Greek nationalism became a growing force. In 1821–2 the Greeks rebelled against the Turks and declared their independence, but this was only recognised after years of war in the 1829 treaty of Adrianopolis. The new state gradually expanded its frontiers to the present day state, incorporating the Ionian islands, Thessaly and Crete, at the expense of Turkey and her Balkan neighbours. Following general dissatisfaction, in 1924 the army proclaimed a republic, although in 1935 the monarchy was restored.

Despite a desire to remain neutral in the Second World War, Greece was invaded by Italy and Germany, and in response a strong resistance movement developed. In 1946 the country became embroiled in a bitter civil war until the communists were defeated in 1949 by General Papagos. His party brought some industrialisation and prosperity, until instability returned in the 1960s. In 1967 a group of army colonels took power and established a dictatorial regime led by Georgios Papadopoulos. The King was deposed and a republic proclaimed in 1973. The crisis which erupted over the invasion of Cyprus by Turkey in 1974 saw the end of the colonels' regime, and a gradual return to democracy and more prosperity. This was also helped by Greece becoming a member of the European Community.

The main industries are shipping and tourism. Agriculture still employs about 20 per cent of the population and fruit, olive oil and tobacco are exported.

The population of Greece is 10.1 million and the Greek language has its own alphabet of 24 letters still bearing some relationship to Ancient Greek. The majority of Greeks are Orthodox Christian, the Greek and Roman churches having split in 1054.

Spring and autumn weather is the most pleasant, while the summer is hot and dry. Winters are mild in Crete and Rhodes and cooler as one moves north as well as inland. The prevailing winds of summer are northerly. The seasonal wind of summer, called *etesian* in Greece because of its seasonal character, but better known by its Turkish name *meltemi*, sets in about May and lasts until September. It blows at its strongest in July and August when it can reach force 7 and even 8 on occasions. Violent storms occur only in winter, February being a particularly bad month, but overall the weather is pleasant and extreme conditions are rarely known.

Entry Regulations

Ports of entry

Mainland: Alexandroupolis 40°51′N 25°57′E, Gerakini (Halkidiki) 40°16′N 23°26′E, Glifada 37°52′N 23°44′E, Igoumenitsa 39°30′N 20°15′E, Itea 38°26′N 22°25′E, Kavala 40°55′N 24°25′E, Lavrion 37°42′N 24°04′E, Perama 37°59′N 23°25′E, Piraeus 37°56′N 23°38′E, Preveza 38°57′N 20°45′E, Volos 39°21′N 22°56′E, Thessaloniki 40°38′N 22°56′E, Ivira and Dafni (Agion Oros) 40°13′N 24°13′E, Elefsina 38° 02′N 23° 33′E, Stillis (Lamia) 38°54′N 22°37′E.

Peloponnese: Egion 38°15′N 22°05′E, Githion 36°45′N 22°34′E, Kalamata 37°00′N 22°07′E, Katakolon 37°39′N 21°20′E, Korinthos 37°55′N 23°00′E, Nafplion 37°40′N 22°48′E, Patras 38°15′N 21°44′E, Pilos 36°55′N 21°42′E, Drepanon (Ahaia) 37°32′N 22°55′E.

Ionian Islands: Argostoli (Cephalonia) 38°12′N 20°29′E, Ithaki(Vathi) 38°22′N 20°44′E, Corfu Port 39°37′N 19°57′E, Dassia (Corfu) 39°38′N 19°55′E, Gouvia (Corfu) 39°39′N 19°51′E, Zakinthos 37°47′N 20°54′E.

Aegean Islands: Halkis (Evia/Euboea) 38°27′N 23°36′E, Chios 38°23′N 26°09′E, Kimassi (Evia/Euboea) 38°50′N 23°28′E, Kos 36°53′N 27°19′E, Lesvos (Mitilini) 39°06′N 26°05′E, Limnos (Mirina) 39°52′N 25°04′E, Mikonos 37°27′N 25°20′E, Milos (Adamas) 36°43′N 24°27′E, Patmos 37°18′N 26°35′E, Rhodos (Mandraki) 36°27′N 28°14′E, Samos (Pithagorion) 37°45′N 27°00′E, Samos (Vathi) 37°45′N 26°58′E, Siros 37°26′N 24°57′E, Skiathos 39°09′N 23°29′E, Thira (Santorini) 36°25′N 25°25′E.

Crete: Iraklion 35°16′N 25°09′E, Hania 35°31′N 24°01′E, Souda 35°29′N 24°09′E, Kali Limenes 34°56′N 24°50′E, Agios Nikolaos 35°11′N 25°43′E.

Procedure on arrival

The Greek courtesy flag must be flown and also it should be in good condition, as torn or frayed flags are regarded as a sign of disrespect. Clearance must be done with port authority, customs and health as well as immigration and currency control. The ship's papers will be inspected by the port authority, then customs will issue a transit log. At subsequent ports this transit log may be inspected by the port authority, mainly in the large ports and occasionally in smaller harbours. The port authorities may also want a passenger and crew list on departure from each port. Where there is no port authority, local police or customs officials may wish to see the log. Sometimes the log is kept until departure from a port.

Customs

Firearms must be declared.

Cats and dogs require health and rabies inoculation certificates issued in the country of origin, not more than 12 months previously for dogs, six months for cats, and not less than six days before arrival. Birds also need a health certificate.

The yacht, its permanently installed equipment and personal possessions are exempt from duty. Major portable items, such as TVs, video recorders, tape decks or diving equipment, must be itemised on the transit log or they will be liable for duty.

Immigration

A passport is not required by holders of identity cards from Austria, Belgium, France, Germany, Italy, Luxemburg, Netherlands, Switzerland and British Visitors Passports.

A visa is not required by nationals of West European countries, Andorra, Anguilla, Antigua, Argentina, Australia, Bahamas, Barbados, Bolivia, Brazil, Canada, Colombia, Costa Rica, Cyprus, Dominican Republic, Ecuador, El Salvador, Gambia, Grenada, Hong Kong, Israel, Japan, South Korea, Liechtenstein, Macau,

Malawi, Malta, Mexico, Morocco, New Zealand, Nicaragua, Paraguay, Peru, St Kitts and Nevis, Seychelles, South Africa, Tanzania, Tunisia, Uruguay and USA.

Nationals of Kuwait, Oman, Qatar and UAE can obtain visas on arrival.

Visas must be issued in advance for all other nationalities.

Extensions of visas can be obtained from the nearest police station or Aliens Department.

Nationals of Albania, Bulgaria, China, Czechoslovakia, Hungary, North Korea, Poland and Romania must register within 48 hours of entry with the Aliens Department.

Entry will be refused if there are Turkish Cyprus stamps in the passport.

Transit log

This is completed in Greek and English with details of the yacht, crew, fuel and other provisions. The log authorises the yacht to sail in Greek waters for its period of validity. The log must be produced when requested and must also record any crew changes. After six months the log can be renewed for another six months. After the initial 12 months, further 12 month extensions can be obtained, and repeated as long as a yacht stays in Greece, independent of the period of stay given to individuals. Up to 12 months, the importation is classed as temporary. After 12 consecutive months tax is payable and the tax receipt will be required by customs on application for an extension. The tax must be paid in US dollars at any branch of the Bank of Greece. The tax is US$15 per foot LOA and covers harbour and light dues.

Crew and passengers on board a yacht are considered by the authorities to be in transit, and the transit log only authorises day visits inland, the nights being presumed to be spent on board. The harbour master and immigration should be notified if travelling away from the yacht overnight or if an individual leaves Greece by other means such as by air. These changes have to be noted in the transit log and entry and exit stamps put into the passport. Individual passports are not stamped on entry into Greece by yacht, nor is this required for departure with the same yacht. However, if leaving by another means, these stamps are required by immigration at the point of exit.

On departure from Greece, the transit log must be returned to customs at the port of exit. If the yacht is being left in Greece for the winter, the transit log should be handed in to customs and a new one issued when returning to the yacht. A photocopy of the log should be shown to immigration officials when leaving the country by other means.

Documentation

Foreign yachts must be properly registered. Occasionally visiting captains have been asked to produce a certificate of authority showing that the navigation lights conform to the requirements of the International Regulations for Preventing Collisions at Sea. Such a certificate can be obtained from the builder or company which fitted out the yacht.

Restrictions

Fishing is forbidden with scuba gear and is only permitted with a snorkel in undeveloped areas. Scuba diving is restricted in Greece. Permission should be sought locally before diving.

Chartering by foreign yachts from Greek ports is illegal and is punishable by heavy fines.

Canals

Corinth Canal: Opened in 1893, the canal separates mainland Greece from the Peloponnese. It has a length of 4 miles and a depth of 26 feet (8 metres). The canal is state owned, the canal authority being the Corinth Canal SA. The cut is too narrow for ships to pass each other, so one must get permission to proceed. There are waiting areas at both ends. Pilotage is not compulsory.

The pilot service will supply a declaration form, which must be completed and returned to the control tower at the east entrance, where payment is made. Payment is calculated on the net tonnage recorded on the original registration certificate of the vessel. If only gross tonnage is shown, the fees are calculated as 80 per cent of the gross tonnage. If neither tonnage is on the registration certificate, the length of the vessel will be the basis for the calculation.

A vessel can only enter the canal when a permit has been granted by the Canal Service. A blue flag by day and a white light by night indicates entrance is permitted. A red flag by day and two vertical white lights by night show that entry is prohibited.

The fees in 1990 were as follows:

Net tonnage	Length (metres)	Fee (DRA)
0–10	0–10	10.700
10.1–20	10.0–15.00	24.500
20.1–50	15.0–	38.150
50.1–100		60.050

The above fees do not include VAT of 18 per cent, nor towing or pilot expenses and are valid for only one crossing.

More details can be obtained from the Corinth Canal Company, 88 Hippocratous Street, Athens.

Evripos Canal: Between Euboea (Evia) Island and the mainland, the bridge only opens at slack tide or when ships can pass with a following tide, as there is a very strong current at other times. There are no tolls for the opening of the Halkis bridge.

Lefkas Canal: This canal separating the island of Lefkas from the mainland has existed since ancient times. It is used mainly by local craft as a short cut to nearby Ionian islands. It has been dredged to a minimum depth of 15 feet (4.5 metres). There is no toll. The canal opens on the hour from 0800 to 2200.

Fees

There is a stamp duty on the transit log and sometimes a fee for the log.

There is an annual tax of US$15 per foot LOA for yachts staying over 12 months.

Small harbour fees in ordinary ports. Marina fees are calculated on LOA or tonnage.

Facilities

The recent expansion in yachting has been accompanied by a parallel development in facilities. Although some of those who know Greece from before may not regard this expansion as a blessing, their alarm is unfounded, as none of the picturesque ports have been ruined by the construction of pontoons in centuries old harbours. Most marinas have been built inside newly built breakwaters or reclaimed land and in most islands yachts still either come stern-to the existing quay, if there is space, or stay at anchor. Most of the new marinas are on the mainland and this is also where the best repair facilities are.

The greatest concentration of facilities is in the Athens–Piraeus area, where there are several boatyards with hauling out facilities and a full range of repair services. Permission is required from the port police to haul out a yacht and also when returning it to the water. Haul-out facilities are available at Alimos, Aretsou, Flisvos, Glifada, Mandraki, Lavrion, Patras, Porto Carras and Zea.

Marine equipment is difficult to find anywhere outside of the Athens area where charts are also available. Essential spares may need to be ordered from abroad and, although possible, duty-free importation can be complicated and time consuming. Even if one insists that spare parts are for a yacht in transit, customs officials at the airport may insist on a tax of up to 80 per cent of the value. VAT (value added tax) is also charged on items imported for repairs or fitting out while in Greece and for services provided. Spares and equipment are normally charged 33 per cent tax.

Diesel fuel is widely available, usually on the dock in marinas and most ports. Foreign yachts buy fuel at a transit price, so one must show a foreign currency exchange receipt to cover the amount bought. Stations that sell fuel for foreign yachts are marked by blue and yellow diagonal stripes on the quay. Smaller amounts can be bought without formalities from ordinary stations. Water is available in most ports, but usually one has to pay. In summer in some of the smaller islands it may be difficult to obtain any large quantity of water, so one should try and arrive with full tanks from the mainland. Provisioning is generally good and fresh locally grown produce is available everywhere.

Further Reading

Greek Waters Pilot
The Aegean
The Ionian Islands to the Anatolian Coast
Mediterranean Cruising Handbook
The Blue Guide to Greece
The Greek Islands

ISRAEL

Israel is a small country on the Eastern Mediterranean shore, but one with a wealth of history and culture. A symbol for three of the world's major religions, this country has always been hotly disputed.

The coast is low with no natural harbours or anchorages and visiting yachts have the choice of only a few marinas and ports. An unexciting coastline, stringent security controls and recurring internal problems have kept most cruising yachts away from this interesting country, where yachting facilities have been steadily improving to cater for an expanding resident boating community. The few foreign yachts who make the detour to reach Israel during a cruise of the Eastern Mediterranean are rewarded with the opportunity to visit many of the well-known ancient sites. A sojourn in Israel also provides a unique opportunity to experience and perhaps understand some of the reasons for the continuing conflict in the Middle East.

Country Profile

Lying between Africa and Asia on the edge of Europe, this region has had many peoples move back and forth across it throughout its history. Inhabited from earliest times it was known as Canaan and from 1220–1200 BC the Hebrews conquered the country, developing a monarchy with Jerusalem as its capital. After King

Solomon's death his kingdom split into Israel and Judah, was invaded by the Assyrians, and the Israelites scattered. The region was made a province of the Roman empire in 64–63 BC, with some autonomy until the First and Second Revolts against the Romans saw them destroy Jerusalem, and enslave or exile the Jews. In the fourth century the Byzantine Emperor Constantine encouraged the development of Christianity, and many pilgrims travelled to what became known as the Holy Land. The Arabs, adherents of the new religion preached by Mohammed, invaded in the seventh century ending Byzantine rule.

When in the eleventh century the Ottoman Turks captured Jerusalem and refused to cooperate with visiting Christian pilgrims, the Pope called for a liberating crusade. Crusaders came from all over Europe and occupied Jerusalem. The Christian kingdom of Jerusalem lasted until the thirteenth century, after which the Mamelukes of Egypt took over until the Ottoman Turks made it part of their empire in 1517. In the seventeenth and eighteenth centuries Jewish

The Wailing Wall in front of the Mosque of the Rock, two of the major religious sites of Jerusalem.

immigration and settlement in Palestine increased, especially from Eastern Europe. Later Jewish nationalism developed, with the growth of the Zionist movement and the idea of a Jewish state.

In the First World War the Allies sought Arab and Jewish support to topple the Ottomans, although promises for Jewish aspirations remained vague. After the war Britain occupied Palestine as a League of Nations mandate. The 1920s and 30s saw many Jews immigrate, and Jewish–Arab relations deteriorate, often into violence. The British tried unsuccessfully to control immigration in an attempt to keep racial tension down, and the Zionist movement carried out terrorist attacks against Britain. The state of Israel was declared unilaterally in 1948, following the withdrawal of British troops. Since then the surrounding Arab countries have been in conflict with the country which they call Palestine. In 1979 some peace came to the area when Israel and Egypt signed a Peace Treaty, but since 1987 the Palestinian revolt (Intifadah) and Jewish settlement in the Occupied Territories have kept up tension.

Industry in Israel is increasingly important for the economy. Agriculture produces enough for domestic

Practical Information

LOCAL TIME: GMT + 2. Summer time GMT + 3.

BUOYAGE: IALA A

CURRENCY: New shekel (NIS) of 100 agorot. US$ are also used. Payments made in foreign currency are exempt from 15 per cent Value Added Tax (VAT). VAT refunds can be obtained by presenting the receipts of purchases made in foreign currency to a bank before departure.

BUSINESS HOURS
These vary a lot, depending on religion. The Jewish Shabbat from sunset Friday to sunset Saturday means that on Friday afternoon and Saturday, most shops, offices and places of entertainment are closed. Public transport also does not run, Haifa being an exception.
Banks: hours vary, but generally open Sunday to Tuesday, Thursday 0830–1230/1600–1730. Monday, Wednesday 0830–1230. Friday and the eve of holy days 0830–1200.
Business: September to May 0730–1600 Sunday to Thursday, 0730–1230 Friday. June to August 0730–1430 Sunday to Thursday, 0730–1230 Friday. Muslim businesses close Friday, Christian businesses on Sundays.
Shops: 0800–1300, 1600–1900 Monday to Thursday, 0800–1400 Friday.
Government offices: September to May 0700–1300 Sunday to Thursday, 0730–1430 Friday. June to August 0730–1430 Sunday to Thursday, 0730–1300 Friday.

ELECTRICITY: 220 V, 50 Hz

PUBLIC HOLIDAYS
Many of the Jewish holidays are variable.
February/March: Purim – Carnival
February/March: Feast of Passover Holocaust Day
April/May: Independence Day
May/June: Shavuot
September/October: Rosh Ha-Shanah, Day of Judgement
Yom Kippur, Day of Atonement
October: Sukkot
October: Simhat Torah
December/January: 8 days of Hanukkah
Muslim and Christian holidays are kept by those sections of the population.

COMMUNICATIONS
International calls can be made from main post offices.
Collect calls can be made from public phones. International operator: dial 18/03. Public phones need tokens. International telephone office: 7 Mikve Yisrael St, Tel Aviv. Open Sunday to Thursday 0800–1800, Friday 0800–1400. Tel Aviv's main post office: 132 Allenby Road on corner of Yehuda Ha Levi St, open Sunday to Thursday 0700–2000, Friday 0700–1400.
Emergency: police 100, ambulance 101, fire service 102.
Most international flights for European and North American destinations leave from Tel Aviv airport.

MEDICAL
Medical care is of a high standard.

DIPLOMATIC MISSIONS
In Tel Aviv:
Egypt: 54 Babel St, off ibn Gevirol St. Sunday to Thursday 0900–1100 for visa applications. Can be collected 1200–1300 the same day.
Canada: 220 Hayarkon St. ☎ (3) 228122.
United Kingdom: 192 Rechov St. ☎ (3) 249171.
United States: 71 Hayarkon St. ☎ (3) 654338.

needs as well as for export. The tourist industry is developed, and US aid remains considerable. However, the country has had very high inflation, and the economy is not helped by the costly military budget and a lack of mineral resources or water supply.

The population of Israel is 6 million, over half of which are Jews of very mixed cultures and national origins. The rest are mainly Palestinian and concentrated in East Jerusalem, the West Bank and the Gaza area. Hebrew is the national language, but Arabic is spoken by the Palestinians. Also spoken is Yiddish, which is a combination of Hebrew and medieval German, and Ladino, which derives from Hebrew and Spanish. English is widely spoken and many other languages are spoken by recent immigrants. Judaism as practised by Jews in Israel covers many facets from the most orthodox to the most liberal. Some of the Palestinian Arabs are Christian, although the majority are Muslim. Many Christian denominations have a presence in the capital Jerusalem, which has several holy sites for Jews, Christians and Muslims. Israel is also a centre for the Baha'i faith.

The climate is generally temperate, the winters being cool and rainy, the summers hot and dry. In summer, winds along the coast alternate between land and sea breezes.

Entry Regulations

Ports of entry
Haifa 32°49'N 35°00'E, Ashdod 31°49'N 34°38'E, Eilat 29°33'N 34°57'E, Tel Aviv Marina 32°05'N 34°46'E.

Procedure on arrival
When 40 miles from the coast, a position report with the yacht details and ETA should be sent via VHF radio to the Ministry of Transport. The ports of Haifa, Ashdod and Eilat work on Channel 14 or 16, while Tel Aviv Marina can only be contacted on Channel 16.

On approaching the coast yachts are normally met by an armed patrol boat and asked for details of the yacht and crew. The patrol boat usually accompanies the yacht to the port of entry. Sometimes the yacht is boarded for inspection while still offshore. On arrival yachts are met by customs and immigration. The yacht may be searched for arms or explosives.

Customs

Firearms must be declared.

Dogs, cats and birds need a veterinary health certificate issued in the country of origin. Dogs over three months old need a rabies vaccination certificate issued between one year and one month before arrival. If the yacht carries more than two of any of these animals and other species of animal, an import permit issued by the Director of Veterinary Services is required. A written application must be received not less than 10 days before the planned arrival of such animals.

Immigration

No visa is required for nationals of Austria, Bahamas, Barbados, Belgium, Bolivia, Colombia, Costa Rica, Denmark, Dominican Republic, Ecuador, El Salvador, Fiji, Finland, France, Greece, Guatemala, Haiti, Holland, Hong Kong, Iceland, Jamaica, Japan, Liechtenstein, Luxembourg, Maldives, Mauritius, Mexico, Netherlands Antilles, Norway, Paraguay, Surinam, Swaziland, Sweden, Switzerland, Trinidad and the United Kingdom.

A visa is issued on arrival to nationals of Argentina, Australia, Brazil, Canada, Central African Republic, Chile, Germany, Italy, New Zealand, San Marino, South Africa, Spain, Uruguay, and US citizens born after 1 January 1928. There is no charge for this visa. Irish citizens get a visa on arrival but have to pay a fee. Nationals of Cyprus, Germany (born before 1 January 1928) and Yugoslavia must obtain a visa in advance but no fee is charged. Other nationalities must apply for visa in advance, and pay a fee. A transit visa valid for five days, obtainable in advance from Israeli diplomatic missions, can be extended on arrival for a further 10 days.

Normally a three-month stay is granted on arrival. After three months, one can apply for a visa or extension of a visa at a Ministry of the Interior office. This extension is usually for a further three months and costs US$10. There is no fee for Benelux citizens. Office hours 0800–1200 Sunday to Thursday. Monday, Wednesday open 1400–1500.
Tel Aviv: Shalom Meyer Tower, 9 Ahad Ha'am St.
Haifa: Government Building (opposite Municipality), 11 Hassan Shukri St.

Important note If one is planning to visit Arab countries or countries who do not recognise Israel, one may be refused entry to those countries if possessing an Israeli stamp in one's passport. Therefore one should request the Israeli immigration officer not to stamp the passport on arrival and departure. The officials are aware of this problem and usually provide a loose leaf of paper to slip in the passport, which can be stamped. However, if applying for an extension after the initial three months, this will automatically be stamped in the passport. Equally one may be refused entry into Israel if one has stamps from certain Arab states in one's passport.

Cruising permit

This must be applied for within 30 days of arrival.

Restrictions

There are several areas prohibited to yachts. Information on these areas is obtainable from chart suppliers and is drawn on Navy charts, which are available in every marina.

Health

Typhoid and polio vaccinations are recommended.

Fees

Overtime is payable on weekends and public holidays. Harbour fees are calculated on length. There are light fees.

Facilities

Although not a prime cruising destination, Israel's yachting facilities are slowly expanding as more Israelis discover the pleasures of sailing. The largest sailing community is in Tel Aviv, where the best facilities are concentrated and Atarim Marina offers a good range of services including fuel and water on the dock. There are two chandleries with a limited selection close by and marine charts are also available locally. There are various workshops in the area, including haul-out by crane (25 tons). A whole range of repairs can be undertaken, such as engine, electronic, fibreglass or sail repair. There is a new marina at Jaffa, situated close to Tel Aviv.

Haifa offers a similar range with haul-out facilities, various workshops and docking facilities at the local yacht club. There is also a marina at Akko, north of Haifa. Some limited facilities are also available at Eilat, Israel's port on the Red Sea, which has a small yacht harbour.

Fuel is available in all ports and LPG bottles can also

be filled. Provisioning is very good in the larger centres, although imported goods are expensive. Locally produced fruit and vegetables are more reasonable and are among the best to be found in the Mediterranean.

Further Reading

Mediterranean Cruising Handbook
The Blue Guide to Israel

ITALY

Italy has well over 5000 miles of coastline, surrounded by the Tyrrhenian, Adriatic, Ligurian, Ionian and Mediterranean Seas. Off the west coast there are many small islands and the two large islands of Sardinia and Sicily. The coastline is very varied from the Italian Riviera right down to the south, being mountainous in some areas and low-lying in others. The west coast can be extremely crowded in the summer, especially in the north. July and August are the months to avoid, but in the spring and autumn the coasts are more peaceful and the weather can be very pleasant.

Once the undisputed domain of power boating, many Italians have now discovered the beauty of sailing and to cope with this insatiable demand many marinas have been built, particularly along the Italian Riviera. South of Rome sailing yachts are not so common. The east coast of Italy has been less endowed by nature and is less popular for cruising, even the local sailors often preferring to cruise in neighbouring Yugoslavia. Italy's best cruising spots are spread around the rim of the Tyrrhenian Sea where groups of islands alternate with attractive harbours on the mainland. Some of the most picturesque anchorages are on Sardinia, while close to the Straits of Messina one can either anchor in the shadow of Stromboli or within sight of Mount Etna. Everywhere in Italy there is a lot to see ashore and the proximity of ports or marinas to all tourist attractions makes it easy to visit the main points of interest without leaving the boat for more than a few hours.

Country Profile

The Italian peninsula's earliest inhabitants were Ligurian and Illyrian peoples, and later Etruscans, Greeks and Gauls settled. From the middle of the fourth century BC Rome dominated the peninsula, and expanded to form an empire which at its height stretched around the Mediterranean and north as far as England. The empire declined from the second century AD, and Rome itself fell under waves of barbarian invasions from the east from the fifth century onwards.

The Frankish empire dominated in the eighth century, and was followed by a confused period until the tenth century, when Otto I united the crowns of Germany and Italy into the Holy Roman Empire. Southern Italy was later conquered by the Normans, while semi-independent city-states developed in the north and centre. The power of both the Empire and the Papacy declined, leaving the peninsula divided. By the fifteenth century five main states had emerged, the duchy of Milan, the republics of Florence and Venice, the Papal States, and the kingdom of Naples. Economically prosperous, they fostered the arts as the Renaissance emerged as a new cultural force.

With the Italian Wars (1494–1559) rivalry between small Italian states was intensified by the rivalry of France and Spain, until France abandoned her claims to parts of Italy. Thereafter Spain and the Counter-Reformation dominated Italy until the eighteenth century, when Hapsburg Austria gained Milan and Naples. At the end of the century Napoleon invaded, and by 1810 had extended French control over the whole peninsula. The Congress of Vienna of 1815 restored Sardinia to the House of Savoy, and the rest of Italy to Austrian influence.

Italian nationalism and the idea of unification grew rapidly, although there was little success until Piedmont, ruled by Victor Emmanuel II and prime minister Cavour, won victories over Austria in 1859 and gained Lombardy. Central Italy and Naples voted for union with Piedmont and in 1861 the kingdom of Italy was proclaimed. Venice and Rome were acquired, and the latter became the capital of the new state.

In 1915 Italy entered the First World War on the side of the Allies, and in 1919 gained some territory from Austria. A fascist government was formed in 1922 under Benito Mussolini, and a totalitarian state was gradually imposed. In 1936 the Rome–Berlin Axis was formed with Nazi Germany, and Italy entered the Second World War on the side of Germany. Mussolini was overthrown in 1943 following heavy defeats and social unrest. An armistice was signed with the Allies and war declared on Germany. After the war a republic replaced the monarchy, but was weakened by instability until the 1950s, when under the Christian Democrats the economy made a spectacular recovery. A strong left-wing opposition developed and from 1968 political instability returned with a quick succession of governments, until eventually the political parties

Practical Information

LOCAL TIME: GMT + 1. Summer time GMT + 2 from the last weekend in March to the last weekend in September.

BUOYAGE: IALA A

CURRENCY: Lira (L). The maximum amount of lira that can be imported or exported is L200,000.

BUSINESS HOURS
Banks: 0830–1330, 1500–1600 (afternoon opening varies) Monday to Friday.
Business: 0830–1330 Monday to Friday.
Shops: 0830/0900–1300, and 1530/1600–1930/2000 (Northern Italy takes a shorter lunch break, but closes earlier).
Government offices: 0830–1345 Monday to Friday.

ELECTRICITY: 220 V, 50 Hz

PUBLIC HOLIDAYS
1 January: New Year's Day
6 January: Epiphany
Easter Monday
25 April: Liberation Day
1 May: Labour Day
15 August: Assumption
1 November: All Saints
8 December: Immaculate Conception
25, 26 December: Christmas
There are also local feast days on the day of the patron saint.

COMMUNICATIONS
Phone booths need special tokens (*jettone*) or take 100 and 200 lira coins. Tokens can be bought from post offices, tobacconists and bars. International direct dialling access code is 00.
Mail is very unreliable and slow, although private addresses or marinas are better than poste restante.
Poste Restante: c/o Post Office and adding FERMO POSTA to the name of the locality. Delivery is made at central

post office on presentation of passport and payment of a fee.
Emergency: dial 113.
There are regular international flights from most major cities, such as Rome, Milan, Turin, Genoa, Naples, Venice and Palermo.

MEDICAL
EC citizens have access to health care on a reciprocal basis. Private medical treatment is expensive.

DIPLOMATIC MISSIONS
In Rome:
Australia: Via Alessandria 215, 00198 Rome. ☎ (6) 832721.
Canada: Via Zara 30, 00198 Rome. ☎ (6) 440-3038.
New Zealand: Via Zara 28, 00198 Rome. ☎ (6) 440-2928.
United Kingdom: Via XX Settembre 80A, 00187 Rome. ☎ (6) 475-5441.
United States: Via Veneto 119/A, 00187 Rome. ☎ (6) 46741.

reached a compromise with Communists and Christian Democrats in power together. Through the 1970s the country suffered from right- and left-wing terrorist activity especially by the Red Brigade. In 1987 a new coalition government came to power.

Italy is traditionally an agricultural country with industry concentrated in the north centred on Milan and Turin. There is still a division between the poorer, more rural south and the industrial north. The economy is diverse, the manufacturing industry being well known for quality production in cars, domestic appliances and household goods. Italian goods have a reputation for style in fashion, furniture and many other items.

The population is 57.5 million and the language Italian, although there are some dialects in Sicily, Naples and Sardinia. The majority are Roman Catholic and the capital is Rome, where the Roman Catholic Church has its headquarters in the Vatican City, an autonomous state.

The climate varies from north to south and between the islands. The north can have cold winters, while the south can be extremely hot in summer. Generally the coastal areas have a Mediterranean climate. The summers are hot and dry along the coast. The prevailing winds of summer are NW, although in many areas there is a daily pattern combining land and sea breezes.

Entry Regulations

Ports of entry

There is such a large number of ports and marinas both on the mainland and in the offlying islands that only those where foreign yachts normally clear in have been listed. Most of these are close to cruising routes.

Mainland: Ancona 43°36′N 13°31′E, Anzio 41°27′N 12°38′E, Bari 41°08′N 16°53′E, Brindisi 40°39′N 17°59′E, Chioggia 45°13′N 12°17′E, Civitavecchia 42°06′N 11°48′E, Fiumicino 41°46′N 12°14′E, Genoa 44°25′N 8°55′E, Imperia 43°53′N 8°02′E, La Spezia 44°07′N 9°50′E, Naples 40°51′N 14°16′E, Ravenna 44°25′N 12°27′E, Reggio di Calabria 38°07′N 15°39′E, Salerno 40°41′N 14°46′E, San Remo 43°49′N 7°47′E, Taranto 40°27′N 17°12′E, Trieste 45°39′N 13°48′E, Venice 45°26′N 12°20′E.
Sardinia: Alghero 40°34′N 8°19′E, Arbatax 39°56′N 9°42′E, Cagliari 39°12′N 9°05′E, Carloforte 39°09′N 8°19′E, Olbia 40°55′N 9°34′E, Porto Cervo 41°08′N 9°34′E.
Elba: Porto Azzuro 42°46′N 10°24′E.
Sicily: Catania 37°31′N 15°06′E, Gela 37°04′N 14°15′E, Marsala 37°48′N 12°26′E, Messina 38°12′N 15°34′E, Palermo 38°07′N 13°22′E, Porto Empedocle 37°17′N 13°32′E, Siracusa 37°03′N 15°18′E, Trapani 38°02′N 12°31′E.

Procedure on arrival

Clearing in with the proper authorities is essential to avoid the possibility of fines or even the impounding of the offending yacht. On arrival in a port of entry, one must clear with the port captain, who will issue a transit log (constituto). One also has to clear with customs and immigration.

Officials are very unlikely to come to a yacht, so the captain must report to their offices. Yachts have got into trouble for failing to report to the authorities.

The captain may be asked to show a certificate of competence; other documents needed are the registration certificate and third-party liability insurance.

The transit log may have to be shown at subsequent ports. On departure from Italy the transit log must be handed in to the port captain in the last port, as well as clearing customs and immigration.

Customs

Firearms must be declared on arrival. The penalty for non-declaration is imprisonment.

Dogs and cats need a health certificate, which must be in Italian as well as the language of the country of origin. This can be obtained from the local veterinary inspector of the Ministry of Agriculture and should state that the animal is free from disease and has been vaccinated against rabies not less than 20 days and not more than 11 months prior to the date of issue of the health certificate. Animals under 12 weeks old do not have to have a rabies vaccination, but must be examined on arrival.

Immigration

No visa is required for a stay of up to three months for nationals of EC countries, other West European countries, Australia, New Zealand, the USA and many other countries. Extensions can be obtained from the police.

Cruising permit

A transit log or cruising permit (constituto) is issued by the port captain (Capitaneria) on arrival. The document is issued to all visiting yachts provided they have proof of a valid third-party liability insurance. All visiting yachts must pay a sojourn tax (tassa di stazionamento). The payment must be made at a post office and the receipt shown to the office issuing the permit. The fee is calculated daily per ton and is double for motor boats. It is advisable to pay in advance for longer periods, as the rates are reduced by one third for a two month period, by half if paying for four months and by two thirds for 12 months. Failure to pay the tax or cruising without a valid permit can result in the yacht being impounded.

The permit is valid for 12 months. A yacht remaining longer than one year may be liable for import duty or seizure. When the permit expires, the yacht must leave Italy, then re-enter and get a new permit.

Changes in crew, departure and re-entry must be recorded on the permit by a port official. If the yacht is left in Italy in the care of a marina or boatyard, one can obtain a tax exemption for up to one year.

Insurance

It is illegal for yachts to cruise in Italian waters without valid third-party insurance. An Italian translation of the insurance certificate will be needed, so one should try and arrive with such a translation, which should be supplied by the insurance company. The insurance must be with a company having reciprocal arrangements with a recognised Italian insurance company. Proof of insurance is needed to obtain the transit log, and may have to be shown in subsequent ports. Yachts which do not have insurance will not be allowed to leave the harbour until they obtain it. Insurance can be obtained locally from an Italian insurance company.

Health

Seafood should not be consumed in areas of heavy pollution.

Charter

It is illegal for foreign yachts to charter in Italy. However, if one arrives with a charter party from abroad one can obtain the transit log in the usual way. Neither the charter party nor the crew may be changed while in Italian waters.

Facilities

With a large resident boating population and also a considerable boat-building industry of its own, yachting facilities in Italy are of a very high standard. Purpose-built marinas or docks for yachts are available almost everywhere and the only deterrent can be the high docking fees charged in some places, some of the highest being those at Porto Cervo in Sardinia.

The best repair facilities are in the north-west of the country where most marinas are concentrated. There are boatyards all around Italy's coasts and for any repair or haul-out one is never too far away from help. Marine supplies and spares, particularly more common makes of diesel engines or outboards, are widely available, although everything is found more easily in the north. Essential spares that are not available locally can be imported free of duty. Fuel and water are available in most ports and LPG containers can also be filled in most places although an adaptor may be necessary. Provisioning is good everywhere and most towns have a fresh produce market with a wide selection of fruit and vegetables. Because of the mild winters in the south of the country, fresh produce is available all year round.

Further Reading

Italian Waters Pilot
Adriatic Pilot
The Tyrrhenian Sea

LEBANON

Before being torn apart by civil war, Lebanon was one of the most popular tourist destinations in the Eastern Mediterranean. This beautiful country was also popular with cruising yachts and there used to be a regular movement of small boats between Cyprus and Lebanon. Now the country is definitely off-limits, and any yacht attempting to enter Lebanese waters will probably be immediately intercepted by an Israeli or other patrol boat. Cruising yachts are well advised not only to avoid sailing to Lebanon, but also to try and keep as far away from the Lebanese coast as possible. Another good reason for avoiding Lebanon while the present situation continues is the danger of being abducted by an extremist group, as many of the hostages taken in Lebanon have been innocent foreigners, including a family cruising on a Belgian yacht.

Country Profile

The modern state of Lebanon emerged out of the Ottoman Empire at the end of the First World War. In the inter-war period it was under French mandate, and gained full independence during the Second World War. An important commercial centre with a strategic position in the Middle East, its government was quite stable and westernised. However, the Muslims, who make up 50 per cent of the population, felt excluded as it was the right-wing Christians who held the power. Adding to the tension was the immigration of many Palestinian refugees displaced from Israel. In 1958 a Muslim rebellion occurred and the United States intervened to put this down. In the mid-1970s complete civil war broke out, which continues to rage. The situation has been exacerbated by the intervention of Syrian and Israeli forces, both countries using the Lebanese conflict in their own interests, without regard for the suffering caused to the local population.

A mainly agricultural country, income used to be derived from tourism and trade, but the continuing war is a tremendous drain on the economy.

The population is about 2.5 million, who are Arabic speaking, although both English and French are spoken, especially in Beirut. There are both Muslim and Christian communities and the population is divided along religious lines. The capital Beirut was once a cosmopolitan and prosperous city described as the Paris of the Middle East. Now it lies in ruins with shelled and burnt out buildings and streets covered in rubble.

The pleasant climate used to be Lebanon's main attraction as the weather is mostly sunny. The summers are hot and dry, while the winters are cool and occasionally rainy.

LIBYA

Libya has a long stretch of coastline on the southern shore of the Mediterranean between Egypt and Tunisia. The official name of Libya is the Socialist People's Libyan Arab Jamahariya, meaning the state of the masses. The 1969 revolution established a regime based on Arab socialism and tolerating no outside

---

Practical Information (Lebanon)

LOCAL TIME: GMT + 3	*DIPLOMATIC MISSIONS* United Kingdom: Middle East Airlines	*HARBOURS* Tripoli 34°28′N 35°50′E, Jounieh 33°59′N
BUOYAGE: IALA A	Building, Jal el Dib, East Beirut. ☎ (1) 416-112/410-573.	35°39′E, Beirut 33°54′N 35°31′E, Sidon (Saida) 33°34′N 35°22′E, Tyre (Sour)
COMMUNICATIONS There are flights from Beirut to various European and Middle East destinations.	Also: Shamma Building, Raouche, West Beirut. ☎ (1) 812-849/812-851. United States: Avenue de Paris, Beirut. ☎ (1) 361-800.	33°28′N 35°12′E, Selaata 34°16′N 35°39′E. The main port used in the past was Jounieh, approximately 8 miles north of Beirut, which has a small marina type yacht harbour.

interference, under the rule of Colonel Gaddafi. In 1977 a Jamahariya was declared, which is a combination of democracy and extreme Islam. Since the 1960s massive oil resources have brought the country great wealth. The government actively discourages tourism and entry formalities are very difficult.

The same rules apply to cruising yachts as to ordinary tourists and, whatever their means of travel, foreign visitors are not welcome. Cruising yachts are therefore strongly advised to avoid Libya and to keep well out of its territorial waters when sailing past its shores. Should there be an emergency which forces a yacht to call at one of the Libyan ports, an attempt should be made to contact the authorities on VHF Channel 16 as soon as one enters Libyan territorial waters. As there is a Libyan law which does not permit foreign ships to retain Israeli flags, stores or literature pertaining to Israel on board, even if these are part of the vessel's navigation equipment, such as Sailing Directions, any such incriminating items should be disposed of before entering a Libyan port.

Every visitor needs a visa in advance, which is difficult to obtain. Essential information in one's passport must be printed in Arabic. It should be noted that with a Libyan stamp in one's passport, one may have considerable problems going to some other countries, especially the United States. Entry is refused to Israelis, South Africans and those with passports containing stamps from either of these places.

Diplomatic missions
United Kingdom: British Interests Section Italian Embassy, Shara Uahran 1, Tripoli. ☎ (21) 33191.

MALTA

A small archipelago in the middle of the Mediterranean, Malta is a very popular tourist destination. The Republic of Malta consists of three islands, the largest, Malta, being the economic and administrative centre and most heavily populated. Gozo is smaller and picturesque, with the prehistoric temple of Ggantija, 5500 years old, while Comino is a very small island between the other two. All three islands are dry, mostly treeless, with rocky coasts. Maltese culture is a mixture of Catholic, Arab and the influence of the Knights of St John who were based there for two hundred years and whose cross became Malta's emblem.

Malta was an important yachting centre before the Balearics, Costa del Sol and Greece became such popular cruising destinations. Malta's convenient location, excellent harbours and good range of repair facilities ensured its leading position for many years until the authorities started imposing various restrictions which cruising sailors resented. Many yachts left never to return and cruising yachts deliberately bypassed Malta.

Recently a concerted effort has been made to reverse this trend and yachts are once again discovering the attractions of Malta. Its mild and pleasant winters make it a perfect wintering spot and as the repair facilities are being brought up to their former high standards, Malta is again a good place to refit a yacht between seasons. Malta's position almost in the centre of the Mediterranean makes it an ideal jumping off point for many other cruising grounds and an increasing number of European yachts make their base on the island. Fortunately there is more to Malta than just its repair and maintenance facilities, as besides the impressive Valetta harbour, there are many delightful anchorages around the islands.

Country Profile

Malta was inhabited from early times, first by the Phoenicians and Greeks, then ruled over by Carthage until the third century BC, when it became part of the Roman Empire. St Paul and St Luke were shipwrecked there in AD 58 when on their way to Rome. After the decline of the Roman Empire, Malta was ruled by Byzantium, the Arabs and then the Normans, who were established in nearby Sicily. The population remained Muslim until the mid-thirteenth century, when non-Christians were expelled and the Arab presence eliminated.

In the sixteenth century Malta became the home of the Knights of the Order of St John of Jerusalem, after they had been driven out of Rhodes by Sultan Suleiman the Magnificent. The Knights resisted all attempts by the Turks to conquer the island, notably in the Great Siege in 1562. The Knights ruled Malta until the end of the eighteenth century, when the islands were fought over by Britain and France until declared British in 1814. Internal self-government was granted in 1821, but political crises led to the constitution being suspended. Malta was badly bombed during the Second World War when the islands were used as a British naval base. Full independence came in 1964 and a republic was declared ten years later. In 1979 the British closed their naval base.

Until 1979 the main income was millions of pounds that Britain paid to use the facilities on the island. Since then shipbuilding, tourism, agriculture and light industry are the main money earners.

The Maltese population of 360,000 are mainly

Catholic and speak Maltese, which is a Semitic language in origin, having 80 per cent Arabic and 20 per cent Romance elements. English and some Italian are also spoken. The capital is Valletta, founded at precisely 2 p.m. 28 March 1566 to prevent any enemies from gaining the strategic Mount Sciberras as they had done in the Great Siege.

The climate is similar to North Africa, with extremely hot, dry summers and mild winters. Prevailing winds throughout the year are north-westerlies. When the hot sirocco wind blows from the south, it comes laden with dust.

Entry Regulations

Ports of entry
Marsamxett Harbour (Lazzaretto Creek) and Grand Harbour 35°54'N 14°31'E.

Procedure on arrival
Yachts must not stop anywhere before a port of entry, or they risk being fined. Valletta Port Control must be contacted on VHF Channels 12 or 16 (24-hour watch) before entering the harbour. During office hours, yachts must proceed to the guest berth in Lazzaretto Creek at the marina. Outside office hours clearance is done in the commercial port, Grand Harbour. It is not advisable to enter Marsamxett harbour at night.

Lazzaretto Creek: The guest berth is located on the south side of Manoel Island. The yacht should come alongside and customs and immigration officials will come to complete clearance formalities. After clearance, a yacht will be allotted a berth in the marina, or a reservation can be made before arrival. Marina fees must be paid in advance.

Grand Harbour: The Customs House is in Dockyard Creek on the port side. It is possible to come alongside.

Procedure on departure
Outward clearance is obtained from the customs and immigration offices on Manoel Island. Outside of office hours, one has to go to the Customs House in Valletta. A receipt for the payment of berthing fees must be obtained first in order to clear out. Customs

Malta's Marsamxett Harbour (Malta National Tourist Office).

Practical Information

LOCAL TIME: GMT + 1. Summer time GMT + 2 last Sunday in March to last Sunday in September.

BUOYAGE: IALA A

CURRENCY: Maltese pound (M£). One cannot import more than M£50 and export more than M£25.

BUSINESS HOURS
Banks: 0830–1230 Monday to Friday, 0830–1200 Saturday (October 1 to June 14), and 0800–1200 Monday to Friday, 0800–1130 Saturday (June 15 to September 31).

Business: 0830–1245/1430–1730 Monday to Friday and 0830–1200 Saturday.
Shops: 0900–1300/1530–1900 Monday to Saturday.
Government offices: 0800–1700 winter, 0800–1330 summer Monday to Friday.

ELECTRICITY: 240 V, 50 Hz

PUBLIC HOLIDAYS
1 January: New Year's Day
10 February: Feast of St Paul
Good Friday
31 March: National Day
1 May: May Day
15 August: Assumption Day
13 December: Republic Day
25 December: Christmas Day

EVENTS
Carnival
Good Friday processions.

COMMUNICATIONS
International direct dialling is possible from public phones.
There are international flights from Valletta to various European and North African destinations.

DIPLOMATIC MISSIONS
Canada: 103 Archbishop St, Valetta. ☎ 233121.
Egypt: House of the 4 Winds, Hastings.
United Kingdom: 7 St Anne St, Floriana. ☎ 233134.
United States: Development House, St Anne St, Floriana. ☎ 623653.

will require a crew list. It is possible to clear out on a Friday if leaving the following Sunday. Duty-free stores can be obtained before departure – they will be loaded under the supervision of a customs officer, and will be sealed until departure from Maltese waters. After loading duty-free goods, the yacht must leave within 24 hours.

Customs
Firearms will be taken into custody on arrival and returned prior to departure, or sealed on board if there is a suitable locker.

Yachts with animals on board cannot come alongside or stern-to and must anchor off. Landing animals is strictly prohibited, even with proper health certificates. As it is illegal to bring animals into Malta, the animal may be destroyed.

Immigration
Visas are not required for nationals of Commonwealth countries, West European countries, Bulgaria, Egypt, Hungary, Japan and the United States.

Visas are required by all other American, African and Asian nationalities, obtainable from Maltese or British diplomatic missions abroad.

Immigration officials do not stamp the passports of persons arriving by sea, so if leaving by air, it is necessary to notify the port police, who will stamp passports.

Yachts may remain an indefinite amount of time in Malta, but the length of time people may stay depends on immigration requirements.

Cruising
Yachts no longer have to return each night to Valletta as was the case previously. However, if planning to cruise around the archipelago and stop overnight elsewhere, customs should be notified and their permission obtained before leaving the marina. A permit is not needed if only planning to cruise between sunrise and sunset from Valletta. Valletta Port Control must be kept informed on VHF Channel 12 of the movement of the yacht while away from the marina.

The Maltese Task Force patrols the islands and keeps an eye on yacht movements.

Diving
It is necessary to obtain a diving permit from the Department of Health if planning to scuba dive in Maltese waters. The permit costs M£1 and one needs a medical certificate, two photographs, a logbook, and a certificate of qualification as an amateur diver. The permit must be shown if having diving tanks filled in Malta. Spearfishing without a licence is strictly forbidden, and the penalty is a heavy fine. Diving is prohibited in some areas and these are listed on the permit. Any archaeological findings must be reported to the authorities.

Fees
Clearance is a 24-hour service, but some government offices charge overtime after 1330 in summer and after 1700 in winter. Harbour fees were 50c/metre/week, multihulls 75c/metre/week in 1990.

Facilities

Malta has been blessed by nature with one of the best natural harbours in the Mediterranean and the decline of its traditional role as a Navy base and shipping centre has led to the development of its yachting facilities, which are already among the best in the region. Marina facilities are still being expanded and new pontoons and docks have been installed in the two creeks leading off Marsamxett harbour. Comprehensive repair facilities are also available with several boatyards offering a full range of services, haul-out, maintenance and refits. There is a good selection of marine supplies with all major manufacturers of marine equipment being represented locally. Several companies specialise in the maintenance of yachts left unattended in Malta for longer periods, as an increasing number of European owners have their yachts permanently based there. Provisioning is good and duty-free stores are also available to yachts in transit.

Further Reading

Mediterranean Cruising Handbook
Yachting in Malta

MONACO

Monaco is a small independent principality lying on the southern coast of France, surrounded by the French department of the Alpes Maritimes. Most people know it for its palace, casino and Grand Prix. The Grimaldi family have ruled Monaco since the thirteenth century, the state's independence being recognised by France in 1512. Unlike other small countries in Europe, Monaco was not absorbed by a larger state, although always remaining within the French sphere of influence. A customs union was created between Monaco and France in 1865. Rainier III, prince since 1949, introduced constitutional reforms in 1962. The principality is a prosperous tourist and business centre, with low taxes and no income tax. Of the 28,000 inhabitants, only around 20 per cent are Monégasques.

Immigration

There are no customs controls at the frontiers of France and Monaco. However, all foreigners entering Monaco must have the necessary documents (passport or identity card) and visas, if these are required to enter

France. A stay of up to three months is allowed, after which permission must be obtained from the nearest French consulate to be resident in France, followed by a request for residence permission in Monaco.

Procedure on arrival

There is only one port and yachts should go to the marina at Fontvielle, not the old harbour which is unprotected from the east. Fontvielle 43°44′N, 7°25′E is a fully equipped marina with good services and repair facilities.

MOROCCO

Situated on the north-west shoulder of Africa, Morocco is in some ways the bridge between Africa and Europe. All the main cities lie along the fertile coast, while behind Marrakesh stand the Atlas mountains, which were thought in ancient times to hold up the heavens. The Sahara desert stretches along the south, while to the north are the narrow Straits of Gibraltar.

In spite of its strategic position close to the sailing routes between Europe, the Mediterranean, Madeira and the Canary Islands, Morocco has done very little to develop its yachting facilities. Most of the large ports have a yacht club and there are a certain number of locally owned yachts, but the facilities do not compare with those of the neighbouring countries. Formalities are also complicated and foreign sailors are still regarded with a certain degree of suspicion. Although the coastline and harbours offer limited cruising, the attractions ashore, such as the old quarters and markets of some ports or the country beyond them, may make a visit to Morocco worthwhile.

Country Profile

Morocco was a Berber society from early times, its peoples being the agricultural Masmouda, the nomadic Sanhaja and the Zenata horsemen of the steppes. Over the centuries the country has been invaded by Carthage, Rome, Spain, Portugal and the Arabs, the latter having the most lasting effect. In the eleventh and twelfth centuries AD a Berber dynasty unified the Maghreb and Andalucia into a vast empire and only in 1492 with the fall of Moorish Granada did this link with Spain end. In the sixteenth century a religious revival and reunification came under the Saadi dynasty, driving out the Portuguese traders on the coast and attacking Spain. In the following century the Alaouite dynasty came to power and still rules

Practical Information

LOCAL TIME: GMT. Summer time GMT + 1 April to October.

BUOYAGE: IALA A

CURRENCY: Dirham (DH) of 100 centimes. It is illegal to take DH in or out of the country. It is also difficult to change DH back into foreign currency on departure.

BUSINESS HOURS
Sunday is a holiday; some shops also close on Fridays.
Banks: winter 0815–1130/1415–1630 Monday to Friday; summer 0830–1130/1500–1700 Monday to Friday; during Ramadan 0930–1430.
Business and shops: Tangier 0900–1100/1600–2000; rest of the country 0900–1200/1500–1800; during Ramadan 1000–1500.
Government offices: winter 0830–1200/1430–1800 Monday to Friday, 0800–1300 Saturday (summer afternoons open 1600–1900); during Ramadan 1000–1500.

ELECTRICITY: 110/220 V, 50 Hz

PUBLIC HOLIDAYS
1 January: New Year's Day
3 March: Coronation Day
1 May
9 July: Youth Festival
18 November: Independence Day
Variable Muslim holidays:
Ras el Am (New Year's Day)
Ashoura (Memorial Day)
Mouloud (Prophet's birthday)
Start of Ramadan
Eid el-Seghir
Eid el-Kebir
Hijra
NB: Mosques cannot be visited by non-Muslims.

COMMUNICATIONS
There is an international telephone office in Casablanca. Elsewhere telephone calls have to be made at the post office.
Post offices: 0830–1800 in large towns; elsewhere they close 1200–1500.
There are international flights to Europe and elsewhere from Casablanca, Tangier, Rabat, Fez, Agadir and Marrakesh. There are flights to the Canary Islands from Agadir and Casablanca. There are ferry services to Southern Spain.

MEDICAL
Casablanca has a good public hospital. Medical facilities are adequate in the larger cities.

DIPLOMATIC MISSIONS
In Rabat:
Algeria: 8 rue d'Azrou. ☎ (7) 24215.
Canada: 13 bis rue Jaafar As-Sadiq. ☎ (7) 713-75.
Egypt: 31 Charia Al Jazair, Place Abraham Lincoln.
Mauritania: 6 rue Thami Lam Souissi.
Senegal: 11 Avenue de Marrakesh. ☎ (7) 26090.
Spain: 3 rue Mohammed el Fateh.
Tunisia: 6 Avenue de Fas. ☎ (7) 25644.
United Kingdom: 17 Blvd de la Tour Hassan. ☎ (7) 20905.
United States: 2 Avenue de Marrakesh. ☎ (7) 622-65.
In Casablanca:
United Kingdom: 60 Blvd d'Arifa.
United States: 8 Blvd Moulay Youssef.

today. Europeans were kept out and throughout the eighteenth and nineteenth centuries the country remained impervious to change. However, increasing numbers of European traders and explorers eventually forced the sultans to open up to trade. Great power rivalry let Morocco retain its independence until the early twentieth century when the country was divided into Spanish and French protectorates. This provoked a nationalist religious revival, but only after the Second World War did these feelings emerge more strongly. Mohammed V of the Alaouite dynasty became king and in 1956 independence was achieved.

A continuing problem has been that of the Western Sahara. Morocco annexed part of it after Spain withdrew, which gave the monarchy popularity at home, but worsened the country's relations with Algeria. A liberation movement is still active in the Western Sahara.

Military spending on the Saharan conflict is a burden on the economy. Phosphates are the main export and tourism is increasing rapidly. Wheat and citrus fruit grow in the fertile coastal areas and much livestock is kept. However, much of the population is poor and illiterate. Many Moroccans have emigrated, especially to France, and remittances sent home by workers overseas are important to the economy.

The population numbers 24 million, being mainly Arab in urban areas and Berber in the more rural regions. There is also a long-established Jewish community. The majority are Muslim, but there are also some Christians and Jews. Arabic is the main language, while French is widely spoken, as well as some Berber dialects. The capital Rabat, on the Atlantic coast, replaced the old capital Fez at the start of the twentieth century.

On the coast the climate is one of hot summers and mild winters. Westerly winds predominate on the North African coast in winter, while most of the summer the winds are ENE. On the Atlantic coast summer winds are mostly northerly.

Entry Regulations

Ports of entry

Nador 35°17'N 2°56'W, Al Hoceima 35°15'N 3°54'W, Tangier 35°47'N 5°48'W, Kenitra 34°16'N 6°35'W, Mohammedia 33°43'N 7°22'W, Casablanca

33°37'N 7°36'W, El Jadida 33°16'N 8°31'W, Jorf
Lasfar 33°07'N 8°38'W, Safi 32°18'N 9°15'W,
Agadir 30°25'N 9°38'W.

Procedure on arrival

All crew members, including the captain, are supposed
to remain on board until formalities have been completed, but in practice the captain may have to go
ashore to look for the officials in order to report the
yacht's arrival and request clearance. He should report
first to customs, who will require an inventory and a
crew list. Customs often keep the ship's papers until
departure. An entry declaration must be filled in at the
Capitainerie office (Port Captain's office). Health
control is done by Santé Maritime and a complete
maritime health declaration must be made. One must
also clear with immigration, who often keep passports
until departure. One should be prepared for delays in
the return of documents. Yachts must check in with
the port captain and police at each port visited. Occasionally photographs may be taken of the boat and
crew by officials.

Tangiers: It is possible to come alongside the dock
inside the small boat harbour, which is crowded with
fishing boats. If the boat is not visited by customs and
immigration on arrival, the captain must take the
passports and ship's papers to the various offices all
located within the harbour area.

Casablanca: Entry formalities can be easily done at the
yacht club, as both customs and police have an office
there.

El Jadida: The captain should go ashore with the
passports and ship's papers and visit customs, immigration and port captain's office, all of which are in the
harbour area.

Agadir: One should contact Port Control on VHF
Channel 16 and ask permission to come alongside the
commercial dock for clearance. The ship's papers must
be presented to the port captain who may retain them
during the yacht's stay in port. Similarly, the port
police will retain passports and issue special passes for
access through the harbour gates.

Essaouira: This small port 65 miles south of El Jadida
is not an official port of entry, but yachts may call there.
All formalities are accomplished at the harbour gate,
where the captain must present passports and ship's
papers.

Customs

Firearms must be declared on arrival and will be either
sealed on board or kept in custody until departure. The
penalty for non-declaration of firearms is decided by a
military tribunal.

Animals need valid vaccination certificates; if not
possessing these, vaccination will be carried out on the
spot at the owner's expense and the animal put under
observation.

A yacht may remain in Morocco for a temporary
importation period of three months. Extensions are
possible, but the yacht then may become eligible for
duty.

Immigration

A three months stay is normally given.

Visas are not required for citizens of West European
countries, except Portugal, Netherlands and Belgium.

French and Spanish nationals are allowed unlimited
stay, but they must report to police within three
months of arrival.

Other nationalities, including USA, Canada, Australia, Japan and New Zealand, need visas which
should be obtained in advance.

Visas allow up to 90 days stay with two entries.
Extensions can be obtained from the local police, but
one needs a letter of recommendation from one's own
embassy and one must apply within 15 days of arrival.

People may be refused entry if their passport has an
Israeli stamp in it. South African and Israeli nationals
are refused entry.

Health

Hepatitis, polio and typhoid inoculations recommended.

Fees

Overtime is charged outside of office hours (0800–
1800) on weekdays, all day Sunday and public holidays.

Port charges and pilotage fee if over 50 tons.

Restrictions

There are areas prohibited to yachts and these are
mentioned in the Notices to Mariners. If in doubt, one
should check with the port captain before leaving for
the next port, particularly in the south of the country.

Travel south of Tan Tan into the Western Sahara
needs special permission from the military authorities.

Facilities

Provisioning is good in all major ports, although
imported goods are expensive. The fresh produce
markets are good everywhere, while the one in Tangiers is excellent. In most places fuel must be carried in
jerrycans from a fuel station. In some ports men calling
themselves 'shipkeepers' offer their services. They will
deal with everything and also ensure that nothing is
stolen off the yacht.

Repair facilities in the bigger ports are adequate and there are small boatyards in both Tangiers and Casablanca which have dealt with yachts in the past and carried out simple repairs.

Casablanca: There are a number of workshops, which have attained a certain degree of expertise as they have dealt with the French Transat des Alisées every three years during the last decade. However, the general lack of facilities and other considerations have forced the organisers to abandon the Casablanca start of this transatlantic race in 1990.

The yacht club lies in the south corner at the base of the mole. It is possible to moor the boat at one of the club buoys. The yacht club welcomes visitors and charges a daily fee for the use of its facilities. Water is available on the club dock, but its quality is questionable. Fuel is available by jerrycan. Repair facilities in town are adequate as there is a large fishing fleet and there is the usual range of workshops and small boatyards. Simple electronic repairs can be done with the help of one of the yacht club members.

El Jadida: Lying approximately 50 miles SW of Casablanca, there is a good anchorage off the harbour entrance, but no protection from the NW swell, which is common in winter.

There is a small harbour, but this is only accessible to shallow drafted vessels. The dinghy can be left at the yacht club, which has no facilities except a restaurant. There is good provisioning in town and an excellent fresh produce market.

Agadir: One can anchor off the yacht club, which welcomes visitors. The dinghy can be left at the yacht club pontoon. Water can be obtained at the same dock, which has sufficient depth at high tide. There is good provisioning in town.

Further Reading

Africa on a Shoestring

ROMANIA

Situated in Eastern Europe with a small outlet to the Black Sea and the river Danube separating it from the Balkans, Romania has always been at the crossroads of East and West. As the only Latin people in Eastern Europe, Romanians have always regarded themselves as different from their neighbours, but nearly half a century of communist rule has virtually destroyed traditional life. The profound changes that are sweeping through the former Soviet empire may help return Romania to the European fold.

The Black Sea coast is flat and lacks natural harbours and anchorages, so from the cruising point of view, Romania has very little to offer with the possible exception of cruising the Danube Delta, one of the few remaining wildlife sanctuaries in Europe. The Danube itself is navigable along most of its length and yachts have successfully cruised down the Danube from Austria through Czechoslovakia, Hungary, Yugoslavia, Bulgaria and Romania. Sailing the river in the opposite direction is difficult and slow because of the strong current.

Country Profile

The state of Dacia was fairly developed when conquered by the Romans in AD 106 and it remained a province of the empire until the third century AD, to be followed by invasions by Visigoths, Huns, Lombards and Avars. In the sixth century Slavs settled, and then Bulgarians, while in the eleventh century Hungary conquered Transylvania. From the late thirteenth century the principalities of Wallachia and Moldavia were established, becoming vassals of the Ottoman Empire. After the battle of Mohacs in 1526 Transylvania also fell under Ottoman rule.

The three regions were briefly united at the turn of the sixteenth century under Michael the Brave, but in 1691 the Hapsburgs annexed Transylvania, and the Turks hardened their grip over the rest of the region. In the nineteenth century revolutions against Turkish rule failed, and the principalities were for a time jointly occupied by the Turks and Russians. Moldavia and Wallachia were united as Romania in 1861, but only some years later in 1878 was Romania recognised as an independent kingdom.

Joining the First World War on the side of the Allies in 1916, at the peace settlement Romania gained Dobruja, Banat, Bukovina and Transylvania. King Carol II established a dictatorial regime from 1930, until deposed in 1940 by Antonescu who allied with Germany, and entered the war against the Soviet Union in 1941. An armistice was signed with the USSR in 1944 and King Michael ruled until forced to abdicate in 1947. The communists came to power and a people's republic was proclaimed.

In 1965 Nicolae Ceauşescu became General Secretary of the communist party, and thereafter his increasingly repressive rule dominated the country. In 1989 he was overthrown by a revolution and executed, and the Front for National Salvation took power provisionally, then winning free elections in

Practical Information

LOCAL TIME: GMT + 2. Summer time GMT + 3 from early April until the end of September.

BUOYAGE: IALA A

CURRENCY: Leu (plural Lei) of 100 bani

BUSINESS HOURS
Banks: 0900–1200. Exchange facilities in hotels.
Shops: 0900–1800
Government offices: 0700–1500 (0730–1530) Monday to Friday, 0730–1200 on alternate Saturdays.

ELECTRICITY: 220 V, 50 Hz

PUBLIC HOLIDAYS
1,2 January: New Year's Day
1,2 May: Labour Days
23,24 August: Liberation Day

COMMUNICATIONS
International telephone calls can be made only from the Telephone Company, open 24 hours in main cities. There are regular international flights from Bucharest to many European capitals, also some destinations in Asia, Africa and North America. There is also a network of internal flights.

MEDICAL
Nationals of certain countries are entitled to free medical care in an emergency. The standards in most hospitals are below the normal European standards.

DIPLOMATIC MISSIONS
In Bucharest:
Canada: Strada Nicolae Iorga 36. ☎ (0) 506580.
United Kingdom: Strada Jules Michelet 24. ☎(0) 111634.
United States: Strada Tudor Arghezi 7–9. ☎ (0) 124040.

May 1990. The political situation still remains unstable.

The economy is dominated by metallurgical, petrochemical and mechanical heavy industry. The agricultural sector is mainly state-owned and produces largely wheat, maize and sugar beet. Under Ceauşescu a policy of austerity was imposed to try and combat Romania's large foreign debt, and the economy geared to export, while the population had to cope with constant shortages. This also affected the tourist industry on the Black Sea coast, which declined.

The population is 23 million, the majority being Romanian, but with a 2 million minority of Hungarians living mainly in Transylvania. There are also an estimated 2 million gypsies, the largest gypsy population in Europe. The German minority has dwindled in recent years due to emigration and a similar exodus has reduced the Jewish and Greek communities which used to be sizeable. Other minorities are Armenian, Turkish and Lippoveni, who are Russians inhabiting the Danube Delta area. Romanian is a Latin language with some Slav and Turkish elements. Minorities speak their own languages and many Transylvanians speak Romanian, Hungarian and German fluently. French and English are also widely spoken as foreign languages. The majority are Orthodox Christian, but there are also Catholics and Lutherans. The capital is Bucharest.

The climate is typically temperate with hot summers and cold winters. The winds along the Black Sea coast are very much influenced by the surrounding landmass and in summer there is a daily pattern of land and sea breezes. An onshore breeze comes up around midday and usually dies by dusk to be followed by a land breeze during the night.

Entry Regulations

Ports of entry
Constanta 44°10′N 28°39′E, Sulina 45°09′N 29°39′E.

Procedure on arrival
The recent political changes in Romania have removed some of the restrictions applied to visiting yachts.
Constanta: If wishing to clear in at Constanta one should make for the small boat harbour, Port Tomis, about half a mile north of the main commercial harbour. The boat will be visited by customs and immigration, after which the captain has to go into the main harbour and clear with the Port Authority. The ship's papers will be kept until departure.
Sulina: It is also possible to clear in at the port of Sulina, at the mouth of the Danube. One can tie up to the main wharf to clear with customs. Navigating in the river can be very difficult because of the strong current.

Customs
Firearms must be declared and will be detained.

There are no restrictions on animals, but as there is rabies in Romania, pets should be vaccinated.

Immigration
At the time of writing, all foreign visitors need a visa, which can be obtained on arrival. Visas can also be obtained from Romanian missions abroad, such as the consulate in Istanbul.

Fees
Visa fee, which must be paid in convertible foreign currency. Harbour fees.

Danube–Black Sea Canal

Cruising yachts may use this Canal, which starts near Constanta and bypasses the Danube Delta. There are certain height restrictions both in the Canal and on the Danube and most yachts will have to lower their masts before entering the Canal.

Facilities

Facilities for yachts are practically non-existent. Simple repairs can be undertaken in workshops in either Constanta or Sulina. There are very few local yachts and most of them are kept in Port Tomis. Any of their owners would be the best source of information and advice regarding any repairs that are needed. Provisioning is very limited, although foreign sailors may use a special store within the compound of the commercial harbour where certain items are available if paid for in foreign currency. Diesel fuel can only be bought in jerrycans from a station in town.

Further Reading

Improbable Voyage

SPAIN

With coasts on both the Atlantic and the Mediterranean, there are four main areas in Spain for cruising, which are all very different. The Atlantic coast is in two sections either side of Portugal, the north-west coast bordering the Bay of Biscay and the smaller south-west coast of Andalucia from the Portuguese border to the Straits of Gibraltar. From Gibraltar the Mediterranean coast stretches the length of the Iberian peninsula to France and the fourth cruising area is the Balearic Islands.

The most attractive natural cruising areas of Spain are situated at its extremes, the north-west Atlantic coast and the Balearics, the islands being one of the Mediterranean's prime yachting centres. Nature has been generous in these places creating many natural harbours, secluded coves and pretty anchorages. Elsewhere man has had to make his own contribution and as well as old harbours, many attractive new ports have been created, especially along the southern Mediterranean coast, where there are marinas placed at strategic intervals, so that one is never more than a few hours' sail away from the next harbour. There is a lot to see both inland as well as in the ports along the coast in a country of rich culture, where the relaxed Spanish way of life still can be sampled in the many waterfront cafes and restaurants. It is possible to navigate some of the rivers, such as the Guadalquivir where one can sail as far as Seville. The southern ports are popular wintering spots, due to the mild winter weather.

During the last decade Spain's Mediterranean coast and islands have seen a tremendous development in yachting facilities with new marinas being built everywhere. Initially the development was needed to cope with the demands of foreign sailors, many of whom based their yachts permanently in Spain. With the exception of a few traditional sailing centres such as Mallorca, Barcelona and Cadiz there was little local interest in yachting in Spain, but this is rapidly changing as Spaniards come to enjoy standards of living comparable to those of their partners in the European Community.

Country Profile

The Iberian peninsula was inhabited from Stone Age times, and in the first millennium BC the Celts invaded and mingled with the native Iberians. Phoenician and Greek colonies were established along the coasts. The Carthaginians conquered Spain in the third century BC, but were expelled by the Romans who spread their control over the whole peninsula. After the decline of the Roman Empire, Vandals and Visigoths overran the country and in AD 711 the Moors invaded from North Africa. Spain was gradually reconquered by the Christians from the north, and in 1479 the kingdoms of Castile and Aragon were united under Ferdinand V and Isabella I. In 1492 the Moors were driven from their last stronghold in Granada, and in the same year Christopher Colombus sailed to the New World and claimed it for Spain. The Spaniards explored the Americas over the next century, mainly in search of gold and silver, and established a vast empire.

Spain reached the height of her power in the sixteenth century under Charles V who inherited both the Spanish and Hapsburg thrones. After this, Spanish domination of Europe was slowly eroded, especially by the War of the Spanish Succession (1701–14) after Charles II of Spain died heirless and Louis XIV of France tried to place his own grandson on the throne. Spain lost her European possessions and the succession went to the French Bourbons. In 1808 Napoleon placed his brother Joseph Bonaparte on the Spanish throne, but the Bourbon Ferdinand VII was restored in 1814. His reactionary rule, however, led to the loss of the Latin American colonies.

In the nineteenth century the country was troubled by conflict between the royalists and republicans, and

Practical Information

LOCAL TIME: GMT + 1. Summer time
GMT + 2 April to September.

BUOYAGE: IALA A

CURRENCY: Peseta. The maximum that
can be imported is 100,000, and no more
than 20,000 may be exported. Up to
50,000 pesetas worth of foreign currency
can be exported.

BUSINESS HOURS
Banks: 0900–1400 Monday to Friday,
0900–1300 Saturday.
Business: 0900–1845 winter,
0900–1400/1630–1900 summer, Monday
to Friday.
Shops: 0800/0900–1200, 1400–1800/2000
Monday to Saturday.
Government offices: 0900–1300,
1600–1900 Monday to Saturday.

ELECTRICITY: 110/220 V, 50 Hz

PUBLIC HOLIDAYS
1 January: New Year's Day
6 January: Epiphany
19 March: St Joseph's Day
Maundy Thursday, Good Friday
1 May
Corpus Christi
18 July: National Day
25 July: St James' Day
15 August: Assumption
12 October: Columbus Day
1 November: All Saints' Day
8 December: Immaculate Conception
24, 25 December: Christmas

COMMUNICATIONS
International direct dialling is possible
from public phones, which have
instructions in English. International
dialling access code 07 and a second
dialling tone is obtained. Cheaper rates
after 2000.
There are also telephone offices with
metered booths in major tourist centres.
Post office (correo): telegrams, telex
and fax services as well as poste
restante (lista de correos).
There are international flights to
European destinations from all major
centres. Madrid international airport has
regular flights to all parts of the world.
There is also an excellent network of
internal flights, both within peninsular
Spain, the Canaries and Balearics.

DIPLOMATIC MISSIONS
In Madrid:
Australia: Paseo de la Castellano.
☎ (1) 279-8501.
Canada: Edificio Goya, Calle Nuñez de
Balboa 35, Apartado 587.
☎ (1) 431-4300.
United Kingdom: Calle de Fernando el
Santo 16. ☎ (1) 419-0200.
United States: Serrano 75.
☎ (1) 276-3400.

---

after the war with the United States in 1898 Spain lost Cuba, the Philippines and Puerto Rico. Strong anarchist and nationalist movements developed and in 1923 Primero de Rivera led a coup and established a military dictatorship. The growth of republicanism resulted in the overthrow of the Bourbon monarchy in 1931, but the new republic was faced with strong opposition from the Church and landowners. Civil war broke out in 1936 when the Falangists under General Franco rose against the Popular Front government. In 1939 Franco established a dictatorship, which remained neutral in the Second World War although friendly to the Axis powers. Spain was declared a monarchy in 1947 with Franco the regent for life. Franco died in 1975, succeeded by King Juan Carlos I, and gradually the country returned to democracy. Spain is a member of NATO and the European Community.

Since 1975 the Spanish economy has grown and been liberalised. Agriculture still remains of considerable importance, but industry and services have developed. A traditional trade deficit is helped by tourist revenues. Entry into the Common Market has meant some adaptation, and Spain remains one of the less developed members of the European Community.

The population numbers 40.2 million and most Spaniards are Catholic. Castilian Spanish is the official language and is spoken by virtually everyone in Spain.

Catalan is the second major language and is spoken in the Catalonia region centered on Barcelona. The Galician and Basque languages are in common use in those regions. The capital of Spain is Madrid.

The climate varies greatly from the Atlantic north coast, which is wet and cool, to the Mediterranean south and east, where summers are very hot and winters mild. The winds are just as varied, the north coast coming under the influence of Atlantic weather systems, with south-westerly to north-westerly winds predominating in winter and northerly winds in summer, although land and sea breezes can be experienced inshore. This is also the case along the south-western coast during summer, while the rest of the year, winds are either easterly or westerly. Alternating sea and land breezes are also characteristic of the Mediterranean coast. The eastern coast and Balearics are occasionally affected by the mistral, a N or NW wind which can rapidly reach gale force.

Entry Regulations

Ports of entry
Because of the large numbers of ports of entry as well as marinas which have customs offices where entry formalities can be completed, only the main ports and marinas are listed which are close to Spain's frontiers

and are more commonly used by foreign yachts to clear in.

Atlantic coast: San Sebastian 43°28′N 30°48′W, Santander 43°28′N 3°46′W, Bilbao 43°17′N 2°55′W, Gijon 43°33′N 5°40′W, El Ferrol 43°28′N 8°16′W, La Coruña 43°23′N 8°22′W, Bayona 42°57′N 9°11′W, Vigo 42°14′N 8°40′W, Ayamonte 37°13′N 7°22′W, Huelva 37°07′N 6°49′W, Puerto Sherry 36°36′N 6°13′W, Cadiz 36°30′N 6°20′W, Algeciras 36°07′N 5°26′W.

Mediterranean coast: La Duquesa 36°21′N 15°14′W, Puerto Banus 36°29′N 4°57′W, Málaga 36°41′N 4°26′W, Motril 36°43′N 3°31′W, Almería 36°50′N 2°30′W, Cartagena 37°35′N 0°58′W, Alicante 38°20′N 0°29′W, Denia 38°50′N 0°07′E, Valencia 39°27′N 0°18′W, Tarragona 41°06′N 1°14′E, Barcelona 41°21′N 2°10′E, Palamos 41°50′N 3°08′E.

Balearics: Ibiza 38°54′N 1°28′E, Palma de Mallorca 39°33′N 2°38′E, Andraitx 39°33′N 2°24′E, Alcudia 39°49′N 3°08′E, Mahón 39°52′N 4°19′E.

Procedure on arrival

The captain should proceed ashore and clear customs (Aduana) and immigration (Guardia Civil or Policia Nacional) at a port of entry. Normally officials then come to inspect the boat. In subsequent ports where Guardia Civil and/or customs officials are stationed, the clearance procedure may be repeated, although this varies from place to place. Sometimes the local yacht club or marina inform the authorities about the arrival of foreign yachts and many marinas have their own customs office. After having cleared into Spain, the procedure at subsequent ports seems to depend on the attitude of local officials. However, one should be prepared to show all relevant documents whenever asked. One may be asked for registration papers, crew lists, certificate of competence and proof of marine insurance. Once cleared, yachts are free to stop in ports and anchorages where there are no officials.

If staying in Spain over 90 days without leaving, a special customs permit (permiso aduanero) must be obtained from customs. Otherwise, yachts can leave and on re-entry will be given another 90 days.

Procedure on departure

One should clear with immigration and customs on departure from Spain. Customs will record the date of departure on the customs permit if one has one. This permit can be used again if re-entering Spain within the period of its validity. Each arrival and departure must be noted by customs on the permit.

Customs

Firearms and animals must be declared.

Customs permit

If intending to remain longer than 90 days, or if wishing to leave the yacht in Spain, a customs permit should be obtained on arrival. This permit allows a yacht to be temporarily imported, without paying import duty, for up to six months in one calendar year. The permit is valid until 31 December, regardless of when the permit was issued. Only non-residents of Spain, who are not working in the country, are eligible for the permit. In order to be regarded as a non-resident, residents of European and Mediterranean countries must not exceed a stay of six months in each calendar year, while nationals of the USA and other countries must not exceed eight months in each calendar year. The yacht must not be used for commercial purposes while in Spain.

An extension to the permit of six months is possible by applying to customs. Four further extensions, each of six months, can be obtained, but for these 10 per cent duty must be paid on the value of the yacht, the owner of the yacht must still be non-resident, and must change a certain amount of foreign currency into pesetas. In order to prove continuing non-residency, non-residents must have their passports stamped in order to show that they have not spent more than 90 days in Spain at any one time while the boat was permanently there. It appears to be no longer necessary to place a yacht under Customs seal to avoid paying tax when the owner leaves the country for a long period of time. As the regulations are being changed, it is advisable to check with Customs on arrival.

Immigration

Most nationalities are given 90 days stay on entering Spain. Visas are required for stays longer then 90 days, to be obtained in advance from a Spanish embassy or consulate abroad.

US citizens are allowed a six month stay without a visa and EC citizens are allowed a three month stay with no visa, although this will change as Spain becomes a full member of the EC. Nationals of Israel and South Africa require visas.

Often the immigration official does not stamp passports of people entering on yachts, but if planning to leave Spain by another means of transport, an entry stamp (entrada) will be needed.

Charter

Foreign yachts can charter in Spain under certain conditions. Charter vessels must not exceed 22 metres LOA nor carry more than 12 passengers. They must comply with the international regulations for the safety of life at sea and have an insurance to cover both crew and passengers. A special permit must be obtained from the local maritime authorities (Comandancia de Marina) and also a licence from customs. Yachts will be granted a five month period (extendable for two further periods of five months) in which to charter. If such vessels are engaged in any kind of fishing, proper licences must be obtained both for the passengers and crew.

Fees

Overtime is not normally charged, as all formalities are completed during normal working hours and yachts are not expected to clear at other times.

Harbour fees are charged in most ports if there are any facilities provided for yachts.

Facilities

Although there are marinas all around Spain's coasts, comprehensive repair facilities are only available in the most important yachting centres. The prime yachting centre is Palma de Mallorca, where several companies specialising in marine work have set up base. Facilities in the Balearics generally are probably the best to be found anywhere in Spain. Another centre with good facilities is Barcelona and the surrounding area. There are also good facilities along the Costa del Sol.

Facilities outside the Mediterranean are not so easily available. On the south Atlantic coast there are good facilities at the new Puerto Sherry near Cadiz. On the north coast the best range is to be found at La Coruña where the yacht club can be particularly helpful. Most marinas have haul-out facilities, usually by travelift, while in many ports there are slipways dealing with fishing boats.

Marine supplies and spares are not as widely available as one would expect in a country with such a large boating community, both local and foreign. There are chandleries with a good selection in the main sailing centres, but in smaller ports and marinas the availability of spares is limited.

Yachts in transit can import spares and equipment duty-free, but the procedure is not simple. The owner must lodge a cash deposit with the local customs office equal to the value of the imported goods. This is returned when the goods have been placed on the boat under customs supervision. In the absence of a customs officer, the document must be signed by the police before the deposit is returned. In some places it may be necessary to employ the services of a shipping agent.

Spanish charts are available from the Navy office (Comandancia de Marina) in major ports or the Hydrographic Institute in Cadiz. Now that value added tax is charged on diesel fuel bought by yachts, the fuel must be obtained from marinas and not from fishermen's pumps on quays. LPG gas (butane) is widely available and filling stations are located in all major ports. Provisioning is good everywhere and local fresh produce is of very good quality, although its availability may depend on the season.

Most Spanish yacht clubs are exclusive social clubs, where visitors are not particularly welcome. Those which have docking facilities operate on a commercial basis charging visitors marina fees. Dress etiquette is strict and a sloppy appearance is frowned upon.

Spanish North Africa

Ceuta and Melilla are Spanish enclaves on the north coast of Morocco, administered as city provinces of Spain. Also Spanish are the small islands of Alhucemas, Chafarinas and Penon de la Gomera. The cities became Spanish in the fifteenth century, when the Moors were expelled from the Iberian peninsula and remained Spanish when Morocco became independent in 1956. Ceuta and Melilla are important military bases. Visa requirements are the same as for Spain.
Ceuta: There is a small yacht harbour which has pontoons, although it is not very protected from swell. It is a good place for provisioning as the prices are reasonable. Diesel also is cheaper than on the Spanish mainland and Morocco as the town is duty free.
Melilla: Lying several hundred miles east along the Moroccan coast from Ceuta, Melilla is not as large. A yacht club is located inside the fishing port, where berthing is provided for visiting yachts.

Canary Islands

As the Canary Islands are an autonomous overseas region of Spain, they are dealt with separately on page 110.

Further Reading

Atlantic Spain and Portugal
Foreign Cruising Notes 2
Imray's Foreign Port Forms
East Spain Pilot
Mediterranean Cruising Handbook
Balearic Islands Yachtsman's Directory
Cruising Association Handbook

SYRIA

Syria lies on the coast of the Eastern Mediterranean, which used to be called the Levant as the sun rose there. Its capital Damascus is reputed to be the city which has been continually inhabited for the longest period in the world, and were it not for the xenophobic attitude of the present regime, Syria would be an interesting country to visit. Unfortunately the present political situation keeps this country off the track for yachts, although every year a few cruising boats brave the official barriers and call at one of the Syrian ports. The coast lacks natural harbours, and the country is only worth visiting for the ancient sites to be found inland or such medieval landmarks as the Crusader castle Krak des Chevaliers.

Country Profile

In earliest times the Levant coast was a flourishing trading centre, and Damascus has been a thriving city since 5000 BC. Part of the Persian, Greek and Roman empires and then under the Arabs from the seventh century, the city was sacked by the Mongols, then annexed by the Turks and relegated to the role of a rather unimportant province in the Ottoman Empire. The city of Damascus was liberated from the Turks by the troops of the Arab revolt led by Lawrence of Arabia during the First World War. Syria was placed under French mandate, until independence was achieved at the end of the Second World War. Syria's postwar history has been marked by conflict with Israel. The country has fostered links with the USSR rather than the West. Syria has intervened in the Lebanon conflict since 1976.

The Arabic population of 9.6 million are Muslim. Some French is spoken as well as Arabic.

The climate is of the Mediterranean type with hot dry summers and mild winters, especially along the coast. The prevailing winds of summer are westerly. A day breeze usually comes up at noon and lasts until sunset.

Entry Regulations

Ports of entry
Lattakia 35°31′N 35°46′E, Banias 35°14′N 35°56′E, Tartous 34°54′N 35°52′E.

Procedure on arrival
Port Control should be contacted prior to arrival on VHF Channel 16. Lattakia is Syria's main port and as its officials are used to dealing with foreign vessels, this is the best port to enter.

Immigration
Visas must be obtained in advance from Syrian consulates or embassies abroad. A letter of recommendation from one's own embassy is required if the visa is not obtained in one's country of residence. Visitors are given a stay of 15 days on arrival. Visas are difficult to obtain, particularly by nationals of certain countries, such as the United States. Entry is refused to Israeli nationals or to anyone with an Israeli stamp in their

Practical Information

LOCAL TIME: GMT + 3

BUOYAGE: IALA A

CURRENCY: Syrian pound (S£) of 100 piastres

BUSINESS HOURS
The working week is Saturday to Thursday, Friday being the day of rest.

ELECTRICITY: 110 V, 50 Hz

PUBLIC HOLIDAYS
1 January: New Year's Day

8 March: Revolution Day
Easter*
17 April: Independence Day
1 May: Labour Day
Martyrs Day*
Prophet's Day*
Ramadan*
23 July: Egyptian Revolution Day
Adha Bayram*
Muslim New Year
1 September: Libyan Revolution Day
6 October: Tishrin Liberation
25 December: Christmas Day
*Variable

COMMUNICATIONS
There are flights from Damascus to

Middle East, Asian, North African and European destinations.

DIPLOMATIC MISSIONS
In Damascus:
Australia: 128/A Farabi St, Mezzeh District. ☎ (11) 664317/662603.
Canada: Sheraton Hotel, Omayyad Square. ☎ (11) 229300.
United Kingdom: British Interests Section of the Australian Embassy, Quarter Malki, 11 Mohammed Kurd Ali St, Imm Kotob. ☎ (11) 712561.
United States: Abu Rumaneh, Al Mansur St, No.2. ☎ (11) 333052.

passport. Any evidence of a previous visit to Israel is sufficient reason to be forced to leave the country. Visitors must change US$100 on arrival.

Further Reading

Southern Turkey, the Levant and Cyprus

TUNISIA

Facing the Mediterranean with both its north and east coasts, Tunisia lies between Algeria and Libya. The main towns and good beaches, which are Tunisia's main tourist asset, are situated on the fertile east coast. The country's long association with France has left a noticeable influence in Tunisia's culture and way of life.

Of all the North African countries, Tunisia has approached yachting in the most systematic way. Realising the considerable revenue that can be generated by cruising yachts, the Tunisian government has encouraged the setting up of a chain of marinas and yacht harbours conveniently spaced along Tunisia's entire coast, from Zarzis in the south-east to Tabarka in the west. All ports are within reach of colourful towns and the boat can be left in safety to visit the interior. All this, plus the relatively low prices of the marinas have recently turned Tunisia into a popular cruising destination, especially for wintering. For those wishing to get a taste of Africa, without actually leaving the Mediterranean, Tunisia is undoubtedly the best choice.

Country Profile

The original inhabitants of North Africa were the Berber, named from the Roman 'barbari'. Therefore the Europeans called the Maghreb, which is present-day Tunisia, Morocco and Algeria, the Barbary coast. In 814 BC Queen Dido fled from Tyre with her followers, establishing the new city of Carthage. Legend says she set fire to herself rather than marry a local prince, while Virgil recounts 700 years later that this was due to the loss of Aeneas sailing back from Troy. It has been said that the island of Jerba was the Land of the Lotus Eaters in Homer's *Odyssey*.

Leaving legends aside, after the fall of Tyre, Carthage prospered and dominated much of the Mediterranean. This great maritime power was eclipsed by the rise of Rome and Carthage was finally destroyed. It was in this struggle with Rome that the Carthaginian general Hannibal took his elephants over the Alps. After the Romans came the Vandals, and then Byzantium ruled over the country. The seventh century brought the Arab invasions and the spread of Islam throughout the region. Following the defeat of the Moors in Spain, many settled in northern Africa, both craftsmen and seafarers. Some took to piracy and attacked Christian ships sailing in the Mediterranean. Tunisia was claimed in the sixteenth century both by the Barbarossa pirates, under Ottoman suzerainty, and Spain, and the country passed from being a Spanish protectorate to a Turkish military province. Throughout the eighteenth century piracy continued to bring wealth to the coast.

In the nineteenth century France invaded from Algeria, on pretext that the Bey's rule was bankrupt and corrupt. Tunisia eventually became a French protectorate, and many French people settled in the country. After the Second World War a guerilla war was waged until independence was granted in 1957 under Habib Bourguiba. Since the 1960s the government has kept close links with Western states.

Tunisia has seen rapid economic growth and is a relatively prosperous country. Income comes mainly from petroleum, olive oil and phosphates. The country has made efforts to industrialise, but agriculture remains important. Tourism is an increasing source of revenue. Unemployment is a problem and many Tunisians work abroad, especially in France and Libya.

The population is almost 7 million and is of a mixture which reflects the region's past history, of Arab, Roman, Greek, Spanish, Sicilian, French, Berber and black African origins. In the south the nomadic Bedouin still follow their traditional life. The main languages are Arabic, Berber and French, the latter being used in education, commerce and administration. Tunis is the bustling modern capital. The majority of the population are Muslim, with Christian and Jewish minorities.

Inland the climate can be very hot in summer, but the winters are mild. Spring and autumn are the best times. Westerly winds prevail along the north coast, but in summer they are usually interrupted by the daily alternating land and sea breezes. Along the east coast the prevailing winds of summer are SE. The occasional sirocco arrives with gale force winds from the south, but is usually short lived.

Entry Regulations

Ports of entry
Tabarka 36°58′N 8°45′E, Bizerte 37°16′N 9°53′E, Sidi Bou Said 36°52′N 10°21′E, La Goulette 36°49′N

Practical Information

LOCAL TIME: GMT + 1

BUOYAGE: IALA A

CURRENCY: Tunisian dinar (D) of 1000 millimes (M). The import and export of dinars is illegal. One should only change as much as needed because it is difficult to change back. Exchange receipts should be kept.

BUSINESS HOURS
Sunday is normally a holiday, although some keep Friday as a day of rest.
Banks: summer 0800–1100 Monday to Friday; winter 0800–1100/1400–1615 Monday to Thursday, 0800–1100/1330–1515 Friday; during Ramadan 0800–1130/1300–1430 Monday to Friday.
Business: winter 0830–1200/1500–1800 Monday to Friday; summer 0730–1200/1600–1830 Monday to Friday.
Shops: 0830–1200 winter/1500–1800; summer 1600-1900.

Food shops: 0700–1300/1530–2100 all year.
Souks (markets): 0830–1900 all year.
Government offices: winter 0830–1300/1500–1745 Monday to Thursday, 0830–1300 Friday, Saturday; summer 0700–1300 Monday to Saturday.

ELECTRICITY: 110/220 V, 50 Hz

PUBLIC HOLIDAYS
1 January: New Year's Day
18 January: Anniversary of the Revolution
20 March: Independence Day
9 April: Martyr's Day
1 May
1 June: Victory Day
25 July: Anniversary of the Republic
3 August: President's Birthday
13 August: Women's Day
3 September: Commemoration Day
15 October: Evacuation Day
Variable holidays: Mouloud, Eid el-Seghir, Eid el-Kebir, Ras El Ham El Hejeri, Achoura

COMMUNICATIONS
Telecommunications Centre, 29 rue Gamal Abdel Nasser, Tunis for overseas calls, open 24 hours.
Post office adjacent in rue Charles de Gaulle.
There are frequent international flights to many European, Middle East and North African destinations from Tunis and flights from Sfax to Malta and Paris. Internal flights link the main cities of Tunis, Monastir, Sfax and Gabes.

DIPLOMATIC MISSIONS
In Tunis:
Algeria: 136 rue de la Liberté.
Canada: 3 rue du Sénégal, Place Palestine. ☎ (1) 286577.
Egypt: 16 Rue Essayouti, El Menzeh. ☎ (1) 230004.
Morocco: 39 Rue 1 Juin. ☎ (1) 288063.
United Kingdom: 5 place de la Victoire. ☎ (1) 245100.
United States: 144 Avenue de la Liberté. ☎ (1) 282566.

10°18′E, Kelibia 36°50′N 11°07′E, El Kantaoui 35°52′N 10°36′E, Sousse 35°50′N 10°39′E, Sfax 34°44′N 10°46′E, Gabes 33°55′N 10°06′E, Djerba (Houmt Souk) 33°53′N 10°52′E, Zarzis 33°30′N 11°07′E.

Procedure on arrival
On arrival at a port of entry, all persons must remain on board until the formalities are completed. Customs require a list of dutiable goods and often wish to see the yacht's insurance papers. They will issue a cruising permit which is valid for three months and renewable for another three months in a one year period. One must also clear with police (immigration), and the harbour master (marine marchande) to whom harbour dues have to be paid. In subsequent ports officials may want to see the permit and will request crew lists.

Procedure on departure
When leaving each port, one should pay the harbour fees and check out with the port police, who will want to know the yacht's next destination.

On departure from Tunisia, the permit must be surrendered to customs. It is also necessary to clear with immigration on departure from Tunisia.

Customs
Firearms must be declared to customs on arrival.

Dogs and cats must have health certificates and certificates of vaccination between one and six months old.

Immigration
No visas are needed for up to a four month stay for citizens of Germany and the USA.

No visas are needed for up to a three month stay for citizens of West European countries, Barbados, Canada, Chile, Ghana, Gambia, Iceland, Japan, Malta and Turkey.

Citizens of Bulgaria may stay for up to two months with no visa, while citizens of Greece, South Korea and Hong Kong one month with no visa.

Algerians and Moroccans do not need a visa.

Other nationalities must obtain a visa in advance.

On arrival, passports are stamped by the police for three months, renewable for another three. One must notifiy the authorities of any crew changes.

Cruising permit
A cruising permit (triptique), obtainable on arrival when clearing in, is now compulsory. The permit is valid for six months and is issued free of charge. If

leaving the yacht in Tunisia, but departing the country by other means, the permit must be returned and customs will put the yacht in containment, during which time one cannot cruise, although crew can remain on board. When wishing to cruise again, one must obtain a new permit. If a yacht is left in Tunisia in the care of a marina or boatyard while the owner is abroad, the validity of the permit can be extended. If one stays over the six months without putting the boat into containment the boat becomes liable for duty.

Fees
Harbour dues

Restrictions
The commercial port of Ghannouch 1.5 miles north of Gabes is prohibited to yachts.

Fishing with scuba gear is forbidden.

Facilities

Yachting facilities are the best in North Africa and as good as in many other parts of the Mediterranean. There are now either new marinas or docks for yachts inside existing harbours along the entire Tunisian coast from Zarzis to Tabarka. There are marinas at Port Kantaoui, Sidi Bou Said, La Goulette and Monastir. La Goulette is nearest to the capital Tunis, while Sidi Bou Said is within walking distance of the ruins of Carthage. There are haulout facilities at Kantaoui, La Goulette, Monastir and Sfax, where there are also boatyards with a reasonable range of repair facilities. The best facilities are at Sidi Bon Said. Marine supplies are not widely available, but a new chandlery was due to open at Monastir in 1990. Provisioning is good everywhere, particularly in Monastir, which has some French-type supermarkets. There are street markets everywhere with a very good selection of fresh produce. In most places fuel is available on the dock, otherwise it can be ordered from a nearby station. LPG bottles can be filled in most ports.

Further Reading

Mediterranean Cruising Handbook
Africa on a Shoestring
Tunisie Plaisance
The Bridge and Galley Guide to Tunisia

TURKEY

Boasting a long coastline in the Eastern Mediterranean, the Sea of Marmara and the Black Sea, Turkey is almost surrounded by water. Spanning the two shores of the Bosporus and Dardanelles at the meeting point of Europe and Asia, Turkey cannot be labelled as either European or Asian. It is a melting pot of different cultures and civilisations, every one of which has left its indelible mark on the country and many of whose remains can still be seen, from Troy to Ephesus and Byzantium. This latter city became first Constantinople, and then, as Istanbul, the centre of the vast Ottoman Empire. One of the less praiseworthy legacies from these imperial days is a cumbersome bureaucratic apparatus, whose unwieldy methods are the only thing which can spoil the pleasure of sailing in this country, which has so much to offer for cruising.

Most cruising yachts sail in the south-west of the country, although the Sea of Marmara is also worth exploring and a sail through the heart of Istanbul is an exhilarating experience. Negotiating the crowded waters of the Bosporus can be nerve-racking at times, while the Black Sea coast of Turkey is less accessible partly because of prohibited areas.

Although lacking the profusion of islands of its Greek neighbour, this is more than made up for by a generous coastline indented by so many bays and coves that one can almost always pick a pretty anchorage within minutes of deciding to drop the anchor. Although the number of yachts cruising Turkey is almost doubling every year, many places are still uncrowded, especially out of the high season and particularly on the southern shore, from Marmaris to Antalya and beyond. In some of the places along that coast, the boat can be anchored in sight of a 2000 year old Lycian tomb and a short walk ashore may lead to a well preserved amphitheatre hidden in the hills. It is memories like these, and not the Byzantine formalities, which make a cruise in Turkey an unforgettable experience.

Country Profile

Turkey was part of the classical world and the Trojan Wars were fought on what is now Turkish soil. During the classical era much of the Asia Minor coast was part of Greece. The Christian Byzantine empire, which succeeded Rome, had its capital at Constantinople, later to become Istanbul under the Ottoman Turks. Towards the end of the thirteenth century the Ottoman state was founded in Asia Minor by Osman I

Practical Information

LOCAL TIME: GMT + 3. Summer time GMT + 2.

BUOYAGE: IALA A

CURRENCY: Turkish lira (TL), sometimes called a Turkish pound. Exchange receipts should be kept for reconverting TL on departure and also as proof that any large purchases, such as a carpet, have been bought with legally exchanged foreign currency. Not more than $US100 of TL can be exported.

BUSINESS HOURS
Although a Muslim country Sunday is the day of rest, but may be different in local areas. In summer in Aegean and Mediterranean regions some places may be closed in the afternoons.
Banks: 0830–1200, 1330–1700 Monday to Friday.
Shops: 0900–1300/1400–1900 Monday to Friday, 0900–1300 Saturday.
Government offices: 0830–1200/ 1300–1730 Monday to Friday.

ELECTRICITY: 220 V, 50 Hz

PUBLIC HOLIDAYS
1 January: New Year's Day
23 April: Independence Day, Children's Day
1 May: Spring Festival
19 May: Atatürk's Commemoration Day, Youth and Sports Day
30 August: Victory Day
28, 29 October: Republic Day
Variable religious holidays: Ramadan (called Ramazan in Turkish) Seker Bayrami
Kurban Bayrami.

COMMUNICATIONS
International direct dialling phones: Milletlerarasi.
Post offices have phone booths, which take tokens only.
Post office (PTT): 0830–1200/1300–1700 Monday to Friday.
Some services such as telephone are available in some cities and tourist resorts until 2400 and 0900–1900 Sundays.
Poste Restante at main post offices.
Address should be: name (surname first), Postrestante, Merkez Postahane, City, Turkey.
There are international flights from Istanbul and Ankara to most parts of Europe and elsewhere. There are several flights from Izmir and Antalya to European destinations and many charter flights in the summer.

MEDICAL
Treatment in public hospitals is inexpensive, but standards are not very high.

DIPLOMATIC MISSIONS
In Ankara:
Australia: Nenehatun Cad. 83, Gazi Osman Pasa. ☎ (4) 136-1240/3.
Canada: Nenehatun Cad. 75, Gazi Osman Pasa. ☎ (4) 136-1275/9.
United Kingdom: Sehit Ersan Cad. 46/A, Cankaya. ☎ (4) 127-4310/5.
United States: 110 Atatürk Blvd. ☎ (4) 126-5470.

In Istanbul:
United Kingdom: Mesrutiyet Cad. 34, Beyoglu, Tepesbasi. ☎ (1) 144-7450.
United States: Mesrutiyet Cad. 104-8, Tepesbasi. ☎ (1) 143-6200/9.

and expanded its territory in the fourteenth century through Asia Minor, into Thrace, capturing Adrianople and Bulgaria. The following century saw further expansion, and in 1453 Mehmed II captured Constantinople. The empire reached the height of its power under Suleiman I (1520–66), whose realm stretched from Hungary and the Balkans to south Russia, throughout Asia Minor to the Persian Gulf and across North Africa as far west as Algeria. However, after a decisive defeat at Lepanto in 1571, and unsuccessful sieges of Vienna in 1529 and 1683, the empire had reached its limit.

The new powers of Austria and Russia challenged Ottoman dominance in the Balkans, especially Russia which sought to expand at Turkish expense. The nineteenth century saw states in the Balkans and Mediterranean gain independence from an empire weakened by financial difficulties and lack of reform. The Balkan wars of 1912–13 lost nearly all Turkish territory in Europe. Dissatisfaction with the regime grew, and in 1909 the nationalist Young Turks came to power. In the First World War Ottoman Turkey fought on Germany's side and on defeat was occupied by the Allies and a harsh treaty imposed. In 1922 Mustafa Kemal led the overthrow of the Sultanate, renegotiated the peace settlement, and established a republic. Under the presidency of Kemal, known as Atatürk, a modern, westernised Turkey was created as a smaller, more nationally united state.

Neutral during the Second World War, after the war Turkey joined NATO. Civil troubles in Turkey in 1970–72 saw the army intervene to restore order, and in 1980 there were worse disturbances involving Marxist and Muslim opposition groups as well as Kurdish separatists, leading to the military dissolving parliament and banning political parties. In 1983 civil government was restored and elections were held in 1987, although Turkey's application to join the European Community has been turned down due to Turkey's record on human rights.

Industry is concentrated in the west of the country, while the east remains undeveloped. Agriculture is the traditional mainstay, employing 60 per cent of the workforce. There are some mineral resources of coal, oil and iron ore. Many Turks work abroad, especially in Germany, and remittances from abroad are important to the economy.

The population is over 50 million, of which 90 per cent are ethnic Turks. Kurds form the largest minority in the east of the country and there are also Arabs, Georgians, Bulgarians and some Greeks and Armenians.

Turkish is an Ural-Altaic language of the same origins as Finnish and Hungarian. Kurdish and Arabic are also spoken. Many also speak German or English. Most people are Muslim with small minorities of Jews, Greek Orthodox and Syrian Monophysites. The Turks are not quite so fundamentalist as other Muslims and mosques can be visited provided shoes are removed, women cover their heads and arms and men do not wear shorts. Modesty of dress is important outside of tourist areas.

Ankara, which is a new city, has been the capital since 1923. However, Istanbul is still the largest city and a commercial and cultural centre. Istanbul is a spectacular city, spread over two continents, and there is much to see from the Blue Mosque to the Grand Bazaar.

The climate is very varied, but generally can be described as Mediterranean, with hot summers and mild winters. The Black Sea has more extremes and is more humid. The Aegean coast in summer is under the influence of the northerly *meltemi* wind, which blows from about May until the end of August and at its peak can be very strong. Lighter winds prevail along the south coast where nights are usually calm. During the rest of the year, winds are variable.

Entry Regulations

Ports of entry
Canakkale 40°09′N 26°25′E, Bandirma 40°21′N 27°58′E, Istanbul 41°00′N 28°58′E, Akcay 39°35′N 26°56′E, Ayvalik 39°19′N 26°41′E, Dikili 39°05′N 26°53′E, Izmir 38°26′N 27°08′E, Cesme 38°19′N 26°20′E, Kuşadasi 37°52′N 27°14′E, Güllük 37°15′N 27°38′E, Bodrum 37°02′N 27°25′E, Datça 36°43′N 27°41′E, Marmaris 36°51′N 28°16′E, Fethiye 36°38′N 29°06′E, Kas 36°11′N 29°38′E, Finike 36°18′N 30°09′E, Kemer 36°35′N 30°34′E, Antalya 36°53′N 30°42′E, Alanya 36°32′N 32°01′E, Anamur 36°01′N 32°48′E, Tasucu 36°19′N 33°53′E, Mersin 36°48′N 34°38′E, Iskenderun 36°36′N 36°10′E, Samsun 41°18′N 36°20′E, Trabzon 41°00′N 39°45′E.

Procedure on arrival
On arrival, one must clear with immigration and customs at an official port of entry. Marinas in ports of entry normally have a reception office, where all officials are represented. The customs will issue a transit log, on which details of the yacht, crew, itinerary, passports, customs declaration, health clearance and so on are entered. Sometimes customs inspect the boat, and clearance also must be done with health and the harbour master, who may request a fee for light dues. Officials are particular about the Turkish courtesy flag, which must be flown from the correct position between 0800 and sunset.

In subsequent ports the authorities may wish to see the transit log. There are some regional differences in customs formalities. In the past, some captains have been asked to produce a certificate of competence when clearing and if unable to do so, the yacht was not allowed to leave port.

It is recommended to avoid zigzagging between Turkish and Greek waters. Both countries insist on arrival from abroad to be made only at an official port of entry.

Dardanelles: Yachts sailing in either direction must call at Canakkale to complete transit formalities, even if they have already cleared into Turkey in another port.

Procedure on departure
On departure, Section V of the transit log must be completed and returned to customs. One must also clear out with immigration. If Turkey is left in an emergency, without having been able to clear out correctly, the completed Section V should be handed in to a Turkish consulate abroad within one month, otherwise the offending yacht cannot return.

Customs
All types of firearms must be declared.

Animals require a recent health certificate from the country of origin. A rabies vaccination certificate must show that the animal received the vaccination between 15 days and six months before arrival in Turkey.

Antiques cannot be exported. If carpets are bought, the customs will require to see proof of purchase.

Although the people of Turkey as a whole are extremely hospitable, some of their customs officers leave much to be desired. The formalities are cumbersome and time-consuming and the officials quite unhelpful. Getting the customs duty waived on yacht equipment that has been ordered from abroad is also a lengthy and frustrating procedure, so it might be easier to try and bring any equipment needed into Turkey as personal luggage. In such a case it is advisable to have a copy of the ship's papers as well as some form of proof that the yacht has been left temporarily in Turkey.

Immigration

A visa is issued on arrival for a stay of up to three months to nationals of the following countries: Austria, Belgium, France, Germany, Greece, Italy, Luxembourg, Malta, Netherlands, Switzerland, Spain, Portugal, Liechtenstein, Australia, Bahamas, Bahrain, Barbados, Belize, Canada, Turkish Cyprus, Denmark, Djibouti, Fiji, Finland, Gambia, Grenada, Hong Kong, Iceland, Iran, Ireland, Jamaica, Japan, Kenya, Korea, Kuwait, Mauritius, Monaco, New Zealand, Norway, Oman, Quatar, San Marino, St Lucia, Saudi Arabia, Seychelles, Singapore, Sweden, Trinidad and Tobago, Tunisia, United Arab Emirates, United Kingdom, USA and the Vatican.

A visa is issued for up to two months stay for nationals of Romania and Yugoslavia.

A visa is issued for up to 15 days for Malaysians.

All other nationalities need visas in advance.

Nationals of Taiwan, Greek Cyprus, North Korea and South Africa may only obtain a visa after providing certain references.

If staying longer than three months one has to apply for a residence permit and must prove adequate financial means. It is easier to leave and return after a reasonable period of time, re-enter Turkey and obtain a further three months, than to apply for an extension.

Transit log

An official transit log is required for all yachts cruising in Turkey. The log is issued at the first port of entry and is valid for one year, after which it must be renewed unless wintering or leaving Turkish waters. Yachts can remain in Turkey for up to two years for maintenance or wintering. Certain ports are licensed for the storage of yachts for a two to five year period, (five years is allowed if one uses the yacht at least once every two years).

The proposed itinerary of the yacht is listed in the log, and any changes must be noted, as well as any changes of crew. Yachts can cruise between destinations noted in the log.

The transit log has provision for only one minor crew change. For subsequent non-family changes a new log must be obtained. The owner should be on board and can be accompanied by his family. Family members with different surnames, such as married daughters, may be required to provide proof of their relationship with the owner to qualify as family. No more than four different co-owners are allowed. Within a one year period the owner may be accompanied by non-paying guests twice a year for 10 days maximum each time, or one lot of guests can visit for one period of 20 days. After this, either the yacht must leave Turkish waters and not return for one year or pay the charter fee. Failing to observe this can risk the penalties of breaking Turkish law. If the guests are staying for the entire 20 days period, after 10 days one must get a new log. The captain has to get a new transit log from the port where the crew change occurred.

The regulations are complicated, but the Turkish authorities are very concerned about clandestine chartering in Turkish waters. For this reason, yachts carrying non-family guests which leave and re-enter Turkish waters are considered to be operating commercially, and may be liable to be charged a considerable fee on re-entry.

A great deal of confusion surrounds the regulations concerning restrictions imposed on foreign yachts cruising in Turkey, which are suspected of chartering. A change of crew, even if these are friends of the owner, is sometimes interpreted by some harbour masters as being equivalent to the arrival of a charter party. As a consequence, the yacht in question may be required to buy a new transit log or pay the charter fee despite the owner's protestations. Yachts that are crewed by friends, who are not members of the same family, may also have to pay the charter fee if they spend more than 20 days in Turkey.

Transit logs lose their validity on departure from Turkey, on wintering, and on change of captain. In the case of a temporary exit from Turkey for a period not exceeding seven days, the log may be left behind with the authorities at the port of exit to be re-used on return. However, some authorities insist on issuing a new log in spite of this seven day rule.

Some of these restrictions, especially those applying to non-family crew and the 20 day rule, have been so unpopular with genuine cruising boats that many are now keeping their visits to Turkey to the minimum time allowed. Because Turkey is determined to expand yachting in its waters, it is likely that the authorities will modify some of these restrictions, so it is advisable to check the latest position when clearing in at the first Turkish port.

Wintering

Special formalities must be completed if the yacht is to be left unattended in Turkey and the crew leave the country by other means. The forms are available from marina offices and must be stamped by customs. The passports must be stamped if leaving by other means than by yacht, as the police do not normally stamp passports of people entering by yacht and these stamps are necessary to leave the country overland or by air.

Charter

Foreign yachts used for commercial purposes and private foreign yachts without their owners on board must pay the following fees which include the cost of the transit log: 0–10 metres US$400, 10–18 metres US$600, 18–25 metres US$800, 25 metres and over US$1200. These fees must be paid before one is allowed to sail to another Turkish port. The fee is payable in a convertible foreign currency or Turkish lire. Foreign yachts are not allowed to transport passengers from a foreign port to a Turkish port.

Health
Hepatitis, polio and typhoid vaccinations are recommended.

Fees
A fee is charged for the transit log. There are also light dues, and a charter fee if applicable.

Overtime charges seem to vary from place to place, so if at all possible it is advisable to clear in and out during office hours on normal working days.

Restrictions
Prohibited areas for yachts are: no anchoring at the entrance and exit of the Dardanelles (Canakkale Bogazi, especially Gokceada and Bozcaada, region of Kumkale, Mehmetcik, Burnu, Ani, Korfezi); the zone north of the Bosporus, Gulf of Izmir, isles of Uzin and Hekim; the Bay of Karaagac; Oludeniz, Fethiye; parts of the ports of Mersin and Iskenderun.

Taking archaeological souvenirs can lead to confiscation of the yacht.

Diving is permitted in certain areas, but only with amateur scuba gear. Fishing is permitted for sport in certain areas, but there is a minimum size for fish caught and also the amount per person is controlled.

Facilities

Yachting facilities are constantly improving and those in the major centres are of a good standard. There are several marinas, the best being at Kuşadasi, Kemer, Bodrum and Marmaris. Atakoy Marina was recently opened near Istanbul. Apart from the usual services of fuel and water, these marinas also have good repair facilities as well as haul-out facilities. Fuel is available in all larger marinas, but in smaller places it may have to be carried in jerrycans. Water is available everywhere. LPG (butane) bottles can be filled locally in a few places, otherwise the empty container may have to be sent to Izmir. Although not a major yachting centre, Izmir is the best place for more difficult repair jobs, including those on electronic equipment. Reasonable repair facilities are also available in Istanbul, but they are spread out and difficult to find without local help.

Turkish charts can be obtained from the Hydrographic Office in Istanbul or some of the chandleries. Marine equipment is in rather short supply with only a few chandleries with a limited selection in the largest marinas. Spare parts for diesel and outboard engines are more easily available. Provisioning is generally good and there are grocery stores in most marinas or supermarkets in nearby towns. Fresh produce markets are excellent everywhere in Turkey.

Further Reading

Turkey and the Dodecanese Cruising Pilot
A Pocket Guide to the South East Aegean
The Aegean, A Sea Guide to its Coasts and Islands
The Ionian Islands to the Anatolian Coast
Turkish Waters Pilot
Mediterranean Cruising Handbook
Cruising Guide to the Turquoise Coast of Turkey

USSR

The Union of Soviet Socialist Republics, more commonly called the Soviet Union, is a federation of 15 republics, as well as a number of autonomous regions. The largest country in the world, it stretches from Europe across northern Asia to the Bering Straits and in central Asia south to its borders with Iran, Afghanistan and China. It has coastlines on the Black Sea, Baltic Sea and Arctic Ocean as well as the Bering Sea, Sea of Okhotsk and Sea of Japan in the Pacific.

Perestroika has added another country to the international cruising circuit and formalities in the Soviet Union have been getting simpler as the authorities become used to dealing with foreign yachts. The opening up of the Soviet Union in the late 1980s after seven decades of a closed border policy has been embraced with great enthusiasm by cruising sailors, scores of yachts making their way to the Black Sea or Baltic ports as soon as it became known that they would be allowed to visit the country. Although formalities are being eased and restrictions lifted, a trip to the Soviet Union still requires careful preparation and one cannot expect officials to change their attitudes overnight. Many ports are still closed to foreign yachts and day sailing or coastal cruising are allowed in only a very few places.

From the cruising point of view, the Soviet Union has three main areas which can be visited, all very different in their own ways. The most attractive area is the Black Sea coast, which offers a great variety from the Danube Delta in the west bordering Romania, to

Practical Information

LOCAL TIME: Leningrad, Odessa: GMT + 3; Far East GMT + 12.

BUOYAGE: IALA A

CURRENCY: Rouble of 100 copecks

BUSINESS HOURS
Banks: 0900–1300 Monday to Friday.
Business: 0900–1800 Monday to Friday.
Shops: 0800–1900 Monday, 0800–2100 Tuesday to Saturday.
Government offices: 0700/0730–1700/1730 Monday to Friday, also some Saturday mornings.
Inflot offices: 0800–1730 Monday to Friday.

ELECTRICITY: 220 V, 50 Hz

PUBLIC HOLIDAYS
1 January: New Year's Day
8 March: International Women's Day
1, 2 May: Labour Days
9 May: Victory Day
7 October: Constitution Day
7, 8 November: Anniversary of the Revolution

COMMUNICATIONS
International calls have to be made through an operator and even then it is difficult to make a call.
The mail service is rather unreliable.
There are regular international flights from Moscow to all parts of the world and less frequent flights from Leningrad. A comprehensive internal network links all major cities with Moscow.

MEDICAL
Medical care is good and emergency treatment is free.

DIPLOMATIC MISSIONS
In Moscow:
Australia: Kropotkinsky Pereulok 13.
☎ (095) 244-5011.
Canada: Starokonyushenny Pereulok 23.
☎ (095) 241-9155.
New Zealand: Ul. Vorovskovo 44.
☎ (095) 290-3485.
United Kingdom: Morisa Toreza 14.
☎ (095) 231-8511.
United States: Ul. Chaykovskogo 19-23.
☎ (095) 252-2451.

In Leningrad:
United States: Ul. Petra Lavrova St 15.
☎ (812) 274-8235.

the spectacular Georgian coast in the east. In the centre is the Sea of Azov, an unknown body of water to which access is still prohibited.

The main attraction on the Baltic coast is the historic city of Leningrad, built on the banks of the River Neva and considered the most beautiful Soviet city. The cruising area west of Leningrad comprises the three Baltic republics of Estonia, Latvia and Lithuania, whose independence as individual states will undoubtedly result in their opening up completely to cruising.

The Soviet Far East is more remote and less accessible to cruising yachts, as several sensitive areas, such as the entire port of Vladivostok, are closed to foreign shipping. Weather considerations would probably deter most cruising yachts from sailing to the Arctic ports, which involves a long detour around the whole of Norway.

Country Profile

The first civilisations in the region were those of the Scythians and Sarmatians, while from the third century AD Goths, Huns and Avars invaded. Around the ninth century the eastern Slavs settled in the Ukraine. At the same time the Russian state originated under the Varangians and adopted Greek Orthodoxy, although their kingdom declined and Russia was conquered by the Mongols in the thirteenth century. In the fifteenth century the Muscovite principality developed into a strong state under Ivan III, ending

Mongol supremacy. The seventeenth century saw a period of political and social troubles, with opposition to the autocratic rule of the Czar from the nobles and Cossacks as well as invasions by Poland and Sweden. Russia expanded towards the Pacific, and the nobles' rights over serfs increased to the point of slavery.

Under Peter I an era of westernisation and modernisation began, St Petersburg became the new capital and Russia expanded into both the Baltic and Balkan regions. Under Catherine II Russia became a leading European power, continuing an expansionist policy with the partition of Poland and acquisition of the Crimea. Unsuccessfully invaded by Napoleon in 1812, Russia took a leading role in the peace settlement of 1814–15. The 1860s saw Alexander II bring in some liberal reforms and the serfs were emancipated in 1861. Rapid industrialisation occurred at the end of the nineteenth century followed by the growth of socialist and revolutionary movements. Russia's policy in the Far East led to war with Japan in 1904–5, while at home revolution forced the Czar to allow the formation of a parliament with limited powers.

In 1915 Russia entered the First World War but heavy losses and defeats turned feelings against Czar Nicholas II. Revolution broke out in February 1917, and the Czar abdicated. The provisional government was in turn overthrown by the Bolsheviks led by Lenin. The new regime only established full control in 1921 after the Red Army defeated the White armies and Polish forces which had attacked in the west. In 1922 the Union of Soviet Socialist Republics was officially established. On Lenin's death in 1924 a leadership struggle ended with Joseph Stalin gaining power. State repression increased and the 1930s saw a series of political purges carried out by the secret police. In 1939 a non-aggression pact was signed with Germany and the USSR annexed part of Poland and the Baltic states. Germany invaded the Soviet Union in 1941, but was pushed back by a counter-offensive in 1943–5, the Red Army reaching Berlin in 1945. After the war relations with the West deteriorated into the Cold War and only after Stalin's death in 1953 was there some *détente*. Mihail Gorbachev became head of the communist party in 1985, and his policies of liberalisation saw a much freer atmosphere grow in the Soviet Union, although economic problems still continue to be massive. Relations with the West have greatly improved.

The Soviet Union is the second largest power in the world and has tremendous natural resources to call on plus a highly developed heavy industry. It is less developed in electronics, automobiles and consumer items. Although having a vast agricultural production, it has suffered shortages, often due to inefficient centralised planning. At the time of writing the Soviet Union is undergoing economic upheaval and reorganisation.

The population is 274 million, of which 52 per cent are Russian, 16 per cent Ukrainian and the rest a mosaic of different races, nationalities and languages from Lithuanian, Latvian and Estonian to Uzbek, Kazak, Tartar, Georgian, Moldavian, Armenian and Azerbaijanian. Besides Russian, which is the official language, there are 18 other languages which are spoken by more than a million people, plus many more minor languages. Religious activity has not been encouraged by the Communist regime but is still practised, varying with the ethnic group, most Russians being Orthodox, the Baltic Republics Roman Catholic and the Central Asian republics Muslim. The Armenian church is one of the oldest Christian churches, and there is also a large Jewish community.

The climate varies greatly in this vast country, from the subtropical in the southern republics to Arctic conditions in the northern regions. Conditions along the coasts are less harsh although even in the Baltic, winters can be very cold with freezing temperatures for several months.

Summer weather in the Baltic is very pleasant with long days and good sailing breezes. Winters along the Black Sea coast are milder and resorts on the Georgian coast have a Mediterranean climate. The summers are very hot and because the Black Sea is virtually landlocked, the winds alternate between land and sea breezes.

Entry Regulations

Ports of entry

Foreign yachts are only allowed to visit ports which are designated 'open' for foreign vessels. Only the most important ports are listed below, although with the gradual opening up of the Soviet Union, it may be possible to obtain permission to visit other ports as well.

Baltic Sea: Leningrad 59°53′N 30°13′E, Tallinn 59°27′N 24°46′E, Riga 56°58′N 24°06′E, Klaipeda 55°43′N 21°07′E, Kaliningrad 54°43′N 20°13′E.

Black Sea: Odessa 46°29′N 30°45′E, Sevastopol 44°37′N 33°22′E, Yalta 44°30′N 34°10′E, Sochi 43°35′N 39°44′E, Sukhumi 43°10′N 41°02′E, Poti 42°09′N 41°39′E, Batumi 41°39′N 41°39′E.

Sea of Japan: Nakhodka 42°45′N 133°04′E.

Procedure on arrival

Foreign yachts must arrive in the USSR with visas for each crew member obtained in advance and landfall must be made at one of the ports specified in the visa. Either a hosting yacht club or the official shipping agency Inflot should be informed of the ETA of the yacht, so that the authorities can be alerted. One may be intercepted by a patrol boat on entering Soviet waters.

Leningrad: The 36 mile long main shipping channel is through the Kronstadt Passage and Morskoy Canal. Leningrad Radio can be contacted on 2182 kHz or Port Control on VHF Channel 16 or 26. Yachts clear at the passenger terminal, where there is a customs office. The terminal is located on the Korabelny Channel. After formalities are completed yachts normally go to one of the yacht clubs.

Odessa: Entry formalities can be completed at the Odessa Yacht Club, sometimes referred to as the Black Sea Yacht Club, which is located 1.5 miles south of the commercial harbour. The entrance into the yacht basin is marked by large concrete blocks and there is more water on the starboard, north side of the entrance. Everyone must remain on board until cleared by customs and immigration. The yacht club will inform the officials, who will come to complete clearance formalities.

Customs

Firearms must be declared and may be detained during the yacht's stay in port.

There are no restrictions on animals.

Immigration

All nationalities must obtain a visa in advance. On the cruising routes there are convenient Soviet missions in

Helsinki, Nicosia (Cyprus) and Istanbul, where visas can be obtained. The 'open' ports that a yacht wishes to visit must be mentioned on the visa application. An individual permit is needed to visit each port. Yachts arriving without visas for all crew members may be turned away.

An official invitation from one of the better known yacht clubs, such as Leningrad, Odessa or Tallinn, can be a great help in obtaining a visa to visit the USSR by yacht. It may be quite difficult to get a visa without such an invitation. When writing to one of these yacht clubs, one should give full details of the captain, crew and the yacht as well as the intended itinerary, including ETA and ETD. Once the invitation is received, the visa application must be made at a Soviet embassy or consulate abroad.

To simplify matters on arrival, it is recommended to advise the hosting yacht club of your ETA, as the club will most probably arrange customs and immigration clearance. The Inflot Shipping Agency deals with formalities and should also be contacted in advance:

Leningrad Inflot Shipping Company, Gapsalskaya ul. 10, Leningrad 198035. ☎ 251 1238, Telex 121505.
Odessa Inflot Shipping Company, Vakulenchuka pl. 1, Morskoy Port, Odessa 270004. ☎ 293 3781, Telex 232824 & 232714.
Black Sea Shipping Company, Odessa. Telex 412677A BSSC SV.
Central Yacht Club, Leningrad, Petrovskaia, Kosa 7, ☎ 235 7217
Odessa Yacht Club, Otrada Beach, Odessa.

Fees

Harbour and agency fees can be very high and are payable in convertible foreign currency.

Facilities

Provisioning can be quite difficult as the yacht clubs are out of town, particularly the one in Odessa. Although food shortages are not as severe as in the past, shopping can be time-consuming. There is usually a good selection of fresh produce which is better quality in the markets than in the state-owned shops. Water is readily available, but the quality is sometimes questionable, so it should be treated. Fuel is difficult to obtain, although it may be possible to order some via a yacht club who have their own quota.

Yacht building is gathering pace as there is a great demand for cruising boats. Although not up to western standards, repair facilities are good, as local mechanics are used to having to improvise when spares

are not available. Marine supplies and spares are almost non-existent and should not be relied upon. Ordering essential spares from abroad and clearing them through customs can take a very long time.

YUGOSLAVIA

The Socialist Federal Republic of Yugoslavia is made up of six republics: Bosnia-Hercegovina, Montenegro, Croatia, Macedonia, Slovenia and Serbia, and two autonomous provinces within the Serbian Republic, Vojvodina and Kosovo. Yugoslavia has less than 400 miles of coastline along the Adriatic Sea, from the Albanian border in the south to the Italian in the north, but over 700 offshore islands. Mountains and plateaux make up three quarters of the country, in many places coming right down to the sea and forming a spectacular background.

Overshadowed for many years by the Greek islands, which were both better known and more easily accessible, Yugoslavia has only come into its own as a major cruising area in the 1980s. This popularity has been accompanied, or perhaps spurred on, by the rapid development of a considerable number of marinas strategically placed along the coast and on some of the offlying islands. The coastline is indented with innumerable bays and coves along its entire length, from the spectacular Gulf of Kotor in the south to the rugged beauty of the Pula peninsula in the north. There are many picturesque harbours on the mainland, while the islands abound in scenic anchorages.

Country Profile

Yugoslavia is a modern state, as the various nations that compose it have always been dominated by one empire or another throughout the history of this region. In 1918, out of the ruins of the Ottoman and Austro-Hungarian Empires, the Kingdom of the Serbs, Croats and Slovenes was formed, its frontiers fixed by the peace settlement after the First World War. A parliamentary system of government was adopted, but in 1929 King Alexander I established an authoritarian regime. At this time the country was renamed Yugoslavia. In 1934 Alexander was assassinated by a Croat extremist and was succeeded by his brother Peter II.

Occupied by Germany during the Second World War, the resistance movement was very strong, part of it led by the royalist nationalist Mihailovic, and the rest by the Communist Tito. In 1945 a republic along Communist lines was set up under Tito's leadership.

Practical Information

LOCAL TIME: GMT + 1

BUOYAGE: IALA A

CURRENCY: Dinar of 100 para. Foreign currency can be changed into dinars or dinar cheques. A discount is given in many restaurants if paying with the latter. In 1990, a new dinar worth 1000 old dinar, was issued to combat inflation. Care must be taken not to confuse the new notes with the old.

BUSINESS HOURS
Banks: 0700–1900 Monday to Friday, 0700–1300 Saturday, some may close earlier.
Shops: 0800–1200/0600–1100, 1600/1730–2000 Monday to Friday, until 1500 on Saturdays, although many stay open all day.
Government offices: 0700–1500 Monday to Friday.

ELECTRICITY: 220 V, 50 Hz

PUBLIC HOLIDAYS
In all of Yugoslavia:
1, 2 January: New Year
1, 2 May
4 July: Veterans Day
29, 30 November: National Day

National holidays of the various Republics:
Serbia: 7 July
Montenegro: 13 July
Slovenia: 27 April, 22 July, 1 November
Croatia: 27 July
Bosnia and Hercegovina: 27 July, 25 November
Macedonia: 2 August, 11 October

COMMUNICATIONS
International direct dialling is available to most countries. There are regular

international flights from Belgrade and also some of the popular tourist destinations such as Dubrovnik, Split and Rijeka.

MEDICAL
Countries with a reciprocal agreement are entitled to treatment for a minimum fee, the same as Yugoslavs. One should obtain a certificate from one's own country stating this entitlement.

DIPLOMATIC MISSIONS
In Belgrade:
Australia: Cijika Ljubina 13.
☎ (11) 624655/632261.
Canada: Kneza Milosa 75.
☎ (11) 644666.
United Kingdom: Generala Zdanova 46.
☎ (11) 645055/645034.
United States: Kneza Milosa 50.
☎ (11) 645655.

The country went its own way, breaking relations with Stalin in 1948 and taking a role as leader of the non-aligned states. The Soviet Union renewed relations under Khrushchev in 1955. Following the growth of Croat nationalism in the 1970s, in 1974 a new constitution strengthened the rights of the federal republics. Since Tito's death in 1980, the country has experienced various problems in holding together its constituent nations and ethnic minorities and there is the possibility that the federation may break up.

Previously an agricultural country, industry developed under the socialist regime. The northern part of the country is more developed and prosperous than the south. Tourism has become an important source of revenue. Yugoslavia has a large foreign debt and unemployment is a problem as well as severe inflation. Many Yugoslavs work abroad.

The population is 22.5 million. The main nationalities are Serbian, Croatian, Macedonian, Montenegrin and Slovene. There are also minorities of Albanians, Hungarians, Turks, Slovaks, Romanians, Bulgarians and Ruthenians. The main language is Serbo-Croat, which is a Slavonic language, but every republic has its own official language. Some Italian and German is spoken along the coast. A Latin script is used in the north and cyrillic in the south. The capital is Belgrade, which is also capital of Serbia, the dominant republic of the country. Orthodox Christian, Catholic and Muslim are the main religions.

The climate varies according to the region. On the coast it is of the Mediterranean type with hot, sunny summers and mild winters. In winter, storms along the coast can be severe and the weather is wet. The winds in summer are mostly onshore, mainly NW breezes setting in about noon and dying down by nightfall. The best season for visiting Yugoslavia is from April to October.

Entry Regulations

Ports of entry
Koper 45°33′N 13°44′E, Umag 45°26′N 13°31′E, Porec 45°13′N 13°36′E, Rovinj 45°05′N 13°38′E, Pula 44°53′N 13°50′E, Rasa 45°02′N 14°04′E, Rijeka 45°19′N 14°26′E, Mali Losinj 44°32′N 14°28′E, Senj 45°00′N 15°14′E, Zadar 44°07′N 15°14′E, Sibenik 43°44′N 15°54′E, Split 43°30′N 16°27′E, Korcula 42°48′N 17°27′E, Dubrovnik 42°38′N 18°07′E, Hercegnovi 42°27′N 18°32′E, Bar 42°05′N 19°05′E, Piran 45°32′N 13°34′E, Metkovic 43°06′N 17°33′E, Kardejevo 43°02′N 17°25′E.
Summer only (May 1–October 31): Izola 45°33′N 13°40′E, Novigrad 44°11′N 15°56′E, Primosten 43°35′N 15°56′E, Budva 42°17′N 18°51′E, Hvar 43°10′N 16°50′E, Kotor 42°25′N 18°46′E, Lastovo 42°45′N 16°50′E, Vij 42°04′N 16°11′E.

Procedure on arrival

In the event of a storm or emergency, yachts may enter any Yugoslav port, otherwise they must go to an official port of entry. Yachts have been fined for not going first to a port of entry.

On arrival, one should wait for officials to come to the yacht for clearance. If no one arrives after a while the captain should report to the police for passport control, as well as customs and harbour master, the crew remaining on board until clearance is complete.

Documents needed are the registration certificate, certificate of competence, insurance certificate, crew lists, radio licence, and a list of all dutiable items such as alcohol, tobacco and movable objects not part of the yacht's equipment such as cameras, portable radios or the outboard engine. Some fees will have to be paid on the spot, so it is advantageous to have some dinars already before arrival.

Customs

Firearms must be declared on arrival and will be sealed and checked again when leaving Yugoslav waters. All details of the firearms must be entered on the cruising permit.

Radio equipment must be declared and an operator's permit shown.

Dogs and cats need a veterinary certificate showing rabies vaccination between 15 days and six months previously. All animals need a general health certificate.

Yachts left behind for the winter can be bonded by customs. For periods of absence of up to 20 days, the yacht can be left in the care of a marina without being bonded.

Immigration

Visas are not required for nationals of: Algeria, Argentina, Austria, Belgium, Bolivia, Botswana, Bulgaria, Chile, Costa Rica, Cuba, Cyprus, Czechoslovakia, Denmark, Eire, Finland, France, Germany, Holland, Hungary, Iceland, Italy, Japan, Luxembourg, Malta, Mexico, Morocco, Monaco, Norway, Niger, Philippines, Poland, Portugal, Romania, San Marino, Seychelles, Sri Lanka, Spain, Switzerland, Liechtenstein, Sweden, Tunisia, Turkey and United Kingdom. All others require entry visas.

Citizens of countries with whom Yugoslavia has diplomatic relations may obtain an entry visa on arrival.

Cruising permit

A cruising permit is compulsory and is issued on arrival at the port of entry. The permit is issued by the harbour master and it must be stamped by both him and customs. The cost of the permit is calculated on the tonnage and horsepower of the vessel and is the same for both short- and long-term visits. The cost of a cruising permit for a year is approximately £100 to £150 (US$200 to US$300).

The permit lasts for the calendar year, up to December 31, and covers any number of exits and entries, but each re-entry must be made at a port of entry and the permit stamped each time by the harbour master and customs. A new permit is required if there is a change of captain, but not for crew changes.

The permit decal bearing the year of issue should be displayed on the yacht in a prominent place. After entry into the country, officials may wish to see the permit at subsequent ports or marinas. The permit allows a yacht to cruise along the whole coast including the islands, except for certain prohibited areas.

Fees

Overtime is charged after 1500 and at weekends. There are harbour fees and a cruising permit fee.

Restrictions

Areas prohibited to yachts are listed on the cruising permit. These include the Gulf of Kotor (certain areas next to defence establishments in the outer part of the gulf) as well as other areas. Yachts must keep a minimum distance from the shore of Brioni Island, near Pula, where the President of Yugoslavia has a summer residence.

Places where underwater activities are forbidden are also listed on the permit. Further details on such areas are given on charts and in the National Guide to the Adriatic published by the Adriatic Club of Yugoslavia.

If sailing towards Yugoslavia from the south, one should keep well out of Albania's 12 mile territorial limit, as it is carefully patrolled and yachts that have strayed too far inshore have been escorted into an Albanian port by a patrol boat. Foreign yachts may not take passengers or goods between Yugoslav ports. Changes of crew, regardless of nationality, are permitted.

Facilities

In spite of the large number of marinas, repair facilities and specialised marine work are not widely available. The best workshops as well as haul-out facilities are at Dubrovnik and Zadar, where there is a large resident boating population. Marine equipment and spares are in short supply and may have to be imported. It is usually possible to have the duty waived on such items, but this is a complicated procedure and spares are better brought in as personal luggage.

Fuel in most marinas is available on the dock and if paid for in foreign currency, the price does not include duty. In most other ports, fuel has to be carried in jerrycans and in some places may not be available at all. LPG containers can be refilled at INA Plin stations in the larger ports. Water may be rationed during the summer in some of the smaller islands, so a good reserve should be carried on board. Yugoslav charts are available from the harbour master's office in all major ports.

Provisions are available in most places, but the selection varies and there are occasional shortages of certain items. It is therefore advisable to arrive with a well-stocked boat. Fruit and vegetables are plentiful particularly in the bigger ports where there are open-air markets. An ongoing inflation causes wide fluctuations in the price of supplies, but prices are generally lower than in neighbouring Italy. While inflation remains so high, only small amounts of money at a time should be changed into dinars.

Further Reading

Adriatic Pilot
The Adriatic
National Guide to the Adriatic.

2 Northern Europe

A relatively short cruising season and inconsistent weather limits Northern Europe to being a cruising destination for yachts sailing from neighbouring countries. However, the Baltic Sea has started attracting more yachts from outside of the area as new cruising grounds open up in Poland, the Baltic republics and the Soviet Union.

Yachting is well developed in the Nordic countries who have their own considerable boating community. The traditional links between these countries are strong and yachts flying one of the Nordic flags enjoy many concessions when cruising in other Nordic countries. The rules affecting visiting yachts from other countries are stricter, particularly those concerning onboard stores. For a long-distance cruising yacht this can present serious problems, as the same duty-free allowances apply to foreign nationals arriving by sea as to ordinary tourists coming by land or air. As the allowances are extremely low, it is essential that yachts arrive with a minimum of dutiable stores on board or they could be asked to pay hefty duties.

The major drawback of a cruise in this area is the short sailing season which lasts from June until the end of August. The weather during summer is pleasant and the days are very long with the sun hardly setting in the northern regions. Mooring facilities are good almost everywhere and the yachting associations of Nordic countries have laid down their own moorings which may be used by visitors. Repair facilities are generally good and each country has at least one major yachting centre where more difficult repair jobs can be undertaken.

There are various opportunities for inland cruising, in the lakes and rivers of Sweden or the extensive river and canal systems in Germany, the Netherlands and Belgium. While the inland waterways of Holland or Sweden have great attractions, the busy canals and rivers of continental Europe are generally unsuited for cruising yachts and should be avoided.

Northern Europe is a region of very civilised cruising, but there is a price to pay for this quality of life and even basic provisions can be very expensive. Compensating for this, the Nordic countries have a reputation for extending a very hospitable welcome to visiting sailors and English is widely spoken.

BELGIUM

Situated between France and the Netherlands, Belgium has only a short coastline facing the English Channel and the North Sea. This lack of both coast and natural harbours do not make Belgium an appealing cruising destination. This is not helped by the difficulty of making landfall on the Belgian coast, which is fringed by sandbanks running parallel to the coast. Most foreign cruising yachts visit Belgian ports as a convenient place to stop while sailing north or south through the English Channel or are British yachts on a cross-channel trip. A few visiting yachts use the inland waterway system, which is connected to the extensive European canal network.

Country Profile

This region was originally inhabited by the Celtic Belgae, then was conquered by the Romans and later invaded by the Franks and Vikings. During the Middle Ages small independent principalities developed, while the towns became important commercial centres known especially for their textiles. Under the rule of the House of Burgundy and later the Hapsburgs, the Belgian provinces came under Spanish rule along with the Netherlands.

In 1572 the northern provinces rebelled against King Philip and became independent as the United Provinces, while the southern states remained under Spain. In 1713 they were incorporated into the Austrian Hapsburg Empire. Briefly occupied by France, they proclaimed their independence in 1790 only to be overrun again by their neighbour. Remaining part of France until 1815, Belgium and the Netherlands were then united under the rule of William of Orange. Dissatisfaction with his rule led to the Belgians declaring independence and finally in 1831 the neutral kingdom of Belgium was recognised by the European Great Powers.

The new state established itself rapidly and in the European scramble for African colonies, acquired the Belgian Congo. Although remaining neutral during both World Wars, Belgium was twice occupied by Germany.

In 1948 the Benelux customs union was formed with the Netherlands and Luxembourg and later Belgium joined NATO and the European Community. In 1977 the country was divided into three regions, Flanders, Wallonia and Brussels.

Belgium has an export-based economy, with only a small domestic market. Service industries are dominant, although there is a small manufacturing industry and agricultural sector.

The population is 10 million and the country is very densely populated. There is some tension between the Flemish, who are the majority, and the French speaking Walloons. The Flemish live mainly in the north, the Walloons in the south and there is a small German minority in the east. French, Flemish and German are spoken, being official languages in their respective regions. The population is mainly Roman Catholic, with small Jewish and Protestant minorities. The capital is Brussels, which is one of the main centres of the European Community and NATO, and various other international institutions and companies have their headquarters there.

The climate is mild, humid and wet. The prevailing summer winds are northerly. During the rest of the year winds are mostly W or SW and most winter gales

Map 4: Northern Europe

+++++ Canal

Practical Information

LOCAL TIME: GMT + 1; Summer time GMT + 2 April to September.

BUOYAGE: IALA A

CURRENCY: Belgian franc (BF)

BUSINESS HOURS
Banks: 0900–1630 Monday to Friday.
Business: 0830–1730 Monday to Saturday.
Shops: 0900–1830 Monday to Saturday.
Government offices: 0900–1700 Monday to Friday.

ELECTRICITY: 220 V, 50 Hz

PUBLIC HOLIDAYS
1 January: New Year's Day
Easter Monday
1 May: Labour Day
Ascension Day
Whit Monday
21 July: National Holiday
15 August: Assumption Day
1 November: All Saints Day
11 November: Armistice Day
25 December: Christmas Day

COMMUNICATIONS
International dialling access code 00.
Public telephones take 5 franc coins.
Dial 987 for an English-speaking operator for long-distance collect calls.
Telegrams can be sent from telegraph offices, open 24 hours.
Brussels is the only large international airport with flights to many destinations worldwide.

MEDICAL
There is no national health service so treatment can be expensive. Some West European countries have reciprocal arrangements for free emergency treatment.

DIPLOMATIC MISSIONS
In Brussels:
Australia: Guimard Centre, Rue Guimard 6–8. ☎ (2) 2310500.
Canada: Avenue de Tervuren 2. ☎ (2) 7356040.
New Zealand: Blvd du Regent 47–8. ☎ (2) 5121040.
United Kingdom: Britannia House, Rue Joseph II 28. ☎ (2) 2179000.
United States: Blvd du Regent 27. ☎ (2) 5133830.

are from the SW. The sea often breaks over the outlying sandbanks especially when the wind blows against the tide.

Entry Regulations

Ports of entry
Antwerp 51°14′N 4°25′E, Nieuwpoort 51°09′N 2°43′E, Ostend 51°14′N 2°55′E, Zeebrugge 51°20′N 3°12′E.

Procedure on arrival
Yachts are normally boarded on arrival by the maritime police (immigration) and customs. One may be asked to show a VHF radio licence, a copy of the International Regulation for the Prevention of Collisions at Sea, and tide tables. Yachts must be equipped with sufficient safety equipment, and have their name and home port clearly marked on the stern.

Customs
No licence is required for the importation of hunting and sporting firearms, but these should be licensed in one's own country. Two sporting guns, with a maximum of 100 cartridges per gun can be temporarily imported duty-free. These must be declared to customs on arrival for inspection.

Cats and dogs require a valid rabies vaccination

certificate. The vaccination must have been made at least 30 days before the date of arrival in Belgium.

Foreign yachts remaining more than two months in Belgium must obtain a registration plate, as all Belgian yachts have, and pay navigation dues. Further details can be obtained from the Bureau de Perception des Droits de Navigation. The registration plate costs 360 BF and allows a vessel to stop on navigable waterways or to use their tributaries. There is a restricted registration plate for 100 BF.

Immigration
Visitors must have a passport valid at least three months beyond their proposed departure date.

Visas are not required for nationals of the following countries provided they do not stay more than three months in any six month period: European Community, Andorra, Argentina, Australia, Austria, Bolivia, Brazil, Brunei, Burkina Faso, Canada, Chile, Colombia, Costa Rica, Cyprus, Ecuador, El Salvador, Finland, Guatemala, Honduras, Iceland, Israel, Jamaica, Japan, South Korea, Liechtenstein, Malawi, Malaysia, Malta, Mexico, Monaco, New Zealand, Nicaragua, Niger, Norway, Panama, Paraguay, Peru, San Marino, Singapore, Sweden, Switzerland, Togo, United States, Uruguay, Vatican City, Venezuela, Yugoslavia.

All other nationalities require visas, normally issued for three months. For these nationalities, visas for the countries to be visited before and after the visit to Belgium must be obtained prior to application for a visa.

Navigation

When motorsailing, a black cone with its apex down must be hoisted in the rigging. Port entry signals must be obeyed, due to the very heavy shipping traffic in and out of ports.

Inland waterways

Navigation is freely allowed on the Belgian waterways, although there are regulations one should be aware of. There are maximum speed limits on many of the canals and rivers. Vessels must not sail within 20 metres (60 ft) of the banks on the River Meuse and the Ghent–Terneuzen canal, and within 8 metres (25 ft) on the Lys and the Brussels–Charleroi canal. Full details of the regulations can be obtained in the booklet *Dispositions reglementant la police et la navigation*, available from the offices at the locks. Information is also obtainable from the Ministère des Travaux Publics.

Foreign yachts arriving in Belgium by one of the canals must report to the first navigation tax office, to complete an entry declaration. On departure an exit declaration must also be signed at a navigation tax office. These offices are situated at the locks.

Facilities

The best facilities are concentrated in the ports of Ostend, Zeebrugge and Nieuwport, all of which have yacht clubs and docking facilities. Most repair facilities are available, as well as chandlery, fuel and provisions. There are also good facilities at Antwerp, where there is access to the inland waterways.

Further Reading

Inland Waterways of Belgium
North Sea Harbours and Pilotage
Cruising Association Handbook
North Sea Passage Pilot
The Ministère des Travaux Publics has published a map of the inland waterways.

DENMARK

Denmark juts up towards the Scandinavian peninsula from the north-west edge of Europe and is made up of the Jutland peninsula and many islands. Over five hundred make up the Danish archipelago providing excellent cruising opportunities. The islands are scattered over a relatively small area and distances between harbours are never more than a few miles. The most popular cruising area is the archipelago south of the larger islands of Fyn and Sjaelland. In the northern part of Jutland are the perfectly sheltered waters of Limfjord, connecting the North Sea to the Kattegat. A more convenient point of access for yachts coming from the south is the Kiel Canal, which avoids a long detour around the north of Denmark and leads straight into the heart of the Danish archipelago. The Sound between Denmark and Sweden is the main waterway between the North Sea and the Baltic, so there is very heavy shipping in this area.

Country Profile

Denmark has been populated from neolithic times and was one of the most developed areas in the Bronze Age. The Vikings from the region which is now Denmark and Norway became known and feared for their raids and pillaging of the coasts of Western Europe. In the tenth century Denmark was unified and gradually Christianity spread through the country. The marauding lessened, but Danish kings ruled England for some years in the eleventh century. In 1397 the Union of Kalmar brought Denmark, Norway, Sweden, the Faeroes, Iceland and Greenland under the rule of the Danish king. In the sixteenth century this Union broke up and the next two hundred years saw wars with several countries including Sweden, Denmark's main rival in the Baltic.

In the eighteenth century Denmark had a period of economic expansion. It administered Greenland, which became a colony in 1814. From this time Denmark started losing its territories. It had to cede Norway to Sweden at the end of the Napoleonic Wars, as Denmark had been an ally of France. Later war with Austria and Prussia lost Denmark her southern provinces of Schleswig and Holstein. In 1918 Iceland gained independence, although it was still under the Danish crown until 1953. Neutral in the First World War, during the Second World War Denmark was occupied by Germany, although King Christian X remained in the country and encouraged the resistance movement that developed.

The monarchy's powers were limited in 1849, when

Practical Information

LOCAL TIME: GMT + 1, Summer time GMT + 2 from late March to September.

BUOYAGE: IALA A

CURRENCY: Danish Krone (Dkr) of 100 ore

BUSINESS HOURS
Banks: 0930–1600 Monday to Friday, to 1800 Thursdays.
Business: 0900–1630 Monday to Friday.
Shops: Monday to Thursday 0900–1700, 0900–1900/2000 Friday, 0900–1300/1400 Saturday.
Government offices: 0900–1630 Monday to Friday.

ELECTRICITY: 220 V, 50 Hz

PUBLIC HOLIDAYS
1 January: New Year's Day
Maundy Thursday, Good Friday and Easter Monday
4th Friday after Easter: Prayer Day
Ascension Day
Whit Monday
5 June p.m.: Constitution Day
24 December p.m.
25 December: Christmas Day

COMMUNICATIONS
International dialling access code 009.
Reverse charge calls, 0015 to Europe, 0016 outside of Europe.
Emergency: dial 000.

There are flights to all European and many worldwide destinations from Kastrup International airport near Copenhagen.

MEDICAL
There is free emergency treatment for most West European nationals.

DIPLOMATIC MISSIONS
In Copenhagen:
Australia: Kristianagade 21.
☎ (1) 262244.
Canada: Kr. Bernikowsgade 1.
☎ (1) 122299.
United Kingdom: Kastelsvej 36–40.
☎(1) 264600.
United States: Dag Hammarskjolds Alle 24. ☎ (1) 423144.

a liberal constitution was adopted. In the early twentieth century, the growth of the working class brought the socialists into power. During the interwar years the social democrats introduced many social reforms and dominated the political scene until the 1970s. The country has enjoyed prosperity and joined the European Community in 1973. During the 1980s the conservatives became the leading political party.

Cereals are grown on the plains and there is much pastureland for livestock, the main exports being pork, beef and dairy products. The fishing industry is also important. Industry is developed in the major towns. Unemployment and a foreign debt are problems, although living standards are high.

The population is 5.1 million and is mainly Lutheran. As well as Danish, Faroese, Greenlandic and German are spoken in some areas. The capital is Copenhagen.

Denmark has a temperate climate and the winters are cold. The sailing season is limited to the summer, which can be fairly wet, although enjoying long days. The prevailing winds in summer are westerly and this is also where most gales come from. Because of the surrounding landmass, the winds can be variable and the weather also changes with little warning.

Entry Regulations

Ports of entry
Jutland: Esbjerg 55°28′N 8°26′E, Frederikshavn 57°26′N 10°33′E, Fredericia 55°34′N 9°45′E, Haderslev 55°15′N 9°30′E, Holstebro (Struer) 56°30′N 8°36′E, Horsens 55°51′N 9°52′E, Kolding 55°30′N 9°30′E, Randers 56°28′N 10°03′E, Skive 56°34′N 9°02′E, Sonderborg 54°55′N 9°47′E, Thisted 56°57′N 8°42′E, Vejle 55°43′N 9°33′E, Ålborg 57°03′N 9°55′E, Århus 56°09′N 10°13′E.
Funen (Fyn): Odense 55°25′N 10°23′N, Svendborg 55°03′N 10°37′E.
Sjaelland: Copenhagen 55°42′N 12°37′E, Elsinore 56°02′N 12°37′E, Kalundborg 55°41′N 11°05′E, Korsør 55°20′N 11°08′E, Koge 55°27′N 12°12′E, Naestved 55°14′N 11°45′E.
Lolland: Rodbyhavn 55°39′N 11°21′E.
Falster: Nkobing 54°46′N 11°52′E.
Bornholm: Ronne 55°06′N 14°42′E.

Procedure on arrival
Yachts arriving from Greenland, EC or Nordic countries, with nothing to declare, do not have to report to customs on arrival. Others should proceed to a port of entry and report to customs. The captain may be asked for proof of ownership, or a letter authorising the use of the boat. It should be noted that duty-free allowances are very small and amounts over this are declarable. Customs do check yachts, so if in doubt it is advisable to report to customs. Immigration must be cleared on arrival and departure.

Customs
Firearms must be declared.

Animals can be landed, but dogs taken ashore 1 April to 1 September must be kept on a leash.

Yachts may remain in Denmark without paying duty for three months within a six month period which begins with the yacht's arrival in any Nordic country.

The importation of dairy products is restricted.

The duty-free allowance is only $\frac{1}{4}$ litre of spirits or 3 litres of fortified wine, 4 litres of wine and 60 cigarettes per person. If a yacht has a large amount of dutiable goods in excess of the allowed limits, the stores must be placed under customs seal and re-exported aboard the yacht. A deposit must be paid, which will be refunded after departure from Danish waters by returning the certificate supplied by the Danish customs office, after it has been stamped by customs on arrival in the next country confirming that the same amount of goods are on board.

Immigration

Nationals of EC countries do not need a visa and can stay for an unlimited time. However, after six months they must apply for a resident's permit.

US, Canadian, Australian and New Zealand nationals are amongst those who do not need a visa for up to a three-month visit, after which a visa must be obtained. An extension can be obtained from the police, but later one will not be allowed back for a further six months. At present the visa requirements are being reviewed and may be removed for more countries.

Navigation

Shipping traffic between the North Sea and the Baltic is heavy and vessels must use the correct lane in traffic separation zones. These are in operation in the northern part of the Sound between Elsinore and Hälsingborg in Sweden, at the Great Belt between Korsør and Sprogoe by Hatter Barn and the Baltic Sea south of Gedser. In Danish waters the Transit Route for very large vessels runs from the Skaw to the Moen SE light vessel north-east of Gedser. In some areas larger ships on the Transit Route are confined by depths to Deep Water Routes; these can be found in the Great Belt east of Samsoe, along the east coast of Langeland, and north-east of Gedser. Yachts should avoid the Transit and Deep Water Routes as the depth conditions do not allow large vessels much room to manoeuvre. Attention should also be paid to port entry regulations and signs.

Restrictions

Prohibited areas are military firing areas, information on which is contained on Danish charts and in the Danish Notices to Mariners. Also marked on Danish charts as restricted are several small uninhabited islands, which are protected areas for seabirds and other wildlife and should not be landed on between 1 April and 1 June. On some of these islands there are signs forbidding landing.

Fishing

Foreign visitors may only use simple hand gear for fishing. Harpoons, traps and nets are forbidden. Permission should be obtained from the owners of the fishing rights before fishing in rivers or estuaries.

Facilities

Fuel is available in most ports and some yacht harbours have their own fuelling dock, although these are more common in fishing harbours. LPG containers can be refilled in the larger centres. Provisioning is excellent throughout Denmark and the quality of food is among the best in the world. Marine supplies are available in all yachting centres, although the prices are very high.

Yachting facilities are good throughout the country and there are either marinas or fishing harbours with mooring facilities for yachts conveniently situated within a short distance of each other. The harbours get very crowded in summer and it is customary to raft up extensively, often several boats deep. The Danish Yachting Association has mooring buoys (marked with 'DS' in black letters) in 23 harbours in Limfjord, the east coast of Jutland, SE coast of Fyn and south coast of Sjaelland. Visiting sailors may use such buoys for a maximum of 24 hours free of charge. The maximum load must not exceed 15 tons and two yachts may use the same buoy if their combined weight does not exceed this limit.

The best repair facilities are concentrated in and around Copenhagen where there are several marinas, the best known of which is Langelinie close to the centre of the capital. Also close to Copenhagen is the marina at Svanemoellen. There are also good facilities Århus and Ålborg, the latter in Limfjord.

Danish charts are produced by the Royal Danish Administration of Navigation and Hydrography in special editions for yachts. It is essential to have good charts for the smaller channels. The Danish Yachting Association (Idraettens Hus, 2605 Broendby) publishes an annual handbook with details of rates and facilities for Danish harbours called *Händbog for Tursejlere*. Several local tourist associations also publish leaflets for yachtsmen, which are available from Danish Tourist Association offices.

Further Reading

Händbog for Tursejlere
Baltic South West Pilot
With Pleasure Craft in Scandinavia
Cruising Association Handbook

FINLAND

Finland, known as Suomi to its inhabitants, is situated in the far north-east of Europe and is one of the largest countries on the continent. From the rolling agricultural lands of the south the land rises towards the hills and huge forests of the north and the peatlands and treeless fells of Lapland. Finland has, at the last count, some 62,000 lakes, and nearly 3000 miles of coastline, off which lie thousands of islands including the Åland archipelago.

Cruising opportunities in Finland are infinite, either through the many islands or on the lakes, the larger of which are navigable. With a reputed 6500 islands, the offlying Åland archipelago is a world in itself. Unfortunately the sailing season is very short, usually from about the end of May until September, although the summer days do benefit from almost perpetual daylight. With a highly developed and top quality boat building industry, many foreign visitors only sample the cruising delights of Finland when they arrive to take delivery of their new boats and then sail them to warmer waters.

Country Profile

Little is known about the first inhabitants, who arrived in Stone Age times, although the present-day Lapps are probably their descendants. Between two and three thousand years ago the Finno-Ugrian tribes moved west into what is now Hungary, and north-west into Estonia and Finland. The tribes were well established when Christianity spread across the land around the tenth century. Sweden was a continual aggressor in the following centuries and gradually Finland came under the control of the Swedish kings.

The rise of Russia as a great power led to an expansionist policy westwards, and the 1808–9 war led to Finland being incorporated into the Russian empire as a Grand Duchy. Although having some measure of autonomy, a policy of russification was followed and Finnish national resistance to this grew. The Russian Revolution was the chance the Finns had been waiting for and an independent Finland was declared in December 1917, recognised by the Soviet Union three years later.

The interwar years saw a conflict with Sweden over the possession of the Åland Islands, which were eventually awarded to Finland by the League of Nations.

In November 1930 Stalin declared war on Finland after being refused his demands of territory. The Finns fought back fiercely, but despite aid from Sweden they had to cede much of Karelia to the Soviet Union. From 1941 the Finns fought with Germany against Russia, until an armistice with the latter was declared in 1944. After the war Finland had to pay considerable reparations to the Soviet Union, but the country rebuilt itself and embarked on a strong non-aligned policy as an active member of the United Nations, although concluding pacts of mutual assistance with the Soviet Union. A coalition of centre parties has dominated the political scene since the war.

Around 65 per cent of Finland is forest, and one of its main resources are forest products, especially paper. Only the south is cultivated, due to the harsher climate further north.

Finland is a sparsely inhabited country with a population of 4.9 million. Finnish and Swedish are the two official languages, and Lappish (or Saame) is a semi-official language. The majority speak Finnish as their mother tongue, although there is a large Swedish speaking minority. English is widely spoken. Lutheran and Orthodox Christian are the two main religions. The capital since 1812 is Helsinki.

Much of the country lies north of the Arctic Circle, however the influence of the Baltic Sea keeps the climate milder than other countries on the same latitude. The sailing season is limited to the summer when the winds are variable. The surrounding landmass affects the winds which can be light in summer.

Entry Regulations

Ports of entry

Eckerö 60°13'N 19°35'E, Hamina 60°34'N 27°11'E, Hanko 59°49'N 22°58'E, Haukipudas 65°11'N 25°21'E, Helsinki 60°10'N 24°57'E, Inkoo 60°03'N 24°01'E, Kalajoki 64°17'N 23°55'E, Kaskinen 62°23'N 21°13'E, Kemi 65°44'N 24°34'E, Kokkola (Ykspihlaya) 63°50'N 23°06'E, Kotka 60°28'N 26°57'E, Kristiinankaupunki (Kristinestad) 62°16'N 21°19'E, Lappeenranta 61°04'N 28°15'E, Loviisa 60°27'N 26°14'E, Langnas 60°07'N 20°18'E, Maarianhamina (Marienhamn) 60°06'N 19°56'E, Naantali 60°28'N 22°01'E, Oulu 65°00'N 25°28'E, Parainen 60°17'N 22°18'E, Pietarsaari (Jakobstad) 63°41'N 22°24'E, Pori 61°29'N 21°48'E, Porvoo Malaalaiskunta 60°23'N 25°40'E, Raahe 64°41'N 24°29'E, Rauma 61°08'N 21°30'E, Tammisaari 59°59'N 23°26'E, Tornio 65°51'N 24°09'E, Turku 60°27'N 22°15'E, Uusikaupunki 60°48'N 21°24'E, Vaasa 63°06'N 21°37'E.

Practical Information

LOCAL TIME: GMT + 2. Summer time GMT + 3 from the end of March to the end of September.

BUOYAGE: IALA A

CURRENCY: Markka (Fmk/FIM) of 100 pennies

BUSINESS HOURS
Banks: 0930–1600 Monday to Friday.
Shops: 0900–1800 Monday to Friday, 0900–1400 Saturday.
Government offices: 0800–1600 Monday to Friday.

ELECTRICITY: 220 V, 50 Hz

PUBLIC HOLIDAYS
1 January: New Year's Day
Epiphany
Good Friday, Easter Monday
Saturday before Whit Sunday
May Day Eve and Day
Ascension
Midsummer's Eve and Day
1 November: All Saints Day
6 December
24–26 December: Christmas

COMMUNICATIONS
International directory enquiries 92020. For long-distance calls within Finland, dial the area code with the prefix 9. To book a call to other countries dial 92022, to the Soviet Union 82027.
Post offices 0900–1700 Monday to Friday, until 1800 in winter.
Emergency: dial 008/000 (also for emergencies at sea).
VHF Channel 16 should be used to contact the coastal rescue services, or channel 11A.

There are many international flights to worldwide destinations from Helsinki and flights to other Nordic countries from Turku.

MEDICAL
State hospitals charge reasonable fees for treatment. Private hospitals are more expensive. Certain West European countries have reciprocal agreements for free treatment.

DIPLOMATIC MISSIONS
In Helsinki:
Canada: Pohjois Esplanadi 25B.
☎ (0) 171141.
United Kingdom: Uudenmaankatu 16-20.
☎ (0) 647922.
United States: Itainen Puistotie 14A.
☎ (0) 171831.

Procedure on arrival

Foreign yachts arriving in Finland must keep to the customs routes, which are channels from the open sea to where there are pilot stations. They must report immediately to the nearest port of entry for customs and immigration formalities. No other routes may be taken, nor should anyone land or come aboard before customs clearance has been completed.

A yacht registered in one of the Nordic countries, maximum 30 tons net, arriving in Finland from another Nordic country, with no dutiable stores, is not required to complete customs clearance. Yachts exempted from customs and passport control should follow the customs route until their arrival at a coastguard or pilotage station. Arriving from Sweden, the normal customs routes may be followed, but also the fairways passing Enskar on Eckero and the Valsorarna islands can be used.

Immigration clearance must be done on arrival and departure. On departure the certificate of clearing into Finland must be presented. Crew requiring visas must present an itinerary with their ETAs.

Customs

Firearms are prohibited.

If a yacht is to be left in Finland for the winter and the crew leave the country by other means, it may be necessary to pay import duties.

Animals must have rabies vaccination certificates, issued between 30 days and 12 months previously.

Animals arriving from rabies-free countries (Sweden, Norway, Iceland, United Kingdom, Ireland) do not need this, as long as they did not visit a country with rabies. All animals should have a valid health certificate.

Excess amounts of alcohol, tobacco and other dutiable goods, must be declared to customs on arrival.

A maximum of 15 kg (33 lb) of foodstuffs may be imported, of which no more than 5 kg (11 lb) may be edible fats, no more than 2.5 kg (5 lb) butter and no more than 8kg (18 lb) tinned meat or meat products.

Immigration

Citizens of Denmark, Iceland, Sweden and Norway only need proof of citizenship to enter Finland. A British Visitor's Passport, and national identity cards from Austria, Belgium, Germany, France, Liechtenstein, Luxembourg and Switzerland are accepted for a maximum of three months' stay. All other nationalities require valid passports.

Visas are not required for the nationals of West European countries, Algeria, Argentina, Australia, Bahamas, Barbados, Bolivia, Botswana, Brazil, Bulgaria, Canada, Chile, Colombia, Costa Rica, Cyprus, Czechoslovakia, Dominican Republic, Ecuador, El Salvador, Malaysia, Fiji, Gambia, Grenada, Guatemala, Honduras, Hungary, Israel, Ivory Coast, Jamaica, Japan, Kenya, South Korea, Lesotho, Malawi, Mauritius, Mexico, Morocco, New Zealand, Nicaragua, Niger, Panama, Peru, Romania, Seychelles, Singapore, St Vincent and the Grenadines,

Suriname, Swaziland, Tanzania, Trinidad, Tunisia, Uganda, the United States, Uruguay, Vatican City, Yugoslavia and Zambia.

All foreigners wishing to stay in Finland for more than three months or to work must obtain a visa, except nationals of Denmark, Iceland, Norway and Sweden.

Restrictions

Special permission is needed for voyages through or stops in restricted military areas. The Ministry of Defence are reconsidering the present regulations on this, which will be decided by the summer of 1990.

The general fairways, marked on charts, which lead through restricted areas may generally be used without permission by foreign vessels for a direct passage without stopping. Yachts must remain within these fairways unless one has special permission to leave them. A foreign vessel may only stop in a restricted area in case of emergency. Yachts may anchor for not more than 48 hours within a restricted area at special designated anchorages and moorings. Permission to stay within a restricted area or to move outside of a fairway must be applied for to the Military Area Headquarters or local Frontier Guard (Coast Guard) authorities.

In some areas there is a speed limit, and in others anchoring and going ashore is prohibited. These areas are marked on charts and signs are posted along the shore.

Foreign yachts are not allowed to sail through the Saimaa Canal.

The Finnish Coast Guard have the right to stop and search all pleasure boats in Finnish territorial waters. The code flag L is the stopping sign, which may be given visually or by sound.

Navigation

Customs routes and general fairways must be used. The sailing lanes must be followed and these are clearly marked on the charts issued by the Finnish National Board of Navigation, and on reduced size charts. Short or overnight stays and stopovers due to adverse weather are allowed outside of the sailing routes. Yachts may only stop at yacht harbours, anchorages or holiday sites. Yachts leaving the sailing routes must give consideration to other vessels.

The public has the right of free access to outdoor areas, as well as the duty to preserve and not to interfere with nature. One should not anchor close to an inhabited stretch of shore nor land without the owner's permission. Fires should not be lit ashore nor any garbage be thrown overboard.

Fishing

All fishing requires an official licence, which may be obtained at any post office. Also permission must be obtained from the owner of the fishing rights. Most waters in Finland are under private ownership. Information on local fishing regulations can be obtained from tourist offices, and restrictions on fishing gear and times will be given when applying for the licence.

ÅLAND ISLANDS

These islands are semi-autonomous and some of the regulations applicable in Finland may differ. The flag of the Åland Islands is a red cross with a yellow border on a light blue field. The islands have some 15 visitors' harbours and there are many public jetties where temporary stops can be made. Full details may be found in the National Board of Navigation's *Sailing Charts for Åland*, which also contains charts. Natural harbours outside of inhabited areas should only be used in emergencies and the landowner's permission asked to anchor. Fishing is only allowed with permission from the owner of the fishing rights, and a fishing licence must be bought, available at shops, service stations and fishing associations. Fishing from the shore is not allowed from 15 April to 15 June.

Facilities

Provisioning is very good in all ports, as well as on the larger islands where there are villages or holiday resorts. Fuel is available in all ports. Most coastal towns have visitors' harbours and yacht clubs usually have a few berths reserved for visitors. The standard of services varies and repair facilities are available only in the largest ports. With a developed boat-building industry, producing some of the best yachts in the world, repair facilities are of a high standard. The most comprehensive range of repair facilities are to be found in and around the capital Helsinki. Other yachting centres are at Turku, Vaasa and Pietarsaari, the latter being the home of the famous Swan Yachts. Good facilities are also available in Åland with several marinas, the largest in the capital Mariehamn.

Further Reading

With Pleasure Craft in Scandinavia
National Board of Navigation Yacht Charts for Åland
Finnish Cruising Club handbook of anchorages in Åland and the south coast

GERMANY

Germany occupies a central position in Europe with coasts on both the North and Baltic Seas. The most important navigable rivers in continental Europe, the Rhine and the Danube, also flow through German territory.

Although one of the most active sailing nations in Europe, Germany is not a cruising destination and even most German sailors prefer to do their cruising away from home. One such popular area is the IJselmeer in the Netherlands, which is reputed to have more resident German yachts than locally owned ones. Cruising opportunities on the North Sea coast are rather limited and the restrictions imposed on cruising in some of the German Frisian Islands have reduced the destinations even further, although the opening up of former East Germany is adding a hitherto unknown corner of the Baltic to the German cruising portfolio. The most attractive part is the island of Rügen and the surrounding area in the Greiswalder Bodden.

The only contact many visiting yachts have with Germany is the Kiel Canal, the convenient shortcut from the North Sea to the Baltic. Those with more time on hand may be tempted to sail up the narrow estuaries to the old Hanseatic ports of Hamburg, Bremen or Lübeck.

Country Profile

The region was settled by Germanic tribes after the collapse of the Roman Empire. Saxony was gradually conquered by the Franks, and the eastern part of Charlemagne's empire divided in 843, the Kingdom of the East Franks, became the nucleus of the German state. Large feudal duchies developed while the frontiers were attacked by Magyars, Norsemen and Slavs.

In the tenth century the Holy Roman Empire was formed, uniting the crowns of Germany and Italy. In 1273 a Hapsburg was elected Holy Roman Emperor, and the dynasty expanded its territories, although it was unable to establish centralised rule in a region where over 350 small states were endlessly fighting one another.

In the sixteenth century Hapsburg Austria consolidated its power, but the Protestant Reformation split Germany into the Catholic south and the Lutheran north. Religious conflict was followed by the Thirty Years War (1618–48) which completed Germany's devastation, and established a loose confederation of small principalities under the Emperor's nominal rule. The eighteenth century saw the rise of Prussia as a powerful state and German culture flourished. The Holy Roman Empire was finally destroyed during the Napoleonic wars, and in 1815 a German Confederation was formed, dominated by Austrian and Prussian rivalry. Nationalism was a growing force, but the 1848 revolution saw the liberal Frankfurt Parliament fail to unify the country. Austria dominated the Confederation until Otto von Bismarck, in charge of Prussian policy, achieved unification excluding Austria.

In 1871 the German empire was established under the rule of the Prussian Hohenzollern dynasty. Rapid industrialisation followed, and a colonial expansionist policy brought Germany into conflict with Britain and France. At the start of the First World War Germany invaded Belgium and France, then Poland, Romania and Serbia. After the German defeat in 1918 a social democratic revolution established the parliamentary Weimar Republic. Some economic recovery was made, but thwarted by the world depression which led to mass unemployment. The 1930s saw the rise of the national socialist party, and its leader Adolf Hitler established a totalitarian regime. Germany's expansionist foreign policy led to the outbreak of the Second World War, when much of Europe was defeated and occupied.

Eventually Germany surrendered in 1945, and the country was occupied by the Soviet Union, United States, France and Britain. The onset of the Cold War led to this division hardening, and in 1949 the Federal Republic (West Germany) and the Democratic Republic (East Germany) were formed. West Germany fostered links with Western Europe, joining NATO and the European Community, and made a rapid economic recovery, while East Germany remained under the Soviet sphere of influence. In 1989 the East German Communist party relinquished power, and arrangements for the union of the two Germanies began.

West Germany made a spectacular recovery after the Second World War, becoming one of the leading economic powers in the world. It has a market economy, with a large proportion of its industry geared to export. The agricultural sector is small, but provides much of the domestic need. Service industries are also important. East Germany was the most industrialised of the East European states, having a centralised economy with much of its agriculture collectivised.

The German-speaking population is 80 million, with a small Danish minority. Catholicism is stronger in the south and Protestantism in the north. Since the old capital Berlin was divided into occupied zones after the war, Bonn took over the function of capital in the Federal Republic of Germany.

Practical Information

LOCAL TIME: GMT + 1. Summer time GMT + 2 March to September.

BUOYAGE: IALA A

CURRENCY: Deutsch mark (DM) of 100 pfennig (pf)

BUSINESS HOURS
Banks: 0900–1300, 1500–1600 Monday to Friday, Thursday 0900–1300, 1500–1730.
Business: 0830–1700 Monday to Friday.
Shops: 0800/0900–1830 Monday to Friday, 0830–1400 Saturday.
Government offices: 0900–1230, 1400–1700 Monday to Friday.

ELECTRICITY: 220 V, 50 Hz

PUBLIC HOLIDAYS
1 January: New Year's Day
Good Friday, Easter Monday
1 May: Labour Day
Ascension Day
Whit Monday
17 June: Day of German Unity
19 November: Prayer Day
25–26 December: Christmas

COMMUNICATIONS
International dialling access code 00.
There are regular international flights from Hamburg, Frankfurt, Berlin, Düsseldorf and München.

MEDICAL
Most European countries have a reciprocal agreement with Germany for free emergency treatment.

DIPLOMATIC MISSIONS
In Bonn:
Australia: Godesberger Allee 105–7.
☎ (228) 81030.
Canada: Godesberger Allee 119.
☎ (228) 810060.
New Zealand: Bonn-Center H.1. 902 Bundeskanzlerplatz. ☎ (228) 228070.
United Kingdom: Friedrich Ebert Allee 77. ☎ (228) 234061.
United States: Deichmannsaue.
☎ (228) 3390.

In Hamburg:
Canada: Europa Carton AG, Spitalerstrasse 11. ☎ (40) 30901.
United Kingdom: Harvestehuder Weg 8a.
☎ (40) 446071.
United States: Alsterufer 27.
☎ (40) 441061.

Germany has a temperate climate, with warm summers and cold winters. The coastal areas are generally milder than inland in the winter. In the North Sea the predominating winds are SW or W. The incidence of gales is low in summer but increases in spring and autumn. Gales usually veer from SW to NW producing cross seas. Winds on the Baltic coast are variable.

Entry Regulations

Ports of entry

Bremerhaven 53°33′N 8°35′E, Brunsbüttel 53°54′N 9°08′E, Cuxhaven 53°52′N 8°42′E, Emden 53°21′N 7°11′E, Flensburg 54°48′N 9°26′E, Hamburg 53°33′N 9°58′E, Kiel 54°19′N 10°08′E, Norddeich 53°38′N 7°10′E, Rostock 54°05′N 12°07′E, Stralsund 54°19′N 13°06′E, Travemunde 53°58′N 10°54′E, Wilhelmshaven 53°31′N 8°09′E, Wismar 53°54′N 11°28′E.
Frisian Islands: Borkum 53°35′N 6°40′E, Norderney 53°42′N 7°10′E.

Procedure on arrival

On arrival, the Q flag must be flown, unless arriving from an EC or Scandinavian country. Yachts must be registered. The captains of foreign yachts may have to show a certificate of competence, although the rules stipulate that this is not compulsory if such a certificate is not required in the country where the vessel is registered. A radio operator's certificate is compulsory. Duty-free stores must be declared to customs. Immigration must be cleared on arrival and departure.
Kiel Canal: If passing through the Kiel Canal, but not visiting Germany, the 3rd substitute pennant must be flown.

Customs

Firearms must be declared and will be sealed on board.
   Animals must have valid health certificates.
   Pleasure craft may remain in Germany for up to one year without paying duty.

Immigration

Nationals of other EC countries, the USA, Canada and most European countries do not need visas for up to three months, after which time a resident's permit must be obtained.
   With the reunification of Germany, visa regulations may change, so one should check the requirements, especially if planning to visit the East German Baltic coast.

Restrictions

There are strict anti-pollution regulations in force throughout Germany, but particularly in the Baltic Sea. The disposal of garbage anywhere in the Baltic is forbidden. Degradable foodstuff can only be disposed of overboard more than 12 miles from shore. Special containers are provided in all ports for the disposal of garbage and used oils.

Navigation

When motorsailing, a black cone with its apex pointing downwards must be displayed – failure to do so can result in instant fines. Yachts must carry on board the German collision regulations (Seeschiffahrtsstrassenordnung) and the Kiel Canal Rules. The latter can be obtained at the Canal.

Any vessel over 15 tons is considered a merchant ship and must carry a pilot through most state waterways unless one has a Master's Certificate. Harbour authorities will help to make any arrangements for this.

Children under 16 years may not steer a vessel under way in German waters and in certain rivers this minimum age is 21 or 23. Motor boats and sometimes sailing yachts require special permission to use some inland waterways.

KIEL CANAL

The 100 km (60 miles) long Nord–Ostsee-Kanal (North Sea–Baltic Sea Canal) has strict rules which must be observed by yachts transiting it. A set of the rules, in German (Merkblatt für die Sportschiffahrt auf dem Nord–Ostsee-Kanal), can be obtained at either end of the Canal. The height limit is 39.6 metres (129 ft) and there is a speed limit of 15 km/h (8 knots). Yachts are expected to make the transit under power and although sailing is permitted in certain parts, tacking is forbidden and the engine must be on standby.

1. Because of the high amount of radio traffic, the traffic control office or lock-keepers should only be called on VHF radio if absolutely necessary. Transiting vessels must monitor the correct frequencies permanently.
2. Yachts without a pilot may use the canal only during daylight hours, except in the approaches to the yacht harbours at Brunsbüttel and Holtenau. When waiting at locks, yachts must stay behind commercial vessels.
3. Yachts may moor only in the following places within the limits of the canal:
   Brunsbüttel yacht harbour (km 1.8)
   Waiting area north side of Brunsbüttel (km 2.7)
   Waiting area at Dückerswisch (km 20.5) – one night only
   Waiting area before Gieselau lock (km 40.5).
      Note: foreign yachts which have duty-free stores on board may only stop here if already cleared by customs.
   Waiting area at Obereider Lake (Rendsburg harbour) (km 66)
   Waiting area at Borgstedter Lake (km 70)
   Dock at Flemhuder Lake (km 85.4) – one night only
   Holtenau yacht harbour (km 98.5)
   In an emergency, yachts may also moor behind the dolphins intended for larger vessels.
4. The light signal applicable to yachts at the end locks are:
   Single red light: entry forbidden.
   Flashing white light: proceed.
   Three vertical red lights: all vessels must stop.
5. Yachts unable to use their engine or without an engine may be towed through at the owner's expense.
6. Yachts without radar must stop in reduced visibility.

Facilities

The best facilities are concentrated around the main sailing centres at Hamburg, Kiel and Bremen. Extensive repair facilities are available in all these places and also a comprehensive range of marine supplies. Marinas and small boatyards are spread around the entire coastline and also in the rivers and estuaries. Fuel, water and LPG are easily available and so are provisions.

Further Reading

Frisian Pilot
Baltic Southwest Pilot
Cruising Association Handbook

NETHERLANDS

Facing the North Sea between Belgium and Germany, the Netherlands or Low Countries certainly deserve their name. Much of the country is so low that to prevent the encroaching of the sea has always been a battle, and gradually a system of dykes were built to protect the land. Holland is only one province of the Netherlands and it is not correct to call the whole country by that name.

In the Netherlands one is never too far away from water and the centre of the country is occupied by the IJsselmeer, formerly called Zuidersee, until it was dammed off from the sea. Most cruising is concentrated in the IJsselmeer, Wadden Sea and Frisian Islands, an area of sand dunes, intricate channels and picturesque ports. The western part has deeper water and a keeled yacht has access everywhere, whereas a shallow draft is essential in the eastern part. At IJmuiden one can pass through a lock to reach the IJsselmeer and Amsterdam. Another excellent cruising ground is Zeeland, in the south-west, which can be reached via the Walcheren Canal at Vlissingen or through the locks on the Oosterschelde. Cruising along the North Sea coast is more challenging on account of the strong tides, sand banks and onshore winds. From Vlissingen in the south-west to Delfzijl in the north-east, there are several good yacht harbours in which to shelter in case of bad weather. The Frisian Islands have many sheltered harbours on the east side facing the Wadden Sea, which are good starting points to explore the liquid world of the Netherlands.

Country Profile

This region was already peopled by Celtic and Germanic tribes when conquered by the Romans in 57 BC. Overrun by Germanic invasions in the fourth century, later Saxons and Franks settled in different parts. The ninth century brought Norman invasions and the country was divided into feudal duchies, earldoms and bishoprics, then fiefs of the Holy Roman Empire. The twelfth and thirteenth centuries saw the rapid growth of the towns, their prosperity based mainly on the cloth trade. By the fifteenth century, royal marriages, inheritances and purchases led to the area being united under the Duke of Burgundy, and later brought under Spanish rule. During the sixteenth century there was economic expansion, and the ideas of the Protestant Reformation spread. In 1555 Philip II became the new king of Spain and the Netherlands, and his absolutist anti-Protestant policy led to the Calvinist, prosperous northern provinces rebelling. After a long struggle aginst Spain in 1648 the United

Festival of Sail in Amsterdam. (Netherlands Tourist Office).

Practical Information

LOCAL TIME: GMT + 1. Summer time GMT + 2 from the end of March to the end of September.

BUOYAGE: IALA A at sea, and the ISIGNI system in inland waters.

CURRENCY: Gulden (guilder/florin, Fl) of 100 cents

BUSINESS HOURS
Banks: 0900–1700 Monday to Friday.
Business: 0830–1730 Monday to Friday.
Shops: 0830/0900 to 1730/1800 Monday to Friday, some until 1900–2100 Thursday or Friday, smaller ones close 1300–1400. Half day closing during week, often Mondays.
Government offices: 0830–1730 Monday to Friday.

ELECTRICITY: 220 V, 50 Hz

PUBLIC HOLIDAYS
1 January: New Year's Day
Good Friday, Easter Monday
30 April: Queen's Day
5 May: Liberation Day
Ascension Day
Whit Monday
24–26 December: Christmas

COMMUNICATIONS
International dialling access code is 09, then wait for a second tone.
Post offices open 0830–1700 Monday to Friday, some also 0830–1200 Saturday. Amsterdam has a very busy international airport with flights to almost everywhere in the world.

MEDICAL
There are reciprocal agreements for free treatment with other European countries.

DIPLOMATIC MISSIONS
In The Hague:
Australia: Konninginnegracht 23–24, 2514 AB. ☎ (70) 63 0983.
Canada: Sophialaan 7. ☎ (70) 61 4111.
New Zealand: Mauritskade 25, 2514 HD. ☎ (70) 346 9324.
United Kingdom: Lange Voorhout 10, 2514 ED ☎ (70) 64 5800.
United States: Lange Voorhout 102. ☎ (70) 62 4911.

In Amsterdam:
United Kingdom: Koningslaan 44, 1075 AE. ☎ (20) 76 4343.
United States: Museumplein 19. ☎ (20) 79 0321.

Provinces were eventually recognised as an independent country.

The United Provinces later became known as the Netherlands and they made rapid economic progress, becoming a leading maritime power. They established a vast commercial empire in the East Indies, South Africa and Brazil. However, wars with neighbouring powers weakened the state and the eighteenth century led to a decline. France overran the country, forming first the Batavia Republic, then the Kingdom of Holland. In 1814 the Treaty of Paris united the Netherlands and Belgium as an independent entity, but in 1830 Belgium broke away.

A liberal constitution was introduced in 1848. Wilhelmina became Queen in 1890, her reign lasting nearly sixty years. The Netherlands were neutral in the First World War, and occupied by Germany in the Second. After the war the Netherlands enjoyed an economic recovery. Juliana succeeded as Queen in 1948, until her abdication in 1980 in favour of her daughter Beatrice. The Netherlands are a member of Benelux, NATO and the European Community.

Overseas commerce has always been important, and continues to dominate the economy, half the national product being exported. Electrical, food processing, chemical and natural gas industries or service industries such as finance are the main employers of the working population. Agriculture is intensive, often on reclaimed land, mainly raising livestock, and the flowers and market gardening for which the country is renowned.

The population is 14.5 million and is concentrated around the main towns. Amsterdam is the commercial capital, but The Hague is the parliamentary and legal capital. Dutch is the official language, but English is widely spoken. There are both Protestants and Catholics, as well as several other denominations.

The climate is normally temperate, and rainfall is frequent all year round. Temperatures are rarely above 18°C (65°F) in summer or below 7°C (45°F) in winter. The prevailing winds are W or SW and most gales also come from those directions.

Entry Regulations

Ports of entry

Vlissingen (Flushing) 51°27′N 3°35′E, Breskens 51°24′N 3°34′E, Veerhaven (De Maas/Rotterdam) 51°54′N 4°29′E, Scheveningen 52°06′N 4°16′E, IJmuiden 52°27′N 4°35′E, Den Helder 52°58′N 4°47′E, Terneuzen 51°20′N 3°49′E, Terschelling 53°22′N 5°13′E, Vlieland 53°18′N 5°06′E, Lauwersoog 53°25′N 6°12′E, Delfzijl 53°20′N 6°54′E.

Some ports have customs only in the summer months, such as Roompot Sluis and Oost Vlieland.

Procedure on arrival

One must report on arrival and departure to the nearest customs office. This is strictly enforced. On arrival the customs will issue a certificate of entry, which is valid for a maximum of 12 months. During this period a yacht may leave and re-enter the Netherlands, showing the certificate on each re-entry. Foreign yachts must be registered. Any person steering a vessel capable of more than 9 knots must have a certificate of competence.

Vlissing: The port is entered through a set of lock gates and there is a marina close to the lock.

Scheveningen: The marina is located in fishing harbour no. 2. The port authorities should be contacted on VHF Channel 14 for permission to enter the harbour.

IJmuiden: There can be a strong tidal stream at the entrance. Yachts can moor in the canal near the South Lock.

Den Helder: Yachts can moor in the Royal Naval Yacht Harbour.

Delfzijl: A new yacht harbour is in operation some three miles south of the old harbour entrance.

Customs

All firearms must be licensed, and a copy of the licence carried. There may be restrictions concerning signalling pistols.

Animals must have a valid health certificate.

The yacht may not be sold, rented or borrowed while in the Netherlands, unless the appropriate taxes have been paid. Yachts may stay up to 12 months, after which time they must leave the country but can re-enter after a few days, obtaining a new certificate of entry. Otherwise they become liable for VAT (Value Added Tax).

Immigration

Nationals of the United States, Canada, the United Kingdom, Australia, New Zealand and most European and Commonwealth countries do not need a visa for a stay up to three months.

South African nationals need a visa.

Navigation

Shipping traffic is very heavy along the coast. A very busy shipping route is via the Hook of Holland over the New Waterway to Rotterdam, and there is no yacht harbour in this port. In a strong westerly wind and outgoing tide from the New Waterway there can be a high tidal sea.

Inland waterways

Access to the inland waterways is from the ports of Veerhaven and the IJmuiden locks. From Den Helder there are connections via the Noord-Hollands Canal and the Zaan with Amsterdam. There is no access from Scheveningen.

There are no speed limits on the larger rivers (except the Maas), the IJsselmeer, the open-sea channels in Zeeland, the Waddenzee and the coastal waters. However, there are speed limits in force on the canals and lakes, varying between 5 and 9 knots in different areas, which should be checked. Motorboats capable of travelling at more than 9 knots must be registered. This can be done at most larger post offices for a fee, showing proof of identity. In some areas local permission must also be obtained to travel at greater speeds.

On many of the canals and rivers yachts must keep to starboard and have their engines prepared for use. If motorsailing on the waterways, yachts are required to display forward a black cone, apex downwards.

Landing on some islands in the inland waterways is restricted. There are also restrictions concerning draft and height. However, there are certain routes that can be taken by yachts with high fixed masts without encountering any bridges. These are in the western and northern parts of Holland, such as from Vlissingen to Delfzijl.

Yachts are required to have on board a copy of the Inland Waters Police Regulations, which are in force on most of the inland waters, the Zeeland channels (except the Western Scheldt, where its own shipping regulations apply), the IJsselmeer, and the Waddenzee. On the Dutch Rhine, the Waal and the Lek the Rhine Route Police Regulations are in force.

The Inland Waters Police Regulations are available in Part I of the *Almanak voor Watertourisme*, in Dutch only. Part 2 contains tide tables, opening times of bridges and locks, and other essential details.

Fishing

There are certain regulations regarding fishing in the Netherlands and a permit must be bought. Regulations must be respected concerning closed seasons, areas where fishing is permitted, types of rods which can be used and types of fish which can be caught.

Facilities

As can be expected in a water-based nation with a great maritime past, boating facilities are good everywhere. There are shops in all the small ports and fuel is available in most marinas and harbours on the dock. Along the coast there are marinas with repair facilities at Vlissingen and Breskens, both of which are convenient if coming from the south. There are good facilities also in Zeeland, particularly at the marinas at Zierikzee and Colijnsplaat. Good facilities are also available at Den Helder, with smaller marinas and a limited range of repair facilities at Terschelling and

Vieland. Across the Wadden Sea on the mainland, Harlingen is a picturesque port with good facilities. In the north, best facilities are at Delfzijl, which is reached by sailing up the Ems.

Further Reading

Almanak voor Watertourisme, Parts 1 and 2, from ANWB offices (Royal Netherlands Touring Club) and some bookshops.
ANWB also publishes charts of the inland waters.
Small craft charts published annually by the Dutch Hydrographic Office. There is a special chart of the Province of Friesland, regularly updated.
Inland Waterways of France also has main routes in the Netherlands.
Frisian Pilot
IJsselmeer Harbours
Cruising Guide to the Netherlands
North Sea Harbours and Pilotage
Cruising Association Handbook
North Sea Passage Pilot

NORWAY

Norway occupies the western side of the Scandinavian peninsula, a mountainous forested land, with deep dramatic fjords cutting into the coast. The wild grandeur of the fjords gives Norway one of the most beautiful sceneries in the world. A chain of islands stretching parallel to the western coast and extending almost as far as the North Cape provide sheltered waters for cruising. The majestic fjords are less suited for cruising as the anchorages are extremely deep and the winds alternate between flat calms and violent gusts blowing almost vertically down the sides of the sheer cliffs.

Country Profile

From the eighth to the eleventh centuries the Vikings reigned supreme in the coastal regions of north-west Europe, often terrorising the coasts of the British Isles, France and Greenland. Through their voyaging the Norsemen came in contact with the rest of the world and Norway gradually developed into a state. Christianity spread through the area in the tenth and eleventh centuries. In the thirteenth century Norway expanded westwards and established control over the Faeroes, Orkneys, Shetlands and Greenland. Norwegian vessels were roaming the North Atlantic five

centuries before Columbus sailed the much more benign route to the continent which later became known as America.

The Union of Kalmar of 1397 brought Norway under Danish rule and Norway remained under Danish control for three centuries. The eighteenth century saw the Norwegian economy expand and wood, metal and fish were exported. In the 1814 Treaty of Kiel, Denmark ceded Norway to Sweden, and despite resistance the Norwegians were forced to accept it. In the nineteenth century parliamentary rule was gradually established, and after a plebiscite Norway gained independence in 1905. Social reforms were introduced, and in 1935 working-class strength brought the Labour party to power. Norway was occupied by Germany from 1940 to 1945, and after the king and government fled, Major Quisling, a Nazi supporter, ruled the country. After the war the Labour party were in power until 1965, since when there have been various governments, mainly of a moderate centre coalition. In 1972 the Norwegians voted in a referendum against Norway's proposed entry into the European Community.

Agriculture is centred in the southern region and livestock raising is the most important activity. Forestry, fishing and shipping industries are important, while large North Sea gas and oil deposits have brought a considerable income in recent years.

The population is 4 million. Apart from Norwegians, Finns and Sami (Lapps) live in the northernmost region of Finnmark. Norwegian and Lappish are spoken, and the majority of the population is Lutheran. The capital is Oslo, situated at the head of a large fjord in the south of the country.

The climate is milder on the coast due to the Atlantic influences, but it is still very cold in winter. The winter coastal temperatures average 4 to 10°C (40–50°F), and minus 18° to 1°C (0–35°F) inland. In summer the coast is around 13–15°C (55–60°F), and inland 18–21°C (65–70°F). The weather is generally rainy and changeable on the western coast, while less rainy and more predictable in the south-east. Northerly winds prevail in summer along the coast, while in winter there is a predominance of southerly winds. Winds strengthen during the afternoons.

Entry Regulations

Ports of entry

All ports are ports of entry except those in military areas. Frequently used ports only are listed below.
Bergen 60°24′N 5°19′E, Haugesund 59°25′N 5°16′E, Stavanger 58°58′N 5°44′E, Egersund

Practical Information

LOCAL TIME: GMT + 1. Summer time
GMT + 2 from the end of March to the
end of September.

BUOYAGE: IALA A

CURRENCY: Norwegian Kroner (Kr,
NEK) of 100 ore. Up to 5000 Kr may be
exported.

BUSINESS HOURS
Banks: Monday to Friday 0815–1500
(1530 in winter), Thursday 0815–1700.
Business: 0800–1600 Monday to Friday,
0900–1300 Saturday.
Shops: 0900–1600/1700 Monday to
Friday, 0900–1800/2000 Thursday,
Saturday 0900–1300/1500.
Government offices: 0800–1500 Monday
to Friday.

ELECTRICITY: 220 V, 50 Hz

PUBLIC HOLIDAYS
1 January: New Year's Day
Maundy Thursday, Good Friday and
Easter Monday
1 May: Labour Day
17 May: Constitution Day
Ascension Day
Whit Monday
25, 26 December: Christmas

COMMUNICATIONS
International dialling access code is 095.
International calls can be made from any
public phone.
Page 16 of the telephone directory gives
explanations in English, while various
emergency numbers are given in the
front.

Post office: 0800–1600/1700 Monday to
Friday, Saturday 0800–1300.
The main international airport with
flights worldwide is Oslo, but there are
also international flights from Stavanger
and Bergen.

MEDICAL
There is a reciprocal agreement with
certain West European countries for
medical treatment in the Norwegian
Health Service.

DIPLOMATIC MISSIONS
In Oslo:
Canada: Oscar's Gate 20. ☎ (2) 466955.
United Kingdom: Thomas Heftyesgate 8.
☎ (2) 552400.
United States: Drammensveien 18.
☎ (2) 448550.

58°27′N 6°00′E, Mandal 58°02′N 7°28′E, Kristiansand 58°09′N 8°00′E, Lillesand 58°15′N 8°23′E,
Oslo 59°54′N 10°43′E, Fredrikstad 59°12′N
10°57′E, Tonsberg 59°16′N 10°25′E, Moss 59°26′N
10°40′E.

Procedure on arrival

Yachts from Nordic countries do not need to make a
customs declaration provided they are not carrying an
excess of dutiable stores and equipment and do not
remain in Norwegian waters more than six months.
Yachts from other countries should report immediately on arrival at a port of entry. Customs clearance is
not strictly necessary if one has nothing to declare, but
is advisable. The captain should report to customs and
show the ship's documents and passports. Customs
must be cleared at a quay in the main harbour before
moving to a berth for yachts. Immigration must be
contacted on arrival and both immigration and
customs must be cleared on departure.

Customs

Firearms must be declared. All firearms must have a
licence from the country of origin. Firearms must be
re-exported within three months, if not an application
for a permit must be made.

The importation of birds and other animals is prohibited as Norway is rabies-free. If coming from a
rabies-free country, the animals must be kept in isolation for the first 30 days after arrival. Thereafter an
import permit must be obtained from the Ministry of
Agriculture.

Only up to 10 kg (22 lb) of agricultural products are
allowed to be imported, of which 3 kg (6.6 lb) may be
meat and processed meat products from other Nordic
countries. Tinned meat from all countries is allowed
but fresh fruit, vegetables or dairy products are restricted imports.

There are strict restrictions on the import of
alcohol and a heavy tax is imposed for excess
amounts. For persons over 20 the allowance is 1 litre
of spirits and 1 litre wine *or* 2 litres of wine and 2
litres of beer. A deposit must be paid on excess
amounts and the items placed under seal until leaving
Norwegian waters. This deposit will be refunded on
proof from foreign customs that the yacht has arrived
in the next country.

Yachts may remain for up to one year, after which
Value Added Tax must be paid. If wishing to lay up the
boat, permission from customs must be obtained first
and it may be necessary to have a bond from a bank.
The vessel may only be used by the person to whom
clearance is given and cannot be used for commercial
purposes. For non-resident owners who remain more
than five months in Norway, the yacht is permitted to
stay for six months.

Immigration

No visas are needed for stays of up to three months by
nationals of most European countries, the USA,
Canada, Australia and New Zealand. Nationals of
South Africa, Hong Kong, Poland, the Soviet Union
and several African, Asian and Middle East countries
are among those who need to obtain a visa in advance.

Extensions can be obtained from the police, but then the person will not be allowed back for a further six months.

Fishing

Anyone over 16 years old fishing for salmon, sea trout, sea char or freshwater fish in waters on common land must pay an annual fee at any post office. A local fishing licence is also compulsory and this can be obtained from sports shops, kiosks and tourist offices. The licence only covers a certain area, and can be bought for a day, week, month or whole season. Restrictions are normally stated on the licence. Live bait is forbidden.

Fishing seasons vary from district to district.

Sea fishing with rod or hand lines is open to anyone, and no fishing fee must be paid, unless fishing for salmon, sea trout or sea char. The closed season for these fish is 5 August–31 May.

Foreigners may only use hand gear such as rods or jigs. Nets and similar devices may not be used.

Restrictions

Yachts must stay in the sailing lanes marked on the charts. Sailing close to military areas is prohibited, such areas being marked on charts and usually indicated by signposts on the shore.

There are various conservation areas for sea birds along the coasts, access to which is prohibited between 15 April and 15 July, including the surrounding sea for 50 metres.

The shoreline in anchorages is normally privately owned and one should ask the owner's permission first before landing.

No fires may be lit on shore from 15 April to 15 September.

No garbage may be thrown overboard and toilets can be pumped out only well away from harbours and sailing lanes.

Fees

Overtime is charged on customs clearance at weekends.

Flag etiquette

The courtesy flag must be flown from sunrise to sunset only. It is considered very discourteous to leave the flag flying after sunset.

Facilities

Provisioning is good everywhere, but the price of food is very high. Fuel is available in all ports. LPG con-tainers may be refilled only in the main centres such as Oslo, Stavanger and Bergen, and it may be necessary to have the right adaptor. Sets of small craft charts are available containing details of interest to cruising yachts which are not found on ordinary charts.

The widest range of repair facilities are in the main yachting centres such as Oslo, Stavanger and Bergen, which also have the best docking facilities. Good facilities are also available at Kristiansand, where most repairs can be undertaken and there also is a chandlery and sailmaker. There are docking or mooring provisions for visiting yachts in all ports, although occasionally a dock may be privately owned and permission to use it should be obtained first.

Further Reading

Norwegian Cruising Guide
Guest Harbours in Norway
Cruising in Norwegian Waters
With Pleasure Craft in Scandinavia

POLAND

Poland lies on the southern shores of the Baltic Sea wedged between Germany and the Soviet Union, two countries whose territorial ambitions have shaped most of Poland's recent history. Poland was the first East European country to rid itself of Communist rule by democratic means and also put an end to Soviet domination. The process, which started in Poland in the early 1980s, has had reverberations, not only in Europe but all over the world.

Of all the Communist countries in Europe, Poland was the first to allow its sailors to cruise away from home. Although most limited their sailing to neighbouring Baltic countries, a few Polish yachts sailed as far as the Caribbean and some even around the world. Cruising in Poland itself is limited to the two sailing areas around the ports of Szczecin and Gdynia, the former in the estuary of the river Oder, the latter on the western shore of the Gulf of Gdansk.

Country Profile

Although Poland has been inhabited since 3000 BC, the country's history really began in the fifth century when Slavs settled between the Oder and Elbe rivers. After Christianity came to the area a duchy was established, which later divided into several duchies in the twelfth century. The Teutonic Knights took

Practical Information

LOCAL TIME: GMT + 1. Summer time GMT + 2 end of March to end of September.

BUOYAGE: IALA A

CURRENCY: 1 zloty (zl) of 100 grozy. A daily minimum of US$15 must be spent on food and accommodation, for which vouchers are obtained from Polish National Tourist Offices, which can then be cashed. All receipts of purchases should be kept to show customs on departure. The amount of foreign currency imported must be declared and the amount exported must be less than that imported. In some of the larger towns there are shops where foreigners can make purchases with convertible foreign currencies, preferably US dollars.

BUSINESS HOURS
Banks: 0900–1330 Monday to Saturday.
Business: 0830–1530 Monday to Friday.
Shops: 1100–1900 Monday to Saturday.
Government offices: 0800–1500 Monday to Friday.

ELECTRICITY: 220 V, 50 Hz

PUBLIC HOLIDAYS
1 January: New Year's Day
Easter Sunday, Easter Monday
1 May: Labour Day
Corpus Christi
22 July: National Holiday
1 November: All Saints Day
25 December: Christmas Day
26 December: Boxing Day

COMMUNICATIONS
International calls can be made from telephone offices and are cheaper from 1600 to 0600.

Telegrams can be sent from post offices and by telephone.
There are flights to many destinations worldwide from Warsaw. There are also flights from Gdansk to Hamburg.

MEDICAL
The medical service is good and not too expensive; however, medicines are scarce and expensive.

DIPLOMATIC MISSIONS
In Warsaw:
Australia: Etonska 3/5, Saska Kepa.
☎ (22) 176081.
Canada: Ulica Matejki 1/5.
☎ (22) 298051.
United Kingdom: Aleja Roz No 1.
☎ (22) 281001.
United States: Aleje Ujazdowskie 29/31.
☎ (22) 283041.

advantage of this division to conquer East Prussia and cut off Poland's access to the Baltic. The fourteenth century brought some unity to Poland under Casimir III and later Lithuania was united with Poland, and parts of White Russia and the Ukraine were absorbed. In the first half of the sixteenth century during the reigns of Sigismund I and II, Poland prospered, with economic growth and the development of a humanist culture and religious tolerance. However, after 1572 conflicts between the monarchy and the nobles embroiled the country in civil war which, coupled with wars with Russia, Turkey and Sweden, saw Poland lose territory and her great power status.

Poland's neighbours continued to intervene in her internal affairs, culminating in the partition of Poland between Russia, Prussia and Austria. From 1807–13 Napoleon formed the Grand Duchy of Warsaw, but this was abolished by the Congress of Vienna in 1815 and the land redistributed between the powers. Polish resistance and uprisings throughout the nineteenth century were repressed and many Poles emigrated. However, the independence movement remained strong, and came to the fore in the First World War.

In 1918 Poland was re-established as an independent republic, and given access to the Baltic through the Polish Corridor. Frontier disputes caused fighting with the Germans, Czechs, Russians and Ukrainians until 1921. Non-aggression pacts were signed with both the USSR and Germany in the 1930s, but the

secret Molotov–Ribbentrop agreement provided for the division of Poland. This occurred following Germany's invasion of Poland in 1939, the immediate cause of the outbreak of the Second World War. After the war the Communists gained power and a Soviet type republic was formed. In the 1970s Western finance was sought to modernise the economy, but economic problems continued. Dissatisfaction found an outlet when in 1980 the free trade union Solidarnosc (Solidarity) was formed. A year later martial law was imposed by General Jaruzelski and Solidarity was banned, but by the end of the 1980s restrictions were eased and in 1989 a non-Communist government was elected.

Heavy industry remains important to the economy, mainly iron, steel, chemicals and textiles. The main agricultural products are cereals, potatoes and sugar beet, the private sector in agriculture being quite sizeable. Poland's foreign debt continues to be a burden on the economy. Shortages and high inflation are major problems.

The population is 41.6 million, being mainly Polish with small Ukrainian and Byelorussian minorities. Polish is spoken and the majority are Roman Catholic with an Orthodox minority. Warsaw is the capital.

Winters are very cold, with snow and ice from November to March. June to August are the hottest and driest months. In summer the days are long and the Baltic coast can have pleasant variable breezes.

Entry Regulations

Ports of entry
Gdynia 54°32′N 18°33′E, Szczecin 53°25′N 14°33′E.

Procedure on arrival
Gdynia: Yachts should moor at the harbour master's quay on arrival for clearance. The ship's papers will be retained until departure. One should also clear with customs and immigration. One must return to the harbour master's quay for clearance on departure when the yacht may be searched.

Customs
Firearms must be declared.

Immigration
Visas must be obtained in advance and are valid for three months. If intending to visit more than one port, a multiple-entry visa must be obtained. At the time of writing, nationals of most countries still need a visa, but this is expected to change in the near future. A Polish embassy or consulate should be contacted for advice.

Facilities

Provisioning is reasonable, although there are occasional shortages. Fresh produce is widely available in summer. Best yachting facilities are at Szczecin and Gdynia, where there are considerable local boating communities. Better repair facilities are available at Szczecin, where there is an established boat-building industry, most of the yachts being produced for export. There are many yacht clubs and sailing associations which would be good sources of information if help is needed.

SWEDEN

Up in the north-west corner of Europe, Sweden forms half of the Scandinavian peninsula. The tongue of Sweden divides the Baltic from the North Sea and the country's two coasts offer an infinite variety of cruising. On the west coast the most attractive cruising area is from the Norwegian border to Göteborg, while on the east coast the most picturesque region is the Stockholm archipelago and the area to the south of it. To these should be added the various inland waterways, the best known being the Göta Canal, a scenic route which allows a yacht to sail from one side of Sweden to the other without the necessity to drop its mast. There are secluded anchorages and pretty villages throughout southern Sweden, making it one of the most attractive cruising destinations in Europe.

Country Profile

Inhabited from prehistoric times, the early peoples traded with the rest of Europe and from the eighth to tenth centuries the Swedish Vikings raided Russia and the surrounding region. Christianity spread only around the twelfth century, and gradually the Swedish nation developed, with Stockholm becoming the capital.

In the Union of Kalmar in 1397, Sweden came under Danish rule. Opposition to this grew and in the sixteenth century Gustave Vasa expelled the Danes and was elected king, creating a strong modern state. Sweden became a dominant European power, reaching its height under Gustave II Adolphus, when the country led the Protestant cause in the Thirty Years War. In 1660 the Danes were forced to cede the south of Sweden, leaving Sweden to dominate the Baltic region. However, the Northern War (1700–21) was costly, and Sweden lost all its German and Baltic territories except Finland. The eighteenth century saw the development of the Swedish economy and culture, until the monarchy restored its absolute rule in 1789, quashing the liberalisation in progress. Finland was ceded to Russia in 1808, while on the other hand Norway returned to Swedish rule from 1814 to 1905. The nineteenth century was a period of modernisation and liberalisation of the economy and politics, and in 1888 a free trade system was adopted.

In Gustave V's reign (1907–50) Sweden enjoyed an unprecedented prosperous period. With the Social Democratic party dominating politics, advanced social and political legislation was implemented. Sweden remained neutral during both world wars. In 1975 a new constitution was adopted, making King Charles XVI Gustave only a figurehead monarch. Social Democrat Olaf Palme was prime minister 1976–82 during a social and economic crisis, followed by a period of liberal and centralist government. Olaf Palme was assassinated in 1986.

Half the land is covered in forest so the timber industry is important, as are iron ore deposits. The main industries are mechanical, electrical and engineering. Agriculture is mainly for domestic consumption, producing cereals, potatoes and raising livestock. External trade is important, largely with the European Community.

The population numbers 8.3 million. Besides Swedes there are communities of Finns, Lapps, Yugoslavs,

Practical Information

LOCAL TIME: GMT + 1. Summer time
GMT + 2 from the end of March to the
end of September.

BUOYAGE: IALA A

CURRENCY: Swedish Krona (Skr, Kr,
SEK) of 100 öre.
Besides banks, money can also be
exchanged at 'Forex' exchange offices,
and at post offices showing the 'PK
Exchange' sign.

BUSINESS HOURS
Banks: 0930–1500 Monday to Friday
(some until 1730 in larger cities).
Shops: 0900–1800 Monday to Friday,
0900–1300/1600 Saturday. Shops close
earlier on days before public holidays.
Government offices: 0800–1600 Monday
to Friday.

ELECTRICITY: 220 V, 50 Hz

PUBLIC HOLIDAYS
1 January: New Year's Day
6 January: Epiphany
Good Friday, Easter Monday
1 May: Labour Day
Ascension
Whit Monday
21 June: Midsummer Day
1 November: All Saints Day
25, 26 December: Christmas

COMMUNICATIONS
International dialling access code 009.
International calls can be made either
from telephone offices, Tele or
Telebutik, open until 2100 or dial direct
from payphones.
Emergency: dial 90 000 (free from
payphones).
Post offices: 0900–1800 Monday to
Friday, Saturday 1000–1300.
There are international flights worldwide
from both Stockholm and Göteborg.

MEDICAL
Certain European countries have
reciprocal agreements with Sweden for
emergency treatment. The casualty
department at a hospital is called
Akutmottagning or Vardcentral in more
remote areas.

DIPLOMATIC MISSIONS
In Stockholm:
Australia: Sergels Torg 12.
☎ (8) 24 4660.
Canada: Tegelbacken 4, 7th floor.
☎ (8) 23 7920.
New Zealand: Arsenalsgatan 8C
☎ (8) 23 3790.
United Kingdom: Skarpogatan 6–8.
☎ (8) 67 0140.
United States: Strandvagen 101.
☎ (8) 63 0520.

Norwegians and Greeks. Swedish is the main language, although many speak English. The majority are Lutherans. The capital is Stockholm.

The climate is temperate due to the Gulf Stream, and the summers are pleasant. Winters are cold, the temperatures around freezing. Summer arrives only in June and the sailing season rarely lasts beyond the end of August, but has the advantage of long summer nights. The winds in summer are variable and mostly light.

Entry Regulations

Ports of entry

Customs Places P = passport control points by which foreigners may enter and leave Sweden.
F = frontier crossing points by which foreigners may enter and leave Sweden when travelling to and from Denmark, Finland, Sweden and Norway.
North Coast: Haparanda F 65°46'N 23°54'E, Luleå P 65°35'N 22°10'E, Piteå F 65°19'N 21°30'E, Skellefteå F 64°44'N 20°57'E, Umeå P 63°50'N 20°16'E, Örnsköldsvik P 63°16'N 18°43'E, Härnösand P (no customs facilities) 62°38'N 17°56'E, Sundsvall P 62°25'N 17°20'E, Hudiksvall F 61°43'N 17°07'E, Söderhamn 61°19'N 17°06'E, Gävle P 60°40'N 17°10'E.
Stockholm Archipelago: Norrtälje F (no customs) 59°54'N 18°42'E, Kapellskär F 59°43'N 19°05'E, Stockholm P 59°19'N 18°03'E, Sandhamn P (no customs) 59°17'N 18°55'E, Södertälje P 59°12'N 17°38'E, Nynäshamn P 58°54'N 17°57'E.
East Coast: Oxelösund P 58°40'N 17°07'E, Norrköping P 58°36'N 16°12'E, Söderköping P (no customs) 58°29'N 16°20'E, Västervik P 57°45'N 16°39'E, Oskarshamn F 57°16'N 16°27'E, Kalmar P 56°40'N 16°22'E.
Gotland: Slite P 57°42'N 18°49'E, Visby P 57°39'N 18°17'E.
South Coast: Karlskrona (and Dragsö) P 56°10'N 15°36'E, Ronneby P 56°10'N 15°18'E, Karlshamn P 56°10'N 14°52'E, Sölvesborg F 56°03'N 14°35'E, Åhus F 55°56'N 14°19'E, Simrishamn P (report to nearest communication centre) P 55°33'N 14°22'E, Ystad P 55°26'N 13°50'E, Trelleborg P 55°22'N 13°09'E, Malmö (and Limhamn) P 55°37'N 13°00'E, Landskrona P 55°52'N 12°50'E, Helsingborg (and Råå) P 56°03'N 12°41'E, Höganäs F 56°12'N 12°33'E, Mölle P (no customs) 56°17'N 12°30'E.
West Coast: Halmstad P 56°40'N 12°51'E, Falkenberg F 56°53'N 12°30'E, Varberg F 57°06'N 12°15'E, Göteborg P 57°42'N 11°57'E, Marstrand P (no customs) 57°53'N 11°35'E, Skärhamn F (report to nearest communications centre) 57°59'N,11°33'E, Stenungsund P 58°05'N 11°49'E, Lysekil P 58°16'N 11°26'E, Uddevalla P 58°21'N 11°55'E, Kungshamn and Smögen F (report to nearest communications

centre) 58°22′N 11°14′E, Strömstad P 58°56′N 11°10′E.

Communications Centres
North Coast: Haparanda ☎ 0922-129-49, Umeå 090-241-60, Härnösand 0611-790-82.
Stockholm Archipelago: Furusund 0176-8000-01/800-17, Stockholm 08-789-76-39/789-76-40.
East Coast: Gryt 0123-401-14/401-15.
Gotland: Visby 0498-102-45.
South Coast: Karlskrona 0455-110-63, Malmö 040-731-30/731-38/12-43-30, Heesingborg 042-17-08-02.
West Coast: Göteborg 031-63 71 50, Kungshamn 0523-307-55.

One can also contact the centres direct on VHF Channel 16 (except Haparanda).

Procedure on arrival
Yachts from other Nordic countries do not have to notify customs on arrival in Sweden, but yachts from countries outside the Nordic countries must report to customs, in a place which has a customs office, before stopping anywhere else. If visiting Göta Älv or going through the Göta Canal, one must report to the customs office before entering. Yachts may be intercepted by customs in the customs area for inspection. If arriving at a customs place outside of office hours, one must report by telephone to the nearest communication centre.

Foreign nationals may only enter and leave Sweden at passport control points, or (if travelling to or from Denmark, Finland, Iceland, Norway) via a frontier crossing point.

The customs will want a declaration of provisions and other goods on board. Also the yacht should be registered.

On departure from Sweden, yachts must make a verbal report to customs and clear passport control.

Customs
Firearms must be declared on arrival and may be retained until departure.

Animals may not be brought into Sweden without special permission. Unless one has an import permit, cats and dogs will immediately be sent out of Sweden at the owner's expense. Dogs and cats may be imported from Norway and Finland with a veterinary certificate.

Visitors may bring in up to 15 kg (33 lb) of food of which no more than 5 kg (11 lb) may be edible fats (not more than 2.5 kg butter) and up to 5 kg (11 lb) fresh fruit and vegetables. No fresh, smoked or frozen meat may be imported, although tinned meat is permitted. No potatoes may be brought in.

Goods which may not be imported freely must normally be presented for customs clearance, put into bond or taken out of the country again. In some cases the goods may be kept on board if a cash deposit is paid for the duty owing, which will be refunded if the goods are re-exported under customs supervision within three months. This does not apply to alcohol and tobacco, only the specified amounts of which can be kept on board, which are 1 litre of spirits, 1 litre of wine, 2 litres of beer and 200 cigarettes per person. Excess of this amount will be taken ashore and returned only on departure from Sweden.

Temporary importation
Foreign flagged yachts owned by non-residents of Sweden may be temporarily imported, exempt from duty, for up to one year. The yacht must be taken out of the country within one year. If one wishes to leave the yacht, whether for the winter or other reasons, and to leave Sweden by other means, a deposit must be left with customs equal to the amount of duty that would have to be paid if the yacht remained in Sweden longer than 12 months. If the yacht subsequently leaves before the 12 months are up, the deposit will be returned. The local customs authorities reserve the right to modify these requirements.

Only vessels over 75 tons, bound for non-Nordic countries, may take on board duty-free tobacco and alcoholic products.

Immigration
No visas, but valid passports are required for stays of up to three months for nationals of most countries, including EC countries, USA, Canada, Australia and New Zealand. Extensions can be obtained from local police stations. Persons entering Sweden from another Nordic country need only a document showing that they are a citizen of Denmark, Finland, Iceland or Norway.

Restrictions
Restricted areas are clearly marked on charts, as well as by signs on the shore. In protected and controlled areas foreign yachts must remain within the channels marked on the charts. In some parts of such areas anchoring or mooring is prohibited, and in others foreign yachts may not stay longer than 24 hours. Known prohibited areas are around Göteborg, the naval base at Karlskrona and parts of the southern approaches to Stockholm. Other restricted areas are protected wildlife reserves and at certain times of the year, especially spring and early summer, access is forbidden. The restricted areas are strictly enforced.

Laws are strict concerning the littering of the sea and

shore. Garbage, oils, petrol or harmful substances must not be discharged into the water and in many places toilets must also not be pumped out.

Fishing

Scandinavians can fish for recreation on Sweden's coasts, but non-Scandinavians must have special permission from the county board or county police where they intend to fish. Fishing is not permitted in private waters, except in certain areas where a special permit is needed. There are various regulations on closed seasons and permitted fishing tackle. Spearfishing is not permitted.

Inland waterways

There are various canals linking rivers and lakes which give access to the interior of the country. The Göta Canal crosses Sweden from Göteborg to Mem, a distance of about 200 miles, passing through canals, the Göta River and several lakes. Fees must be paid for locks and harbour dues, and are quite high. Swedish charts are essential. As there are no fixed bridges, the canal can be navigated without dropping the mast.

There are also the canals of Falsterbo, Dalslands, Arvika and Vaddo, and the Lake Malaren near Stockholm may also be navigated. There are maximum draft as well as height restrictions on some of these canals.

Facilities

Provisioning is easy everywhere with the exception of the remoter areas and in many places it is possible to come alongside a dock close to a grocery store. Fuel is not so widely available away from the larger centres. LPG containers can only be filled with the proper adaptor and this can only be done in some of the major towns.

There are only a few marinas, although mooring facilities are available everywhere. Most moorings belong to the Swedish Cruising Club, are painted red or blue and can also be used by foreign visitors either for short stays in daytime or for the night. Private moorings may also be used, either with permission, or if the absent owner has left a prominent green card indicating the berth is free. The biggest marinas are in Stockholm (Vasahamn) and Göteborg, and this is also where most repair facilities are located.

The standard of repair work is good throughout Sweden, but it may be difficult finding repair facilities in the more remote areas. For any major repair it is best to head for one of the larger yachting centres where almost everything is available.

The Swedish Tourist Association publishes a brochure about visitors' harbours in Sweden, called *Swedish Guest Harbours*, while plans of ports and anchorages on the east and south coasts, *Seglarhamnar pa Ostkusten*, are published by the Swedish Cruising Club. *Batsport-kort* are Swedish charts reproduced on small scale, available in most Swedish bookshops.

Further Reading

Baltic Southwest Pilot
Swedish Guest Harbours
Batsport-kort
Seglarhamnar pa Ostkusten
With Pleasure Craft in Scandinavia

3 Western Europe and North Atlantic Islands

The islands of the North Atlantic have served throughout history as stepping stones for new discoveries and the routes of former explorers have been taken up by modern sailors. The southern islands – Bermuda, the Canaries, the Azores and Madeira – are visited every year by hundreds of cruising yachts on their way east or west across the Atlantic. The northern islands attract fewer cruising yachts from afar, although countries like the United Kingdom and Ireland have their own large boating communities. This is also the case with France, which has coastlines on both the Atlantic and Mediterranean, with excellent facilities on both sides.

An increasingly popular cruise undertaken by many European sailors is a circumnavigation of the North Atlantic. By taking advantage of the prevailing weather conditions, this is easily accomplished, by sailing south to Madeira and the Canaries with the Portuguese trades of summer, west with the NE trade winds of winter and back east with the westerlies, or anti-trades, of higher latitudes. These weather patterns are due to a permanent feature of the North Atlantic, the area of

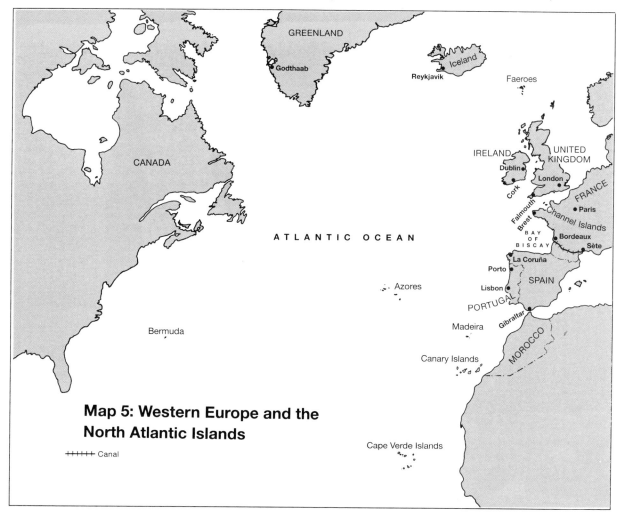

Map 5: Western Europe and the North Atlantic Islands

+++++ Canal

atmospheric high pressure situated near the Azores, whose name it bears. Because of its influence on sailing conditions over such a large area of the North Atlantic, the position of the Azores high must be watched carefully especially when planning an Atlantic crossing in either direction.

The sailing season in the northern islands is strictly for the summer, whereas the southern islands, being on the transatlantic circuit, have certain peak periods. Madeira and the Canaries are busiest between September and November when yachts prepare to cross to the Caribbean, while Bermuda and the Azores are busiest in May and June, when the movement is in the opposite direction. In the entire region, only Bermuda is affected by tropical storms, the hurricane season extending from July to November, with September being the most dangerous month. Although occasionally a hurricane may track eastwards, none of the other islands fall within the hurricane zone.

The best facilities are to be found in Britain and France, two of the world leaders in yachting, where there are several centres offering a full range of repair services. Facilities are also good in the most frequented islands, particularly Gran Canaria and Bermuda. Outside of these countries, repair facilities can only be described as adequate.

THE AZORES

Reputed to be the fabled Atlantis, the nine islands of the Azores lie in mid-Atlantic 900 miles off the coast of Portugal and 1800 miles from Bermuda. These volcanic islands have a scenic landscape of cones and craters, where the rich soil grows lush vegetation, both subtropical and temperate, with vividly coloured flowers growing everywhere among green fields.

Most yachts choose to stop in the Azores on their

Horta Marina.

way east across the Atlantic, although some call on their way west or when sailing from the South Atlantic towards Northern Europe. Although hundreds of yachts call every year, very few of them cruise around the islands and the majority stop only in Horta, on the island of Faial, one of the perennially favourite places of long-distance sailors. With their secluded bays, uncrowded anchorages and protected harbours, the rest of the Azores are still waiting to be discovered as a cruising destination in their own right. Besides their natural beauty, the relaxed pace of life in the islands is their main appeal. The islanders are as hospitable to visiting sailors as they were to Joshua Slocum, one of the first to call there in 1895.

Country Profile

The islands were uninhabited when, under the instigation of Prince Henry the Navigator, they were discovered by the Portuguese early in the fifteenth century, although they were known in ancient times. The Portuguese soon settled the islands and cultivated the land, and settlers came both from the Portuguese mainland and the Low Countries, the latter being Flemings fleeing religious persecution. The Azores became an important port of call for ships and Angra, with its natural harbour, became the leading town. Christopher Columbus stopped at Santa Maria on his first return voyage, and João Fernandez Labrador sailed west with Cabot's fleet and sighted the land now bearing his name.

When Spain occupied mainland Portugal in 1580, Dom Antonio, claimant to the Portuguese throne, fled to Terceira to organise his opposition. The islands fiercely resisted the Spanish invasion, but eventually Spain took control of all of them, and used them as a stopping-off point for ships returning from South America with treasure. When Portugal regained independence in 1640 the islands were each ruled by an independent governor, until in 1766 a central government was set up in Terceira. The latter supported the Liberals during Portugal's constitutional struggles in the early nineteenth century, and following the Liberal Revolution of 1832 the Azores were made a province of Portugal with three districts centred around the main ports of Horta, Angra and Ponta Delgada. Ships remained an important source of income and employment, especially the American whalers which took on many islanders as crew, due to their whaling expertise. Gradually, however, through the nineteenth century the number of ships calling declined. In 1895 the Azores were granted limited autonomy, but they remained poor and economically

dependent on Portugal, although with the laying of transatlantic cables from Faial, they became an important link in international communications. During both World Wars the islands were important bases for the Allies, and there is still a US base on Terceira. The Portuguese Constitution of 1976 made the Azores an autonomous region of Portugal with its own assembly and regional government.

The Azorean economy is mainly agricultural, the most important crops being cereals, fruit and vines, with cattle and dairy products. Fishing has recently expanded. Whaling was once an important source of income, the islanders hunting whales from small open boats, but this has recently ceased due to the whaling moratorium. There is a small tourist industry and the US air base on Terceira brings some income.

The population numbers 245,000. Many Azoreans have emigrated to North America, Brazil and Bermuda. Portuguese is the main language, although English, Spanish and French are widely understood. The majority are Roman Catholics. Ponta Delgada on São Miguel is the capital of the autonomous region.

The climate in the Azores is dominated by the mid-Atlantic area of high pressure which bears their name. The position of the Azores high varies with the season, being more northerly in the autumn and more southerly in the spring, usually lying to the S or SW of the islands. In winter the area can be stormy and very wet, while in the summer the Azores high can be stationary with prolonged periods of calm weather.

Entry Regulations

Ports of entry
Ponta Delgada (São Miguel) 37°44′N 25°40′W, Horta (Faial) 38°32′N, 28°38′W, Santa Cruz (Flores) 39°27′N 31°07′W, Angra do Heroismo (Terceira) 38°39′N 27°13′W, Praia da Vitoria (Terceira) 38°44′N 27°03′W, Vila do Porto (Santa Maria) 36°56′N 25°09′W, Vila das Velas (São Jorge) 38°40′N 28°13′W, Vila da Praia (Graciosa) 38°40′N 28°13′W.

Procedure on arrival
The Q flag should be flown at the first port of entry into the Azores, unless coming from Portugal or Madeira, when customs clearance need not be done. Yachts must clear in at one of the ports of entry where a transit log will be issued by the port authority. Clearance should also be done with customs (Alfandega) and immigration. In all ports of call in the Azores visited subsequently, the transit log must be taken along and presented to the local Guarda Fiscal

Practical Information

LOCAL TIME: GMT –1. Summer time GMT April to September.

BUOYAGE: IALA A

CURRENCY: Portuguese escudo of 100 centavo, written 00$00

BUSINESS HOURS
Banks: 0830–1145, 1300–1445 Monday to Friday.
Shops: 0900–1230, 1400–1800 Monday to Friday, Saturday morning.
Government offices: 0900–1200, 1400–1700.

ELECTRICITY: 220 V, 50 Hz

PUBLIC HOLIDAYS
1 January: New Year's Day
Good Friday
25 April: National Day

1 May: Labour Day
Corpus Christi
Whit Monday: Autonomy Day
10 June: Portugal Day
15 August: Assumption
5 October: Republic Day
1 November: All Saints Day
1 December: Restoration of Independence Day
8 December: Immaculate Conception
25 December: Christmas Day
There are also municipal holidays

EVENTS
Horta: Sea Week (Semana do Mar) starting first Sunday in August, a local festival including yacht races.

COMMUNICATIONS
Area codes for Faial (Horta) 92, São Miguel (Ponta Delgada) 96. International dialling access code 097.

International calls can be made from post offices, hotels and some public phones, including Café Sport, Horta. Stamps can be bought from post offices or where a 'correio' sign is shown. There are regular flights to Lisbon from São Miguel, Faial and Terceira. There are also occasional flights to Boston from Terceira, especially in the summer. There are frequent flights between all islands except Corvo, is linked by ferry.

MEDICAL
Emergency treatment is free to all. EC residents will not be charged for a hospital bed, but non-EC nationals may pay. For non-emergency consultations, a nominal fee is charged.

DIPLOMATIC MISSIONS
United States: Avenida Infante Dom Henrique, Ponta Delgada. ☎ (96) 22216.

office. In larger ports, the Port Authority (Capitania) should also be visited, and sometimes the Policia Maritima.

Horta Marina: On arrival yachts should berth alongside the reception quay (minimum depth 10 ft). The marina office is open 0800–1200, 1300–2000 (seven days a week in the high season April to June). The offices of Policia Maritima and Customs (Alfandega) are next to the marina office on the same quay, open 0800–1230, 1400–2000. The marina office should be visited first and will give instructions where to berth once clearance is completed. Yachts arriving after office hours should wait at the reception quay until the next morning.

On departure, one should first pay the marina fees, then take the receipt to the Guarda Fiscal and the Capitania for outward clearance.

Ponta Delgada: There is a small dock on the west side of the commercial harbour used by visiting yachts. The Guarda Fiscal office, within the port compound, should be visited first, followed by the Policia Maritima. Yachts are normally met on the dock by an officer, who ensures that there is no contact with other boats before formalities are completed. This is normally done during office hours, although the Guarda Fiscal office is open 24 hours. Customs is in town.

Angra do Heroismo: The Guarda Fiscal and Policia Maritima are by the Porto Pipas mole. With permission, yachts may come alongside there for short periods to clear if there is space.

Customs

Firearms must be declared.

There are no restrictions on animals being allowed ashore, but a rabies inoculation certificate is required.

Yachts may stay for a six-month period before becoming liable for duty.

Immigration

Visas are not required for citizens of Western European countries, Canada and the USA. Other nationalities may need to obtain a visa in advance. Persons travelling on a yacht in transit are normally granted a visa on arrival which is valid for a limited period. Those who require a visa and arrive without one should attempt to clear in at one of the major ports of entry.

Cruising permit

A transit log (Livrete de Transito) is issued by the Capitania or Delegaoes Maritimas on arrival. All subsequent movements of the yacht are recorded in this log until departure. Yachts must clear in and out of all ports, including harbours on the same island. If arriving from Madeira, the same transit log may be used, but if arriving from mainland Portugal, a new log is usually issued.

Facilities

Yachting facilities are concentrated in the two main ports of Horta and Ponta Delgada, which cater well for day-to-day needs, but whose repair facilities are barely adequate. Limited repair facilities are available in Angra do Heroismo and Praia da Victoria on Terceira, the yacht club in Angra being particularly helpful to visiting yachts.

Provisioning in the islands is limited with a better selection on the islands of São Miguel, Terceira and Faial. Limited supplies are available on the other islands, although local fresh produce is available everywhere. Water and fuel is also available in all ports, the latter usually having to be brought in jerrycans from filling stations.

Horta: With over 700 yachts calling every year at this well-organised and pleasant marina, repair facilities are getting better, but still only minor repairs can be undertaken locally. There are no proper hauling out facilities in Horta, although a crane can be hired in an emergency and the yacht lifted out onto the main wharf. There is a repair yard run by the port authority and also several workshops in town which can undertake engine, electrical, radio, metalwork and sail repair. There is a small chandlery with a limited selection. Fuel and water are available in the marina and LPG bottles can also be filled. There are several supermarkets and a daily fresh produce market.

Ponta Delgada: Less facilities are available in the capital, although a marina is planned. In the meantime, most repair facilities are concentrated around the fishing dock where there is a crane and some small workshops. Fuel is available at the fuelling berth and water is laid on at the floating pontoon used by visitors. There are several supermarkets in town providing the best provisioning in the Azores and there is also a daily fresh produce market. The small yacht club in the port is very helpful.

Further Reading

The Atlantic Islands
Silverman's *Guide to the Azores* is mostly outdated and inaccurate.

BERMUDA

Bermuda is an archipelago of over 150 small islands and islets, the largest linked together by causeways and bridges into a fish hook shape. The existence of coral islands so far north and only 600 miles off the East Coast of the USA is explained by the warm waters of the Gulf Stream which bathe Bermuda and account for its mild climate.

One of the most popular landfalls in the North Atlantic, Bermuda has welcomed weary mariners for over three centuries. Although it has little to offer in the way of cruising, Bermuda attracts over 1000 yachts every year who stop here to rest and reprovision after a long passage, or simply to turn around at the finish of one of the many ocean races which run from the US East Coast. Bermuda is well geared to cope with these transient sailors, most of whom arrive from the Caribbean in April and May, some on their way to Europe, others to the USA. Later in the autumn Bermuda sees another influx as yachts make their way south from the USA to the Caribbean.

The well sheltered St George's Harbour provides a restful anchorage from which to explore this neat and tidy little country. Such exploring is best done by land, particularly by those who are short of time and treat their stop in Bermuda as a brief but enjoyable interlude. The alternative anchorage is in Hamilton, but as all yachts have to clear in first at St George's, few bother to sail out afterwards and around the island to thread their way through the reefs to Hamilton harbour. It is easier by bus.

Country Profile

Bermuda was discovered early in the sixteenth century and named after the Spaniard Juan Bermudez. So many ships were lost on the islands and the reefs around them, that they became known as 'Isles of the Devil'. Generally they were given a wide berth, and were only settled in the seventeenth century following a misadventure. In 1609 the *Sea Venture*, a flagship under the command of Sir George Somers on an expedition to Virginia, was wrecked during a hurricane. This event lies behind the plot of Shakespeare's *The Tempest*, as the playwright's patron was the Earl of Southampton, a major shareholder in this Virginia Company. After surviving on the islands for some time and building two new ships, the group continued their voyage but soon returned and the Virginia Company was granted the islands by Royal Charter. In 1612 English settlers founded St George's, bringing in slaves, but the settlement was never profitable, and in 1684 Bermuda was taken over by the Crown as a colony.

The inhabitants remained more interested in the sea than the land. During the American War of Independence the population stole gunpowder from St George's to send to the rebels in exchange for food. Bermuda was also a popular base for privateers and pirates, later becoming an important base and dockyard for the British Navy. With the advent of the steamship, tourism developed and this increased

Practical Information

LOCAL TIME: GMT - 4. Summer time GMT - 3 May to October.

BUOYAGE: IALA B

CURRENCY: Bermuda dollar (BD$) on a par with US$. The latter is widely accepted.

BUSINESS HOURS
Banks: 0930–1500 Monday to Friday, 1630–1730 Fridays
Shops: 0900–1700 Monday to Saturday.
Business and government offices: 0930–1730 Monday to Friday (some close 1300–1400 and Thursday afternoons).

ELECTRICITY: 110 V, 60 Hz

PUBLIC HOLIDAYS
1 January: New Year's Day
Good Friday
Monday nearest to 24 May: Empire Day
Monday nearest second Saturday in June: Queen's Birthday
Thursday and Friday before first Monday in August: Cup Match and Somers Day
11 November: Remembrance Day
25, 26 December: Christmas

EVENTS
International Race Week, April–May.
Newport to Bermuda Ocean Yacht Race, June of even years.
Blue Water Cruising Race, June of odd years.
Biennial Multihull Race, June of odd years.
Single-handed Race, June of odd years.
Trans-At Yacht Race, May of odd years.

COMMUNICATIONS
Area code 29+ for numbers beginning with 2, 3, 5, 7 and 23+ for those beginning with 4, 6, 8.
Cable & Wireless: International calls, telex and fax.
Main post office: Church and Parliament Streets, Hamilton.
Bermuda Harbour Radio (call sign ZBM) maintains a continuous watch on Channel 16. As well as dealing with arriving yachts, it is the Airsea Rescue Coordination Centre for the Bermudan area, and is in contact with the US and Caribbean Coast Guards. Weather information and warnings are broadcast on Channel 27.
Weather Information for departure may also be obtained from the US Naval Oceanography Command Facility by phoning 293-5491 giving name, name of yacht and destination. A Yacht Pre-Sail Weather Packet can be arranged by the weather office 12 hours in advance and collected from Main Gate Office, US Naval Air Station.
Local weather: ☎ 977 (Bermuda Telephone Co.) or ☎ 293-5212 (Naval Station recording).
There are flights from Bermuda to London, Canada and the USA.

MEDICAL: King Edward VII Hospital in Paget East, outside Hamilton.

DIPLOMATIC MISSIONS
United States: Vallis Building, 58 Par La Ville Rd, Hamilton. ☎ 295-1342.

---

further after the First World War, especially with the establishment of airlinks. During the Second World War Bermuda was used as a US military base and still is today. In 1968 a new constitution gave the country internal self-government. Bermuda is one of the oldest of Britain's self-governing dependent territories.

Tourism is the main industry, and special legislation makes Bermuda a tax haven and business centre. Bermudans enjoy a very high standard of living having the highest per capita income in the world. Pressure on the land is considerable, and there is little agriculture apart from that for domestic consumption.

The English speaking population is 58,000, the majority being of African origin, with about 40 per cent of other origins, mainly European. Hamilton is the capital. Anglican and Roman Catholic are the largest of 40 different churches and religious communities.

The Gulf Stream makes the climate subtropical, with mild winters and warm humid summers. The Azores high dominates the summer months, bringing steady NE winds. June to November is the hurricane season with September the most dangerous month, although the majority of these storms pass to the west of Bermuda.

Entry Regulations

Port of entry
St George's Harbour 32°23′N, 64°40′W.

Procedure on arrival
All yachts arriving in Bermuda must clear in at the Yacht Clearing Facility at Ordnance Island, St George's Harbour, open 24 hours. St George's is entered through the Town Cut channel. Yachts stopping elsewhere will be escorted to St George's and may be fined by Customs. After clearance yachts may then proceed to Hamilton or elsewhere in the archipelago.

The Harbour Radio Station must be contacted prior to arrival on VHF Channel 16 giving approximate time of arrival and any special requirements. The station is on call 24 hours on 500 KHz, 2182 KHz and VHF Channel 16. A 24-hour radar watch is also kept and unidentified vessels are called up, especially if they approach too close to the reef. The radio station will direct a yacht where to berth and how to proceed for clearance. The Q flag must be flown. The captain should have ready two crew lists and two store lists showing details of consumable stores. The customs boarding officer normally carries out immigration and health formalities as well. Customs normally monitor VHF Channel 64.

Immigration

Visas are required in advance for nationals of East European countries, Argentina, Cuba, Haiti, Iran, Iraq, Jordan, Kampuchea, Laos, Lebanon, Libya, Mongolia, North Korea, Vietnam, China, Philippines, South Africa and Syria and are obtainable from a British embassy or consulate. Visas are not required if any of the above are permanent residents of the USA or Canada.

The period of stay is decided by the admitting immigration official, and is usually three to four weeks. Extension applications can be made at the Immigration Department.

Persons who require visas to enter other countries they are sailing to after Bermuda must already have them. This applies particularly to yachts leaving Bermuda for the USA.

All visitors arriving by air are required to show a return air ticket. To avoid this for crew members arriving or leaving by air on one-way tickets, the captain or owner of a yacht must write to the Chief Immigration Officer, Department of Immigration, Ministry of Home Affairs, POB HM 1364, Hamilton HM FX (☎ 809 295-5151) well in advance giving the name, address and nationality of any crew member, also details of the airline, flight number and date of arrival plus $10 (US or Bermudan $) for the landing permit. The latter will be sent to the captain and it permits the purchase of a one-way ticket (otherwise travel agents or airlines will not issue one). The permit must be shown on entry. If time is short, the captain can telephone with the crew details. In such cases the crew may have to buy a return ticket, but once the permit is issued, one can get a validation from the Chief Immigration Officer to allow a refund to be obtained.

When arriving by yacht and leaving by air, crew must have written proof from the owner or captain of their means of departure. The responsibility to ensure that such crew leave the island rests with the captain.

Customs

All firearms and ammunition must be declared on arrival to the customs officer, who will either impound them until departure or seal them on board. Firearms include spear guns, Verey pistols and flare guns.

Animals arriving without an import permit will be restricted to remaining on board, as Bermuda has no quarantine facilities. To obtain an import permit one should apply as far in advance as possible to the Director of the Department of Agriculture & Fisher-ies, POB HM 834, Hamilton HM CX (☎ 809 236-4201). Application forms are also available from any Bermuda tourist office. The animal must also have a general health certificate, and for dogs and cats, proof of a recent rabies vaccination, unless coming direct from the UK.

All medically prescribed drugs and medications must be declared on arrival.

Fruit and vegetables from other countries are prohibited imports.

Yachts can stay up to six months, after which time customs will impose a duty of 33.5 per cent on the yacht's value.

Fees

An arrivals tax of $20 per person is charged, including children.

Berthing and anchorage

One may anchor in both St George's and Hamilton harbours. In St George's there are some berths available at Somers Wharf, Hunters Wharf (east), and the north side of Ordnance Island. There is limited space, but the berths are free and there is no time limit. In Hamilton, yachts are restricted to the yacht club, boatyards and marinas.

Restrictions

Berthing for yachts is prohibited at all commercial docks except in an emergency.

No spearfishing permitted.

Facilities

Although there is a boatyard, slipway and some repair facilities in and around St George's, the development of the Marina Real del Oeste in the former naval dockyards has attracted some workshops to that area. Located on Ireland Island, at the opposite end of Bermuda to St George's, the new marina is adjacent to a boatyard and marine workshop with its own slipway. Although existing repair and service facilities are dispersed all over Bermuda rather than being grouped together, virtually everything one may need is available on the island even if it may take some time to find it. Marine supplies or essential parts that are unavailable can be ordered from the USA to which there are several flights every day.

Provisioning in St George's is reasonable with several supermarkets. Fuel and water are also available locally. For charts and marine supplies one has to go to the Pearman Watlington Marine Centre in Hamilton.

Further Reading

Yachtsman's Guide to the Bermudan Islands
The Bermuda Department of Tourism publish a very useful Information Sheet for yachts, which can be obtained from: Bermuda Department of Tourism, POB HM 465, Hamilton HM BX.

THE CANARY ISLANDS

The Canary Islands consist of seven main islands and many smaller ones lying off the African coast, 300 miles south of Madeira. These high volcanic islands on the Atlantic seismic ridge lie near to Africa, a combination of factors which explains the varied scenery, from sandy deserts to lush mountain valleys, pine forests to snow-capped Mount Teide on Tenerife, rising 12,000 feet (3700 metres) out of the ocean. The Canary Islands are a continent in miniature.

The seven islands of the archipelago are well spaced out so that it is only a day's sail between most of them. The logical route for most yachts arriving from the north is to visit Lanzarote and Fuerteventura first

The wild west coast of Gran Canaria.

before sailing to Gran Canaria, then Tenerife, La Gomera, El Hierro and La Palma.

Traditionally the Canaries have been the logical jumping-off point for yachts crossing the Atlantic to the Caribbean, ever since Columbus started the fashion 500 years ago. The route pioneered by Columbus cannot be bettered and from November to January the islands are full of yachts preparing for their Atlantic crossing.

While for some it is a quick provisioning stop, other cruising yachts take advantage of what the islands have to offer and leave Europe at the end of summer, so that they can spend a couple of months cruising the Canaries. The facilities for yachts have increased and improved dramatically in recent years and more cruising yachts are now spending longer in the islands and some are permanently based there. Also on the increase is the number of yachts sailing down from Europe to spend the winter months in the Canaries' pleasant climate.

Country Profile

The early population were known as Guanches, probably descended from Berbers who came over from

Practical Information

LOCAL TIME: GMT. Summer time GMT
+ 1 March to September

BUOYAGE: IALA A

CURRENCY: Spanish peseta (Pta) of 100
centavos

BUSINESS HOURS
Banks: 0900–1330 Monday to Saturday.
Business: 0800–1600 Monday to Friday.
Shops: 0900–1300, 1600–2000 Monday to
Saturday. Some large department stores
0900–2000.
Government offices: 0800–1400 Monday
to Friday.

ELECTRICITY: 220 V, 50 Hz

PUBLIC HOLIDAYS
1 January: New Year's Day
6 January: Epiphany
19 March: St Joseph
Maundy Thursday, Good Friday
Corpus Christi
18 July: National Day
25 July: St James
15 August: Assumption
12 October: Columbus Day

1 November: All Saints Day
8 December: Immaculate Conception
25 December: Christmas Day

EVENTS
Carnival (Las Palmas de Gran Canaria
and Santa Cruz de Tenerife).
Corpus Christi, floral carpets are laid
down in many towns.
ARC Transatlantic Rally starts last
Sunday in November.

COMMUNICATIONS
Area code for Gran Canaria,
Fuerteventura and Lanzarote 28, for
Tenerife, La Palma, Gomera and El
Hierro 22.
International dialling from public
phones. International dialling access
code 07, followed by a second dialling
tone.
Telefonicas: group of telephone booths
with an attendant who charges you after
the call is made.
Faxes can be sent and received at main
post offices.
    There are many flights, both regular
and charter, from Tenerife, Gran
Canaria and Lanzarote to all parts of

Europe with links to the rest of the
world. There are regular flights between
the islands. Tenerife, Gran Canaria and
Fuerteventura are linked by fast
hydrofoil. Gomera has no airport and is
linked by ferry to Tenerife.

MEDICAL
There are medical facilities in all
islands. There are also special clinics
catering for foreigners in most tourist
areas.

DIPLOMATIC MISSIONS
In Las Palmas de Gran Canaria:
Brazil: Nicolas EstéVanez 18.
☎ 277534.
Cape Verde Is: Arco 16. ☎ 241135.
France: Nestor de la Torre 12.
☎ 242371.
Germany: Franchy Roca 5. ☎ 275700.
Morocco: Mesa y Lopez 8. ☎ 292859.
Mauritania: Rafael Davila 10. ☎ 234833.
Senegal: Edificio J.O.P. Dto 101.
☎ 265069.
United Kingdom: Edificio Cataluña,
C/Luis Morote 6. ☎ 262508.
United States: Franchy Roca 5.
☎ 271259.

North Africa. The islands were known to both the Greeks and the Romans and the first recorded expedition was sent by King Juba of Mauritania in 60 AD. At one time they were called the Fortunate Islands, due to the ease of life on the islands. The Roman writer Pliny, in describing the islands, called one of them Canaria from the Latin word for dog 'canis', due to the number of large wild dogs roaming the island. Originally applied to Gran Canaria, the name later came to be used for the whole archipelago.

After the Roman era, the Canaries were largely forgotten until several Genoese and other European expeditions explored the islands in the thirteenth and fourteenth centuries, mainly as raiding parties for slaves with no interest in settlement. This changed when the Norman knight Juan de Bethencourt, serving Spain, subdued Lanzarote in 1402, then Fuerteventura and Hierro. The Guanches put up a fierce fight and La Gomera resisted conquest for 80 years. Gran Canaria, Tenerife and La Palma were even more difficult conquests and only in 1495 was the last Guanche resistance crushed. Three years before that Columbus sailed to the Canaries and left on his voyage to the New World from La Gomera. The new routes

pioneered by Columbus opened up the Atlantic Ocean and had a big impact on the Canaries. They developed as a repair and provisioning centre for westbound vessels and many merchants and traders settled in the islands. Although attacked by pirates, the Dutch and the English, the islands remained under Spanish control and in 1823 the Canaries became a full Spanish province.

Thriving on trade, in the mid-nineteenth century the islands were declared a free trade area and they have remained a duty-free zone ever since. The Canary Islands now form an autonomous region of Spain with their own parliament. They are divided into two provinces, the eastern province, Las Palmas, which includes Gran Canaria, Lanzarote and Fuerteventura and the western province, Tenerife, which includes Tenerife itself, La Gomera, La Palma and El Hierro. Due to rivalry between the two main islands, the government sits alternately in the provincial capitals of Las Palmas de Gran Canaria and Santa Cruz de Tenerife.

Tourism is the main industry and has contributed to the economic boom that the islands have enjoyed. Tourism appears to have almost reached saturation point and has experienced a slight drop-off in recent years. Agriculture is still important, especially market gardening, fruit, wine and some dairy products. There is a large fishing industry, with fleets based on every island.

The resident population is 1.5 million with a tourist population of 5 million a year. The Canary Islanders are proud of their differences from the mainland Spanish, whom they call 'peninsulares', many of whom have settled in the islands. The Spanish-speaking population is mainly Catholic.

Despite its position close to the tropics, the Canaries are not too hot in summer, 21–29°C, pleasantly warm in winter, 15–20°C, and can be regarded as an all-year cruising ground, which has earned them the title of Land of Eternal Spring. The frequency of gales is low and the islands are not affected by hurricanes. In the trade wind belt, the prevailing wind is north-easterly.

Entry Regulations

Ports of entry
Arrecife (Lanzarote) 28°57′N 13°33′W, Puerto Rosario (Fuerteventura) 28°30′N 13°51′W, Las Palmas de Gran Canaria (Gran Canaria) 28°09′N 15°25′W, Santa Cruz de Tenerife (Tenerife) 28°29′N 16°14′W, San Sebastian (Gomera) 28°05′N 17°07′W, Puerto de la Estaca (El Hierro) 24°47′N 17°54′W, Santa Cruz de la Palma (La Palma) 28°40′N 17°45′W.

Procedure on arrival
A yacht is supposed to call at one of the above ports of entry first, but in practice a yacht can arrive at any port in the Canaries provided the authorities are informed of the yacht's arrival. On arrival the captain should report to the port authority or marina office who will advise on the correct procedure and, in the case of the marinas, will contact the relevant authorities. As an overseas province of Spain, the Canaries are administered as a military zone, and although in the larger ports a civilian authority is in charge, in the smaller places it is still the naval Ayudantia de Marina who are responsible. This can be confusing as the Ayundantia, Port Police and Guardia Civil all wear different uniforms. In practice the formalities are very simple; a brief visit to the relevant office when the ship's papers should be shown and a crew list handed in. The Canaries are a duty-free area, so yachts are not expected to clear customs.

Most yachts arriving from overseas clear in at one of the following three ports:
Arrecife: The capital of Lanzarote has two ports used by yachts. The more northerly is the fishing harbour

Puerto Naos where two pontoons have been installed for visiting yachts. In the old port of Arrecife yachts tie up to the wall inside the breakwater. In the approaches to both ports attention must be paid to the outlying reefs. Formalities are completed at the Policia Nacional, on the waterfront, almost opposite the causeway to the old fort.
Las Palmas: Arriving yachts should tie up at the Texaco dock for berthing instructions. Formalities are completed in the port office (Junta del Puerto) and captains are very rarely asked to visit any other office.
Santa Cruz de Tenerife: Yachts berth in the fishing harbour (Darsena Pesquera) north of the city. The port office should be contacted in the large shed. The captain should then take passports and papers to the main port authority office in town.

There are no restrictions on yacht movements in the Canaries, although papers may be checked at subsequent ports. Clearing out in the Canaries is not compulsory, however it is advisable as most countries do wish to see an outward clearance form on arrival.

Customs
There are no restrictions on firearms or animals in the Canaries. However, customs are concerned about drug trafficking, especially from North Africa, and although they appear to be easy-going, they do keep a close eye on yacht movement.

Equipment and spare parts can be imported free of duty provided they are clearly marked as being for a yacht in transit. The use of an agent can speed up the extrication of these goods from the airport.

A yacht remaining more than six months continuously in Spanish waters is liable for import duty or seizure until this is paid. One can obtain a customs permit (permiso aduanero) for a yacht not based in Spain, valid for a further six months in a 12-month period.

It is possible to lay up a boat in which case the authorities must be informed and the boat is sealed. Duty is not then liable. This is possible at Pasito Blanco and Mogan (both on Gran Canaria).

Immigration
Nationals of most European countries, the USA and Canada do not need visas for up to a three-month stay. Other countries may need to apply for a visa in advance from a Spanish embassy or consulate. This does not appear to be applied strictly to yachts, provided the person also leaves the islands by yacht.

Passports of crew are not normally stamped on arrival, but if crew members wish to leave by air, it is essential to get their passports stamped, as otherwise they might be turned back from the airport.

Fees
There are no overtime fees as clearance is done during office hours.

Facilities

Yachting facilities in the Canaries are constantly improving and repair facilities are good, particularly on Gran Canaria. There are yacht clubs on most islands but as they are primarily social clubs, visitors are not particularly welcome.

Gran Canaria: The widest range of facilities is concentrated in the capital Las Palmas, which has a yacht harbour administered by the port authority. There are various repair workshops in the Cebadal industrial estate, close to the commercial harbour. A sailmaker operates in town. There are several chandleries, although their selection is rather limited and essential spares may have to be ordered from abroad. Charts, both Spanish and British, are available from Premanaca. There is no hauling out facility for small yachts, although there is a shipyard handling larger boats.

Provisioning in Las Palmas is the best in the Canaries with several supermarkets and daily fresh produce markets. LPG bottles can be filled and fuel is available in the yacht harbour.

Gran Canaria's south coast has several good marinas at Pasito Blanco, Puerto Rico and Puerto Mogan. There are haul-out facilities at all of them as well as at the fishing harbour Arguineguin. Provisioning is best in the latter, while Puerto Mogan has a good chandlery.

Tenerife: Facilities in Santa Cruz de Tenerife are limited and yachts berth in the fishing harbour to the north of the city. There are some repair facilities in the port itself and in town.

Provisioning is good but because of the distance to the port is not convenient. There is fuel and water on the dock. Better docking as well as some repair facilities are in the marinas at Radazul, Puerto de Guimar, Los Gigantes and Puerto Colon. The boatyard at Los Cristianos also has haul-out and repair facilities.

Lanzarote: Most facilities are in the capital Arrecife, around the commercial Puerto Naos. A small industrial estate in the neighbourhood provides a good range of services. Provisioning is good with supermarkets and daily market. Fuel, water and LPG are available in the commercial harbour. There are also small marinas at Puerto Calero and Playa Blanca, with limited facilities.

Fuerteventura: There is a small marina with haul-out and some repair facilities at El Castillo and limited repair facilities in the capital Puerto Rosario.

There are only basic facilities in the islands of La Gomera, El Hierro and La Palma, with the exception of Santa Cruz de la Palma, which has good provisioning and some repair facilities.

Further Reading

Canary Islands Cruising Guide
Atlantic Islands
Cruising Guide to the Eastern Caribbean, Vol. 1: Transatlantic Cruising Guide.

CAPE VERDE ISLANDS

The Cape Verde Islands are a volcanic archipelago lying near the coast of West Africa, although the islands' culture reflects its Portuguese colonial past more than its geographical position. The islands' climate tends to be very dry, the scenery is rather bleak and they have had severe drought problems in the 1970s and 1980s. There are 10 main islands, of which São Tiago, with the capital Praia, is the most important. Mindelo, the second largest town and the main harbour, is on São Vicente. The group divides into Barlovento (Windward group) and Sotavento (Leeward group).

The Cape Verdes are conveniently placed close to the best sailing route from the Canaries to the Caribbean and ships on transatlantic voyages have always found them a useful stopover, although now modern yachts call instead of square riggers and steamers. Most cruising yachts are on their way to the Caribbean, a few to Brazil or West Africa, particularly Senegal and Gambia. Some people have enjoyed cruising the islands more extensively, rather than just viewing them as a stop on the way to somewhere else. Facilities are basic in the Cape Verdes, but that seems to be made up for by the friendliness of their inhabitants.

Country Profile

The islands were not populated when the Portuguese discovered them in 1456. At that time they were green with vegetation, hence the name 'verde'. The Portuguese returned six years later and founded the capital of Ribeira Grande on São Tiago. Slaves were brought from West Africa to work on the plantations that were established. The islands' strategic position made them

Practical Information

LOCAL TIME: GMT -1

BUOYAGE: IALA A

CURRENCY: Cape Verde escudo (CVE) of 100 centavos. Local currency cannot be imported or exported.

BUSINESS HOURS
Banks: 0800–1200 Monday to Thursday. Business: 0800–1200, 1430–1800 Monday to Friday, 0800–1200 Saturday. Government offices: 0800–1200, 1430–1800 Monday to Friday, 0800–1130 Saturday.

ELECTRICITY: 220 V, 50 Hz

PUBLIC HOLIDAYS
1 January: New Year's Day
20 January: National Heroes Day
8 March: International Women's Day
1 May: Labour Day
1 June: International Children's Day
5 July: Independence Day
12 September: Nationality Day
25 December: Christmas Day

COMMUNICATIONS
International calls can be made from most post offices. International telegrams can be sent from larger post offices. Sal Island has the only international airport, where jets refuel on flights between Europe and South America or Africa. There are direct flights to Lisbon and a weekly service to Boston. All the other islands except Ilha Brava have domestic airports for internal flights.

MEDICAL
Hospitals: Rua Martines Pidjiguita, Praia; Avenida 5 de Julho, Mindelo. Treatment is very expensive. There are limited stocks of medicines at pharmacies.

DIPLOMATIC MISSIONS
There are representatives in Praia for Brazil, France (for French Guiana visas), Portugal, Senegal, Belgium, Netherlands and Norway.
United States: Rua Hoji Ya Yenna 81, Praia. ☎ 553 and 761.

a base for the slave trade to the Americas. Some prosperity was enjoyed, but in the mid-eighteenth century a series of droughts hit the islands. These were due to an imbalance in the environment, brought about by deforestation and the introduction of goats that ate the ground vegetation. Thousands of Cape Verdeans perished in droughts in the eighteenth and nineteenth centuries and many emigrated to New England, to work in the whaling trade.

With the rise in the number of liners crossing the Atlantic the archipelago became an important coaling station for ships. The droughts continued, however, and little help was forthcoming from Portugal. After the Second World War a joint independence movement was started by Cape Verdeans and Guinea-Bissau, another Portuguese colony. After fourteen years of guerilla warfare, independence was achieved in 1975, following the toppling in Portugal of the Salazar regime.

Since then both Portugal and the United States have given the islands aid. As the lack of rain continues to be a major problem, much of the aid goes into projects such as planting trees and building dykes and water-retaining walls. Money sent by Cape Verdeans abroad is important to the economy, for as many Cape Verdeans live overseas as on the islands. Salt mining on Sal and Maio and fish exports are other sources of income.

The islands have a total population of approximately 340,000 people of mixed African and Portuguese descent. Although the official language is Portuguese, amongst themselves Cape Verdeans usually converse in Crioulo, a local dialect closely related to Portuguese.

The majority are Roman Catholics.

Rainfall is limited to a few downpours between late August and October, although there are years with little or no rain. The NE trade winds are at their strongest in the first months of the year, when they sometimes arrive laden with dust from the Sahara, which can seriously affect visibility.

Entry Regulations

Ports of entry
Mindelo 16°53′N 25°00′W, Praia 14°54′N 23°31′W, Sal 16°45′N 23°00′W.

Procedure on arrival
Mindelo: The town is in Porto Grande Bay, which is one of the best harbours in the archipelago. If there is space, one can tie up to the central dock in the inner harbour to clear in. One can come alongside or else anchor off, and immigration and port officials visit soon after arrival. One should not go ashore until cleared. Yachts must fly the courtesy flag, if a yacht does not possess one, they must buy one from the port captain. The captain must sign a form that absolves the port authority from responsibility in case of theft from the yacht. Ship's papers and passports will be held by the authorities whilst in the harbour, although a passport can be temporarily reclaimed to change travellers cheques. Yachts can clear out up to 24 hours before departure.
Praia: One should anchor in the western part of the

harbour, although sometimes there is space alongside the commercial dock, where it is easier to clear in, rather than take the officials by dinghy to the boat. One should not go ashore until visited by customs and immigration.

Sal: This is the only other island where yachts can clear in. Usually customs and immigration formalities are completed at the international airport. Palmeira has a sheltered anchorage. One should fly the Q flag and the captain should check in with the police in Almeria. The police hold passports until departure.

Customs

Firearms and animals must be declared to customs.

Immigration

Those on yachts making a short visit are issued visas on arrival. Photographs are needed for these visas. Visitors intending to spend longer in the islands need to obtain a visa in advance. In this case visas are required by all nationalities except Guinea-Bissau. There are Cape Verdean diplomatic missions in Algeria, Canary Islands, Guinea, Italy, Netherlands, Portugal and Senegal or one can apply direct to: Ministerio de Negocios Estrangeiros, Direccão de Immigracão, Praia, writing in Portuguese. Where there is no Cape Verde mission, one should contact the Portuguese embassy. Visa applications need two photos and a vaccination certificate for yellow fever and cholera.

Health

Malaria prophylaxis may be necessary in São Tiago. There is tuberculosis throughout the archipelago.

Fees

Immigration fee for a visa. Clearance fee CVE 55 in and out.

Warning

Charts may be inaccurate, especially near Ilha da Boa Vista, which is now believed to be 2 miles east of its charted position. There are several wrecks and offlying reefs not marked on the charts, especially off the east coast of the island.

Theft appears to be a problem in Mindelo and visitors are advised to employ a local watchman, usually one will be recommended by the port captain.

Facilities

Provisioning is limited on all the islands and most food is imported and expensive. There are fresh produce markets in Mindelo and Praia, which vary in variety and quality with the seasons.

Mindelo: This is where most yachts go for a quick refuelling stop. There is a small yacht club, Clube Nautico, where visitors are welcome, and the members can help with repairs. Although not geared up to deal with yachts, the two boatyards, Internave and Onave, can handle some basic repairs and have hauling out facilities. There are no marine supplies except equipment used by fishing boats sold at hardware stores. Butane gas bottles can be refilled at ENACOL.

Praia: Water and fuel are not easily available as the suppliers prefer to sell larger quantities than those required by yachts. Fuel can be bought in jerrycans from a filling station. Water can be ordered by truck load and shared out amongst several boats. Permission is usually granted to come alongside the commercial dock to take on larger quantities of fuel or water. Gas bottles can be filled at a filling station out of town best reached by taxi. There is a small boatyard near the harbour for local fishing boats, which can tackle simple repair jobs. There are also various workshops in town, as well as a small chandlery.

Sal: There is only a small shop and bakery in Palmeira, but Almeria has better supplies. Fuel and water can be bought from the fish freezing plant at Palmeira.

Further Reading

Atlantic Islands
Cruising Guide to the Eastern Caribbean, Vol. 1: Transatlantic Cruising Guide

CHANNEL ISLANDS

'Fragments of Europe dropped by France and picked up by England' is how Victor Hugo, in exile there, described these islands lying close to Brittany but part of the United Kingdom. This cluster of five islands and many smaller islets is divided into two regions. The Bailiwick of Jersey comprises the largest island, Jersey, and its islets, while the Bailiwick of Guernsey includes Guernsey, Alderney, Herm and Sark. The Bailiwicks have their own parliaments and are proud of their autonomy, which was granted to them by King John in 1204. In many ways the culture of the islands is closer to Normandy than the United Kingdom.

The Channel Islands are a popular cruising destination both with French and British sailors, who find here some of the most hazardous sailing conditions in Europe, as well as a very special atmosphere ashore.

Practical Information

LOCAL TIME: GMT. Summer time
GMT + 1 from March to October.

BUOYAGE: IALA A

CURRENCY: Pound sterling (£) of 100
pence. The Channel Islands have their
own money also in circulation.

BUSINESS HOURS
Banks: 0930–1530 Monday to Friday
(some open Saturday mornings).
Business: 0900–1730 Monday to Friday.
Shops: 0900–1730/1800 Monday to
Friday; some close Thursday afternoons.
Government offices: 0900–1730 Monday
to Friday.

ELECTRICITY: 240 V, 50 Hz

PUBLIC HOLIDAYS
1 January: New Year's Day
Good Friday and Easter Monday
May Day
9 May: Liberation Day
Spring Bank Holiday
Summer Bank Holiday
25, 26 December: Christmas

COMMUNICATIONS
International dialling access code 010.
Operator 100, International operator 155.
International calls can be made from
public phones in booths and post offices.

Many public phones use phone cards,
which can be bought in post offices or in
shops where the card sign is shown.
Emergency: dial 999.
Post offices open 0830–1700 Monday to
Friday, 0830–1200 Saturday. The
Channel Islands have their own stamps.
There are frequent flights to Britain and
some to Europe. There is also a ferry
service.

MEDICAL
Medical advice and emergency
treatment can be obtained free of charge
at general hospitals, but visitors must
pay for consultation with a doctor and
any medicines prescribed.

The main hazards are strong tidal streams, concealed rocks and poor visibility. Summer weather is generally settled, but at any other time it can change very quickly. There is complete shelter in St Peter Port in Guernsey and St Helier in Jersey. There are many good anchorages in offshore winds on all the islands and the smaller ones provide an interesting alternative to the busy main ports.

Country Profile

During the period of Roman expansion into northern Europe, Gauls sought refuge on the islands. Later Britons settled, eventually being driven out by the Norsemen, who also settled in France and gave their name to Normandy. When in 1066 the Normans led by their Duke William invaded England, the Channel Islands were already part of Normandy, but remained loyal to the English throne when in 1204 the French captured Normandy. King John, one of William's successors, in recognition for this loyalty, granted the islands their special status within the Kingdom of England. A troubled period of two hundred years followed as the French repeatedly tried to capture the islands. At the request of Edward IV, in 1483 the Pope declared the islands neutral, which brought a more peaceful era.

During the English Civil War Jersey supported the Royalist cause, and Guernsey the Parliamentarian, almost losing its privileges when the monarchy was restored. The Channel Islands became prosperous, largely due to privateering and smuggling, especially after they ceased to be neutral in 1689. Before the

Royal Navy was established, the islands maintained a fleet of privateers that harassed Spanish, Dutch, French and American shipping. The French tried again unsuccessfully to gain the islands. During the French Revolutionary and the Napoleonic Wars fortifications were strengthened. However, the islands were finally invaded and occupied during the Second World War by the Germans.

After the war, the economy developed, agriculture was diversified, tourism encouraged, and the islands found a new role as a leading offshore banking and financial centre. The population numbers 60,000. Languages spoken include English, a Norman patois, and French.

The winds during summer alternate between NW and NE. At other times, SW winds are more frequent and this is also the direction of most gales. More than strong winds, the main danger in the islands are the extremely strong tidal streams, the notorious Alderney Race reaching 8 knots on occasions.

Entry Regulations

Ports of entry
Alderney: Braye 49°43′N 2°12′W.
Guernsey: St Peter Port 49°27′N 2°32′W, Beaucette Marina 49°30′N 2°29′W.
Jersey: St Helier 49°11′N 2°07′W, Gorey 49°12′N 2°01′W.

Procedure on arrival
Although the Channel Islands are Crown Dependencies, they are not part of the United Kingdom and

customs requirements are strict. The Q flag must be flown and it is necessary to report to customs when arriving from anywhere outside of the islands, which includes both the United Kingdom and France. It is also necessary to report to customs when moving from one administrative area to the other, such as from Guernsey to Jersey. On arrival, normally the port control staff will give the captain customs and immigration declaration forms that must be completed as soon as possible. No one except the captain may go ashore until these have been completed.

St Peter Port: Port Control monitors VHF Channel 12. Visitors should call about one hour prior to arrival to receive berthing instructions. One of the port launches normally meets arriving yachts and directs them to a berth. A red light on the pier at the port entrance indicates large vessels are under way, and only boats of 15 m (49 ft) or less may enter or exit if keeping clear of the main fairways. Do not anchor or berth without the prior permission of the harbour master.

Beaucette Marina: The harbour office monitors VHF Channels 16 and 80 seven days a week and should be contacted prior to arrival or if having difficulties in entering.

St Helier: Port Control monitors VHF Channel 14 and should be contacted before arrival. There are traffic lights controlling the entrance into the main harbour. A green light shown on Victoria pierhead means that a vessel may enter, while a red light allows vessels to leave only. Access into La Collette basin is possible at all times, although there are some draft restrictions. La Collette is used as a waiting area to proceed into St Helier Marina.

Customs

The landing of animals is strictly prohibited from vessels arriving from anywhere other than the UK, Republic of Ireland, Isle of Man or other Channel Islands. If arriving from other countries than these, animals must be securely confined below deck during the yacht's stay. Any animal found ashore or not confined will be detained and may be subject to six months quarantine or destroyed, and the captain prosecuted. Unless given express permission by a customs officer, no vessel with an animal on board may moor alongside or in the marinas.

Excess duty-free stores will be sealed. There is no sales tax in the islands.

Immigration

Requirements as for the United Kingdom. Immigration must be notified of any persons leaving or joining vessels which are arriving from or departing to places other than the UK or other Channel Islands.

Facilities

Being the favourite offshore cruising area for British yachts as well as a traditional tax-free shopping destination for the French, the Channel Islands have made an effort to improve their yachting facilities. There are now several new marinas and facilities in the old ones have also been upgraded. Repair facilities are generally good, although those in Guernsey have overtaken Jersey in the range of services offered. As a low tax area, items may be imported duty-free with minimal formalities. Most UK discount chandlers can offer overnight tax-free delivery. Provisioning is good in all centres, although many shops close for the weekend and spirits cannot be bought on a Sunday.

Virtually all repairs are available in St Peter Port in or around the marina. There are haul-out facilities and several chandleries offering a complete range of equipment including charts. Fuel is available on the dock. On Jersey repair facilities are centred in or around St Helier Marina, where there is a boatyard with its own chandlery, capable of any kind of repair. The Royal Channel Islands Yacht Club and the St Helier Yacht Club are particularly welcoming to visiting sailors.

Further Reading

Normandy and Channel Islands Pilot
Brittany and Channel Islands Cruising Guide
Channel Islands Pilot
Cruising Association Handbook
Channel Islands – Insight Guide

THE FAEROES

The Faeroe Islands (Føroyar in Faeroese) are a small group of islands with a surface area of 540 square miles situated in the North Atlantic between Scotland and Iceland. They are a self-governing dependency of Denmark. The Faeroes were settled by the Vikings in the ninth century and came under Danish rule in 1380. They were granted autonomy in 1984. The population of 35,000 speak Faeroese, a Norse dialect akin to Icelandic, as well as Danish. English is widely understood. The capital and main port is Thorshavn on the island of Streymoy, which is the largest of the group. The smaller islands are very distinctive with precipitous cliffs and steep hills. Some of the coasts are broken by fjords providing spectacular scenery.

The weather is often unsettled and visibility is frequently poor when the land may be obscured by fog or drizzle. The incidence of summer gales is similar to

Practical Information (The Faeroes)

LOCAL TIME: GMT

CURRENCY: Danish and Faeroese Krone

PUBLIC HOLIDAYS
1 January: New Year's Day
Maundy Thursday, Good Friday and Easter Monday

Fourth Friday after Easter: Prayer Day
Ascension Day
Whit Monday
Olavsoka Eve and Day
24 December afternoon
25 December: Christmas Day
Half-day holidays are taken on Workers Day, Flag Day and a Mourning Day for those lost at sea.

COMMUNICATIONS
There are air links to Copenhagen, and a weekly ferry to the Shetlands.

DIPLOMATIC MISSIONS
There is an honorary British consul in Thorshavn.

other places on the West European seaboard. Sudden squalls may be experienced inside the fjords. In the summer months the long daylight hours may be enjoyed, the weather is fairly mild due to the Gulf Stream and winds are often light.

Entry Regulations

Ports of entry
Eysturoy: Fuglafjordur 62°15′N 6°49′W.
Bordoy: Klaksvik 62°14′N 6°35′W.
Streymoy (Strømø): Thorshavn (Torshavn) 62°00′N 6°45′W, Vestmanna (Vestmanhavn) 62°09′N 7°10′W.
Suduroy: Tvoroyri 61°33′N 6°48′W, Vagur 61°28′N 6°48′W.

Procedure on arrival
Normally the police board a yacht on arrival and give customs clearance, but if not, the captain should contact customs at a port of entry.

Thorshavn Port Control monitors VHF Channel 16 and the working channel is 12.

Customs
The Faeroes are dry islands and no alcoholic drinks can be purchased, but yachts are allowed small quantities on board for their own use (one bottle of spirits per person, slightly more of wine).

Navigation
The Faeroe courtesy flag should be flown not the Danish. The flag shows a red cross with a small blue border (like the Danish white cross), on a white field.

Overhead cables cross the fjords and sounds between the islands and give a reading on radar similar to a ship.

Tidal streams run very strongly both around and between the islands, being significantly stronger at the equinox, when the tidal race may reach 11 knots in

places. At the entrance to the fjords a combination of wind and tide can create a big sea, while inside the fjords if a strong tide is running one can navigate close to the steep-to sides where counter-eddies may be found. Information on dangerous overfalls and races as well as on the direction of the tides can be found in *Tidal Current around the Faeroe Islands*, which has an English translation of essential information and is available in the Faeroe Islands.

Facilities

There are shops in all the main ports and a super-market in Thorshavn, so provisioning is not a problem. Fuel and water are available in Thorshavn, Tvoroyri and Klaksvik and other fishing ports. There are no special facilities for yachts and any marine supplies available are those for fishing boats. However, basic repairs can be carried out using the extensive repair and shipbuilding facilities provided for the fishing fleets.

Further Reading

Cruising Association Handbook

FRANCE

Blessed with both an Atlantic and a Mediterranean coastline, France has more variety to offer the cruising sailor than any other European country, from the tidal creeks and shallow estuaries of Brittany to the chic ports of the Côte d'Azur and the stark beauty of the island of Corsica. France is one of the leading sailing nations in the world and its top sailors are as well known to the general French public as its best soccer players. The booming French boatbuilding industry, which was the first to put well-designed cruising boats into mass production, has been instrumental in bringing cruising within the reach of a wider market. A sustained construction programme has resulted in a string of marinas along the entire Mediterranean coast to cater for the thriving sailing community.

For the visiting sailor, each side of France has its special attractions. The Atlantic coast calls for more attentive navigation, but brings its rewards in the many natural harbours and inlets. Although spectacular, this coast can be dangerous as there are many offlying hazards, strong tidal streams and frequent gales. This is more than made up for by such attractive ports as Morlaix, St Malo or Lézardrieux. The western coast divides into three distinct areas, the most popular and picturesque being the Brittany coast, which has many navigable rivers and the Morbihan inland sea. The central area to the Gironde has several offlying islands as well as the great rivers, the Loire and the Gironde, which lead into the inland waterways. The

Sanary-sur-Mer, one of the smaller ports of the French Riviera.

low-lying area stretching to the Spanish border is the least appealing as a cruising destination.

In some ways, Mediterranean France is more suited to those who prefer to find their pleasures ashore. Sailing into such glittering places as St Tropez, Cannes or Antibes is an experience that cannot be repeated and it is worth the long detour just to spend some time among the most beautiful collection of yachts in the world. For a good taste of Mediterranean France, the island of Corsica offers a wide selection of ports ideally to be visited outside of the peak summer season as it is a favourite holiday destination for French sailors.

Country Profile

Remains have been found in France of the earliest prehistoric human settlements. In historic times, the first settlers were of Ligurian and Iberian stock, followed in the sixth century BC by the Gauls, a Celtic people. Gaul was conquered by the Romans and from

Practical Information

LOCAL TIME: GMT + 1. Summer time
GMT + 2 last Sunday in March to last
Sunday in September.

BUOYAGE: IALA A

CURRENCY: French franc (FF) of 100
centimes (FF)

BUSINESS HOURS
Banks: 0900–1200, 1400–1600 Monday to
Friday, closed either Saturday or
Monday. They close early the day before
a bank holiday.
Food shops: 0700–1830/1930.
Other shops: 0900–1830/1930 (many
shops close all or half-day Monday;
some open on Sunday mornings,
especially bakers and food shops; in
smaller towns shops close for lunch
1200–1400/1500 on weekdays).
Hypermarkets: 0800–2000/2100 Monday
to Saturday.
Government offices: 0830–1200,
1400–1800 Monday to Friday.

ELECTRICITY: 220 V, 50 Hz

PUBLIC HOLIDAYS
1 January: New Year's Day
Easter Sunday and Monday
Ascension Day
8 May: Victory Day

Whit Monday
14 July: Bastille Day
15 August: Assumption Day
1 November: All Saints
11 November: Remembrance Day
25 December: Christmas Day
Nearly all of France is on holiday in
August.

COMMUNICATIONS
International dialling access code 19.
There are no area codes for France, but
there are two zones, Paris and the rest
of France. The access code for the other
zone is 16. If dialling Paris from the
provinces zone code 1 must be dialled
after 16. Within a zone just the number is
dialled.
International calls can be made from
public payphones, most of which take
phonecards (télécarte) obtainable from
post offices. In some post offices there
are telephones where one can make a
metered call.
Post offices open 0800–1900 Monday to
Friday (0800–1200, 1400–1700 in smaller
towns), 0800–1200 Saturdays.
Emergency: Fire 18, Police 17, Operator
13.
There are flights worldwide from
international airports at Charles de
Gaulle and Orly in Paris, and Bordeaux,
Lyon, Marseille, Nice and Toulouse.

MEDICAL
Certain European countries have
reciprocal arrangements with France for
emergency cover.

DIPLOMATIC MISSIONS
In Paris:
Australia: 4 Rue Jean Rey, 75724.
☎ (1) 40.59.33.00.
Canada: 35 Avenue Montaigne, 75008.
☎ (1) 47.23.01.01.
New Zealand: 7 Leonardo da Vinci,
75116.
☎ (1) 45.00.24.11.
United Kingdom: 35 rue du Faubourg St
Honoré, 75383. ☎ (1) 42.66.91.42.
United States: Avenue Gabriel, 75382.
☎ (1) 42.96.12.02.
In Bordeaux:
United Kingdom: 15 Cours de Verdun,
33081. ☎ 56.52.28.35.
United States: 22 Cours du Marechal
Foch, 33080. ☎ 56.52.65.95.
In Marseilles:
United Kingdom: 24 Avenue du Prado,
13006. ☎ 91.53.43.32.
United States: 9 Rue Armeny, 13006.
☎ 91.54.92.00.

---

the resulting Gallo-Roman civilisation the French language and institutions developed. After Rome's downfall Burgundians and Visigoths settled in the south, and Franks in the north. The latter extended their rule over the whole country, and a centralised monarchy developed with the Carolingian dynasty, especially under Charlemagne. In 843 his empire was divided, and the monarchy weakened by a strong feudal nobility and numerous Viking raids on the northern coast.

From the tenth to the fourteenth centuries, royal power was gradually consolidated, while commerce, culture and Christianity thrived. External affairs were dominated by the ongoing conflict with England, who claimed much of French territory, resulting in the Hundred Years War (1328–1440). By the end of the war England retained only Calais and the French monarchy had established its authority over both the

Church and the nobles. A strong modern state evolved and with the addition of Brittany in 1491, its frontiers were nearly that of present-day France.

The Protestant Reformation led to religious wars in France until the Protestant Henry IV, the first of the Bourbons, accepted Catholicism and brought religious tolerance and prosperity to the country. After his death royal absolutism reached its peak, with Louis XIV's long reign (1643–1715), which was the age of French classicism that influenced all of Europe. A series of expansionist wars weakened French finances, a problem that escalated during the eighteenth century, while the monarchy continued its absolute rule despite the growing current of ideas for reform and liberty. Then in 1789 the Revolution overthrew the old order, the king was executed and the First Republic established.

France became engaged in numerous wars in Europe,

and Napoleon Bonaparte rose to power becoming Emperor and dominating Europe until his defeat in 1814–15. During the nineteenth century there was much industrialisation, and the middle and working classes sought to have a say in politics. Their aspirations led to another revolution in 1848, establishing the Second Republic. Three years later the Second Empire under Napoleon III took a more absolutist line, although some reforms were carried out in its later years. The Empire toppled following France's 1870 defeat by Prussia and the Third Republic was formed.

In the First World War France suffered heavily, both in men lost and economically, and peace was followed by an era of inflation, economic depression, and political instability. A policy of appeasement was followed towards Nazi Germany, but in 1940 France was invaded and the Third Republic fell. The Vichy government signed an armistice soon afterwards. A strong resistance movement developed, and after the war Charles de Gaulle, leader of the Free French, came to power in the Fourth Republic. In 1958 the Algerian crisis returned de Gaulle to power, and the Fifth Republic was established, giving the President greater powers. In 1981 the socialist François Mitterand was elected President.

The service industries, such as administration, commerce, banking, transport and armed forces employ around 60 per cent of the population, while agriculture only 8 per cent and industry under a third. Traditional industries have declined, whereas more modern ones such as the car manufacturing, aeronautical engineering, electrical and chemical industries are thriving. France is the leading agricultural country of the EC, producing mainly wheat, wine, meat and dairy products. There is some unemployment, while the trade balance is helped by revenues from tourism.

The population numbers 55.2 million, mainly French, but there are also some Arab and African populations in major cities.

Paris is the capital of France. French is the main language and regional languages such as Provençal, Basque or Breton are only spoken by a few. The majority of the French are Roman Catholic.

The climate differs significantly between the Atlantic and Mediterranean coasts and so do sailing conditions. On the Atlantic side, the climate is temperate and the sailing season lasts from late spring to the autumn. The prevailing winds of summer are northerly, becoming SW when a system of low pressure comes in from the Atlantic. The strongest winds also come from the SW. Winds along the Mediterranean coast and Corsica are more variable, the strongest wind being the mistral, a northerly wind which occurs regularly and often reaches gale force.

Entry Regulations

Ports of entry

Channel/North Sea: Dunkirk 51°03′N 2°21′E, Gravelines 50°59′N 2°08′E, Calais 50°58′N 1°51′E, Boulogne 50°44′N 1°37′E, Le Touquet-Etaples 50°31′N 1°38′E, Abbeville 50°06′N 1°51′E, Dieppe 49°56′N 1°05′E, Le Havre 49°29′N 0°07′E, Caudebec-en-Caux 49°32′N 0°44′E, Le Tréport 50°04′N 1°22′E, Fécamp 49°46′N 0°22′E, Honfleur 49°25′N 0°14′E, Caen 49°11′N 0°21′W, Cherbourg 49°38′N 1°38′W, Granville 48°50′N 1°36′W, St Malo 48°39′N 2°01′W, Le Légué-St Brieuc 48°32′N 2°43′W, Paimpol 48°47′N 3°03′W, Morlaix 48°38′N 3°53′W, Roscoff 48°43′N 3°59′W.

Atlantic: Brest 48°23′N 4°29′W, Quimper 47°58′N 4°07′W, Douarnenez 48°06′N 4°20′W, Lorient 47°45′N 3°22′W, Vannes 47°39′N 2°45′W, La Trinité-sur-Mer 47°35′N 3°01′E, Concarneau 47°52′N 3°55′W, St Nazaire 47°16′N 2°12′W, Nantes 47°14′N 1°34′W, Les Sables d'Olonne 46°30′N 1°48′W, La Rochelle 46°09′N 1°09′W, Rochefort 45°56′N 0°58′W, La Tremblade 45°46′N 1°08′W, Le Château d'Oléron 45°53′N 1°12′W, Royan 45°38′N 1°02′W, Bordeaux-Bassens 44°50′N 0°34′W, Pauillac-Trompeloup 45°12′N 0°45′W, Blaye 45°07′N 0°40′W, Le Verdon 45°33′N 1°05′W, Arcachon 44°40′N 1°10′W, Bayonne 43°30′N 1°29′W, Ciboure 43°23′N 1°41′W, Hendaye-Béhobie 43°22′N 1°46′W.

Mediterranean: Port Vendres 42°31′N 3°07′E, Port la Nouvelle 43°01′N 3°04′E, Sète 43°24′N 3°42′E, Marseilles 43°20′N 5°21′E, Port St Louis du Rhône 43°23′N 4°49′E, Port de Bouc 43°24′N 4°59′E, Toulon-la Seyne 43°07′N 5°55′E, Bandol 43°08′N 5°45′E, Cassis 43°13′N 5°32′E, Hyères 43°04′N 6°22′E, La Ciotat 43°10′N 5°36′E, Le Lavandou 43°08′N 6°22′E, Sanary 43°07′N 5°48′E, St Mandrier 43°05′N 5°55′E, St Tropez 43°16′N 6°38′E, St Maxime 43°18′N 6°38′E, Fréjus-Saint Raphael 43°25′N 6°46′E, Cannes 43°33′N 7°01′E, Antibes 43°35′N 7°09′E, Nice 43°42′N 7°17′E, Menton-Garavan 43°46′N 7°30′E.

Corsica: Ajaccio 41°55′N 8°44′E, Bastia 42°42′N 9°27′E, Porto-Vecchio 41°36′N 9°17′E, Propriano 41°40′N 8°54′E, Calvi 42°35′N 8°48′E, Ile Rousse 42°39′N 8°56′E, Bonifacio 41°23′N 9°06′E.

River ports

Seine: Rouen

Moselle: Metz, Thionville

Rhine: Strasbourg, Lauterbourg, Beinheim, Gambsheim, Ottmarsheim, Huningue, Neuf-Brisach.

Procedure on arrival

On arrival in France, the captain should report to customs at a port of entry with the ship's registration papers and passports. In some places customs will visit the boat on arrival. Customs may also inspect yachts up to 12 miles off the coast. The port captain (Capitainerie) should also be contacted.

Yachts must have a proper certificate of registration, the originals must always be kept on board as photocopies are not accepted. For British yachts the French authorities will accept the Small Ships Register, issued by the Royal Yachting Association, but not the International Certificate for Pleasure Navigation also issued by the RYA. They are very strict about registration certificates, and some boats have been fined for not having a satisfactory document.

Customs

Firearms must be declared.

Cats and dogs must have an anti-rabies vaccination certificate and health certificate stating if they come from a rabies-free country. Other animals must be inspected by a health official on arrival. Animals under three months old are not allowed. A maximum of three dogs and/or cats may be brought in.

Temporary Importation of Yachts: Foreign yachts may be temporarily imported into France for six months of any year, either in one or several visits, without paying duty. This is allowed for up to a period of three years, after which the yacht must be exported to another country before returning to France, or the tax must be paid. Temporary importation is on condition that the boat is not used for commercial purposes during its stay, and used only by the person who originally imported the yacht into France. A yacht under temporary importation may be left in France for 12 months provided that for six months the vessel is put in bond and the registration papers left with customs. Otherwise, after six months the yacht must leave France for six months. Only the owner is eligible to keep the yacht in bond in France after six months, a non-owning captain has to export the yacht after six months.

Boats which are borrowed, chartered or owned by companies can be brought into France under temporary importation, but only if the same person who brought the vessel in remains in charge and takes it out of the country again. Anyone borrowing a yacht must have a letter from the owner stating that permission has been given for the yacht to be used in his or her absence. Crew changes are allowed while in France only if the same person remains in charge. The only changes of owner or captain allowed are on privately owned yachts, where the person in charge may hand over control to a member of the immediate family, namely spouse or children, who must not be resident in France. A co-owner may hand over to another co-owner, who is listed as such on the ship's papers. Delivery crews may bring in a yacht for the owner to take over, or sail a yacht out of France on behalf of an owner, as long as a proper delivery agreement is made, which the authorities may wish to see. The yacht being delivered is not allowed to stop anywhere else in France except its entry and exit points, unless forced to by weather conditions.

Yachts may not be lent, hired or sold while in French waters while under temporary importation. Those in breach of any of these conditions, will be liable for tax on the value of the yacht.

If cruising in France's Mediterranean waters, owners of foreign yachts who wish to remain longer than six months can obtain a permit (titre de séjour) from French customs, which is valid for one year. This exempts yachts from having to give up the registration papers to customs and put the yacht into bond after the six month period is up. Application for the permit should be made in the port where the yacht is normally kept. Customs will want to see the registration certificate and identity papers. Company-owned yachts must also show the company statute, and proof that the user of the yacht holds the majority of the company shares. The permit can be renewed after one year. This permit simplifies matters if wishing to winter on the French Mediterranean coast.

Chartering: Only bareboat charters are permitted and if the yacht is foreign owned, proper formalities must be completed. Taking on paying crew is not permitted, as this is considered to be chartering. If a yacht has paying passengers, this must be declared to customs on arrival in France, the yacht imported and TVA (Value Added Tax) of 18.6 per cent of the yacht's value must be paid.

Immigration

Nationals of the European Community, Andorra, Austria, Canada, Cyprus, Finland, Iceland, Liechtenstein, Monaco, Norway, Sweden, Switzerland and the United States do not need visas for up to a three month stay. A British Visitors Passport is acceptable instead of a full passport. All other nationalities need visas which must be obtained in advance.

Inland waterways

There are various canals which cross France, still used by commercial traffic as well as yachts. The Atlantic and Mediterranean are connected by a canal route of 314 miles (503 km) with 139 locks, from Bordeaux on the River Garonne, to Castets where the Canal Latéral à la Garonne runs to Toulouse, from where the Canal du

Midi leads to Sète in the Mediterranean. Other canals and river systems go into the heart of Brittany, through the centre of Paris, the eastern part of France and the Rhône river to the Mediterranean. The Northern France waterway can be entered at Dunkerque, Calais, Gravelines or St Valéry-sur-Somme, while the Brittany Canal runs from the English Channel to the Bay of Biscay through 63 locks from St Malo via Dinas, Rennes, Redan and the River Vilaine.

Normally no charge is made for the use of the waterways, with a few local exceptions. Yachts must unstep their masts, which can be done at the seaports before entry into the canals, there usually being facilities which specialise in this operation. There are certain maximum restrictions, the most important being the draft, which is normally 6 ft (1.80 metres) on the main waterways from the English Channel to the Mediterranean. The Canal du Midi has a minimum depth of 5′4″ (1.60 metres) while the canals in Brittany have a maximum draft of 4 feet (1.20 metres). A yacht drawing up to 10 feet (3 metres) with a maximum height restriction of 20 feet (6 metres) may be taken up the Seine as far as Paris. On all other canals and rivers, the maximum headroom is 11 feet (3.50 metres) and in some places as little as 8 feet (2.50 metres). There are variations and the level of water can be greatly reduced following a dry winter. The maximum speed limit is 16 mph/25 kmh on the rivers, 3.7–6.25 mph/6–10 kmh on the canals. Chemical toilets and holding tanks are compulsory. The French Tourist Office should be contacted for a list of 'chomages' (stoppages), obtainable from the end of March onwards, which details any canals or locks closed for repairs during the year.

Facilities

France prides itself on having the best cuisine in the world and the quality of food is excellent everywhere. Supplies are easily available and on the outskirts of every town there are huge hypermarkets, which have an immense selection of foodstuffs and other goods. Water and fuel are available in all ports and most marinas have their own fuelling dock. LPG is widely available as it is used by many French households, but for longer stays in France it may be advisable to change over to the French system of bottles.

With the most developed yacht building industry in Europe, yachting facilities generally are of a high standard. Marinas have been built along the entire Mediterranean coast and in many places, particularly in the older ports, special docking arrangements have been made for yachts. Many ports and marinas are full

to capacity and during the summer season it can be extremely difficult to find space.

Chandlery and repair facilities are widely available and small repairs can be undertaken in most ports. For more complicated or specialised jobs it is best to go to one of the major centres, where there are established boatyards and specialist companies offering a complete range of repair facilities. On the Atlantic coast, the best centres are at St Malo, Ouistreham (near Caen), Cherbourg, Brest, La Trinité, La Rochelle, Le Havre, Lorient and Bordeaux. In the Mediterranean, excellent facilities are at Antibes, in the St Tropez–Cogolin area, Toulon and Marseilles, although the latter deals mainly with commercial shipping. In Corsica, the main port of Ajaccio has the best facilities on the west coast and Bastia on the east coast.

Further Reading

North Biscay Pilot
South Biscay Pilot
South France Pilot (6 Volumes)
North France Pilot
North Brittany Pilot
Normandy and Channel Islands Pilot
Brittany and Channel Islands Cruising Guide
French Pilot (Vols 1–4)
Mediterranean Cruising Handbook
Shell Pilot to the English Channel, Vol. 2: French Coast
Votre Livre de Bord (Mer du Nord – Manche–Atlantique)
Votre Livre de Bord (Méditerranée)

For the French Canals:
Carte–Guide Navigation Fluviale
Cruising French Waterways
Inland Waterways of France
French Inland Waterways
Cruising Association Handbook
North Sea Passage Pilot

GREENLAND

Lying close to North America, but administered by Denmark, Greenland, also known as Kalaallit Nunaat, is the world's largest island. Lying mostly within the Arctic Circle, much of the land is under ice and in places the ice cap is over 2 miles deep. Greenland is undoubtedly the most challenging cruising destination in the North Atlantic and every year a few yachts brave the elements to explore this wild and beautiful island during the all too short summer season. The deeply

Practical Information

LOCAL TIME: GMT - 3

BUOYAGE: IALA A

CURRENCY: Danish krone (Dkr) of 100 ore

BUSINESS HOURS
Banks: 0930–1600 Monday to Friday, to 1800 Thursdays.
Business: 0900–1630 Monday to Friday.
Shops: Monday to Thursday 0900–1700, 0900–1900/2000 Friday, 0900–1300/1400 Saturday.
Government offices: 0900–1630 Monday to Friday.

ELECTRICITY: 220 V, 50 Hz

PUBLIC HOLIDAYS
1 January: New Year's Day
Maundy Thursday, Good Friday and Easter Monday
Fourth Friday after Easter: Prayer Day
Ascension Day
Whit Monday
5 June afternoon: Constitution Day
24 December afternoon: Christmas Eve
25 December: Christmas Day

COMMUNICATIONS
There are flights from Nuuk airport (Godthaab) to Reykjavik in Iceland, from where international connections can be made.

MEDICAL
There is a hospital at Godthaab and dispensaries in all ports.

DIPLOMATIC MISSIONS
Canada: Nuna Air, PO Box 800, 3900 Godthaab. ☎ 299-25411.

indented coasts offer an infinite variety of anchorages in the steep sided fjords or among the myriad islands.

Country Profile

Greenland was discovered in AD 982 by the intrepid Norseman Eric the Red and rediscovered in the sixteenth century by the explorers Davis and Hudson. The island was colonised by the Danes from 1721 and came under their direct control in 1729. In 1953 Greenland was incorporated into Denmark, but from 1979 has enjoyed a great deal of internal autonomy. In 1985 the population voted to leave the European Community, which Greenland had previously joined as part of Denmark. Because of its strategic position, Greenland is the site of several air bases.

The economy is based on fishing and cryolite mining with income from the air bases. The population of 51,000 is concentrated on the south-west coast, being mainly Eskimo, with a European minority. Danish and Greenlandic are spoken and most people are Lutheran. The capital is Godthaab, or Nuuk in Eskimo.

The weather is cold all year round and the winters are particularly harsh with some ports being icebound until well into the summer. Temperatures are low even in the summer months. The prevailing winds in the southern part are S or SW, while easterly winds predominate further north. Winds are light and variable in summer. Depending on latitude, the midnight sun is visible from the end of May until the end of July.

Entry Regulations

Ports of entry
Angmagssalik 65°35′N 37°30′W (August to November navigation period), Christianshaab 68°49′N 51°11′W (May to November), Egedesminde 68°43′N 52°53′W (May to December), Faeringehavn 63°42′N 51°33′W (year round), Frederikshaab 62°00′N 49°40′W (year round), Godhavn 69°15′N 53°33′W (May to December), Godthaab 64°10′N 51°44′W (year round), Holsteinsborg 66°57′N 53°41′W (year round), Jakobshavn 69°13′N 51°06′W (May to November), Julianehaab 60°43′N 46°02′W (year round, only ice-strengthened vessels January to July), Marmorilik 71°08′N 51°17′W (May to October), Nanortalik 60°08′N 45°15′W (August to December), Narssaq 60°54′N 45°59′W (September to December), Narssarssuaq 61°09′N 45°26′W (May to October), Sukkertoppen 65°25′N 52°54′W (year round), Umanak 70°41′N 52°08′W (July to October), Upernavik 72°47′N 56°09′W (June to November).

Procedure on arrival
Contact the port authorities well in advance of arrival for special permission to enter the ports, if possible 24 hours beforehand.

Customs
The importation of firearms is forbidden.
Animals shall be confined on board.

Immigration
The same visa requirements apply as for Denmark, which in brief means that nationals of EC and Nordic

countries do not need a visa, while those of the USA, Canada, Australia and New Zealand are among those who can stay up to three months without a visa. In some ports the crew may only be allowed to land with permission from the Port Authority who will issue shore passes.

Restrictions
The military areas of Gronnedal Fladestation (naval base), Thule Air Base and Sondre Stromfjord Air Base are prohibited for yachts. All military areas must be avoided.

Ice conditions
Icecontrol ☎ 3 52 44.

Some of the harbours are accessible all year round, but many are only accessible during the summer, and even then ice-strengthened vessels are recommended. There are ice booms placed across the harbour entrances at Jakobshavn, and one should confirm with port authorities that these booms are slackened off before entering.

Facilities

Provisions are available only in the larger settlements and the best supplies are to be found in the capital Godthaab. It is also here that the best range of repair facilities is available. Limited repair facilities are also available at Holsteinsborg and Jakobshavn, which also have slipways. Fuel and water are available in all ports.

ICELAND

Isolated in the North Atlantic with Greenland its only neighbour, Iceland consists of one main island and numerous smaller ones. Iceland is a country of stark beauty, of mighty glaciers, hissing geysers, boiling lakes and live volcanoes. Visited by only the most intrepid yachts during its short summer, a passage to Iceland and the subsequent cruise along its rugged coasts offers an experience difficult to match anywhere else in the North Atlantic.

Country Profile

In the ninth century AD Norsemen and Irish came to settle on the island and in 930 the Althing, an assembly of free men, was formed. The Althing is considered to be the oldest democratically elected assembly in the world. In the tenth century Icelanders settled Greenland and sailed across to North America. Norway took control of Iceland in the thirteenth century, and then fell under Danish rule taking Iceland with it. Denmark established a trade monopoly for which Iceland suffered. In the eighteenth century the population was decimated by smallpox, volcanic eruptions, and a terrible famine. The nineteenth century saw a revival, as both free trade and the Althing were re-established. Autonomy was achieved in 1903, and in 1918 the independent kingdom of Iceland was formed, although still under the Danish Crown. In 1944 the Republic of Iceland was proclaimed, which made economic agreements with the Scandinavian countries. It also joined NATO and in 1958 the United States took control of Iceland's defence. In 1958–61 the 'Cod Wars' broke out with England, after Iceland extended its coastal fisheries limit from 4 to 12 nautical miles.

The raising of sheep is important, but the fishing industry is the mainstay of the economy. The population is 240,000, half of whom live in the capital Reykjavik. The language is Icelandic and most people are Lutheran.

In spite of the closeness to the Arctic Circle, the climate is not too harsh and summers are relatively mild, mainly because of the warming waters of the Gulf Stream. The average temperatures are 10°C in summer and 1°C in winter. Prevailing winds are from the SE or E. Summer winds are often light and calms are common.

Entry Regulations

Ports of entry
Reykjavik 64°08′N 21°54′W, Akranes 64°19′N 22°05′W, Isafjördur 66°05′N 23°06′E, Saudarkrokur 65°45′N 19°36′W, Siglufjördur 66°12′N 18°52′W, Akureyri 65°41′N 18°03′W, Husavik 66°03′N 17°22′W, Seydisfjördur 65°15′N 13°55′W, Neskaupstadur 65°09′N 13°41′W, Eskifjördur 65°05′N 13°59′W, Vestmannaeyjar 63°26′N 20°16′W, Keflavik 64°00′N 22°33′W, Hafnarfjördur 64°04′N 21°55′W.

Procedure on arrival
The captain must inform customs of the yacht's arrival. Customs will give clearance to all places within Iceland. No cruising permit is required, however yachts must obtain from customs a permit to temporarily import the vessel for exemption from duty.
Reykjavik: Port Control should be contacted on VHF Channel 12 for berthing instructions.

Practical Information (Iceland)

LOCAL TIME: GMT

BUOYAGE: IALA A

CURRENCY: Icelandic krona (Kr/IKr) of 100 aurar

BUSINESS HOURS
Banks: 0915–1600 Monday to Friday, until 1800 on Thursday.
Shops: 0900–1800 Monday to Thursday, 0900–1900/2000 Friday, 0900–1100/1200 Saturday (shorter hours in smaller communities).
Government offices: 0800–1700 Monday to Friday.

ELECTRICITY: 220 V, 50 Hz

PUBLIC HOLIDAYS
1 January: New Year's Day
Maundy Thursday, Good Friday and Easter Monday
First day of summer (end April)
1 May: Labour Day
Ascension Day
Whit Monday
17 June: National Day
August Bank Holiday
24–26 December: Christmas
31 December: New Year's Eve

COMMUNICATIONS
There are public phone boxes only in main towns. There are payphones in post offices, shops and service stations.
Operator: dial 02.

Post office 0900–1700 Monday to Friday, 0900–1200 Saturdays.
There are international flights from Reykjavik to many European cities, Greenland, the Faeroes and the USA.

MEDICAL
There are hospitals in all major ports and several hospitals in Reykjavik.

DIPLOMATIC MISSIONS
In Reykjavik:
Canada: Suduriandsbraut 10.
☎ (1) 25355.
United Kingdom: PO Box 460, 121 Reykjavik. ☎ (1) 15883.
United States: Laufasvegur 21.
☎ (1) 29100.

Customs

Firearms must be declared on arrival and remain under seal while in Iceland. If one does not want to have firearms under seal, one can apply for special permission to be granted by the police.

The importation of animals is prohibited. In special cases, the Minister of Agriculture will authorise an import permit on condition that strict conditions are fulfilled, for example long- or short-term quarantine. Otherwise animals must remain on board.

Immigration

Visas are not required for nationals of EC or Nordic countries, United States, Canada, Australia or Japan who can spend three months in any nine month period. All other nationalities need visas.

Fees

Overtime fees are charged 1700–0800 Monday to Friday, and all of Saturday and Sunday.

Facilities

Provisioning is best in Reykjavik as there is a more limited selection in the smaller places. The price of food is high everywhere. Although there are not many local yachts, repair facilities are relatively good, particularly in active fishing harbours such as Reykjavik, Isafjördur and Olafsvik. A feature along the Icelandic shores are orange huts, set up as refuges for shipwrecked sailors. Every hut has some emergency supplies and a radiotelephone.

IRELAND

The North Atlantic island of Ireland is made up of two political units, the independent Republic of Ireland, also known as Eire, and the smaller region of Northern Ireland, which is part of the United Kingdom. Ireland has a coastline of nearly 3000 miles with many deep and sheltered bays.

Described by some sailing authors as one of the finest cruising grounds in the world, the only missing element to put Ireland at the top of the table is better weather. At least this is more than made up for by a profusion of perfectly sheltered anchorages.

Ireland's three coasts are very different and in their variety they cater for every requirement. The east coast is the most easily accessible for yachts coming from the United Kingdom, but Ireland's real beauty lies on its southern and western coasts. The most popular cruising area is between Cork and the Dingle Peninsula with an abundance of snug harbours and picturesque anchorages. The wilder west coast is more exposed and the distances between sheltered harbours are greater. Some 200 islands lie scattered off the west coast of Ireland and only a handful are inhabited. While the east and south-western coasts have a sizeable local boating population and also attract a number of cruising yachts, the west of Ireland is less frequented.

Country Profile

In the fourth century AD the Celts settled in Ireland and eventually the small rival kingdoms of Ulster,

Connacht, Meath, Leinster and Munster developed. In the early fifth century St Patrick brought Christianity to the island, and in the sixth to seventh centuries Ireland became a flourishing cultural and religious centre. Irish monks travelled and established important monasteries on the mainland of Europe.

The seventh to eleventh centuries saw the country suffer from Viking raids and invasions. Political disunity due to rivalry between the Irish kingdoms was exploited by the Anglo-Normans, and in 1175 King Henry II imposed English rule on Ireland. In 1541 Henry VIII took the title of King of Ireland, and his religious reforms provoked revolt amongst the Catholic Irish. Irish land was confiscated by the English crown and given to English gentry in retaliation, while Protestant Scots settled in Ulster. In the eighteenth century some legislative autonomy was gained. The influence of the American and French revolutions led to rebellion at the end of the eighteenth century, but in 1800 the Act of Union united Ireland and England. The potato famine of 1846–8 plunged the island into misery, and caused a mass emigration.

Nationalism continued to be strong, until in 1914

Quiet cruising on the south coast of Ireland.

the Home Rule Act was passed, but its implementation was delayed until after the First World War. A nationalist rising of 1916 was repressed and guerilla warfare followed. Then in 1920 the six counties of Ulster were incorporated into the United Kingdom, and a year later the Irish Free State was formed. Civil war resulted between the provisional government and those opposing the partition of Ireland. Eventually some calm was established, and efforts made at developing the country. In 1937 a new constitution was adopted, and the name changed to Eire. The Irish Republican Army (IRA), which was formed during the First World War to fight partition, was outlawed in 1939. Neutral during the Second World War, Eire became the independent Republic of Ireland in 1948 and joined the European Community in 1972.

The six counties of Ulster, known as Northern Ireland, have remained part of the United Kingdom, although there is some internal autonomy. Following widespread civil disturbances in 1969, the British army was sent in to re-establish order and still remains there. The outlawed IRA continues its guerilla activities. The situation shows no signs of a solution.

Livestock is an important resource, and agriculture in general plays a major role in the economy. There is

Practical Information

LOCAL TIME: GMT. March to September GMT + 1.

BUOYAGE: IALA A

CURRENCY: Punt (Ir£) of 100 pence. Not more than Ir£150 may be exported.

BUSINESS HOURS
Banks: 1000–1230, 1330–1500 Monday to Friday, most until 1700 on Thursdays.
Business: 0900–1300 Monday to Friday, 1400–1730.
Shops: 0900–1730/1800 Monday to Saturday. Late shopping 2000/2100 Thursdays and/or Fridays in many towns. Early closing days in some smaller towns.
Government offices: 0900–1730 Monday to Friday.

ELECTRICITY: 220 V, 50 Hz

PUBLIC HOLIDAYS
1 January: New Year's Day
17 March: St Patrick's Day
Good Friday (not a public holiday but observed in most parts of Ireland)
Easter Monday
4 June: June Holiday
6 August: August Holiday
29 October: October Holiday
25 December: Christmas Day
26 December: St Stephen's Day

COMMUNICATIONS
Post offices open 0900–1730 Monday–Friday, 0900–1300 Saturday. There are frequent flights from Dublin and Cork to the UK and regular flights

from Dublin and Shannon airports to European and North American destinations.

MEDICAL
There are reciprocal agreements with many West European countries for free emergency treatment.

DIPLOMATIC MISSIONS
In Dublin:
Australia: Fitzwilton House, Wilton Terrace. ☎ (01) 761-517.
Canada: 65 St Stephen's Green. ☎ (01) 781-988.
United Kingdom: 31/33 Merrion Road. ☎ (01) 695-211.
United States: 42 Elgin Road, Ballsbridge. ☎ (01) 688-777.

some industry and tourism, although a trade deficit and unemployment are problems.

The population is 3 million, although the tradition of emigration continues. Irish (Gaelic) and English are spoken.

The majority of the population are Roman Catholic, with a minority of Anglicans. In Northern Ireland the majority are Protestant, although there is a sizeable Catholic minority. The capital of Ireland is Dublin on the east coast.

Ireland has a mild humid climate influenced by the Gulf Stream. Rainfall is very heavy all year round on the western coast. Strong winds and gales are most frequently from the SW and are very common in winter. The weather is generally very changeable. The prevailing winds are westerly. Higher seas are encountered off the west coast than in any other neighbouring area.

Entry Regulations

Ports of entry
Dublin 53°21′N 6°13′W, Dun Laoghaire 53°18′N 6°08′W, Wicklow 52°59′N 6°02′W, Dundalk 54°00′N 6°23′W, Drogheda 53°43′N 6°21′W, Carlingford 54°03′N 6°11′W, Greenore 54°02′N 6°08′W, Waterford 52°07′N 6°57′W, New Ross 52°24′N 6°57′W, Dungarvan 52°05′N 7°36′W, Wexford 52°20′N 6°27′W, Cork Harbour (Crosshaven and Cobh) 51°54′N 8°28′W, Kinsale 51°42′N 8°30′W, Baltimore (summer only) 51°27′N 9°24′W,

Skibbereen 51°33′N 9°16′W, Bantry 51°42′N 9°28′W, Castletown Bere 51°39′N 9°54′W, Glengariff 51°43′N, 9°33′W, Youghal 51°56′N 7°50′W, Limerick 52°40′N 8°38′W, Tralee 52°16′N 9°46′W, Galway 53°16′N 9°03′W, Westport 53°48′N 9°32′W, Sligo 54°16′N 8°28′W, Ballina 54°07′N 9°10′W, Moville 55°11′N 7°02′W, Ballyhoorisky 55°15′N 7°46′W.

Procedure on arrival
Yachts must fly the Q flag, and notify customs whether having dutiable stores on board or not. At night, a red light over a white light, not more than six feet apart, must be shown. On arrival the customs office should be contacted, or if no customs officer is available, the local police (Garda). The harbour master must also be notified. All dutiable, restricted and prohibited items must be declared to customs. The officer in charge of the port of departure must be notified of details of the yacht, its destination and name of the captain

Customs
Firearms must be declared. The importation of firearms and ammunition is prohibited unless a licence is granted by the Minister for Justice.

Importation of animals is prohibited except from the United Kingdom, where the animal must have been resident for at least six months, unless accompanied by a licence from the Department of Agriculture. Animals from other countries must be secured on board and not taken ashore.

Yachts should be registered. Yachts may be laid up

for one winter, but customs permission should be obtained first.

Yachts may be temporarily imported by a non-resident for private use for up to one year before becoming liable for import charges. Under temporary importation a yacht may not be hired, sold or lent to a resident, nor used for any other purpose than the importer's private use. If the owner wishes to employ a resident as captain of the yacht, customs approval must be sought; if permission is granted, the captain may not use the yacht for his own private use, nor may he import the yacht unless acompanied by the non-resident owner.

Excess dutiable stores will be placed under customs seal on arrival; these, and stores shipped from bond, must not be consumed in port without prior permission from customs and on payment of duty. They may be used while cruising Irish waters but duty must then be paid on the quantity consumed in the subsequent port. Yachts laid up or remaining longer must pay all duty owed on dutiable stores, or deposit the stores in a State Warehouse, or have them sealed on board, in which case a bond must be given by the captain or owner.

There are restrictions on the import of meat and meat products, poultry and poultry products, plants and plant products including vegetables.

Immigration
Nationals of West European countries, Central and Southern American countries except Colombia, Bolivia and Peru, also Australia, Bahamas, Barbados, Botswana, Canada, Fiji, Gambia, Israel, Jamaica, Japan, Kenya, South Korea, Malawi, Malaysia, Mauritius, Nauru, New Zealand, Sierra Leone, Singapore, South Africa, Swaziland, Tanzania, Tonga, Trinidad & Tobago, Uganda, United States of America, Western Samoa, Yugoslavia, Zambia and Zimbabwe do not require visas.

Fees
Overtime is charged on Sundays, public holidays and outside working hours 0800 to 2000 on weekdays.

Light dues must be paid by yachts over 20 tons normally kept or used outside of Ireland, the United Kingdom or Isle of Man. These dues are £2.10 per 10 tons for every period of 30 days or less, with a minimum payment of £7.

Facilities

Provisioning in all ports on the east and south coast is good and there are several marinas scattered about. As one moves west, supplies become scarcer and the boat should be well provisioned with food, fuel and water.

Repair facilities for yachts range from excellent in such major yachting centres as Cork Harbour to virtually non-existent in some of the smaller ports. The facilities at Crosshaven are possibly the best in Ireland and a whole range of repair services is available, including travelift, workshops, rigger and sailmaker. Further east, repair facilities are also available at Youghal and Waterford. There are several marinas and repair facilities in and around the capital Dublin, the best centres being at Dun Laoghaire, Howth and Malahide. A useful source of help are the many yacht clubs dotted about the coasts, the most famous among them being the Royal Cork Yacht Club, founded in 1720 and considered the oldest yacht club in the world. Most yacht clubs have moorings for visitors who are generally made welcome everywhere.

Further Reading

South and West Coast of Ireland Sailing Directions
North and East Coast of Ireland Sailing Directions
Lundy, Fastnet and Irish Sea Pilot (Vols 2 and 3)
Cruising Association Handbook

MADEIRA

Madeira lies in the Atlantic some 300 miles off the African coast. Only two islands of this volcanic archipelago are inhabited, the largest, Madeira Grande, which gives its name to the whole group, and Porto Santo to the north-east. The smaller islands of the main group are Ilha Chao, Ilha Deserta Grande, and Ilheu de Bugio. The Ilhas Selvagem, on the northern fringe of the Canary Islands, are a wildlife refuge administered by Madeira, and yachts wishing to visit them need permission from the authorities in Madeira.

The Madeiran archipelago is one of those places whose geographical position means that it is always visited by yachts en route to somewhere else and not as a destination in its own right. Yet these islands have much to be enjoyed and many transatlantic sailors regard Madeira with special affection. The majority of yachts arrive in Madeira during October and November on their way to the Canary Islands and the Caribbean, while some leave direct from the main port Funchal to cross the Atlantic. There has also been an increase in the number of American boats cruising the Atlantic circle of Bermuda, Azores, Madeira and Canary Islands during the summer, while Madeira has also become a popular port of call in the spring, for yachts returning to Europe after wintering in the Canaries.

Country Profile

Legend says that Madeira was part of the lost kingdom of Atlantis. The islands were already known to the Phoenicians, but the Portuguese rediscovered them early in the fifteenth century. The islands were uninhabited and covered in dense forest, hence the name, which means Island of Timber. Settled by the Portuguese, prosperity soon came with the cultivation of sugar cane and wine production. Christopher Columbus lived on Porto Santo for several years after he married the daughter of the island's governor.

The islands were briefly ruled by Spain, during the period when they also occupied the mainland of Portugal. Many foreign traders settled on the island and became involved with the development of the wine trade. With the growth in the numbers of ships calling for provisions, Madeira wine rapidly became popular and sought after in many countries. It was not only for the wine, but for other fresh provisions that trading vessels and passenger ships called at Madeira, which was a very popular port of call for British ships

Visitors' quay at Funchal.

on their voyages to all parts of the globe. It is the lush vegetation and profusion of fruit and flowers which have accounted for the island's enduring charm and Madeira has been a destination for the discerning tourist since the early twentieth century. Madeira is an autonomous region of Portugal, although in recent years there have been some calls for independence.

Agriculture is important on this fertile island, and sugar cane, bananas, sweet potatoes and fruit are grown. Orchids are one of Madeira's specialities. The tourist and fishing industries also contribute to the economy.

The Madeirans were originally Portuguese, mixed with Moors, Jews, Italians and Africans. Many Madeirans have emigrated, especially to Brazil. The majority are Roman Catholics. Portuguese is the official language, although many understand Spanish, French and English. The capital Funchal is a pleasant city with attractive mosaic pavements and whitewashed buildings in the Portuguese colonial style.

The islands have a pleasant and mild climate all year round, the air temperature rarely falling below 16°C (60°F) in winter or rising above 22°C (72°F) in summer. Due to the influence of the Gulf Stream the

Practical Information

LOCAL TIME: GMT. Summer time GMT + 1 March to September.

BUOYAGE: IALA A

CURRENCY: Escudo ($) of 100 centavos

BUSINESS HOURS
Banks: 0830–1145, 1300–1445 Monday to Friday.
Business: 1000–1200, 1400–1800 Monday to Friday.
Shops: 0900–1300 Monday to Saturday, 1500–1900 Monday to Friday.
Government offices: 0900–1200, 1400–1700 Monday to Friday.

ELECTRICITY: 220 V, 50 Hz

PUBLIC HOLIDAYS
1 January: New Year's Day
Good Friday
25 April: National Day
1 May
Corpus Christi
Whit Monday: Autonomy Day
10 June: Camoes Day
1 July: Discovery of Madeira
15 August: Assumption
21 August: Municipal Holiday (Funchal)
5 October: Republic Day
1 November: All Saints
1 December: Independence Day
8 December: Immaculate Conception
25, 26 December: Christmas

COMMUNICATIONS
International calls and telex at the main post office, Avenida Zarco, Funchal, separate entrance, open 0830–2400 Monday to Friday, 0900–1230 Saturday. Smaller post offices also have phones from where international calls can be made.
The main post office 0830–2000 Monday to Friday, 0900–1230 Saturday. There is a special counter for post restante and the post office has its own customs department at the airport for incoming parcels.
Stamps can also be bought from newsagents and shops where a green 'correio' sign is displayed.
There are regular international flights from Madeira and Porto Santo.

MEDICAL
Health Services Information centre for visitors, Rua das Pretas 1, Funchal.

DIPLOMATIC MISSIONS
In Funchal:
United Kingdom: Avenida Zarco 2.
United States: Avenida Luis Camoes, Block D, Apartment B.

water temperature similarly varies only between 17° and 21°C (63–70°F). The prevailing winds are north-easterly and all the ports and anchorages are sheltered from this direction. Only the more variable winds of winter and the passage of lows across the North Atlantic can cause problems, otherwise Madeira can be visited virtually all year round.

Entry Regulations

Ports of entry
Funchal (Madeira) 32°38'N 16°54'W, Porto Santo 33°03'N 16°19'W.

Procedure on arrival
Funchal: The small boat harbour inside Funchal harbour is run as a marina, but virtually all spaces on the pontoons are reserved for local craft and visiting yachts are obliged to tie up alongside the harbour wall, often rafted three to four deep. All offices are located in the marina, where formalities are completed during normal working hours. The first office to visit is Guarda Fiscal, followed by Policia Maritima and finally the marina office. The Guarda Fiscal will issue a transit log to yachts arriving from outside of Madeira. Even if coming from Porto Santo, the clearance procedure must still be completed. On departure the marina office and all other officials must be visited.

Porto Santo: There are some pontoons for yachts in this large harbour. Formalities are normally completed during office hours. The captain should report to the Port Captain's office on the north side of the harbour, as well as the Guarda Fiscal and the Policia Maritima. Even if arriving from Funchal and already possessing a transit log, one still has to report to all these offices.

Customs
Firearms must be declared. Animals are not permitted to land.

Immigration
No visa is needed for up to 60 days stay for Western European nations, the USA, Canada, and many others. For extensions one has to apply at the Foreigners Registration Service.

Transit log
This is issued to all yachts at either port of entry by the Guarda Fiscal, and must be presented to the authorities when visiting any other island. Even if possessing a transit log from mainland Portugal or the Azores, clearance must still be done on arrival in Madeira. A new transit log may be issued.

Fees
There are no overtime fees as clearance is done in working hours. There are harbour fees.

Restrictions

The uninhabited Ilhas Selvagem are administered from Madeira and as they are a wildlife reserve access to them is prohibited. Yachts who wish to stop must obtain special permission from the authorities in Madeira.

Facilities

Funchal: Shopping is good as there are several supermarkets and one in the marina itself which is open seven days a week. There is also an excellent fresh produce market. LPG bottles can be refilled locally and Camping Gaz bottles can be either exchanged or bought. For diesel fuel there is a filling station in Funchal marina. Elsewhere it must be transported by jerrycan from filling stations. There is a small chandlery opposite the marina.

There are various engineering shops in Funchal, although because there are not many local yachts, repair facilities are rather limited and everything revolves around the yacht club (Clube Naval do Funchal). Visiting yachtsmen are welcome at the club, which is rather far from the harbour, although the club maintains a base next to the marina. It is here that yachts can be lifted out of the water. For hauling out, local yachtsmen usually hire a 35-ton crane. For all emergency repairs, it is advisable to contact the club, which can advise visiting yachtsmen with the names of local specialists.

Porto Santo: Water and electricity are laid on to the pontoons and there are showers at the end of the dock. The main town of Porto Santo is a long walk from the harbour, but there one can find a fresh fish and produce market, bakery and two small supermarkets. There are only basic repair facilities in Porto Santo and for any work it is best to sail over to Funchal. There are no facilities or provisioning on any of the other adjacent islands.

Further Reading

Atlantic Islands
Cruising Guide to the Eastern Caribbean, Vol.1: Transatlantic Cruising Guide

PORTUGAL

Portugal occupies the western part of the Iberian peninsula with a coastline on the Atlantic Ocean. A nation of seafarers, the Portuguese started the age of discovery in the fifteenth century. Portuguese ships sailed beyond the known horizons to discover first the route around Africa to India and then around the world. Portugal's isolation in the past from Spain and the rest of Europe has produced a distinctive culture and language. Little remains of the once mighty empire except Macao and the Atlantic islands of Madeira and the Azores, which enjoy an increasing degree of autonomy and therefore have been dealt with separately in this book.

From the cruising point of view, mainland Portugal divides into two distinct areas, the west and the south. The ports on the west coast are situated mostly in estuaries or rivers often with bars at the entrance. Among them, the most interesting landfall is the capital Lisbon set on the River Tagus, which can be navigated right up into the centre of the city. The Algarve coast in the south has better weather and easier approaches to its small picturesque ports.

Country Profile

Portugal was originally inhabited by Iberian tribes who came into contact with Phoenicians, Greeks and Romans, the latter making the country part of their empire until the fifth century AD. The entire Iberian peninsula was overrun by Visigoths and then the Moors in the eighth century. The Portuguese kings had expelled the Moors by the eleventh century and an independent kingdom was established, its borders basically those of present-day Portugal. Portugal was unified into a state earlier than most European nations.

In the fifteenth century Prince Henry the Navigator initiated voyages of discovery into the Atlantic and along the African coast, then to the East Indies. Vasco da Gama found the sea route to India, and prosperity came with Portuguese monopoly of the spice trade. Gradually Portugal established a maritime empire. Rivalry with Spain was intense and the two countries eventually concluded a treaty, which laid out their spheres of influence. In 1580 the country was occupied by Spain and independence was only restored in 1640. By then France, England and the Netherlands were overtaking the Portuguese in maritime strength and Portugal went into decline as it failed to establish a productive economy of its own.

During the nineteenth century civil wars, economic crises, and political and constitutional conflicts kept the country weak. In 1910 the monarchy was over-thrown in a revolution, but strife continued and a fascist regime was established under Antonio de Olive-ira Salazar in the 1930s. After the Second World War the colonies pushed for independence and several prolonged and costly wars were fought in Africa. In 1974 the almost bloodless 'Carnation Revolution' overthrew the dictatorship and the military regime was replaced with civil government and democracy.

Portugal has predominantly an agricultural economy, but industry is developing in such fields as textiles. Portugal hopes to gain considerably from its recent membership of the European Community.

The population numbers around 10 million. Portu-guese is the main language. Of Latin origin, it sounds very different from other Latin languages, although written the similarities are obvious. The majority of the population are Catholic, but there are also Prot-estant and Jewish minorities. The capital is Lisbon (Lisboa), 10 miles from the Atlantic on the north bank

Belem Marina in Lisbon close to the monument of Henry the Navigator.

of the River Tagus, which opens into the Mar de Palha (Sea of Straw). The area has been settled since the time of the Phoenicians and the town became the capital in 1260. After an earthquake in 1755, the city was rebuilt on a grand scale.

The climate is mild and varies slightly, being cooler in the north and warmer in the south. The prevailing winds of summer are northerly. The Portuguese trades commence in about April and last until September. On the Algarve coast the northerly winds of summer are often replaced by land and sea breezes. Most gales occur in winter, when the prevailing winds are west-erly. Due to their location some harbours are inaccessi-ble in strong onshore winds.

Entry Regulations

Ports of entry
All Portuguese ports, including Viana do Castelo 41°41′N 8°50′W, Porto 41°09′N 8°37′W, Lisbon 38°44′N 9°07′W, Lagos 37°05′N 8°40′W, Vilamoura 37°04′N 8°07′W, Faro 37°01′N 7°55′W.

Practical Information

LOCAL TIME: GMT. Summer time GMT + 1 from the end of March to the end of September.

BUOYAGE: IALA A

CURRENCY: Escudo ($) of 100 centavos. Foreign currency exceeding 30,000 escudos must be declared on arrival. 5000 escudos is the maximum that may be exported or imported.

BUSINESS HOURS
Banks: 0900–1130, 1400–1530 Monday to Friday.
Business: 1000–1200, 1400–1800 Monday to Friday.
Shops: 0900–1300 Monday to Saturday, 1500–1900 Monday to Friday (food shops stay open later and on Sundays).
Government offices: 0900–1700 (close for lunch 1200–1400).

ELECTRICITY: 220 V, 50 Hz

PUBLIC HOLIDAYS
1 January: New Year's Day
25 April: Revolution Day
1 May: Labour Day
10 June: Portugal Day
15 August: Assumption
5 October: Republic Day
1 November: All Saints
1 December: Independence Day
8 December: Immaculate Conception
25 December: Christmas Day

COMMUNICATIONS
International calls can be made from metered booths in telephone offices in major towns.
Emergency: dial 115.
Post offices open 0900–1230, 1430–1800 Monday to Friday.
There are regular international flights from Lisbon, Porto and Faro to most

European destinations. There are also flights to America, Africa and Asia from Lisbon. There are daily flights to the Azores and Madeira.

MEDICAL
Many European nationals can get free emergency treatment if their country has reciprocal arrangements with Portugal.

DIPLOMATIC MISSIONS
In Lisbon:
Australia: 4th floor, Avenida da Liberdade 244. ☎ (1) 52-3350.
Canada: Avenida da Liberdade 144/56. ☎ (1) 3474892.
United Kingdom: Rua São Domingo à Lapa 35-37. ☎ (1) 66-1191.
United States: Avenida das Forcas Armadas. ☎ (1) 72-5600.

In Porto:
United Kingdom: Avenida da Boavista 3072. ☎ (2) 68-4789.

Procedure on arrival

Immediately on arrival the port captain (Capitania) must be contacted. The office should be visited with the ship's papers, including registration certificate, radio licence, passports and detailed crew lists. The port captain will issue a transit log (livrete de transito) after which clearance must be done with the immigration (Guarda Fiscal) and customs (Alfandega). A small fee has to be paid for the transit log, so it helps to have a few escudos on arrival.

Lisbon: The approaches to the River Tagus (Rio Tejo) are straightforward and one should keep to the marked channel as there are a few shallows in the approaches. Doca de Santo Amaro is the best place to come to clear in, but the authorities do not insist that a boat is taken there.

The basin lies past the two marinas, just beyond the suspension bridge which has a clearance of 70 metres (220 feet). The basin, which is usually full of naval craft and harbour launches, is close to customs, immigration and harbour police offices. From one of the other basins, it is best to take a taxi or the electric train to Alcantara station, which is right by the port police and customs building.

Porto: There is a bar at the entrance to the River Douro and the entrance is dangerous in strong winds or with a heavy swell. The deep water channel is on the north side. For clearance, it is best to come alongside

the commercial quay (Cais de Estiva), on the north side of the river close to the Luis I bridge.

Vilamoura: Vilamoura Radio monitors VHF Channels 16 and 20 and works on Channel 62. The wide entrance leads into an outer basin used mainly by local fishing boats, from which a narrower entrance leads to the marina. For clearance, yachts must come alongside the reception dock on the port side in front of the control tower.

Procedure on departure

On departure the captain should clear out at the same offices, particularly if leaving Portugal for a foreign destination. On departure from Portugal, the transit log must be stamped by both the Capitania and the Guarda Fiscal. Customs need only be cleared on arrival and departure from Portugal and not between ports. If arriving from or continuing on to the Azores or Madeira, customs clearance does not have to be obtained as both these island groups are administered by Portugal. However, on arrival in those places the Capitania must be contacted as normal, and a new transit log may be issued.

Customs

Firearms must be declared on arrival.

All animals need an international vaccination certificate.

A yacht is permitted to remain in the country for up to one year before it becomes liable for import duty. After six months, a circulation tax is payable for the calendar year. To avoid payment of circulation tax and import duties, a yacht may leave Portugal and re-enter after a reasonable period.

Duty-free goods in excess of the limits allowed are permitted as long as they remain on board.

Permission must be obtained from customs before landing any equipment, even for repair.

Immigration

Visas are not required for citizens of West European countries, Canada and the USA. Other nationalities may need to obtain a visa in advance. Persons travelling on a yacht in transit are normally granted a visa on arrival, which is valid for a limited period. Nationals who require a visa and arrive without one should attempt to clear in at one of the major ports. Visitors are normally allowed a 60 days stay.

Visa extensions can be obtained from the Foreigners Registration Service, Avenida Antonio Augusto de Aguiar 18, Lisbon (or regional offices).

Cruising permit

All yachts are issued with a transit log (livrete de transito) on arrival. All subsequent movements of the yacht are recorded in the log until departure. Crew changes must be noted in the transit log. Yachts must clear in and out of all ports with the Capitania and the Guarda Fiscal, who will stamp the log. Procedure varies greatly from port to port – sometimes an official of the Capitania will come out to the boat, sometimes he must be looked for. The log is valid for one year, or until the yacht leaves Portugal.

Fees

A small fee is charged for the transit log.

Facilities

Provisioning is generally good and fresh produce particularly is of good quality. Fuel is available in all major ports. Repair facilities, with a few exceptions, are below the standards of neighbouring countries. The best repair facilities are concentrated in the three areas which have a local boating community: the capital Lisbon, Porto on the west coast and the large Vilamoura marina on the Algarve.

Lisbon: Facilities for visiting yachts are very basic and the limited number of pontoon spaces in the two marinas are always taken up by local craft. There are four different basins used by yachts, all of them

situated on the north bank of the river. Coming from seaward the first is Doca de Bom Succeso, immediately past Torre de Belem. There are no special places allocated for visitors. Further upstream, past the monument to Henry the Navigator, is Doca de Belem. Visitors should tie up initially by the fuel station opposite the entrance. For a small fee visitors can use the facilities of the Associaciâo Naval de Lisboa (Sailing Association) which has its base there. The club secretary is also the best person to consult concerning any repair. There are various workshops in Belem and also a small chandlery, but the selection is limited. Charts are available at the Hydrographic Institute.

Porto: Repair facilities for yachts are limited and either the local yacht club or the port captain's office are the best source of information on the facilities available. Most workshops are for commercial vessels, but they could work on a yacht if necessary.

Vilamoura: This large and well-run marina is very popular among North European sailors as it is a good place to leave the boat for long periods, especially if planning to set off across the Atlantic and not go into the Mediterranean. The marina offers all usual services with fuel at the reception dock. Repair facilities are the best in Portugal with a complete range of engine, sail, electrical, electronic and fibreglass repair. Carpentry and metalwork can also be done here. There is a 30-ton travelift as well as a drying out grid.

Further Reading

Atlantic Spain and Portugal
Cruising Association Handbook

UNITED KINGDOM

The United Kingdom of Great Britain and Northern Ireland incorporates the three countries of England, Scotland and Wales, the six counties of Ulster in Northern Ireland as well as several smaller island groups such as the Scillies, Orkneys and Shetlands. The Isle of Man, situated in the Irish Sea, has a special status and enjoys a certain degree of autonomy. The Channel Islands enjoy even greater autonomy, and are therefore treated separately.

With hardly anywhere over fifty miles from the sea, the British Isles has always been a maritime nation and produced some of the greatest sailors and navigators in history, a tradition which has continued into the modern age, when British cruising yachts were among the first to penetrate the furthest corners of the world. Sailing is a national pastime in Britain and the proportion of yachts per head of population is among the highest in the world. The most popular cruising areas are the Solent and Isle of Wight, the south west counties of Devon and Cornwall, East Anglia and the west coast of Scotland. The British Isles provide a vast cruising ground with plenty of variety, the greatest drawback being the weather, which rarely ensures enjoyable cruising conditions for more than a few days at a time. Most visiting yachts limit their cruising to the south coast, where there is an abundance of yachting facilities, but also an abundance of local craft, resulting in crowded harbours. There are many cruising attractions and more space to be found elsewhere.

Country Profile

The original inhabitants were of Iberian origin and later Celts settled the island. The Romans invaded and established the province of Britannia, the Celts fleeing west to North Wales and north to what the Romans called Caledonia, both areas successfully resisting Roman expansion. The inhabitants of Caledonia were called Picts and this area was also settled by the Scots, a Celtic tribe originating in Ireland.

After the collapse of the Roman Empire, Germanic tribes – the Angles, Saxons and Jutes – settled, driving the remaining Celts into Wales and Cornwall. From the eighth century the Danes were constant raiders and established settlements on the east coast. Danish kings ruled in the tenth and eleventh centuries, then a Saxon dynasty was re-established, but this fell to a Norman invasion in 1066.

After several weak kings and the Hundred Years War with France, it was only in the fifteenth and sixteenth centuries under the Tudors, Henry VII, Henry VIII and Elizabeth I, that a strong modern state was forged. Wales was united with England while Scotland remained an independent kingdom until Queen Elizabeth died without an heir. Then the Stuart King James VI of Scotland became James I of England and united the two kingdoms. Scotland has still kept many of its own laws and institutions.

Under Elizabeth I there had been an era of maritime exploration and economic expansion. Following her reign, under the Scottish Stuarts, there were conflicts between Parliament and the monarchy, civil war, and eventually parliamentary supremacy was accepted, which limited the power of the ruling monarch.

The Hannoverian dynasty came to the throne in 1714 and a period of internal stability followed, although Britain was involved in European wars and an ongoing rivalry with France. Britain's maritime power, trade, commerce and colonisation prospered. Despite the loss of the American colonies following the War of Independence, Britain gained Canada and India and continued to expand her empire. The Industrial Revolution at the end of the eighteenth century heralded an era of economic development and prosperity, which peaked in the 60 year reign of Queen Victoria in the nineteenth century.

The prosperity did not reach down to the working

La Aventura *sailing on the river Dart in the west of England.*

Practical Information

LOCAL TIME: GMT. Summer time GMT + 1 from March to October.

BUOYAGE: IALA A

CURRENCY: Pound sterling (£) of 100 pence

BUSINESS HOURS
Banks: 0930–1530 Monday to Friday (some close 1630 weekdays, some open Saturday mornings).
Scottish Banks: 0930–1230, 1330–1530 Monday to Thursday, 0930–1530 Friday.
Business: 0900–1730 Monday to Friday.
Shops: 0900–1730/1800 Monday to Friday; some early closing Wednesdays, some close 1900/2000 Thursdays, Fridays.
Government offices: 0900–1730 Monday to Friday.

ELECTRICITY: 240 V, 50 Hz

PUBLIC HOLIDAYS
England and Wales:
1 January: New Year's Day
Good Friday and Easter Monday
May Day
Spring Bank Holiday: Last weekend in May
Summer Bank Holiday: Last weekend in August
25, 26 December: Christmas
Scotland:
2 January.
Easter Monday is not a holiday.
Northern Ireland:
17 March: St Patrick's Day
12 July: Battle of the Boyne

COMMUNICATIONS
International ☎ access code 010.
Operator 100, International operator 155.
International calls can be made from public phones.
Many use phone cards, which can be bought in post offices or in shops where the card sign is shown.
Emergency: ☎ 999.
Post offices open 0900–1730/1800

Monday to Friday, some 0900–1200 Saturday.
London's Heathrow and Gatwick airports are among the busiest in the world with flights to all international destinations. There are also flights to many destinations from Belfast, Birmingham, Edinburgh, Glasgow, Manchester and Newcastle.

MEDICAL
National Health Service treatment may be free for nationals of countries that have reciprocal agreements with Britain.

DIPLOMATIC MISSIONS
In London:
Australia: Australia House, The Strand WC2B 4LA. ☎ (071) 379-4334.
Canada: Macdonald House, 1 Grosvenor Square, W1X 0AB.
☎ (071) 629-9492.
New Zealand: New Zealand House, Haymarket, SW1Y 4TQ.
☎ (071) 973-0366.
United States: 24/31 Grosvenor Square, W1A 1AE. ☎ (071) 499-9000.

---

classes, who began to find their voice. Gradually a series of social and democratic reforms were introduced. The First World War resulted in a major loss of life and seriously weakened the economy, which took time to recover. During the Second World War, Britain again made a major war effort at great cost to the economy, although helped later by the United States. In 1945, the newly elected Labour government carried out a large-scale policy of nationalisation and social reform. In the post-war years Britain followed a policy of granting independence to the majority of its former colonies, although most remained within the British Commonwealth. The period of prosperity enjoyed in the 1950s and 60s gave way to inflation and high unemployment. The Conservative party has been in power since 1979 and has followed a monetarist policy with denationalisation and curbing government spending.

There has been a decline of traditional industries such as shipping, steel, textiles and coal, and the regions where these were concentrated suffer heavy unemployment. The chemical and electronic industries have expanded and the south-east region is more prosperous. North Sea oil and gas, and service industries offset the trade deficit. Agriculture is intensive and still plays an economic role.

The population is 57 million, of which the majority are English (Anglo-Saxon) with large Celtic minorities, Welsh, Scots and Irish. There are sizeable West Indian and Asian communities in larger cities, as well as of Chinese, Cypriot, Arab and African origins. Apart from English, Welsh is spoken in Wales and Gaelic in Scotland and Ireland. Church of England Protestantism is the established church, while most other denominations and religions are represented. While London is the capital of the United Kingdom, Edinburgh is the Scottish capital, Cardiff is capital of Wales and Belfast capital of Northern Ireland.

The climate is mild and temperate, being greatly influenced by the Atlantic and Gulf Stream. Rainfall is heavier on the western coasts. The spring, from March to May, can be cool and wet, while summer, from June to September, can be warm. The weather is very changeable, although occasionally there are long spells of pleasant weather when a system of high pressure remains stationary over the British Isles. Depressions tracking east across the Atlantic bring strong SW winds, usually of gale force. The prevailing winds of summer are NE, although SW winds predominate throughout the year and this is also the direction of most gales. Strong tides make navigation around the British Isles particularly difficult.

Entry Regulations

Ports of entry

The following ports have Customs offices, which should be contacted by telephone or radio telephone to advise Customs of a yacht's arrival and to request pratique.

* These numbers are of Customs offices which should be contacted by radiotelephone.

† Free telephone calls can be made to these Customs offices from telephones ashore dialling 100 and asking for FREEFONE CUSTOMS YACHTS.

Aberdeen (0224 586-258*), Ardrossan (0294 63017), Avonmouth† (0272 826451*), Ayr (0292 262088*), Barnstaple† (see Plymouth*), Barrow (0229 27104*), Barry (see Cardiff), Beaulieu (see Lymington), Berwick (0289 307547*), Blyth (0670 361521*), Boston† (0205 63070/63080*), Bradwell† (see Ispwich*), Brightlingsea† (see Ipswich*), Brighton† (see Southampton*), Bristol (see Avonmouth*), Brixham† (see Plymouth*), Buckie (0542 32254), Burham-on-Crouch† (see Ipswich*), Burnham-on-Sea (see Bridgwater*), Campbeltown (0586 52261), Cardiff† (0222 399123*), Chatham† (see Dover*), Christchurch (see Lymington*), Colchester† (see Ipswich*), Combwitch (see Bridgwater or Watchet*), Corpach (see Fort William*), Dartmouth† (see Southampton*), Dover† (0304 202441*), Dundee (0382 22412), Edinburgh (031 554 2421), Elgin (0343 7518), Ellesmere Port† (see Liverpool*), Exmouth† (see Plymouth*), Falmouth† (see Plymouth*), Faversham† (see Dover*), Felixstowe† (see Ipswich*), Fishguard† (see Cardiff*), Fleetwood† (03917 79211*), Folkestone† (see Dover*), Fort William (0397 2948), Fowey† (see Plymouth*), Fraserburgh (0346 28033 or Peterhead 0779 74867), Glasgow (041 445 1364), Glasson Dock (see Heysham*), Goole† (0405 4112*), Gravesend (London Port)† (see London*), Great Yarmouth† (see Ipswich*), Greenock (0475 28311), Grimsby† (0472 45441*), Hamble†(see Southampton*), Hartlepool (0429 63131), Harwich† (see Ipswich*), Heysham† (see Liverpool*), Holyhead† (0407 2714*), Hoylake (see Liverpool*), Hull† (0482 796161*), Immingham† (0469 74748*), Invergordon (0349 852221), Inverness(0463 231608), Ipswich† (0473 219481*), Itchenor† (see Southampton*), King's Lynn† (see Ipswich*), Kirkcudbright (see Stranraer*), Kirkwall (0856 2473*), Lancaster (see Heysham*), Larne† (0232 752511*), Lerwick (0595 4040*), Littlehampton (see Shoreham*), Liverpool† (051 933 4292*), London Port† (071 626 1515 ext. 5861/5864*), Lossiemouth (see

Elgin*), Lowestoft (see Great Yarmouth*), Lydney (see Sharpness*), Lymington† (see Southampton*), Macduff (0261 32217), Maldon† (see Ipswich*), Milford Haven† (see Pembroke*), Minehead (see Watchet*), Montrose (0674 74444/74469), Mostyn† (see Liverpool*), Newhaven† (see Southampton*), North Shields (0632 579441*), Oban (0631 63079*), Padstow† (see Plymouth*), Par (see Fowey*), Penzance† (see Plymouth*), Peterhead (0779 74867*), Plymouth† (0752 669811*), Poole† (see Southampton*), Porlock (see Watchet*), Port Edgar (Inverkeithing 0383 412475*), Portpatrick (see Stanraer*), Portsmouth† (see Southampton*), Preston (see Fleetwood*), Ramsgate† (see Dover*), Royal Docks (London Port, including St Katherine's Yacht Haven)† (see London*), Rye† (see Dover*), Salcombe† (see Plymouth*), Scarborough (0723 366631*), Scunthorpe† (0724 860404*), Sharpness† (0453 811302/811513*), Sheerness† (see Dover*), Shoreham† (see Southampton*), Silloth (see Workington*), Southampton† (0703 229251*), Southend-on-Sea† (0702 547141* or see London), Southport (see Liverpool*), Stranraer (0671 2718*), Sunderland (0783 657113*), Swansea† (see Cardiff*), Teignmouth† (see Plymouth*), Thames Haven (London Port)† (see London*), Tilbury Docks† (see London*), Torquay† (see Plymouth*), Trent (see Scunthorpe*), Walton-on-the-Naze† (see Ipswich*), Watchet† (see Plymouth*), Wells† (see Ipswich*), West Mersea (see Colchester*), Weston-super-Mare (see Avonmouth*), Weymouth† (see Plymouth*), Whitby (0830 1700 Monday to Friday, 0947 602074 other times see Scarborough), Whitehaven (see Workington*), Whitstable† (see Dover*), Wick (0955 3650*), Wisbech† (see Ipswich*), Woodbridge† (see Ipswich*), Workington (0900 4611*), Yarmouth, Isle of Wight. (see Cowes*).
Northern Ireland: Ardglass† (0232 752511*), Belfast† (0232 752511*), Coleraine† (0232-752511*), Kilkeel† (see Belfast*), Larne† (see Belfast*), Londonderry† (see Belfast*), Portavogie† (see Belfast*), Warrenpoint† (see Belfast*).
Isle of Wight: Cowes †(0703 229251*).
Isle of Man: Douglas (0624 74321*).
Orkney: Kirkwall (0856 2473*).
Shetlands: Lerwick (0595 4040*).
Isles of Scilly: St Marys (0720 22571*).
Isle of Lewis: Stornoway (0851 3626/3576).

Procedure on arrival

On entering UK territorial waters (12 miles offshore), the yellow Q flag must be flown until customs formalities have been completed. At night the flag should be illuminated. Failure to fly the flag is an offence and may lead to prosecution and a fine of up to £400. Yachts are liable to be searched by customs officers at any time while in UK territorial waters.

Yachts arriving from abroad, including the Channel Islands and the Republic of Ireland, must clear customs except as specified below under *UK Yachts*. All non-residents must also clear immigration when arriving from outside the UK, Channel Islands, Republic of Ireland or the Isle of Man. Often the customs officer will also complete immigration procedure. If there are animals or birds on board or any illness, health clearance must be obtained. The captain should contact the port health authority or local authority responsible for port health control by radio, 4 to 12 hours before arrival and if this is not possible immediately on arrival. Until health clearance is given no one except officials may board the vessel nor anyone leave. On arrival in a place where there is a customs house, the captain must notify customs in person or by telephone. Notification must be made within two hours of arrival, unless arriving between 2300 and 0600, when arrival need not be notifed until 0800 the following morning provided there are no birds or animals on board. Failure to notify the arrival within two hours is an offence and can lead to a fine of up to £400. If notifying by telephone, in some areas the freephone system can be used, elsewhere a message may have to be left on a telephone-answering machine, with the yacht name, time of arrival, location of the yacht and if there are animals on board. Radio telephones can be used to notify arrival while the yacht is still at sea. Freephone facilities (marked †) are only available on land. All persons must await clearance on board. Goods must not be landed until customs clearance is complete.

UK Yachts: UK-based yachts carrying UK residents, with no animals and no dutiable or VAT liable goods on board who have departed the UK less than one year previously and are returning from an EC country do not have to report to Customs. The captain should deliver the completed section of the form obtained on departure from the UK to the customs office on arrival, or post it in a post office box or customs post box. The form should be completed before entering UK territorial waters (12 miles).

Foreign Yachts: For non UK-based yachts clearance by customs entails completing form C1329, reporting the yacht's arrival, making a temporary importation declaration, and a declaration of all goods for all persons on board. Part of this form must be retained for obtaining outward clearance. On arrival, all dutiable goods must be declared including tobacco and alcoholic drinks.

Departure: Part II of form C1329 must be returned to the customs office in the place of departure, having filled in the Notice of Intended Departure. This may be given personally or deposited in a customs post box or posted in a post office box and addressed to the customs office for the port from which the yacht is about to depart. The form should arrive at customs before the expected time of departure, preferably up to 48 hours before.

Non-residents must clear immigration before departure, unless going to the Channel Islands, Republic of Ireland or the Isle of Man.

Customs
Firearms and ammunition, including gas pistols and similar weapons, may not be imported.

Animals and birds must be restrained at all times, and kept confined below deck. They must not come into contact with other animals or be landed. Animals and birds may not be imported into the UK without a licence. All animals will be placed in quarantine for six months at the owner's expense, immediately on arrival. The landing of a cat, dog or other rabies-susceptible animal from the Republic of Ireland, Channel Islands or the Isle of Man is not restricted provided that if the animal originated from outside of those places, it has served its full quarantine period. If on leaving the UK one intends to return with the animal, a licence must be obtained from the Ministry of Agriculture, Fisheries and Food before departure allowing the animal or bird to land at certain designated ports before entering quarantine.

Prohibited imports include meat, poultry and many other animal products; plants and produce, including potatoes and certain other fruit and vegetables; certain articles made from endangered species including fur, ivory and reptile leather.

Radio transmitters, such as portable VHF radios, which are not approved for use in the UK, may not be operated.

Duty and Value Added Tax (VAT)
Duty and VAT are payable on stores in excess of personal duty-free allowances. These will either be sealed on board and the seal not broken until departure from UK waters, or released on payment of duty, or put into bond until re-exportation arrangements are made or duty paid.

If a yacht is laid up in UK waters any dutiable, taxable stores remaining must be paid for, or placed in bond. Sometimes the stores can be sealed on board and a refundable deposit paid.

Temporary importation
Private yachts may be temporarily imported duty-free by a visitor to the UK, provided that the importer is not

resident in the UK, that the yacht is exported when the importer next leaves the UK, or when the yacht has been in the UK for up to a total of six months in any 12 month period. Only the importer or person authorised can use the yacht and the yacht must not be lent, hired or sold in the UK. Equipment and spare parts for a temporarily imported vessel may also be imported duty-free. The local customs office should be contacted for details.

In theory all yachts are liable for VAT on importation. There are various exemptions and conditions pertaining to this and also to the exemption from VAT of yachts purchased in the UK for export. Full details can be found in two booklets published by Her Majesty's Customs & Excise, 'Notice to Owners and Persons responsible for Pleasure Craft not based in the United Kingdom' (8A) and 'Notice to Owners and Persons Responsible for Pleasure Craft based in the United Kingdom' (8).

Departure

Duty-free goods may be loaded on board if prior application is made. Further details on shipping stores or to re-ship previously landed surplus duty-free stores may be obtained from local customs offices. Stores shipped under bond, or on which repayment of customs dues is claimed, may be sealed on board, not to be used until out of UK waters.

VAT chargeable goods may be zero-rated when supplied as stores for foreign-going vessels, provided that orders are given in writing, the goods are delivered direct to the vessel and a receipt for the goods is given to the supplier.

Immigration

Nationals of EC countries do not need a visa for up to three months stay. Visas are not required for nationals of Commonwealth countries, except for Bangladesh, Ghana, India, Nigeria, Sri Lanka and Pakistan who require visas. Nationals of all European countries do not require visas except for Albania, Bulgaria, Czechoslovakia, Hungary, Poland, Romania, Turkey and the USSR. Nationals of all Asian, African and American countries do not require visas except for Bahrain, Cuba, Haiti, Israel, Ivory Coast, Japan, Kuwait, South Korea, Niger, Quatar, South Africa, and the UAE. Visas must be obtained in advance from a British embassy or consulate. Persons requiring visas who arrive in the UK without one will be refused entry. Permission to enter is at the discretion of the immigration officer at the point of entry – he has the power to refuse entry even if one has a visa, although for those on a tourist visit with sufficient funds for their stay, entry is normally straightforward.

Argentinian nationals no longer require visas.

Facilities

Provisioning is good throughout the country. Fuel is available in most ports. LPG containers of non-UK standard are difficult to refill and for longer stays it is advisable to change over to the British (Calor gas) type bottles. Camping Gaz is widely available in camping and hardware stores. Marine supplies are also widely available with the best stocked chandleries being concentrated on the south coast and in London. Charts and marine publications are stocked by all major chandleries.

Mooring facilities vary both in quality and availability. In some of the fishing and commercial harbours these can be very basic. Not all yacht clubs have their own moorings, but when they do a place can usually be found for a visiting member of an overseas club. There are nearly 150 purpose-built marinas scattered about the coasts of Great Britain and Northern Ireland. Starting in 1991, all marinas will operate on VHF Channel 80, which is monitored during normal working hours. Most marinas keep a number of berths for visiting yachts. Many have chandleries and also repair facilities, as well as slipways or travelifts. The most comprehensive range of repair facilities is to be found in the area between Southampton and Portsmouth where the biggest names in the British yachting industry are concentrated. It has been said that whatever cannot be fixed there probably cannot be fixed anywhere else in the world.

Further Reading

East Coast Pilot Guide from Ramsgate to the Wash
Solent (Selsey Bill to Needles)
Scottish West Coast Pilot
South England Pilot (several volumes)
Shell Pilot to the English Channel, Vol. 1
Clyde Cruising Club: Sailing directions for Scotland,
Hebrides, Orkney and Shetland Islands (several volumes)
Bristol Channel and Severn Pilot
West Country Cruising
Yachtsman's Pilot to West Scotland (several volumes)
The West: A Sailing Companion to West Coast of Scotland
Channel Harbours and Anchorages
Cruising Association Handbook
North Sea Passage Pilot

4 West Africa and South Atlantic Islands

With the exception of Senegal and the Gambia, the west coast of Africa is largely bypassed by cruising yachts and hardly any venture south of the Ivory Coast. This is the main reason why none of the countries between the Gulf of Guinea and Namibia were included in this book, but also because it was felt that for the time being most of those countries are best avoided. According to reports received from commercial ships as well as travellers in the region, the conditions that prevail in those countries, the cases of piracy, corruption, crime and diseases, as well as the total lack of facilities, should deter anyone from visiting them, particularly as by yacht one is more vulnerable than if travelling in an organised group. However, for a taste of West Africa, no place is better suited to explore by yacht than Senegal and the Gambia, whose rivers and estuaries provide an excellent cruising ground without the dangers and difficulties associated with the countries lying further south.

A completely different picture awaits the sailor at the southern tip of the continent where great changes are underway. After many years of isolation, South Africa may soon rejoin the international fold, while its former dependency, Namibia, has recently joined the ranks of independent nations. For the adventurous sailor, the islands of the South Atlantic are interesting destinations each in its own particular fashion. St Helena and Ascension have a long history of being welcome stops on the trade wind route to the equator, whereas the main attraction of Tristan da Cunha and the Falkland Islands is their very remoteness. With the exception of South Africa, where Durban and Cape Town have yachting facilities of international standards, facilities in all other places in the region are either limited or non-existent.

ASCENSION ISLAND

A mountainous peak rising over 3000 metres (9840 ft) from the floor of the Atlantic Ocean, Ascension is a dormant volcanic island like Tristan da Cunha and the Azores on the mid-Atlantic volcanic ridge. Lava flows have formed a barren twisted landscape. The 34 square mile island is a communications centre for Cable & Wireless, the BBC, NASA and the US Air Force. As a traditional port of call for ships on the Cape of Good Hope route, the few yachts that sail on this route sometimes stop at Ascension although they are not encouraged to do so. Only a brief stop is allowed by the authorities, who obviously resent the intrusion and wish to see these uninvited guests on their way as quickly as possible. Apart from being a useful stop in an emergency, as well as a break on a long passage, Ascension holds few attractions. The anchorage is uncomfortable, provisions are hard to come by and there is little to see ashore except satellite dishes and huge antennas. One cannot even drown one's sorrows, as there are no pubs, bars or restaurants. A sad place for a sailor indeed.

Country Profile

The island was discovered in 1501, and visited on and off by sailors who took turtles and eggs for food, and left goats behind. Ascension became a well-known stopping point for ships, but was only settled in 1815, when Britain feared attempts to free Napoleon from St Helena. The settlement developed and labourers came from the Gold Coast as well as freed slaves. After Napoleon's death in 1821, the island was used as a naval supply base and convalescent home for sailors. At the end of the century the Eastern Telegraph Company, now Cable & Wireless, landed a submarine cable, which marked the end of the island's isolation from the outside world. Ascension had been administered by the British Navy, but in 1922 St Helena took over this administration, while Eastern Telegraph took control on behalf of St Helena. The Americans arrived in 1942 to fortify this unprotected vital communications centre, and constructed the Wideawake Airfield, named after the thousands of wideawake terns which settle there for breeding. During the Second World War planes refuelled here on the route from Brazil to Africa. In the 1950s the United States established a missile tracking station and a NASA earth station, which tracked the Apollo missions.

Communications projects are the dominant factor in the economy. St Helenians come to Ascension to work. Income also comes from the sale of stamps. The water supply is always a concern, due to the low annual rainfall and since 1967 distilled water has been used. The main language of the 300 inhabitants is English and Georgetown is the capital.

The climate is tropical, hot and dry. The island is under the influence of the SE trade winds for most of the year.

Entry Regulations

Ports of entry
Clarence Bay, Georgetown 7°56'S 14°25'W.

Procedure on arrival
Yachts should anchor in the area north of the Pierhead, in a position which does not obstruct ships arriving, departing or unloading cargo. Yachts must not tie up to any buoy or mooring in Clarence Bay. Landing is

Map 6: West Africa and the South Atlantic Islands

Practical Information

LOCAL TIME: GMT

BUOYAGE: IALA A

CURRENCY: St Helenian pound (£) of 100 pence

BUSINESS HOURS
Government offices: 0800–1630 Monday to Saturday.

ELECTRICITY: 240 V, 50 Hz

PUBLIC HOLIDAYS
1 January: New Year's Day
Good Friday and Easter Monday
Ascension Day
Queen's Birthday
Whit Monday
August Bank Holiday
25, 26 December: Christmas

COMMUNICATIONS
Cable & Wireless office for international calls.
Only military aircraft use the airport, mostly belonging to the US Air Force. Civilian passengers are only taken in a serious emergency with the approval of the military authorities.

MEDICAL
There is a hospital with limited facilities.

permitted only at Pierhead steps. No advance notice is required of arrival, but at the earliest opportunity the captain must report to the Police Office, who also act as immigration officials, with the yacht's details, crew list and passports. This must be done within working hours, as no yachts are attended to outside of normal working hours. The crew must wait on board if a yacht arrives outside of these hours.

Crew may not leave a yacht at Ascension.

It is not allowed to clear out on the day before departure, so one should plan on leaving on a normal working day.

Customs

Firearms must remain on board. Animals must remain on board and are not allowed ashore.

Immigration

A landing permit is issued on arrival and no visas are needed.

Yachts may normally only stay 48 hours. The crew may come ashore between 0700–1900, unless they have a special police pass to stay until 2300. No one may stay ashore overnight.

In exceptional circumstances, if for example repairs need to be done, yachts may stay up to a maximum of 72 hours.

Immigration will hold passports until departure.

Health

Yellow fever vaccination certificates are required if coming from some African countries.

Fees

There is an immigration fee.

Medical insurance must be taken out at £3 per day. Personal insurance cover already held will not be accepted.

There is a landing fee of £5 per person and £2.50 for children under 15.

Restrictions

Yachts are not allowed to anchor anywhere except Clarence Bay.

Facilities

There are no public bars, cafes, restaurants, nor public transport or taxis on the island. Fresh produce and other provisions are sometimes in short supply and may not be available for yachts even if on sale to the islanders. Water can be scarce at times, so it may not be freely available. Only minor repairs can be effected, although in a serious emergency one may be able to enlist the help of the military who operate some workshops.

Further Reading

St Helena including Ascension Island and Tristan da Cunha

FALKLAND ISLANDS

The Falkland Islands, also known as Islas Malvinas, are a British colony in the South Atlantic. The archipelago is made up of two groups of over 700 islands, East Falkland (Isla Soledad) and its adjacent islands, and West Falkland (Gran Malvina). The islands lie about 480 miles north-east of Cape Horn. Port Stanley is the main town, where most people live, and the rest of the country is called the 'camp'.

The Falklands used to be an important port of call for sailing ships on the Cape Horn route and the hulks of abandoned square riggers scattered around Port Stanley harbour bear silent witness to that glorious era and its magnificent ships. Some of them, such as

Practical Information

LOCAL TIME: GMT - 4

BUOYAGE: IALA A

CURRENCY: Falklands pound (£). This is not legal tender in the UK, but pounds sterling can be used in the Falklands. Money can be exchanged at the Standard Chartered Bank, Ross Road, Port Stanley. Falklands £s cannot be changed for sterling or other currencies outside of the islands. One can cash personal British cheques with a cheque guarantee card, but credit cards cannot be used.

BUSINESS HOURS
Government offices: 0800–1200, 1315–1630.

ELECTRICITY: 240 V, 50 Hz

PUBLIC HOLIDAYS
1 January: New Year's Day
Good Friday
Queen's Birthday
14 June: Liberation Day
October Bank Holiday
Anniversary of the Battle of the Falkland Islands
25, 26 December: Christmas

COMMUNICATIONS
Cable & Wireless for international telephone calls, telegrams and telex. The Town Hall, Ross Road, houses the post office and government offices. Other government offices are in the nearby Secretariat.
There are two RAF Tristar flights a week from Britain via Ascension Island.

MEDICAL
There is a good hospital at Port Stanley.

Jhelum and *Charles Cooper*, have been there for a century, while the *Vicar of Bray* is the last survivor of the California Gold Rush fleet. The Falklands' traditional role as a convenient stop for reprovisioning has been resuscitated in the last few years by modern yachts, some sailing the classic Cape Horn route, but most being on their way to or from the Straits of Magellan, Tierra del Fuego and the Chilean canals, which are becoming an increasingly popular cruising destination. Only a few have sufficient time to stop long enough in the Falklands to cruise these wild and windswept islands. Although access is restricted in some areas, either for military reasons or because some islands are nature reserves, most of the islands can be visited and a glimpse caught of their spectacular wildlife with large colonies of penguins, sea lions and elephant seals. The weather is the greatest impediment to cruising, as it can change rapidly and without warning, but there are many protected anchorages, so that one is never too far from shelter.

Country Profile

The first recognised sighting of the islands was in 1598 by a Dutchman. At the end of the seventeenth century the Englishman Strong landed, and named Falkland Sound. French seafarers christened the islands Iles Malouines after their homeport St Malo and later under Spanish influence the name became Islas Malvinas. In the eighteenth century France established a small colony at Port Louis, which two years later was ceded to Spain. The island became a penal colony and a military garrison was stationed there. At the same time Britain established an outpost on Saunders Island, West Falkland, which was expelled in 1770 by Spain,

restored after the threat of war, but then later abandoned. During the South American wars of independence at the start of the nineteenth century, Spain also left the islands. Authority was re-established in 1820, when the United Provinces of the River Plate, later to become Argentina, claimed Port Louis. This settlement was destroyed by a US warship after the colonists arrested some American sealers. The Argentinian force was expelled by Britain, and the islands then became a dependency of Britain until the Argentines, still laying claim to the islands, invaded in April 1982. After a brief conflict Britain recaptured the islands. Recently relations between the two countries have been improving, although Argentina has not formally given up her claim.

In 1986 a 150 mile fisheries protection zone was declared and licence fees from Asian and European fleets have quadrupled the islands' revenue. Improvements have been made in education, infrastructure and social benefits. Aid from Britain is important. The land is devoted to sheep grazing, the wool being exported to the UK. A British military force of about 2000 personnel has been stationed on the islands since the war.

The 1900 inhabitants are of British origin, about two-thirds being born in the Falklands. English is the only language.

The climate is temperate, although changeable. Westerlies are frequent, often strong, and their yearly average is 17 knots. Summer winds are more northerly in direction and this is also where the worst gales come from, usually with very little warning. Another local phenomenon occurring during strong westerly winds are the willywaws, violent gusts of wind which are felt in the lee of the islands and in some of the passages between them.

Entry Regulations

Ports of entry
Port Stanley 51°39′S 57°43′W.

Procedure on arrival
Port Stanley: One should report one's ETA in advance to the authorities on VHF Channel 12. All yachts must enter at Port Stanley, where clearance formalities are completed. Yachts anchor in the inner harbour, but to clear in it is usually possible to come alongside the wharf. The yacht will be inspected by officials and the captain notified of prohibited areas within the Falklands.

Fox Bay East: This is a port of entry for vessels over 50 tons and certain restrictions apply to yachts intending to clear there. The authorities insist that anyone intending to clear at Fox Bay must give at least one week's notice. Vessels clearing in at Fox Bay must also bear the cost of return fares for customs officials to fly out from Port Stanley.

Customs
Firearms must be declared to authorities, but may be kept on board.

Animals must remain on board, unless quarantined ashore with permission of the Veterinary Department.

Immigration
The following nationalities do not need visas: EC countries, Australia, Andorra, Austria, Canada, Cyprus, Finland, Iceland, Israel, Japan, Liechtenstein, Malta, New Zealand, Norway, San Marino, Sweden, Switzerland, the USA, Uruguay and dependencies of the UK.

At the time of writing Argentinian yachts are not allowed entry. Yachts of any flag arriving from Argentina should not have Argentinians on board. However, travel restrictions for Argentinians are changing and the current situation should be checked with a British Embassy.

Yachts may stay up to 30 days, unless given permission by the harbour master to stay longer.

Fees
Harbour dues are paid for an initial one-month period and are £40 for yachts under 15 tons, £150 for yachts 15–50 tons.

Entry fee £20, clearance fee £20, pilot fee £35 (£15 paid to pilot).

Overtime is charged outside of working hours; customs have a minimum 2 hour charge: £15 per hour, £25 per hour from midnight to 0600, £30 per hour Saturday, Sunday and public holidays.

Minefields
These are left from the 1982 war, but are clearly marked and fenced off. They are mainly areas around Port Stanley, Port Howard, Fox Bay and Fitzroy.

Facilities

Provisioning is good, as the local shops are well stocked and there is also some fresh produce grown locally. Fuel and water are available. The Falkland Islands Company has a 60-ton slip and can do some repairs. There is also a government slip. Some provisions, mainly locally grown vegetables and meat, may be obtained in the other settlements. There are also some facilities in Fox Bay East, on West Falkland.

Further Reading

Falkland Island Shores
South American Handbook

THE GAMBIA

Surrounded on all sides by Senegal with only a narrow outlet to the Atlantic Ocean, The Gambia is a thin ribbon of land stretching along the Gambia river. The 300-mile long river is the heart of this small country, which rarely exceeds 20 miles in width. The river can be navigated for a long distance inland, which a few yachts have done in recent years. The bird and wildlife is prolific and there are many villages along the river banks, where it is possible to stop and barter for food.

For the ordinary tourist The Gambia's prime attraction are the vast stretches of undeveloped beaches, while upriver is the much visited village of Juffure, from where the main character in the *Roots* book was abducted and taken as a slave to America. Other interesting sites are the Abuko nature reserve and the Wassau burial sites, whose huge stone columns are said to be at least 1200 years old.

Country Profile

The region has been inhabited at least since AD 750. Islam was introduced during the time when it was part of the empire of Mali. The Portuguese were the first European visitors in 1455 and they introduced groundnuts and cotton. In the sixteenth and seventeenth centuries England established a garrison and slaving post at Fort James, while France had a trading

Practical Information

LOCAL TIME: GMT

BUOYAGE: IALA A

CURRENCY: Gambian dalasi (GAD) of 100 bututs. Certain African currencies cannot be exchanged. All foreign currency must be declared on arrival.

BUSINESS HOURS
Banks: 0800–1300 Monday to Thursday, 0800–1100 Friday, Saturday.
Business: 0800/0900–1500 Monday to Thursday (closed for lunch), 0800/0900–1300 Friday, Saturday.
Shops: 0800/0900–1200, 1400–1700 Monday to Thursday, 0800/0900–1300 Friday, Saturday.
Government offices: 0800–1500 Monday to Thursday, 0800–1300 Friday, Saturday.

ELECTRICITY: 220 V, 50 Hz

PUBLIC HOLIDAYS
1 January: New Year's Day
18 February: Independence Day
Good Friday, Easter Monday
Eid el-Fitr
1 May: Labour Day
Eid el-Adha
15 August: Assumption
Mouloud
25, 26 December: Christmas

COMMUNICATIONS
Cable & Wireless: Mercury House, Telegraph Road, Banjul for telephone calls and telex. Telephone calls also from Gamtel Company. The telephone network connects through operators to the Senegalese network.
Post office: 0800–1300 Monday to Friday, 0800–1100 Saturday.

There are regular flights to London and African cities, plus charter flights to European destinations from November to April.

MEDICAL
Royal Victoria Hospital
Westfield Clinic (private)
German Clinic, Pipeline Road

DIPLOMATIC MISSIONS
In Banjul:
Senegal: Buckle Street.
United Kingdom: 48 Atlantic Road, Fajara. ☎ 95133.
United States: Pipeline Road, Fajara. ☎ 932856.
Also represented are France, Germany and Mauritania (a letter of recommendation from one's own embassy is needed if applying for a Mauritanian visa).

post across the river. There was rivalry between them for slaves, ivory and gold and eventually The Gambia was awarded to Britain in the Treaty of Versailles at the end of the eighteenth century. Slavery was abolished in 1807, and British ships patrolled the coast trying to enforce the ban. The Gambia was administered from Sierra Leone until 1888 when it became a British Crown Colony. Very little was done by Britain to develop the country.

Independence was gained in 1965 and The Gambia became a republic seven years later. There was a military coup in 1981, but this was ousted with the aid of Senegalese troops. A Confederation called Senegambia lasted from 1982 to 1989. The Gambia has some economic problems, but is politically stable.

The economy depends on groundnuts, which are the main crop, and efforts to diversify have not been very successful. Tourism brings some income. There is a large trade deficit.

The population is 800,000 and the land is densely populated. The Mandinka are descendants of rulers of the old Mali empire and live mostly inland, while the Wolof live mainly in Banjul. There are also Fulani and ten other ethnic groups. Most of the population are Muslim, with some Animist and Christian minorities. English is the official language, but Mandinka, Fula, Wolof, Jola and Serahule are also spoken.

Originally called Bathurst, Banjul the capital was founded in 1816 on the tip of the peninsula at the river mouth, which is in fact an island.

The climate is tropical with two distinct seasons. The dry and more pleasant weather is from November until May, while the remainder is the wet season. The hottest months are from February to May. The winds are variable throughout the year, with the strongest winds in September and October.

Entry Regulations

Ports of entry
Banjul 13°27′N 16°34′W.

Procedure on arrival
The average depth in the channel is 30 ft (9 metres). Vessels should keep all buoys to starboard when entering. Port Control keeps a continuous watch on VHF Channel 16 on weekdays and should be contacted prior to arrival. If arriving after 1300 on Friday, one will have to wait until the following Monday to clear.

Yachts normally proceed to the government wharf for inspection by the various officials, but this can only be done at high tide, as the wharf almost dries out at low tide. The captain should then visit the harbour master at the Port Authority building in Wellington Street, then immigration in Anglesea Street, customs and finally health. Although the officials are very friendly, the formalities tend to be time-consuming. It has been recommended to hire a taxi and guide to do the rounds of the various offices.

Customs
Firearms and animals must be declared.

Immigration
For a stay of up to three months no visas are required from nationals of Commonwealth countries, members of the Economic Community of West African States, Belgium, Denmark, Germany, Greece, Italy, Ireland, Spain, Finland, Iceland, Norway, Netherlands, Senegal, Sweden, Tunisia, Turkey and Uruguay. Normally seven days are granted on arrival and this can be extended to up to three months at the Immigration Office, Anglesea and Dobson Street, Banjul. Other nationals including citizens of the United States and Japan must obtain visas in advance.

British embassies issue Gambian visas in countries with no Gambian representative. The British embassy in Dakar issues visas the same day.

Health
Yellow fever vaccination is required and malaria prophylaxis recommended.

Facilities

There is good provisioning in Banjul, where there are several supermarkets. Fresh produce is also available. Fuel is available in the harbour from the Con Oil fuel barge. Some repairs can be made at the shipyard run by the port authority which also has a slipway. The Gambia Sailing Club in Banjul has some sailing enthusiasts who organise regular races and will help visitors if needed.

Further Reading

Africa on a Shoestring
West Africa, A Travel Survival Kit

IVORY COAST

The Ivory Coast or La Côte d'Ivoire lies on the northern shore of the Gulf of Guinea in West Africa. Until not long ago it was regarded as the most stable regime in the region and has tried to build up its tourism as an alternative to the agriculture-dominated economy. The capital Abidjan is a pleasant modern city and most yachts who visit the Ivory Coast rarely go anywhere else, apparently content with Abidjan's transplanted French ambience.

Country Profile

As the European colonial powers extended their influence throughout Africa and especially along the coast, France became interested in establishing a trade monopoly in this region and therefore signed treaties with several local chiefs, giving France the right to trade freely in the area. Towards the end of the nineteenth century France took outright control of the region. A cash crop economy was rapidly established and the local inhabitants were used as labour on the predominantly French-owned plantations.

After the Second World War discontent grew amongst the Ivorians, who demanded a greater say in local administration, and 1948–9 saw violent demonstrations, which were repressed by the French authorities. Independence was finally achieved in 1960, under the Presidency of Felix Houphouet-Boigny, a founder member of the independence movement. France has remained quite involved with the Ivorian economy, and until the mid-1980s many French expatriates worked there, but these have been gradually replaced with Ivorians. Government efforts to introduce austerity measures have led recently to widespread discontent and an attempted coup.

The population is 10.5 million, composed of over 60 tribes, the main one being the Baoulé. There are also many expatriate workers from neighbouring African states, as well as France and Lebanon. French is the official language and also spoken are five main African languages, among them Dioula, Baoulé and Bete. The majority of the population follow traditional beliefs, while a quarter are Muslim and 16 per cent Christian. Abidjan is still the commercial capital and main port, but the political capital since 1986 has been the former village of Yamoussoukro, the birthplace of President Houphouet-Boigny.

The climate in the south of the country is hot and humid with a high rainfall. The north is drier, November to April being the dry season and May to October the rainy season. October to May is the most pleasant time. The winds are light throughout the year, the prevailing winds being SSW Force 2 to 3. The weather has been described as perfect for all year round sailing.

Entry Regulations

Ports of entry
Abidjan 5°18′N 4°00′W.

Practical Information (Ivory Coast)

LOCAL TIME: GMT

BUOYAGE: IALA A

CURRENCY: West African franc (CFA). A maximum of CFA 20,000 may be exported.

BUSINESS HOURS
Banks: 0800–1130, 1430–1630 Monday to Friday.
Shops: 0800–1200, 1430–1830 Monday to Friday, close 1730 on Saturdays.
Government offices: 0800–1200 Monday to Saturday, 1430–1700 Monday to Friday.

ELECTRICITY: 220 V, 50 Hz

PUBLIC HOLIDAYS
1 January: New Year's Day
Easter Monday
1 May: Labour Day
Ascension
Whit Monday
Korite (end of Ramadan)
15 August: Assumption
Tabaski (Eid el Kebir)
1 November: All Saints
7 December: National Day
25 December: Christmas Day

COMMUNICATIONS
The main post office (PTT) is by the railway station in Le Plateau, Abidjan. The international airport at Abidjan has regular flights to several European and African cities.

DIPLOMATIC MISSIONS
In Abidjan:
Canada: Immeuble Trade Center, 23 Avenue Nogues, Le Plateau, CP4101. ☎ 322009.
United Kingdom: 3rd floor, Immeuble Les Harmonies, Boulevard Carde and Avenue Dr Jamot, Le Plateau. ☎ 226850.
United States: 5 Rue Jesse Owens. ☎ 320979.

Procedure on arrival

Yachts should try and come to the main dock to clear customs and immigration. If there is no space, yachts normally anchor at Carena, close to the centre of town, or at the local yacht club (Centre de Voile Abidjanaise).

Customs

Firearms and animals must be declared.

Immigration

No visas are required for a stay up to three months for nationals of Belgium, Denmark, Finland, France, Germany, Italy, Luxembourg, Norway, Netherlands, Sweden, United Kingdom and francophone African states. All other nationals need visas.

There are Ivorian representatives in Paris, Dakar, Rabat, Algiers and Tunis.

Health

Yellow fever, cholera vaccinations and malaria prophylaxis are recommended.

Facilities

Although yachting facilities are virtually non-existent, the local yacht club welcomes visitors and may be able to help in an emergency. There are various workshops in the industrial zone south of the city. Provisioning is good and if anchored off the yacht club, it is a short walk to Gare Lagunaire, from where a ferry goes to the shopping centre. Fresh produce is best at the central market in Treichville, which is the African part of

Abidjan, as opposed to Le Plateau which is more French.

Apart from the anchorage off the yacht club, there is also good shelter in the lagoon, which can be navigated for a long distance but only by shallow drafted yachts, as the depths are less than 4 ft (1.20 metres).

Limited facilities are available at Grand Lahou, which has a small boat club at the end of a long inlet. Provisions are available and also some repairs at a workshop, which also does welding. Minimal facilities only are available at Sassandra and Grand Bassam, the former colonial capital.

Further Reading

West Africa, A Travel Survival Kit

MAURITANIA

Stretching along the west coast of Africa between Morocco and Senegal, a large part of Mauritania is the Sahara Desert. The republic is based on an Islamic socialist constitution and a traditional Muslim society, and does not particularly encourage tourism. Its long coastline has very few natural harbours and the never-ending sandy beaches are its most remarkable feature. For those in search of solitude this might be sufficient attraction, but otherwise the country has very little to offer the cruising sailor.

Practical Information

LOCAL TIME: GMT

BUOYAGE: IALA A

CURRENCY: Ouguiya of 5 khoums. The import and export of local currency is forbidden. The ouguiya is pegged to the West African franc (CFA). Foreign currency must be declared on arrival. Ouguiyas cannot be exchanged outside Mauritania.

BUSINESS HOURS
Working hours: 0800–1200, 1400–1600/1800. Closed Fridays. Banks: 0730–1430 Sunday to Wednesday.

ELECTRICITY: 220 V, 50 Hz

PUBLIC HOLIDAYS
1 January: New Year's Day
26 February
1 May: Labour Day
25 May: Africa Liberation Day
28 November: Independence Day
Also variable holidays: Mouloud, Korite (end of Ramadan), Tabaski (Eid el Kebir), First Moharem.

COMMUNICATIONS
There are regular flights from Nouakchott to Las Palmas de Gran Canaria, Casablanca and Paris. Flights from Nouadhibou also go to Las Palmas and Casablanca as well as to Budapest and Moscow.

MEDICAL
There is a hospital in Nouakchott.

DIPLOMATIC MISSIONS
United States: BP222, Nouakchott, ☎ 52660.
There is also a French embassy, where visas for Senegal can be obtained as there is no Senegalese mission in Nouakchott.

Country Profile

Mauritania once enjoyed some prosperity, lying on the trade route between the Maghreb and West Africa. During the nineteenth century the country was added to France's large colonial possessions in West and Central Africa.

Independence from France was gained in 1960 when French West Africa was broken up. When Spain abandoned its colony in the Western Sahara, Mauritania divided the region with Morocco, but the burden of war with the Polisario guerillas seeking independence for the region led to the abandonment of Mauritania's claims to the Western Sahara, although Morocco continues occupation.

The production of iron ore for export is the mainstay of the economy, although efforts have been made to diversify. Foreign aid remains important and much food is imported. With the exception of the iron mines, the country is very undeveloped and many people still lead an existence bordering on the primitive. Slavery was only officially abolished in 1980 and a rigid feudal system still survives in remote communities.

There are 2 million inhabitants, being Moors and African. Ethnic conflict is an ongoing problem between 'white' and 'black' Moors and the Africans. Arabic and French are the official languages and some local languages are also spoken. The majority of the population are Muslim. The capital is Nouakchott, situated north of the port.

Most of the land has a harsh desert climate. The climate is better along the coast where the prevailing winds are northerly. The rainy season is from July to September, when it sometimes rains heavily. A strong swell is often felt along the coast from January to March.

Entry Regulations

Ports of entry
Nouadhibou 20°54′N 17°03′W, Nouakchott 18°02′N 16°02′W.

Procedure on arrival
Nouadhibou: This is the main commercial port. The port authority (Etablissement Maritime) should be contacted on arrival on VHF Channel 16 for instructions. There is an inner quay where a yacht can come alongside for clearance. The yacht may be searched.
Nouakchott: The port authority (Etablissement Maritime) should be contacted on VHF Channel 16. The main wharf in the port is some four miles south of the capital. This port is not protected in bad weather and if there is too much swell, a boat should put to sea.

Customs
Firearms and animals must be declared.

Immigration
Visas are required by all nationals except the French.
There are Mauritanian representatives in Paris, Algiers, Dakar, Rabat and Las Palmas.

Health
Yellow fever vaccination is required.

Facilities

The only repair facilities available are at Nouakchott where there is a shipyard which may take on work on a yacht in an emergency. Fuel is available in both ports and also some basic provisioning. Water should be treated.

Further Reading

Africa on a Shoestring

NAMIBIA

The latest country in Africa to gain independence, Namibia lies on the south-west coast of the continent and as a German colony used to be known as South West Africa. The easternmost area is part of the Kalahari desert, while the Namib desert stretches along the west coast. Most of the coast is inhospitable desert, but inland are many national parks and unusual dramatic scenery.

Yachts sailing this part of the Atlantic usually stop at Luderitz, an old German colonial town surrounded by the encroaching Namib desert. It is a convenient stop on the way north from Cape Town. The winds are usually favourable and so is the Benguela current, which sweeps up the western coast. The detour shortens the distance to St Helena and, if time permits, also gives a chance to visit some of the interior of this fascinating country, which was for so long in the grip of a guerilla war.

Country Profile

The Portuguese were the first Europeans to sail along the Namibian coast in the fifteenth century on their way around the Cape of Good Hope. Other sailors to pass this way were American whalers in the late eighteenth century. Only at the end of the nineteenth century was a more permanent interest shown when Namibia became a German colony, except for the Walvis Bay enclave which was annexed by Britain. The indigenous tribes fought to preserve their independence and rebelled early in the twentieth century. Repression was fierce and nearly all the Herero tribe were annihilated. Germany relinquished her colonies at the end of the First World War and South Africa was given a League of Nations Mandate to rule South West Africa, continued after the Second World War as a United Nations Mandate.

In the 1950s nationalism and opposition to South African rule grew. SWAPO (South West Africa People's Organisation) was formed in 1960 and mounted a guerrilla war against the South Africans, which gradually escalated. In 1966 the United Nations changed the country's name to Namibia and cancelled the Mandate, but the South African government continued to administer the country and industry was dominated by a white minority. Finally South Africa agreed to negotiations and eventually to withdraw from Namibia. Early in 1990 the Namibians held elections, voted for a black government and independence was gained. Namibia has since been accepted into the Commonwealth.

Namibia is rich in minerals, uranium, copper, lead, zinc and diamonds. Until independence these were mined by foreign multinational and South African companies. The economy has been severely affected by international sanctions, although the lifting of these should have a positive effect. The areas which have suffered most were fishing and agriculture, and prior to independence unemployment was high.

The population is 1,040,000, being mainly Bantu with a small white minority. Afrikaans and English were the official languages until independence. However, Bantu is the main language spoken with some German and Khoisan. The majority of the population are Christian.

The weather is usually hot, although it is milder on the coast. Rainfall is unreliable. Winds are mostly from

Practical Information

LOCAL TIME: GMT + 2

BUOYAGE: IALA A

CURRENCY: South African rand was still in use at the time of writing, but this is expected to change.

PUBLIC HOLIDAYS
1, 2 January: New Year
Good Friday, Easter Monday
1 May: Labour Day
Ascension
First Monday in September: Settlers Day
10 December: Human Rights Day
25, 26 December: Christmas

COMMUNICATIONS
There are flights from Luderitz and Walvis Bay to Cape Town.

DIPLOMATIC MISSIONS
These are to be established.

the south. The cold Benguela current produces misty conditions close to the coast and up to about 5 to 10 miles offshore.

Entry Regulations

Ports of entry
Luderitz 26°38'S 15°09'E, Walvis Bay 22°57'S 14°30'E.

Procedure on arrival
Luderitz: This is a safe harbour in all weathers and the approaches are straightforward. One should contact the harbour master or Dias Point Lighthouse on VHF Channel 16 asking permission to enter the harbour. If arriving at night it is best to raft up to one of the tugs until the morning. Yachts can come alongside the commercial wharf for clearance. Customs, immigration and the harbour master's office are on the quayside.

Immigration
Visas are not needed by citizens of Austria, Canada, France, Japan, Ireland, Italy, Nordic countries, United Kingdom, USA, USSR, and some African countries.

Facilities

In Luderitz the local yacht club welcomes visiting sailors and its facilities are available to visitors. Provisions are available from a selection of supermarkets and water and diesel fuel can be obtained in the harbour. There are some repair facilities here (the port is used by fishing boats working this area of the South Atlantic) and at Walvis Bay.

Further Reading

Africa on a Shoestring

ST HELENA

The island of St Helena lies halfway between Africa and South America, with her two dependencies of Ascension over 700 miles to the north-west and Tristan da Cunha 1500 miles to the south-west. St Helena has only one harbour called The Anchorage. The rest of the coast is towering rocky cliffs backed by green slopes climbing up to the summit of Mount

Acteon at 2683 feet (818 metres). St Helena became known all over the world when chosen as the place of exile of Napoleon Bonaparte, and Longwood House where he lived for six years is now a museum. One of Britain's last remaining colonial possessions, an English way of life mixes with the influence of the climate and origins of the inhabitants.

St Helena's popularity as a port of call for passenger liners has now been taken over by sailing yachts, a large number of which stop there every year. A warm welcome awaits the visiting sailor ashore in Jamestown, the island's only settlement.

Country Profile

The island was discovered in 1502 by a Portuguese fleet returning from India, but was kept a secret by them, so as to keep it as a port of call for Portuguese ships on that route. In 1516 a Portuguese deserter, Fernando Lopez, stowed away on a ship, but got off at St Helena and lived there for 30 years. Then the island had lush vegetation and fruit trees, which were destroyed by wild goats left by ships. By the end of the sixteenth century a little community had established itself, and the island became known to the rest of the world. Despite Dutch efforts to claim the island, in the mid-seventeenth century the English East India Company set up base there, to protect their interests against Dutch and Spanish privateers and warships. A settlement grew in James Valley, plantations were cultivated and African slaves brought in as labour. A Dutch invasion in 1673 was foiled by Black Oliver, a slave who knew the island well and who led the English counter-attack.

In 1815 St Helena received its most famous visitor, when Napoleon Bonaparte was brought there as a prisoner, remaining with a mini-imperial French court until his death in 1821. It marked a period of prosperity for the island with the influx of naval and military personnel, but this faded after Napoleon's death. Slavery was abolished in 1832, and two years later St Helena became a Crown Colony. The British government used the island as a base for the campaign against the slave trade, and many freed slaves settled on the island. Joshua Slocum, the first single-handed circumnavigator, called there on *Spray* in 1898.

Towards the end of the nineteenth century, the opening of the Suez Canal saw the number of visiting ships fall, and many islanders left the island. The start of the twentieth century brought another brief period of activity, when 6000 prisoners from the Boer War were brought to St Helena. The development of a flax growing industry, which lasted until the 1960s, helped

Practical Information

LOCAL TIME: GMT

CURRENCY: St Helenian pound (£) of 100 pence. Credit cards are not accepted on the island, only cash or travellers' cheques.

BUSINESS HOURS
Government offices: 0830–1600 Monday to Friday.

ELECTRICITY: 240 V, 50 Hz

PUBLIC HOLIDAYS
January 1: New Year's Day
Good Friday and Easter Monday
Queen's Birthday
St Helena's Day
Whit Monday
August Bank Holiday
December 25, 26: Christmas

COMMUNICATIONS
Radio St Helena 1511 kHz/194 m, VHF Channel 16. There are regular communications with the UK and St Helena's dependencies.
Cable & Wireless: telex and telegrams.

MEDICAL
There is a small general hospital in Jamestown, also a dental surgery.

the shaky economy, especially during the two World Wars.

Many islanders work on the US base on Ascension, but unemployment remains a problem. Some have emigrated to Britain. There is a small fishing industry and also some revenue from the sale of stamps, the rest being made up by British aid.

The total population, most of whom live in Jamestown, numbers 5300. The islanders call themselves Yamstocks, from the diet of yams the slaves used to live on. They are a mixture of Portuguese, Dutch, English, Malay, Goanese, Madagascan, East Indian, African, Chinese, Boer, American whalers and perhaps some of Napoleon's entourage, to name only a few of the people who have contributed to the St Helenian ethnic mix. English is the main language, although there is also a local dialect. Various Christian denominations are represented.

The climate is tropical, but cooled by the SE trades, and the cold Benguela current from the Southern Ocean. The weather is warm and occasionally humid, but it varies within the island and it is sometimes foggy or misty.

Entry Regulations

Port of entry
Jamestown 15°55′S 5°43′W.

Procedure on arrival
St Helena Port Control should be called on VHF Channel 16 for anchoring details. Do not use any moorings unless directed to do so, as they are all privately owned.

Formalities are simple, but should be done in working hours. No overtime is charged, but clearance on weekends is only done by arrangement. All persons must remain on board until cleared by the harbour master, customs and police.

Customs
Firearms will be held in custody by the police until departure. Spearguns and scuba gear will be impounded for the duration of the stay. There are strict laws for the protection of the underwater environment, but visitors who wish to dive can do so with the local island club, which can be joined on a temporary basis.

Animals are not allowed ashore and will be shot on sight if found ashore.

A declaration of bonded stores is required.

Immigration
A landing permit is issued on arrival for up to 12 months by the immigration officer. No visas are required.

Health
Yellow fever vaccination is required if coming from some parts of Africa.

Fees
Immigration fee is £5 for adults, £2.50 for children, harbour fees £10, health £1, light dues £5.

Facilities

Commuting ashore by dinghy was always a problem due to the bad surge at the landing pier, so a local fishing company has started a 24-hour launch service for visiting yachts. A booklet containing tickets for 40 passages can be bought for a few pounds. There are showers near the landing steps.

Water can be taken in jerrycans from an outlet on the main dock. Diesel fuel can be bought by jerrycan from a fuel station in town, or arrangements can be made for a 44 gallon (200 l) drum to be delivered to the quayside. Visiting boats are not allowed to come alongside the dock so all fuel has to be transported by launch or dinghy.

Yachting facilities are scarce, but a modest selection of fresh provisions can be obtained for the onward passage. It is advisable to arrive in St Helena with a well-stocked boat and only expect to buy a few fresh provisions locally. Simple repairs can be carried out at the workshop dealing with the local boats.

Further Reading

St Helena including Ascension Island and Tristan da Cunha

SENEGAL

The best known and most visited country by cruising sailors in West Africa, Senegal was once the centre of French West Africa and Dakar one of the most sophisticated African cities. The French influence is still noticeable and the mixture of the two cultures has produced some interesting results in music, painting and even cuisine.

The country is mostly flat except for some mountains in the far south-east and east. Several rivers, some of which are navigable for some distance inland, flow into the sea. These rivers and the offlying islands are Senegal's main cruising attraction, which brings a few cruising yachts to this part of the world every year. The most interesting area is the Casamance, a labyrinth of creeks and islets south of the river Gambia, which is populated by millions of migratory birds during the dry season.

Country Profile

This area has been inhabited since at least 1300 BC, one of the earliest inhabited areas of West Africa. Under successive kingdoms, it was part of the Ghana empire in the ninth to the eleventh centuries and the Mali empire in the thirteenth to fourteenth centuries. During this period Islam spread across the region. Droughts in the Sahara drove various peoples, the Wolof, Serer, Fulani and Toucouleur, south into Senegal.

In 1444 the Portuguese arrived and set up a trading post on La Gorée Island off Dakar. This became a slave trade centre and over the next 150 years intensive slave trading was carried out. The British, Dutch and French also arrived and there was rivalry between the European powers for the region. Finally the French, who had founded the town of St Louis, captured La Gorée and penetrated into the interior, becoming masters of the area. When the slave trade was banned, the French developed agriculture and followed a policy of assimilation of the local population. At the end of the nineteenth century, the Senegalese had limited French citizenship and sent deputies to the French parliament.

French West Africa covered a vast area as far as the Niger and Dakar was its capital. In the twentieth century nationalism grew and after the Second World War, Léopold Senghor, a poet educated in France, led the independence movement, wanting to form a strong federal union. However, individual countries preferred to remain separate and in 1960 French West Africa dissolved into nine separate republics. Senghor became President of Senegal until he stepped down in 1980, when Abdou Niouf took over.

The economy of Senegal is mainly agricultural, with groundnuts being the main crop. Some income is also derived from fishing, phosphates and tourism. There is a trade deficit and much food has to be imported. There is considerable foreign aid.

The population is 6.7 million, with about one-third being Wolof, the largest ethnic group. Other peoples are Serer, Diola, Fulani, Toucouleur and Mandinka. Unlike other parts of Africa, there is a high degree of homogeneity among the ethnic groups, as language and religion are shared. Most understand Wolof and practise their own brand of the Muslim faith. French is also spoken and widely used by officials. Dakar has been the capital since 1958. South-west of the port is the city centre, where administration and businesses are based.

The climate is tropical with a rainy season between July and September. The winter months, from November to March, have more pleasant weather. The prevailing winds are northerly, although occasionally from December to May a dust laden *harmattan* blows from across the desert. Drought is sometimes a problem north of the Gambia river.

Entry Regulations

Ports of entry
Dakar 14°41′N 17°25′W, Ziguinchor 12°35′N 16°16′W.

Procedure on arrival
Dakar: The port authority should be contacted on VHF Channel 16 for instructions. There is a new fishing harbour where yachts may berth if there is space.
Ziguinchor: This port lies 33 miles up the Casamance

Practical Information

LOCAL TIME: GMT

BUOYAGE: IALA A

CURRENCY: West African franc (CFA)

BUSINESS HOURS
Banks: 0800–1130/1430–1630 Monday to Friday.
Business and government offices: 0800–1200/1430–1800 Monday to Friday, 0800–1200 Saturday (except government).

ELECTRICITY: 220 V, 50 Hz

PUBLIC HOLIDAYS
1 January: New Year's Day
1 February
4 April: National Day
Easter Monday
1 May: Labour Day
Korite (end of Ramadan)
Ascension Thursday,
Whit Monday
Tabaski (Eid el Kebir)
15 August: Assumption
1 November: All Saints' Day
Mouloud (Prophet's birthday)
25 December: Christmas Day

COMMUNICATIONS
International calls can be made from Telesenegal, 6 rue Wagare–Diouf, Dakar: 0700–2400.
Telegrams can be sent from the post office.
There are international flights from Dakar to most African capitals and some European cities.

MEDICAL
Hôpital Principal, Clinique Hubert, both in Dakar.

DIPLOMATIC MISSIONS
In Dakar:
Canada: 45 Avenue de la République. ☎ 239290.
Cape Verdes: 1 rue de Denan. ☎ 211873.
France: BP 4035. ☎ 210181.
Gambia: 11 rue de Thiong. ☎ 214476.
United Kingdom: 20 rue du Docteur Guillet. ☎ 237392.
United States: BP 49, Avenue Jean XXIII. ☎ 214296.
All neighbouring countries are represented in Dakar and so it is possible to obtain the necessary visas.

---

river. There is a depth of 15 ft (5 metres) over the bar at the river entrance, after which the minimum depth in the navigable channel is 30 ft (9 metres). The middle channel is marked by buoys, but the river should only be navigated in daylight. Yachts can come alongside a wharf in the main port, which is on the southern bank of the river.

Customs
Firearms must be declared.
Animals need anti-rabies vaccinations as well as a health certificate.

Immigration
Visas are not required by nationals of Belgium, France, Germany, Italy, Luxembourg and the Netherlands. Other EC countries do not need a visa if spending up to a maximum of one week. All other nationals need a visa obtained in advance. Visas are not issued on arrival.
There are Senegalese consulates in all neighbouring countries, otherwise visas are issued by French embassies. There are Senegalese missions in Algiers, Banjul, Tunis, Rabat, Nouakchott and Las Palmas de Gran Canaria. Entry is refused to South Africans and Zimbabweans.

Health
Vaccination against yellow fever is obligatory and against cholera recommended. Malaria prophylaxis is also recommended.

Facilities

Provisioning is good in Dakar, where there are several supermarkets. Fresh produce is available in Dakar from an open-air market near the port. The capital also has reasonable repair facilities with various workshops being located in the Medina industrial estate, north of the city. Marine equipment is non-existent, but some of the bigger engine manufacturers are represented locally and have a limited range of spares. Some provisions are also available in Ziguinchor, but only the minimum can be expected in smaller places. Fuel is only available in Dakar and Ziguinchor.

Further Reading

West Africa, A Travel Survival Kit
The Travellers Guide to West Africa

SOUTH AFRICA

The Republic of South Africa lies at the southern tip of the African continent, its shores washed by the Indian and Atlantic Oceans. Much of the interior is a high semi-arid plateau, the veld, while the narrow plain along the long coast is rugged, more fertile and with a subtropical climate. An important shipping centre for more than five centuries ever since the Portuguese discovered the route to the Indies around the Cape of

Good Hope, the old sailing route is now only used by cruising yachts, most of whom are on passage from the Indian Ocean to the Atlantic.

The number of yachts calling at South African ports has diminished in recent years, partly because more circumnavigators prefer to reach Europe via the Red Sea and Suez Canal, but also because of South Africa's international isolation as an apartheid state. The recent changes and the gradual dismantling of apartheid will probably lead to the reinstatement of South Africa as a sailing destination and such prestigious international events as the Whitbread Round the World Race may call again at Cape Town. Such changes will please the many sailors who have visited South Africa in the past and were always warmly welcomed by the local sailing community.

The country's convenient position and excellent yachting facilities make it a natural stopover, added to which are the many nature reserves that make South Africa an interesting place to visit. One major drawback is the weather and sailing conditions, the waters around the tip of Africa being among the most dangerous in the world.

Yacht basin in Durban. (South Africa Tourist Board).

Country Profile

The oldest inhabitants of the Cape area were the Bushmen and the Khoi-Khoi or Hottentots. By the thirteenth century several Bantu tribes had settled in the region, being forced to move gradually south and west to find new grazing lands. The Portuguese were the first Europeans to visit the Cape, when they discovered the route to India at the end of the fifteenth century. Only in the mid-seventeenth century were efforts made by Europeans to colonise the land, when the Dutch East India Company became interested in the area for a supply of slaves and raw materials, as well as a stopping point for ships. Dutch settlers came and gradually moved inland, forming a close-knit Boer society, with their own dialect called Afrikaans. Tension rose between the Bantu tribes and the Boer farmers, and this burst into violent conflict in the eighteenth century.

In the early nineteenth century Britain took over the colony from the bankrupt Dutch East India Company. Then British settlers started arriving, pushing the Xhosa off their land, and conflicting both with the African tribes and the Boers who resented the new regime, especially after the British abolished slavery in

Practical Information

LOCAL TIME: GMT + 2

BUOYAGE: IALA A

CURRENCY: Rand of 100 cents. Import or export is limited to R100.

BUSINESS HOURS
Banks: 0900–1530 Monday, Tuesday, Thursday, Friday, and 0900–1300 Wednesday, 0900–1100 Saturday.
Business: 0800/0830–1630/1700 Monday to Friday.
Shops: 0800–1700 Monday to Friday.
Government offices: 0800/0830–1630/1700 Monday to Friday.

ELECTRICITY: 220 V, 50 Hz

PUBLIC HOLIDAYS
1 January: New Year's Day
6 April: Founders Day
Easter Week
31 May: Republic Day
10 October: Kruger Day
16 December: Day of the Vow
25, 26 December: Christmas

MEDICAL
There are hospitals in all major centres and the standards are very good.

COMMUNICATIONS
Direct dialling to Europe and North America.
Post offices open 0800–1700 Monday to Friday, 0830–1200 Saturday.
There are flights from Cape Town to London and Brazil, but most of the international flights leave from Johannesburg.

DIPLOMATIC MISSIONS
In Pretoria:
Australia: 4th floor, Mutual and Federal Building, 220 Vermuelen St.
☎ (12) 325-4315.
Canada: 5th floor, Nedbank Plaza, Church and Beatrix Sts, Arcadia.
☎ (12) 28-7062.

United Kingdom: (July to December) 255 Hill St, Arcadia. ☎ (12) 433-121.
United States: Thibault House, 225 Pretorius St. ☎ (12) 284-266.

In Cape Town:
United Kingdom: (January to June) 91 Parliament St. ☎ (21) 467-220 (consulate: 12th floor, Southern Life Centre, 8 Riebeeck St. ☎ (21) 253-670).
United States: Broadway Industries Centre, Heerengracht, Foreshore.
☎ (21) 214-280.

In Durban:
United Kingdom: 10th floor, Fedlife House, 320 Smith St. ☎ (31) 052-920.
United States: Durban Bay House, 29th floor, 333 Smith St. ☎ (31) 324-737.

Mozambique does not have diplomatic relations with South Africa, but visas may be obtained from the Mozambique Trade Mission, 73 Market Street, Johannesburg. ☎ (11) 234-907.

1834. The Africans were caught between the Boers and British, being no match for superior European firepower, and already weakened by years of intertribal warfare. Tension between the Boers and the British led to the formation of the autonomous Boer republics of the Orange Free State and Transvaal.

At the turn of the century British efforts to gain control over the Boer republics led to the Boer Wars, and eventually Britain gained control over the whole country. In 1910 the Union of South Africa was established, with the white minority holding power. The first apartheid laws were passed to control black workers in the rich gold and diamond mines. After the Second World War a rise in Afrikaaner nationalism brought the National Party to power in 1948, and they reinforced the apartheid system, denying the black majority any political voice. The African National Congress was formed to campaign for the rights of black South Africans, but many of its leaders were imprisoned in the 1960s and the ANC was banned. Nelson Mandela became the best known among the imprisoned leaders and a symbol of resistance.

In 1962 the Union of South Africa became an independent republic and left the Commonwealth. Martial law was established following riots in 1985–6 and severe repression followed, which led to several Western states imposing economic sanctions. Recently some efforts have been made towards reform, led by the release from prison of Nelson Mandela and the legalisation of the ANC. These moves point the way to a future solution and the gradual dismantling of the apartheid system.

South Africa has the strongest economy on the African continent, although racial tension is a threat to prosperity. The country is rich in important precious and rare mineral resources, such as gold, diamonds, chrome, titanium, uranium, coal and iron. Industry has mainly been developed for the domestic market. The Mediterranean type climate around the Cape has made agriculture important. South Africa also has the geographic advantage of controlling the route around the Cape.

The population is 32.5 million of which 72 per cent are Bantu, 15 per cent of European descent, mainly Afrikaaner with some British, 9 per cent mixed race and 4 per cent Indian, who were originally brought in as indentured labourers by the British in the nineteenth century. Afrikaans and English are spoken, plus several African languages, Xhosa and Zulu being the main ones. The majority are Christian. The Indians are mainly Hindu, and there are also Muslims, Jews and those who follow traditional African beliefs. Pretoria is the administrative capital, while Cape Town is the home of the legislative assembly.

The climate varies greatly between the coastal regions and inland, and also between the Atlantic and Indian Ocean coasts. Generally, it can be described as temperate in the Cape area and tropical in the rest of the country. The prevailing winds of summer are SE, replaced in winter by W or NW winds. Gales are frequent and in summer depressions come up from the Southern Ocean accompanied by cold gale force winds. Conditions are particularly bad when such gales blow against the SW flowing Agulhas current.

Entry Regulations

Ports of entry
The ports of entry are listed in the order of the route from the Indian to the Atlantic Ocean.

Richards Bay 28°48′S 32°06′E, Durban 29°52′S 31°02′E, East London 33°02′S 27°55′E, Port Elizabeth 33°58′S 25°38′E, Mossel Bay 34°11′S 22°10′E, Cape Town (Table Bay) 33°55′S 18°26′E, Saldanha Bay 33°03′S 17°56′E.

Procedure on arrival
The captain must report to the nearest customs office within 24 hours of arrival. If a yacht arrives from abroad at a port other than a port of entry, the captain must immediately report to the port captain, and clear at an official port of entry within 24 hours. One must also clear with Port Health on arrival. Formalities on arrival are complicated and time-consuming. Yachts must check in and out with customs, immigration and port captain in each port. It is also necessary to obtain coastal clearance to sail between ports and the authorities must also be informed if a yacht goes out for a day sail even if returning to the same port.

Richards Bay: Yachts should moor in the small boat harbour for clearance with customs and immigration. Formalities are simpler than in other South African ports. After clearance yachts can use the facilities of the Zululand Yacht Club. Often the Navy or police will send out a boat to pilot a yacht into the port.

Durban: Durban Harbour Radio can be contacted to inform the Authorities in advance of one's arrival. Yachts should berth at the international jetty for clearance with customs, immigration and port authority. All formalities are completed ashore. Customs are located in the Ocean Terminal building. The Port Liaison Office must be visited on the 10th floor, Port

Control Building. The Point Yacht Club has a few spaces for visitors, who may use the club facilities after clearance is completed.

Cape Town: The Royal Cape Yacht Club deals with all yacht movement within Table Bay Harbour, so they must be contacted first on VHF Channel 16 and not the port authority. The movement of shipping around the harbour is indicated by lights on the port captain's office, red (Ben Schoeman Dock), green (Duncan Dock) and orange (Victoria Basin). A flashing light signifies a ship is entering port and a steady light that one is leaving. Yachts should keep to starboard when entering the harbour. The yacht basin and yacht club are located at the SE end of Duncan Dock. The captain must clear with customs, situated at the main gate, and immigration (Room 535, Customs & Excise Building, outside the Adderley Street Customs Gate). On departure one must clear first with the yacht club in order to get a clearance certificate, then immigration, harbour revenue (Room 340, Customs & Excise Building) and finally customs who require the yacht club clearance certificate.

Saldanha Bay: The port captain should be contacted on VHF Channel 16 for permission to enter and leave the harbour, as well as when crossing the shipping channel between Saldanha and Langebaan. If the port captain is notified that clearance is required on arrival, the relevant officials will be informed so as to meet the yacht at the yacht club, which is located in the NW of the bay, north of President Jetty.

Port Owen: Port Owen Marina stands by on VHF Channel 10. The marina is located up the Berg river in St Helena Bay. It is advisable to enter the river at high tide. Although not a port of entry, the marina staff can arrange transport to Saldanha for clearance.

Customs
Firearms will be sealed by customs on board if this is possible. Otherwise firearms will be removed and bonded until departure.

Animals must obtain the necessary certificate from the State veterinary officer in the harbour area. This will permit the movement of the animal within the harbour area.

There is no limit on the length of time a foreign yacht may stay in South Africa.

Immigration
Visas are required by all nationalities except the United Kingdom, Switzerland and Ireland. Most nationalities are issued with a three month visa. For yachts sailing towards South Africa, there are South African embassies only in Port Louis (Mauritius) and St Denis (Réunion), but visas can be obtained from South

African trade missions in many southern African nations. It may also be possible to get a Temporary Residence Permit as owner of a yacht by proving ownership, and as crew by possessing an air ticket home or equivalent funds.

If one has a South African stamp in one's passport, it is very difficult to visit other African countries. One may be refused entry, or alternatively, nationalities who do not normally require visas for a particular country will have to obtain them in advance. If asked, South African immigration officials will stamp a separate piece of paper, which can be removed on departure.

Any crew leaving the country by other means than by yacht must inform immigration and must possess a valid air ticket to their own country or equivalent funds. Immigration must also be notified if a South African national joins the yacht for a cruise while in South African waters.

Health
A yellow fever vaccination certificate may be requested if arriving from some African countries. Malaria prophylaxis is recommended.

Fees
Clearance is a 24-hour service, but overtime is charged after 1630 on weekdays, all day public holidays, and weekends.
Harbour fees: Visiting yachts not moored at a commercial berth are normally allowed a free stay of 30 days in port from arrival day to departure day inclusive. After this, fees must be paid which increase the longer the period spent. These are reasonable for the first three months, double for the following three months, and so on. A yacht leaving and then returning to the same port within six months will continue where they left off and will not get another 30 days free.

Yachts staying at commercial berths have to pay port fees.

There are sometimes fees for using yacht club moorings, or for temporary membership of the club, but some yacht clubs give this free for certain periods up to one month for visiting foreign yachts.

Pilotage service is free.

Restricted areas
The diamond producing areas off Oranjemund are off limits to yachts.

Yachts may not enter or anchor within an area one mile wide around the high security prison Robben Island. In an emergency, however, yachts can anchor in Murray's Bay in the NE of the island, but must first contact Robben Island Port Control on Channel 16 for permission to enter the one mile zone.

Anchorage is allowed at Dassen Island, but landing is forbidden.

There is a naval base in Simon's Town, False Bay, and yachts must arrange permission to enter the bay in advance with the False Bay Yacht Club, or contact the Navy on VHF Channel 16 for permission to enter.

Facilities
Yachting facilities throughout South Africa are of a high standard and as there are yacht clubs in most ports, the clubs are the best source of information on local conditions. The yacht clubs like to be contacted in advance by those wishing to use their facilities. It is not normally allowed to live aboard a yacht, but a concession is made for visiting foreign yachts as a temporary privilege. Most yacht clubs, such as those at Cape Town, Durban and Richards Bay, have their own hauling facilities or work closely with a local boatyard. For any major repair, Cape Town and Durban have a complete range of services: electronic, electrical, sail-making, rigging, refrigeration, diesel and outboard engines, metal, fibreglass and woodwork.

Fuel and water are easily available and provisioning in all major centres is very good. LPG containers can be filled in Durban and Cape Town. Yacht clubs are also convenient places to leave the boat while visiting the interior.

The Zululand Yacht Club in Richards Bay is a good place from which to visit the Windy Ridge Reserve, while Kruger Park can be easily reached from the Point Yacht Club in Durban. For those who are concerned about the difficult passage from Durban to Cape Town, Chris Bonnet of the Durban Sailing Academy presents regular slide shows for visiting sailors in which he explains the best tactics to apply in these stormy waters.

Further Reading
Welcome to Durban
Harbour and Yacht Club Regulations and facilities in the Cape Province
Africa on a Shoestring

TRISTAN DA CUNHA

The remote South Atlantic island of Tristan da Cunha came to the world's attention in 1961, when a volcanic eruption forced the entire population of 241 to be evacuated to Britain. Other islands nearby are the

Practical Information

LOCAL TIME: GMT

CURRENCY: St Helenian pound (£)

BUSINESS HOURS
Government offices: summer 0800–1230, 1330–1600 Monday to Friday, winter 0830–1230, 1330–1630 Monday to Friday.

PUBLIC HOLIDAYS
1 January: New Year's Day
Good Friday and Easter Monday
Queen's Birthday
Whit Monday
August Bank Holiday
25, 26 December: Christmas

COMMUNICATIONS
There are regular radio communications with St Helena and the UK.
Tristan has no airport and ships call at most three times a year on supply runs from the UK, St Helena and Cape Town. The occasional fishing boat stops at the island for provisions.

MEDICAL
There is a small hospital.

small, uninhabited Inaccessible, Nightingale, Gough, Middle and Stoltenhoff Islands. Since 1938 all the islands have been administered by St Helena, 1500 miles to the north. South Africa is the same distance to the east.

Tristan da Cunha is almost circular, the core of a volcano with steep cliffs plunging into the sea. On the north west corner is a small habitable plateau, and the settlement of Edinburgh. The volcano's summit is bleak and often snow-covered from June to October, although the lower slopes are greener. The islanders have retained a simple way of life and little has changed over the years.

The anchorage is completely unprotected and a heavy swell is constant, worst in a north-westerly. The small boat harbour has only about 3 feet of water and a heavy surge from the constant swell. Yachts can rarely stay for very long, even if they want to. Yet in spite of all the difficulties, every year this remote community is visited by a few intrepid yachts.

Country Profile

In 1506 the Portuguese Admiral Tristao da Cunha reported the first sighting of the island. No landings, however, were attempted until the Dutch came the following century, and only in 1810 was a settlement established, when three Americans made their base there. A few years later England claimed the island as part of the defence of St Helena, primarily to guard against Napoleon's unlikely escape. A small garrison was established and fortifications were built. Corporal William Glass, who had been stationed there during this time, returned to settle with his wife and a few others after the garrison was abandoned, and from these beginnings the community grew. Deserters from ships, American whalers and castaways came and went. In 1876 the island was declared a British territory. The islanders grew enough to eat and to trade with passing

ships. Occasional trips were made to Nightingale Island to collect guano, penguin eggs and petrel carcasses for lamp oil. The islanders still make this trip twice every year.

In the early twentieth century life was hard, and fewer ships visited, sometimes a whole year passed without a ship calling. Nevertheless the community survived, being 200 strong in 1939. During the Second World War a small meteorological and wireless station was built on the island and manned by the Royal Navy. The most dramatic event in Tristan da Cunha's history occurred when the volcano erupted in 1961. The evacuated islanders lived for a couple of years in England, but most of them returned as soon as the island was safe again. The lava had formed a natural breakwater and in 1967 the small boat harbour was built.

After the war a crayfish industry was developed, with a factory for canning and freezing the tails. Income is also derived from fishing royalties, the sale of stamps and aid from Britain.

The population numbers around 300, most of whom can trace their descent back to the very first settlers. Seven family names are shared among the islanders. English is the language spoken.

The climate is temperate, with moderate rainfall and high humidity. The wind is strong most days, and gales are frequent all year round.

Entry Regulations

Port of entry
Edinburgh 37°03'S 12°18'W.

Procedure on arrival
One should anchor off Edinburgh settlement. Radio Tristan will contact the yacht on VHF Channel 16. The yacht is first boarded by the doctor for a health inspection. Immigration formalities are completed at

the police station ashore, where Sergeant Glass, a direct descendant of the first settler of the same name, holds most public functions, including those of immigration officer, port captain and post master.

Customs
Firearms and animals must be kept on board and not landed. There are restrictions on the import of alcohol.

Immigration
No visas are required.

Restrictions
Landing is prohibited on Gough, Inaccessible, Nightingale, Middle or Stoltenhoff Islands.

Fees
Overtime is charged by arrangement. There is a landing fee of £3 per person.

Facilities

In spite of its remoteness, yachts are usually able to obtain some basic provisions, as the islanders grow some vegetables, mainly potatoes. The islanders are very adept at all kinds of repairs and have helped yachts in the past. Basil Lavarello, the manager of the lobster freezing factory, is a qualified marine engineer and is the best person to approach for advice and help.

Further Reading

St Helena including Ascension Island and Tristan da Cunha

5 Caribbean

The islands of the Caribbean are undoubtedly the most popular cruising destination in the world. This is particularly true of the Eastern Caribbean, an area which attracts an increasing number of cruising yachts, while the resident charter fleets are forever expanding. In some parts, such as the Virgin Islands, charter yachts are already in the majority, although in the Leeward and Windward Islands the scene is still dominated by cruising boats. Another area rapidly gaining in popularity are the islands off Venezuela, both those belonging to that country and the ABC Islands, Aruba, Bonaire and Curaçao. By contrast, the Greater Antilles are either off the cruising track or, as in the case of Jamaica and Haiti, are usually deliberately avoided.

The popularity of the Eastern Caribbean is well deserved as the winter weather is mostly fine, the trade winds reliable and the facilities are being continually improved to cope with a constant demand. The sailing season lasts from the end of November until June, by which time the prudent sailor should be on his or her way to a hurricane-free area. The peak hurricane season is from August until October and while the majority of cruising yachts leave the area, some stay behind planning on finding shelter in a hurricane hole should a hurricane come their way. Several years of relative peace created a false sense of security, shattered in 1989 by hurricane Hugo which devastated several islands and destroyed hundreds of boats. Even known hurricane holes did not provide the hoped for protection in the face of a storm of unprecedented violence.

The weather during winter, particularly from Christmas until the end of April, is very good, with steady easterly winds and not much rain. Usually winds are NE at the beginning of winter and become SE with the approach of summer. The hurricane season lasts from June through November, the most dangerous period being from the middle of August until the end of September. The whole region can be affected by hurricanes with the exception of the southern part, Trinidad and the islands off Venezuela, where tropical storms are extremely rare.

Provisioning is better in the major centres, however, most islands have shops with a reasonable selection and fresh produce is widely available. Although most islands have air links with the outside world, direct flights to Europe or North America are only available from some islands, so crew changes are best planned for such places as Barbados, Martinique, Guadeloupe, Antigua, Trinidad, Grenada, Puerto Rico or St Martin.

With thousands of yachts plying up and down the island chain, one is never too far away from a good supply point or repair facilities. Although in most islands mooring is still on one's own anchor, the number of purpose-built marinas is growing steadily, with the highest concentration in the Virgin Islands to St Martin area. For any major repair work one should head for one of the islands having a yachting centre which can offer a complete range of services, such as the Virgin Islands, St Martin, Antigua, Guadeloupe, Martinique, St Lucia or Isla de Margarita.

In the fight against drug trafficking in the area, the island nations have made an agreement with the US government, which gives the US Coast Guard permission to stop and search any vessel regardless of registry in Eastern Caribbean waters without a search warrant. Some of the island Coast Guards also may stop and board vessels in their respective territorial waters.

ANGUILLA

Anguilla is the most northern of the Leeward Islands in the Eastern Caribbean and one of the least developed. Long and flat, this coral island was named 'eel' in Spanish.

Anguilla's brief claim to fame occurred in 1969 when the small island was invaded by a British expeditionary force accompanied by a posse of London policemen. This is probably the only instance in which London bobbies have been used as an occupying force and their presence on the island was greeted with delight by the Anguillans. The crisis came to a head after Anguilla declared its independence from St Kitts & Nevis.

Anguilla's main attraction is her isolation and although distances to neighbouring Caribbean islands are very small, the changes that have occurred elsewhere have largely left Anguilla untouched. There are several delightful bays both on the south and north coasts of Anguilla, while those in search of blissful solitude can do no better than the Prickly Pear Cays and Dog Island, north of Anguilla.

Country Profile

Although discovered by Columbus in 1493, Anguilla was only settled in the middle of the seventeenth century by the English and remained under their influence thereafter, except for a brief period of French rule at the end of the eighteenth century. Throughout the nineteenth century Anguilla was closely associated

with St Kitts, but in 1967 it refused to join with St Kitts & Nevis as an associated state. To calm the crisis British troops and police were sent in. In 1971 Britain established Anguilla as a separate administrative unit and now the island has internal self-government, while remaining a British dependency.

The lack of rainfall makes agriculture difficult, but some of the best fishing grounds in the Caribbean are

found in the area. Salt-farming also contributes to the economy, both salt and fish being exported. Many of the population work abroad, although recently the tourist trade has been cautiously expanded.

The population numbers 7500, mostly of African origin, as well as a number of European descent. The language is English. The Valley is the main centre. Of nine different religious denominations, Protestantism has the most followers. The climate is semi-tropical, dry but pleasant with an average temperature of 27°C (80°F).

Entry Regulations

Ports of entry
Road Bay 18°12′N 63°06′W, Blowing Point 18°12′N 63°06′W.

Procedure on arrival
Road Bay: One should clear first with immigration, at the police station near the dinghy dock, then with customs who can be found by the big ship dock and from whom the cruising permit must be purchased. Because of the serious concern over drug traffic, yachts must be sure to clear in properly. Failure to do so could result in a fine, and the boat being confiscated.

If staying less than 24 hours, one can clear in and out at the same time.

Blowing Point is used mainly by commercial shipping.

Customs
Firearms should be licensed and must be securely locked on board, under the captain's control only.

A valid veterinary certificate must be shown for all animals.

There is no specified time limit on how long a yacht may stay.

Immigration
US citizens need only have proof of identity.

No visas are required by nationals of EC countries, Commonwealth countries, Finland, Iceland, Japan, Liechtenstein, Norway, Sweden, Switzerland, Tunisia, Turkey, Uruguay, United States and Venezuela. All other nationals require visas.

Cruising permit
All foreign boats are required to have a cruising permit, issued by customs. The cost of the permit depends on tonnage and the duration of a visit, for example a boat from 5 to 20 tons for a week would pay EC$125. The permit can be obtained on arrival and is only required if cruising. If staying in Road Town only

Map 7: The Caribbean

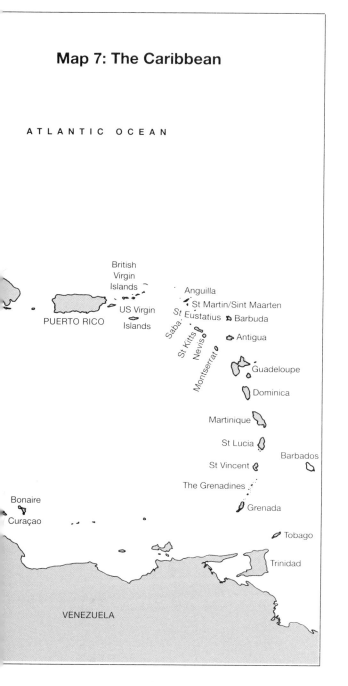

Practical Information

LOCAL TIME: GMT - 4

BUOYAGE: IALA B

CURRENCY: East Caribbean dollar (EC$).

BUSINESS HOURS
Shops: 0800–1200, 1300–1600 Monday to Friday.
Banks: 0800–1200 Monday to Friday, 1500–1700 Fridays only.
Government offices: 0830–1200, 1300–1600 Monday to Saturday except Thursdays 0830–1200. Officials 0700–2400 at Blowing Point.

ELECTRICITY: 110 V, 60 Hz

PUBLIC HOLIDAYS
1 January: New Year's Day
10 February: Freedom Day
Good Friday and Easter Monday
30 May: Anguilla Day
Whit Monday
Second Saturday in June: Queen's Birthday
First Monday in August: Emancipation Day
First Thursday in August
First Friday in August: Constitution Day
19 December: Separation Day
25, 26 December: Christmas

EVENTS
August: Yacht race

COMMUNICATIONS
Cable & Wireless for international telephones and telex.
The main post office is in The Valley: 0800–1200, 1300–1530 Monday to Friday, and 0800–1200 Saturday.
International flight connections have to be made in Antigua, Sint Maarten or San Juan (Puerto Rico), to all of which there are regular flights.

a cruising permit need not be bought. It also counts as a clearance certificate and with it one need not check out with customs in order to leave Anguilla.

Fees

An overtime fee of EC$30 is charged at Blowing Point after 2400 and on public holidays, and at Road Bay outside of official hours and on Sundays and holidays. There is also a cruising permit fee.

Restrictions

There is a prohibited area in Little Bay, following a line from a point 18°04′03.5′′N and 63°04′15.7′′W extending south to a point 18°13′57.6′′N and 63°04′15.7′′W turning east to a point 18°13′57.6′′N and 63°04′12.5′′W.

Anguillan waters are all protected as a national park and spearfishing and the collection of coral and shell-fish are prohibited.

Facilities

As yachting is neither encouraged nor restricted, repair facilities are very basic and for any serious repair one has to go to neighbouring St Martin.

Further Reading

Cruising Guide to the Leeward Islands
Caribbean Islands Handbook

ANTIGUA & BARBUDA

Antigua occupies a central position in the popular Caribbean cruising ground of the Lesser Antilles. Antigua administers two other islands: Barbuda, 30 miles to the north, with its only settlement at Codrington, and small uninhabited Redonda, 35 miles to the south-west.

Antigua has been blessed by nature with a beautiful coastline and by the British Admiralty with one of the most picturesque harbours in the world. English Harbour is an enclosed bay that offers protection in all kinds of weather, which is why it was used as a hurricane hole by the British West Indies fleet for nearly two centuries. English Harbour, and particularly Nelson's Dockyard, have been saved for posterity by the foresight of a British yachtsman who stopped there during a world cruise shortly after the Second World War, fell in love with the island and never sailed on. Due to the tireless efforts of Vernon Nicholson, the derelict port with crumbling buildings underwent a gradual metamorphosis and Nelson's Dockyard is now the undisputed centre of Caribbean yachting. The old sail lofts, powder rooms, rope walks and officers' quarters have been restored and given new roles to play, while a museum housed in the former Admiral's Residence helps bring to life this harbour's fascinating history.

Over 2000 yachts pass through English Harbour each year, many of them charter boats based in the area. Most cruising boats arrive towards the end of the winter season, in April and May, as they make their way home either to Europe or North America. They are joined by hundreds of racing enthusiasts who congregate in Antigua at the end of April for the annual Antigua Sailing Week which brings together the cream of Caribbean yachting and signals the end of the Caribbean sailing season.

Antigua's coastline is dotted with secluded coves and attractive bays and once away from the bustle of English Harbour the solitude of some anchorages is quite surprising. On the north coast, near Parham Harbour, is Crabbs Marina and there are plans for another marina to be built on Antigua's north east coast. Further along on the East Coast is Mamora Bay, the secluded base of St James's Club. Visiting sailors can anchor in the bay or ask permission to use the dock.

Those in search of absolute solitude can sail to Antigua's smaller sister, Barbuda, a coral island surrounded by a maze of reefs that over the centuries have claimed over 200 ships. Although modern charts and good sunlight reduce the hazards, the area should be treated with caution as coral growth has made even recent charts not entirely reliable.

Country Profile

In the pre-Columbian era, the Siboney inhabited Antigua, at least as far back as 2400 BC, followed by the Arawak Indians. Columbus visited the island on his second voyage in 1493, naming the island after the Church of Santa Maria de la Antigua in Seville. The English were the first to settle in 1632, and apart from a very brief French occupation, the islands remained a British possession until independence. As on many Caribbean islands, sugar cane was introduced, and slaves from Africa brought in to work the plantations. In the seventeenth and eighteenth centuries English Harbour was developed as a major naval base, and Horatio Nelson spent much time there during his command of the Leeward Islands Squadron.

In 1967 Antigua, Barbuda and Redonda gained internal self-government, becoming first an associated state with Britain, then fully independent in 1981.

Once a major part of the economy, the sugar industry has declined, suffering especially from droughts in the arid climate. Many of the plantations have been turned to forest and pasture. There is some export of cotton and fish. However, industry is lacking, and unemployment high. Tourism plays a major role in the economy and tourist facilities are being expanded.

The population of 80,000 is mostly of African origin, with only 2 per cent of European descent. St John's on the west coast is the capital. English is spoken and the majority are Protestant with a minority

English Harbour, Antigua.

Practical Information

LOCAL TIME: GMT - 4.

BUOYAGE: IALA B

CURRENCY: East Caribbean dollar
(EC$).

BUSINESS HOURS
Banks: 0800–1300 Monday to Friday,
1500–1700 Friday only.
Bank of Antigua: 0800–1200 Saturday.
Shops: 0900–1630 Monday to Friday
(some close early Thursdays),
0900–1300 Saturdays.

ELECTRICITY: 220 V, 50 Hz

PUBLIC HOLIDAYS
1 January: New Year's Day
Good Friday, Easter Monday
First Monday in May: Labour Day
Whit Monday

Second Saturday in June: Queen's
Birthday
1 November: Independence Day
25, 26 December: Christmas

EVENTS
Antigua Sailing Week, April/May.
Midsummer Carnival, July/August.

COMMUNICATIONS
Cable & Wireless for international
telephone calls, telex, telegrams and
fax: St Mary's Street, St John's:
0700–2200 Monday to Friday, 0700–1400
Saturday, 1600–2000 Sunday;
Dockyard Market, English Harbour:
0830–1630 Monday to Friday.
Public phones can be used for collect
and credit card calls.
VHF: Channel 68 is used as the calling
frequency by all coastal stations,
including repair companies, taxis and
restaurants, so use of this channel as a

working frequency is not permitted in
Antiguan waters. It is strongly advised
that an alternative channel is used as
soon as contact is made on Channel 68.
Mail is held at the following places:
Nicholson's Yacht Charter, English
Harbour
Seagull Yachts, Falmouth Harbour
English Harbour Post Office
Crabbs Slipway & Marina
There are regular flights from Antigua to
other Caribbean destinations, Canada,
USA and Europe, principally London.

DIPLOMATIC MISSIONS
In St John's:
United Kingdom: 38 St Mary's St.
☎ 462-0008.
United States: Queen Elizabeth Highway.
☎ 462-3505.
Venezuela: Cross and Redcliffe Sts.
☎ 462-1570.

---

of Roman Catholics. Antigua has a tropical climate, but is very dry with a rainy season from September to November. The hurricane season is from July to November.

Entry Regulations

Ports of entry
English Harbour 17°00′N 61°46′W, St John's 17°07′N 61°52′W, Crabbs Marina 17°08′N 61°46′W, Codrington (Barbuda) 17°38′N 61°49′W.

Procedure on arrival
The Antigua Port Authority clearance form must be completed and clearance shown from last port of call. Ship's papers and passports also have to be shown.
English Harbour: One should anchor in the bay (Freeman's Harbour) and hoist Q flag. The captain only should go ashore with all documents to clear. All offices are located in the old Officers' Quarters building, where customs, immigration and the Park department have to be visited, open 0800–1800 daily. On departure from English Harbour, harbour fees must be paid at the Paymaster to collect the port clearance certificate. This should then be presented to the immigration officer, with the ship's papers and passports.
Crabbs Marina: On arrival the captain should go to the customs and immigration office opposite the

chandlery (open 0830–1630 weekdays). No one else must go ashore until formalities are completed.
St John's Harbour: The port facilities are at the outer end of the peninsula running west into the middle of the harbour and its use is restricted to commercial vessels. The inner harbour, between the deepwater port and town waterfront, is used by small local craft with less than 6 feet draft. Clearance is done at the Port Authority offices in the deepwater dock on the north side of the harbour, 0800–1200, 1300–1600 weekdays, closes 1500 Friday.

Customs
Firearms must be registered with the police on arrival.
Animals are not allowed ashore and must remain on board at all times.

Immigration
No visas are required by nationals of EC countries, Commonwealth countries, Finland, Iceland, Japan, Liechtenstein, Norway, Sweden, Switzerland, Tunisia, Turkey, Uruguay, the United States and Venezuela. All other nationals require visas in advance. South Africans are not allowed entry.
On arrival, immigration will issue a visa for the duration of one's stay. It is advisable to request more than the intended time, as extensions must be obtained from the capital St John's and can cost as much as US$100.
If crew leave the boat in Antigua, they must have a

valid airline ticket out of the country; it is the captain's responsibility to provide this ticket for all persons leaving.

Fees

Port entry, depending on length, from US$2 (up to 20 feet) to $12 (120–150 feet).

Cruising permit from US$8 (up to 20 feet) to $20 (120–150 feet) per month. One can buy an annual cruising permit to avoid paying the charge at every entry. All boats in Antiguan waters must have a valid cruising permit, which should be obtained on entry and enables one to go anywhere in Antiguan waters, including Barbuda. The permit is still valid if the yacht leaves Antigua and returns within the period of the permit.

Mooring fees in English Harbour and Falmouth Harbour are less for anchoring than for at the dock and are calculated per foot per day, week or month. If the fees are not paid in advance the daily rate is charged.

Dockyard entry is EC$5 per person, valid for duration of stay.

No overtime fees, except at St John's, where they are about EC$20. There are no harbour fees in St John's.

English Harbour regulations

The navigation channel from Fort Berkley to the inner harbour must be kept free. One can either anchor off the channel, or come stern to the quay. There is a dinghy speed limit of 4 knots, and all old fuel and oil must be disposed of in the special containers provided.

Restrictions

The coastline between Pillars of Hercules and entrance to Mamora Bay is protected and no fishing of any type is allowed in this area.

Coast guard

The Coast Guard stand by on VHF Channel 68 and 16. A boat can be searched either on entry into port from foreign waters or with a signed search warrant from a magistrates court.

Charter

If intending to charter, one must apply for an official licence from the Chief Marine Surveyor/Examiner in St John's Harbour. ☎ 462-1273.

Facilities

Because of Antigua's long-standing involvement with yachting, service and repair facilities are of a high standard and almost anything can be fixed on the island. Most specialised firms are concentrated within walking or rowing distance of English Harbour. Foremost among them is Antigua Slipways, which undertakes all kind of boat repair and has a well-stocked chandlery. Electronic repair is undertaken by the Signal Locker in English Harbour and there are also two sailmakers nearby. Seagull Yacht Service in Falmouth Harbour is a marine engineering service. Crabbs Marina on the north coast operate a full service yard, chandlery and 50-ton travelift. The Map Shop in St John's has a good supply of British and US charts for the North Atlantic and South Pacific.

All companies in the English Harbour area undertaking yacht or equipment repair monitor Channel 68 and this is the quickest and surest way to obtain help if anything needs to be done on the boat.

BARBUDA

All the population live in the town of Codrington. Customs and immigration are located in the boat harbour, about three miles south of Codrington, and can be called on VHF Channel 16. Outward clearance can be obtained here, but if entering, they cannot issue a cruising permit and one would have to remain in the small boat harbour. A valid cruising permit should be obtained in Antigua before going to Barbuda. Codrington village has a post office, telephone service and limited provisioning. Palaster Reef is a national park and no fishing with a speargun or rod is permitted. There are virtually no repair facilities in Barbuda and only a limited selection of supplies can be obtained there.

REDONDA

A 1000 foot high rocky island with sheer cliffs, the only decent anchorage is on the south-west coast.

Further Reading

Afloat, The Mariner's Guide to Antigua and Barbuda
A Cruising Guide to the Caribbean and the Bahamas
Caribbean Islands Handbook
Cruising Guide to the Eastern Caribbean, Vol. 2
Cruising Guide to the Leeward Islands

ARUBA

Westernmost of the ABC islands, Aruba is a convenient last stop for yachts heading for Panama. A new marina became operational recently and has brought a welcome change to an island which until then had lacked decent yachting facilities.

Practical Information

LOCAL TIME: GMT - 4

BUOYAGE: IALA B

CURRENCY: Aruban florin of 100 cents. The Antillian guilder is not accepted as an equivalent, and has to be exchanged in banks. The US$ and Venezuelan bolivar are widely accepted.

ELECTRICITY: 110 V, 60 Hz

BUSINESS HOURS
Banks: 0800–1200, 1330–1600 Monday to Friday, some stay open during the lunch hour.

Shops: 0800–1830 Monday to Saturday, some close for lunch. A few open on Sundays or holidays when cruise ships are in port.

PUBLIC HOLIDAYS
1 January: New Year's Day
Carnival Monday
Good Friday, Easter Monday
18 March: National Day
30 April: Queen's Day
1 May: Labour Day
Ascension Day
25, 26 December: Christmas

EVENTS
Carnival, February or March
24 June: St Johns Day
6 December: St Nicolas Day

COMMUNICATIONS
International telephone calls, telegrams and telexes from the Government Telegraph and Radio Office in the Post Office Building, Oranjestad. There is also an ITT office at Boecoetiweg 33. Emergency: dial 115. There are flights from Aruba to Amsterdam, Bonaire, Curaçao, Sint Maarten, Puerto Rico and several US and South American destinations.

MEDICAL
There is a modern hospital.

DIPLOMATIC MISSIONS
Colombia: Smith Blvd 52. ☎ 21206.
Venezuela: Lacle Blvd. ☎ 21078.

No longer part of the Netherlands Antilles, Aruba broke away from the other five islands in 1986 to become an autonomous member of the Kingdom of the Netherlands. The Hague is now only responsible for defence and foreign affairs, and the Queen is represented by a Governor. The island has the same status as the Netherlands Antilles and will gain complete independence in 1996.

Protestantism. Dutch is the official language, but English and Spanish are widely spoken, as well as the local language Papiamento.

Aruba lies outside the hurricane belt and has a dry climate. Temperatures are higher from August to October, although there is not a great difference to the cooler months, which are from December to February.

Country Profile

Arawaks populated this island when the Spanish first landed in 1499, but it was the Dutch who established rule over the island and resisted all challenges from other European powers. Early in the nineteenth century gold was discovered, but exploitation of it had ceased by 1916. In 1929 an oil refinery was built, at that time the largest in the world, and its closure in 1985 was a shock to the Aruban economy. Tourism was rapidly developed as a cure, and recently efforts have been made to establish Aruba as an offshore business centre. Aid from the Netherlands, however, is still vital to the economy. The island has three ports, of which only the capital Oranjestad, which is sheltered behind a reef, is suitable for yachts.

Aruba is one of the few Caribbean islands where descendants of the indigenous population, the Arawaks, still live. The population of 68,000 also includes those of Spanish and Dutch origin as well as many recent immigrants. A wide range of religions are practised including Roman Catholicism, Judaism and

Entry Regulations

Port of entry
Oranjestad 12°31'N, 70°00'W.

Procedure on arrival
Oranjestad: Yachts can enter either through the northern or southern opening in the reef. Aruba Port Control should be called on VHF Channel 16, who will advise where to tie up at a dock and wait for officials. As Aruba has broken its ties with the Netherlands Antilles, the correct courtesy flag is that of the Netherlands.

Customs and immigration offices are by the harbour.

Customs
Dogs and cats are only allowed entry with valid rabies and health certificates. Animals arriving from South and Central America are not allowed to land.

Oranjestad is a free port and therefore no customs restrictions apply.

Immigration

US and Canadian citizens need proof of identification only, all others need a valid passport. Proof of adequate funds may also be required to be shown.

Facilities

Besides the new marina in Oranjestad, there are two yacht clubs where visitors may sometimes use the moorings. Down the coast from Oranjestad, near Spanish Lagoon, is the Aruba Nautical Club, which has berths, fuel, water and electricity. Members of other yacht clubs may use the facilities, but should check in advance. Between Oranjestad and Spanish Lagoon is the Bucuti Yacht Club which also has docking space and a few other facilities. Provisioning is best done in Oranjestad, where there is a good selection of fresh produce and one is moored conveniently by the town centre.

Further Reading

A Cruising Guide to the Caribbean and the Bahamas
Caribbean Islands Handbook

BAHAMAS

Over 700 islands and 2400 uninhabited cays make up the Bahamas, its name coming from the Spanish 'baja mar', meaning shallow sea. The coral and limestone archipelago stretches south-east from Florida for nearly 500 miles.

In the world of cruising, the Bahamas stand out as a totally different experience. These low islands surrounded by clear waters of exquisite colours and unbelievable transparency have a charm all of their own. The distinctive features are the large shallow banks and coral reefs which, although a hazard to shipping, provide excellent diving and underwater scenery. The shallow depths and strong tidal currents that occur call for very attentive navigation.

The proximity to the USA has profoundly affected the islands, particularly those closest to Florida, which are visited by large numbers of tourists, cruise ships and yachts. Outside of the main tourist centres, however, the Bahamas have changed little and the slow pace of life in the outer islands is their enduring charm. Unfortunately this isolation and yet relative closeness to the USA has turned the Bahamas into a convenient transit point for drug traffickers. As the Bahamian authorities are unable to police their vast territory, the

task of surveillance is often taken over by the US Coast Guard who keep track of all sea and air movement between the Bahamas and the mainland. As they cannot tell the difference between a smuggler and a genuine cruising yacht, they treat everyone with suspicion. Boats are often stopped and searched on their way to the USA, an unpleasant experience that unfortunately one has to put up with in the relentless war being waged against drug trafficking. Some cruising boats have also been caught unwillingly in the dangerous drugs game when they were seized by gangs, the crew disposed of and the boat used for an illegal run. Although such incidents have been very rare, it is prudent to sail in company if possible and avoid spending the night alone in remote anchorages.

Country Profile

On 12 October 1492, Christopher Columbus made his first landfall in the New World on the island of San Salvador. At that time the Bahamas were inhabited by the peaceful Lucayans, who were to disappear as a people within a few years, as the Spanish deported most of the population to work in the gold and silver mines in Hispaniola and Cuba. Once plundered of their only resource, people, the Spanish left the islands alone.

From the time of the first settlement in 1629 by Protestant settlers from Bermuda escaping religious persecution, the Bahamas have remained under British rule until 1973 when they became a fully independent nation. With the development of merchant shipping between the New World and Europe, piracy became common with such renowned figures as Blackbeard finding the deserted islands and reefs perfect hiding places. At the end of the American War of Independence many loyalists fled to the Bahamas and established cotton plantations, which met with little success in the poor soil. The descendants of the slaves brought over to work on these plantations, emancipated in 1838, form the majority of the inhabitants today.

The geographical position of the Bahamas has always influenced its history, from being a refuge for gun-runners during the American Civil War to making the fortune of those running liquor to the USA during the Prohibition era. This aspect continues today with the islands being a large transhipment area for illegal drugs on their way to the USA. The conditions which suited the seventeenth century pirate work equally well for the twentieth century drug baron.

Over 3 million tourists visit the Bahamas every year and the majority of the population is employed in the tourist industry, which is the backbone of the

Practical Information

LOCAL TIME: GMT - 5. Summer time
GMT - 4 April to October.

BUOYAGE: IALA B.

CURRENCY: Bahamas dollar (B$),
which is on a par with the US dollar. US$
are widely accepted.

BUSINESS HOURS
Banks in Nassau: 0930–1500 Monday to
Thursday, 0930–1700 Friday. Banks in
Freeport: 0900–1300 Monday to Friday,
1500–1700 Friday.
Shops: 0900–1700, or 1000–1800,
Monday to Friday. Some close Friday or
Saturday afternoons.
Government offices: 0900–1730 Monday
to Friday.

ELECTRICITY: 110 V, 60 Hz

PUBLIC HOLIDAYS
1 January: New Year's Day
Good Friday, Easter Monday
Whit Monday
10 July: Independence Celebrations
First Monday in August
12 October: Discovery Day
1 November: State Day
25, 26 December: Christmas

EVENTS
February: Miami–Nassau Yacht Race
March: Miami–Nassau Sailing Race
July–August: Goombay Holiday
December 26, January 1: Junkanoo

COMMUNICATIONS
There is a public telephone, cable and
telex office open 24 hours in the
Telecommunications Building on East St,
Nassau. International calls can be made
from metered booths at telephone

offices on all major islands.
There are many international flights
from Nassau and several to US and
Canada from Freeport. There are also
daily flights to Miami from Georgetown
on Great Exuma. All inhabited islands
are linked to Nassau by internal flights.

MEDICAL
The Princess Margaret Hospital in
Nassau is the main facility, but most of
the inhabited islands have a clinic.
Contact the Coast Guard in an
emergency.

DIPLOMATIC MISSIONS
In Nassau:
Canada: Out Island Traders Bldg.
☎ 323-2123.
Haiti: Marlborough St. ☎ 322-2109.
United Kingdom: Bitco Bldg. ☎ 325-7471.
United States: Queen St. ☎ 322-4753.

economy. The absence of income tax and strict bank secrecy laws have made the Bahamas a tax haven and important financial centre. The government has made efforts to develop other areas of the economy, particularly agriculture, to help meet domestic demand.

The total population of the islands is 235,000, largely of African origin with a minority of English and American origin. Only 30 of the islands are inhabited and 75 per cent of the population lives on New Providence Island, location of the capital Nassau. The outer islands are known as the Family Islands. English is the main language. There are many religious denominations, mainly Christian, particularly Anglican and Roman Catholic. The Bahamian climate is very pleasant, lying on the edge of the anticyclone belt. The hurricane season is July to November.

Entry Regulations

Ports of entry
Abaco: Walker's Cay 26°32'N 76°57'W, Green Turtle Cay 26°45'N 77°20'W, Marsh Harbour 26°40'N 75°05'W, Sandy Point 26°01'N 77°24'W.
Andros: Nicholl's Town 25°07'N 78°02'W, San Andros 24°43'N 77°47'W, Fresh Creek 24°41'N 77°50'W, Mangrove Cay 24°13'N 77°36'W, Congo Town.
Berry Islands: Great Harbour Cay 25°44'N 77°49'W, Chub Cay 25°44'N 77°49'W.

North Bimini: Alice Town 25°20'N 76°29'W.
Cat Cay: Cat Cay Club 25°33'N 79°18'W.
Eleuthera: Harbour Island 25°34'N 76°40'W, Hatchet Bay 25°20'N 76°29'W, Governor's Harbour 25°12'N 76°15'W, Rock Sound 24°53'N 76°16'W, Cape Eleuthera (sometimes) 25°12'N 76°15'W.
Exuma: George Town 23°34'N 75°49'W.
Grand Bahama: West End 26°42'N 78°59'W, Freeport Harbour 26°31'N 78°47'W, Lucaya Marina 26°29'N 78°38'W, Xanadu Marina 26°29'N 78°42'W.
Inagua: Matthew Town 20°57'N 73°41'W.
New Providence: Any marina in Nassau 25°04'N 77°21'W.
Ragged Island: Duncan Town 22°12'N 75°44'W.
San Salvador: Cockburn Town 24°03'N 74°32'W.
Although Abrahams Bay on Mayaguana Island is not listed as an official port of entry, yachts coming from the east have been able to stop there, although they had to clear in at an official port of entry later on.

Procedure on arrival
Entry into the Bahamas must be made at one of the official ports of entry. The Q flag should be flown within three miles of the port and no one should go ashore until pratique has been granted. Officials are supposed to come to the yacht, but in some smaller islands the captain will have to go ashore to find them. Crew must remain on board until clearance is completed. A health declaration, inwards report and crew

lists must be completed by the captain.

Penalties are severe (fines, imprisonment, confiscation of the boat) for not clearing customs.

Clearance must be done on arrival, and in major ports officers are on call at all hours; in such places one is not allowed to anchor off and wait until morning, to avoid overtime charges. The Bahamas can be transited without clearing in until one arrives at a port of entry at a convenient time, but during transit one cannot anchor overnight or enter a port. In the outer islands normally the customs officer handles all formalities, but in Nassau both the customs and immigration officials must be seen.

Movement of vessels is strictly controlled in Nassau, where all yachts are required to clear with Nassau Harbour Control (VHF Channel 16) when entering, leaving and even changing position within the harbour.

If chartering a boat in the Bahamas, one can clear in and out at the airport. No cruising permit (transire) is needed nor must customs be cleared to cruise the Bahamas, although an onward ticket must be shown.

Customs

Firearms must be declared and listed on the ship's declaration. Personal firearms are permitted as part of a ship's equipment on board visiting yachts in Bahamian waters, but cannot be used and must remain locked on board throughout the stay. After three months, these become liable for duty and a permit must be obtained from the police.

A permit costing $10 from the Ministry of Agriculture and Fisheries is required for any animals on board. Cats and dogs need a valid anti-rabies certificate, issued from ten days to nine months previously.

Foreign boats remaining in the Bahamas after six months must notify customs and special arrangements made. They will be subject to an import tax of 22.5 per cent of their value. Spare parts imported for visiting foreign boats are subject to duty ranging from 12.5 to 35 per cent.

Immigration

US and Canadian citizens can enter with proof of identity only for a stay of up to three weeks. A valid passport is necessary for longer visits. Nationals of Commonwealth and West European countries are among the many who do not require visas.

Nassau on New Providence Island (Ministry of Tourism, Bahamas).

Cruising permit (transire)

This is issued on arrival and gives permission to visit all other islands. The transire must be presented to officials if requested at any port visited. The permit must be retained until the cruise is finished and handed back at the port of exit. Only one cruising permit may be issued per trip, but it is valid up to six months. If for any reason one is not able to clear out, the transire should be posted back from the next destination.

Fees

If a yacht arrives within office hours, there is no charge except sometimes the transport costs of the officer to the entry point. Arriving outside of hours, overtime has to be paid. This is one and a half times the officer's hourly rate (one hour minimum) between 0600–0900, 1730–2200 weekdays, 0600–2200 Saturdays. It is double from 2200 to 0600 any day, all day Sundays, and public holidays. If a port has both a customs and an immigration officer, both must be paid overtime. Charges can be minimised by arriving within working hours on weekdays.

Restrictions

No marine life at all may be captured in the national marine parks, Exuma Cays Land and Sea Park, Peterson Cay National Park (Grand Bahama) and Pelican Cays (Abaco). Elsewhere, fishing regulations are strict. On arrival a fishing permit should be requested from the customs officer; this is required by any foreign vessel fishing in Bahamian waters for non-commercial purposes. Fishing may only be done with a hook and line, no more than six lines are allowed, and spears, fish traps, nets (other than landing nets) and spearguns (apart from the Hawaiian sling) are prohibited. Scuba gear may not be used for fishing. The maximum catch of kingfish, dolphin fish and wahoo is six in total per person and no more than 20 pounds of scalefish, plus ten conch or six crawfish per person. The latter may only be caught in season (1 August to 31 March) and females with eggs must be left. Turtles, coral or sea mammals must not be taken, nor any species that are undersize. It should be noted that the Royal Bahamas Defence Force regularly patrols sensitive areas and has the power to inspect any boat they suspect of flouting either these regulations or the drug laws. They monitor VHF Channel 16.

Facilities

Almost everything is available in Nassau, which has several marinas, chandleries and repair facilities. Fuel and other marine supplies are also easily available and so are provisions. There is an excellent fresh produce market at Potter's Cay. *The Yachtsman's Guide to the Bahamas* gives details of facilities available not only in Nassau, but throughout the islands.

Another popular destination with good facilities is Freeport on Grand Bahama Island. The main port is geared to dealing primarily with commercial vessels, so visiting yachts might find it more convenient to clear in at nearby Lucayan or Xanadu Marinas. Facilities at both are good and most repairs can be undertaken locally. In the outer islands Georgetown in Great Exuma is slowly establishing itself as a yachting centre where minor repairs can be effected. Basic supplies are available and also charts for the Bahamas. There is also a daily fresh produce market. Any parts that are not available locally can be obtained from either Nassau or Florida to which there are frequent flights.

Further Reading

Yachtsman's Guide to the Bahamas
A Cruising Guide to the Caribbean and the Bahamas
Bahamas: Insight Guide
Cruising Guide to the Abacos and the Northern Bahamas
The Gentleman's Guide to Passages South

BARBADOS

As the most easterly of the Lesser Antilles, Barbados is a comparatively flat island and to windward of all the other islands. It is the nearest landfall for yachts crossing the Atlantic on the traditional trade wind route. The windward position of Barbados means that few yachts attempt to beat their way against the prevailing trade winds from the other islands of the Lesser Antilles to visit this island which has little to offer from the cruising point of view.

The cruising yachts that call in Barbados usually arrive after a long passage either from the Canaries or Cape Verdes across the North Atlantic or when sailing up from Brazil and the South Atlantic and make a stop before sailing on elsewhere.

Despite having a developed tourist industry which benefits from the island's good airlinks, little has been done for those arriving by sea and facilities in Carlisle Bay, the main anchorage, are very basic. The only cruising area is along the sheltered west coast, where most of the tourist development lies, but permission from the authorities to do this is not simple to obtain.

After almost 3000 miles of Atlantic Ocean, most boats make their landfall on the SE coast of Barbados,

Practical Information

LOCAL TIME: GMT - 4

BUOYAGE: IALA B

CURRENCY: Barbados dollar (BDS$)

BUSINESS HOURS
Banks: 0800–1500 Monday to Thursday,
0800–1200, 1500–1700 Friday.
Shops: 0800–1800 Monday to Saturday.
Business and government
offices: 0730–1630 Monday to Friday.

ELECTRICITY: 120 V, 50 Hz

PUBLIC HOLIDAYS
1 January: New Year's Day
Good Friday
Easter Monday

1 May: Labour Day
Whit Monday
First Monday in August: Emancipation
Day
First Monday in October: UN Day
30 November: Independence Day
25, 26 December: Christmas

EVENTS
Crop Over Festival: July, at the end of
sugar harvest.
Mount Gay Regatta: Boxing Day, three
days of yacht racing.

COMMUNICATIONS
Overseas calls, telex and fax from
Barbados External Telecommunications
(BET).

There are international flights from
Grantley Adams airport to the USA,
Canada, Europe, South America and
many Caribbean destinations. There are
connecting flights from international
flights to the smaller Caribbean islands.

DIPLOMATIC MISSIONS
Canada: Bishops Court, Hill Pine Rd,
Bridgetown. ☎ 429-3550.
United Kingdom: Roebuck St,
Bridgetown. ☎ 436-6694.
United States: Broad St, Bridgetown.
☎ 436-4950.
Venezuela: El Sueno, Worthing.
☎ 426-5466.

---

which is easily detectable at night by the strong loom of the airport lights. The east coast, exposed to the Atlantic breakers, is wild with strange rock formations along its beaches and should be given a wide berth.

Country Profile

The pre-Columbian population of Barbados were probably Arawaks, eventually driven out by the warlike Caribs. The island was named Bearded Island – Isla de los Barbados – by the Portuguese, after the bearded fig-trees found growing there. Pedros a Campos, the Portuguese explorer, landed here in 1536 on his way to Brazil, but the first settlers in the seventeenth century were English. By then the island was uninhabited, although why the Amerindians left is not known. Jamestown, near the present-day Holetown, was the first settlement, founded in 1627. A year later the rival Bridgetown, eventually to become the capital, was established. Tobacco, cotton and sugar cane crops were developed, and thousands of slaves brought over from Africa. Barbados grew into a flourishing colony and centre for maritime trade, and through the eighteenth and nineteenth centuries the influx of English settlers continued. Due to its position it never changed hands unlike its Caribbean neighbours and remained British throughout. Barbados became independent in November 1966.

Sugar was always the cornerstone of the economy, and remains important today. Sugar, molasses, syrup and rum are exported. There is some light industry.

Tourism in recent years has increased greatly, and is an important source of employment on this relatively affluent island.

The population is 280,000, mainly descendants of mixed African and European origin. There is a small white minority of English origin. English and Bajan, a dialect, are spoken. Of more than 70 religious denominations, the largest is Anglican. Barbados has a tropical climate, although as the island is further south, it rarely is hit by hurricanes. June to January is the rainy and humid season.

Entry Regulations

Port of entry
Bridgetown 13°06′N, 59°38′W.

Procedure on arrival
Clearance can only be done in the Deepwater Harbour north of Bridgetown. On approach, yachts should call the signal station on VHF Channel 12 (call sign 8PB) and will be advised where to proceed. Once permission is given, the yacht should go into the Deepwater Harbour and unless advised to the contrary come alongside the Cross Berth, in the southern corner. One should stay in radio contact while entering the harbour to ensure no other vessel is manoeuvring, as the harbour frequently has cruise ships berthed there. The Q flag must be flown until clearance is complete. The captain only should proceed to clear customs, health and immigration in the Customs Examination Hall

behind the Cross Berth, from 0600–2200 seven days a week. If arriving outside these hours, yachts are directed to anchor in the Quarantine anchorage in Carlisle Bay and the crew should not go ashore. The following morning the yacht must proceed into the Deepwater Harbour as outlined above.

After entry formalities are complete, a yacht may anchor in Carlisle Bay or berth in the Careenage in the centre of town. Docking space in the Careenage is limited and permission to berth there must be obtained from the harbour master at the Barbados Port Authority (☎ 436-6883).

Permission has to be obtained from customs, preferably requested on arrival, if wishing to cruise or anchor along the coast away from Carlisle Bay.

On departure, the port authority's clearance must be obtained first in order to get customs clearance. Outward clearance is valid for 24 hours after it has been granted. A vessel must proceed directly to sea from the Deepwater Harbour after receiving outward clearance.

Customs
Firearms must be licensed and declared immediately to customs on arrival. They will be kept in custody until departure. Penalties for non-declaration or possessing an unlicensed firearm are severe.

Animals are not allowed to land.

Chartering is forbidden for foreign yachts.

Immigration
Nationals of Western European and Commonwealth countries, Brazil, Canada, Colombia, the USA and Venezuela, do not need visas. Other nationals are granted a short stay on arrival. Those needing a visa in advance are nationals of Eastern European countries, India, Pakistan and South Africa (the latter may have problems getting a visa). Extensions are difficult to obtain, so on arrival one should state the maximum time one intends to stay. Extensions must be applied for at the immigration office in the harbour (open 0830–1630), cost BDS$12.50, and are time-consuming to obtain.

Immigration must be notified of any crew changes. Crew flying in must have a letter from the captain confirming that they will be leaving by yacht. They may still have difficulties with immigration officers at the airport if an onward air ticket cannot be shown, so it is advisable for the captain to meet crew and take the ship's papers along. If any crew are disembarking after the yacht has been cleared, they must go with the captain to inform immigration. If transferring to another vessel, both captains must go with the crew member.

Fees
Small light dues calculated by tonnage, unless under 5 tons. Stamp duty on both entry and exit amounts to BDS$50 in total.

Facilities

As the number of locally owned yachts is relatively small, there are few facilities aimed specifically at the yachting market, although the arrival of the ARC fleet for four years brought some improvement in the repair facilities. There are two chandleries in the capital Bridgetown, which have a limited selection of marine hardware. Mannings stock charts and cruising guides for the Caribbean and are the only place to undertake rigging work, as they have both the wire and a swaging press. As Barbados is a relatively developed island, electrical, electronic, refrigeration, metal-working workshops and other facilities are found even if not catering primarily for yachts. Most engine repair, both diesel and outboard, can be done on the island as all major manufacturers are represented locally. The only hauling-out facility is in the commercial harbour by arrangement with the Port Authority, but this is a complicated and costly operation. Sail repair can be done via the Barbados Yacht Club, which welcomes visitors and can be of help in an emergency.

Further Reading

A Cruising Guide to the Caribbean and the Bahamas Caribbean Islands Handbook

BONAIRE

The stunning underwater scenery is the chief attraction of this easternmost of the ABC islands and anyone with even the smallest interest in diving should use their stay to best advantage. Bonaire is ranked as one of the top three dive spots in the world and as a result the whole island is a protected marine park.

Bonaire is less densely populated than its neighbour Curaçao and also less developed. The slow pace of life on the island and its relaxed population have an enduring charm. For visiting sailors the attraction also lies in the better than average repair and service facilities. A much needed marina was created by dredging a channel through to a salt pond close to the capital Kralendijk.

Practical Information

LOCAL TIME: GMT - 4

BUOYAGE: IALA B

CURRENCY: Antillean guilder of 100 cents. US dollars may be accepted and sometimes the Venezuelan bolivar.

BUSINESS HOURS
Banks: 0930–1200, 1400–1600 Monday to Friday.
Shops: 0800–1200, 1400–1800 Monday to Saturday, and for a few hours on Sundays, if there are cruise ships in port.

ELECTRICITY: 110/130 V, 50 Hz

PUBLIC HOLIDAYS
1 January: New Year's Day
Good Friday and Easter Monday
30 April: Queen's Birthday
1 May: Labour Day
Ascension
Whit Monday
6 September: Bonaire Day
15 December: National Day
25, 26 December: Christmas

EVENTS
Carnival in February or March

COMMUNICATIONS
There is a telecommunications office on J.A. Abraham Blvd, Kralendijk.
There are flights from Bonaire to Aruba and Curaçao, and also to New York and Miami.
DIPLOMATIC MISSIONS
Venezuela: Breedestr. Kralendijk.
☎ 8275.

Country Profile

The island was discovered along with Aruba and Curaçao in 1499 by the Spaniard Alonso de Ojeda. At that time an Arawak tribe, the Caiquetios, lived there, and although many did not survive, they managed to retain their identity on Bonaire until the end of the nineteenth century. The Dutch took the island in 1636 and the ABC islands changed hands several times as the European powers fought for colonies in the Caribbean, although from 1816 Dutch rule was firmly established. After the Second World War demands for more autonomy grew stronger, and in 1954 the Netherlands Antilles were granted full internal autonomy.

Lacking natural resources and a good harbour, Bonaire was never as prosperous as Curaçao. The economy is fairly diversified, with salt, textiles and rice on the traditional side, and oil transhipment and radio communications more modern sources of income. Tourism is an important foreign exchange earner. The island's population numbers 10,000, of mixed Arawak, European and African descent. They speak Dutch and Papiamento. English and Spanish are also widely spoken.

Entry Regulations

Ports of entry
Kralendijk and Bonaire Marina 12°09′N 68°17′W.

Procedure on arrival
Kralendijk: Yachts clearing in must come to the customs dock. The customs office is open 24 hours a day seven days a week and no overtime is charged. Next one must visit the immigration office located a short distance from the port in the police building. After clearance one is free to anchor.
Bonaire Marina: This is a small marina just north of Kralendijk, where clearance by customs can also be done.

Customs
All firearms are impounded until departure, including flare guns and spearguns.

To either buy or import equipment duty free one has to fill in a special form obtainable from the customs office. Customs sometimes insist on inspecting the boat before departure to see that the item is still on board.

Immigration
A three-month visa is usually granted on arrival although nationals of certain countries may be required to check with immigration every two weeks or every month. Visas can be extended for a further three months.

Restrictions
Due to the marine park status of the island, spearfishing is forbidden and marine life of any description may not be removed or destroyed.

Facilities

Bonaire Marina has a large travelift and good repair facilities. Propane bottles can be filled by leaving them at the local petrol station from where they are sent to Curaçao and returned about one week later. If bound for Curaçao, it is better to wait to refill gas bottles and fuel tanks there as it is more convenient and cheaper than in Bonaire.

There are several good supermarkets in Kralendijk and although the selection might be better in Curaçao, the advantage of shopping in Bonaire is that everything is very conveniently situated. The biggest supermarket is Cultimara and there are several shops which sell case lots at a reduced price.

Further Reading

A Cruising Guide to the Caribbean and Bahamas
The Bonaire Marine Park Guide
Caribbean Islands Handbook

BRITISH VIRGIN ISLANDS

The Virgin Islands are an archipelago comprising hundreds of small islands and cays situated between Puerto Rico and the Leeward Islands. The western part, having some of the larger islands, is US territory, while the eastern half is a British dependency. The language and currency are shared, but the US Virgin Islands are more developed and culturally different. The largest British islands are Tortola, Virgin Gorda, Jost van Dyke and Anegada, the latter being slightly set apart, while the former are grouped together around the Sir Francis Drake channel.

There are few island groups in the world which are better suited for cruising than the Virgins. They are scenically beautiful, there are countless bays, coves and anchorages, the waters are sheltered from the strong trade winds and navigation is never taxing. With so many convenient hideaways and access channels it is not surprising that the islands became a favourite base for the pirates and buccaneers who in days gone by were roaming the surrounding seas in search of bounty. It is exactly these same features which attract modern-day sailors to these shores and the British Virgins are now the largest bareboat charter centre in the world. For this reason they are often less attractive to the long-distance cruising sailors, who prefer the less crowded islands of the Caribbean.

Country Profile

The original inhabitants were Arawaks and Caribs. Visited by Columbus on his second voyage, he named the islands after St Ursula and her 11,000 virgin warriors who died rather than submit to pagan assault. Soon after their discovery, the Virgin Islands' strategic position rapidly turned them into a popular stop for vessels plying between Europe and America. The Caribs, pirates and privateers all harassed the Spanish settlements and ships from the Spanish Main returning laden with gold and silver. Infamous figures such as Henry Morgan and Sir John Hawkins operated in this area and the Virgin Islands were the inspiration for R. L. Stevenson's *Treasure Island*.

As Spanish power waned, colonisation by other European nations became more serious and several countries fought over the islands. At the end of the seventeenth century England annexed Tortola, then Virgin Gorda and Anegada. Plantations were established and slaves brought in for labour. Civil government over the islands was minimal. With the slump in sugar cane and slave rebellions leading to their emancipation, economic problems occurred with a resulting labour shortage. After 1956 the British Virgin Islands became separately administered from the rest of the British West Indies, and developed more links with the US Virgin Islands. Today the British Virgin Islands have internal self-government, but remain a British colony.

Much of the land is cultivated, mostly for fruit and vegetables, yet reliance on food imports means there is a high cost of living. Tourism is very important and is just about at saturation point. Tax privileges have prompted the islands' growth as an offshore business centre. English is spoken and most people are Protestant. The capital is Road Town on Tortola, the largest island in the British Virgin Islands, where about half the total population of 12,000 lives.

Entry Regulations

Ports of entry
Tortola: Road Harbour 18°25'N 64°37'W, Sopers Hole 18°23'N 64°42'W.
Jost van Dyke: Great Harbour 18°27'N 64°45'W.
Virgin Gorda: Virgin Gorda Yacht Harbour 18°27'N 64°26'W.
There are two other entry points, Port Purcell and Beef Island Airport, but yachts are not supposed to enter or clear at these.

Procedure on arrival
Ship's papers, passports and last clearance must be shown, and an inward manifest and/or outward manifest, and crew list completed. It should be noted that the British Virgin Islands and the US Virgin Islands require full customs clearance out and in when sailing between them. If, however, one's stay is short, one may be able to clear in and out at the same time.

Practical Information

LOCAL TIME: GMT - 4

BUOYAGE: IALA B. The BVI changed over to the IALA B system in 1984. However, some buoys were just painted over and have been reported as revealing their original colours after a few years. Privately maintained buoys may not be as reliable as those looked after by the Coast Guard.

CURRENCY: US dollar (US$).

BUSINESS HOURS
Banks: 0900–1400 Monday–Friday, also 1600–1730 on Fridays.
Shops: 0900–1700 Monday–Friday.
Government offices: 0830–1630 Monday–Friday.

ELECTRICITY: 110 V, 60 Hz

PUBLIC HOLIDAYS
1 January: New Year's Day
Second Monday in March: Commonwealth Day
Good Friday
Easter Monday
Whit Monday
Second Monday in June: Queen's Birthday
1 June: Territory Day
Beginning of August: Festival (Monday, Tuesday, Wednesday)
21 October: St Ursula's Day
14 November: Prince Charles' Birthday
25, 26 December: Christmas

EVENTS
Easter Festival, on Virgin Gorda
BVI Spring Regatta, on Tortola, March–April

COMMUNICATIONS
International telephone calls, telex and fax at Cable & Wireless, centre of Road Town.
Emergency: dial 999.
There are flights to other Caribbean destinations but no direct flights to Europe or the USA. Connections are usually made in Antigua or Puerto Rico.

Road Harbour: Customs and immigration are at the government dock at Road Town. One should anchor off the dock and check in with customs and immigration before proceeding elsewhere. One can also clear at Nanny Cay Marina, which should be called on VHF Channel 16 first for berthing instructions as one cannot anchor there. Customs and immigration are inside the marina.

Sopers Hole: Offices are at the ferry dock at West End. Ferries from the US Virgin Islands stop here, which can mean clearance takes longer if a ferry arrives.

Great Harbour: Customs and immigration offices are in the same building by the dock.

Virgin Gorda: Offices are in the yacht harbour; one should contact the harbour master first on radio to arrange berthing.

Customs

Firearms are not allowed to be kept on board and must be surrendered to Customs until departure. This law is strictly enforced.

For animals a valid health certificate issued at least two weeks prior to arrival must be shown, plus a valid anti-rabies certificate (dogs and cats) and proof that the animal is free from disease. No animals can be landed without a permit and must remain secured on board at all times. A permit may be obtained from the Department of Agriculture in Road Town by giving full details (species, sex, age, colour, country of origin, owner's name and address, means of arrival). A charge of US$5 per animal is made by customs at the time of clearance and all certificates must be presented at the

same time. The penalty for breaking the law is a fine and impounding of the animal.

Immigration

No visas are required for nationals of Commonwealth countries, Belgium, Denmark, Finland, France, Greece, Iceland, Italy, Liechtenstein, Luxembourg, Netherlands, Norway, San Marino, Spain, Sweden, Switzerland, Tunisia, Turkey, Uruguay and the United States, if visit does not exceed six months. Nationals of Germany and Venezuela do not require visas if visit does not exceed one month. All other nationals require visas.

Normally a 30 day stay is given on arrival. Extensions cost US$10 per passport. All members of the crew must be present to clear immigration.

Charter

If a yacht is chartered complete with crew, the captain and crew are not required to pay a cruising fee, but the charter guests are. On a bareboat charter, everyone on board is required to pay the daily cruising fee.

BVI registered boats pay US$2 per person per day (December 1 to April 30), and 0.75c (May 1 to November 30). Foreign registered boats pay a fee of US$4 per person per day all year round. Visiting crewed charter boats also have to pay a departure tax of US$4 per person. These charges only apply to yachts that are chartering.

Fees

Harbour dues and ships' dues make up a charge of

about US$7 to US$15, depending on the size of the boat.

Overtime must be paid for customs clearance outside 0830–1530 Monday to Friday, 0830–1230 Saturdays.

Fishing

Non-residents must obtain a recreational fishing permit in order to fish in BVI waters.

Facilities

Virtually all facilities are concentrated on Tortola, particularly around Road Town, where there are several marinas. There is a large marina at Nanny Cay with a travelift, chandlery and extensive repair facilities. A smaller marina at Sopers Hole has its own slipway, whereas nearby West End Slipways offer a wider range of repair facilities including a 200-ton marine railway.

Virgin Gorda Yacht Harbour has full marina facilities, a 60-ton lift as well as good provisioning. Only basic facilities are available on Jost van Dyke at Great Harbour. On all small islands only basic provisions can be bought, so it is best to fully provision in one of the larger centres.

Further Reading

Yachtsman's Guide to the Virgin Islands
Caribbean Islands Handbook
A Cruising Guide to the Caribbean and the Bahamas

CAYMAN ISLANDS

The Cayman Islands are a British Crown Colony lying south of Cuba and west of Jamaica. Known mainly for their flag of convenience seen flying at the stern of the occasional yacht, the Caymans are very much off the cruising track.

Grand Cayman, lying some 80 miles west of its smaller sisters, has several anchorages and also a well protected marina inside a shallow lagoon. Little Cayman and Cayman Brac ('bluff' in Gaelic) are less developed and even less visited by cruising yachts than the main island. Grand Cayman's chief attraction is its underwater world, which can be described as a diver's paradise. The sea surrounding the island is a marine park and conservation area.

Country Profile

The islands were first sighted by Columbus on his last voyage to the Americas. First named Las Tortugas after the large numbers of turtles frequenting the islands, later they were called Caymanas from the Carib word for the marine crocodile found there. The turtles became a popular source of fresh meat for ships' crews sailing the Caribbean.

The first settlers were English, probably deserters from Oliver Cromwell's army, which was fighting Spain for control of nearby Jamaica. The islands were ceded to Britain in 1670 and in the following century became a popular base for pirates, Spanish privateers having driven off the early English settlers. Scottish fishermen were the next to come and settle on the islands. In 1788 ten merchant ships, a convoy from Jamaica, were wrecked off Grand Cayman and all aboard were saved by the islanders. In return King George III promised the islanders exemption from taxation. The islands were dependencies of Jamaica until the independence of the latter in 1962, when the islanders chose to remain as a direct dependency of Britain.

The original settlers were fishermen, seamen and farmers. Now the islanders enjoy a high standard of living as the Cayman Islands are a tax haven, and major offshore finance and banking centre. Tourism has also developed considerably. The English speaking population of mixed African and European descent is 25,000, most of whom live on Grand Cayman. The capital is Georgetown. Many Christian denominations are practised on the island.

The island is cooled by the prevailing north east trades, so the mean winter temperature is 24°C and in the summer 26–29°C. The winter northerlies make most anchorages untenable, when shelter must be sought either off the south coast or inside North Sound. The hurricane season is June to November.

Entry Regulations

Ports of entry
Grand Cayman: Georgetown 19°18′N 81°23′W.
Cayman Brac: Creek 19°45′N 79°44′W.

Procedure on arrival
Port Security should be called on VHF Channel 16, which is monitored 24 hours a day. They will notify customs and immigration and keep one informed regarding boarding of the yacht. In Georgetown yachts are normally asked to come alongside the commercial dock for clearance.

Practical Information

LOCAL TIME: GMT - 5

BUOYAGE: IALA B

CURRENCY: Cayman Islands dollar
(CI$)

BUSINESS HOURS
Banks: 0900–1430 Monday to Thursday,
0900–1300/1430–1600 Fridays.
Government offices: 0800–1700 Monday
to Friday.

ELECTRICITY: 110 V, 60 Hz

PUBLIC HOLIDAYS
1 January: New Year's Day
Ash Wednesday

Good Friday, Easter Monday
Third Monday in May: Discovery Day
Monday in June following Queen's
official birthday
First Monday in July: Constitution Day
Monday in November following
Remembrance Sunday
25, 26 December: Christmas

EVENTS
Pirates Week: last week October.
Batabano: Carnival weekend, last week
of April.
Cayman Brac has 'Brachanal' the
following Saturday.
Million dollar month: June, sport-fishing
tournament.

COMMUNICATIONS
International phone booths, telex,
telegram, fax at Cable & Wireless,
Anderson Square, 0815–1700.
There are flights from Grand Cayman to
Kingston (Jamaica) and several US
cities.

MEDICAL
Good health care is available in George
Town Government Hospital and other
clinics.
Cayman Islands Divers have a
recompression chamber behind Cayman
Clinic, off Crew Road, Georgetown.

DIPLOMATIC MISSIONS
United States: Cayside Galleries,
George Town. ☎ 98440.

Customs

Firearms are held by customs for the duration of the yacht's stay, unless a yacht is fitted with a proper safe, which can be sealed. Spearguns and their parts may not be imported nor used without a licence.

There are no restrictions on animals.

Immigration

No visas are required for a stay of up to six months by nationals of West European countries, the Commonwealth, Israel, Japan, South Africa and the United States. If a visa is required it can be issued on arrival.

Health

Malaria still occurs occasionally and there are lots of mosquitoes and sandflies.

Fees

Overtime fees are payable on weekdays after normal working hours and from noon Saturday to midnight Sunday.

Marine parks regulations

The Cayman Islands have a particularly rich marine life, and so strict regulations are in force to protect its beauty. Many indigenous species are protected including sea turtles, iguanas and orchids. In the Marine Parks and Environmental Zones no marine life at all may be taken, although one may fish outside protected areas. There are permanent moorings on the west coast of Grand Cayman which is a popular diving area.
Anchoring: Yachts are to use fixed moorings only. Boats of less than 60 feet may anchor in sand, as long as

no grappling hook is used and no coral is touched. Anchoring is permitted in designated anchorage areas and in replenishment zones.

The main restrictions are as follows:

Damaging coral by anchor or chains is prohibited.
No marine life may be taken while scuba diving.
No corals or sponges may be removed.
A spear gun or seine net may not be used without a licence from the Cayman Marine Conservation Board, and then only in certain areas.
The export of live fish and other marine life is prohibited.
Fishing with gill nets or poison is prohibited.
Dumping anything at all in the sea is prohibited.
All yachts need a holding tank.

Lobster: The closed season is February 1 to July 31. Only spiny lobster may be taken and six-inch tail length is the minimum size. There is a catch limit of five per person or 15 per boat per day, whichever is less.
Conch: There is a catch limit of 15 per person or 20 per boat per day, whichever is less. No one may buy or receive more than 20 conch from Cayman waters per day.
Grouper: Certain areas off the east end of each of the islands are protected for grouper spawning.
Penalties: A maximum fine of $5000 and one year in jail can be applied for contravening the regulations. Confiscation of the boat and other equipment may also be ordered. The protected areas and marine parks are clearly marked while full-time officers enforce the rules and can arrest offenders.

Facilities

There are various repair facilities in Georgetown including two chandleries; the one on Eastern Avenue also stocks charts. Propane bottles can be filled at a fuel station on Walker Road. A boatyard on the south side of North Sound has a travelift and some repair facilities. Fuel and water can be obtained at Governor's Marina, also in North Sound, which has the usual marina services.

There are few facilities on Little Cayman and Cayman Brac, although the latter has a commercial harbour where some provisions can be obtained and some repairs could be made in an emergency.

Further Reading

A Cruising Guide to the Caribbean and the Bahamas
Caribbean Islands Handbook

CUBA

Largest of the Caribbean islands, Cuba is mountainous, with rich soils, forests, mineral resources and a spectacular coastline. World-famous for its cigars and its revolution, it is another example of the wide diversity of the Caribbean nations.

The possibilities of cruising in Cuba have been fairly limited until recently, when the country began encouraging tourists to visit the island. In the past a few non-American yachts have visited the island every year, especially from those countries which always maintained diplomatic relations with Cuba. In more recent years the number of yachts has increased, although experiences seem to vary greatly, some yachts managing to cruise along the coast with little restriction, while others have had to visit the country by land, their yachts being confined to their port of entry. Fortunately the situation is changing rapidly and cruising is expected to open up in Cuba. New marinas built for sports fishermen have made life easier, and at present any sailor following the correct procedures should expect few problems.

Cuba has been blessed with countless natural harbours and once the country re-opens to cruising, it will quickly become a popular destination. Because the island runs in a general SE–NW direction and the prevailing winds are easterly, ideally one should sail along Cuba's coasts in a counterclockwise direction. The US still maintains a military base at Guantanamo Bay on the SE extremity of the island. This port should only be entered in an absolute emergency.

Country Profile

When discovered by Columbus in 1492 during his first voyage, the island was populated by Arawaks. Conquered by Diego Velazquez early in the sixteenth century, African slaves were introduced by the Spanish and soon replaced the Arawaks. The following century saw a long struggle for freedom and some autonomy from Spain was gained after the 1868–78 rebellion, when slavery was abolished. The United States, seeking to expand their influence in the Americas, became involved in the rebellion of 1895–8, which led to war with Spain, in which the latter was defeated. Cuba was then ruled by the US military until independence in 1901, and even after that the US continued to play a active role in Cuban affairs. The 1920s and 30s were dominated by the dictatorship of Gerardo Machado, toppled by a military coup led by Fulgencio Batista. The latter remained in power with US protection until 1959, when after three years of guerilla warfare, Fidel Castro ended Batista's rule. Castro's socialist policies turned Cuba from the US to the Soviet sphere of influence. In 1961 the Bay of Pigs invasion attempt by anti-Castro Cubans was defeated. The Cold War reached its peak with the Missile Crisis of 1962, when the USA refused to let the Soviet Union install nuclear missiles in Cuba. After this crisis the regime hardened, although more recently tensions have eased with the changing international climate.

Cuba is one of the leading producers of sugar in the world, although efforts have been made to diversify the economy. Agriculture is the dominant industry. Coffee and citrus fruits are important exports, and tourism is slowly growing. Some aid comes from the USSR, but the country has a large foreign debt.

The capital of Cuba is Havana, in which one fifth of the 10 million Spanish-speaking population lives. The majority are of Spanish origin, about 12 per cent are black, and a small minority Chinese. Catholicism still is the main religion, although it is mostly of the Marxist influenced 'liberation' type. Sects such as 'santeria', a mixture of popular Catholicism and the Yoruba belief, also have a considerable following.

The climate is subtropical with November to April, the cooler dry season, being the most pleasant. The rest of the year is often humid, rainy and very hot and the hurricane season is from June to November.

Entry Regulations

Ports of entry
North Coast: Santa Lucía (Pinar del Río province) 22°41′N 83°58′W, Hemingway Marina (Barlovento)

Practical Information

LOCAL TIME: GMT - 5

BUOYAGE: IALA B

CURRENCY: Cuban peso, of 100
centavos. US dollars are accepted by
hotels and some official institutions.
Exchange receipts should be kept to be
able to change back Cuban pesos on
departure, up to US$10.

BUSINESS HOURS
Banco Nacional de Cuba: 0830–1200,
1330–1500 Monday to Friday, 0830–1030
Saturday.

Shops: 1230–1930 Monday to Saturday.
Government offices: 0830–1230,
1330–1730 Monday to Friday,
some offices open Saturday morning.

ELECTRICITY: 110/230 V, 60 Hz

PUBLIC HOLIDAYS
1 January: Liberation Day
2 January: Victory of Armed Forces
1 May: Labour Day
25, 26 and 27 July: Revolution Days
10 October: War of Independence Day

EVENTS
Carnival in July

COMMUNICATIONS
Telegrams can be sent from all post
offices in Havana.
Collect calls are not permitted.
The postal service is very slow.
There are flights from Havana to several
Central and South American and
European cities.

DIPLOMATIC MISSIONS
Canada: 518 Calle 30, corner of Av. 7,
Miramar. ☎ (7) 2-6421.
United Kingdom: 101–103 Calle Carcel,
La Habana Vieja. ☎ (7) 61-5681.
US interests at the Swiss embassy: Calle
Calzada, between Calle L and Calle M,
Vedado. ☎ (7) 32-0551.

23°01′N 82°45′W, Gaviota Marina (Varadero, Pta. Hicacos) 23°03′N 81°12′W, Chapelin Marina (Varadero, Canal de Chapelin) 23°03′N 81°12′W, Paso Malo Marina (Varadero, Lag. Paso Malo) 23°03′N 81°12′W, Playa Santa Lucía (Camagüey province, Nuevitas) 21°33′N 77°16′W, Bahia Naranjo Marina (Holguín province) 21°07′N 75°53′W.
South Coast: Punta Gorda (Bahia de Santiago de Cuba) 19°59′N 75°52′W, Ancon (S.Spiritus province, Trinidad) 21°45′N 79°59′W, Jagua (Bahia Cienfuegas) 22°08′N 80°27′W, Cayo Largo (Archipelago de los Canarreos) 22°58′N 83°10′W.
Isla de la Juventad (Isla de Pinos): Colony 21°55′N 82°46′W.

Procedure on arrival

Recommended ports of entry for yachts are the Hemingway Marina at Barlovento (10 miles east of Havana), as well as the other marinas and Cayo Largo. All these have tourist facilities and are used to clearing in yachts. If entering at one of the other ports, which have no tourist services on site, one should request the services of the Tourist Office (Empresas Turisticas). Formalities may take longer in these ports as they may have to refer the matter to Havana. The commercial port of Havana should not be entered as it has no provision for clearing yachts.

As soon as Cuban territorial waters are entered 12 miles off the Cuban coast a yacht must contact the port authorities or coastguard on VHF Channel 16 or HF 2128KHz. The various authorities operate as follows: HF(SSB) 2760KHz Red Costera Nacional (coastguard net), 2790KHz Red Turistica (tourist

net); VHF Channel 68 port authorities, Channel 19 tourist services.

The following details should be communicated: name of yacht, flag, port of registry, last port of call, intended port of arrival in Cuba with approximate ETA, type of yacht and number of people on board. The captain will then be given instructions to proceed. A vessel may be sent out to escort the yacht into port. Channel 16 is also monitored by the marinas and they will also provide assistance. In no circumstances should one attempt to arrive unannounced or anchor in a bay.

Once moored in port one must wait for the officials to arrive and no one must go ashore until clearance is complete. Although entry formalities are lengthy with much paperwork, the officials are usually good natured and it all adds up to the excitement of visiting this country which for so long has been off limits.

Hemingway Marina: Most visiting yachts try and enter at the new large Hemingway Marina which is receiving an increasing number of foreign yachts. There is a check-in dock in the entrance channel to the marina and clearance formalities are completed here, after which a yacht is assigned a place in the marina.

Customs

If a yacht is staying a long time in one of the marinas, firearms will be impounded by the Coast Guard (Guarda Frontera). If the yacht is cruising along the coast, the firearms will be sealed on board, placed under the responsibility of the captain. The seals and arms will be inspected when clearing out.

Animals must have health certificates and anti-rabies

vaccinations. No animal may be landed without a permit from the health authority (Filosanitario) which requires a minimum two week quarantine period and costs US$25.

All plant, animal and meat products that are not canned must be declared to the health authorities on arrival. Reasonable quantities of canned meat, dairy or vegetable produce can be imported for the crew's own consumption.

The yacht can remain as long as the length of the tourist card issued to the crew and indefinitely if based permanently in one of the marinas.

Immigration

A tourist card (tarjeta de turista), but not a visa, is required by most visitors, if visiting Cuba for tourist purposes. It is recommended that this card is obtained in advance from Cuban embassies or consulates. However, the only countries in the Caribbean area where there are Cuban missions are Guyana, Mexico, Panama and Nicaragua. If arriving without a visa or tourist card, permission is granted on arrival for a 72-hour stay. Otherwise one can apply for a tourist card on arrival, valid for 15 days, which is renewable. Nationalities without visa-free agreements must get visas in advance, which can take time. If travelling on a visa, on arrival one should go to the immigration office to register and obtain an exit permit. Some Latin American countries will not admit someone with a passport stamped in Cuba, but if asked, Cuban officials will not stamp passports. It appears that the US government cannot stop its citizens from visiting Cuba, but for the time being it may be advisable for US citizens not to have their passport stamped in Cuba. A US citizen was heavily fined in 1990 for having visited Cuba several years previously.

Cruising permit

Once initial clearance is completed and if all crew members have tourist cards, a coastwise cruising permit (despacho de navegación – costera) can be obtained from the Coast Guard. This clearance permit will specify the areas the yacht wishes to visit and the length of time planned for the cruise. Although the clearance permits a yacht to cruise and anchor along the coast, if any of the ports of entry mentioned above are entered, one has to go through a clearance procedure again.

Fees

Entry or exit clearance fee is US$10 during normal working hours (0800–1700 weekdays). Clearance outside of these hours is charged as follows: weekdays 1700–2400 US$25, 0000–0800 US$35; Saturdays, Sundays and public holidays 0700–2400 US$25, 0000–0800 US$35.

A tourist card issued on arrival costs US$8, which can be extended at US$5 per extension.

Restrictions

It is forbidden to land at unauthorised places along the coast and also to take any other person on board the yacht apart from those on the crew list.

Scuba diving can only be done through the Tourist Office with an official instructor. Spearfishing is prohibited and no marine life, flora, fauna or any other object may be taken from the sea.

No archaeological objects should be removed, defaced or exported.

Facilities

Yachting is still in its infancy and as there are very few locally owned sailing boats, repair facilities are limited. The situation is somewhat better in the Havana area where workshops dealing with commercial craft and fishing boats may be persuaded to effect a repair on a yacht. Except for a few makes of diesel and outboard engines, spare parts are unobtainable.

Water and electricity are laid to the berths in the new marinas. Diesel fuel is also available. General provisioning is not easy as ration books are required to buy food in most places outside of Havana. Foreigners can only buy provisions at special shops where purchases have to be made in foreign currency. These shops are located in tourist resorts and the diplomatic area of Havana.

The Hydrographic Institute can supply nautical charts of Cuba at the port of entry if requested prior to arrival. These can be ordered from Empresa TECNOTEX, Habana. Telex 51-1039 TECTEX CU. The Institute also has other aids to navigation such as leaflets on buoyage and maritime signs of Cuba.

Further Reading

*A Cruising Guide to the Caribbean and the Bahamas
Caribbean Islands Handbook*

Practical Information

LOCAL TIME: GMT - 4

BUOYAGE: IALA B

CURRENCY: The Antillean guilder of 100 cents. The US dollar is widely accepted and sometimes the Venezuelan bolivar.

BUSINESS HOURS
Banks 0800/0830–1200, 1300–1600, 1330–1600 Monday to Friday.
Shops: 0800–1200, 1400–1800/1830 Monday to Saturday. Some stay open at lunchtime.

ELECTRICITY: 110/130 V, 50 Hz

PUBLIC HOLIDAYS
1 January: New Year's Day
Good Friday and Easter Monday
30 April: Queen's Birthday
1 May: Labour Day
Ascension
Whit Monday
15 December: National Day
25, 26 December: Christmas

COMMUNICATIONS
All American Cables and Radio Inc. offer telecommunications services.
There are flights to Aruba and Bonaire, Sint Maarten, Puerto Rico, Amsterdam, and US and South American cities.

DIPLOMATIC MISSIONS
In Willemstad:
Colombia: Scharlooweg 112. ☎ 614663.
Ecuador: Breedestr. 46. ☎ 613222.
Panama: Mahaalweg 26. ☎ 35292.
Peru: Pietermaai 20B. ☎ 611212.
United Kingdom: Erieweg 23. ☎ 70744.
US: J.B. Gorsiraweg 1. ☎ 613066.
Venezuela: de Ruyterkade 58. ☎ 613100.

CURAÇAO

Known worldwide for the orange liqueur named after it, Curaçao is the largest of the islands in the Netherlands Antilles off the coast of Venezuela. Curaçao is a very dry island, with a barren landscape and an excellent natural harbour at Schottegat.

The island is a favourite stop for yachts en route to Panama. Most yachts who stop here arrive from Bonaire and the contrast between the two islands is quite striking, particularly the capital Willemstad, which is a true metropolis by Caribbean standards. In spite of the increasing number of modern buildings, the waterfront buildings have an Old World charm redolent of Amsterdam. Although it is not too comfortable to linger in Willemstad after clearing in, the big ships continually moving in and out of this busy port are a sight to behold. Many yachts choose the protected anchorage at Spanish Water while Kleín Curaçao, an uninhabited island to the south-east, is a more solitary spot.

Country Profile

The first inhabitants of the island were Arawaks, who left remains of villages and cave drawings. Although the Spanish were the first Europeans to visit Curaçao, they showed little interest in anything except the Arawaks who were transported to Hispaniola as slave labour. The Dutch were the first to develop the island, attracted by Curaçao's protected natural harbour and the island's strategic position for trade. The Dutch West India Company was established, which panned salt and traded slaves from Africa. Despite challenges from other colonial powers, the Dutch retained their rule over the island. During the eighteenth century Curaçao became a centre for pirates, American rebels, Dutch merchants, Spaniards and Creoles. After a brief English occupation during the Napoleonic Wars, the island was restored to the Dutch in 1816 and became a free port. Since the creation of the Netherlands Antilles in 1954, Curaçao has had full internal autonomy, and is the administrative centre for the whole group, which remains part of the Netherlands.

Following the discovery of oil in Venezuela, a refinery was established on Curaçao. Today oil is still the linchpin of the economy, despite a recent recession, recovery from which is gradually taking place. Curaçao is also an important offshore financial centre and tourism a developing industry.

The population of 165,000 consists of a mixture of about 40 different nationalities, a result of the island's history as a thriving trading port. Curaçao is noted for its religious tolerance and a variety of religions freely celebrate their festivals there. Dutch is the official language, but English and Spanish are also widely spoken as well as the unique Papiamento.

Entry Regulations

Ports of entry
Willemstad 12°07'N 68°56'W, Spanish Water 12°09'N 68°17'W.

Procedure on arrival
The VHF working channels in Curaçao are 12 and 14.
Willemstad: At the centre of Willemstad is St Anna Bay, through which all ships pass into the large Schottegat Harbour, past the floating pedestrian bridge which opens for vessels. One should tie up at

the commercial dock on the starboard side of St Anna Bay, which is near customs and immigration. The port authorities will give berthing instructions. The immigration office is on the quayside next to the post office, not to be confused with the immigration counter at the post office which is for immigrants not yacht crews. As tying up to the dock in Willemstad for clearance is both uncomfortable and dangerous on account of the heavy wash of the constant commercial traffic, many yachts prefer to clear at Spanish Water.

Spanish Water: One should anchor off Sarifundy's Marina, west of the Curaçao Yacht Club. Officials will visit a yacht for clearance, if one telephones from the marina on arrival. One can take a bus to Willemstad to clear immigration. The entrance into Spanish Water is sometimes difficult to locate and should not be attempted at night.

On departure one has to contact immigration only, not customs. After having cleared out of Curaçao to sail to Aruba one is technically not allowed to stop anywhere en route, although the authorities do not seem to mind genuine overnight stops.

Customs

Firearms must be declared to customs, and will be removed for the duration of the stay.

Duty paid on equipment will be refunded on departure.

Immigration

A three-month visa is usually granted on arrival, although nationals of certain countries may be required to check with immigration every two weeks or every month. Visas can be extended for a further three months.

Restrictions

The area from Jan Thiel Bay, SE of Willemstad, to East Point, is an underwater park. Permanent moorings are provided to protect the coral from damage and using one's own anchor is prohibited. No harpoons or spearguns are allowed.

Facilities

Curaçao has good haul-out and repair facilities. Willemstad is more convenient than Spanish Water for provisioning and repair. There is a wide selection of goods and US-style shopping centres out of town. Fresh produce can be bought at the floating market from boats which come over from Venezuela. Fuel and bottled gas are reasonably priced, as Curaçao has its own oil refinery. The Curaçao Yacht Club's facilities

are available to foreign visitors. Berthing space is limited, but water and fuel are available from the jetty for a small fee, and there is a slipway.

Further Reading

A Cruising Guide to the Caribbean and the Bahamas
Caribbean Islands Handbook

DOMINICA

The island of Dominica, known as the Commonwealth of Dominica to distinguish it from the Dominican Republic, is one of the most mountainous of the Windward Islands. Seen from afar, this forest-clad island presents a forbidding face with its lofty peaks brushing the rain clouds that frequently shed their load to make this the lushest island in the Caribbean. Unable to compete with the beauty of her neighbours' anchorages, it is Dominica's interior that is her main attraction.

There are various hikes for the energetic leading into the interior. One of the most interesting inland trips is to Trafalgar Falls where one can bathe in a cascade of hot sulphur water. More arduous is the hike to the Boiling Lake, which is another volcanic phenomenon. A more sedate glimpse of Dominica's varied interior can be gained by making a dinghy trip up the Indian River, which is easily reached from the anchorage in Prince Rupert Bay.

Dominica's wild interior allowed a group of the indigenous Carib population to escape extermination and the remaining Carib settlement on the east coast is open to visitors. The Caribs called Dominica 'Waitukubuli' meaning 'tall is her body', a fair description of this beautiful island which is often bypassed by cruising yachts because of the impression that they might be in danger if stopping there. Although there have been a few instances of theft from unattended yachts, Dominica is as safe as any other Caribbean island and if basic precautions are taken, as in any other part of the world, one's stay can be both satisfying and enjoyable.

Country Profile

Dominica was sighted by Christopher Columbus on Sunday, 3 November 1493. It was inhabited by the warlike Caribs, who fiercely resisted both French and English for possession of the island. The two powers

Practical Information

LOCAL TIME: GMT - 4

BUOYAGE: IALA B

CURRENCY: East Caribbean dollar (EC$)
BUSINESS HOURS
Banks: 0800–1200 Monday to Friday,
1500–1700 Friday also.
Shops: 0800–1300, 1400–1600 Monday to
Friday and 0800–1300 Saturdays.
Government offices: 0800–1300,
1400–1700 Monday, closing at 1600
Tuesday to Friday.

ELECTRICITY: 220/240 V, 50 Hz

PUBLIC HOLIDAYS
1 January: New Year's Day
Carnival, Monday and Tuesday before
Ash Wednesday
Good Friday and Easter Monday
Labour Day
Whit Monday
First Monday in August: Emancipation
Day
3 November: Independence Day
25, 26 December: Christmas

COMMUNICATIONS
International telephone calls can be
made from Cable & Wireless on the

corner of Old Street and Hillsborough
Street.
The Anchorage Hotel offers telephone,
telex and fax services. They can be used
also as a mail drop (P.O.B. 34, Roseau).
The post office in Roseau is on the
corner of Castle Street and Cartwheel
Road.
Emergency: dial 999.
There are flights to other Caribbean
islands such as Barbados, Antigua, St
Lucia or Martinique, from where
connections have to be made for flights
to Europe and North America.

finally came to an agreement in 1805 and France ceded Dominica to England in return for a payment. However, situated between the French islands of Martinique and Guadeloupe, French influence has persisted on the island. Dominica was neglected in the nineteenth century and only in the 1930s were efforts made to build roads and open up the interior. Further development came in the 1950s and 60s, with the expansion of agriculture and house building. In 1967 Dominica became self-governing and full independence was achieved in 1978.

Agriculture is the most important sector of the economy. Coffee was the major export in the nineteenth century until struck by disease, to be replaced by lime-growing, an important supply to the Royal Navy in the prevention of scurvy. In the 1930s bananas became the chief export, along with coconut oil, cocoa and citrus fruit. The devastation caused by hurricanes David and Allen in 1978–9 was followed by some reconstruction of roads, hotels and the airport, but Dominica remains one of the poorest islands in the Caribbean. As for so many of its neighbours, the expansion of tourism provides some economic hope, although in Dominica there is a desire to temper tourist expansion to prevent the destruction of the 'Nature Island' of the Caribbean. The lack of beaches means tourism is low key.

Of the 84,000 inhabitants, the majority are of African descent. A small number of Caribs, the original population, live on a reservation on the east side of the island. English and Creole French are spoken, and Protestant and Roman Catholic are the main religious denominations. Roseau is the capital. Dominica is a rainy island, especially June to October, while the hurricane season from July to November should be avoided.

Entry Regulations

Ports of entry
Roseau 15°17′N 61°24′W, Portsmouth 15°32′N 61°23′W.

Procedure on arrival
Roseau: Customs and immigration are in the deepwater port. Arriving yachts should try to contact Dominica Port Authority on VHF Channel 16 for permission to anchor off the deepwater port; if there is no reply, one can wait offshore and send someone ashore with papers. Alternatively one can anchor off the Anchorage Hotel one mile south of Roseau, and make arrangements to clear from there.
Portsmouth: (Prince Rupert Bay) The captain should go ashore to obtain clearance. The customs and police are in a pink building behind the old jetty. Crew lists and clearance from last port are needed. Immigration formalities should be done at the police station.

On arrival, one should ask for a cruising permit to cover all the places one intends to visit. A cruising permit is needed to go from Roseau to Portsmouth.

Clearing out can be done the day before departure.

Customs
Firearms should be declared.

Immigration
Nationals of East European countries require visas in advance.

Fees
Overtime is charged outside of office hours (0800–1200, 1300–1600 Monday to Friday). EC$5 departure tax per boat.

Facilities

Repair facilities are very basic, although there are a few mechanics in Roseau who can undertake repairs on diesel engines. The Anchorage Hotel provides a few facilities and repairs for visiting sailors. Water can be taken from their dock and fuel carried in jerrycans from a nearby fuel station. A similar service is offered by the Castaways Hotel further up the coast. Immediately north of Roseau, at Canefield, the owner of the Shipwreck Bar does fibreglass work and outboard engine repair. Provisioning in Roseau is reasonable, there are supermarkets and a fresh food market, while Portsmouth has a good market on Saturdays.

Further Reading

Cruising Guide to the Leeward Islands
A Cruising Guide to the Caribbean and the Bahamas
The Caribbean Islands Handbook
Cruising Guide to the Eastern Caribbean, Vol. 2

DOMINICAN REPUBLIC

One of the Greater Antilles, the island of Hispaniola, of which the Dominican Republic occupies the eastern two-thirds, is a mountainous island, cut by deep valleys and sometimes troubled by earthquakes. The other third of the island is Haiti, culturally very different to the Dominican Republic where the Hispanic culture dominates.

Described by Christopher Columbus as 'the fairest land human eyes have ever seen', until not so long ago, this beauty was denied to cruising sailors as yachting was not encouraged by the authorities in Santo Domingo. The situation is very different now; foreign yachts are welcome in most places and facilities are steadily improving, although entry formalities are still cumbersome and lengthy. Most yacht traffic takes place along the north coast as yachts make their way either east or west between the USA and the Virgin Islands or Lesser Antilles.

Because of the prevailing NE winds, the south coast offers more protected anchorages, although the more scenic bays are on the wild and rugged north coast. The capital Santo Domingo lies at the mouth of a heavily polluted river and although the city itself, the oldest in the New World, is very attractive, facilities for visiting yachts leave much to be desired. A better alternative is Boca Chica in Puerto de Andrés where one can use the facilities of the local Club Nautico.

The north coast, although scenically spectacular, only offers a handful of sheltered anchorages and as it is usually difficult to cover the distances between them in one day's sail, cruising here needs careful planning. There is no doubt that this coast is best enjoyed if heading westward, otherwise the continuous beating into the trades can mar the pleasure of discovering this unspoilt area. The best northern anchorages are to be found between Puerto Plata and Manzanillo Bay. However, the most attractive area is at Samana Bay where a large resort is expected to be completed shortly, although the area is still largely undeveloped and one may come across a group of humpback whales who migrate south to the bay area for the breeding season.

Country Profile

Arawaks were living on the island when Columbus visited it during his first voyage. The island was settled by the Spanish until 1697 when the French gained control of the western half. In 1804 the independent republic of Haiti was founded in the west and the Haitians plundered the eastern Spanish half of the island. Sovereignty remained in dispute until finally in 1844 the Dominican Republic was founded. After a brief return to Spanish rule from 1861–5, and then a period of instability, the Dominican Republic was annexed by the United States from 1916 to 1924. In 1930 Rafael Trujillo Molina, head of the army, took control with US support, beginning a ruthless dictatorship. He remained in power until his assassination in 1961. Economic problems are the dominant political issue, with violent demonstrations occurring in the 1980s against economic hardship. One of Trujillo's associates, Joaquin Balaguer, was elected president for his fifth term from 1986 to 1990.

Agriculture dominates the economy, sugar being the main crop, although efforts are being made to diversify. Other produce is coffee, bananas, tobacco and cocoa. There is some mining of bauxite, gold and silver, while tourism is growing in importance as a foreign exchange earner.

The population is 6.7 million. The majority are a mixture of African and Spanish origins, and Spanish is spoken. Santo Domingo is the capital. Most of the population are Roman Catholics, with a Protestant minority.

The Dominican Republic lies in the outer tropical zone, so there is little temperature variation between summer and winter. The varied relief of the large island means a diverse climate, from warm and tropical to arid and more temperate.

Practical Information

LOCAL TIME: GMT - 4

BUOYAGE: IALA B. Lights are reported to be unreliable in some parts of the country.

CURRENCY: Dominican peso (RD$) of 100 centavos. US$ travellers' cheques or banknotes are preferred as other currency travellers' cheques may not be accepted.

BUSINESS HOURS
Banks: 0830–1230 Monday to Friday.
Business: 0800–1200, 1400–1700 Monday to Friday.
Some offices and shops: 0900–1700 Monday to Friday, 0800–1300 Saturday.
Government offices: 0730–1430 Monday to Friday.

ELECTRICITY: 110 V, 60 Hz.

PUBLIC HOLIDAYS
1 January: New Year's Day
6 January: Epiphany
21 January: Our Lady of Altagracia
26 January: Duarte Day
27 February: Independence Day
Good Friday
Corpus Christi
1 May: Labour Day
16 August: Restoration Day
24 September: Our Lady of Las Mercedes
25 December: Christmas Day

COMMUNICATIONS
Codetel operates local and international calls. The Codetel office in Santo Domingo is Av 30 de Marzo 12, near Parque Independencia, open 0800–2200 (there are other offices in the city), for international calls, telex and fax.
Main post office, Santo Domingo, is Calle Emiliano Tejera, opposite Alcazar

de Colon, open 0700–1300, 1400–1600 Monday to Friday, some hours on Saturday. For overseas mail, it is recommended to use 'entrega especial' (special delivery), available for a small extra charge at a separate window at post offices.
There are international flights to various Caribbean, North and South American and European destinations from both Santo Domingo and the new international airport at Puerto Plata.

DIPLOMATIC MISSIONS
In Santo Domingo:
Canada: Mahatma Gandhi 200.
☎ 689-0002.
Haiti: Calle Cub Scout 11. ☎ 562-5731.
United Kingdom: Independencia 506.
☎ 682-3128.
United States: Calle César Nicolas Penson. ☎ 682-2171.

Entry Regulations

Ports of entry
North coast: Manzillo Bay 19°43′N 71°45′W, Puerto Plata 19°49′N 70°42′W, Puerto Duarte (Samana) 19°12′N 69°26′W.
South coast: La Romana 18°25′N 68°57′W, San Pedro de Macoris 18°26′N 69°18′W, Santo Domingo 18°28′N 69°53′W, Haina 18°25′N 70°00′N.

Procedure on arrival
If possible, one should arrive during working hours, 0800–1700. Fly the Q flag and wait to be boarded, as it is illegal to land before clearance. Usually a port official will come with customs and immigration officers. All boats are searched. The ship's papers, passports and clearance certificate from last port should be presented. Then a visitor's card for each person must be obtained. In some ports not used to yachts, clearance is more complicated than elsewhere in the Caribbean.

Yachts must clear from port to port, and see customs on each arrival, but there is no charge for this. Clearance papers must be obtained from each port. Note that many ports are closed to foreign yachts, unless one has special permission. Permission should also be obtained from the Port Authority to cruise outside of the ports.

Customs
Firearms are checked by the boarding officer. One should have certificates of ownership.

Immigration
No visas are required for nationals of Argentina, Aruba, Austria, Costa Rica, Denmark, Ecuador, Finland, Germany, Israel, Italy, Japan, Luxembourg, Liechtenstein, Netherlands, Netherlands Antilles, Norway, Spain, Sweden, Switzerland and the United Kingdom. All others, including citizens of the United States (Puerto Rico and USVI included) and France and its dependencies, need to purchase a tourist card (US$10), from consulates or tourist offices. East European nationals must obtain a visa in advance.

Health
Cases of ciguatera have been reported on the north coast between Samana and Puerto Plata.

Fees
Overtime fees are payable if clearing outside office hours, or if special paperwork is required.

Facilities

The best facilities are in the capital Santo Domingo which are put to the test every four years during the

Ruta de Descubrimiento transatlantic yacht race from Palos in Spain. Reasonable facilities are also available in La Romana, which is the base of a large fleet of sportsfishing boats and has two well-equipped marinas. On the north coast, a new marina with full facilities is due to open at Estero Balsa, near Puerto Manzanillo. There are adequate facilities at Puerto Plata which has seen a steady increase in yacht traffic in recent years, although a dangerous surge can affect the harbour during northerly winds. Fuel is delivered to the dock, where water is also available. There is good provisioning in town and propane bottles can be filled locally. Only basic repair facilities are available at Samaná where there is fuel and water on the dock and a good fresh produce market.

Outside of the large industrial centres, repair facilities for yachts are virtually non-existent although minor repairs can be dealt with by ordinary workshops.

Further Reading

Caribbean Islands Handbook
A Cruising Guide to the Caribbean and the Bahamas
The Gentleman's Guide to Passages South

GRENADA

The most southerly of the Windward Islands, Grenada or the 'Spice Island' is gradually rejoining the fold of Caribbean cruising destinations after the turmoil of a Marxist-Leninist regime and a US-led invasion. A beautiful island with lush mountains and silvery beaches, Grenada was for many years a sailors' favourite. Situated conveniently close to the Grenadines, with which it is linked by its smaller sisters Carriacou and Petit Martinique, Grenada is the usual turning-point north for a cruise among the Windward Islands.

Carriacou is the largest of the Grenadines and was once a great sugar-growing island. Relatively undeveloped, it is attractive with its green hills, sandy beaches, and sheltered natural harbours such as Tyrell Bay. On Carriacou customs and beliefs of African origin have been preserved, as seen in the annual Big Drum Dances and Tombstone Feasts. A Scottish tradition has also survived in the hand-built schooners which are raced in August in the Carriacou Regatta.

Petit Martinique, island of mystery, with a reputation as a smuggling centre, is not often visited by yachts cruising the popular nearby Grenadines, which belong to St Vincent, as this means having to sail down to Carriacou to clear in and then sail back.

Country Profile

The Caribs who originally lived on Grenada called it Camerhogue. Then the Spanish first gave it the name of Concepción and later changed it to Granada after the town in Spain, becoming Grenada under French influence. Carib hostility prevented European settlement until the seventeenth century, when the French settled near present-day St George's. After a period of peaceful coexistence, the Caribs were exterminated, and those who survived threw themselves into the sea on the north coast at Morne des Sauteurs (Caribs' Leap). Under the French a plantation economy was introduced, African slaves were brought in, and the population grew. As elsewhere, the English challenged the French and Grenada was ceded to England in 1763. First tobacco and indigo were grown, then cotton, coffee and sugar, and later cocoa, nutmeg, cloves and mace were introduced, earning Grenada the name of Spice Island.

Full independence was granted in 1974, but five years later a coup overthrew the corrupt government of Eric Gairy. The New Jewel Movement established a Marxist-Leninist government led by Maurice Bishop, which moved close to Cuba and other communist countries, and thus attracted the suspicion of the USA. In 1983 Bishop and some of his followers were murdered after a power struggle and soon afterwards a joint US-Caribbean force invaded to restore order. Since then links with the USA have grown stronger.

Agriculture is important to the economy and the main exports are nutmeg, bananas and cocoa. Recently tourism has been expanding, partly due to the new international airport.

The population is 120,000. English is the main language and some French patois is spoken. Unlike other islands which have had a mixture of French and English rule, the French influence has not retained much strength except in the patois and place names.

The picturesque St George's, situated in a large natural harbour on the SW corner of the island, is the capital. The old town lies around the inner harbour, which is known as the Carenage. Most Grenadians are Roman Catholic or Protestant.

The climate is tropical. The hurricane season lasts from June to November, but most hurricanes pass to the north of the island.

Practical Information

LOCAL TIME: GMT - 4

BUOYAGE: IALA B

CURRENCY: East Caribbean dollar
(EC$)

BUSINESS HOURS
Banks: 0800–1200/1400 Monday to
Friday, 1430–1700 Friday.
Shops: 0800–1145, 1300–1545 Monday to
Friday, 0800–1145 Saturday.
Government offices: 0800–1145,
1300–1545 Monday to Friday.

ELECTRICITY: 220/240 V, 50 Hz

PUBLIC HOLIDAYS
1 January: New Year's Day
7 February: Independence Day
Good Friday and Easter Monday
Labour Day
Whit Monday
Corpus Christi
First Monday in August: Emancipation
Day
Carnival Monday
Thanksgiving Day
25, 26 December: Christmas

EVENTS
Carriacou Regatta, first week in August
Carnival, second week in August

COMMUNICATIONS
Grenada Telephone Co. (Grentel), in St
George's, behind Cable & Wireless, for
long distance telephone calls.

Cable & Wireless, Carenage, for fax and
telex.
Post Office, Carenage, St George's
0800–1145, 1300–1530 Monday to
Thursday, to 1630 on Fridays. Saturday
mornings.
There are flights to various Caribbean
destinations and also to London, New
York and Miami.

DIPLOMATIC MISSIONS
In St George's:
United Kingdom: 14 Church Street.
☎ 440-3536.
United States: The Belmont.
☎ 440-1731.
Venezuela: Archibald Avenue.
☎ 440-1721.

Entry Regulations

Ports of entry
Grenada: St Georges 12°03′N 61°45′W, Prickly Bay 12°00′N 61°45′W, Grenville 12°07′N 61°43′W, and Secret Harbour (from 1991).
Carriacou: Hillsborough 12°29′N 61°30′W.

Procedure on arrival
The Q flag should be flown. Documents to be prepared are ship's papers, three crew lists, passports, a ship's stores list, health declaration and the clearance from the previous port.

Clearance must be obtained for voyages both coastwise or foreign. If planning to cruise in Grenada one should ask for a cruising permit from customs when clearing in – no charge is made for this.

Grenada Coast Guard and Grenada Yacht Services stand by on VHF Channel 16 0800–1600, while the Port Control and Spice Island Marine Services have a 24-hour watch.
St George's: Customs are in the Grenada Yacht Services building south of the Carenage. All yachts will be boarded by customs on arrival.
Carriacou: One can clear in here if coming from the north, but one still has to clear again in Grenada.

Customs
Firearms must be declared to customs and will be sealed on board in a proper locker or kept ashore in custody until departure. A receipt will be issued.

Animals may not be landed unless they have a health certificate and local permit from the veterinary officer. Cats and dogs need a valid anti-rabies certificate.

Medicines such as morphine in the medical stores must be declared.

Yachts are allowed to stay for an indefinite period, being initially granted three months on arrival, which is easily renewable.

Immigration
South Africans and nationals of East European countries must obtain a visa before arrival.

Fees
Overtime fees are higher on Sundays and public holidays. EC$20 overtime is charged for clearance outside 0800–1200, 1300–1600 (1700 on Fridays) on weekdays, and all day Saturday and Sunday and holidays. Some officials may work until 1700–2000 before charging overtime, depending on location. In some cases there will also be a transportation charge.

A small charge is made for the crew list form if one does not provide one's own.

Restrictions
Yachts may not anchor within 200 metres of any beach, including Grand Anse, Prickly Bay, Grenville, Carriacou and Petit Martinique. It is prohibited to pump bilge or waste into the water, and marine toilets may not be used within 200 metres of the beaches. There are toilets ashore at both marinas and the yacht clubs.

Facilities

Grenada's facilities are split between St George's and Prickly Bay. The long-established Grenada Yacht Services operate a marina with the usual services as well as dry docking facilities. Some small repair firms, including metal work and refrigeration, have set up shop in and around GYS. According to some reports, the GYS docking installations are in urgent need of repair and the marina is very run down. The situation is much better in Prickly Bay where the establishment of various charter operations has brought about a marked improvement in repair and service facilities. Spice Island Marine Services have the best facilities in Prickly Bay.

Fuel and water can be taken on at the dock in both places. Provisioning is good with several supermarkets and the fresh produce market in St George's is one of the best and most colourful in the Lesser Antilles. There are garbage facilities ashore at both yacht marinas, the yacht club, and the main towns and villages.

Further Reading

Sailor's Guide to the Windward Islands
Caribbean Islands Handbook
Cruising Guide to the Eastern Caribbean, Vol. 3

GUADELOUPE

The largest of the Leeward Islands, Guadeloupe is a Département d'Outremer (Overseas Department) of France and its inhabitants are French citizens. The department includes the neighbouring islands of Les Saintes, Marie-Galante, and La Désirade as well as St Barts and St Martin. Guadeloupe is a butterfly-shaped island. Basse-Terre to the west has impressive scenery, black beaches, gorges, waterfalls and forests, and La Soufrière a still active volcano, while to the east lies the lower Grande-Terre, more developed with its white beaches and tourist resorts. The two butterfly wings are separated by the Rivière Salée, which is navigable by shallow draft boats.

The proximity between French-speaking Guadeloupe and English-speaking Antigua invariably leads to comparisons between these two rival yachting centres. While there is not much difference in the type and quality of services offered, where Guadeloupe scores is in the blend of French sophistication and Caribbean *joi de vivre* that has produced an atmosphere unmatched in any of the English-speaking Caribbean islands. The French influence has mixed with the African heritage to form a distinctive and rich culture seen in the music, cuisine and especially Carnival.

From the cruising sailor's point of view, Guadeloupe comes close to perfection. The island and her dependencies offer everything a sailor could wish for, from secluded anchorages to the latest marinas, first-class repair facilities, good provisioning as well as an excellent cuisine suited to all pockets.

Country Profile

The Caribs called the island Karukera, 'Land of beautiful waters'. Arawak archaeological finds indicate they had an advanced culture, but the Caribs who followed them were fiercer and less developed. Columbus came in 1493 and named the island Santa Maria de Guadalupe de Estremadura. Spain showed little interest in settling the island, and Carib hostility put off attempts by other countries. In 1635 a French expedition of colonisation had some success, despite conflict with the hostile Caribs. The island was briefly occupied by England, but the Treaty of Paris in 1763 returned Guadeloupe to France.

The French Revolution brought an unsettled period, Victor Hugues' rule even echoing France's bloody Terror, although slavery was briefly abolished. Emancipation of the slaves was finally achieved in 1848 largely due to Victor Schoelcher, now regarded as a national hero. In the second half of the nineteenth century indentured labourers were brought in from East India to cope with the labour shortage and social conflicts arose between various races, with resulting demands for independence. Despite equal status with Martinique, Guadeloupe is poorer and less developed and politics tend to be radical. A pro-independence movement has grown in Guadeloupe, while St Barts and St Martin are more conservative.

Agriculture is an important part of the economy, especially sugar and bananas, the latter being the main export. Vegetables are increasingly grown, especially for domestic comsumption to combat the large amount of food imports which makes the cost of living high. There is some industry, especially around Pointe-à-Pitre. Tourism has developed, boosting the economy, yet unemployment is a problem.

The 337,000 inhabitants are a mixture of French, African and Indian descent. French is the official language, although Créole is spoken everyday. Most of the population are Roman Catholic. Situated between the sea and La Soufrière, Basseterre is the administrative centre and capital. It is very picturesque, being one of the oldest French colonial towns in the Caribbean,

Practical Information

LOCAL TIME: GMT - 4

BUOYAGE: IALA B

CURRENCY: French franc, US$ often accepted.

BUSINESS HOURS
Banks: 0800–1200 weekdays, 1500–1700 Friday afternoons.
Shops: 0800–1200, 1430–1700 Monday to Friday, morning only on Saturday.
Government offices: 0730–1300, 1500–1630 Monday and Friday.
0730–1300 Tuesday to Thursday.

ELECTRICITY: 220 V, 50 Hz

PUBLIC HOLIDAYS
1 January: New Year's Day
Good Friday and Easter Monday
1 May: Labour Day
Ascension
Whit Monday
14 July: Bastille Day
21 July: Schoelcher Day
15 August: Assumption
1 November: All Saints Day
2 November: All Souls Day
11 November: Armistice Day
25 December: Christmas Day

EVENTS
Carnival starts in February with the climax on Ash Wednesday, when Vaval, the Carnival king, is symbolically burnt on the stake.

COMMUNICATIONS
Post office and telephones: Blvd Hanne, Pointe-à-Pitre.
Phone cards can be bought for public phone booths, with direct dialling.
Emergency numbers: police 82 00 05, nautical assistance 82 91 08, medical centre 82 98 80/82 88 88.
There are flights from Pointe-à-Pitre to the Caribbean, and cities in South America, Canada, the USA and France.

MEDICAL
There is a good medical system.

DIPLOMATIC MISSIONS
Dominican Republic: rues St-John Perse et Frebault, Pointe-à-Pitre.
Most diplomatic representations are in Martinique.

founded around 1640. In Petit Cul-de-sac Marin, the bay to the south, lies Pointe-à-Pitre, the largest city and economic centre of Guadeloupe.

The climate is tropical, in the trade wind belt. The height of the land means frequent rainfall. July to September is the highest danger period for hurricanes and Guadeloupe took some of the worst damage during hurricane Hugo in September 1989.

Entry Regulations

Ports of entry
Pointe-à-Pitre 16°13′N 61°32′W, Basseterre 16°02′N 61°45′W, Deshaies 16°18′N 61°48′W, Saint François 16°15′N 61°16′W.

Procedure on arrival
Pointe-à-Pitre: The main customs offices are at 6 Quai Foulon.
Basseterre: There are customs offices both by the main dock in town and in the marina. Open 0800–1200, 1400–1800 Monday to Friday.
Iles des Saintes: It is possible to clear into these islands by going to the local gendarmerie, although one still has to clear in again on arrival in Guadeloupe.

Customs
Non-French nationals on a tourist visit to Guadeloupe for less than 185 days can import two hunting guns and 100 cartridges for each. Other firearms are not permitted. All weapons should be declared.

Animals need a health certificate, and dogs and cats need a valid anti-rabies vaccination certificate.

The yacht is considered to be temporarily imported and duty is waived for a period of six months within a 12-month period on condition that no work is done either ashore or chartering. The yacht can be left in bond with customs if one leaves the department, and this is not included in the six-month period.

Immigration
Visas are required by nationals from South Africa, Bolivia, Cuba, Haiti, Honduras, El Salvador, Dominican Republic, Turkey and English-speaking Caribbean islands. Any non-EC citizen staying longer than three months needs an extended visa.

Charter
This is illegal in French territory, although transit with non-French passengers is allowed.

Fees
Port tax is payable depending on length of stay and size of yacht. No customs charges are made for EC countries and US yachts, although yachts from some other countries may have to pay some fees calculated by day and tonnage.

Facilities

Yachting facilities in Guadeloupe are excellent. There are several marinas (ports de plaisance) and as Guadeloupe has been chosen as the finish of several transatlantic races from France, repair and service facilities are of a high standard.

Pointe-à-Pitre has a protected harbour and an excellent marina complex (Marina Bas du Fort). All services are available in the marina complex as well as a large selection of marine supplies in several chandleries and specialised shops. There is a 27-ton travelift in the marina and two slipways at a boatyard nearby. Provisioning is of a very high standard.

Basseterre has good repair facilities, most of them concentrated around Marina Rivière Sens. There are various repair shops and a chandlery with a reasonable selection. There is a good fresh produce market in town and a large supermarket on the outskirts.

The small fishing harbour of St François has a municipal marina offering the usual services, but only a limited range of repair facilities. Only basic facilities are available in Deshaies.

Further Reading

Cruising Guide to the Leeward Islands
A Cruising Guide to the Caribbean and the Bahamas
Caribbean Islands Handbook
Cruising Guide to the Eastern Caribbean, Vol. 2

HAITI

The island of Hispaniola in the Greater Antilles is divided between Haiti and the Dominican Republic, both very different from each other. The Republic of Haiti occupies the western third of the island which is very mountainous, hence the name Haiti, which means 'high ground'. Haitian culture is a rich mixture of African and French, and Haitians are proud of being the first black republic in the world.

Decidedly off the cruising track, the relatively few who visit Haiti by yacht find the experience either appalling or delightful. While people eventually get used to the poverty of most Haitians, it is the exasperating bureaucracy that turns most cruisers off. At least there are some compensations. One is the stunning scenery, while the other is the tasty cuisine, as despite nearly two centuries of separation, the French heritage still makes itself felt.

As in the case of Haiti's eastern neighbour, the Dominican Republic, cruising is best done from east to west as particularly during winter the strong trade winds make eastbound passages difficult. Therefore Haiti is best left for a return voyage from the Carib-

bean. If that is not possible, it is undoubtedly easier to make one's way east along Hispaniola's southern coast than beating along the rugged north coast.

If coming south from the Bahamas, the most convenient and interesting landfall is at Cap Haitién, as it allows a glimpse into this fascinating country's turbulent past. Above the town of Milot stands the Citadelle, a huge fortress built by self-proclaimed king Henri Christophe, at the cost of some twenty thousand lives. At the base of the trail leading to the Citadelle stand the ruins of Sans Souci, the imperial palace of one in a line of ruthless dictators that have ruled this unfortunate country. A contrasting glimpse into Haiti's present can be gained by visiting the daily market in Cap Haitién, a colourful experience not to be missed.

The southern cruising route leads towards the capital Port-au-Prince, past several attractive harbours, none of which offer all-weather protection. Port-au-Prince lies at the head of the Gulf of Gonave and is a city of contrasts like the country itself. Beyond Cape Tiburon at Haiti's SW extremity, there are several attractive anchorages with the most scenic surroundings in the Baie des Cayes.

Country Profile

On his first voyage Columbus landed on the north coast and established the first European settlement in the New World, which was destined to be wiped out by the Tainos, who were the indigenous inhabitants of the island. Later the Tainos were eliminated by disease, war with the settlers and slavery, which led to a labour shortage. This was filled by bringing in large numbers of African slaves to work on the plantations. The Spanish neglected the western half of the island for the more profitable east and the vacuum was filled by the French, Dutch and English, while pirates had hiding places along the coasts from where they attacked the Spanish treasure fleets. In the seventeenth century France gained the upper hand and made the region the colony of Saint Domingue and soon it was the largest sugar producer in the French West Indies.

The French Revolution sparked off discontent and a slave rebellion was led by Toussaint L'Ouverture, the unrivalled black leader who drew up a constitution and declared himself Governor General. A year later he was captured and thrown into prison in France where he died. Napoleon wanted to reintroduce slavery, but this provoked an uprising and the French were driven out, the rebels declaring independence in 1804 under the new name of Haiti.

The following century saw further revolutions and

Practical Information

LOCAL TIME: GMT - 5

BUOYAGE: IALA B

CURRENCY: Gourde of 100 centimes.
US currency also circulates.

BUSINESS HOURS
Banks: 0900–1300 Monday to Friday.
Shops: 0700–1600 (1 hour later
October–April).
Government offices: 0700–1200,
1300–1600 (October to April 0800–1200,
1300–1800).

ELECTRICITY: 110 V, 60 Hz

PUBLIC HOLIDAYS
1 January
2 January: Glorification of Heroes
Mardi Gras
14 April: Americas Day
Good Friday
1 May
18 May: Flag and University Day
22 May: Sovereignty Day
Corpus Christi
Ascension Day
15 August: Assumption
8 October: Death of Henri Christophe
17 October: Death of Dessalines
24 October: UN Day
1 November: All Saints Day
18 November: Armed Forces Day
5 December: Discovery of Haiti
25 December: Christmas Day

EVENTS
Carnival, three days before Ash
Wednesday

COMMUNICATIONS
In Port-au-Prince the Teleco office is in
rue Pavée, and the post office is in Place
des Nations Unies.
There are flights from Port-au-Prince to
several Caribbean destinations, North
America and Paris.

DIPLOMATIC MISSIONS
In Port-au-Prince:
Canada: c/o Bank of Nova Scotia, Route
de Delmas. ☎ 22358.
United Kingdom: 21 Ave Marie Jeanne.
☎ 21227.
United States: Boulevard Harry Truman.
☎ 20200.

conflicts until in 1915 the United States intervened, bringing some order to the country. Opposition to this occupation led to a revolt from 1918 to 1920 and some 2000 Haitians were killed. The USA withdrew in 1934, leaving a poor and overpopulated country. After various crises in the 1950s François Duvalier (Papa Doc), a black nationalist, was elected President. He established a repressive rule with an armed militia and thousands were killed or fled the country. In 1971 his son Jean-Claude (Baby Doc) inherited the Presidency. Discontent arose and in 1986 Baby Doc was forced to flee to France. Establishing a civil government has proved difficult, with high aspirations for change amongst Haitians, and the 1990 elections led to disturbances.

Haiti is probably the poorest country in the Western Hemisphere. It is overpopulated, lacks raw materials and the mountainous terrain is difficult to cultivate. Problems have been worsened by low agricultural productivity, low prices in world markets and hurricane damage. Coffee is the most important crop. There is a little industry and commerce, which is concentrated in the Port-au-Prince area. Tourism declined in the 1980s with the political troubles.

The population is 5.5 million, the majority being of African origin, but many are mulattos of mixed French and African descent. Conflict in the past has often been between the African and mulatto sections of the population. The languages spoken are French and Créole. Voodoo, a spirit religion with its origins in Africa, exists alongside Christianity, the population being nominally 90 per cent Catholic, 10 per cent Protestant.

The climate is tropical. It is cooler and drier from December to March, and on the coast, which is cooled by sea breezes. The hurricane season lasts from June to November.

Entry Regulations

Ports of entry
Port-au-Prince 18°33′N 72°21′W, Cap-Haitién 19°46′N 72°12′W, Gonaives 19°27′N 72°42′W, Port-de-Paix 19°57′N 72°50′W, Miragoane 18°28′N 73°06′W, St Marc 19°07′N 72°42′W, Jacmel 18°13′N 72°31′W, Les Cayes 18°11′N 73°44′W, Jérémie 18°39′N 74°07′W, Petit Goave 18°26′N 72°52′W, Fort Liberté 19°41′N 71°51′W.

Procedure on arrival
Entry can only be made at an official port of entry. Clearance from the last port must be shown and five crew lists are needed. A cruising permit must be obtained from the port captain (Capitainerie).

Customs
Firearms must be declared, and an authorisation for their possession must be shown to the police, plus a description of the firearms and the reasons for possessing them. Firearms must be kept on board.

Animals must be declared to customs.

Immigration

All nationalities need a visa prior to arrival with the exception of Austria, Argentina, Belgium, Canada, Denmark, Germany, Israel, Liechtenstein, Luxembourg, Netherlands, Norway, Monaco, Sweden, Switzerland, the United Kingdom (including Northern Ireland) and the United States.

A 90 day stay is usually given which may be extended.

Cruising permit

A 'Permis de Navigation' must be obtained from the Capitainerie at the port of entry. This permit is necessary to allow free access to all ports in Haiti.

There is no limit on the length of time a yacht may stay as long as one remains in contact with the authorities.

Security

During any periods of political unrest, it is wise to go out only in the daytime.

Health

Malaria prophylaxis is recommended. There is a red alert on AIDS.

Fees

Customs $11, Immigration $11, Health $11. Port charges of $50 per day are charged if berthed alongside a quay. Light dues.

Facilities

Facilities in Haiti are generally poor, although it is possible to have some work done in the commercial harbours. If planning to cruise in Haiti one should carry all essential spares as practically nothing is available locally. A few ports have fuel on the dock, but in most places fuel must be either carried in jerrycans or ordered in drums and delivered by truck. Water is available everywhere, but should be treated. There is good provisioning with fresh fruit, vegetables and fish, but imported goods are scarce.

Further Reading

A Cruising Guide to the Caribbean and the Bahamas
Caribbean Islands Handbook
The Gentleman's Guide to Passages South

JAMAICA

Part of the Greater Antilles, Jamaica is one of the largest islands in the Caribbean. Lying south of Cuba, this mountainous and scenic island is known worldwide as the birthplace of reggae music.

This island of stunning beauty with its hundreds of miles of coastline and abundance of natural harbours has all the ingredients of a perfect cruising destination. Unfortunately the high level of crime, muggings and theft keeps most yachtsmen away. The often unfriendly or aggressive attitude of officials has not helped matters either, even if such attitudes can perhaps be justified by the relentless fight against drug traffic into which cruising yachts have become unwillingly entangled. While the present situation remains unchanged it is doubtful that the number of visiting yachts will increase significantly.

Country Profile

The name Jamaica comes from the Arawak word 'Chaymaka', meaning well-watered. Arawaks were the original inhabitants before the arrival of Christopher Columbus in 1494. Soon afterwards the first Spanish settlement was established and the Arawaks did not survive long. In 1525 Santiago de la Vega, now Spanish Town, was founded and was for a long time Jamaica's capital. The seventeenth century saw England stake its claim and capture the island from Spain. A plantation economy was developed with English and Irish settlers, based on slave labour, and Jamaica became England's main sugar-producing colony. In the early days pirates such as Henry Morgan used the island as a base.

The competition of sugar-beet meant that the cane sugar industry suffered in the nineteenth century; economic and social problems continued into this century, provoking disorders. Rival trade union movements arose, the Jamaica Labour Party and the People's National Party, whose rivalry has dominated politics since the 1944 Constitution and universal suffrage were introduced. After a brief membership of the West Indies Federation, Jamaica celebrated independence in 1962. The 1970s saw a phase of socialism and links with Cuba, followed by a more conservative period. Recently the socialists have returned to power.

Once a prosperous island, Jamaica has been in recession since 1973. The bauxite mining and alumina refining industries, although still important, have declined. A large part of the land is cultivated, mostly

Practical Information

LOCAL TIME: GMT - 5

BUOYAGE: IALA B

CURRENCY: Jamaica dollar (J$). One may have problems changing local currency back on departure, the best method being to take the outward clearance papers to the airport at Kingston or Montego Bay.

BUSINESS HOURS
Banks: 0900–1400 Monday to Thursday, 0900–1200, 1430–1700 Friday.
Shops: 0900/0930–1600/1730 Monday to Saturday. Shops close at 1300 on Wednesday in downtown Kingston, and on Thursday in uptown Kingston.
Offices: 0830–1630 Monday to Friday. Government offices: 0800–1700 Monday to Thursday, 0800–1600 Friday.

ELECTRICITY: 110 V, 50 Hz

PUBLIC HOLIDAYS
1 January: New Year's Day
Ash Wednesday
Good Friday
Easter Monday
End of May: Labour Day
First Monday in August: Independence Day
Third Monday in October: National Heroes' Day
25, 26 December: Christmas

EVENTS
Sun Splash, annual reggae festival mid-August.
A week of celebrations around Independence Day.

COMMUNICATIONS
Jamaica Internal Telecommunications Ltd, open 24 hours for cables, telephone calls, fax and telex.
There are international flights from both Kingston and Montego Bay to Caribbean and North American cities and London.

DIPLOMATIC MISSIONS
In Kingston:
Canada: Royal Bank Building, 30 Knutsford Road. ☎ 926-1500.
United Kingdom: Trafalgar Road. ☎ 926-9050.
United States: 2 Oxford Road. ☎ 929-4850.

for sugar and bananas, the main exports. Tourism, as elsewhere in the Caribbean, is the leading foreign exchange earner. However, unemployment remains very high, with its accompanying problems of poverty and crime. There has been and still is a high level of emigration away from the island, formerly to the United Kingdom and now to the USA.

Kingston is the capital. The population is 2.5 million, of which the majority are of African descent, but there are also minorities of East Indian, Chinese, Lebanese and European origins. English is spoken and also the local dialect 'Jamaica Talk'. There are various religions, with a Protestant majority, some Roman Catholics as well as Jews, Muslims, Hindus and Baha'i. Rastafarianism has a significant following.

The climate is tropical and humid, and Jamaica lies in the hurricane zone. The hurricane season lasts from June to November.

Entry Regulations

Ports of entry
Kingston 17°58′N 76°48′W, Montego Bay 18°28′N 77°56′W, Ocho Rios 18°25′N 77°07′W, Port Antonio 18°11′N 76°27′W.

Procedure on arrival
The captain should provide customs with a detailed itinerary and they will then issue a cruising permit (transire). The authorities must be notified every time one moves to another port. A yacht can only go where is stated on the transire. Yachts are monitored and if checking in late or making unauthorised stops will be fined. Yachts clearing in from foreign ports may not be allowed to dock until given permission by customs. Foreign registered boats that have already cleared into Jamaica must notify customs within 24 hours of arrival in another port. According to recent reports formalities in Jamaica are difficult and time-consuming.
Port Antonio: One should anchor off the Admiralty Club or moor at a club dock with the Q flag flying and officials will come to the yacht.

Alternatively Huntress Marina, which monitors Channel 16, can help and may even persuade the officials to clear an incoming yacht at their dock.
Montego Bay: Customs and immigration officials are located at the boat dock when a cruise ship is in the harbour, at other times one must go to the airport. If one has firearms, the officials will come to the Montego Bay Yacht Club. Occasionally yachts have been cleared at the yacht club after customs were duly notified. However, these policies seem to change frequently, so it may be advisable to contact the port authority or customs first and ask about the correct procedure.
Kingston: Yachts should anchor off the customs dock at Port Royal with the Q flag flying and wait to be boarded by officials.
Ocho Rios: Port authority and customs have to be contacted on VHF Channel 16. One will have to anchor in this open harbour.

Customs

Firearms must be declared and will be kept in the custody of customs until departure.

Animals must be properly documented.

Yachts may stay up to six months.

Immigration

No visas are required for nationals of Commonwealth countries, Austria, Belgium, Denmark, Finland, Iceland, Eire, Israel, Italy, Luxembourg, Mexico, Netherlands, Norway, Spain, Sweden, Switzerland, Turkey, Germany and the United States for up to six months. All other nationalities require visas.

Fees

Overtime is charged after 1600 Monday to Friday and at weekends for customs and immigration.

Security

Security is a problem and no yacht should be left unattended. It is advisable not to carry valuables or much money when ashore.

Facilities

Repair facilities in Jamaica can only be described as adequate and workshops willing to undertake an urgent job can only be found with local help. There are two marinas in the Kingston area and both have reasonable facilities, being used mainly by locally owned boats. The Royal Jamaica Yacht Club maintains a marina-type facility about 12 miles from Kingston where visitors belonging to reputable clubs are always welcome. Morgan's Harbour Club at Port Royal has similar docking facilities, as well as fuel and water.

At Port Antonio, Huntress Marina has the best facilities and the staff are very helpful. Also the East Jamaica Anglers Association maintains a dock and some facilities which can be used by visitors. Similarly at Montego Bay the Montego Bay Yacht Club has an excellent facility, which may be used by members of other yacht clubs.

Further Reading

A Cruising Guide to the Caribbean and Bahamas
Caribbean Islands Handbook

MARTINIQUE

Martinique is the main island of the French Antilles and the most northerly of the Windward Islands. Volcanic in origin, in the north-west of the island Mount Pelée is still active. 1902 saw the last major eruption, which completely destroyed the capital St Pierre and brought Martinique to the attention of the world. The Atlantic side of this mountainous and lush island is rugged and rough, while the west coast is more sheltered, with beaches and pleasant anchorages.

Most yachting facilities are concentrated around the capital Fort-de-France which is the largest city in the Windward Islands and has a distinctly European flavour. Yachting facilities are on a par with those in Guadeloupe, with which Martinique has an ongoing rivalry.

Country Profile

The origin of the name Martinique is disputed, coming either from the Carib 'Madinina', island of flowers, or Saint Martin as named by Columbus after he saw the island in 1493. He only landed there in 1502, on his fourth voyage. Arawaks were the original inhabitants, 2000 years ago, probably exterminated by the fiercer Caribs who inhabited the island when the Europeans arrived. First to be interested in settling the island were the French and conflict with the Caribs was resolved with a treaty in 1660, but the Indians quickly died out. African slaves were then brought over to work on the sugar cane plantations.

All through the seventeenth and eighteenth centuries the French and English fought over their colonial possessions, until the 1763 Treaty of Paris established French control of Martinique and Guadeloupe in return for relinquishing claims on other territories. The French Revolution encouraged the slaves to fight for freedom, so landowners persuaded the English briefly to occupy the island to prevent this. During the Napoleonic wars the English Navy captured Diamond Rock off the coast and commissioned it as a ship, from where for 18 months it proceeded to harass the French. Slavery was abolished in 1848 and the resulting labour shortage led to indentured labourers being brought in from India and China. Martinique became a French department in 1946 and the inhabitants are full French citizens.

Agriculture has always been important to the economy, although the sugar industry has declined as elsewhere in the Caribbean. Rum exports remain important, as well as pineapples and bananas. High food imports mean the cost of living is expensive. The

Practical Information

LOCAL TIME: GMT - 4

BUOYAGE: IALA B

CURRENCY: French franc. US$ are sometimes accepted.

BUSINESS HOURS
Banks: 0730–1800 Monday to Friday, until 1300 on Saturday.
Shops: 0900–1200, 1500–1800 Monday to Saturday.
Government offices: 0800–1730 Monday to Friday, with a lunch break.

ELECTRICITY: 220 V, 50 Hz

PUBLIC HOLIDAYS
1 January: New Year's Day
Mardi Gras, Carnival
Ash Wednesday
Good Friday, Easter Monday
1 May: Labour Day (Fête du travail)
Ascension
Whit Monday
14 July: Bastille Day
21 July: Victor Schoelcher Day
15 August: Assumption
1 November: All Saints Day
11 November: Armistice Day
25 December: Christmas Day

EVENTS
Sailing Week, early April
Carnival

COMMUNICATIONS
Phone cards for public phones can be bought from post offices, newsagents and some shops.
PTT office, rue Antoine Siger, has coin and card telephones.
Post offices are open 0700–1800 weekdays and Saturday mornings. The main post office is on Rue de la Liberté, Fort-de-France.
There are flights from Fort-de-France to Caribbean destinations, Montreal, Toronto, Miami and several cities in France.

DIPLOMATIC MISSIONS
In Fort-de-France:
United States: 14 Rue Blenac.
☎ 719301.

French government spends a lot on social services, but unemployment and a trade deficit are problems. Efforts, however, have been made to develop industry, and tourism is expanding.

The 350,000 cosmopolitan Martiniquais are a mixture of French, African and Asian origins, speaking French, as well as Créole which combines French and African languages. Most of the islanders are Roman Catholics.

The island has a high rainfall due to the mountains, June to November being the wet season. The high humidity is made tolerable by the steady trade winds. July to November is the hurricane season.

Entry Regulations

Ports of entry
Fort-de-France 14°38′N, 61°04′W, Marin 14°28′N 60°53′W, St Pierre 14°44′N 61°11′W.

Procedure on arrival
Yachts in Fort-de-France should anchor away from the ferry dock in the north-east side of the bay as the ferries are always coming and going. For clearance, yachts can come stern-to the YSM dock. Customs and immigration are in a hut by the dock, open daily 0800–1100, 1500–1730.

Initial clearance can be done in Marin and St Pierre, but one must check in again with customs on arrival in Fort-de-France. If one cannot find the customs officer

at Marin, one can leave the Q flag up and visit customs in Fort-de-France by taxi.

Outward clearance must be from Fort-de-France.

Customs
Firearms must be declared.

Anti-rabies certificates are needed for cats and dogs.

As in all other French territory, yachts staying over six months in a consecutive 12 month period become liable for import duty, although if leaving the boat in bond and flying out of Martinique, for which special permission from customs must be obtained, this period is suspended until one's return.

Immigration
Visas are required for nationals of South Africa, Bolivia, Cuba, Haiti, Honduras, El Salvador, Dominican Republic, Turkey and English-speaking Caribbean islands.

Any non-EC citizen planning a stay over three months will need a visa. In theory all non-EC citizens need a visa, but this is not applied to those arriving and leaving on the same yacht. Non-EC nationals should have a visa if planning to fly in or out of Martinique.

Fees
Most nationalities including the USA and EC countries pay nothing, but some others are charged a fee on a daily rate according to tonnage. No overtime is charged as clearance can only be arranged in office hours.

Facilities

Although the anchorage in front of Fort-de-France gets very crowded at times, at least everything is available ashore. There are good repair facilities, several well-stocked chandleries and all major engine manufacturers are represented locally. There are boatyards with slipways or travelifts. Also there are several large supermarkets as well as a good fresh produce market.

Marina de Cohe is a small marina north of Fort-de-France with its own dry dock and repair facility.

Anse Mitan is the main tourist centre of Martinique and a popular spot with yachts. Marina Pointe du Bout is close by and the complex surrounding this marina offers various repair facilities, chandleries and supermarkets.

Both St Pierre and Marin have only basic facilities.

Further Reading

Sailors Guide to the Windward Islands
Caribbean Islands Handbook
Cruising Guide to the Eastern Caribbean, Vol. 3

MONTSERRAT

This picturesque little island in the Leeward Islands is a useful navigation mark for yachts plying between Antigua and Guadeloupe, very few of whom bother to make the detour to stop by in Montserrat. The island has no natural harbour, although there are a few pretty anchorages on its relatively sheltered west coast. As in the case of its northern neighbours, Nevis and St Kitts, it is Montserrat's interior that attracts most sailors. The island is known sometimes as the 'Emerald Isle' – as much for the strong Irish influence as the lush vegetation – and three mountain ranges covered in rain forest dominate the island. There are waterfalls, mountain streams, hot springs and fumeroles, nature trails and that rare but increasingly welcome phenomenon in the English-speaking West Indies, decent restaurants with good cuisine.

The usual winter anchorage is off Plymouth, which is also the capital. Although the west coast offers protection from prevailing winds, it is the swell that sometimes makes the anchorages untenable and should this occur one must be prepared to move up or down the coast in search of better protection.

Country Profile

A few Caribs lived on the island when Columbus sighted it on his second voyage in 1493, naming it after the well-known abbey in Spain. In the first half of the seventeenth century, Montserrat was settled by Irish Catholics and the island became a refuge for Catholics fleeing persecution both in Ireland and Virginia.

A sugar plantation economy was developed based on slave labour. In 1768 on St Patrick's Day some slaves rebelled and all of them were executed; today the rebels are celebrated as freedom fighters. During the seventeenth and eighteenth centuries the French invaded several times, but never succeeded in permanently wresting Montserrat from British rule. In 1967 the island became self-governing as a Crown Colony of Britain.

Tourism is the largest earner of foreign exchange, and there has been an influx of foreign residents. A few small industrial concerns have been established. However, the economy has only recently started to pick up, not helped by the havoc wreaked by hurricane Gilbert.

The population is 12,500, the majority being of African descent. A considerable number of retired Americans, Canadians and Britons live on the island. English is the main language and most people are Protestant or Catholic. Plymouth, with many attractive Georgian buildings, is the capital, lying on the sheltered west coast.

The climate is tropical with a low humidity. June to November is the hurricane season.

Entry Regulations

Port of entry
Plymouth 16°42′N 62°13′W.

Procedure on arrival
Arriving in Plymouth one should anchor off the yacht club or north of the main dock. Customs are located in the area near the main dock. After clearing customs, one must visit immigration at the police station in town.

If one contacts customs on the radio, they may come over to Old Road Bay for an extra fee.

Clearance from the previous port must be submitted to the port authority.

Customs
Firearms must be kept sealed on board.

Animals must stay on board until they have been checked by the veterinary officer.

Practical Information (Montserrat)

LOCAL TIME: GMT - 4

BUOYAGE: IALA B

CURRENCY: East Caribbean dollar
(EC$)

BUSINESS HOURS
Banks: 0800–1300 Monday to Thursday,
0800–1200, 1500–1700 Friday.
Shops: 0800–1200, 1300–1600 except
0800–1300 Wednesday, either
0800–1200,1300–1530 or 0800–1300
Saturday.

Government offices: 0800–1200,
1300–1600 Monday to Friday.

ELECTRICITY: 110/220 V, 60 Hz

PUBLIC HOLIDAYS
1 January: New Year's Day
17 March: St Patrick's Day
Good Friday, Easter Monday
2 May: Labour Day
June: Queen's Birthday
Whit Monday
First Monday of August: Emancipation
Day

23 November: Liberation Day
25, 26 December: Christmas
31 December: Festival Day

COMMUNICATIONS
Cable & Wireless, Church St, has fax,
telex and international telephones.
Main post office, Strand St, 0815–1555
Monday to Friday and 0815–1125
Wednesday and Saturday.
For international flights, connections
must be made in Antigua.

Yachts can stay indefinitely in Montserrat without paying duty.

Immigration

No visas are required for nationals of Commonwealth countries, Belgium, Denmark, Finland, France, Greece, Iceland, Italy, Liechtenstein, Luxembourg, Netherlands, Norway, San Marino, Spain, Sweden, Switzerland, Tunisia, Turkey, Uruguay, US citizens (if visit does not exceed six months), Germany and Venezuela (if visit does not exceed one month). All other nationals require visas.

Cruising permit

One needs coastwise clearance to visit all other anchorages, and one must not go to any bay without a customs permit. One can apply for this permit from customs on arrival and it will be granted for a certain period. If wishing to stay longer one can return and get an extension.

Fees

Overtime is charged after 1600 on Mondays, Tuesdays, Thursdays and Fridays, after 1130 on Wednesdays and Saturdays and all day on Sunday. Rates for customs overtime are EC$16 and EC$21.

There is a EC$5 port tax on departure. There are plans to charge for the cruising permit.

Facilities

With virtually no local yachts, facilities are very basic. There is a small boatyard, which may be able to undertake some repair work. Air Studios should be approached for emergency electric or electronic repair. Water can be taken on at the pier in Plymouth for a charge of EC$20. Texaco will deliver fuel to the same dock, but only in a minimum amount of 200 gallons. Texaco will also fill gas bottles. There are several supermarkets in Plymouth with a good selection of imported goods, although tending to be expensive, and also a good fresh produce market.

Like everywhere else in the neighbouring islands, there are plans for a marina development in Montserrat. The proposed site is at Cars Bay (also known as Carr's Bay) on the north-west coast.

Further Reading

Cruising Guide to the Leeward Islands
Caribbean Islands Handbook

NETHERLANDS ANTILLES

The Netherland Antilles are part of the Kingdom of the Netherlands, but have full internal autonomy. Politically one unit, the islands form two groups geographically. One group (often called the three S's), Sint Maarten, Saba and Sint Eustatius (Statia), are in the Leeward Antilles, while the second group, Bonaire and Curaçao, lie off the Venezuelan coast. The latter, with neighbouring Aruba, which is a separate political unit within the Netherlands, are also commonly called the ABC islands. To complicate matters further, the northern half of the island of Sint Maarten is Saint Martin, part of the French overseas department of Guadeloupe.

Unique to the ABC islands is the local language, called Papiamento, which is a mixture of Spanish, Portuguese, Dutch, English and some African and Indian dialects. Dating back at least to the early eighteenth century, this unusual language is in everyday use and there are both books and newspapers published in it.

The ABCs lie outside the hurricane belt and are therefore popular as a cruising ground for yachts trying to avoid the dangerous season further north. The ABC islands are also a useful stop en route to Panama.

Each Dutch island has its own distinctive character and they are so proud of their individuality, that they have been treated separately in this book:

PUERTO RICO

Puerto Rico is the most easterly island of the Greater Antilles. From the high mountain range in the interior, the land plunges down past coastal plains to the Puerto Rico Trench north of the island, which is 30,190 feet (9200 m) below sea level. Included within the US Commonwealth of Puerto Rico are the small islands of Mona to the west, and Vieques and Culebra to the east.

Frequented mainly by US cruising boats on their way to or from the Virgin Islands and Lesser Antilles, Puerto Rico has so far failed to become part of the cruising circuit, whose playground remains the islands to the east. Among the relatively few who venture west past the Virgins, even less bother to go beyond Vieques and Culebra to visit the main island. The main reason for this reluctance is that once committed to sailing to Puerto Rico, one has either to carry on west or fight one's way back east, a prospect not enjoyed by many cruisers. The same manner of thinking also affects the local Puerto Rican sailors who seldom venture east past Culebra. As can be expected on an increasingly prosperous island like Puerto Rico, yachting is well developed, although sailing yachts are still in the minority.

For the cruising sailor who does sail beyond the attractive outposts of Vieques and Culebra, there are a number of ports on each coast, those on Puerto Rico's south coast being both more plentiful and better protected. On the northern coast, only San Juan offers total protection from the prevailing NE winds. A busy and noisy port, the capital is a good place to reprovision and Old San Juan is an attractive well-preserved city from Puerto Rico's colonial past.

Culebra is geologically part of the Virgin Islands. The island is quietly beautiful and tourism not too developed. Dewey is the chief town, known as Culebra to the locals. Culebra was badly hit by Hurricane Hugo, when scores of boats were destroyed in the anchorage, which was previously considered to be a hurricane refuge.

Country Profile

Christopher Columbus landed on the island in 1493, accompanied by Juan Ponce de León. At that time Arawaks were the inhabitants of Borinquén, as they called it. Ponce de León, attracted by stories of gold, returned 15 years later and established the first settlement. Later the settlers moved to the site of present-day Old San Juan. Puerto Rico was one of the first parts of the Caribbean to be colonised. Columbus had named the island San Juan Bautista, after St John the Baptist whose symbol, the lamb, may still be seen on the flag. León named the new settlement's harbour 'Puerto Rico' and at some point island and port swapped names.

Puerto Rico was important to Spain as gold had been discovered on the island and the local population were used as slave labour to work in the gold mines. The island lay in a prime location between Spain and her American empire, and attacks by other maritime powers were frequent. During the seventeenth century more settlers came, and plantations were established, growing sugar, and later tobacco and coffee. At the end of the Spanish-American war in 1898, Spain ceded Puerto Rico to the United States. In 1917 the island ceased to be a colony and Puerto Ricans became US citizens, the islands becoming a US Commonwealth in the 1950s. Today many Puerto Ricans would like their island to become a full US state.

Federal laws apply, although not income taxes, a major incentive for US businesses to come to Puerto Rico. Since becoming a Commonwealth, industrialisation has been extensive, to replace the monoculture of sugar. Agriculture is still important as is tourism. However, US budget cuts have caused economic problems, and large numbers of the population have emigrated to the United States.

The population is 3.3 million, being mainly Roman Catholic. Spanish is the first language, although English is widely spoken. The capital is San Juan.

Rain is heavier on the northern coastal plain of Puerto Rico and the climate is more arid in the south. The hurricane season is June to November.

Practical Information

LOCAL TIME: GMT - 4

BUOYAGE: IALA B

CURRENCY: United States dollar (US$)

BUSINESS HOURS
Business and government
offices: 0700–1200, 1300–1600 Monday to
Friday.

ELECTRICITY: 110 V, 60 Hz

PUBLIC HOLIDAYS
1 January: New Year's Day
6 January: Three Kings Day
11 January: De Hostos birthday
* Third Monday in
February: Washington's Birthday
* 22 March: Emancipation Day
Good Friday
16 April: José de Diego's Birthday

* Last Monday in May: Memorial Day
30 June: St John the Baptist Day
4 July: Independence Day
17 July: Muñoz Rivera's Birthday
25 July: Constitution Day
27 July: Dr José Celso Barbarosa's
Birthday
First Monday in September: Labour Day
* 12 October: Columbus Day
* Fourth Monday in October: Veterans'
Day
19 November: Discovery Day
Last Thursday in
November: Thanksgiving Day
25 December: Christmas Day
* Half-holidays. Any holiday that falls on
a Sunday will be observed the following
Monday. US holidays are observed as
well as local Puerto Rican ones.

EVENTS
The festival of St John, the island's
patron saint, is the most important
holiday.

COMMUNICATIONS
P.R. Telephone Co.: overseas calls can
be made from the former ITT office,
Parada 11, Av Ponce de León, Miramar,
and the airport.
Blue Pages in the phone book are in
English for tourists.
Post office in Hato Rey, Av Roosevelt.
There are many international flights
from San Juan to Caribbean, European,
North and South American destinations.

DIPLOMATIC MISSIONS
In San Juan:
Dominican Republic: Edificio Avianca
Santurce. ☎ 725-9550.
Haiti: 654 Muñoz Riviera Hato Rey.
☎ 753-0825.
Honduras: Sky Tower 2-D Borinquen
Gardens, Rio Pedras. ☎ 790-3263.

Entry Regulations

Ports of entry
Culebra 18°18′N 65°17′W, Ponce 17°58′N 66°39′W, San Juan 18°28′N 66°07′W, Mayaguez 18°12′N 67°07′W, Guanica 17°58′N 66°55′W, Playa de Fajardo 18°20′N 65°38′W.

Procedure on arrival
US Customs numbers: Fajardo 863-0950, Mayaguez 832-0308, Ponce 842-3195, San Juan 791-0220, 791-0222.
Culebra: Most yachts coming from the US Virgin Islands enter here. One should anchor off the main town of Dewey, which is in the narrowest part of the isthmus. The customs office is in town, halfway across the isthmus.
Ponce: A four-mile journey into town must be made to do the clearance formalities. Entry procedure is complex and takes time.
San Juan: One should notify customs and immigration on arrival, which can be done by telephone from the Club Nautico or marina. This is preferable to going to the Customs House, where the officials are busy with cruise ships and commercial vessels. They prefer to come and clear yachts at the club or the marina.
Mayaguez: This is the largest port on the west coast – it is commercial, but a convenient port of entry. One

should go to the commercial dock and phone customs or clear at the customs office on the main street.
American yachts coming from the US Virgin Islands must clear customs on arrival in Puerto Rico the same as other yachts.

Immigration
All non-US residents must obtain a visa in advance. Canadians may not need a visa, but should check this before arrival. A multiple entry visa should be requested, especially if cruising from the US Virgin Islands or other US territory.

Cruising permit
This should be obtained in the US Virgin Islands, where it is issued free, otherwise a fee will be charged for it on arrival in Puerto Rico. Customs must be notified when a yacht arrives at each subsequent port or anchorage after the first port of entry even when possessing a permit.

Fees
Overtime is charged outside of working hours Monday to Saturday from 0900–1600.

Restrictions
Ensenada Harbour lies within a restricted area and may be closed during military activity, as there is a US

Navy base at Roosevelt Roads. In the Puerto Nuevo area there are artillery and small-arms ranges extending 10 miles to seaward, although these are seldom used. The western end and parts of the south coast of Isla Vieques are also restricted naval areas.

No garbage may be taken ashore: it must be disposed of outside of Puerto Rico. San Juan does have some garbage removal facilities, but these are not found elsewhere on the island.

Facilities

With a large fleet of local craft, although predominantly motor yachts and sport-fishing boats, facilities are of a high standard and there are many marinas dotted around Puerto Rico's coastline. The best facilities are in and around San Juan, where there are several small shipyards, which can handle yachts and do major repair work. There are also several chandleries in San Juan and the selection of marine supplies is good. Whatever is not available can be flown within 48 hours from mainland USA.

Facilities are of a similar standard in Ponce, Puerto Rico's second city, where the Ponce Yacht and Fishing Club has a reputation of welcoming visiting sailors. The club facilities, including a travelift, may only be used by visitors if they are not being used for work on club members' craft. The usual repair facilities can be found in all commercial ports, such as Mayaguez and Fajardo, and fuel and water are normally available on the dockside. This also applies to Culebra, where repair and yachting facilities are gradually improving, especially after the devastation caused by Hurricane Hugo. A good place to haul-out is Isleta Marina to the east, where a boatyard offers repair facilities.

Further Reading

A Yachtsman's Guide to the Greater Antilles
A Cruising Guide to the Caribbean and the Bahamas
Caribbean Islands Handbook
The Gentleman's Guide to Passages South

SABA

Saba is one of the northern islands in the Netherland Antilles. No other Caribbean island could better the saying that 'small is beautiful' than Saba. An extinct volcano only two miles in diameter, the island rises sheer out of the sea to a lofty peak of 3084 feet (940 m).

Its small size does not offer much protection from the prevailing swell but the slight discomfort at anchor is more than made up for by the delights experienced ashore. There are well-protected anchorages at Well's Bay and Ladder Bay on the west coast, while the entry formalities have to be completed at Fort Bay, which is on the SW point of the island. Fort Bay offers better protection in strong NE winds, while the previous anchorages are to be preferred in SE winds.

Until not so long ago Saba's interior was completely inaccessible and the sole way to reach the island's only villages, fittingly called Bottom, Windwardside and Hell's Gate, was to land at Ladder Bay and negotiate the 800 steps cut into the rock. Although the building of a road was deemed an impossible task by civil engineering experts, the Sabans proved them wrong by building one themselves. This amazing feat of stamina and determination was finished in 1958 and runs almost all the way around the island. With the same determination a small airport was built on the only flat area possessed by this rugged island. The villages are neat and picturesque and visitors are treated to a view of a tranquil life that has all but disappeared elsewhere. There are no beaches but the underwater scenery is remarkable. The construction of the airport, the road to the harbour in Fort Bay, and later a pier, brought in tourism on a small scale and the tourist boom of Sint Maarten is spreading over to Saba. Saba has become a duty-free area like Sint Maarten.

Entry Regulations

Port of entry
Fort Bay 17°37′N 63°15′W.

Procedure on arrival
One should proceed ashore and clear with the harbour master at the government building near the pier. Hours are 0800–1700 Monday to Saturday. There is a small charge depending on the size of the boat. One can check in and out at the same time, even if staying a few days. A yacht is allowed to anchor in one of the other anchorages and then visit Fort Bay by land or dinghy to clear.

Restrictions
All the waters around Saba were made a national marine park in 1987 and anchoring is restricted to sandy areas where the coral will not be damaged. Spearfishing and the taking of coral or shells is prohibited. Marine Park officials patrol the anchorages and welcome yachts.

Practical Information (Saba)

LOCAL TIME: GMT - 4

BUOYAGE: IALA B

CURRENCY: Netherlands Antilles
guilders or florins.

BUSINESS HOURS
Banks: 0830–1300 Monday to Friday,
plus 1600–1700 Friday.
Shops: 0800/0900–1200, 1400–1800.

ELECTRICITY: 110 V, 60 Hz

PUBLIC HOLIDAYS
1 January: New Year's Day
Good Friday and Easter Monday
30 April: Queen's birthday
Labour Day
Ascension Day
Whit Monday
1 November: All Saints Day
Early December: Saba Day
15 December: Kingdom Day
25, 26 December: Christmas

COMMUNICATIONS
International calls can be made from the
telephone office.
There are flights to Sint Maarten, where
connections can be made to Europe,
North America and Caribbean
destinations.

MEDICAL
There is a medical centre on the island.

Facilities

There are no facilities available. Fuel can be taken in jerrycans from the fuel station at the Fort Bay anchorage. Some provisioning can be done in Windwardside, which has the better shops of the two settlements.

Further Reading

Cruising Guide to the Leeward Islands
Caribbean Islands Handbook

ST BARTS

In the northern group of the Leeward Islands, Saint-Barthélemy, commonly known as St Barts, is linked administratively to St Martin within the French overseas department of Guadeloupe. St Barts is an attractive island, relatively unspoiled by tourism, with white sandy beaches and volcanic hills. The picturesque harbour of Gustavia is a favourite port of call for cruising sailors who come here to provision their boats with duty-free goods. The island is surrounded by several bays and small islets, but it is in Gustavia where all the action is.

Country Profile

Christopher Columbus named the island San Bartolomé after his brother's patron saint. The French were the first to settle in the mid-seventeenth century, mostly emigrating from Normandy and Brittany. After a period of French rule, it was ceded to Sweden at the end of the eighteenth century in exchange for trading rights in the port of Göteborg. Le Carénage,

present-day Gustavia, became a free port, which together with its neutrality during the great power conflicts brought prosperity and peace. The sea has always been a source of income; men-of-war, traders and pirates called and the island was used as a transhipment point for both plunder and legitimate goods. During the American War of Independence St Barts acted as a base for American privateers and American goods. Transhipment still remains an economic activity today. In the last part of the nineteenth century, after a referendum, St Barts was returned to France. The French had remained the predominant influence and today one can still see old women in the traditional white starched Breton bonnets.

St Barts relies on its free port status, its anchorages and beaches for revenue. Trade and fishing are also important. Of the 3500 inhabitants, most are of French descent and some Swedish, there being only a small percentage of people of African origin. The French that is spoken still has traces of seventeenth century dialect. Roman Catholicism and Protestantism are the main denominations. The islanders are French citizens with full rights. Gustavia is the capital, a colonial town with a French atmosphere, although named after a Swedish king.

Entry Regulations

Port of entry
Gustavia 17°55′N 62°50′W.

Procedure on arrival
It is possible to stop in anchorages outside of Gustavia before checking in.
Gustavia: Proceed ashore to the port authority with papers and passports, open 0730–1230, 1500–1700 Monday to Friday, 0830–1230 Saturdays, and on

Practical Information (St Barts)

LOCAL TIME: GMT - 4

BUOYAGE: IALA B

CURRENCY: French franc, although US$ are widely accepted as on St Martin.

BUSINESS HOURS
Banks: 0800–1200, 1400–1600 (only in Gustavia).
Shops: 0800–1200, 1430–1700 Monday to Friday; morning only on Saturday.

ELECTRICITY: 220 V, 50 Hz

PUBLIC HOLIDAYS
1 January: New Year's Day
Good Friday and Easter Monday
1 May: Labour Day
Ascension
Whit Monday
14 July: Bastille Day
21 July: Schoelcher Day
15 August: Assumption
1 November: All Saints Day
2 November: All Souls Day
11 November: Armistice Day
25 December: Christmas Day

EVENTS
Carnival
24 August: St Barts Day

COMMUNICATIONS
International dialling access code 19.
Public phones use phone cards which can be bought in the post office and some shops.
There are flights to Guadeloupe, St Croix, St Martin, St Thomas and San Juan (Puerto Rico) for connections to Europe and North America.

Sundays 1030–1230 (during November to May).
Port authority monitors VHF Channels 16 and 13.

Customs

As a free port, St Barts does not have customs regulations.

Immigration

Visas are required by nationals of South Africa, Bolivia, Cuba, Haiti, Honduras, El Salvador, Dominican Republic, Turkey and English-speaking Caribbean islands. Any non-EC citizen staying longer than three months will need an extended visa.

Because of the duty-free status of St Barts, visa regulations are less strictly enforced than on Guadeloupe or Martinique.

Restrictions

Anchoring is not permitted in Baie St Jean. Water-skiing or jet-skiing is prohibited within 350 metres of any beach. No water sports are allowed inside Gustavia harbour.

Fees

Port dues are payable in the main harbour of Gustavia and they are collected by a roving harbour patrol. The daily fees depend on length and location, being lowest if anchoring in the outer harbour, higher in the inner harbour and if coming stern-to the quay. One is charged per night of stay depending on the length of boat.

Facilities

Fresh water can be bought from the port authority. Provisioning in town is adequate and the best buy

continues to be duty-free spirits, although most other goods are more expensive than in the other French-speaking islands.

Fuel can be obtained from the commercial dock. Camping Gaz is available but gas bottles with US fittings cannot be filled. There are water, showers, toilets and garbage disposal at the yacht dock. Only basic repair facilities are available.

Further Reading

St Martin/Sint Maarten Area Cruising Guide
Cruising Guide to the Leeward Islands
Caribbean Islands Handbook

ST EUSTATIUS (STATIA)

St Eustatius, affectionately known as Statia, lies north of St Kitts in the Leeward Island chain. The island's only anchorage is off the main village of Oranjestad, in Oranje Baai, which is an open roadstead where the swell usually makes itself felt. Statia is a free port, like its sister islands in the Netherlands Antilles Saba and Sint Maarten.

Country Profile

It is difficult, if not impossible, to imagine that this tiny island was once the commercial hub of the West Indies. During the American War of Independence, when the loyal British colonies were forbidden to trade with the rebel Americans, Dutch Statia made best use

Practical Information (St Eustatius)

LOCAL TIME: GMT - 4

BUOYAGE: IALA B

CURRENCY: Netherlands Antilles guilders or florins

BUSINESS HOURS
Banks: 0830–1300 Monday to Friday, plus 1600–1700 Friday.
Shops: 0800/0900–1200, 1400–1800.
Many Statians are Seventh Day Adventists and the shops they run are closed on Saturdays.

ELECTRICITY: 110 V, 60 Hz

PUBLIC HOLIDAYS
1 January: New Year's Day
Good Friday and Easter Monday
30 April: Queen's birthday
Labour Day
Ascension Day
Whit Monday
All Saints Day
16 November: Statia Day
15 December: Kingdom Day
25, 26 December: Christmas

COMMUNICATIONS
International calls can be made from the telephone office.
There are flights to Sint Maarten, from where connections can be made to Europe, North America and Caribbean destinations.

MEDICAL
There is a hospital on the island.

of its neutrality and traded with everyone without asking questions. The small population became very rich and Statia was known as the Golden Rock. Today, 16 November 1776, the date of the first firing in the world of an official salute to the new Stars and Stripes, is celebrated as Statia Day. Later when Britain declared war on the Netherlands, Admiral Rodney sacked Statia and confiscated its wealth. In more recent times Statia has become a forgotten corner of the Dutch Empire and most of its impoverished population have emigrated to other countries. Farming, fishing and trading have been the traditional industries and more recently oil storage and a refuelling facility have helped the economy of the poorest of the Netherlands Antilles. Tourism is expanding and bringing a little prosperity, Statia being a tourist destination for discriminating travellers, who enjoy the tranquillity of a small place off the beaten track.

Entry Regulations

Port of entry
Oranjestad 17°29′N 62°59′W.

Procedure on arrival
Proceed ashore and check in with immigration and the harbour master at the head of the big pier, the office being normally open 0800–1600 with a lunch break.

Facilities

There are hardly any facilities available and even fuel and water have to be taken in jerrycans. Basic supplies can be bought in Oranjestad as well as locally produced vegetables.

Further Reading

Cruising Guide to the Leeward Islands
Caribbean Islands Handbook

ST KITTS AND NEVIS

Part of the Leeward Islands in the Lesser Antilles is the Federation of St Christopher (the popular name St Kitts is more often used) and Nevis. St Kitts is a green, mountainous island with a low-lying peninsula to the south east while Nevis is smaller and circular, rising to a volcanic peak over 3000 feet (984 metres) high with a dramatic crater at the top. As well as politically united, the two islands are linked by a submarine rock base, separated by the two mile wide waters of the Narrows.

So near and yet so far from the English-speaking Lesser Antilles, St Kitts and Nevis are rather off the cruising track. Some people avoid them because they do not fancy a tough return beating against wind and current to more popular Antigua. Others are put off by the frustrating requirement to clear in and out for every move around the islands. These factors, as well as the absence of docking facilities, have combined to make these islands some of the least frequented in the Lesser Antilles. This is surprising, because although they do not abound in scenic anchorages, the islands themselves are extremely attractive and their interesting past makes visiting ashore a worthwhile experience. As the first English settlement in the Caribbean, St Kitts is of historical interest. There are old relics, ruined forts, grand plantation houses and in Basseterre, the capital since 1727, the best preserved colonial town in the British West Indies. The main town of Nevis, Charlestown, also retains a picturesque

Practical Information

LOCAL TIME: GMT - 4

BUOYAGE: IALA B

CURRENCY: East Caribbean dollar (EC$). US$ also widely accepted.

BUSINESS HOURS
Banks: 0800–1300, also Friday 1500–1700. St Kitts and Nevis National Bank also opens Saturday 0830–1100.
Shops: 0800–1200, 1300–1600; closed Thursday afternoons.
Government offices: 0800–1200 Monday to Friday, 1300–1430 Monday and Tuesday, 1300–1400 Wednesday to Friday.

ELECTRICITY: 230 V, 60 Hz

PUBLIC HOLIDAYS
1 January: New Year's Day
Good Friday, Easter Monday
First Monday in May: Labour Day
Whit Monday
Second Saturday in June: Queen's Birthday with a parade
August Monday
September 19: Independence Day
November 14: Prince Charles' Birthday
25, 26 December: Christmas

EVENTS
Carnival, over Christmas and New Year period on St Kitts.

Culturama carnival on Nevis, July–August, ending the first Monday in August.

COMMUNICATIONS
Cable & Wireless, Cayon St, Basseterre, and Main St, Charlestown, is open 0800–1800 weekdays, 0800–1400 Saturdays, 0600–2000 Sundays and public holidays.
Post offices at Bay Road, Basseterre and Main St, Charlestown, open 0800–1500 except Thursdays when they close at 1100.
There are flights from St Kitts to various Caribbean destinations as well as to Miami, New York and Toronto.

colonial air. For the energetic there are some challenging hikes up to the top of St Kitts or the peak of the Nevis volcano. The promised development of marinas on both islands will undoubtedly change this state of affairs and place St Kitts and Nevis firmly on the Antilles cruising circuit.

Country Profile

Some archaeological remains have been found of the original inhabitants, who suffered a similar fate to those on other islands, perishing at the hands of Europeans, although not without a struggle. They called the island Liamuiga, 'fertile island'. Columbus visited the island on his second voyage and renamed it after St Christopher, the patron saint of travellers. Nevis was originally called Oualie by the Indians, meaning land of beautiful water, and the name Nieves is thought to have been given to the island by Columbus because it reminded him of the white clouds gathered around the snowy peaks of the Pyrenees, Nieves becoming corrupted over the years to Nevis.

St Kitts was the first British settlement in the West Indies, although some French also settled and for a while the island was divided between the two, still reflected in the place names. From their bases in St Kitts both the English and French colonised other Caribbean islands and the relationship was often stormy.

On Nevis the natural mineral baths made the island a popular spa and Horatio Nelson, coming to water his ships, met and married Frances Nisbet, who lived on the island.

From 1816 St Kitts, Nevis, Anguilla and the British Virgin Islands were administered as a single colony until the Leeward Islands Federation was formed. St Kitts and Nevis gained independence in 1983 as a separate Federation.

On St Kitts the nationalised sugar industry dominates the mainly agricultural economy, although efforts are being made to diversify. Nevis grows sea island cotton and coconuts. Tourism is increasingly important, helped by the good airport on St Kitts.

There are 46,000 inhabitants, mostly of African descent, whose first language is English, although some French patois is also spoken. The majority are Protestant.

The islands are in the trade wind belt. There is plenty of rainfall on the hills, but it is less humid on the coast. The hurricane season is from June to November.

Entry Regulations

Ports of entry
Charlestown (Nevis) 17°08′N 62°38′W, Basseterre (St Kitts) 17°18′N 62°43′W.

Procedure on arrival
Charlestown: Anchor off the pier and go first to customs, which is opposite on Main Street, open 0800–1200, 1300–1600 weekdays. Then one should check in with passports at immigration in the police station, to the right down Main Street.
Basseterre: Customs are upstairs in the post office on Bay Road by the ferry dock, open 0800–1630 Monday and Tuesday, and 0800–1600 the rest of the

week, with 1200–1300 being a lunch break. At weekends or holidays the local taxi drivers can help find a customs official. Immigration is upstairs in the police station on Cayon Street, three streets inland from Bay Road.

Customs

Firearms must be declared and usually are bonded on board.

Animals must be quarantined before being allowed entry. An import permit from the Ministry of Agriculture is necessary. Otherwise animals must remain on board.

Immigration

No visas are required for nationals of Commonwealth countries, Belgium, Denmark, Finland, France, Greece, Iceland, Italy, Liechtenstein, Luxembourg, the Netherlands, Norway, San Marino, Spain, Sweden, Switzerland, Tunisia, Turkey, Uruguay, US citizens (if visit does not exceed six months), Germany and Venezuela (if visit does not exceed one month). All other nationals require visas. South Africans are not given visas.

Cruising permit

If one clears in first at Charlestown, one must clear in again at Basseterre and vice versa. On both islands, clearance is normally given only for anchoring in the port of entry, and a cruising permit must be obtained to visit any other anchorages on that island.

If wanting to visit the other island, one must return to customs and get a Boat Pass to go to the other port of entry. Here another cruising permit will have to be obtained, although one does not have to visit immigration again before clearing out.

Fees

Customs charges EC$20, which does not have to be paid again if visiting both islands. The overtime fee is usually EC$5 on both islands for clearance outside of working hours. There is an exit fee at Basseterre.

Facilities

Although only basic facilities were available on both islands at the time of writing, a marked improvement is expected if the projected marina development plans come to fruition. On St Kitts, the Great Salt Pond and surrounding area in the south of the island may be developed into a marina complex, while on Nevis there are plans to build a small marina at Fort Charles, at the southern end of Charlestown. Another development

on Nevis is planned at the old Newcastle harbour, on the NW side of the island near the airport.

For the time being visiting yachts have to put up with what there is, which is very little. Water can be taken on at the dock in Basseterre, but fuel must be either carried in jerrycans or ordered by tanker if the quantity warrants it. The Shell depot in St Kitts will also fill gas bottles. There is a boatbuilding firm near the deepwater harbour in Basseterre which will undertake fibreglass work and general repair. Brooks Boat Company can be contacted on VHF Channel 16, call sign BBC. There is good provisioning in Basseterre, where there are several good supermarkets.

Water is also available on the dock in Charlestown, but permission to come alongside must be obtained from the harbour master. The fuel situation is similar to the one in St Kitts. The Nevis Gas Company will refill gas bottles. There is less selection in provisions than in St Kitts, but there is a good supply of fresh produce, particularly freshly caught fish.

Further Reading

Cruising Guide to the Leeward Islands
A Motoring Guide to St Kitts
Caribbean Islands Handbook

ST LUCIA

This volcanic island in the Windward Islands boasts some of the most spectacular scenery in the Caribbean, which has earned her the name 'Helen of the Caribbean'. The Grand and Petit Pitons peaks rise out of the sea at Soufrière Bay and there are few Caribbean anchorages to match this spot for sheer magnitude. Not far away lies Marigot Bay, a landlocked bay that reputedly hid from sight an entire British fleet during the Napoleonic wars and now shelters one of The Moorings' fleet of charter yachts. However, the main yachting centre of St Lucia is at Rodney Bay close to the northern end of the island, where an excellent marina has been set up in a dredged lagoon. To this one should add that the facilities in the well-protected port of the capital Castries make St Lucia the perfect base from which to explore the rest of the Lesser Antilles.

Recently tourism has become a major revenue earner and yachting plays an important part in this development. The government has actively encouraged the establishment of yachting related businesses, aiming to make St Lucia one of the prime yachting centres in the Caribbean.

Country Profile

Arawaks were probably the first to settle on St Lucia, only to be driven out by the Caribs. The first European sighting remains a matter of controversy and it is disputed that Columbus ever came to the island in 1502 on December 13, which is celebrated as St Lucia's Day, the national holiday. Populated by hostile Caribs, there was little interest by Europeans in settling the island until the 1600s. English efforts to settle failed, then in 1642 the French king granted it to the French West Indies Company. The Caribs continued to resist settlement, and several governors were killed. Twenty years later the English renewed their claim and a struggle for possession commenced between Caribs, French and English, the island changing hands some fourteen times before finally becoming a British Crown Colony in 1814, which it remained until independence in 1979. The majority of settlers, however, were of French origin and the French influence remained strong, still to be seen in the French patois, architecture and place names.

For many years the economy was dominated by

Castries Harbour with Rodney Bay in the background.

sugar, although bananas, cocoa and coconuts have also become important exports. Tourism is now a major earner of foreign exchange.

The population is 140,000. English is the official language but many speak a French patois and most are Roman Catholic.

The island has constant trade winds with only minor differences through the year. December to June is the best time of year, when it is less humid, and there is no risk of hurricanes. The hurricane season is from June to November.

Entry Regulations

Ports of entry
Vieux Fort 13°44'N 60°57'W, Marigot Bay 13°58'N 61°58'W, Castries 14°00'N 60°59'W, Rodney Bay 14°04'N 60°58'W.

Soufrière is soon to open as a port of entry and it may be possible to get permission from the police station there to stay overnight.

Procedure on arrival
On arrival the captain should go ashore to report to

Practical Information

LOCAL TIME: GMT - 4

BUOYAGE: IALA B

CURRENCY: East Caribbean dollar (EC$). US$ also widely accepted.

BUSINESS HOURS
Banks: 0800–1200 Monday to Friday, 1500–1700 Friday.
Shops: 0800–1230, 1330–1600 Monday to Friday, 0800–1200 Saturday.
Government offices: 0830–1230, 1330–1630 Monday to Friday.

ELECTRICITY: 220 V, 50 Hz

PUBLIC HOLIDAYS
1 January: New Year's Day
22 February: Independence Day
Good Friday and Easter Monday
Whit Monday
Corpus Christi
Emancipation Day
Thanksgiving Day
13 December: National Day
25, 26 December: Christmas

EVENTS
Carnival: February.
Flower festivals: La Rose, August; La Marguerite, October.
Aqua Action: yacht match racing, early June.
ARC Finish: December.

COMMUNICATIONS
International telephone calls at Cable & Wireless, Bridge St, Castries, also New Dock Road, Vieux Fort.
The main post office is on Bridge Street, Castries.
There are international flights from Hewannora Airport near Vieux Fort to various European and North American cities, while inter-island flights leave from Vigie airport near Castries.

DIPLOMATIC MISSIONS
United Kingdom: 24 Micons St, Castries. ☎ 22484.
Venezuela: Casa Vigie, Castries. ☎ 24033.

customs. The crew must remain on board until clearance is completed. Customs clearance from last port is required and a local declaration form must be completed in quadruplicate (including animals, duty-free goods, firearms on board).

If staying less than three days, one can clear in and out on arrival. After clearing out, yachts have 72 hours to depart St Lucia, or 24 hours if local or charter boats. If returning to St Lucia, a permit may be obtained from customs before departure, costing EC$25, which allows one to anchor in a place which is not a port of entry, such as the Pitons, before proceeding to a port of entry.

Vieux Fort: The customs office is at the head of the large dock. Clearance may be completed 0800–1600 on weekdays only; at weekends one must clear at Hewannora Airport.

Marigot Bay: The customs office is on the right hand side by The Moorings fuel dock, open 0800–1800 every day.

Castries: Yachts clearing in must come straight to customs dock or, if there is no space, must anchor in the quarantine anchorage to the east of the customs dock. Failure to do so could result in a fine. Customs and immigration officials are available during office hours (0800–1630 weekdays).

Rodney Bay: One should tie up alongside the customs dock in the marina, which is marked by yellow posts. The customs and immigration office is open 0800–1800 every day. There is no docking charge if only coming to clear. The channel leading into Rodney Bay Marina has a maximum reported depth of 8 feet (2.4 metres).

Customs

Firearms must be declared, but no action is taken if staying less than three days, after which they must be sealed on board by a customs officer. Yachts temporarily imported will have weapons held by customs in Castries or possibly by police if a longer permit is obtained.

Animals are not allowed ashore without prior inspection by the veterinary officer, who will then grant permission. Paperwork for the animal should be correct. St Lucia is rabies-free.

A temporary import permit for the yacht for stays of up to three months can be obtained on arrival from customs at Rodney Bay or Marigot Bay. For stays longer than three months a permit can be obtained from the Directorate of Customs in Castries.

Immigration

Visas are not required for nationals of Commonwealth, Scandinavian and EC countries (except Ireland and Portugal), Liechtenstein, Switzerland, Turkey, Tunisia, Uruguay, Venezuela and the United States. Others, for example Iranians, Colombians and South Africans, require a visa in advance.

Normally a six week to two month stay is granted by the customs officer when clearing in, with a further one month extension possible. Extensions may be difficult to obtain and cost EC$25, so stays should not be underestimated. Longer extensions have to be obtained in Castries.

Cruising permit

This is not obligatory, but permission is needed to

move to any different place other than the port of entry. A cruising permit for sailing the coast or visiting other places in St Lucia is best requested when clearing in.

Fees

The port authority charges charter yachts a fee of betwen EC$20 and EC$40 depending on length. Port dues must be paid if clearing in at Castries. Overtime is charged after 1630 Monday to Friday ($10) and all day Saturday ($10) and Sunday, holidays ($15).

Facilities

St Lucia is constantly improving its yachting facilities and several charter companies have their base there, which means that most repair work can be undertaken locally. The marina in Rodney Bay offers the usual facilities with a travelift and boatyard attached to the marina. More comprehensive repair facilities are available at Vigie near the capital Castries where the St Lucia Yacht Services offer a full marina service, repair facilities, a travelift and slipway.

The Moorings charter company maintains a base of operations in Marigot Bay. The company's employees will undertake outside work if not needed to work on their own yachts. Fuel and water are available at their dock and also provisions from their supply store. The Moorings stand by on VHF Channels 16 and 85.

There are only basic services available in Vieux Fort, although some engine repair work can be undertaken at the Goodwill Fishermen's Cooperative. Some supplies as well as fresh fruit and vegetables are also available.

Further Reading

Sailor's Guide to the Windward Islands
Caribbean Islands Handbook
Cruising Guide to the Eastern Caribbean, Vol. 3
A Cruising Guide to the Caribbean and the Bahamas

ST MARTIN

One of the northern Leeward Islands, St Martin is French while Sint Maarten, which occupies the southern half of the same island, is Dutch, part of the Netherlands Antilles. French St Martin is different from its Dutch neighbour, not only in culture, but also in terrain, as the north is hilly and forested compared to the low sandy south. Pic du Paradis is the highest point. Since 1963 St Martin has been part of the French overseas département of Guadeloupe. Both tourism and yachting have developed at a great rate during the last decade. One area where the French half of the island scores high is not surprisingly that of cuisine.

Country Profile

The Caribs were the original inhabitants of this island, which Christopher Columbus probably sighted on St Martin's Day in 1493, hence its name. Spain showed little interest in the island and it was left to the French to settle in the north in the seventeenth century, while Dutch settled in the south. A treaty in 1648 divided the island between France and the Netherlands on the basis of peaceful coexistence, an arrangement which continues to this day.

The economy of St Martin is almost entirely dependent on tourism, with its duty-free shopping, pleasant climate and good beaches. The 8000 inhabitants speak French and are mainly Roman Catholic. Marigot is the capital.

Entry Regulations

Ports of entry

Marigot Bay 18°04′N 63°06′W, Anse Marcel 18°07′N 63°03′W.

Procedure on arrival

One should proceed ashore and report to customs (*douane*) and police (gendarmerie). Yachts are supposed to check with immigration on arrival and departure and also when sailing between the Dutch and French sides of the island.

Marigot Bay: Clear in with immigration at the head of the dock (open daily 0700–1930).

Anse Marcel: Yachts can clear at the port office.

Customs

St Martin is a duty-free island.

Firearms must be declared.

Animals need a health certificate, and dogs and cats need a valid anti-rabies vaccination certificate.

Fees

An immigration fee of US$10 is charged for a yacht with crew, and $20 if carrying a charter party. There is an entry fee.

Immigration

A stay up of up to three months is permitted. Visas are

Practical Information

LOCAL TIME: GMT - 4

BUOYAGE: IALA B

CURRENCY: French franc. US$ are widely used.

BUSINESS HOURS
Banks: 0900–1200, 1400–1500 Monday to Friday.
Shops: 0900–1200/1230, 1400–1800. Monday to Saturday.

ELECTRICITY: 220 V, 50 Hz

PUBLIC HOLIDAYS
1 January: New Year's Day
Carnival, beginning of February
Good Friday and Easter Monday
Ash Wednesday
Labour Day
Ascension
Whit Monday
14 July: Bastille Day
21 July: Schoelcher Day
15 August: Assumption
1 November: All Saints Day

11 November: Armistice Day
25 December: Christmas Day

COMMUNICATIONS
International dialling access code 19.
If calling the Dutch side of the island, dial 3 first and then the number.
Public phones take phone cards, which may be bought from post offices and some shops.
International flights can only be made from the Dutch Sint Maarten airport. The small airport in St Martin only has flights to St Barts and Guadeloupe.

required by nationals of South Africa, Bolivia, Cuba, Haiti, Honduras, El Salvador, Dominican Republic, Turkey and English-speaking Caribbean islands. Any non-EC citizen staying longer than three months needs an extended visa.

As international flights arrive in the Dutch Sint Maarten, crew joining a boat in French St Martin have sometimes experienced difficulties with immigration officials at the airport as they did not have either an onward or return ticket. Captains of yachts expecting crew should contact immigration beforehand to avoid this problem.

Facilities

There are two established marinas and there is a possibility of more to come. Port La Royale, in the north-east corner of Simpson Bay Lagoon, offers the usual marina services, repair and engineering workshops. There are two chandleries in Marigot, a good supermarket and a fresh produce market. Port Lonvilliers marina is the best hurricane hole on the island being completely enclosed and offering protection from every direction. Overall, repair facilities are somewhat better on the Dutch side of the island.

Further Reading

Cruising Guide to the Leeward Islands
Caribbean Islands Handbook

ST VINCENT AND THE GRENADINES

Part of the Windward Islands in the Lesser Antilles, the island of St Vincent plus over 30 Grenadines have always been a popular yachting destination. The long established cruising Mecca of the Caribbean, the Grenadines, have not lost their appeal in spite of the steady increase of sailing pilgrims who flock there. The anchorages might be better in the Virgins, the scenery more stunning in the Leewards, but the affection of discriminate cruisers for the Grenadines remains unswayed. Why this is so is difficult to say, but the fact that the Grenadines have changed so little compared to the rest of the Caribbean is probably the main reason. How much longer this will continue is hard to tell as a fast pace of change has gripped the Caribbean island nations, so it may be only a matter of time before the government of St Vincent jumps on the bandwagon.

Arbitrarily divided by the British Colonial Office, the Northern Grenadines are administered by St Vincent, while the smaller southern group belongs to Grenada. The island of St Vincent itself is not as popular a cruising destination as Bequia and the smaller islands, mainly because of a less friendly attitude. An infinitely warmer welcome awaits sailors in neighbouring Bequia, whose Port Elizabeth in Admiralty Bay is one of the most famous watering holes on the international cruising scene.

Bequia is a true island of sailors and boats. Although there are plans to build an airport on the island, for the moment it is only linked to the outside world by sea. The seafaring tradition is very much alive among today's Bequians, most of whom are descendants of the early Scottish settlers and whaling crews. Boats are still built on the beach, from small fishing boats to 70 ft

Practical Information

LOCAL TIME: GMT - 4

BUOYAGE: IALA B

CURRENCY: East Caribbean dollar
(EC$)

BUSINESS HOURS
Banks: 0800–1200/1300 Monday to
Friday, plus 1400/1500–1700 Friday.
Shops: 0800–1200, 1300–1600 Monday to
Friday, 0800–1200 Saturday.
Government offices: 0800–1200,
1300–1600 Monday to Friday, 0830–1200
Saturday.

ELECTRICITY: 220/240 V, 50 Hz

PUBLIC HOLIDAYS
1 January: New Year's Day
22 January: Discovery Day
Good Friday, Easter Monday
Labour Day
First Monday and Tuesday in July:
Caricom Day and Carnival Tuesday
First Monday in August
27 October: Independence Day
25, 26 December: Christmas

EVENTS
Whitsun Regatta
Carnival

COMMUNICATIONS
Cable & Wireless, Halifax St, Kingstown
for international telephone calls.
Post office, Halifax St, 0830–1500
Monday to Friday, 0830–1130 Saturday.
Frangipani Yacht Services in Bequia:
International telephone calls, telex and
mail service.
St Vincent, Union, Mustique and
Canouan all have airports, but for
international flights to North America or
Europe, connections have to be made in
Barbados, St Lucia or Martinique.

DIPLOMATIC MISSIONS
In Kingstown:
United Kingdom: Grenville St. ☎ 71701.
Venezuela: Granby St. ☎ 61374.

schooners. More than anywhere else in the West Indies, Bequia is the island where sailors feel truly at home.

The other Grenadines all have their special character, from the unspoilt Tobago Cays to exclusive Mustique, retreat of royalty and rock stars.

Country Profile

Caribs inhabited Hairoun, as they called St Vincent, when Columbus visited on his third voyage, and their hostility initially prevented European settlement. In 1675 a Dutch ship carrying settlers and slaves was wrecked on the island and only the slaves survived, mixing with the Caribs. Slaves from neighbouring islands fled to swell this population of 'Black Caribs' of whom some descendants still live on the island.

England and France disputed possession of the island and both occupied it at different times. The French encouraged the Black Caribs against the English, and a fragile peace came only at the end of the eighteenth century when a revolt was crushed, and most of the Black Caribs were deported to Roatán Island, now part of Honduras.

During the nineteenth century labour shortages brought in Portuguese and Indian immigrants. St Vincent became incorporated into the British colony of the Windward Islands. The volcano of Soufrière erupted in 1902, two days after Mount Pelée on Martinique, killing 2000 people and was a blow to an already bad economic situation. The volcano still remains active, its last eruption occurring in 1979. Full

independence was gained the same year.

Crops on the island have suffered from the 1979 eruption, Hurricanes Allen in 1980, and Emily in 1987. The soil is fertile and agriculture is important economically, bananas being the main export. Tourism also contributes considerably to the economy, but there is high unemployment.

The population of 125,000 lives mostly on the coast and in the capital Kingstown, on St Vincent. English is the main language, but some people also speak a Créole patois. The population is predominantly Protestant and Roman Catholic.

The islands lie in the tropical trade wind zone. December to May are the best months, dry, and outside the hurricane season, which lasts from June to November.

Entry Regulations

Ports of entry
St Vincent: Kingstown 13°09′N 61°14′W, Wallilabou Bay 13°15′N 61°17′W (yachts only). A customs office is due to be opened at Young Island Cut.
Bequia: Port Elizabeth 13°00′N 61°16′W.
Mustique: Grand Bay 12°53′N 61°11′W.
Union Island: Clifton 12°35′N 61°25′W.
Canouan: 12°42′N 61°20′W.

Procedure on arrival
Visiting yachts arriving in St Vincent territorial waters must proceed to a port of entry to clear in before stopping in any other port or anchorage.

With Q flag hoisted, one should anchor in the port of entry and the captain only should go ashore. Three crew lists, clearance from previous port, passports and ship's papers will be needed. One should proceed first to the Custom House if in Kingstown, or the Revenue Office in the other islands. Clearance must also be done with the port authorities and immigration.

Kingstown: One should anchor east of the ferry dock. First one should clear in with customs and then immigration, which is in town, and finally the port authority. This can take some time. Because of the lengthy formalities and difficult mooring in Kingstown, some people prefer to clear in at Bequia and visit St Vincent on the schooner *Friendship Rose*, which sails there daily.

Bequia: As Bequia is more used to yachts, clearing in at Port Elizabeth can be done more quickly. In Port Elizabeth customs and immigration are in the same building as the post office, open 0900–1500.

A cruising permit will be granted by customs or Port Department on clearing in, if they are satisfied that the voyage is for cruising purposes only.

Customs

Firearms must be declared on arrival, and can be sealed on board, but if a yacht has no suitable locker, the firearms will be held in the custody of customs or police until departure.

Animals may be inspected by the veterinary officer and are not allowed ashore.

A yacht may stay up to one year subject to immigration requirements provided customs is satisfied that it is a genuine visiting yacht.

Immigration

Nationals of the UK, USA and Canada may enter for up to six months on proof of citizenship. Other nationalities will be normally granted one month on arrival for each visit, which can be extended by application to immigration, or another month gained by re-entry. No nationalities need obtain visas before arrival. South African passport holders will be refused entry.

Fees

Overtime fees for customs are payable outside of working hours, EC$15 Monday to Saturday, EC$20 Sundays and holidays. A departure tax of EC$10 per person is payable except for children under 12.

Fees are payable by yachts that are chartering as follows:

Charter licence: EC$2 per foot per month or EC$12 per foot per year. Yachts over 100 feet $2400 per year.

Day charters: A tax of EC$5 per person per day or part thereof is payable.

Cruising yachts do not pay these licence fees.

Fishing

The use of spearguns or quantity fishing is not allowed unless written approval is given by the Fisheries Department. One can request this permit from customs on arrival.

Trolling and handlining a few fish for one's own consumption is allowed. There is a closed season for lobsters from 1 May to 31 August, and for turtles from 1 March to 31 July. The removal of coral is forbidden.

Restrictions

No swimsuits to be worn in towns or any business place in town or in the streets.

Facilities

Although there are some workshops in the capital Kingstown which can deal with repairs, most yacht services are concentrated in the Young Island Cut and Blue Lagoon area, the latter being the base of the CSY charter company. There is a small boatyard undertaking fibreglass repair and metal work, as well as various workshops specialising in electrical work, rigging and engine repair, both outboard and diesel.

Water and fuel are available at the dock in Blue Lagoon. There is also a supermarket geared specifically for charter clients, while other supermarkets can be found in Kingstown and near the airport. There are various friendly establishments clustered around Young Island Cut catering for the well-being of transient sailors.

Almost on a par with St Vincent's repair facilities are those of Bequia. There is a boatyard and slipway of 100 tons and skilled shipwrights are available for most kinds of work. Others specialise in fibreglass work and sailmaking. There are two chandleries with a good selection of spares and accessories, one also stocking charts. Water and fuel are available from the dock next to the slipway. The range of provisions is less varied than in Kingstown and they tend to be more expensive. Fresh produce can be bought on the waterfront. The traditional meeting point for sailors is the Frangipani bar.

Facilities are rapidly improving on Union Island, where the Anchorage Yacht Club has expanded its docking space and also has a slipway, chandlery and repair facilities. Fuel and water are also available. There are several supermarkets with a reasonable selection in Clifton.

A marina development on the south-west side of Canouan offers fuel, water, Camping Gaz, basic supplies and long-distance telephones. On the other Grenadines facilities are very basic. Only essentials can be obtained in Mayereau, rather less on Petit Saint Vincent and not even that in the Tobago Cays.

Further Reading

Sailor's Guide to the Windward Islands
A Cruising Guide to the Caribbean and the Bahamas
Cruising Guide to the Eastern Caribbean, Vol. 3
Caribbean Islands Handbook
St Vincent and the Grenadines

SINT MAARTEN

Politics has little relation to geography in this small country, for Sint Maarten is part of the Netherlands Antilles, but shares the island with St Martin, which is part of the French département of Guadeloupe. One of the most northerly of the Leeward Islands, Sint Maarten is of arid limestone, its southern part low-lying with coastal lagoons and saltpans. However, Sint Maarten is a developed island, and has some fine beaches. Tourism development has virtually exploded in recent years and the island has become one of the most popular destinations in the Caribbean.

If water tourism develops at the same pace as land tourism, there is no doubt that by the end of the century this island will be the yachting centre of the Caribbean. Already the facilities are of the highest standards and the ones that are in the pipeline, such as the new marinas planned in the Simpson Bay lagoon, will consolidate the island's leading position.

Country Profile

The Caribs were the original inhabitants of this island, which was called St Martin by Christopher Columbus. Spain showed little interest in the island and French settled in the north, while the salt ponds attracted Dutch settlers to the southern coast. A treaty in 1648 divided the island between France and the Netherlands on the basis of peaceful coexistence, an arrangement which continues to this day. Farming, fishing, salt-extraction, and sugar were the main activities of the islanders, although with the abolition of slavery in 1863 the plantations declined. In 1954 the Dutch half, like the rest of the Netherlands Antilles, was granted full self-government while still under Dutch sovereignty.

The economy depends mainly on tourism. The island has very good airlinks, beautiful beaches, a free port status, and is prosperous. Of the 14,000 inhabitants, most are of African or Dutch origin. Many religious denominations are represented. Dutch is the official language, although everyone speaks English. Philipsburg is the capital of the island.

Sint Maarten has a mild tropical climate, with steady easterly trade winds. July to November is the rainy season, while December to June is dry, although conditions vary little, June to November being the hurricane season.

Practical Information

LOCAL TIME: GMT - 4

BUOYAGE: IALA B

CURRENCY: Netherlands Antilles guilders or florins are the official currency, but US dollars are widely accepted. French francs, the currency of St Martin, are not accepted on Sint Maarten.

BUSINESS HOURS
Banks: 0830–1300 Monday to Friday, plus 1600–1700 Friday.
Shops: 0800/0900–1200, 1400–1800. Monday to Saturday.

ELECTRICITY: 110 V, 60 Hz

PUBLIC HOLIDAYS
1 January: New Year's Day
Good Friday and Easter Monday
30 April: Queen's birthday
Labour Day
Ascension Day
Whit Monday
All Saints Day
11 November: St Maarten Day
15 December: Kingdom Day
25, 26 December: Christmas

EVENTS
Easter Carnival mid-April
Sint Maarten's trade wind race

COMMUNICATIONS
Sint Maarten uses the Dutch system, which is different to the French side. If calling the French St Martin dial 06 and then the number.
There is a telecommunications office on Back Street.
There are international flights to Europe, North America and many Caribbean destinations.

Entry Regulations

Port of entry
Philipsburg 18°02′N 63°03W.

Procedure on arrival
On arrival, one should proceed ashore and take passports and ship's papers to the immigration department on Back Street, or the police station opposite.

Immigration
A valid passport is necessary for all nationals, although US citizens need only proof of citizenship. Crew joining a boat have sometimes experienced difficulty with immigration officials if they are unable to show an onward ticket. Captains of yachts expecting crew are advised to contact immigration in advance.

Facilities

Facilities are concentrated in two main locations, on the eastern side of Philipsburg Harbour and in Simpson Bay. There are two marinas in Philipsburg, Great Bay and Bobby's, the latter offering a wide range of services as well as having a 70-ton travelift. Budget Marine is a large chandlery with an excellent selection of marine supplies. All repair work can be dealt with in the Philipsburg area and what is not available there can be found at Simpson Bay. Several charter companies maintain a base at Oyster Pond, which also has a marina. The usual repair and service facilities are available there, although not as extensive as in the other two areas of Sint Maarten.

Further Reading

Caribbean Islands Handbook
Cruising Guide to the Leeward Islands

TRINIDAD AND TOBAGO

The Republic of Trinidad and Tobago lies just off the Venezuelan coast, the most southerly of the Caribbean islands, and regarded by some as the most exotic. Cosmopolitan Trinidad, home of calypso and the steel drum, is famous for its Carnival called De Mas (short for masquerade). Tobago is more peaceful, and was used by Daniel Defoe as the setting for *Robinson Crusoe*, although Alexander Selkirk, on whom the story is based, was in fact wrecked on Juan Fernandez island in the South Pacific.

Being slightly out of the way, Trinidad and Tobago are visited by fewer cruising boats than the islands to the north. Tricky navigation through the current-swept Dragon's Mouth and the restrictions imposed on cruising in the past by the authorities have also contributed to Trinidad's lack of popularity. Recently, however, efforts have been made to encourage tourism, including yachts, and formalities have become much easier. Most yachts sail to Trinidad to be there for Carnival time, when the anchorage off Port of Spain gets very crowded. This is certainly the best time to visit, as the Carnival is one of the most spectacular to be seen outside of Brazil.

Country Profile

The Arawaks and Caribs were the first inhabitants of the islands. On his third voyage Columbus spotted Trinidad, although no one is quite sure whether he named it after the Holy Trinity or the three distinctive peaks on the south-east of the island. Tobago's name is a corruption of tobacco, which was grown there by the Caribs.

Spain used Trinidad as a base to explore South America. Diseases and slavery soon killed off most of the native population. The late eighteenth century saw an influx of French settlers, but Spain ceded the islands to England in 1802. After the abolition of slavery in 1834, the English brought in Indian and Chinese indentured labourers to fill the labour shortage. Immigrants also came from neighbouring islands, North America, Madeira and Europe.

Tobago was first settled in 1641 when the Duke of Courland obtained a royal grant to settle on the island. Later both the Dutch and French occupied the island until it was ceded to England in the eighteenth century.

In 1888 Trinidad and Tobago were united into one Crown Colony and in August 1962 the islands became independent, the country being declared a Republic in 1976.

Agriculture is important and coffee, sugar, cocoa and citrus fruit are cultivated in the fertile soil. Trinidad is rich in mineral deposits including asphalt from the Pitch Lake on the south-west coast. Sir Walter Raleigh found the lake in 1595 and caulked his ships there. Trinidad has oil reserves, which are an important factor in the economy, although after the depression of the oil market in the 1980s, efforts were made to diversify. Tourism is rapidly developing.

The population of Trinidad is 1,195,000, the majority

Practical Information

LOCAL TIME: GMT - 4

BUOYAGE: IALA B

CURRENCY: Trinidad and Tobago dollar (TT$)

BUSINESS HOURS
Banks: 0900–1400 Monday to Thursday, and 0900–1200, 1500–1700 Friday.
Shops: 0800–1600/1630 Monday to Friday, and 0800–1200 Saturday.
Government offices: 0800–1600 Monday to Friday.

ELECTRICITY: 110/220 V, 60 Hz

PUBLIC HOLIDAYS
1 January: New Year's Day
Good Friday and Easter Monday
Easter Tuesday
Whit Monday
Eid el-Fitr (end of Ramadan)

Corpus Christi
19 June: Labour/Butlers Day
First Monday in August: Discovery/Caribbean Day
31 August: Independence Day
24 September: Republic Day
Divali, Festival of lights
25, 26 December: Christmas

EVENTS
Carnival
Phagwah, Spring festival, February/March
Yaum um-Nabi
Hosein festival
Tobago Race Week

COMMUNICATIONS
Main Textel office, Independence Square and 1 Edward Street, operates international telephones, telex, fax, and is open 24 hours (there is also an office in Scarborough).

Main post office, Wrightson Road, Port of Spain, open 0700–1700 Monday to Friday. There are flights from Port of Spain to many destinations in Europe, North America, South America and the Caribbean. There are also flights from Tobago to Miami, New York and Toronto as well as Caribbean destinations.

DIPLOMATIC MISSIONS
In Port of Spain:
Canada: 72 South Quay. ☎ 623-7254.
New Zealand: Geo F. Higgins Building, 233 Western Main Rd, Cocorite. ☎ 622-7020.
United States: 19 Queens Park West. ☎ 622-6371.
United Kingdom: Furness House, 90 Independence Square. ☎ 622-6371.
Venezuela: 16 Victoria Av. ☎ 622-2019.

being of African or Asian origin. Chinese, Portuguese, Syrian, Jewish and Latin American minorities make up Trinidad's very cosmopolitan population. Tobago has 45,000 inhabitants. English is spoken, as well as Spanish, French patois and Hindi dialects. Port of Spain is the capital of Trinidad, and Scarborough is Tobago's main town. Many different religions are practised, among them Roman Catholicism, Protestantism, Hinduism, Judaism, Islam, the syncretist creed of spiritual Baptists, and the Xango cult, which is a combination of African and Asian elements.

The islands have an equatorial climate within the trade wind belt. June to November is the rainy season. The islands are almost out of the hurricane zone.

Entry Regulations

Ports of entry
Trinidad: Port of Spain 10°39'N 61°31'W, San Fernando 10°17'N 61°28'W, Brighton 10°15'N 61°38'W, Pointe-à-Pierre Yacht Club 10°19'N 61°28'W, Point Gourde 10°40'N 61°38'W, Point Tembladora 10°41'N 61°36'W, Point Fortin 10°11'N 61°41'W.
Tobago: Scarborough 11°11'N 60°44'W.

Procedure on arrival
Yachts entering Trinidad territorial waters are advised to call coastguard control on Channel 16 to advise of the yacht's arrival and to give an ETA. Yachts have been boarded by the coastguard or police when passing through the Dragon's Mouth.

All yachts are boarded on arrival by customs who will require details of crew, passengers, animals, firearms and dutiable stores. The harbour master will give instructions as to berthing. Vessels may not be moved from their anchorage without prior approval of the customs officer.
Port of Spain: There is a dock by the health and immigration offices in front of the twin towers, which can be seen on the approach into Port of Spain. One should tie up to this dock for clearance. Customs are a four-block walk away.
Scarborough: One should come to the government dock. Customs can be cleared at Chaguaramas and immigration will come over from Port of Spain if their transport costs are paid.

Procedure on departure
Clearance must be obtained from the harbour master, customs and immigration.

Customs
Firearms and ammunition must be declared on arrival and will be taken by the customs boarding officer and

placed in custody at the central police station. Requests for their return prior to departure must be made to customs at least 24 hours before clearance; failure to do so may result in a delay to departure or departure without the firearms. To keep firearms in one's possession during the stay, it is necessary to apply to the Commissioner of Police for a licence.

Animals must remain on board, and may only land with the permission of the government veterinary officer and customs.

Fruits, plants and plant material must be inspected by a plant quarantine officer before being landed.

Yachts are admitted duty-free for a reasonable period of time.

Immigration
All visitors need valid passports, except US and Canadian citizens who can enter for up to two months with proof of citizenship. Visas must be obtained in advance by nationals of Albania, Bulgaria, People's Republic of China, Republic of China, Cuba, Czechoslovakia, Hungary, North Korea, Poland, Romania, South Africa, the USSR, Vietnam and Yugoslavia.

Entry permits for one month are given on arrival, which can be extended at the immigration office in Port of Spain. This can be time-consuming so it is better to try and get a three month entry permit on arrival if planning to stay longer.

After six weeks visitors must get a tax clearance from the Inland Revenue Office (Edward Street).

Passengers and crew embarking or disembarking from a yacht must notify immigration.

Cruising permit
An actual cruising permit is not required; however, on arrival the captain must notify the authorities of the vessel's intended itinerary to cruise around the islands and permission must be obtained before sailing. Permission must be obtained from customs for any movement of the yacht, from one port or place to another, and to cruise the coast of either Trinidad or Tobago.

Health
A yellow fever inoculation certificate is needed if coming from an infected area in South America.

Fees
On departure one may be charged light dues, which are minimal. Overtime is charged outside of working hours on weekdays and all day Saturdays, Sundays and holidays. Customs charge overtime for boarding TT$97, and clearance TT$86.96. Immigration overtime is TT$100 plus TT$25 for transport if the vessel is berthed outside of Port of Spain.

Port of Spain port authority charges yachts docking in the harbour and for the use of the port facilities there TT$50 a day for the first three days, and TT$30 per day thereafter.

Visas cost TT$100.

The departure tax per person is TT$50.

Restrictions
The tanker ports at Point Fortin and Pointe-à-Pierre, and the cargo port of Point Lisas are prohibited to yachts.

Facilities

There are reasonable repair facilities in Port of Spain and in an emergency it is best to contact the Trinidad Yacht Club for advice. The Club has some docking facilities for visitors, who can become temporary members on payment of a fee. The Mariners Club in Port of Spain has showers, bar and a restaurant. Water and showers are available by the dock in Port of Spain by the immigration offices. Alternatively one can anchor off the city. Provisioning is good. The Trinidad-Tobago Yachting Association at Chaguaramas has various facilities including a 10-ton travelift, but should be contacted in advance. With the new policy of encouraging visiting yachts, facilities are improving.

Only basic facilities are available in Tobago.

Further Reading

*A Cruising Guide to the Caribbean and the Bahamas
Cruising Guide to the Eastern Caribbean, Vol. 3
Caribbean Islands Handbook*

TURKS AND CAICOS

The British dependency of Turks and Caicos consists of about 40 low-lying cays and islands south-east of the Bahamas. Turks Island Passage separates the Turks from Caicos. The windward sides of these islands tend to be cliffs and sand dunes, while the western, leeward coasts are greener. Only a few are inhabited, most of the 9000 inhabitants living on the principal island, Grand Turk. The group is quite a tranquil area, with stunning underwater scenery, which is strictly preserved by conservation laws.

Practical Information

LOCAL TIME: GMT - 4

BUOYAGE: IALA B. Navigation aids are unreliable. In 1989 the government began changing the buoyage system to red right returning (IALA B), replacing the red left returning system.

CURRENCY: United States dollars (US$). Some Turks and Caicos coins are used.

BUSINESS HOURS
Government offices: 0800–1630 Monday to Thursday, 0800–1600 Friday. Lunch break 1230–1400 daily.

ELECTRICITY: 110 V, 60 Hz

PUBLIC HOLIDAYS
1 January: New Year's Day
Good Friday and Easter Monday
Last Monday in May: Commonwealth Day
June: Queen's Birthday
12 June: Constitution Day
Early August: Emancipation Day
October, both variable: Columbus Day and Human Rights Day
9 November: Peacemakers Day
25, 26 December: Christmas

EVENTS
Start of South Caicos regatta on Commonwealth Day
Carnival, end of August

COMMUNICATIONS
Cable & Wireless Offices on Grand Turk and Providenciales for telephone calls. These two islands, as well as South Caicos, have a modern international telephone service, although calls are quite expensive.
The mail system is somewhat inconsistent.
The main international airport is at Providenciales, with flights to North America. There are also flights to Nassau from other islands and to Miami from Grand Turk.

MEDICAL
There is a good hospital in Grand Turk.

The building of a large international airport on Providenciales capable of handling intercontinental jets has thrown this sleepy little country into the modern age. A cosmopolitan mix of expatriates has swollen the ranks of the local population to make Provo, as Providenciales is usually known, an oasis of sophistication in the midst of a watery desert.

The opening of a Club Méditerranée and other exclusive holiday resorts have produced a boom in tourism and yachting facilities are not lagging far behind. Situated conveniently halfway between Florida and the Virgins, the islands provide a useful stop in an emergency, or at least a break during a long passage. For the visiting sailor the main attractions are the clear unpolluted waters that give access to an underwater scenery of rare beauty and also the possibility of diving on some historic wrecks. The flipside of the coin is the tricky navigation among the reefs, sand banks and coral heads, with few navigation aids and those that are in place unreliable. Having nearly lost my previous boat among the Ambergris Cays, I would treat this area with utmost caution.

Country Profile

Arawaks were probably the first inhabitants, although none were left by the mid-sixteenth century. It is disputed whether Columbus sighted the islands first in 1492 or if it was Ponce de León some years later. Both Grand Turk and Caicos have been put forward as the original San Salvador where Columbus made his first landfall and this landfall controversy is still not resolved. From the sixteenth to eighteenth centuries many Spanish ships were lost on the Caicos Banks where the depth falls abruptly from about 3000 to 30 feet.

From the seventeenth century the islands were settled by the Bermudans who farmed salt there. Pirate raids were common, which probably provided the names: 'Turks' referring to the Mediterranean pirates, and 'caiques' their ships. Loyalists fleeing the American Revolution came and settled, establishing cotton and sisal plantations with slave labour. The islands became quite prosperous but competition from abroad meant these crops and salt panning suffered.

During the nineteenth and twentieth centuries the Turks and Caicos were ruled alternately by the British colonies of the Bahamas and Jamaica, but when the latter two became independent, nothing came of integrating the Turks and Caicos and they have remained a British colony. Since 1976 the islands have had internal self-government. Recently political scandal rocked the island group, as members of government were found to be involved in the drugs trade. As a result Britain ruled directly from 1986 until 1988 when a constitutional government was restored.

Natural resources are limited, both in respect of water and fertile soil. The export of lobster and conch generates some revenue. The development of tourism and the growth of offshore companies now contributes an important part of the islands' income.

The inhabitants speak English and are mostly Protestant. Cockburn Town on Grand Turk is the seat of government and the largest population centre.

The islands are hot, although the trade winds make the temperature bearable. Rain is more frequent on the west coast. The hurricane season is June to November.

Entry Regulations

Ports of entry

Cockburn Town (Grand Turk) 21°28'N 71°06'W, Providenciales 21°44'N 72°17'W, Cockburn Harbour (South Caicos) 21°30'N 71°31'W.

Procedure on arrival

Customs should be contacted on arrival on VHF Channel 16. A general declaration must be submitted to customs declaring all persons on board and stores. *Grand Turk:* If the anchorage off Cockburn Town is untenable, one should sail two miles south and anchor off the small dock. Then the harbour master should be called on Channel 16 or one can visit his office by the town dock (the northernmost dock in Cockburn Town anchorage).

Turtle Cove Marina: This marina on Providenciales has a customs service: they should be contacted on Channel 16 and they will send out a pilot boat ($15) to guide one through the reefs to Turtle Pond. They will arrange for a customs official to come down there. The clearing officer here can only give permission for a seven day stay, and in order to obtain a 30-day extension, one must go to the immigration office in the centre of the island (0800–1630 Monday to Thursday, 0800–1600 Friday).

On Providenciales, one can also clear at the Provo Aquatic Centre in Sapodillo Bay (Channel 68), and at Caicos Marina and Shipyard (they arrange for the officials to visit). Call both of these places on VHF for information on approach and entry.

A transire (cruising permit) is needed to visit the other islands. All yachts must also clear with the authorities on departure.

Customs

Firearms must be declared to customs on entry and will be taken into custody until departure.

Animals must remain on board whilst in port and must be declared to customs.

There is no restriction on the amount of time a yacht may stay.

Boats in transit can have parts and equipment shipped duty-free. There are two air freight flights weekly to Florida.

Note that all visiting vessels are subject to search by customs at any time whilst in the Turks and Caicos territorial waters.

Immigration

A visa is not necessary with a valid passport; usually 30 days is granted on arrival, which is renewable once only.

Fees

Overtime fees are charged outside of working hours. This includes work during the lunch break. There are also customs fees and light dues.

Restrictions

Sport fishing without a permit is forbidden, as are spearguns, pole spears, Hawaiian slings and using scuba gear to take any marine life. Lobster may be taken in season (August 1 to March 31) by hand or noose.

Facilities

By far the best facilities are on Providenciales, where there are two marinas, Turtle Cove and Leeward Marina, offering the usual range of services. Access to Turtle Cove through Sellar's Cut is rather difficult, so it is advisable to contact the marina on VHF Channel 16 and ask to be guided in. Most repairs can be undertaken by the Caicos Marina & Shipyard, also located on Providenciales, which operates an 85-ton travelift and offers full repair facilities. They also have a well-stocked chandlery. The yard can be contacted on Channel 16 between 0700 and 1700. Propane bottles can be filled at the Shell station. A large marina is under construction which will become another point of entry into the country.

Facilities on the other islands, including the main island of Grand Turk, are much more limited. Fuel and some provisions can be obtained at Cockburn Harbour, on South Caicos, which is the only commercial harbour in the archipelago. In Grand Turk itself, fuel can be taken on at South Dock while water can be ordered by truck to the dock at the government pier at Governor's Beach, south of Cockburn Town. MPL Enterprises have a store in town with some marine supplies and spare parts and they also undertake engine repair. There is a good supermarket in town. A useful pamphlet which gives details of facilities which are available and can be obtained locally is *Information for Visiting Yachtsmen*.

There is a hurricane hole in the vicinity of Cockburn Town, at North Creek or Columbus Sound, the entrance to which was dredged in 1985.

Further Reading

Yachtsman's Guide to the Bahamas
Caribbean Islands Handbook
Information for Visiting Yachtsmen

US VIRGIN ISLANDS

The US Virgin Islands, lying just east of Puerto Rico, have three main islands, St Thomas, St John and St Croix. Most of the other 65 islands are uninhabited. The islands have long been developed as resorts for American tourists. As a US Unincorporated Territory, the islanders are US citizens, although unable to vote in federal elections.

For most European sailors coming from the Lesser Antilles, St Thomas is their first glimpse of the USA and unfortunately the area around Charlotte Amalie does not present the best image. Scenically the US Virgin Islands are on a par with their British counterpart with the advantage of having superior repair facilities, even if prices are usually those of the US mainland. The islands are a convenient landfall if coming directly from continental USA and also a good point of departure when heading for the USA, either direct or via Bermuda. As a cruising destination in itself, the US Virgin Islands have lost some of their appeal, but as a reprovisioning or emergency repair stop they are almost unbeatable.

Country Profile

The Spanish were the first Europeans to settle the Virgin Islands, but as Spain's maritime power waned, other countries laid claim to the islands. St Croix was settled by the English and Dutch, these being pushed out by the Spanish and then the French. Wars, pirates and religious conflicts all made St Croix militarily and economically unprofitable for the French, and the settlers left. At the beginning of the eighteenth century France sold the island to Denmark. With St Thomas and St John already in Danish hands, by mid-century the Danish West Indies had become a prosperous colony. After the decline in the sugar-cane industry and the abolition of slavery, by the end of the century the economy was in bad shape. When in 1917 the USA showed an interest in acquiring the islands for a Caribbean naval base, Denmark was happy to sell them for $25 million. Nothing much changed until the 1930s, when the collapse of the sugar industry and high unemployment prompted action. Naval rule was replaced by civil government and efforts were made to improve social conditions. Only after the Second World War did the economy take off with a boom in tourism, visitors being attracted by the warm climate and unspoilt islands. This provided employment that continues today as the main source of income, bringing considerable prosperity. There is some industry, an oil refinery on St Croix and other manufacturing industries. Tax incentives have attracted some US investment.

The English-speaking population is around 100,000, mainly of African origin. Charlotte Amalie on St Thomas is the capital, often referred to just as St Thomas. A picturesque town, with a good harbour, the influence of the Danes is still noticeable in the architecture and the traffic still drives on the left. Most religions have some following here, and one of the oldest synagogues in the Western hemisphere is in Charlotte Amalie.

The islands have a very pleasant climate, cooled by the trade winds. From November to April swells on the north coast can be a problem following heavy weather in the North Atlantic. June to November is the hurricane season.

Entry Regulations

Ports of entry
St Thomas Charlotte Amalie 18°23'N 64°56'W, *St Croix* Christiansted 17°46'N 64°41'W, *St John* Cruz Bay 18°20'N 64°47'W.

Procedure on arrival
US Customs telephone numbers: St Croix 773-1011, St John 776-6741, St Thomas 774-9700, Yacht Haven Marina 774-9700.
St Thomas: The captain should go ashore and obtain preliminary clearance at the offices on the western end of the waterfront next to the seaplane landing. Foreign nationals must then go with their completed papers to customs and immigration in town, behind Kings Wharf, in the Federal Building on Veterans Drive.
St Croix: The yacht should berth at the wharf at Gallows Bay and the captain call customs. They will give instructions on how to proceed. Also one should call immigration (814129), who will send an official from the airport. The customs office is above the post office on the waterfront.
St John: The captain should go to the customs office on the waterfront in Cruz Bay.

If a yacht is going on to Puerto Rico it is advisable to obtain a cruising permit in St Thomas, issued free (otherwise on arrival in Puerto Rico a fee is charged). All yachts must clear out with customs before going to Puerto Rico.

Customs
Firearms must be declared and need a permit. For further information on firearms write to the Commissioner of Public Safety, St Thomas, USVI.

Practical Information

LOCAL TIME: GMT - 4

BUOYAGE: IALA B

CURRENCY: United States dollar (US$)

BUSINESS HOURS
Banks: 0900-1430 Monday to Friday,
plus 1530–1700 Fridays.
Government offices: 0800–1700 Monday
to Friday.

ELECTRICITY: 110/120 V, 60 Hz

PUBLIC HOLIDAYS
1 January: New Year's Day
6 January: Three Kings Day
30 January: Roosevelt's Birthday
Mid-January: Martin Luther King Day

12 February: Abraham Lincoln's
Birthday
Mid-February: George Washington's
Birthday
Maundy Thursday, Good Friday, Easter
Monday
31 March: Transfer Day
End of May: Memorial Day
16 June: Organic Act Day
3 July: Emancipation Day
4 July: Independence Day
21 July: Hurricane Supplication Day
First Monday September: Labour Day
12 October: Columbus Day
20 October: Hurricane Thanksgiving Day
1 November: Liberty day
11 November: Veterans Day
Last Thursday in November:
Thanksgiving Day
25, 26 December: Christmas

EVENTS
Carnival week, end April

COMMUNICATIONS
International telephone calls can be
made at AT&T.
Vitelco is the USVI telephone company.
Emergency: dial 922.
There are flights from St Thomas and St
Croix to various US and Caribbean
destinations.

DIPLOMATIC MISSIONS
In Charlotte Amalie:
Dominican Republic: ☎ 775 2640.
United Kingdom: 1 Fortel St.
☎ 774-0033.

Animals should be fully documented with health and anti-rabies certificates.

Note
In their fight against drug traffic, the government of the US Virgin Islands has created Blue Lightning, a strike force to patrol the waters of the US Virgins. Any yachts within territorial waters may be stopped, boarded and searched, and the presence of any illegal drugs on board can result in the yacht being confiscated.

Immigration
All nationalities need a valid US visa, which must be obtained in advance of arrival.

Fees
No fees are charged Monday to Saturday 0800–1700, after which overtime rates apply.

Facilities

Most repair facilities are concentrated around Charlotte Amalie, either in the harbour itself or the immediate vicinity. The old established Yacht Haven Marina complex inside the harbour provides one of the most complete marina service facilities in the Caribbean. Another marina is at Crown Bay and on the western side of the bay is the Haulover Marine Yachting Center, comprising a group of companies providing specialist services such as diesel repair, boatbuilding and sailmaking. There are several more marinas dotted around St Thomas's indented coastline, all offering the usual services.

The only other island having comparable services is St Croix, where St Croix Marina has a 60-ton travelift, chandlery and good provisioning. A similar service is available at Green Cay Marina on the north-east coast. St John Island is largely unspoilt and its facilities, or lack of them, reflect this.

Further Reading

Yachtsman's Guide to the Virgin Islands
A Cruising Guide to the Caribbean and the Bahamas
Caribbean Islands Handbook

6 Central and North America

From the torrid jungle of Panama to the frozen wastes of Alaska, this region encompasses a vast array of cruising areas as well as some of the most famous yachting centres in the world. The coasts of Mexico and Central America are mostly visited by American yachts who have some of the best cruising spots almost on their doorstep. The United States itself has enough cruising attractions to satisfy even the most demanding sailor, which can also be said of Canada, whose western coast is of a beauty rarely matched elsewhere. While the greatest pull of the northern destinations is their scenery, a major attraction of the southern destinations, apart from their exoticism, is the opportunity to visit the remains of some of the great civilisations that once flourished in the region.

The fear of lengthy formalities and corrupt officials has dissuaded many from sailing to Spanish-speaking Mexico and Central America, but this fear is largely unfounded and in many places the officials are often more friendly than those in the USA. However, in Central American countries, some identification should always be carried when ashore. Facilities are not up to US and Canadian standards, but should anything break, help is never too far away and repair facilities are now available in most places frequented by cruising boats.

From a sailor's point of view, the main feature of Central America is the Panama Canal, a wonderful technological achievement whose operation has been largely unaffected by political upheavals in Panama. The transiting of yachts is now more efficient than ever before and passing through the Canal is a rewarding experience. For those whose cruising plans are blocked by continental America, there is always the possibility of crossing from one ocean to the other over land. There are several haulage companies specialising in transporting yachts across the continent at a cost comparable to the fee charged by a delivery crew.

Besides the opportunities provided by coastal cruising, much of North America is also accessible by a large network of rivers and canals. While the Intracoastal Waterway parallels almost the entire east coast of the United States, a system of canals and locks links New York to the Great Lakes, which can also be reached via the St Lawrence River. The Great Lakes are the largest inland cruising area in the world and, as their boating facilities are of the highest standard, they provide a very special cruising destination to anyone looking for something different.

BELIZE

Belize, formerly known as British Honduras, fronts the Western Caribbean Sea and borders on Mexico and Guatemala. The coastlands are low and swampy, with mangroves and lagoons, while forested mountains present a contrast in the south-west of the country. Belize's main attraction lies offshore, a 175 mile long barrier reef, second only in size to the Great Barrier Reef of Australia. Cruising inside the island-dotted reef is a unique experience and the underwater scenery is reputed to be amongst the best anywhere in the world. Between the reef and the coastal strip there are hundreds of uninhabited islands and cays, and therein lies Belize's popularity as a cruising destination. The barrier reef is not broken by many passes and inside the reef navigation is difficult as the sea is shallow and there are not many navigational aids, but the number of secluded anchorages, unsurpassed diving and excellent fishing will ensure Belize's attraction as an alternative to the crowded Eastern Caribbean.

Country Profile

Hidden in the interior of Belize are many ruins of the ancient Mayan empire which flourished in this region from the fourth to ninth centuries, before moving to the Yucatan peninsula. In the mid-seventeenth century, the country was colonised by English settlers from Jamaica with their African slaves who came for the logwood used for textile dyes. The British government tried to secure the protection of these settlers, but did not claim sovereignty over the country. In 1821 both Guatemala and Mexico claimed Belize, claims which were rejected by Britain. In the middle of the century Guatemalan fears over an attack by the USA led to better relations with Britain, and a convention was signed in which Guatemala recognised Belize's boundaries. Belize eventually became a British Crown Colony. Mexico later renounced its claim by treaty although Guatemala, never having ratified the original treaty, sometimes renews its claim to the territory. Independence was gained in 1981, although a British force is still maintained in Belize.

The economy is agricultural and the main concern is how to become self-sufficient in food production, as so

Map 8: Central and North America

Practical Information

LOCAL TIME: GMT - 6

BUOYAGE: IALA B. Many of the navigation lights or marks are reported to be either out of action or missing and therefore night passages should be avoided. Even in daylight the barrier reef area should be navigated with caution.

CURRENCY: Belize dollar (Bze $)

BUSINESS HOURS
Banks: 0800–1300 Monday to Thursday, 0800–1200, 1500–1800 Friday.
Government offices: 0800–1200, 1300–1600 Monday to Friday.
Shops: 0800–1200, 1300–1600 Monday to Thursday, Friday 1600–2100 also, half day Wednesday.

ELECTRICITY: 110/220 V, 60 Hz

PUBLIC HOLIDAYS
1 January: New Year's Day
9 March: Baron Bliss Day
Good Friday, Easter Saturday and Easter Monday
1 May: Labour Day
24 May: Commonwealth Day
10 September: St George's Caye Day
21 September: Independence Day
19 November: Garifuna Settlement Day
25, 26 December: Christmas

COMMUNICATIONS
Belizean Telecommunications Ltd: Bishop St, off Albert St, for telegrams, telephone calls, telex, 0730–2100 Monday to Saturday.
Collect calls can be made to the USA, Canada, Australia and the UK.
Post office: Queen St and North Front St, Belize City.
There are international flights from

Philip Goldson airport, 10 miles from Belize City to US and Central American cities.

DIPLOMATIC MISSIONS
In Belize City:
Canada: 120–A New Road. ☎ (02) 3639.
Mexico: 20 North Park Street.
☎ (02) 45367. Mexican visas can be obtained at the consulate, north of Fort George pier. It is also advisable to purchase the certified crew lists at the consulate as they may be needed when clearing into Mexico.
Panama: Cork Street.
United States: Gabourel Lane and Hutson Street. ☎ (02) 7161.
In Belmopan:
Panama: 7/9 Unity Boulevard.
☎ (08) 22714.
United Kingdom: PO Box 91.
☎ (08) 2146.

much still has to be imported. Labour shortage is another problem, and the immigration of workers is encouraged. The main exports are sugar, citrus fruit and bananas, while timber and fish are also important. Tourism has developed, and there is some light industry. Oil has been found near the Mexican border.

The 176,000 inhabitants are mainly Créole and mestizo, with Indian and Garifuna minorities. The latter are descended from Black Caribs, who were deported from St Vincent in the eighteenth century. They live mostly along the southern coast and speak their own language. English is the official language, but Créole English and Spanish are also spoken as well as a Low German dialect and Mayan languages. Most Christian denominations have followers, the main ones being Roman Catholic, Anglican and Methodist. In 1970 Belmopan, some 50 miles inland, became the new capital replacing Belize City.

The tropical climate can be hot especially February to May, although the prevailing wind helps to keep the coast cooler. During winter months the anchorages are rather exposed to the northers which sweep down across the Gulf of Mexico. The hurricane season lasts from June to November.

Entry Regulations

Ports of entry
Belize City 17°30′N 88°11′W, Punta Gorda 16°06′N 88°48′W.

Procedure on arrival
Customs require four crew lists, four store lists and ship's papers.
Belize City: Clearing in formalities at Belize City, although relatively simple, can take time as some offices are quite far away. Clearance can be accomplished more rapidly if the Belize port captain is called in advance of arrival on VHF Channel 16. One can anchor off the dock in front of the Fort George Hotel flying the Q flag or come alongside the St George Pier, where there is reportedly a depth of 6 feet in some places. If anchored, a customs boat will usually come alongside and the officials will board the boat, but if not, the captain should go ashore to the customs office west of Fort George Hotel. In this case the captain is usually accompanied back to the boat by a customs official for the necessary paperwork. The next office to be visited is immigration, which is in town north of the police station.
Punta Gorda: Entry and exit formalities are reported to be much simpler here.
Ambergris Cay: It is also possible to clear in at San Pedro on Ambergris Cay, but a charge will be made for flying the customs officers to the Cay, which amounts to about US$50. San Pedro is located just south of the Mexican border and therefore convenient for yachts arriving from the north.

Procedure on departure
For clearing out at Belize City it is necessary to

purchase two special clearance forms available from Angelus Press near the police station. The first office to be visited is the port authority, which is quite far and requires a taxi ride. A charge will be made depending on the tonnage of the yacht. Customs must be cleared next, and finally immigration.

Customs

Firearms and ammunition are usually removed and kept in custody by customs until clearing out.

Animals must have a health certificate and anti-rabies vaccination.

The importation of fruit or vegetables is prohibited.

Yachts may remain in Belize for up to six months.

Immigration

Visas are not required for nationals of Commonwealth countries, Canada, Belgium, Denmark, Finland, Greece, Mexico, Netherlands, Norway, Panama, San Marino, Sweden, Switzerland, Tunisia, Turkey, the United Kingdom, the United States and Uruguay. Normally on arrival a 30-day stay is given.

Other nationals require a visa to be obtained in advance. Visas can be obtained from the Belizean consulate, Chetumel, Mexico, valid for 30 days. Extensions may be obtained every 30 days for up to six months at the immigration office, Barrack Rd, Belize City. At the end of six months one must leave the country for at least 24 hours.

Health

Malaria prophylaxis is recommended.

Fees

There is a visa charge of US$5, extensions US$5. The navigation charge is calculated per ton. There is an exit fee.

Restrictions

Nature conservation is a high priority and there are several nature reserves. A permit is needed to hunt or collect any kind of wildlife and this will be granted only if it is for scientific or educational purposes.

It is prohibited to remove or export black coral, turtles or turtle products, to pick orchids in forest reserves, to spear fish in certain areas or while wearing scuba gear and to remove archaeological artefacts.

Facilities

Most of the existing facilities are in Belize City. The anchorage there is an open roadstead and often rolly. Belize City has some repair facilities, good provision-

ing, a limited supply of hardware but very little yachting equipment. Water and fuel are available at the dock. LPG bottles can be filled by taking a taxi to the filling station out of town. Some provisioning and fuel is also available at Moho Cay, north of Belize City, where there is a charter operation. Pyramid Cove Marina on Chapel Cay monitors VHF Channel 68 and gives directions for the shallow pass at the entrance to the cove. There is electricity, water and fuel on the dock. A boat goes once a week for provisions to Belize City. Supplies also arrive on a weekly basis at Placentia, where provisioning is best on Sundays, after the arrival of the boat. There is good provisioning at San Pedro, on Ambergris Cay, which also has daily flights to the mainland.

Further Reading

A Cruising Guide to the Caribbean and the Bahamas
Belize Cruising Guide
South American Handbook

CANADA

Spanning the north of the American continent, Canada has cruising grounds on both the western Pacific coast and the eastern Atlantic coast. The majority of Canadians, however, sail inland on the Great Lakes, which can be reached either by sailing up the St Lawrence river from the Atlantic or through the Erie Canal. Some visiting cruisers like to make the round trip by sailing to Nova Scotia, up the St Lawrence to the Lakes and then back to New York and the US east coast through the Canal.

For the decreasing number of yachts who take the northern route across the Atlantic, the island of Newfoundland, closest point to Europe, is their landfall or springboard. Cruising this northern island is strictly for summer months and even then it can be cold, wet and windy at times. The rewards are a vast choice of anchorages in small bays, harbours and islands and the few cruising boats sailing this far north can find complete isolation in beautiful surroundings. More often visited by foreign yachts is Nova Scotia, the first stop down-east from Maine. Halifax, the main harbour, is a large yachting centre and, like St Johns in Newfoundland, a transatlantic springboard and landfall.

On the Pacific coast British Columbia boasts one of the most beautiful and dramatic cruising grounds in the world with its snowcapped mountains, waterfalls cascading down rugged cliffs, a myriad of islands and

Practical Information

LOCAL TIME: GMT - 5 to - 10

BUOYAGE: IALA B

CURRENCY: Canadian dollar of 100 cents (Can$)

BUSINESS HOURS
Banks: 1000–1500 Monday to Friday, occasionally Saturday.
Business: 0900–1700 Monday to Friday.
Shops: 0930–1900 Monday to Friday, some nights until 2100, 0930–1800 Saturday.
Government offices: 0900–1630 Monday to Friday.

ELECTRICITY: 110/220 V, 60 Hz

PUBLIC HOLIDAYS
1 January: New Year's Day
Good Friday, Easter Monday
Monday before 25 May: Victoria Day
1 July: Canada Day
First Monday in September: Labour Day
Second Monday in October: Thanksgiving Day
11 November: Remembrance Day
25 December: Christmas Day
26 December: Boxing Day
Also provincial holidays

COMMUNICATIONS
Overseas dialling access code 011.
Dial 0 for the operator, 411 for information.
Emergency: dial 911.
Air travel within Canada is extensive, and all major cities have international flights, but particularly Montreal and

Toronto. There are flights to London from both Halifax and St Johns, Newfoundland.

MEDICAL
Emergency medical treatment is available in all hospitals. Canadians have free health care, but visitors must pay, so travel health insurance is recommended.

DIPLOMATIC MISSIONS
In Ottawa:
France: 42 Sussex Drive. ☎ (613) 232-1795.
New Zealand: Suite 801, Metropolitan House, 99 Bank St, K1P 6G3. ☎ (613) 238-5991.
United Kingdom: 80 Elgin Street. ☎ (613) 237-1530.
United States: 100 Wellington Street, K1P 5T1. ☎ (613) 238-5335.

quiet, still fjords. The 100 mile long Vancouver Island protects most of the mainland from the Pacific Ocean and so creates an inland sea. Dotted with islands and spiked with inlets, the absence of swell can provide great sailing conditions.

The most popular cruising area is the Gulf Islands in the south. There are harbours and anchorages on both sides of the Strait of Georgia, which separates Vancouver Island from the mainland. Another good cruising area is at the north of the Strait, where a cluster of islands border the magnificent Desolation Sound. North of this begins the inside passage to Alaska.

A large tidal range and strong currents make for attentive navigation, as do the hazards of floating logs and kelp. All of the area is well charted and tide rips are marked. Fog can be a hazard along this coast and radar a great boon, especially as there is a lot of other traffic – logging tugs, fishing boats, fast ferries to and from the islands and, especially near Vancouver, commercial shipping. The rewards of nature, both in scenery and wildlife, including superb fishing, more than make up for the attentive navigation needed.

Country Profile

The first inhabitants were Indian tribes who probably came over from Asia thousands of years ago. European contact commenced when John Cabot discovered Canada in 1497. Jacques Cartier explored the St Lawrence river in the sixteenth century, claiming it for

France, and Quebec was founded in 1608. French settlement of New France, as the area was called, was slow at first, but increased in the seventeenth century. New France came into conflict with England, who gained Acadia (renamed Novia Scotia) and Hudson Bay, and established a naval base at Halifax. After France's defeat in the Seven Years War, in 1763 the rest of French Canada was ceded to England. New Brunswick province was created following a large immigration of loyalists after American independence.

The provinces of Upper Canada, now Ontario, and Lower Canada, now Quebec, were created and both rebelled in 1837 in protest at England's refusal to establish a parliamentary regime. This revolt was suppressed, but three years later a united Canada was created by the English government and given internal self-government in 1848. The Dominion of Canada was established in 1867, as a Confederation of the provinces of New Brunswick, Novia Scotia, Quebec and Ontario. In the following thirty years the new country expanded its borders to include Manitoba, British Columbia, Prince Edward Island, Alberta and Saskatchewan and border disputes with the United States were resolved regarding Oregon and Alaska.

In the First World War Canada fought with the Allies and became an international power. In 1931 her independence was formally recognised. William Mackenzie King, leader of the Liberal Party, presided over Canadian politics from 1921 until 1948 almost without interruption. Fighting Germany in the Second World War, Canada's war effort pushed her to develop her industry and agriculture. In 1949 Newfoundland became a Canadian province. After the war the Liberal Party dominated politics until 1984, and links with the United States were drawn ever closer, although relations are also important with Britain and other Commonwealth countries, particularly the Caribbean. Demands for greater independence by some of the population of the French-speaking Quebec province is an ongoing problem.

Canada has rich agricultural and mineral resources, and is a leading world producer of wheat, timber, oil and natural gas, iron, lead, zinc, copper, nickel, gold and uranium. The main industries are food processing, timber and metallurgy, while US finance has helped the development of the automobile and chemical industries. The Canadian economy is very closely tied to its neighbour and over half of external trade is with the United States.

The population numbers 25.6 million, mostly of British, French and other European origins, while only about 1.5 per cent are indigenous Eskimo and Indian. Almost half are Roman Catholic, while United Church and Anglican are the next popular among the many religions practised. English and French are the official languages. Canada's capital is Ottawa, located in Ontario on the banks of the Ottawa river.

The climate varies considerably around the country. Atlantic Canada is very cold November to April (minus 10° to 4°C/15° to 50°F), while May to October is mild on the coasts. There are few gales in summer, but the area is affected by fog. In spring and summer up to July, icebergs can be carried into the Newfoundland area.

In Western Canada November to April is temperate on the coast, while May to October is warm and rainy. Northern Canada has subarctic conditions during the winter. The southern area, nicknamed the 'banana belt', is in the rain shadow of Vancouver Island, has milder winters and so cruising is possible all year round, while the northern sector tends to be summer cruising only. Land breezes often dictate the sailing conditions and calms are commonplace. In the summer gales are rare and west or north-westerly winds blow most afternoons.

Entry Regulations

Ports of entry

Newfoundland: St John's 47°34′N 52°41′W, Corner Brook 48°57′N 57°56′W, Fortune 46°54′N 55°38′W, Harbour Grace 47°41′N 53°13′W, Catalina 48°31′N 53°04′W, Argentina 47°18′N 53°59′W, Botwood 49°09′N 55°19′W, Burgo 47°37′N 57°37′W, Harbour Breton 47°29′N 55°48′W, Burin 47°00′N 55°10′W, Grand Bank 47°06′N 55°45′W.

Ontario: Portsmouth Olympia Harbour (west of Kingston) 44°12′N 76°30′W, Toronto 43°38′N 79°23′W, Brockville 44°36′N 75°38′W, Cornwall 45°01′N 74°43′W, Goderich 43°45′N 81°45′W, Welland 42°58′N 79°13′W.

Prince Edward Island: Charlottetown 46°13′N 63°07′W, Summerside 46°24′N 63°47′W.

Nova Scotia: La Have 44°17′N 64°21′W, Lunenburg 44°22′N 64°18′W, Halifax (customs ☎ 426-2071, 0800-2200) 44°38′N 63°33′W, Parrsboro 45°23′N 64°20′W, Pictou 45°41′N 62°43′W, Port Medway 44°08′N 64°34′W, Pugwash 45°52′N 63°40′W, Sheet Harbour 44°51′N 62°27′W.

North West Territories: Frobisher 63°45′N 68°32′W.

New Brunswick: Caraquet 47°48′N 65°01′W, Chatham 47°02′N 65°28′W, Dalhousie 48°04′N 66°22′W, Newcastle 47°00′N 65°33′W, St Andrews 45°04′N 67°03′W.

Quebec: Gaspé 48°50′N 64°29′W, Port Alfred 48°20′N 70°52′W, Rimouski 48°29′N 68°31′W, Rivière du Loup 47°51′N 69°34′W.

British Columbia: Kitimat 54°00′N 128°42′W, Nanaimo 49°10′N 123°56′W, Port Alberni 49°14′N 125°00′W, Woodfibre 49°40′N 123°15′W, Prince Rupert Harbour 54°19′N 130°22′W.

Gulf Islands: Bedwell (South Pender Island, summer only) 49°38′N 124°03′W, Sidney 48°39′N 123°24′W, Nanaimo (Vancouver Island) 49°10′N 123°56′W, North Head Harbour (Grand Manan) 49°10′N 123°56′W.

Procedure on arrival

The local customs office should be contacted prior to arrival, giving the yacht's ETA. If this is not possible, the captain should go ashore on arrival to report the yacht's arrival to customs, by telephone (the customs will then come down to clear the yacht) or by going to the customs office. No one else should go ashore until clearance is complete. Sometimes clearance will be done over the telephone, if coming from the United States. Customs will want to know the boat's name and registration number, last port of call, details of all the crew, how long one is intending to stay, as well as if one has any alcohol or tobacco on board. Firearms and animals must be declared. Immigration must also be cleared.

Customs require a list of ports where one intends to cruise between Canada and the last port and estimated date of departure from Canada. They will then issue a cruising permit, which exempts yachts from clearance at subsequent ports, after the first port of entry. The cruising permit is available only to countries who have reciprocal arrangements with Canada, otherwise customs clearance must be done at every port.

For yachts on their way to or from Alaska, there is a Canadian customs station at Prince Rupert Harbour, open 0600–2000, seven days a week in season and a US Customs office at Ketchikan, open 0800–1700, Monday to Saturday.

Customs

All firearms must be declared on arrival. Firearms such as revolvers and automatic weapons are prohibited. Rifles and shotguns are permitted.

Animals must be declared to customs, and must remain on board. Dogs and cats must have a valid anti-rabies vaccination certificate. Fresh fruit and vegetables cannot be brought into Canada.

Yachts are allowed to remain three months.

Immigration

All nationalities need valid passports, except US citizens who only need valid identification. No visas are required for nationals of the USA, West European countries (except Portugal and Turkey) or Commonwealth countries (except Bangladesh, Gambia, Guyana, India, Jamaica, Kiribati, Nigeria, Pakistan, Sri Lanka, Trinidad and Uganda). Most other nationalities require a visa to be obtained in advance.

Fishing licence

A fishing licence is required in British Columbia, available from most marine service outlets, fuel docks, sporting and hardware stores. The cost of an annual permit for non-residents is Can$35. There are also catch limits.

Traffic

In poor visibility, yachts can contact the local 'Traffic' (VHF Channel 13 or 14) and report their position, route and speed, and receive information on any large ships they may encounter. Fundy Traffic can be contacted on VHF Channel 14 and 21 on the way to St John and will help when visibility is bad. Halifax Traffic on VHF Channel 14 offers similar assistance to yachtsmen.

The Canadian Coast Guard monitors Channel 16.

Fees

Ports normally have 24-hour service, but some may charge overtime for clearance outside of working hours, which can vary. At St John's, overtime is charged for customs clearance between 0000–0800, approximately Can$60 if arrival is after midnight. In some ports customs may only come and clear during their working hours (0800–1700 normally).

Facilities

There are good facilities in all major yachting centres. Marine equipment and fuel is more expensive than in the USA, whereas Canadian charts are cheaper than US charts. Provisioning is very good in larger ports, but only adequate in some of the smaller places.

On the west coast, the best stocks of chandlery and general boat repair facilities are in Vancouver as well as Surrey, one of its suburbs. Particularly north of Vancouver, grocery stores and fuelling stations are far apart and therefore some are mentioned below.

Nanaimo, on Vancouver Island, is a good provisioning place used by the local fishing fleet, so docking space is sometimes limited. There are several marinas in Pender Harbour, with stores, post office and fuel station. Similar services are available at Sullivan Bay on North Broughton Island. Good facilities are available in Prince Rupert, although the place gets crowded when the fishing fleet is in.

On the Atlantic coast, Halifax, in Nova Scotia, has a wide range of repair facilities and services. There are three large yacht clubs in town and visitors can secure free mooring for one week at the Maritime Museum of the Atlantic in the main harbour. Although there are barely any yachting facilities in St John's busy commercial harbour, these are concentrated in Long Pond, a narrow inlet on the west side of the Avalon peninsula. This is also the home of the Royal Newfoundland Yacht Club, which is particularly welcoming to foreign visitors.

Further Reading

Cruising Guide to Nova Scotia Coast
Cruising Guide to British Columbia
Pacific Boating Almanac, Pacific Northwest & Alaska
Cruising the Pacific Coast
Cruise Cape Breton

COSTA RICA

Costa Rica lies between Nicaragua and Panama, enjoys the highest standard of living in Central America and also has the reputation for being the most stable Latin American democracy. Costa Rica has coastlines on both the Caribbean Sea and the Pacific Ocean, the latter being the more attractive for cruising. Compared to its northern neighbours, Costa Rica's indented coastline presents a welcome change and a pleasant cruising ground. The hilly interior and attractive capital

Practical Information

LOCAL TIME: GMT - 6

BUOYAGE: IALA B

CURRENCY: Colon of 100 centimos

BUSINESS HOURS
Banks: 0900–1500 Monday to Friday.
Business and government
offices: 0800/0830–1100/1130,
1300–1500/1530 Monday to Friday and
0800–1100 Saturday.
Shops: 0800–1200, 1300–1800 Monday to
Saturday.

ELECTRICITY: 110 V, 60 Hz

PUBLIC HOLIDAYS
1 January: New Year's Day
19 March: St Joseph
Easter Week, three days

April: Battle of Rivas
1 May
Corpus Christi
29 June: Saints Peter and Paul
25 June: Guanacaste Day
2 August: Virgin of Los Angeles
15 August: Mothers Day
15 September: Independence Day
12 October: Columbus Day
8 December: Immaculate Conception
25 December: Christmas Day
28–31 December, holiday in San José
only

EVENTS
Holy Week: most places are shut during
the week, and everything closes from
Friday to Sunday.
October: Costa Rica Yacht Club Regatta in
Puntarenas, visiting yachts are welcome.

COMMUNICATIONS
Internacional de Costa Rica for
international phone calls.
Collect calls overseas can be made from
special booths in the telephone office.
Instituto Costarricense de Electricidad
and Compania Radiografica for cables,
long-range radio telephone and telex.
There are frequent flights from San José
to the USA and Latin American capitals.

DIPLOMATIC MISSIONS
In San José:
Canada: 6th floor, Edificio Cronos, Calle
3 and Ave. Central, Apartado 10303.
☎ 230446.
United Kingdom: Edificio Centro Colon,
11th floor, Apartado 815. ☎ 215566.
United States: Avenida 3 and Calle 1.
☎ 331155.

San José can be visited from either Puntarenas or Limón.

The most popular port of call is Golfito, rarely missed by cruising boats plying the western coast of Central America. The famous local character is Captain Tom, who has been welcoming visiting yachts for over 30 years and his many guest books bear the names of thousands of sailors who have passed through Golfito during these years. An exciting destination lies 300 miles offshore in the Pacific, the fabled treasure island of Coco. Hundreds of expeditions have been mounted over the years to find the various treasures reputed to have been buried there, but so far nothing has been found. The island's real treasure is its unspoilt nature and Isla del Coco was declared a national park by the Costa Rican government. Even if not looking for treasure, it is worth the detour to watch the birdlife and underwater scenery teeming with fish.

Country Profile

The Caribbean coast was discovered by Columbus in 1502 during his last voyage. Costa Rica means 'rich coast', and there were rumours of vast gold treasures to be found there. Spaniards settled in the interior, where there were already thousands of farming Indians, who were decimated by European diseases. Gradually European settlement expanded, but life was hard and mostly on a subsistence level.

When in 1821 independence from Spain was declared, the country became part of Mexico along with the rest of Central America. Civil war resulted, and the capital moved to San José. In 1840 Costa Rica became a sovereign state; after independence, coffee became a source of prosperity and by the middle of the century exports were considerable. The government offered free land to coffee growers, thus building a prosperous land-owning peasant class. Bananas were introduced at the end of the century and these thrived and became a major crop on both the Caribbean and the Pacific coasts. President Oscar Arias Sanchez won the Nobel Peace Prize in 1987 for his Central American Peace Plan, signed by all five Central American republics but never implemented.

Costa Rica's economy has a good rate of growth, based on the export of coffee, bananas, meat, sugar and cocoa. Industry has grown, mostly in the food processing sector, but also in chemicals and plastics. However, Costa Rica still has a large foreign debt and public sector deficits as government spending on welfare is high.

The 2.6 million inhabitants are mostly white or mestizo and only about 5000 Indians are left in the whole country. Spanish is the main language. There are a number of people of African origin living along the Caribbean coast, especially in Limón, who speak Jamaican English, as their forebears came from Jamaica to work on banana plantations early in the twentieth century. Roman Catholicism is the religion of the majority. The capital is San José.

The Pacific coast of Costa Rica is drier, while the Atlantic coast has heavy rainfall. Both coasts are hot and humid. December to April are the dry months, while May to November are wet, hot and humid. The east coast is under the influence of the NE trade winds during the winter months, but the west coast has light winds and often calms. Costa Rica is rarely affected by tropical storms.

Entry Regulations

Ports of entry

Pacific: Playa de Cocos 10°35′N 85°42′W, Golfito 8°38′N 83°11′W, Puntarenas 9°59′N 84°51′W, Quepos 9°24′N 84°10′W.
Atlantic: Puerto Limón 10°00′N 83°03′W.

Procedure on arrival

Playa de Cocos: This is the first Costa Rican port when coming from the north and is convenient for clearing in. Apart from immigration, one must also clear with customs and the port captain.
Puntarenas: Yachts intending to clear here should anchor first by the town at the end of the peninsula. All offices are close by in the port. After clearance the yacht may proceed up the estuary to the yacht club.
Golfito: The offices of the port captain, customs and immigration are all near the big dock directly in from the channel entrance. Yachts should anchor near the dock, but not come alongside.
Quepos: Clearance formalities are completed at the administration building. The port captain's office is on the banana pier.

Cruising yachts should get a clearance certificate (zarpe) before proceeding from one main port to another.

Customs

Firearms and animals must be declared.

Immigration

Visas are issued on arrival to nationals of most countries. There are no visa requirements for stays of up to 90 days for nationals of most West European countries, Argentina, Canada, Colombia, Israel, Japan, Panama, Romania, South Korea and Yugoslavia.
No visas are required for stays of up to 30 days for nationals of Australia, Belgium, Brazil, Ecuador, Eire, Guatemala, Honduras, Iceland, Monaco, Mexico, New Zealand, Switzerland and the USA. Entry formalities are, however, simplified, if one arrives with a visa obtained in advance from a Costa Rican embassy or consulate abroad.

A passport or at least a certified copy should always be carried.

Health

Malaria prophylaxis recommended.

Facilities

Provisioning is reasonable in Playa de Cocos or at the marina ten miles south in Bahia Potrero, where fuel and water are available on the dock. Best facilities are in Puntarenas where the yacht club is particularly helpful and offers a range of repair facilities including a 20-ton travelift, as well as fuel and water on the dock and 24-hour launch service. The club monitors VHF Channel 6 from 0700 to 1700 every day except Wednesday. There are several marinas in the Puntarenas area, some of which offer repair facilities. There are also good supermarkets and an excellent fresh produce market. Coming from the south, Golfito is an ideal port for repairs and reprovisioning. Puerto Limón, on the Caribbean side, is the main port of Costa Rica. There is good provisioning and adequate repair facilities. Trains and buses run to San José.

Further Reading

A Cruising Guide to the Caribbean and the Bahamas
Cruising Ports: California to Florida via Panama
South American Handbook

EL SALVADOR

El Salvador is a small, highly populated, industrialised country on the Pacific Ocean side of Central America. The volcanic uplands in the interior provide fertile soil for coffee. Violent civil war has affected the country in recent years, and although the situation is showing signs of improvement, many parts of the country should be avoided. Only the western and southwestern regions were considered safe at the time of writing. In recent years yachts have deliberately avoided El Salvador by keeping a good distance off the coast. The few yachts that have called have gone straight to one of the country's two main ports.

Country Profile

El Salvador remained largely isolated from the Spanish conquest of the continent, having no precious metals

Practical Information

LOCAL TIME: GMT - 6

BUOYAGE: IALA B

CURRENCY: Colon (often called peso) of 100 centavos. Only US$80 worth of colones can be changed back when leaving.

BUSINESS HOURS
Business: 0800–1200, 1400–1800 Monday to Friday, 0800–1200 Saturday.
Banks: 0900–1300, 1345–1530 Monday to Friday.
Government offices: 0800–1600 Monday to Friday.
Shops: 0900–1200, 1400–1800 Monday to Friday, 0800–1200 Saturday.

ELECTRICITY: 110 V, 60 Hz

PUBLIC HOLIDAYS
1 January: New Year's Day
Palm Sunday to Easter Monday for government
Maundy Thursday, Good Friday, for banks and commerce
1 May
10 May
Corpus Christi (half day)
5–6 August: St Saviours Day (San Salvador)
15 September: Independence Day
12 October: Discovery Day
2 November: All Souls Day
5 November (half day)
24 December: Christmas Eve (half day)
25 December: Christmas Day

Government offices are also closed 1–6 August, 24–31 December.
Banks closed: June 29, 30, December 30, 31

COMMUNICATIONS
Antel, the state telecommunications company, for telex and telephones.
No collect calls can be made to Europe.
There are some international flights from San Salvador to Miami, San Francisco and Central American cities.

DIPLOMATIC MISSIONS
In San Salvador:
Canada: PO Box 1935.
United Kingdom: Paseo General Escalon 4828. ☎ 240473.
United States: 25 Av. Norte 1230. ☎ 267100.

---

to attract the Spaniards. A small number of Spaniards settled, intermarried with the Indians and raised cattle and subsistence crops. The introduction of coffee at the end of the nineteenth century saw the population and prosperity grow. The prosperity was short-lived and many emigrated due to the shortage of land, and more recently due to the continuing violence.

In 1979 a military coup took place and the president was replaced by a junta. Then in 1980 the civilian José Napoleon Duarte was appointed president, and elected four years later. Political tension increased as dissatisfaction grew and efforts at land reform were unsuccessful. Eventually civil war broke out, in which thousands of people, mainly civilians, were killed, often by right-wing death squads. Despite this, the left-wing guerillas, the FMLN, have remained strong. No breakthrough in the situation has been made, despite the peace plan of 1987 drawn up by President Arias of Costa Rica. A stalemate was reached by 1989, and the conflict and economic problems continue. Support has grown for the right-wing party, and a recent presidential election was won by their candidate.

Agriculture dominates the economy, coffee and cotton being the most important crops, although efforts have been made at diversification. Sugar and maize are increasingly important earners of foreign exchange. Land ownership is concentrated in the hands of a few, and the majority of people live at subsistence level, this being a cause of instability in the past. Industry is growing, and there are small mineral

deposits. US aid is very important to El Salvador's economy.

The 5.33 million inhabitants are mostly mestizo with a small proportion of pure Indian and European. Spanish is the main language, but English is widely understood. The majority are Roman Catholic. The capital is San Salvador, 2230 ft (680 m) above sea level in the centre of the country.

The coast is hot and humid, especially March to May, and is coolest from December to February. December and March may have spells of continuous rain for 2–3 days or even weeks. Water shortages are possible at other times of the year.

Entry Regulations

Ports of entry
Acajutla 13°36′N 89°50′W, Cutuco 13°19′N 87°49′W.

Procedure on arrival
Vessels may not go anywhere else outside of these two ports as the whole coast is a military zone. The port authorities can be contacted on VHF Channel 16. Yachts will be inspected first by a quarantine inspector.
Acajutla: This is the port for the western part of the country.
Cutuco: This is the port for the eastern part. Customs are in 3 Avenida Norte 3.9, and immigration 3 Calle Oriente 2.8.

Customs

An authorisation for firearms must be obtained from the Ministry of Defence.

Animals must have a health certificate. Dogs must have a valid anti-rabies vaccination certificate.

All animal products except sealed, sterilised meat products are prohibited. Animal products from the USA, Puerto Rico, Australia, New Zealand, Japan, Jamaica and Mexico are also exempt.

Fruit is inspected and may be destroyed. Leather products may be subject to disinfection.

Immigration

Visas are required for nationals of the USA, Canada, Australia, New Zealand, Israel and France. Some West European countries do not require visas, but regulations are subject to frequent change. Visas can be renewed for 30 days at immigration.

Health

There is a risk of malaria and dengue fever.

Fees

There is an entrance and exit tax of 6 colones.

Overtime is charged for clearance outside working hours (1200–1400, 1800–0800 weekdays, 1200 Saturday to 0800 Monday, and national holidays).

Restrictions

Literature that may be regarded as subversive may be confiscated or refused entry. Military style clothing is also confiscated.

Facilities

Limited supplies are available in the two main ports, which also have facilities for simple repairs. Of the two, Acajutla has the better range of workshops.

Further Reading

Cruising Ports: California to Florida via Panama
South American Handbook

GUATEMALA

Among the Central American republics, Guatemala stands out as the country which has best preserved the language, customs and character of the original population. This area of Central America used to be the centre of Maya civilisation.

Much of the land is still uninhabited and most settlements are in the highlands. The Pacific coast is narrow, low and featureless, and it is the smaller Caribbean coast which attracts most cruising yachts. The Motagua and Polochic rivers drain into the Caribbean Sea, but it is the Rio Dulce which is the ultimate destination of almost every yacht cruising this part of the world. Yachts that are not hampered by too deep a draft can negotiate the bar at the entrance to the river, after which the river virtually belongs to them. Impenetrable forests come down to the water's edge where almost hidden by the thick foliage are small Indian villages. The river widens into Golfito, a small inland lake and further on the river merges with Lake Izabal, whose entrance is guarded by the fort of San Felipe, now restored according to original plans found in the Spanish archives. There are other rivers on the Guatemalan coast, which are navigable for longer or shorter distances, giving yachts a chance to savour a different kind of cruising.

Country Profile

The Maya civilisation developed about AD 100 and after 200 years of growth entered its 'classic' period, flourishing in an area corresponding to present-day Guatemala, Belize, Honduras and parts of Mexico. Centred on the city state, the Mayans developed mathematics, agriculture, architecture and writing. This civilisation lasted until the tenth to eleventh centuries AD, when the movements of other Indians forced the Mayas to concentrate in the Yucatan peninsula. When the Spaniards arrived, there were only scattered groups of Indians living in the Guatemala area. Some Spaniards settled in the southern highlands and mixed with the people already there. Guatemala City eventually became the administrative centre for all the Central American region, which was ruled by Spain from Mexico City.

Early in the nineteenth century independence movements began to develop, precipitated by the 1820 revolution in Spain. A year later independence was declared in Guatemala City, which became the centre of a federation. For some time this was ruled by the dictator General Morazán, but revolts and warfare broke up the federation. Since then the political history of the whole region has been tempestuous. Guatemala was ruled by a succession of strong dictators, with periods of constitutional government and anarchy between. After the Second World War efforts were made to introduce social reforms. After a coup in 1954 the military took power, and the following years saw great bloodshed as the army crushed those trying

Practical Information

LOCAL TIME: GMT - 6. Summer time GMT - 5 May to August.

BUOYAGE: IALA B

CURRENCY: Quetzal of 100 centavos

BUSINESS HOURS
Banks: 0900–1500 (some have longer hours, but close for lunch).
Business: 0800–1200, 1400–1800 Monday to Friday.
Shops: 0800–1200, 1400–1800 Monday to Friday, 0800–1200 Saturday.
Government offices: 0700–1530 Monday to Friday.

ELECTRICITY: 110 V, 60 Hz

PUBLIC HOLIDAYS
1 January: New Year's Day
6 January: Epiphany
Wednesday of Easter week (half day)
Maundy Thursday, Good Friday, Easter Saturday
1 May
30 June: Anniversary of the Revolution
15 August (Guatemala City only)
15 September: Independence Day
20 October: Revolution Day
1 November: All Saints' Day
24 and 25 December: Christmas Eve and Day
31 December: New Year's Eve
If a holiday falls on a Saturday or Sunday, the following Monday is taken as a public holiday.

COMMUNICATIONS
Guatel for international telephones and cable.
Mail is very slow, slower to the USA and Canada than to Europe.
There are frequent international flights from Guatemala City to most American capitals, flights less frequently to Europe.

MEDICAL
Public hospitals charge a small fee for examinations.

DIPLOMATIC MISSIONS
In Guatemala City:
Canada: Galerias España, 6th floor, 7 Avenida 11–59, Zona 9 ☎ 321411.
United Kingdom: Edificio Centro Financiero, 7th floor, Tower Two, 7a Avenida 5–10, Zona 4. ☎ 321601.
United States: 7–01 Avenida de la Reforma, Zona 10. ☎ 311541.

---

to restore the reforms. The 1980s saw some moves towards democratisation, a new constitution was drafted and presidential elections held in 1985. However, the military remains strong, and civil war is still going on in parts of the country.

Agricultural exports dominate the economy. Industry is growing and there are some oil reserves. The return to democracy, economic growth and improved balance of payments have seen a revival of the tourist industry.

Of the 8.4 million inhabitants, more than half are Indian. There are two distinct cultures, the largely self-supporting indigenous peoples of the highlands, and the Ladino commercial economy in the lowlands. 'Ladino' is a Central American term used to refer to anyone with a Latin culture, who speaks Spanish and wears western clothes, even if they are Indian.

Spanish is the official language, but there are also 20 Indian languages and some 100 dialects. The majority of the population practise a mixture of paganism and Catholicism. Guatemala City is the capital located in the centre of the country at an altitude of 5000 ft (1500 m).

The climate depends very much on the altitude and the coast is hot and humid. The Caribbean coast is occasionally affected by northers in winter. Throughout the year the local prevailing winds are easterly.

Entry Regulations

Ports of entry
Pacific: Champerico 14°18′N 91°56′W, Puerto Quetzal 13°55′N 90°47′W, San José 13°55′N 90°50′W.
Atlantic: Livingston 15°50′N 88°45′W, Puerto Barrios 15°44′N 88°36′W, Santo Tomàs de Castilla 15°42′N 88°37′W.

Procedure on arrival
On arrival yachts are normally visited by customs, immigration, police, health and port captain.
Santo Tomàs: Yachts which have tried to clear in at this commercial port have been directed to Livingston, on the Rio Dulce. As an official port of entry, one should be able to clear in at Santo Tomàs and the reason why boats have been turned away could be the presence of the naval base.
Livingston: Fly the Q flag and the officials will come out to the yacht in office hours (closed 1300–1500), then the captain should go ashore to clear immigration, customs, then lastly the port captain. Access to Rio Dulce is difficult on account of a wide sand bar at the river entrance. Information on the actual depth varies, but it appears that a maximum 6 ft can be carried through at high tide. If in doubt it is advisable to take soundings ahead from a dinghy. As the depth at the pier is only 5 ft it is better to anchor off.

Puerto Barrios: This is Guatemala's main commercial harbour 9 miles from Livingston and the approaches are much easier than for the latter. Entry as well as exit formalities are dealt with quickly, as all offices are within a short walking distance. One should visit customs first, at the large customs building on the waterfront. This should be followed by immigration and port captain.

Puerto Quetzal: This new port was built on the Pacific side to replace the old port of San José. Port Control should be contacted on VHF Channel 16 for instruction on where to berth for clearance. The new port has a service area for yachts.

Customs

Firearms and animals must be declared.

Immigration

Most nationals do not need a visa. Visas are required by some countries, including Canada, Ireland, Australia and the United Kingdom. Visas are usually valid for 30 days and must be used within 30 days of the date of issue, so it is best to obtain them in one of the neighbouring countries, all of whom have Guatemalan missions. Multiple entry visas are available. Visitors have been fined US$10 per day for overstaying their visa.

Some identification should always be carried.

Cruising permit

Cruising yachts intending to spend longer than 90 days in Guatemala must obtain a special permit consisting of a sticker that must be displayed prominently on the boat. The sticker will be attached by the customs officer in the first port of entry. The maximum time one is allowed to remain in the country is six months.

Health

Amoebic dysentery is endemic. Malaria prophylaxis is necessary.

Fees

Immigration 10 quetzals per passport. Customs 70 quetzals.

Facilities

There is good provisioning in Puerto Barrios and a fresh produce market. Water is available from the small dock. Fuel is available from the ferry dock, but there is little depth alongside. Tecno Marine is a small boatyard offering a range of repair services as well as some

marine supplies. They monitor Channel 74 and will advise on entry procedure.

At El Golfete there is a marina on the river catering for visiting yachts where it may be possible to leave the boat to travel inland, either to the capital or the ancient Maya sites. Apart from the usual marina services, repair facilities are basic and provisioning is also more limited than in bigger towns.

There are small boatyards at both Livingston and Puerto San Tomàs with haul-out facilities, but the range of repair services is limited.

Further Reading

A Cruising Guide to the Caribbean and Bahamas
Cruising Ports: California to Florida via Panama
South American Handbook

HONDURAS

Honduras has coastlines on both sides of Central America, while the interior is mountainous and sparsely populated. Its Pacific coast on the Gulf of Fonseca is only about 70 miles long compared to a 400 mile shoreline in the Caribbean. The country's prime sailing attraction is the Bay Islands, a perfect cruising ground whose popularity with yachts has increased steadily in recent years. Roatán, Utila and Guanaja are the main islands of this group of islands, islets and cays which spread over an area larger than the Virgin Islands, with whom their scenic beauty is on a par. For those who find the Eastern Caribbean, and the Virgin Islands in particular, too crowded for their taste, the Bay Islands provide a perfect alternative. Until recently tourism has been low key, but this will probably change following the expansion of Roatán's airport.

The rest of Honduras is less tempting to explore by sea and although the mountainous north coast is scenically attractive, the lack of harbours make cruising along it very difficult, while the western Pacific coast is featureless and uninteresting.

Country Profile

When the Spanish pushed east from Guatemala early in the sixteenth century, they found silver in this newly conquered land. The present-day capital Tegucigalpa, which means silver hill in the local Indian language, was founded as a mining camp in 1578. Gradually Spanish settlements spread along the north coast and this is where most of the population live today. During

Practical Information

LOCAL TIME: GMT - 6

BUOYAGE: IALA B

CURRENCY: Lempita of 100 centavos

BUSINESS HOURS
Banks: 0900–1500 Monday to Friday, 0800–1100 Saturday.
Business: 0900–1200/1400–1800 Monday to Friday, 0800–1200 Saturday, some also open on Saturday afternoons.
On the north coast businesses open and close half an hour earlier than the capital.

ELECTRICITY: 110 V, 60 Hz

PUBLIC HOLIDAYS
1 January: New Year's Day
14 April: Day of the Americas
Maundy Thursday, Good Friday, Easter Saturday
1 May
15 September: Independence Day
3 October: Francisco Morazán Day
12 October: Discovery Day
21 October: Army Day
25 December: Christmas Day

COMMUNICATIONS
Hondutel for international telephone calls and telex.
Post offices open 0700–2000 Monday to Friday, 0800–1200 Saturday.

There are international flights from Tegucigalpa. There is a good network of internal flights, as well as daily flights from the Bay Islands to the mainland.

DIPLOMATIC MISSIONS
In Tegucigalpa:
Canada: Edificio Comercial, Las Castanas, 6th floor, Blvd Morazán. ☎ 314548.
United Kingdom: Edificio Palmira, 3rd floor, Colonia Palmira. ☎ 325480.
United States: Avenida La Paz. ☎ 323120.

---

the nineteenth century US companies developed banana plantations in the northern lowlands and imported labour from the British West Indies and Belize.

Honduras was under Spanish colonial rule until the Central American colonies declared their independence in 1821 and formed a federation under the leadership of Guatemala City. Francisco Morazán led a Honduran army in 1828 in revolt, captured Guatemala City, and took over control of the federation. He introduced many liberal reforms, but was assassinated in 1842. The federation fell apart, and thereafter the history of Honduras as an independent republic was very troubled. Throughout the nineteenth and into the twentieth centuries the efforts of Honduras, El Salvador and Nicaragua to create a political federation came to nothing. From 1969 relations with El Salvador deteriorated, following a dispute over the illegal immigration of Salvadoreans into Honduras. Relations only returned to normal in 1980. In 1987 the Central American Peace Plan was drawn up by the Costa Rican President, but the provisions for US military personnel and Nicaraguan contra forces to withdraw from Honduras were not carried out. The last two elections in Honduras have been won by the Liberal Party.

The Bay Islands (Islas de la Bahia) were ceded to Honduras only in 1859 by Britain, hence their less Latin atmosphere. The people of the Bay Islands are of British origin and many are still English-speaking. They are descendants of Scottish and English pirates, colonists from the Cayman Islands who arrived in the eighteenth century, and some Black Caribs, deported to Roatán from St Vincent at the end of the eighteenth century. Henry Morgan had a lair at Port Royal,

Roatán, and legend says that he is buried on Utila. Also part of Honduras is Swan Island, a former US dependency, which was ceded to Honduras in 1972. The island is a navy base and should be avoided.

Honduras is a poor country, with 25 per cent unemployment, due to low investment, poor harvests and labour disputes. Agriculture is the main economic activity, coffee, bananas and timber being the main exports. Almost half the land is forested. The country has considerable mineral and oil reserves.

The population number almost 5 million. The main language is Spanish, but English is spoken in the north and in the Bay Islands. The majority of the population are Catholic.

Rain is frequent on the Caribbean coast all year round, but heaviest from September to December. The drier months are April to May but these months are very hot. The east and north coasts have strong NE trade winds throughout the winter months. The best time to cruise the Bay Islands is at the end of winter or early spring when the northers of winter are no longer a problem.

Entry Regulations

Ports of entry
Pacific: San Lorenzo 13°25′N 87°27′W, Tela 15°47′N 87°30′W.
Atlantic: Puerto Castilla 16°01′N 86°03′W, Puerto Cortés 15°51′N 87°56′W, La Ceiba 15°47′N 86°45′W.
Bay Islands: Roatán (Coxen Hole) 16°18′N 86°35′W, Utila 16°16′N 86°40′W, Guanaja 16°28′N 85°54′W.

Procedure on arrival

Roatán: Known locally as Coxen Hole, the port of Roatán is the main port of entry in the Bay Islands. The Q flag should be flown to attract the attention of the officials. The boat is usually boarded by the port captain accompanied by a customs officer. A crew list must be handed in as well as the clearance papers from the last port. A 30-day cruising permit is issued which can be easily renewed. Immigration charges a small fee per passport. Visiting yachts are sometimes asked to employ the services of a local agent to carry out the clearance formalities, although this is not compulsory as clearance formalities are fairly straightforward. Yachts heading for the Bay Islands should try and make straight for Roatán, rather than clear at one of the mainland ports as formalities are simpler and officials are used to dealing with foreign yachts.

Utila: Yachts have also cleared in at this island, which although not listed as an official port of entry, has all the usual offices stationed there.

Puerto Castilla: There is an old dock for yachts, as well as a new dock that has recently been constructed. Tie up to either dock and wait to be boarded by the officials.

Guanaja: On arrival, yachts are normally boarded by the local officials. Formalities are completed in town.

Yachts must obtain outward clearance (*zarpe*) before proceeding to the next port.

Customs

Firearms and animals must be declared.

Immigration

No visas are required for nationals of Japan and all West European countries, except France and Germany, who need a tourist card which is issued on arrival. Visas are required in advance for citizens of the USA, Australia, New Zealand and Austria.

A 30-day stay is granted on arrival. Extensions of 30 days, up to six months maximum, can be obtained from immigration offices.

Some identification should always be carried, as the police often do spot checks.

One should not have stamps in one's passport from communist countries or those with which Honduras has no diplomatic relations such as India. If arriving from Nicaragua, all literature, maps and even fresh produce will be confiscated. These requirements will probably be dropped following the change of government in Nicaragua.

Health

Dysentery and stomach parasites are a problem for those travelling inland. Water must be treated everywhere. Malaria prophylaxis recommended.

Fees

Overtime charges are made for clearance outside of working hours. Agent's fees if an agent is used. There is an immigration fee.

Wildlife reserves

All of Utila Island is a sanctuary except for the settlements. Also protected in the Bay Islands are the National Marine Park of Barbareta, West End on Roatán, and most of Guanaja and its surrounding reefs. Other protected islands are: Hog Cays (Cayos Cochinos), off the Caribbean coast, Cayos Zapotillos, Swan Island (Isla del Cisne) and Miskito Cays (Cayos Misquitos) off the Mosquito coast.

Facilities

Provisioning and repair facilities in the mainland ports are barely adequate and for any specialised job it is better to enlist the help of one of the workshops in Roatán, which are used to dealing with yachts. There is good provisioning with many shops and a general market close to the dock in Coxen Hole. Fuel is also available on the dock. Yachting facilities are even better at Port Royal, also on Roatán Island, which has two marinas and a good range of repair facilities. Marine equipment is in short supply, but as yachting services are being expanded, this may change. There are also two small shipyards, with their own slipways, at French Harbour, fuel at the Texaco dock and good provisioning. One can anchor away from the commercial port of French Harbour in West Bight, where French Harbour Yacht Club has drinking water at its dock and other facilities. Guanaja, the easternmost island in the group, also has a reasonable range of supplies, as does Utila. All islands have regular flights to La Ceiba on the mainland.

Further Reading

Cruising Guide to the Bay Islands
Cruising Ports: California to Florida via Panama
Caribbean Islands Handbook

MEXICO

Mexico has many things of interest to offer its visitors, whether they come by air, land or sea: an ancient culture, a vibrant atmosphere unmatched anywhere else in Latin America and a landscape of varied scenery from the high mountains of the interior to the silvery beaches lapped by the Pacific Ocean and Caribbean Sea. The cruising attractions of Mexico are concentrated in two main areas, the Gulf of California (Sea of Cortez) in Baja California on the west coast, and the Yucatan Peninsula on the east coast.

While Baja California's attraction lies primarily in the incredible wildlife that inhabits the limpid waters of the Gulf of California, the Yucatan's temptations lie mostly ashore, among the awe-inspiring ruins of the mighty Mayan empire. For many years the Gulf of California has been the preferred foreign destination of Californian sailors, a place so near and yet so far from their own highly developed state. Equally the Yucatan peninsula and the offlying island of Cozumel have offered almost the same kind of contrast to yachts heading south from Florida, but rapid tourist development is already creating a skyline similar to Acapulco in the formerly deserted beaches, bays and lagoons where for centuries the tallest buildings were those of the Mayan temples.

Less than 400 miles off Mexico's western coast lies a group of islands rarely visited from the mainland except by yachts on passage to the Marquesas. Of the four Islas de Revillagigedo only two, Socorro and

Acapulco Bay (Ministry of Tourism, Mexico).

Clarión, are inhabited, Partida is just a rock, while San Benedicto was parched by a volcanic eruption in 1952. The lack of rainfall has resulted in an arid landscape, which is more than made up for by the spectacular underwater scenery.

Country Profile

Since 2000 BC Mexico has seen thousands of years of continuous civilisation and has over 1000 archaeological sites to show for it. Before the arrival of the Spanish conquistadors, several highly developed and complex civilisations had risen to power and fallen. Huge ceremonial cities were built, the states based on the rule of a small elite over a people tied together by strong family and community ties. By the sixteenth century the flourishing Aztec empire had succeeded the Mayas, with its capital at Tenochtitlan. An estimated 20 million people populated Mexico at this time.

Hernando Cortez, leading a militarily superior force, conquered Tenochtitlan and then slowly the rest of the country, which was then called New Spain. It remained under Spanish control for 300 years. The Indians, used as slave labour, were decimated by

Practical Information

LOCAL TIME: GMT - 5 (east coast), - 6 (Mexico City), - 7 (Baja California).

BUOYAGE: IALA B

CURRENCY: Mexican peso of 100 centavos

BUSINESS HOURS
Banks: 0900–1330 Monday to Friday, open Saturday mornings in some larger towns.
Shops: 0900/1000–1300/1400 and 1500/1600–1900/2000 weekdays.
Government offices: 0800–1500 Monday to Friday.

ELECTRICITY: 110/120 V, 60 Hz

PUBLIC HOLIDAYS
1 January: New Year's Day
5 February: Constitution Day
21 March: Birthday of Benito Juarez
Good Friday (some businesses close
Monday to Thursday of Holy Week)
1 May
5 May: Anniversary of Battle of Puebla
16 September: Independence Day
12 October: Columbus Day
2 November: All Souls Day

20 November: Anniversary of Mexican Revolution
12 December: Feast of Our Lady of Guadalupe (Mexico's patroness saint) is not an official holiday but is often observed
25 December: Christmas Day (most offices are closed from Christmas until 2 January)

EVENTS
There are lots of fiestas all year round, usually religious, with folk dances and fireworks.

COMMUNICATIONS
International calls from a long-distance concessionary (caseta de larga distancia), although these are hard to find.
Dial 09 for an English-speaking international operator.
Collect calls can only be made to the USA, UK and a few European countries. There is a service charge if the call is not accepted or the person is not reached.
International calls are heavily taxed.
There are many flights worldwide from Mexico City and to US cities from other places such as Acapulco.

MEDICAL
Public hospitals are cheap, but not recommended. Both the US and UK embassies in Mexico City have lists of approved doctors. Medical facilities are good in larger cities.

DIPLOMATIC MISSIONS
In Mexico City:
Australia: Plaza Polanco Torre B, Jaime Balmes 11, Col. Los Morales.
☎ (5) 359-7870.
Canada: Calle Schiller 529 (Rincon del Bosque), Colonia Polanco.
☎ (5) 254-3288.
New Zealand: Homero 229, 11570.
☎ (5) 250-5999.
United Kingdom: Rio Lerma 71, Col. Cuauhtemoc. ☎ (5) 207-2089.
United States: Paseo de la Reforma 305.
☎ (5) 211-0042.

In Acapulco:
Canada: Hotel Club Del Sol, Mezzanine floor, Costera Miguel Aleman.
☎ (748) 56-621.

disease, and converted by Catholic missionaries who had followed soon after the conquistadors. Assimilation of the Indians went smoothly in the centre of the country, but the discovery of silver in the north meant the Spaniards pushed into a less welcoming area, where the Indians rebelled against the invasion. The Spaniards loaded vast amounts of silver on to their ships to be sent back to Europe, always under the threat of attack by pirates or privateers.

In 1810 the War of Independence began, and although defeated, guerilla warfare continued until independence was finally gained in 1821. Until the middle of the century the country remained politically unstable, dominated by the struggle between the liberals and the conservatives, while the majority of the people lived in terrible poverty. Territory was lost to the expanding United States, including Texas and present day California and New Mexico. At the turn of the century President Diaz brought some stability and prosperity, but not to the workers or labourers. From 1911–20 revolution and civil war tore the country apart, with Pancho Villa and Emiliano Zapata the popular heroes. Despite fierce conflict, some land reforms were introduced, industry developed, and Mexico's relationship with the USA improved.

Since the Second World War industrialisation has continued, helped by the oil reserves, nationalisation and moves towards democracy. However, little progress has been made on land and agricultural reforms. Many Mexicans seek employment in the United States. Exports to the USA are vital to the economy. Oil has been the main source of income since the 1970s, also minerals and plantation crops. The tourist industry is growing.

The population of Mexico is 80 million. Traditionally the gachupines, Spaniards born in Spain, dominated the country, but were always resented by the criollos, being those of Spanish origin but born in Mexico. The mestizos, mixed Spanish and Indian, forming the bulk of the population, were much poorer, but those who suffered the most were the Indians, comprising 54 different ethnic groups. The situation has not changed a great deal to the present day.

The official language is Mexican Spanish and there are various Indian languages. English is spoken by some, especially those involved in the tourist industry. Roman Catholicism is the religion of the majority. The capital is Mexico City, although the state capitals within the federation are also important, especially after the 1985 earthquake in Mexico City, when decentralisation was spurred on. Mexico City is at a very high altitude, 7347 ft (2240 m) and is built on the site of the former Aztec capital Tenochtitlan.

The climate is often very hot on the coasts, although it is more temperate at higher altitudes and in the north. May to October is the rainy season, and it usually rains in the late afternoon and evening. May is the hottest month. It rarely rains from November to April. Temperatures on the west coast are high all year round, especially in the Gulf of California where the wind is often light. On both coasts the hurricane season runs from June to October, while winter brings the occasional norther and, on the east coast, strong trade winds. The best time to cruise is spring and late autumn.

Entry Regulations

Ports of entry
Pacific: Acapulco 16°50′N 99°55′W, Altamira 22°25′N 97°55′W, Cabo San Lucas 22°50′N 109°55′W, Ensenada 31°51′N 116°38′W, Guaymas 27°54′N 110°52′W, La Paz 24°10′N 110°19′W, Lazaro Cardenas 17°55′N 102°11′W, Manzanillo 19°03′N 104°20′W, Mazatlán 23°11′N 106°26′W, Morro Redondo (Cedros Island) 28°03′N 115°11′W, Tampico 22°13′N 97°53′W.
Islas de Revillagigedo: 18°42′N 110°58′W.
Atlantic: Alvarado 18°46′N 95°46′W, Campeche 19°51′N 90°33′W, Ciudad del Carmen 18°39′N 91°51′W, Coatzacoalcos 18°09′N 94°25′W, Cozumel 20°30′N 86°58′W, Frontera 18°35′N 92°39′W, Isla Mujeres 21°10′N 86°43′W, Progreso 21°17′N 89°40′W, Puerto Madero 14°42′N 92°27′W, Puerto Vallarta 20°37′N 105°16′W, Salina Cruz 16°10′N 95°11′W, San Carlos 24°47′N 112°07′W, Santa Rosalia 27°20′N 112°16′W, Veracruz 19°12′N 96°08′W.

Procedure on arrival
Formalities can be time-consuming, but in the major ports there are maritime agents who will do the formalities for a fee, as well as help to obtain fuel permits. At the first port of entry the captain must visit the port captain (Capitán del Puerto), with the last outward clearance, also immigration (inmigración)

and customs (aduana). As well as the ship's papers, the captain should have four crew lists in Spanish. Crew list forms in Spanish can be obtained before arrival from a Mexican consulate for a fee, or for a similar fee on arrival. A request for consular clearance has to be made in Spanish and this can also be done at Mexican consulates before arrival.

One must also clear in at all subsequent ports, paying visits to the port captain and immigration if they have an office. Crew lists will have to be given to all these officials. The port captain will only sign the permit for outward clearance 24 to 48 hours before departure, and yachts should leave promptly after obtaining their exit permit (zarpe). The following ports also include some minor ports where normally yachts have to check in only with the port captain.
Ensenada: The port captain normally inspects boats on arrival and advises on the required procedure and the order of offices to be visited.
Puerto Escondido: Yachts usually anchor off the beach. The port captain's office is on the waterfront next to the army post.
Huatulco: The port captain comes over every day from Puerto Angel to check the boats.
Cabo San Lucas: The port captain and immigration offices are on the quay next to the fishing boats and outdoor market.
Mazatlán: Yachts anchor off and dinghies can be left at the boating club. Frequent buses stop at the club gate and go into town where the offices of customs, immigration and port captain are situated.
Manzanillo: Yachts anchor outside Las Hadas Hotel or stern-to one of the docks inside the jetty. The captain of any yacht arriving from a foreign port is required to visit the port captain, customs and immigration both when clearing in and out.
Acapulco: Yachts can either anchor outside or come stern-to the dock. The yacht club facilities can be used by visitors and the yacht club can arrange clearance facilities for a fee. Although time-consuming, the formalities are straightforward.
Puerto Madero: This is the last port on the Pacific coast for those going south. The port captain's office is in the building outside the gate to the dock area, which is fenced off.
Cozumel: This island is a favourite place for clearing in or out of Mexico. Recommended anchorages are just off Hotel El Presidente or at San Miguel, on the north side of the commercial dock. The wharf is used by large ferries so one should not come alongside, unless prepared to move off at short notice. The anchorage is uncomfortable in westerlies and strong northers. The port captain's office is on the waterfront, while the customs office is at the airport. Clearing in formalities

tend to be lengthy, as one has to visit several offices around town. The easier alternative is to go directly to the yacht club, which operates a marina and has an agent who deals with all necessary formalities for a fee of approximately $25. Customs and immigration officials usually inspect boats at the yacht club and the port captain also has a representative there. Outward clearance can also be done at the club.

Isla Mujeres: Formalities are relatively simple as all offices are within walking distance. One has to clear in with customs, then the port captain on the front street opposite the ferry wharf; immigration is also on the main road and harbour master next door. A health inspection is sometimes carried out at the local hospital. Occasionally firearms are inspected, but left on board. The Navy sometimes boards vessels in the harbour.

Islas de Revillagigedo: One should clear with the Navy, which has a garrison there, on the main island of Socorro.

Procedure on departure

It is advisable to complete the proper clearing out formalities from Mexico and obtain a clearance certificate (zarpe) from the port captain of the last port of call. Although this document may not be requested when clearing into the next country, one would have to show it if stopped by a Mexican Navy boat while still in Mexican waters. When leaving Mexico one should also clear with immigration and customs. If wishing to stop anywhere in Mexico after clearing out, this should be put on the outward clearance by the relevant official. Even when cruising between two major Mexican ports, it is advisable to ask the official filling out the exit permit to mention on the document any intermediate ports which may be visited (puertos intermedios).

Customs

The only firearms allowed in Mexico are sporting guns which must have a valid Mexican hunting licence, obtained in advance. Other firearms must have a permit, and be declared to the authorities on arrival, who will keep them in custody until departure. The penalties for having an unauthorised gun on board are severe and can led to seizure of the yacht and imprisonment of the captain.

Animals require a veterinary health certificate and cats and dogs also require an anti-rabies vaccination certificate.

The importation of spare parts or equipment from abroad duty free is considerably eased if one has a temporary import permit, which is normally issued at the port of entry.

Immigration

Citizens of Australia, Canada, Japan, Philippines, the United Kingdom, the United States, West European countries and most Latin American countries (except Cuba, Chile and Haiti) require a tourist card. This can be obtained from Mexican consulates, national airlines, or on arrival, although it is advisable to obtain it in advance. Most other countries require a visa, to be obtained in advance.

For US citizens, the tourist card is valid for six months. Other nationalities are normally given 90 days on their tourist card, although if the card is obtained on arrival sometimes only 30 days is granted, so if intending to stay longer one should insist on 90 days or obtain a card in advance. Particularly if coming from Belize it is advisable to arrive in Mexico either with a tourist card or a visa obtained in advance. These can be obtained from the Mexican consul in Belize City.

Renewal of the tourist card can be done in Mexico City at the Secretaria de Gobernación, Dirección General de Asuntos Jurídicos, Avenida Juarez 92, 2nd floor (postal address: CP06500), ☎ 535-2718. If one has proof of possessing US$500 per month of intended stay, renewal of tourist cards and visas, which can take several weeks, can be done at a local immigration office. However, in an emergency a local immigration officer can extend a card for a few days, with telephone approval from Mexico City. A tourist card is needed to leave the country, and if lost it takes about a week to replace.

Health

Water should be treated everywhere in Mexico. Several cruising sailors have contracted parasites either from contaminated water or food which had come in contact with such water, such as salads, fruit or ice cream.

Fees

There is an immigration fee for forms and a fee for the exit permit from customs. Overtime is charged for clearance outside of office hours.

Fishing licence

Each person on board must have a fishing licence, and a licence must also be purchased for the yacht. For a yacht with four crew this will amount to about US$100. Spot checks are made, and simply having fishing tackle on board is considered by the Mexican authorities sufficient reason to have a licence. The licences can be obtained in advance from the Mexican Fisheries Department, 2550 5th Street, San Diego, California 92101, USA.

Restrictions
Turtles are protected and no products made from turtles are allowed to be exported.

Facilities

As the number of yachts visiting Mexico is increasing, so the yachting facilities are improving. All major ports visited by cruising yachts now have a reasonable range of services and most routine repairs can be dealt with locally. In most places there is good provisioning with both supermarkets and fresh produce. Fuel is available almost everywhere, although it can be dirty.

La Paz is a major gathering point for yachts wintering in Baja California and there are excellent repair facilities with three shipyards capable of handling most jobs, and a good marina with a chandlery, fuel and all the usual services.

In Manzanillo fuel and water are available on the dock, good provisioning in the neighbouring town as well as various workshops, engine repair and spares. Also Mexican charts can be bought at the Instituto Oceanigrafico in Las Brisas. At Puerto Vallarta there is a chandlery at the new marina. Opequimar offer a complete range of repair services as well as 30-ton travelift. Acapulco has a very helpful yacht club which offers a wide range of services to visiting yachts.

In Cozumel the yacht club is run as a marina and welcomes visiting sailors, especially during the off season. The mooring fees become prohibitively high during the game fishing season from March to June. There is fuel and water as well as some small workshops which can undertake simple repairs. There are daily air trips to the Maya ruins on the mainland, which can also be reached by taking the ferry to Playa del Carmen and thence by bus or taxi to the ruins.

Isla Mujeres is another place where yachts can be left while visiting the Mayan sites on the Yucatan peninsula. There are good shops in town and some workshops for small repairs. Fuel and water are on the dock.

Further Reading

Crew List for Spanish Speaking Countries, by Larry Baldwin (pads containing sheets of crew lists, and of the initial request for consular clearance into Mexico, and details of the correct procedures)
Charlie's Charts, Western Coast of Mexico
Cruising Ports: California to Florida via Panama
South American Handbook
Fodor's South America

NICARAGUA

Nicaragua is the largest Central American state, lying between Costa Rica and Honduras with coasts on both the Pacific Ocean and the Caribbean Sea. The capital Managua lies on the shores of Lake Managua 30 miles from the Pacific Ocean. The Miskito kingdom encompassing the Caribbean lowlands was a British protectorate until the end of the nineteenth century. Following the Sandinista revolution, the Miskito Indians fought for self-determination, and this coastal area, including the Corn Islands, has been a self-governing region since 1987. English is spoken there and the African influence is noticeable.

For the last few years Nicaragua has been avoided by cruising yachts and for good reason, although with the changing political situation this may well change in the future. The shallow reef-encumbered Miskito coast has many attractive anchorages, but navigation is difficult and even in the past when the area was not off-limits, most yachts restricted their cruising to the more accessible Corn Islands.

Country Profile

Nicaragua was under Guatemalan jurisdiction until it gained independence in 1838. An American William Walker led a famous expedition to Central America in the mid-nineteenth century, setting out to conquer Mexico. Driven into Nicaragua with his bellicose followers, he captured Granada and then took control of the whole country. Walker was elected President and recognised as such by the United States. A Central American coalition fought against him, and he eventually surrendered to the US Navy. A second expedition failed, and in 1860 Walker sailed to Honduras, where he was arrested and executed.

Nicaragua was again invaded in 1912–13 when US marines were sent in to enforce a loan. The nationalists under General Sandino fought against this occupation. The United States appointed Anastasio Somoza supreme commander of the Nicaraguan National Guard, and Sandino was killed. Following the introduction of President Roosevelt's 'Good Neighbour' policy, the United States withdrew and Somoza dominated political life until his assassination in 1956. His son, General Somoza Debayle, followed him as ruler, until he was deposed in 1979. The revolution was led by the Sandinista guerillas (FSLN), who went on to establish a government with Daniel Ortega as President. However, their socialist policies were not welcomed by their neighbours and the US-backed 'contras' mounted a counter-revolutionary war, mainly

Practical Information

LOCAL TIME: GMT - 6

BUOYAGE: IALA B

CURRENCY: Cordoba (C$) of 100 centavos.

BUSINESS HOURS
Banks: 0830–1200/1400–1600 Monday to Friday, 0830–1100 Saturday.
Business and government offices: 0800–1200, 1430–1730/1800 weekdays.

ELECTRICITY: 110 V, 60 Hz

PUBLIC HOLIDAYS
1 January: New Year's Day
Maundy Thursday, Good Friday
1 May: Labour Day
19 July: Revolution of 1979
14 September: Battle of San Jacinto
15 September: Independence Day
2 November: All Souls Day
8 December: Immaculate Conception
25 December: Christmas Day
During most of Holy Week and the Christmas and New Year period businesses and shops close. Holidays falling on Sunday are taken on the following Monday.

COMMUNICATIONS
Telcor for telegraph and telephone calls, open 0700–2200.
There are international flights from Managua to other Central and North American capitals.

DIPLOMATIC MISSIONS
In Managua:
Canada: 208 Calle del Triunfo, Frente Plazoleta Telcor Central. ☎ 24541.
United Kingdom: El Reparto 'Los Robles', Carretera de Masaya. ☎ 71112.
United States: Km 4–1/2 Carretera Sur. ☎ 25494.

from bases in Honduras. The Sandinistas introduced reforms, but both the war and the US trade embargo damaged the economy, one of the main reasons for their defeat in the 1990 elections.

The economy is based on agriculture, the main exports being coffee, cotton, sugar and bananas. Industry expanded in the 1970s, but suffered due to guerilla warfare, floods and drought. Inflation is also a problem, and a new currency was introduced in 1988. At the time of the 1990 elections, the country was virtually bankrupt and dependent on foreign aid.

The 3.5 million inhabitants are mestizo and of Indian and African origins as well as a small number of European origin. Spanish is the main language and most are Roman Catholic.

The climate is humid and hot, December to May being the dry months, while June and October are the wettest. Violent northerly winds occasionally affect both coasts in winter, particularly the Caribbean coast. On this coast the prevailing winds are E or NE, while winds on the west coast are usually light. The coasts are sometimes affected by tropical storms, the season for which lasts from June to October.

Entry Regulations

Ports of entry
Pacific: Corinto 12°28′N 87°11′W, Puerto Sandino 12°11′N 86°47′W, San Juan del Sur 11°15′N 85°53′W.
Atlantic: El Bluff 12°01′N 83°44′W.

Procedure on arrival
Corinto: This is the main port of Nicaragua. Port

control keep 24-hour watch on VHF Channel 16 and should be contacted for instructions concerning clearance.
El Bluff: Yachts should dock at the customs wharf for clearance, where customs and health officials will board.

Customs
Firearms and animals must be declared. A declaration of money and valuables must be made on arrival.

Immigration
Passports must have a validity of at least six months. Proof of adequate funds is sometimes required. No visa is required for up to a 90 day stay for nationals of Central American states, the United States, Canada, Belgium, Denmark, Liechtenstein, Luxembourg, Netherlands, Norway, Finland, Spain, Sweden and the United Kingdom. All others require a visa, to be obtained in advance, valid for arrival within 30 days, for a stay of up to 30 days. Extensions are difficult to obtain.

Foreign visitors used to have to change US$60 on arrival, but this, like many other regulations, may change with the new regime.

One's passport or a photocopy of one's passport should be carried at all times.

Health
Malaria prophylaxis is recommended.

Restrictions
There are sensitive areas, where fighting was a possibility until recently, and special permission was needed to visit them, namely: Solentiname Island, most of the Honduran and Costa Rican border areas, all of the

Atlantic coast including the Corn Islands (Islas del Maíz). To visit the Corn Islands, the Caribbean coast, Bluefields and Puerto Cabezas, a permit must be obtained in Managua.

Facilities

Provisioning is very difficult due to severe food shortages and rationing. Even essential goods are impossible to obtain in some places and this includes fuel. There are simple repair facilities in most ports.

Further Reading

A Cruising Guide to the Caribbean and the Bahamas
South American Handbook

PANAMA

Panama is a country that lies at the world's crossroads, a narrow isthmus which divides the Atlantic from the Pacific Oceans and links the two halves of the American continent. The country is dominated by the Panama Canal and the surrounding Panama Canal Area, at present under US administration, but which will be incorporated fully into Panama on 31 December 1999. Balboa on the Pacific and Cristobal in the Caribbean are the two main ports and gateways to the canal. The port of Cristobal incorporates the town of Colón.

Political uncertainty in Panama in recent years has not affected the operation of the canal, nor the requirements which apply to yachts wishing either to transit the canal or visit other parts of Panama. The main cruising attractions in Panama are the 365 San Blas islands off the Caribbean coast, a popular destination for yachts. The islands are the home of the Cuna Indians and their distinctive handicrafts are a popular buy. A cruising permit is required to visit these islands, but the local Panamanian officials usually treat yachts arriving from the east on their way to the mainland with a certain degree of tolerance.

On the Pacific side, the Las Perlas islands are another unspoilt cruising ground popular with boats en route to the Galapagos and South Pacific islands.

Country Profile

The name Panama means 'abundance of fish' in the local Indian dialect. The San Blas coast was discovered in 1501 by the conquistador Roderigo de Bastidas and Christopher Columbus visited the islands the following year. It was in 1513, however, that the country's fate was decided, when Vasco Nuñez de Balboa crossed the isthmus and sighted the Pacific Ocean. Panama City was founded on the Pacific side and became the starting point for Spanish conquests which fanned out north and south along the Pacific coast. All trade from the Pacific ports had to be taken overland across the isthmus, then heavily escorted ships laden with treasure left for Spain from Puerto Bello on the Caribbean side, returning later with European goods. This route was continually being attacked and in 1671 the pirate Henry Morgan looted and burnt Panama City. Finally in the mid-eighteenth century Spain abandoned the overland route for the one around Cape Horn.

During the Californian Gold Rush, the land route was again used for transport and a railway was built across the isthmus, completed in the mid-nineteenth century at great loss of life. A canal was the obvious solution and Ferdinand de Lesseps, who had successfully built the Suez Canal, started work in 1882. However, this project failed after tropical disease killed thousands of workers. In 1903 Panama declared its independence from Colombia, the fledgling state being promptly recognised by the United States who had been instrumental in its birth. Work on a canal started again under US supervision, but not before the surrounding area had been cleared of the worst diseases. The first passage through the Canal was finally made in 1914. The former Canal Zone was a ribbon of land under US control and included the ports of Cristobal and Balboa. In 1979 the Canal Zone was transferred to Panamanian sovereignty, although the US retain a military presence, have representatives on the Canal Commission and are involved with its day-to-day administration. US involvement in Panamanian affairs came to a head in 1989, when widespread dissatisfaction led to the downfall of President Noriega, who is currently facing criminal charges in the USA.

The Panama Canal is one of the wonders of the modern world and transiting it is a unique experience. The total length of the Canal is 50 miles and runs in a NW to SE direction, which means that the Pacific entrance lies further east than the Caribbean one. It requires about nine hours for the average ship to transit the Canal. Coming from the east a Pacific-bound vessel is raised 85 feet in a series of three steps at Gatun Locks. Each lock chamber is 110 feet wide and 1000 feet long. Gatun Lake, through which ships have to travel for 23.5 miles from Gatun Locks to the end of the Gaillard Cut, is one of the largest artificial lakes in

Practical Information

LOCAL TIME: GMT - 5

BUOYAGE: IALA B

CURRENCY: US dollars (US$). These
are sometimes referred to as balboas.
Panama has no banknotes of its own,
although local coins are in circulation.

BUSINESS HOURS
Banks: variable, usually all morning
Monday to Friday.
Shops: 0700/0800–1200, 1400–1800/1900
Monday to Saturday.
Government offices: 0800–1200,
1230–1630 Monday to Friday.

ELECTRICITY: 220/110 V, 60 Hz

PUBLIC HOLIDAYS
1 January: New Year's Day
9 January: National Mourning

Shrove Tuesday: Carnival
Good Friday
1 May
*15 August (Panama City only)
11 October: National Revolution Day
*1 November: National Anthem Day
*2 November: All Souls Day
3 November: Independence Day
*4 November: Flag Day
5 November: Independence Day (Colón
only)
10 November: First Call of
Independence
28 November: Independence from Spain
8 December: Mothers Day
25 December: Christmas Day
* Official holiday, banks and government
offices close but not businesses.

EVENTS
Fiestas, especially Panama City
Carnival, four days before Ash
Wednesday.

COMMUNICATIONS
Post office in Cristobal, Cristobal
Administration building, corner Av.
Bolivar and Calle 9.
'Republic of Panama' or 'RP' must be
written on letters or they may be
returned.
There are international flights from
Panama City, mainly to the USA and
other Latin American capitals, but also
Madrid and Amsterdam.

DIPLOMATIC MISSIONS
In Panama City:
Canada: Edificio Proconsa, Aero Peru,
Floor 5B, Calle Manuel Icaza, 51 Este
and Avenida 3A Sur, Campo Alegre.
☎ 647014.
United Kingdom: Via España 120, Zona
1. ☎ 230451.
United States: Av. Balboa and Calle 38.
☎ 271777.

the world. It was formed by an earth dam across the Chagres River.

Because of its historical background, no part of the Canal is more interesting than the Gaillard Cut. This portion of the Canal was cut through eight miles of rock under the command of Col. David DuBose Gaillard, whose name it now bears. It was a mammoth task requiring enormous effort and several devastating landslides occurred both during construction and after the Canal was opened. The Pacific-bound ships enter Pedro Miguel Locks at the southern end of Gaillard Cut. Ships are lowered here 31 feet in one step to Miraflores Lake, a small artificial lake which separates the two sets of Pacific locks. Finally, ships are lowered the remaining two steps to sea level at Miraflores Locks, which are slightly over one mile in length. The lock gates at Miraflores are the highest of any in the system because of the extreme tidal variations in the Pacific Ocean.

The Panamanian economy is traditionally founded on income derived from the Canal, services to incoming visitors, Canal employees, and US military personnel. It is now developing tourism, industry and copper mining, while agriculture is also important. Panama's role as an offshore banking centre has suffered from recent political unrest and the country's foreign debt is considerable.

The population numbers around 2.3 million, mostly mestizo, but also of Indian, African and Asian origin.

The Cuna Indians of the San Blas Islands are descendants of the Caribs, who originally peopled much of the Caribbean islands and coasts. The Cunas are one of the few groups to survive the arrival of the Europeans. The San Blas Islands enjoy a measure of autonomy within the state of Panama. Spanish and English are the main languages of Panama and the majority of the population are Roman Catholic. Panama City, two miles from Balboa, is the capital.

The climate is hot and very humid, although cooled by the prevailing easterly winds. The dry season is January to April, and rain can be heavy in October and November. Panama is not affected by hurricanes.

Entry Regulations

Ports of entry
Cristobal 9°21′N 79°55′W, Balboa 8°57′N 79°34′W.
San Blas Islands: Porvenir 9°34′N 78°57′W, Rio Diabolo.

Procedure on arrival
Arriving yachts can clear immigration at either the Panama Canal Yacht Club in Colón if coming from the Caribbean, or at the Balboa Yacht Club if coming from the Pacific. After immigration, one must clear with customs and the port authority, both of which are within a short distance, but are best visited by taxi. The

procedure for transiting the Canal is dealt with separately at the end of this section. At both Balboa and Cristobal, arriving yachts may be boarded by a Panamanian official who will complete all the initial clearance formalities. If the yacht is not boarded, the captain should go ashore, but all others must remain on board until clearance is complete.

Cristobal: Cristobal Signal Station should be contacted on VHF Channels 12 or 16 and the yacht will be directed to proceed to anchor. The captain should go ashore and clear immigration first. The office is in a building to the right of the yacht club, open 0700–1500 Monday to Friday. After-hours clearance can be obtained from the immigration office in Cristobal. Next the captain should go to the Autoridad Portuaria (port authority) to clear into Panama and obtain a cruising permit. The port captain's office is in the Panama Canal Commission building 1105, 3rd floor. If not transiting the Canal, clearance is completed at the port authority. If transiting the Canal, the captain should go to the Canal Admeasurement office.

Balboa: Flamenco Signal Station should be contacted on VHF Channels 12 or 16 upon arrival at the sea buoy. Yachts will be directed to anchor off the Balboa Yacht Club. Occasionally the yacht club launch will come out and the launch operator will direct the yacht to a vacant club mooring if available. On arrival, yachts are normally boarded by a Panamanian Migration and Drug Enforcement Officer. Immigration is completed ashore at the yacht club, open 24 hours.

Porvenir: One should clear with customs and immigration.

Rio Diabolo: One should check in at the police station.

Customs

Firearms must be declared on arrival and will be held in bond until departure.

Dogs need health and anti-rabies certificates and are not allowed to land. All other animals need health certificates.

Immigration

Visas are not required for nationals of Costa Rica, Dominican Republic, El Salvador, Germany, Honduras, Spain, Switzerland and the United Kingdom. 30 days are given on arrival, renewable for another 60 days.

Nationals of the United States, Japan, Australia, Canada, communist countries, India and Pakistan need visas. In the USA, visas can be obtained from: Panamanian Consulate, 201E Kennedy Boulevard, Suite 1400, Tampa, FL 33602, USA, ☎ 813-229-6860. Visitors arriving without a visa are charged US$10 per person.

Cruising permit

On arrival the port authority will issue a cruising permit which costs $20 per month for boats less than 40 ft LOA and $30 for boats over that length. The permit is needed whether transiting the Canal or not. Yachts planning to sail to the San Blas Islands after transiting the Canal should make sure that they receive a cruising permit for these islands. Yachts clearing in Cristobal, who do not intend to stop in Balboa at all, can clear out of Panama in Cristobal, but they must do this one working day before transiting the Canal. Apparently the clearance is free in Cristobal, but costs $25 in Balboa. If intending to stop at Las Perlas, this should be mentioned on the clearance paper by the relevant officer.

Security

In Colón and Cristobal, muggings are a real threat, even in daylight. One should avoid walking anywhere outside of the port and all shopping should be done by taxi. Crime is also a problem in Panama City.

Health

An international yellow fever vaccination certificate is required. If just transiting the Canal, it is not necessary to take anti-malarial precautions, but outside of the Canal Area, malaria prophylaxis is recommended.

Fees

Visa fee of US$10 if a visa is required. Clearance fee. Canal fees (admeasurement fee and transit fee). Cruising permit.

Procedure for Transiting the Panama Canal

After clearing into Panama, the captain must call the Admeasurers Office (☎ 252-4570 Pacific side, ☎ 246-7293 Atlantic side) to make arrangements for admeasurement and to make an appointment to be measured. In Cristobal, the office is on the second floor, Administration Building, No. 1105, and in Balboa, first floor, Building 729. An appointment will be made to visit the boat. If one arrives in the office before noon the measurement can be done the same day; if arriving after 1200, it will be done the next working day (0700–1600 Monday to Saturday). The yacht's tonnage is based on its interior volume in cubic feet divided by 100, and the transit fee is this figure multiplied by $1.46. The minimum fee for admeasuring is $50 for up to 50 tons, and $1 for each additional ton up to 100 tons. Payment must be made in US$ cash.

As well as paying transiting fees and tolls, it is

necessary to make a cash deposit with the Agents Accounts branch to cover any extra expenses which might be charged by the Panama Canal Commission. This is refunded after transit.

After admeasurement, the captain must report to the Canal Operations Captain's Office (Building 910, La Boca on the Pacific side and Building 1105, third floor, Cristobal Administration Building). This officer will explain the requirements needed for the transit, which include four mooring lines not less than 100 feet long and not less than ⅞″ rope, four line-handlers (in addition to the captain), adequate fendering, and the yacht should be able to maintain a minimum of five knots under power. If it becomes apparent at the start of the transit that the yacht is doing less than five knots, it will have to return to the starting point and will be charged for an aborted transit. Yachts with no engines can be towed through the Canal by a Commission launch, all towing charges to be paid by the yacht owner.

The captain will be given a provisional pilot time for the transit. This must be confirmed or changed by calling Marine Traffic Control ☎ 252-4202. Final arrangements must be made no later than 24 hours before the scheduled transit time. Yacht transits begin on Tuesdays and Thursdays, therefore 1200 Monday is the latest time to be scheduled to transit on Tuesday, and 1200 on Wednesday to transit on Thursday. Transits can be arranged earlier and if reconfirmed or cancelled the day before the transit a delay charge will not be made. Yachts normally make the transit in two days, spending a night at Gamboa. The pilot arrives early in the morning, and leaves the yacht for the night, returning the following morning to complete the transit. The yacht will be charged a delay fee of US$275 if the transit is not cancelled before the close of working hours on the day before the scheduled transit or if the yacht is for any reason unable to commence transit. Yachts are required to maintain their transit schedule regardless of weather conditions.

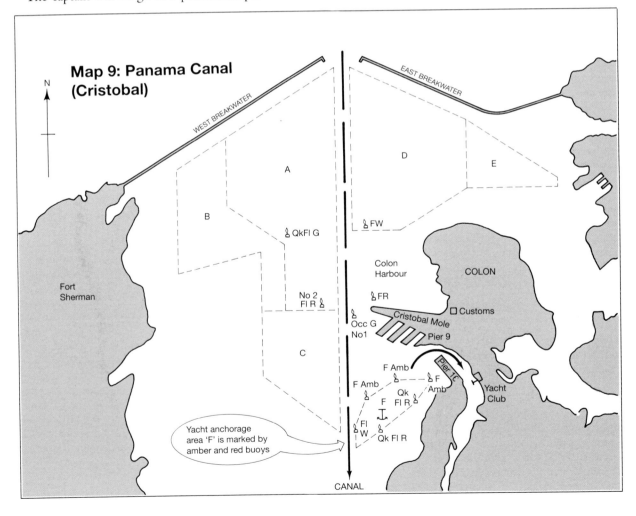

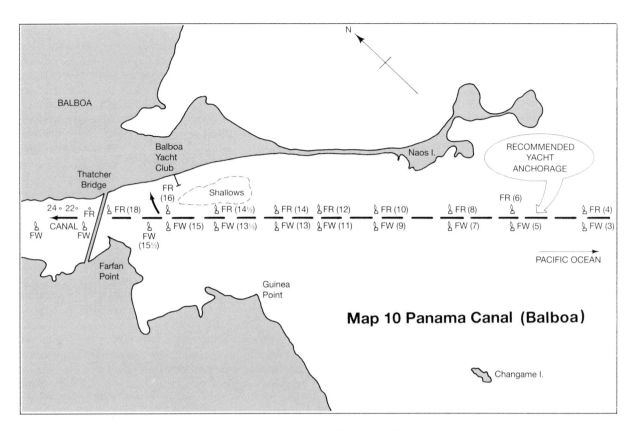

N

BALBOA

Balboa
Yacht
Club

Naos I.

RECOMMENDED
YACHT
ANCHORAGE

Thatcher
Bridge

FR
(16)

Shallows

FR (6)

24 ∘ 22∘   ⚓ FR (18)   ⚓   ⚓ FR (14½)   ⚓ FR (14)   ⚓ FR (12)   ⚓ FR (10)   ⚓ FR (8)   ⚓   ⚓ FR (4)

FR

⚓   ⚓ FW (15)   ⚓ FW (13½)   ⚓ FW (13)   ⚓ FW (11)   ⚓ FW (9)   ⚓ FW (7)   ⚓ FW (5)   ⚓ FW (3)

FW   CANAL ⚓   FW
⚓   ⚓   FW
FW   (15½)

PACIFIC OCEAN

Farfan
Point

Guinea
Point

Map 10 Panama Canal (Balboa)

Changame I.

Types of lockage

There are three different types of lockage in the Canal, and all vessels must be capable of making a centre chamber lockage. Other types are sidewall or alongside a Commission tug. Whether a yacht is assigned a sidewall or centre chamber lockage is decided by the port captain. This depends on hull configuration, protruding railings, awnings, high masts, and anything that could be damaged if made fast to the chamber walls.

Centre chamber lockage: The vessel is held in the centre of the chamber by two bow and two stern lines. Yachts are sometimes rafted together.

Sidewall lockage: Only two 100′ lines are required; lots of fenders will be needed as the walls are rough concrete. Care should also be taken of the rigging which may hit the walls in the turbulence.

Alongside a tug: Two 50′ lines will be required.

Mooring lines

Each yacht must have four line-handlers in addition to a helmsman. All lines, chocks, cleats should be inspected to ensure they are in good condition, as they will be under heavy strain during the transit. The area around the fittings must be clear of gear so that the lines can be efficiently handled.

Yacht clubs

Visiting yachts usually stay at the Panama Canal Yacht Club in Colón on the Atlantic side, or the Balboa Yacht Club on the Pacific side. An alternative to the latter is to anchor off Taboga island, from where one can commute by ferry to Panama City, which takes about two hours. The Panama Canal Yacht Club is reputed to be much more welcoming to visiting sailors than the Balboa Yacht Club. It is open 24 hours a day and its dinghy dock can be used by yachts anchored in the harbour. Those who wish to tie up at the club dock can do so on payment of a daily fee. A fee is also charged for the use of a mooring and launch service at the Balboa Yacht Club. The Pedro Miguel Yacht Club on Miraflores Lake has some repair facilities, and is a half-hour bus ride from Panama City.

Facilities

Provisioning is very good in both Colón and Panama City and there are several supermarkets with a wide selection. There is also a fresh produce market near the railway station in Balboa. Another good fresh produce market is held daily in Margarita, which can be reached by taxi from Colón. There is a wide range of repair facilities at both ends of the Canal with various work-shops capable of dealing with diesel and outboard engines, electronic equipment and sail repair. Either yacht club will advise on the best companies to approach. Both yacht clubs have slipways and there is also a boatyard in Las Minas with haul-out facilities. Charts are available in Panama City.

Facilities in the San Blas and Las Perlas islands are very limited.

Further Reading

Panama Canal Guide for Yachts
South American Handbook
Cruising Ports: California to Florida via Panama

UNITED STATES OF AMERICA

Spanning the North American continent between the Pacific and the Atlantic Oceans, the United States is not a major cruising destination for foreign yachts and with the exception of Canadian boats, the number who visit this great country is comparatively small. Such visitors include European yachts making a detour on the way home from the Caribbean and occasionally a North European yacht which has braved the elements to cross the North Atlantic as part of a summer cruise. Being so remote from any sailing nation, except Canada, the West Coast is even less frequented.

This is rather surprising, as the USA has a lot to offer the cruising sailor, particularly the East Coast, the entire length of which can be cruised from the Florida Keys to Maine. A cruise along this coast has the added attraction of the Intracoastal Waterway, a unique system of canals, rivers and estuaries, which stretches along most of the eastern seaboard offering the chance of sailing up or down the coast in sheltered waters almost within sight of the ocean. For the foreign sailor, Florida is a perfect introduction to the United States and some of its best-known attractions are close by, such as Disneyworld or the Cape Canaveral Space Center. The waterways of the southern states wind their way through old cities, deserted estuaries and silent woods to reach the Chesapeake. This, the largest bay in the USA, has a shore line of thousands of miles and within striking distance of some of America's largest cities are secluded anchorages and snug har-bours. A couple of days sail up the coast, at the confluence of the Hudson and East rivers, lies New York, one of the few cities in the world where one can sail right through its centre. Passing almost within touching distance of Manhattan's skyscrapers and under the many bridges is an experience that cannot be repeated. New York is the gateway to the Great Lakes which can be reached by a system of canals and locks. Alternatively, one can carry on through Long Island Sound to the heart of New England where much of modern America's history was made. Famous sea-farers, whalers and explorers left from these old ports. Finally one reaches the island world of Maine where many summers could be spent exploring the countless bays, rivers and anchorages which stretch all the way to the Canadian border.

Offering less variety, the West Coast's main attrac-tions are concentrated at its two extremes. The most popular cruising area in the Pacific Northwest are the San Juan Islands, an archipelago of some 200 islands, many of which have been declared wildlife reserves or marine parks. Beyond these islands and through Cana-dian waters, the Inside Passage beckons, linking Puget Sound to Alaska, America's ultimate cruising desti-nation. An increasing number of yachts sail to Alaska for the short summer season, either by taking the inside route, or making an offshore detour by stopping first at the Hawaiian Islands. For those avoiding cold and fog, there is all year round sailing in the Pacific Southwest, whether in the San Francisco Bay area or the Channel Islands, off Southern California. Of the eight main islands, Santa Catalina is the best known and most popular. The other islands are less fre-quented and there are countless coves around their precipitous shores. Since some of the Channel Islands are either privately owned or part of the National Park system, a permit to visit them must be obtained in advance by those wishing to go ashore.

Country Profile

The original inhabitants of North America probably came across the Bering Straits from Asia, and spread south through the Americas. The Red Indians, as they later became known, lived in scattered tribes. Their first contact with Europeans was not with Columbus, who only visited the offlying islands of the Caribbean, but with an expedition led by the Norseman Erik the Red, who probably touched on the eastern coast in the tenth century. European settlement began 500 years later, with the French settling in Canada, and the Spanish in Florida.

Throughout the seventeenth century English settle-ment took place, while the French expanded along the Mississippi, founding Louisiana. There was a large emigration from Europe to this New World. Thirteen English colonies were established and antagonism grew between the plantation South, and the bourgeois, puritan North. However, in the eighteenth century they united against both the Indians and the French, although the latter ceased to be a threat after the Treaty of Paris in 1763, when Canada was ceded to England. The French then became an ally of the American colonies in the escalating tension with England, resulting in the War of Independence in 1775–6.

The newly independent Federal Republic grew more confident in the nineteenth century and extended its territory as the western frontier was conquered and settled, Louisiana, Florida and Alaska were purchased and Texas, New Mexico and California were incorporated into the republic. In 1823 President Monroe laid down the US sphere of influence, in which European powers should cease to intervene showing that a new power was emerging on the international scene. The middle of the century saw antagonism growing between the agricultural southern states, which advocated free trade, and the protectionist industrialis-

Rockport, Massachusetts.

ing north, the antagonism aggravated by the question of slavery. The resulting civil war led to the north's victory and the abolition of slavery. The last 30 years of the century saw the country enjoy something of a golden age, with the economy growing to rival the European industrial powers.

In 1917 war was declared on Germany, but immediately after the war, the country returned to its isolationist, protectionist policy. Economic growth continued until the Wall Street Crash of 1929 set off an unprecedented social and economic crisis. Franklin D. Roosevelt introduced a New Deal Policy in an effort to combat the depression. Entering the Second World War in 1941 brought an end to isolationism, as with peace the United States' foreign policy became dominated by opposition to the expansion of the Soviet Union, and communism in general. The 1960s saw the rise of strong civil rights movements calling for an end to racial segregation, and then increasing protests against the war in Vietnam, where the USA had intervened in 1964. Under President Richard Nixon relations improved with China and the Soviet Union, and withdrawal from Vietnam occurred in 1973. The

Practical Information

LOCAL TIME: GMT - 5 (east coast),
GMT - 8 (west coast), GMT - 11 (Alaska).

BUOYAGE: IALA B

CURRENCY: US dollar (US$)

BUSINESS HOURS
Banks: 1000–1500 Monday to Friday.
Business: 0900–1200, 1300–1700 Monday
to Friday.
Shops: 0900–1800 Monday to Saturday.
Government offices: 0900–1200,
1300–1630 Monday to Friday.

ELECTRICITY: 110 V, 60 Hz

PUBLIC HOLIDAYS
1 January: New Year's Day
19 January: Martin Luther King's
Birthday
16 February: George Washington's
Birthday
Easter Weekend
25 May: Memorial Day
4 July: Independence Day
September: Labor Day
12 October: Columbus Day
12 November: Veterans Day
Last Thursday in November:
Thanksgiving Day
25 December: Christmas Day

COMMUNICATIONS
Dial 0 for operator, 411 for information.
Emergency: dial 911 for police and
emergencies.
There are flights to worldwide
destinations from most major cities.
Miami, New York and San Francisco
particularly have many international
connections.

DIPLOMATIC MISSIONS
In Washington DC:
Australia: 1601 Massachusetts Avenue
NW. ☎ (202) 797-3000.
Canada: 501 Pennsylvania Avenue NW.
☎ (202) 682-1740.
New Zealand: 37 Observatory Circle
NW. ☎ (202) 328-4800.
United Kingdom: 3100 Massachusetts
Avenue NW. ☎ (202) 462-1340.

1980s saw a return to an active foreign policy under President Ronald Reagan, and some recovery by the economy, but the trade deficit has remained a burden. In 1989 George Bush became President.

The United States is a vast country with many natural resources and a large agricultural production. It is also the original consumer society and imports much more than it exports, including raw materials, energy sources and finished goods. The service industries are where the majority of the population are employed. Major exports are machinery, chemicals, livestock and fertilisers, electronic equipment and computers.

The population numbers 244 million, the majority of whom are of European origin, mainly English, German, Irish and Italian. Ten per cent of the population is of African origin and there are also large minorities of Hispanics, Chinese and Japanese. There are very few of the Indians who originally populated the continent. The main language is English, but Spanish is increasingly spoken, especially in some areas, Florida, California and New York. A predominantly Christian country, the main denominations are Protestant and Roman Catholic. Washington DC is the federal capital, while each of the 50 states have their own state capitals.

Being such a large country, the climate varies considerably, from cold and temperate in the north to tropical and desert in the south. Hurricanes occur from June to November on both the Atlantic and Pacific coasts. The Gulf of Mexico and the South Eastern seaboard are particularly at risk, although hurricanes have reached up as far as New York on occasion. On the Pacific coast, however, it is rare that a tropical cyclone reaches as far as California. The weather in the Pacific Southwest is warm thoughout the year, most of the rainfall occurring during the winter months with summers being very dry. Winds are mostly westerly, except for the hot dry NE winds, the Santa Anas, that come down the mountains. The Pacific Northwest has colder and wetter weather and cruising is decidedly seasonal, from May to October, with high summer being the best time. Winds are NW or W and many days are foggy.

Entry Regulations

Ports of entry

Yachts arriving in the USA from a foreign port must call first at a customs port or designated place where customs service is available. Those in South Florida are listed below. In other areas if in doubt it is advisable to contact the US Coast Guard on VHF Channel 16 and ask for instructions.

Miami (Florida) Customs District: All yachts arriving in Southern Florida from a foreign port must call at one of 26 designated entry points and report their arrival to US Customs immediately by telephone. At each entry point a special telephone will automatically connect the caller with customs. After answering various questions about the vessel, its crew and itinerary, the captain will be told by a customs officer what to do next. US registered boats are usually told to proceed to their destination, but foreign yachts are normally inspected by customs. These 26 locations are in five areas within the district.

Fort Pierce Area: Harbortown Marina; Sailfish Marina, Stuart; Sebastian Inlet Marina, Sebastian.

Fort Lauderdale Area: Lauderdale Marina; Bahia Mar; Pier 66; Lighthouse Point Marina and Sands Harbor Marina, Pompano Beach; Delray Harbour Club Marina, Delray; Cove Marina, Deerfield Beach.

Key West Area: A & B Marina and Oceanside Marina, Key West; Ocean Reef Club, Key Largo; Tavernier Creek Marina, Tavernier; Boot Key Marina, Marathon (800) 432-1216; Holiday Isle Marina, Islamorada (800) 432-1216.

Miami Area: Matheson Hammock Marina (open sunrise to sunset only); Phillips 66 Marina, Causeway-Watson Island; Miamarina, Bayside (800) 432-1216; Crandon Park Marina, Virginia Key; Sunset Harbor Marina and Bakers Haulover Marina, Miami Beach.

West Palm Beach Area: Sailfish Marina, Palm Beach Shores; Jupiter Marina, Jupiter; Spencers Boatyard, West Palm Beach; Lake Worth Boating Center, Hypoloxo.

Some of these places, such as Pier 66 and Miamarina, allow yachts temporary free dockage while they are clearing.

Customs telephone numbers for other states: (* 24 hours)

Alabama: Mobil (205) 690-2111, (800) 432-1216*.

Alaska: Anchorage (907) 248-3373, (907) 243-4312, Juneau (907) 586-7211*, Ketchikan (907) 225-2254*, Sitka (907) 747-3374*, Skagway (907) 983-2325*, Valdez (907) 835-2355*, Wrangell (907) 225-2254*.

California: Los Angeles (213) 514-6013, (213) 514-6810, (213) 894-4723*, Port Hueneme (805) 488-8574*, San Diego (619) 293-5370, (619) 428-7209*, San Francisco (415) 556-2844, (415) 876-2812, San Luis Obispo (805) 595-2381*.

Connecticut: Bridgeport (203) 579-5606, (800) 343-2840*.

Florida: Ft Myers (813) 768-4318, (813) 228-2385 after 1700, Jacksonville (904) 291-2775*, Panama City (904) 785-4688, (904) 291-2775*, Pensacola (904) 432-6811, (904) 291-2775*, Pt Canaveral (407) 783-2066*, St Petersburg (813) 536-7311*, Tampa (813) 228-2385*.

Georgia: Brunswick (912) 267-2803, (912) 638-4294, (912) 264-4468, Savannah (912) 944-4452, (912) 232-7507, (912) 944-8018.

Illinois: Chicago (312) 686-2131/3.

Louisiana: New Orleans (504) 586-6804*.

Maine: Portland (207) 775-3131, (800) 343-2840*.

Massachusetts: Boston (617) 565-4657, (800) 343-2840*.

Michigan: Detroit (313) 226-3140, Muskegon (616) 722-2913, Port Huron (313) 985-9541, Sault Ste Marie (906) 632-2631.

Minnesota: Crane Lake (218) 933-2321, Duluth (218) 720-5203, Ely (218) 365-3262, Grand Portage (218) 475-2244, International Falls (218) 283-2541, Lake of the Woods (call Pembina, North Dakota).

Mississippi: Gulfport (601) 864-1274, (504) 589-3771*, Pascagoula (601) 762-7311, (504) 589-3771*.

Montana: Great Falls (406) 453-7631.

New Jersey: Newark (201) 645-3760, (800) 221-4265*, Perth Amboy (201) 442-0415, (800) 221-4265*. (If one arrives in New Jersey south of the Manasquan Inlet contact Customs in Philadelphia, Pennsylvania.)

New York: New York City (212) 466-3456, (800) 522-5270*, Albany (518) 472-3456, (800) 522-5270*, Buffalo (716) 846-5901, (716) 846-4311, Ogdensburg (315) 393-2840*.

North Carolina: Morehead City (919) 726-5845/ 3561/2034, Wilmington (919) 343-4616.

North Dakota: Pembina (701) 825-6201.

Ohio: Cleveland (216) 522-4258.

Oregon: Astoria (503) 325-5541, Coos Bay (503) 267-6312, Longview (206) 425-3710*, Newport (503) 265-7746, Portland (503) 221-2871*.

Pennsylvania: Philadelphia (215) 597-4605, (800) 343-2840*.

Maryland: Baltimore (301) 962-2666, (800) 343-2820*.

South Carolina: Charleston (803) 723-1272.

Texas: Brownsville (512) 542-4232*, Corpus Christi (512) 888-3352, (800) 392-3142*, (512) 888-7019 (0800–1700 Saturdays), Freeport (409) 233-3004, (800) 392-3142*, Galveston (409) 766-3624, (800) 392-3142*, Houston (713) 443-3883, (800) 392-3142*, Port Arthur (409) 727-0285, (800) 392-3142*, Port Lavaca (512) 987-2722, (800) 392-3142*.

Vermont: St Albans (802) 524-6527, (800) 343-2840*.

Virginia: Alexandria (703) 557-1950, (301) 953-7454, (202) 566-2321, Newport News (804) 245-6470, Norfolk (804) 441-6741*.

Washington: Aberdeen (206) 532-2030, (800) 562-5934*, Anacortes (206) 293-2331, (800) 562-5943*, Bellingham (206) 734-5463, (800) 562-5943*, Blaine (206) 332-6318, (800) 562-5943*, Everett (206) 259-0246, (800)

562-5934*, Friday/Roche Harbors (206) 378-2080, (800) 562-5943*, Neah Bay (206) 645-2312, (800) 562-5934*, (206) 645-2236, Olympia (206) 593-6338, (800) 562-5934*, Point Roberts (206) 945-2314, (800) 562-5943*, Port Angeles (206) 457-4311, (800) 562-5934*, Port Townsend (206) 385-3777, (800) 562-5934*, Seattle (206) 442-4678*, Tacoma (206) 593-6338, (800) 562-5934*, Vancouver (503) 221-2871*.
Wisconsin: Green Bay (414) 433-3923, Milwaukee (414) 291-3924, Racine (414) 633-0286.

Procedure on arrival

The US Coast Guard have the power to board any vessel within US territorial waters and they frequently do this, particularly off Florida. They can also board any US flag vessel anywhere in the world.

On arrival everyone must remain on board until clearance is completed, except for the captain going ashore to report the arrival of the yacht. After doing this he or she must return on board. Failure to follow the correct procedure on arrival can lead to a $5000 fine and seizure of the offending vessel.

US registered yachts: On arrival in the USA from a foreign port all US yachts must report their arrival to customs immediately, and also report any merchandise acquired abroad that is subject to duty. If an inspection is required, the customs officer will direct the yacht to an inspection area. Otherwise, US yachts are not obliged to make formal entry provided they are not engaged in trade or are violating any laws. Customs do not have to be notified when US boats leave for a foreign port, although as most countries require the last port clearance for their own entry procedure, it is advisable to obtain this before leaving the USA.

Foreign yachts: The captain must report the arrival of the yacht to customs immediately and clear within 48 hours. Documents needed include registration papers, a declaration of both ship's stores and crew's possessions, last port clearance, and a crew list. Clearance must be completed with customs, immigration, health and agriculture. Sometimes the customs officer performs some or all of these other duties. On departure from the USA, yachts must clear out with customs.

Certain countries are eligible for a cruising licence, which exempts them from having to clear in and out at any subsequent US port after entry has been made in the first port of entry. The licence is obtained from customs on arrival and is valid for up to one year. The countries to which this applies are Argentina, Australia, Austria, Bahamas, Belgium, Bermuda, Canada, Denmark, Germany, France, Greece, Honduras, Ireland, Jamaica, Liberia, Netherlands, New Zealand,

Norway, Sweden and the United Kingdom (including Turks and Caicos, St Vincent and the Grenadines, the Cayman Islands, British Virgin Islands, St Kitts and Nevis and Anguilla). This list is subject to change and it includes countries with which the USA has reciprocal arrangements.

Yachts from other countries must obtain a permit before proceeding to each subsequent US port.

Customs

Hunting and sporting firearms may be brought into the USA, provided they are taken out again on departure with any unspent ammunition. All other firearms and ammunitions are subject to restrictions and require an import permit from the Bureau of Alcohol, Tobacco and Firearms (ATF), US Treasury Dept, Washington DC 20520.

Returning US citizens do not require an import permit for firearms they have taken out of the country; however, this previous export must be proven by registering the firearms before departure with either customs or the ATF.

Cats and dogs must be free of diseases communicable to man. Vaccination against rabies is not required for cats and dogs arriving from rabies-free countries. Otherwise, dogs must have a valid rabies vaccination certificate.

Pet birds may be brought in, but will be subject to at least 30 days quarantine on arrival at the owner's expense in a Department of Agriculture facility. These facilities are only available in New York, Miami, San Ysidro, Honolulu, Hidalgo and Los Angeles, and bird owners must enter at one of these six ports of entry. The quarantine must be arranged in advance and the quarantine fee should be paid not later than on arrival.

Further details can be obtained from the US Department of Treasury, US Customs Service, Washington DC 20229, who publish special leaflets: *Importing a Pet Bird*, *Pets*, *Wildlife*.

A foreign visitor may import a pleasure boat into the USA free of duty if it is for his or her personal use. Duty must be paid within one year of the date of importation if the boat is sold or offered for sale or charter in the USA. Boats entered for alterations or repairs, as samples for taking orders or as professional equipment and tools of the trade, may be entered without payment of duty as temporary importation under bond. The length of stay is normally one year and cannot exceed three years.

Immigration

All nationalities require a visa obtained in advance, except Canadians, who require only proof of their citizenship.

Fees

Overtime is charged for customs inspection outside of the official hours 0800–1700 Monday to Saturday, except holidays. After hours an inspection service will be provided at pro rata overtime rates, not to exceed US$25 per boat. If more than one boat is cleared at the same time, the overtime charge is shared between them. For clearance on Sundays and holidays, 1/8 of the officer's daily pay is charged.

There are also fees for formal entry, permit to proceed and clearance.

There is an annual customs user fee of US$25.

Restrictions

It is prohibited to import many food and plant products and yachts are subject to an agricultural inspection on arrival, including those arriving in the US mainland from Hawaii, Puerto Rico and the US Virgin Islands. Meat and meat products, fresh produce and plants are among the items normally confiscated. Bakery products, cured cheeses and canned meat are generally admissible.

Also restricted is the import of any wildlife and fish which are considered an endangered species by the USA, or any of their products. This includes tortoise shell jewellery, leather, whalebone and ivory, coral, skins and furs.

Fishing licence

Licences are required for fishing by the states of Washington and Alaska. There are daily and annual catch limits described in the regulations for each area. Licences are available through most marine service outlets, fuel docks, sporting goods and hardware stores. The approximate cost is as follows:
Washington: non-resident annual licence US$18.
Alaska: non-resident annual licence US$36, non-resident 2 week licence US$20.

An Alaska Fish and Game Licence is required for fishing in National Parks such as Misty Fiords and Glacier Bay.

Pacific Northwest

The Vessel Traffic Service (VTS) on VHF Channel 14 provides a useful service in the Juan de Fuca Strait which is often fogbound and always very busy with traffic.

Visibility is often poor in the Pacific Northwest region, so radar and Loran are useful.

Facilities

Yachting facilities throughout the United States are of a high standard. There are marinas practically everywhere and the only objection visiting sailors might have are the high docking fees. Fortunately almost everywhere there is also a place to anchor at little or no cost and in some ports municipal marinas, docks or moorings are priced at a level affordable by those cruising on a restricted budget.

Provisioning everywhere in the USA is good, fuel is cheap and widely available and most ports have fuelling docks which often also have water. Marine equipment is available in most places, although the selection depends on how much local demand there is.

Repair facilities vary from place to place, being best in major yachting centres. There are too many to mention, but on the East Coast the most important centres where the whole range of repair facilities are available are the areas around the following cities: Miami, Fort Lauderdale, Beaufort/Morehead City, Baltimore, City Island (New York), Newport, Marblehead. On the West Coast: San Diego, Newport Beach, San Francisco, Seattle. In between these places there are countless smaller ports, where one can find boatyards, chandleries and all kinds of workshops.

Further Reading

The Department of the Treasury, US Customs Service, Washington DC 20229, publish leaflets on the various import restrictions, as well as details on import duty.
How to Cruise to Alaska without Rocking the Boat too Much
Northwest Boat Travel
Evergreen Cruising Atlas (Olympia to Skagway)
Cruising the Pacific Coast
Pacific Boating Almanac, Pacific Northwest & Alaska
Cruising Ports: California to Florida via Panama
The Intracoastal Waterway
A Cruising Guide to the New England Coast
A Cruising Guide to the Chesapeake
A Cruising Guide to the Florida Keys
A Cruising Guide to the Maine Coast
Embassy Complete Guide to Long Island
Embassy Complete Guide to Cape Cod and Rhode Island
Cruising Guide: Block Island to Nantucket
Cruising Guide: Long Island Sound

7 South America

The South American continent provides the extremes of cruising conditions, from the trade wind-cooled Caribbean islands of Venezuela to the spectacular wilderness of Tierra del Fuego and the Chilean fjords. The most popular cruising ground for foreign yachts is the Caribbean coast, while other parts of the continent are usually visited by cruising boats as a detour on their way to somewhere else.

Many cruising yachts visit Brazil on their way to the Caribbean, either from the Canaries, Cape Verdes or West Africa, or else on their way north from South Africa. A few yachts have navigated the mighty Amazon, but north-eastern Brazil is the most popular destination, with Carnival in Bahia the main attraction, a worthy substitute for the more famous one in Rio de Janeiro, which some yachts manage to include in their itinerary. Only a few venture further south than Rio, usually on their way to the Straits of Magellan, an area which is gaining in popularity as a cruising destination in its own right. For a return to warmer climes, a sail up the west coast of South America has the advantage of favourable wind and current, although there are few cruising opportunities north of Chile. The desert-like coast of Peru is bare and unappealing, while Ecuador's only attractive area is that surrounding Guayaquil.

Sailing is not a very popular pastime in South America and the largest local boating communities are found in major centres such as Rio de Janiero, Santos, Montevideo, Buenos Aires, Valparaiso, Callao and Guayaquil. This is also where most repair and other yachting facilities are concentrated. Unfortunately these do not coincide with the cruising areas popular with visiting yachts. For most South American destinations one should aim to carry all essential spares and be prepared to be quite self-sufficient. The one notable exception is Venezuela, whose popularity among cruising yachts sailing down from the Lesser Antilles has stimulated the development of marinas, boatyards and other facilities geared specifically for visiting yachts. Another attraction of this area is that it is very rarely affected by hurricanes, making it a good place to spend the summer season.

ARGENTINA

Argentina shares the southern tip of South America with Chile, the Andes mountains forming a natural border between the two countries. Argentine scenery varies from the high Andes and the oases in their foothills where the Spanish first settled, to the forests and plains of the north, the vast central pampas, and remote Patagonia in the south.

Not many cruising yachts brave the elements to visit Argentina, but those who do are attracted to the challenging wilderness of the Magellan Straits and Tierra del Fuego. Yachts coming from the north can get a taste of Argentina in Buenos Aires and the resorts in the Rio de la Plata estuary, where most yachting facilities are concentrated. There are only a few ports along Argentina's long coastline and there is little to see between the Rio de la Plata and the Straits of Magellan.

Country Profile

When the Incas tried to push south from the Andes, the Indians who already lived in the area prevented them expanding any further. The Indians were no more welcoming to the Spaniard Juan de Solis, who landed in present-day Argentina in 1516 and was killed by them. Magellan paid a brief visit in 1520, before his voyage to the Pacific through the straits that bear his name. Early settlement proved difficult due to Indian hostility, causing Buenos Aires, which was founded in 1535, to be abandoned for nearly fifty years. Expeditions were made into the country from Peru and Chile, and eventually towns were founded in the eastern foothills of the Andes.

From the mid-sixteenth century, Peru ruled over all Spanish possessions in South America, but Buenos Aires was not considered important and all trade went via Panama and the Caribbean. At the end of the eighteenth century the Viceroyalty of Rio de la Plata was formed and Argentine confidence grew after repulsing British attacks early in the nineteenth century. In 1816 independence from Spain was declared and José de San Martín led an Argentine army to free first Chile and then Peru. Despite conflict between the central government and the provinces, eventually federalism triumphed, and in the mid-nineteenth century a federal system was established, which still continues today.

The 1930s saw Argentina become one of the world's wealthiest countries, a prosperity based mainly on cattle, and trade made Buenos Aires one of the world's

Cartagena

Caracas

VENEZUELA

Georgetown

SURINAME

Paramaribo

FRENCH GUIANA

COLOMBIA

GUYANA

Cayenne

• Bogota

Buenaventura

St Peter and St Paul

Quito

ECUADOR

Manaus

Amazon River

Belém

Fernando de Noronha Island

Guayaquil •

PERU

BRAZIL

Recife

Callao • Lima

Brasilia

Salvador

Arica •

Rio de Janeiro

Santos

SOUTH PACIFIC OCEAN

CHILE

ARGENTINA

SOUTH ATLANTIC OCEAN

URUGUAY

Valparaiso • Santiago

Juan Fernándes Islands

Buenos Aires • Montevideo

Mar del Plata

Valdivia •

Map 11: South America

Punta Arenas

Ushuaia

Practical Information

LOCAL TIME: GMT - 3

BUOYAGE: IALA B

CURRENCY: Austral of 100 centavos

BUSINESS HOURS
Banks: 1000–1600 Monday to Friday.
Government offices: central area
0700–1300 Monday to Friday;
southern regions 1000–1700 Monday to
Friday.
Shops: 0900–1900 Monday to Friday,
midday Saturdays. Many close for siesta
and reopen around 1700.

ELECTRICITY: 220 V, 50 Hz

PUBLIC HOLIDAYS
1 January: New Year's Day
Holy Thursday, Good Friday
1 May: Labour Day
25 May: Anniversary of 1810 Revolution
10 June: Malvinas Day
20 June: Flag Day

9 July: Independence Day
17 August: Anniversary of José de San
Martín's death
12 October: Columbus Day
8 December: Immaculate Conception
25 December: Christmas Day
31 December: New Year's Eve

EVENTS
The days before Día de la Tradición,
10 November: music and gaucho
parades.
30 December: ticker tape parade in
Buenos Aires.

COMMUNICATIONS
ENTEL offices: international telephone
calls, cables, telex.
Post office: 0800–2000 Monday to Friday,
0800–1400 Saturday. 0800–2400 for
telegrams. Corner of Sarmiento and
Leandro Alem, Buenos Aires.
Poste Restante, State Railways Building,
Av. Maipu 4, Puerto Nuevo district
0800–2000.

Emergency: Police dial 101.
There are frequent international flights
from Buenos Aires. There are regular
flights from Buenos Aires to all major
cities in Argentina, including Ushuaia.

MEDICAL
British Hospital, Buenos Aires, Perdriel 74.
German Hospital Pueyrredon 1658
between Calle Berruti and Calle Juncal.

DIPLOMATIC MISSIONS
In Buenos Aires:
Australia: Avenida Santa Fe 846.
☎ (1) 312-6841.
France: Avenida Santa Fe 846 (Swissair
building).
New Zealand: Avenida Santa Fe 846.
☎ (1) 312-4207.
United States: Colombia 4300, near
Palermo Park. ☎ (1) 774-7611.
British Interests Section at Swiss
Embassy, Luis Agote 2412/52.
☎ (1) 112511. As relations are improving,
the British Embassy may reopen soon.

leading cities. It was largely an elite that enjoyed this affluence and popular discontent led to General Juan Perón becoming President in 1946, his popularity based on an alliance between the army and the working classes. During his rule, and aided by his flamboyant wife Evita, living conditions were improved for the lower classes. However, the military mounted a coup in 1955 and thereafter the country suffered political violence and economic decline. Various regimes succeeded one another, and Perón briefly returned as President. Finally, a military junta took power, establishing a repressive rule, during which thousands of people disappeared. Continuing economic problems and defeat in the Falklands war in the early 1980s brought pressure for democracy, and free elections were held in 1983 and 1989.

Argentina is a rich farming country, and 70 per cent of export earnings still come from agriculture and livestock, although the manufacturing sector is also developing. In the 1980s inflation was a major problem, and a new currency, the austral, was issued. The country has a large foreign debt, and inflation has not been contained.

The population numbers 32 million. In the Buenos Aires province people are mostly of European origin, while in other provinces they are mestizos, a mixture of Spanish and Indian. Few pure Indians are left, most

having been either absorbed or killed in wars with the early settlers. Spanish is the official language, although its pronunciation and some vocabulary are different to Castilian Spanish. English, French and Italian are also spoken. The majority are Roman Catholic. The capital is the sprawling city of Buenos Aires, lying on Rio de la Plata, into which flow the Parana and Uruguay rivers.

The Argentine climate ranges from subtropical in the north to cold temperate in Tierra del Fuego. The central zone is temperate, while Buenos Aires is hot and humid, the summer months December to February being the hottest. In Rio de la Plata the prevailing winds in summer are easterly, while SW winds are more common in winter. They are often accompanied by pamperos, violent SW squalls that affect most of Argentina's coastal waters.

Entry Regulations

Ports of entry
Buenos Aires 34°36′S 58°22′W, Mar del Plata 30°01′S 57°32′W, Puerto Madryn 42°46′S 65°03′W, Puerto Deseado 47°45′S 65°54′W, Santa Cruz 50°80′S 68°23′W, Rio Gallegos 51°36′S 68°58′W, Ushuaia 54°49′S 68°17′W.

Procedure on arrival

The ports of entry listed above are a selection only, as foreign yachts may use any Argentine port to clear in.

Yachts arriving from overseas must clear with the following authorities: naval authority (Prefectura Naval Argentina) where the ship's documents have to be presented, customs (aduanas) and immigration (migraciones).

Buenos Aires: The coastguard should be contacted on VHF Channel 16 for instructions on where to berth for clearance in the busy commercial harbour. After the compulsory quarantine inspection, the customs and immigration formalities are normally completed ashore.

Mar del Plata: Yachts are first cleared by a health officer, followed by customs and Prefectura Naval, whose offices are in town. When clearing out, the captain must again visit the Prefectura Naval office.

Ushuaia: As the Beagle Channel, south of Tierra del Fuego, is claimed by both Chile and Argentina, formalities there are rather complicated. Yachts are asked to either come to the coastguard dock or tie up alongside a patrol boat. Those who wish to go through the Beagle Channel must also clear in and out with the Chilean Navy at Puerto Williams, then at Ushuaia with the Argentine Prefectura Naval, before returning to Puerto Williams to clear again if continuing into Chilean waters. Those who need Chilean visas can obtain them at the Chilean consulate in Ushuaia, situated on the corner of Calle Maipu and Kuanip.

Customs

Firearms must be declared to customs.

Animals must be inspected on arrival by a veterinary health officer and must have rabies vaccination certificates.

Foreign flagged yachts are allowed to be temporarily imported for a maximum period of six months. This can be extended by leaving Argentina for a short period, such as to Uruguay or Chile.

Immigration

Neighbouring South American countries need only identity cards not passports.

No visas are required for nationals of West European countries (except Portugal), Japan, as well as most Western Hemisphere countries, except Cuba. A three-month stay is allowed, which can be extended for another month by immigration.

Nationals of the following countries must obtain a visa before arrival: Australia, Cyprus, Guyana, Iceland, Israel, Jamaica, Morocco, New Zealand, Nicaragua, Panama, South Africa, South Korea, Trinidad and Tobago, Turkey, Venezuela.

One's passport should be carried at all times if travelling inland.

Health

Malaria prophylaxis is recommended, although there is no risk in some areas. Polio and measles vaccinations are recommended.

Fees

Overtime is not charged, except by immigration if called outside of office hours. There are port fees in commercial harbours.

Restrictions

The naval bases of Mar del Plata and Puerto Belgrano (38°54′S 62°06′W) are prohibited areas.

Fishing is only permitted if in possession of a valid permit. The open season for fishing is November to February or March.

Facilities

Most yachting facilities are concentrated around Buenos Aires, where there are several resorts with yacht clubs in the Rio de la Plata estuary, such as San Isidro and Rosario. A yacht club with good facilities is at San Fernando, 20 miles upriver from the capital, where there is a boatyard offering a range of services. Another helpful yacht club is the Club Nautico Mar del Plata, reached through a narrow passage controlled by a swing bridge, on the north side of the main harbour. Visitors can used the club facilities on payment of a daily fee. Some marine supplies are available as well as repair facilities. Fuel is obtainable from the fishing dock in the main harbour. Only basic facilities are available at Puerto Madryn and Puerto Deseado.

Provisioning outside of the Buenos Aires area is adequate and for yachts heading south a good place to reprovision is at Río Gallegos, capital of Santa Cruz province, which is also a convenient place to clear in or out of Argentina.

There is good provisioning, fuel, banks as well as LPG in Ushuaia in Tierra del Fuego, the southernmost town in Argentina. There are some repair facilities, but, generally, visitors are not welcome in the yacht club.

Further Reading

South American Handbook
South America on a Shoestring

BRAZIL

Brazil covers nearly half the area of South America and shares borders with all of the countries except Chile and Ecuador. This vast and varied country is a land of plateaux and plains, huge rivers, rain forests and desert. Much of the interior is still unexplored, although the days of undiscovered Brazil are numbered and the rain forests of the Amazon are threatened with destruction. This unique world of incredible flora and fauna where aboriginal tribes still live a life that has not known change for thousands of years is now on the threshold of extinction.

Brazilian culture is a rich mixture of European, African and Latin American, all of which can be seen in its world-famous Carnival. It is this Carnival which brings many sailors to Brazil, those who arrive from the north sailing for Salvador in Bahia, while those coming from the south have the opportunity to see the greatest show of them all in Rio de Janeiro. In between these two cities, to the north as well as to the south, stretches a long coastline of varied scenery and just as varied climate and weather conditions. There are interesting places to explore all along the coast, but perhaps the best cruising ground is the area between São Sebastião Island and Rio de Janeiro, which has many protected anchorages and attractive scenery, slightly marred by the increasing number of oil rigs. The River Amazon also has an appeal for some cruising sailors and it can be navigated for well over one thousand miles giving the opportunity to see some of the interior of this huge country. For many sailors the first taste of Brazil lies 250 miles offshore on the island of Fernando de Noronha, while another Brazilian outpost in the Atlantic is better avoided, the St Peter and St Paul rocks near the equator, where landing is only possible in the calmest of weathers.

Country Profile

Brazil's first contact with Europe was in 1500 when the Portuguese Pedro Alvares Cabral made landfall, thinking at first it was India. He called it the island of Santa Cruz, not guessing that it was part of the same continent discovered by Columbus further north. Later the country got its present name from the hardwood 'brazil' found in its forests. Portugal developed trading posts along the coast as well as establishing sugar and spice plantations. Efforts to enslave the local inhabitants failed – they either died or fled – and West Africans were brought over to work on the plantations instead. By the seventeenth century Brazil was the largest sugar producer in the world. Then gold

and diamonds were discovered, and a flood of people arrived moving inland to the mines. Gradually settlements were developed further afield and the frontiers expanded.

When Napoleon occupied Portugal, the Portuguese Royal Family fled to Brazil. After Napoleon's defeat, the King's son Dom Pedro I remained in Brazil and became Emperor on the proclamation of Brazil's independence from Portugal in 1822. Despite wars with Argentina and Uruguay, coffee and rubber exports helped prosperity slowly grow. Following an army coup in 1889, a republic was proclaimed.

Brazil's twentieth-century history has been troubled by economic crises, military coups and dictatorships. Being on the side of the Allies in the Second World War favoured the economy. Reformist governments ruled from 1956, despite pressure from the powerful multinational companies, until a military coup in 1964 established a military regime. During the 1980s Brazil moved slowly towards democracy and free elections, but her economic and financial problems remain considerable. The question of land has yet to be resolved, as most is concentrated in the hands of a few landowners and the majority of the peasants are landless. Unemployment and inflation are high. The country has extremes of poverty and riches, while a large foreign debt adds to the burden. Brazil's main exports are coffee, cocoa and sugar. Industry is slowly developing and there are rich mineral deposits of iron, bauxite and manganese.

Brazil's 138.5 million inhabitants are mainly a mixture of Portuguese, African and native Indian, also Dutch and French in the north-east. Nineteenth century immigration from Germany, Italy, Poland and Japan added to the mix. The indigenous Indian tribes of the interior number over 170 cultural groups and speak as many languages. Portuguese is the official language, although it is slightly different to that spoken in Portugal. Catholicism is the religion of the majority of the population, although there are also Indian and African beliefs, and the Candomblé, Macumba and Xango cults. The capital of the federal republic is Brasilia.

Brazil's climate varies greatly. Most of the northern part of the Brazilian coast is under the influence of NE winds which are strongest in the summer between December and February. The rest is in the SE trade wind belt, which predominates from March to August. During the austral winter months the SE trades have a lot of south in them, and sailing down the coast can be difficult. An eye must be kept on the weather, as the winds can change direction suddenly putting a boat on to a dangerous lee shore.

Practical Information

LOCAL TIME: GMT - 3. Summer time GMT - 2, but times of change vary. Fernando de Noronha GMT - 2.

BUOYAGE: IALA B

CURRENCY: Cruzado novo (NCz$). Introduced in 1986 as an anti-inflationary measure, it replaced the cruzeiro (1000 to 1).

BUSINESS HOURS
Banks: 1000–1630 Monday to Friday.
Business: 0900–1800 Monday to Friday. The lunch break is normally between 1200 and 1500.
Shops: 0900–1830/1900 Monday to Friday, 0900–1300 Saturday. Government offices: 0800–1200/1400–1800 or 0800–1700 Monday to Friday.

ELECTRICITY: 220 V, 50 Hz

PUBLIC HOLIDAYS
1 January: New Year's Day
6 January: Epiphany
February Carnival (Mardi Gras)
Good Friday, Easter Monday
21 April: Tiradentes Day
1 May: Labour Day
Corpus Christi
Ascension

7 September: Independence Day
12 October: Our Lady of Aparecida Day
1 November: All Saints' Day
2 November: All Souls' Day
15 November: Proclamation of the Republic
19 November: Flag Day
25 December: Christmas Day

EVENTS
Carnival starts on Friday night, four days before Ash Wednesday, and is celebrated throughout the following days and much of the nights as well. Although Rio Carnival is the most famous, it is celebrated all over Brazil.

COMMUNICATIONS
International operator 000111.
International calls can be made from state telephone company offices, hotels and post offices.
There is a 40 per cent tax on international communications.
Post office (Correios), open 0800–1800 Monday to Friday, 0800–1200 Saturday.
There are frequent international flights from Rio de Janeiro, São Paolo and Salvador, also a wide network of internal flights.

POLTUR
This is a special police unit set up to assist foreign visitors. In Rio de Janiero

the office is at: Avenida Humberto de Campos 315, Leblon. It is open 24 hours.

MEDICAL
Rio Health Collective, Ave das Americas 4430, Sala 303, Barra da Tijuca, 0900–1400, has English-speaking doctors.
The public health system is poor. Private treatment is expensive, so medical insurance is recommended.

DIPLOMATIC MISSIONS
Australia: Casa 1, Conjunction 16, SH15 Q19 Brasilia. ☎ (61) 248-6669.
New Zealand: Rua Hungria 888–6°, São Paulo. ☎ (11) 212-2288.

In Rio de Janiero:
Canada: 35 rua Dom Gerardo. ☎ (21) 233-9286.
France: Av. Presidente Antonio Carlos 58. ☎ (21) 220-4529.
United States: Av. President Wilson 147. ☎(21) 292-7117.
United Kingdom: Praia do Flamengo 284. ☎(21) 552-1422.

In Salvador:
United Kingdom: Av. Estados Unidos, 1109. ☎ (71) 242-1266.
United States: Avenida Presidente Vargas, 1892. ☎ (71) 245-6691.

Entry Regulations

Ports of entry
Manaus (Amazonas state) 3°09′S 60°01′W, Belém (Pará) 1°27′S 48°30′W, Macapá (Amapá) 1°18′S 51°01′W, São Luis (Maranhão) 2°30′S 44°18′, Fortaleza/Mucuripe (Ceara) 3°41′S 38°29′W, Natal (Rio Grande do Norte) 5°47′S 35°11′W, Recife (Pernambuco) 8°04′S 34°52′W, Maceió (Alagoas), 9°40′S 35°44′W, Salvador (Bahia) 12°58′S 38°30′W, Ilheus/Malhado (Bahia) 14°47′S 39°02′W, Vitoria (Espirito Santo) 20°18′S 40°20′W, Rio de Janeiro 22°55′S 43°12′W, Angra dos Reis (Rio de Janeiro) 23°01′S 44°19′W, Itacuruça 22°55′S 43°50′W, Macaé 22°23′S 41°46′W, São Sebastião (São Paulo) 23°48′S 45°23′W, Santos (São Paulo) 23°56′S 46°20′W, Paranaguá (Paraná) 25°30′S 48°31′W, São Francisco do Sul (Santa Catarina) 26°14′S 48°38′W, Florianópolis Island (Santa Catarina), Rio Grande (Rio Grande do Sul) 32°10′S 52°05′W.

Procedure on arrival
Formalities can be very time-consuming everywhere, although officials are generally polite and helpful. Normally yachts are not boarded and the captain has to go into town to find the various offices. The port captain should be visited first (the Brazilian Port Authority is called PORTOBRAS, Empresas Portos do Brasil). After that, one must go to customs and the Federal Police, who deal with immigration. The order of visits is important, as certain forms have to be taken from one office to another. A cruising permit (passe de saida) will be issued at the port of entry by the port captain.
Some yachts have reported having to use a special officially approved agent (despachante), whom one is

introduced to on arrival. The agent takes passports and ship's papers and does the entry formalities for a fee. This usually only applies to the first entry into the country and also depends on local officials.

After having completed the initial clearance at a port of entry, one has to obtain clearance to the next port, although one is allowed to cruise and stop on the way. One should request clearance to the next port 'with stops' (con escala). At every major port en route one has to visit the port authority and Federal Police offices. This is particularly important when one enters a new state. This clearance is strictly enforced, and failure to do so can lead to on the spot fines of up to US$5000.

Rio de Janiero: All clearance formalities must be undertaken in the commercial harbour of Rio de Janeiro, which is not recommended to be entered by yacht, as it is much more convenient to stay in one of the marinas and go to the necessary offices by public transport.

Santos: To clear in, one has to visit various offices in the commercial harbour, but it is better to leave the boat at the Yate Clube de Santos on Ilha de Santo Amaro.

Cabedelo: There is a marina close to Joao Pessoa, capital of Paraíba state. The police visit the marina every day and one can drive with them to check in at Cabedelo where there is also a customs office. The port captain's office must then be visited in Joao Pessoa.

Fernando de Noronha: Although not an official port of entry into Brazil, visiting yachts are allowed to spend a limited time on the island, usually five days. The first day is free, after which a charge is made according to the number of persons on board and the duration of the stay. Arriving yachts must clear with the port captain's office and the Guarda Territorial. Yachts can anchor at Bahia Antonio, from where a bus runs to the main settlement.

Customs

Firearms are retained by customs, until authorisation for their possession is given by the military authorities. The firearms should then be registered with the police.

Animals need a health certificate. Rabies vaccination is available upon arrival.

After six months the yacht must leave the country or it becomes liable to import tax of about 100 per cent of value.

Immigration

Passports must be valid six months from arrival date. A three-month permit is issued initially, renewable on request for another three months from the Federal Police on payment of a fee. Visas are not required by nationals of EC countries (except France), Andorra, Argentina, Austria, Bahamas, Barbados, Chile, Colombia, Ecuador, Finland, Iceland, Liechtenstein, Mexico, Monaco, Morocco, Norway, Paraguay, Peru, Philippines, San Marino, Suriname, Sweden, Switzerland, Trinidad and Tobago and Uruguay.

All other nationalities, including Australian, New Zealand, US and Canadian citizens, need to obtain a visa before arrival, otherwise they risk a fine or deportation.

Health

Yellow fever vaccination certificates are required by those who have been within the last three months in Africa, Bolivia, Colombia or Peru. The certificate must not be more than 10 years old. Those who arrive either without a certificate or who have not been vaccinated will have to be vaccinated in Brazil, which is not always done under the most hygienic conditions.

In rural areas especially, there is the risk of malaria, dengue fever, typhoid, hepatitis and yellow fever, so vaccination or prophylactic treatment is recommended.

Fees

Overtime is charged for clearance outside of office hours on weekdays, and all day on weekends. There are harbour fees and light dues.

Facilities

Provisioning is better in larger cities, although imported goods are both expensive and difficult to come by. There are strict price controls in an effort to curb inflation. This has led to shortages of essential goods and even rationing. Fresh produce is plentiful in most places. Fuel and water are normally available alongside at fishing docks. Diesel fuel is sometimes diluted with petrol (gasolene), but this is marked on the pump. Also petrol (gasolene) is often diluted with alcohol. Propane is available from Supergasbras depots. For cruising in local waters it is best to buy Brazilian Navy charts, which are available in Rio and Bahia. Charts for the Amazon river are available in Belém.

Yacht clubs are usually welcoming to foreign visitors, with the exception of the Rio Yacht Club, where visitors are not at all welcome. Clubs with a large fleet of yachts, often motor yachts, have good repair facilities or access to them.

There are several anchorages and marinas in Rio de Janeiro, one of the most conveniently situated being

Marina Gloria close to Rio's smaller airport. The marina is very crowded with local boats, but space is usually found for visitors. There are repair facilities available as well as a chandlery. Practically everything is available in Rio, but it can take time finding it.

Angra dos Reis, close to Rio, has a huge shipyard which also undertakes work on yachts. The repair facilities are excellent. The yard has a social club, shops and banks in the complex. There is a also a good marina at Bracuhy, 23 miles from Angra.

The yacht club at Niterói welcomes visitors. There are good repair facilities, chandlery and fuel on the club dock.

Santos is close to São Paolo and has a large club, Yate Clube de Santos, on Ilha de Santo Amaro, the base of a large fleet of power boats. As a result, repair facilities are very good with all kinds of workshops and a good chandlery.

Salvador, the capital of Bahia, is a first port of call for many yachts arriving in Brazil. There is a well-stocked market and adequate repair facilities. Near Cabedelo there is a boatyard with a slipway at Praia de Jacaré with moorings for yachts. Everything is available locally – fuel, gas, charts, as well as good repair and haul-out facilities. It is also reputed to be a safe place to leave the yacht while visiting the interior.

Natal is a pleasant port on the NE tip of Brazil with a good yacht club and a range of repair facilities. It is a good place to leave from for the Caribbean.

Belém is a large city 80 miles inland on the south bank of the Para river. The yacht club gives temporary membership. All services and supplies are available.

On the island of Fernando de Noronha only basic provisions can be obtained as well as water from the fisherman's building on the dockside. Diesel can be bought from the fuel station a short distance inland.

Further Reading

South American Handbook
Fodor's Brazil
South America on a Shoestring

CHILE

Chile is a 2600 mile long strip of land between the Andes and the Pacific Ocean, with an average width of rarely more than 100 miles. The northern area is mostly desert, and forms the frontier with Peru, while the crests of the Andes make up the eastern frontier. Around the capital Santiago is a fertile heartland, where most of the population live. To the south are lakes, rivers and forests, down to the southern tip of South America where lies the notorious Cape Horn, the island of Tierra del Fuego, which Chile shares with Argentina, and the Magellan Straits.

An increasing number of cruising yachts are attracted to the islands and channels in the southern part of Chile, a spectacular area with magnificent fjords and imposing glaciers. The major drawback of this beautiful cruising ground, apart from its remoteness, is the weather, which is rarely pleasant. The best time for exploring this part of the world is at the height of the southern summer, from December to March, when the weather is both drier and more settled than at other times. The rest of Chile is rarely visited by foreign yachts, except those on their way to or from the southern fjordland. Chile's offshore possessions in the Pacific, Easter Island and the Juan Fernandez Islands are dealt with separately.

Country Profile

Remains of a pre-Inca civilisation have been found in the north of Chile. When the Incas expanded their empire from their base high in the Andes, they only reached as far as the centre of present-day Chile, their advance being fiercely resisted by the Araucanian tribes. In 1520 Magellan sailed through the Straits on his voyage that was to prove to all doubters that the earth was round. Tierra del Fuego was named 'Land of Fire' by his sailors who spotted the numerous Indian cooking fires glowing on the shores. Fifteen years later a Spanish expedition from Peru searched unsuccessfully for silver and gold. Don Pedro de Valdivia led a later expedition and founded Santiago, but on pushing further south, he was killed by the Araucanians. The Indians continued to resist Spanish encroachment for three centuries.

Under the rule of the Viceroyalty of Peru, a farming colony developed, although often raided by English and French pirates. In 1810 a revolt was led against Spanish rule and an independent republic was formed in 1818. The first Chilean constitution was drafted in 1833, although internal conflict continued to trouble the newly independent state. Chile's victory in the War of the Pacific (1879–83) fought with Peru and Bolivia over the northern desert area which was rich in nitrates, brought only some Chileans considerable wealth. In the early twentieth century the decline of the nitrate trade contributed to an economic crisis, which coupled with continuing social inequalities, led in the 1920s to the rise of powerful socialist and communist parties. Government reforms had little success in stabilising

Practical Information

LOCAL TIME: GMT - 4. Summer time
GMT - 3 October to March.

BUOYAGE: IALA B

CURRENCY: Peso ($)

BUSINESS HOURS
Banks: 0900–1400 Monday to Friday.
Business: 0830–1230, 1400–1800 Monday
to Friday.
Shops: 1030–1930, Monday to Friday,
0930–1330 Saturday (Santiago).
Government offices: 0800–1300,
1500–1800 Monday to Friday.

ELECTRICITY: 220 V, 50 Hz

PUBLIC HOLIDAYS
1 January: New Year's Day
Holy Week (two days)
1 May: Labour Day

21 May: Navy Day
15 August: Assumption
18 September: Independence Day
19 September: Army Day
12 October: Discovery of America
1 November: All Saints' Day
8 December: Immaculate Conception
25 December: Christmas Day

COMMUNICATIONS
International phone calls and telegraph
from ENTEL, Transradio Chilena, and
Compania Internacional de Radio.
Post offices open 0900–1630 Monday to
Friday.
There are regular flights from Santiago
international airport to European and
American capitals. Lan-Chile and
Ladeco Air operate domestic flights to
the main cities and also to Easter Island.
There are airports near the ports of
Iquique, Puerto Montt and Valdivia.

DIPLOMATIC MISSIONS
In Santiago:
Australia: Gertudis Echenique 420,
Las Condes. ☎ (2) 228-5065.
Argentina: Vicuña Makenna 41.
Canada: Avenida Humada 11, Casilla
427. ☎ (2) 696-2256.
New Zealand: Avenida Isidora
Geyenechea 3516, Las Condes.
☎ (2) 231-4204.
United Kingdom: Avenida Concepción
177, Providencia 1800. ☎ (2) 223-9166.
United States: Codina Building,
Agustinas 1343. ☎ (2) 710326.

In Punta Arenas:
Argentina: Consulate at Avenida 21 de
Mayo 1278 (open 1000–1400). It is
possible to obtain a visa for Argentina
here in 24 hours.

the country, and in 1970 a Marxist coalition came to office under Salvador Allende, rapidly polarising the country between right and left. A military coup three years later saw Allende killed and a military junta led by General Pinochet take power, which at the price of severe repression brought some recovery to the economy. In more recent years gradual moves towards democracy have been made and following free elections in 1989 a civilian government was re-established.

Chile remains a leading producer of nitrates and the by-product iodine, as well as other mineral resources. Forestry products are the second largest export. Agriculture, including viniculture, is important, mainly concentrated in the fertile central region.

The population of over 12.5 million are either of European origin or mestizo, a mixture of Spanish and Indian. In some of the rural and mountain areas, there are still a large number of Mapuche, the original inhabitants of this land. The urban areas are populated mainly by descendants of immigrants who came during the nineteenth century. Spanish is the main language and Roman Catholicism the religion of the majority.

October to April are the warmer summer months, while May to October is colder. The Chilean climate varies considerably according to latitude, being dry and hot in the north, wet and windy in the south. The coastal areas are cooled by the cold Humboldt current. In the south, the most settled weather is between December and March, which is dominated by westerly winds. In this area, northerly winds usually bring rain and poor visibility, while southerlies are accompanied by clear skies.

Entry Regulations

Ports of entry
Arica 18°29'S 70°26'W, Iquique 20°12'S 70°10'W, Mejillones 23°06'S 70°28'W, Antofagasta 23°38'S 70°26'W, Valparaiso 33°01'S 71°38'W, Valdivia 39°48'S 73°14'W, Puerto Montt 41°28'S 72°57'W, Castro 42°29'S 73°46'W, Puerto Natales 51°43'S 72°31'W, Punta Arenas 53°10'S 70°54'W, Puerto Williams 55°56'S 67°37'W.

Procedure on arrival
Yachts should first clear with the Navy (Armada de Chile), then immigration police (investigaciones), then customs (aduana).
Valdivia: After entering the Rio Valdivia at Corral, the town of Valdivia, where formalities are completed, lies about 11 miles up the river.
Puerto Williams: Yachts entering the Beagle Channel area should contact the Chilean Navy on VHF Channel 16. Puerto Williams is a naval base, but yachts are welcomed there. One can moor in the western part of the harbour by the old navy gun boat which houses

the Chilean Navy Boat Club. The officials board the yacht for clearance. If wishing to sail the Beagle Channel, it is necessary to clear at Puerto Williams, then at Ushuaia to complete Argentinian formalities, then return again to Puerto Williams.

Customs
Firearms must be declared.

There are no restrictions on animals.

Foreign yachts should obtain a customs exemption certificate on arrival. This is valid for a limited time only and must be renewed before its expiry date.

Yachts are normally allowed to stay up to six months but up to two years is possible.

Immigration
Nationals of most West European countries, Australia, Canada, New Zealand and the USA, plus any countries that have diplomatic relations with Chile, do not require visas for short stays. Visas are required by nationals of France, Mexico and African and East European countries. Visitors are normally given a 90-day visa, which can be renewed for another 90 days. As visa requirements may be changed by the new government, it is advisable to check with a Chilean embassy or consulate before arrival.

Cruising permit
A cruising permit is issued to visiting yachts when clearing into Chile. The permit must be presented to officials at every port of call and is usually retained by the port captain until departure. A detailed itinerary must be submitted. Yachts cruising the southern archipelago have found the officials in Castro to be the most cooperative, not insisting on a precise cruising plan and issuing an open permit valid for two or three months provided a designated port was visited at the end of the proposed itinerary.

Restrictions
Some parts of the Patagonian channels are prohibited to yachts.

Facilities

There are good repair facilities and various workshops in the port area of Valparaiso, which is the port serving Santiago. There is also excellent provisioning in town.

There are several good supermarkets in Valdivia, which also has the usual range of workshops. A good boatyard and sail loft operated by Alwoplast, upriver from Valdivia, provide a good range of repair services including metalwork, carpentry, fibreglass, rigging as well as haul-out. Yachts may also be left there while touring the interior.

Fuel is available in several places along the coast, but as there are no pumps on the dock, it has to be carried in jerrycans. In the smaller southern ports, fuel is available at Puerto Montt, Castro, Quellan, Chacabuco, Calbuco and Ralun.

Provisioning is variable depending on the size of town, but some supplies can be bought in Puerto Montt and Castro. In smaller ports supplies are limited and expensive. There are fresh produce markets with good quality and reasonably priced produce in Valdivia, Puerto Montt and Castro. Even in remoter areas, fresh fruit and vegetables can normally be bought from local farmers, depending on the season. Fishing is excellent everywhere.

In spite of its remoteness, provisioning is surprisingly good at Puerto Williams, where there is a bank, post office, supermarket and fuel which can be delivered by tanker to the dock. Visitors are welcome at the local yacht club, located in a grounded gun boat. If cruising the southern channels, one must carry all essential supplies and spares, as these are almost impossible to obtain south of Valdivia.

Charts can be obtained from the Chilean Hydrographic Office, which also produces an atlas comprising all necessary charts reduced in size. Also useful for the southern area are a set of the Chilean tide and current tables.

Further Reading

South American Handbook
Second Chance, Voyage to Patagonia
South America on a Shoestring

COLOMBIA

Colombia has a coastline on both the Pacific Ocean and the Caribbean Sea. The country is sparsely populated, the majority living on the Caribbean lowlands or in mountain valleys. The eastern part is very remote, linked only by air and river to the rest of the country. The Pacific coast from Ecuador to Buenaventura is a marshy lowland with few settlements and most of the coastal development is on the Caribbean side, which has the large towns of Cartagena, Barranquilla and Santa Marta.

The scenery along the Caribbean coast offers more contrast than any of Colombia's neighbours. From the

Practical Information

LOCAL TIME: GMT - 5

BUOYAGE: IALA B

CURRENCY: Peso ($) of 100 centavos. A maximum of 500 pesos can be exported or imported. One may not be able to reconvert pesos on departure. Travellers' cheques are difficult to change, as reportedly there are many forged American Express travellers' cheques in circulation. It is also difficult to change pounds sterling and US dollars are preferred, particularly smaller notes such as US$20 bills.

BUSINESS HOURS
Banks: 0800–1130, 1400–1600 Monday to Friday, some open until 1630 Fridays, except last Friday of the month when they shut at 1130. Some open 0800–1100 Saturday.
Shops: 0900–1230, 1430–1830 Monday to Saturday.
Business: 0800–1200, 1400–1530/1800 Monday to Friday.
Government offices: 0800–1200, 1400–1800 Monday to Friday.

ELECTRICITY: 120 V, 60 Hz

PUBLIC HOLIDAYS
1 January: New Year's Day
*6 January: Epiphany
*19 March: St Joseph
Maundy Thursday, Good Friday
1 May
*Ascension
*Corpus Christi
*Sacred Heart
*29 June: St Peter and St Paul
20 June: Independence Day
7 August: Battle of Bogotá
*15 August: Assumption
*12 October: Discovery Day
*1 November: All Saints' Day
*11 November: (week of celebration) Independence of Cartagena
8 December: Immaculate Conception
25 December: Christmas Day
*When not falling on a Monday, these are observed the following Monday.

COMMUNICATIONS
Empresa Nacional de Telecomunicaciones: offices in all main cities for international calls.

Collect calls can only be made from private phones.
Surface mail is unreliable.
There are international flights from Bogotá and many internal flights between major cities.

MEDICAL
Emergency treatment in hospitals is free.

DIPLOMATIC MISSIONS
In Bogotá:
Canada: Calle 76, No. 11–52.
☎ (1) 217-5555.
New Zealand: Carrera 5, No. 81–26.
☎ (1) 249-5524.
United Kingdom: Torre Propaganda Sancho, Calle 98, No 9–03.
☎ (1) 218-5111.
United States: Calle 38, 8–61,
☎ (1) 285-1300.

In Cartagena:
Canada: Calle de la Inquisicion No. 33–08, ☎ (59) 648-250.

In Barranquilla:
United States: Calle 77 Carrera 68, Centro Comercial Mayorista.
☎ (5) 457-088.

sand dunes and desert of the Guajira peninsula to the dense forests of Darien, the coast shows an ever-changing face. Not far inland tower the majestic peaks of the Sierra Nevada de Santa Maria crowned by the snow-capped Mount Cristóbal Colón, 18,900 ft (5762 m), which can be seen from far offshore. The contrasts of nature are not the only attractions of this part of the Spanish Main as ashore one is forever reminded of the country's tumultuous past. The forts of Nueva Andalusia and the walled citadel of Cartagena bear witness to the rise and fall of the Spanish Empire.

In spite of persistent reports about the danger of cruising in Colombian waters, mainly because of the risk of being intercepted on the high seas by a drug-running vessel, Colombia has some very attractive cruising grounds. A beautiful landfall is the historic city of Cartagena, whose picturesque harbour is one of the most attractive ports in the New World. There are undoubtedly many rewards for those who cruise Colombia, but caution is certainly called for and it might be safer to cruise in company when in doubtful areas.

Country Profile

Long before Europeans arrived, Caribs lived along the northern coast, while the interior was inhabited by hunters, nomadic tribes, and the Chibchas, skilled goldsmiths who rolled their chief in gold dust every year. The other cultures of the pre-Colombian era also produced amazing goldwork. In 1500 the Spaniards sailed along the northern coast to Panama, and soon afterwards founded the settlements of Santa Marta and Cartagena. Spanish explorers pushed into the interior and Santa Fe de Bogotá was founded in 1538. The initial period of settlement saw strife between rival conquistadors, although some unity was gained in the mid-sixteenth century when the kingdom of Nueva Granada was established. In the eighteenth century this was replaced by a Viceroyalty at Bogotá, independent of the Peruvian Viceroyalty.

Influenced by the French Revolution, an independence movement developed and at the start of the nineteenth century revolts against the Spanish colonial power occurred. When the Spanish government tried to reconquer Venezuela and Nueva Granada, Simón

Bolívar raised an army, crossed the Andes and occupied Bogotá. In 1819 the Republic of Gran Colombia was declared, which included today's republics of Colombia, Venezuela and Ecuador, but the latter two soon broke away leaving Nueva Granada alone, to be named Colombia later in the century.

The newly independent country was divided between Conservatives and Liberals, and civil wars and revolts continued throughout the nineteenth century. In 1885 a centralised constitution was imposed by the Conservatives, and this is still in use today. At the turn of the century there was another civil war and eventually the Liberals were defeated. Relative peace followed until 1948 when civil war broke out once again. It was ended in 1957 by a political truce, the two parties agreeing to divide power equally by means of alternative governments until 1978. In recent years, guerilla groups have been active in the country, especially after the Liberals' victory in the 1986 elections and considerable violence occurred during both 1988 and 1989. The war against the drug barons of Medellin are another violent problem for the government, which is determined to stamp out the production of cocaine.

Agriculture is the most important sector of the economy and coffee Colombia's main export along with some consumer goods. The 1980s saw a growth in mining, especially oil and coal, and also in precious metals, such as emeralds.

The population is over 29 million, a mixture of European, Indian and African origins. Spanish is the main language, and most are Roman Catholic. Bogotá, at 8690 ft (2650 m), is the capital.

The climate varies according to altitude, the coast being tropical, hot and humid. The NE trade winds cool the coast during the winter months, while the summer has much lighter winds. Hurricanes rarely reach as far south as Colombia.

Entry Regulations

Ports of entry
San Andrés 12°33'N 81°41'W, Cartagena 10°25'N 75°32'W, Barranquilla 10°58'N 74°46'W, Buenaventura 3°54'N 77°05'W. Yachts have also been able to clear in at the following ports: Riohacha 11°33'N 72°55'W, Santa Marta 11°15'N 74°13'W.

Procedure on arrival
Yachts must clear in and out between major ports, and will be given an outward clearance (*zarpe*) for the next port. Visiting yachts must clear in with the port captain in each port. Customs and immigration formalities are completed only in the first and last ports.

Yachts clearing in or out of Colombia must use an approved agent to complete the formalities for customs, immigration, port captain and health. On departure, the agent will take the papers and return them with a *zarpe*.

Barranquilla: Arriving yachts should dock wherever possible, then ask for a berthing assignment from the port captain. The yacht clubs have limited space, and anchoring is not possible in the busy river. It may be necessary to come alongside the commercial dock. The port captain's office should be visited first.

Cartagena: The local yacht club, Club Nautico, on the island of Manga, monitors channel 16. It is possible to berth there or to anchor off. The club will contact an agent who brings the various officials.

Riohacha: One should anchor off the pier and wait to be boarded. If the officers do not come out, the captain should go to customs at the far end of the dock. If there is space on the pier it may be possible to go alongside.

Santa Marta: One should come alongside the eastern dock or anchor south of the dock. Officials prefer to board at the dock.

Customs
Firearms must be declared.

Animals need a health certificate and an anti-rabies vaccination certificate.

Immigration
Visas are not required for nationals of Argentina, Austria, Barbados, Belgium, Brazil, Chile, Costa Rica, Denmark, Ecuador, El Salvador, Germany, Finland, Ireland, Israel, Italy, Japan, Liechtenstein, Luxembourg, Netherlands, Norway, Peru, St Vincent and the Grenadines, South Korea, Spain, Sweden, Switzerland, Trinidad, United Kingdom and Uruguay. These nationalities are granted 90 days on arrival.

Other nationalities must obtain a visa, which is issued for up to three months, renewable for one month. Visas are issued within 48 hours at a Colombian embassy or consulate free of charge for nationals of Australia, Canada, Greece, Malta and the United States, and for a fee for those of France, Iceland, New Zealand and Portugal. Some other Caribbean and Latin American countries may also have to pay for the visa. Nationals of all other countries will have to wait for approval from the Ministry of Foreign Affairs and issuing the visa can take up to six weeks.

A Colombian cruising permit and visas can be obtained from any Colombian embassy or consulate in one of the countries in the vicinity, such as Venezuela or Panama. There is a Colombian consulate in Colón in Panama, which is used to dealing with yachts intending to visit Colombia.

Fees

The agent's fee varies between US$60 and US$100 and is negotiable. A deal can sometimes be negotiated with the agent if more than one yacht is cleared in or out at the same time.

Security

Colombia is a major drug-smuggling area, and police and customs are especially active on the north coast, San Andrés Island and in other tourist resorts. Penalties for possession are up to 12 years' imprisonment. Searches are frequent and one should beware of anyone claiming to be a plainclothes policeman. Apparently foreign visitors have also been set up by police with planted drugs, so caution is essential. Walking alone at night is to be avoided as this is dangerous in many towns. The Tourist Office (CNT) will advise on the dangerous areas.

Health

Vaccination against yellow fever is recommended and malaria prophylaxis for the coastal regions, Amazonas and Llanos Orientales region. Hepatitis is common.

Facilities

Provisioning is good along the Caribbean coast, particularly in larger ports, where there are both supermarkets and daily fresh produce markets. Fuel is available everywhere. There are excellent repair facilities at Cartagena, where there is a good boatyard with haul-out facilities and a complete range of services. In town, Avenida Don Pedro Heredia is the best place for non-marine hardware. Charts are available from an agent in Calle Larga near Manga. The naval base has a large sail loft and may be persuaded to do repairs. The yacht club is particularly helpful towards visitors and has marina berths.

There are also good repair facilities at Barranquilla with both haul-out and repair services, but the approaches to the port, which lies on the bank of the River Magdalena, are very difficult. Barranquilla is also considered a high security risk area. Very good facilities are also available on San Andrés Island, both in respect of provisioning and repair.

Further Reading

A Cruising Guide to the Caribbean and the Bahamas
South American Handbook
Fodor's South America
South America on a Shoestring

ECUADOR

Straddling the equator on the west coast of South America between Peru and Colombia, Ecuador is a country of contrasts between coastal plains and rugged mountains. The lowlands of Costa is the main agricultural region of Ecuador and Guayaquil its principal city. Inland is the high Sierra and the eastern Amazon basin. In the central Sierra highlands is the capital Quito, originally an Inca city, which was built on by the Spanish conquistadors.

For cruising sailors Ecuador's main attraction lies several hundred miles offshore in its Archipiélago de Colón, commonly known as the Galapagos Islands. As they form a separate entity and cruising regulations also differ from mainland Ecuador, the Galapagos are described separately in the South Pacific section.

Due to the prevailing winds and currents, the Ecuadorian coast is best cruised from south to north, which most yachts visiting Ecuador rarely do, as usually they sail from the north after having transited the Panama Canal and have to battle against wind and current. The Ecuadorean coast is arid and there are few natural harbours with the notable exception of the estuary of the River Guayas. A convenient stop can be made at Salinas, the westernmost point of Ecuador, where the boat can be left in the care of the local yacht club, while visiting the interior. This is also a good place to leave for the Galapagos Islands.

Country Profile

In the mid-fifteenth century the Incas of Peru expanded into Ecuador and made it part of their empire. Later Pizarro claimed the northern kingdom of Quito, and conquered the city in 1534. When Lima was made the capital of the whole region, Quito was put under the Viceroyalty of Peru. In the eighteenth century African slaves were introduced to work on the coastal plantations. In the early nineteenth century during the struggle for independence, the national hero Antonio José de Sucre defeated the Spanish forces and occupied Quito. Simón Bolívar continued the war of liberation and Ecuador was drawn into a confederation with Venezuela and Colombia. Independence finally came in 1830.

During the nineteenth century Ecuadorean politics were dominated by the struggle between the pro-Church Conservatives and the anticlerical Liberals. From the end of the century the country experienced long periods of military rule. The 1940s and 50s brought a period of prosperity and constitutional rule,

Practical Information

LOCAL TIME: GMT - 5

BUOYAGE: IALA B

CURRENCY: Sucre of 100 centavos

BUSINESS HOURS
Banks and government
offices: 0900–1700 Monday to Friday,
with a one hour break for lunch.
Shops: 0900–1730 Monday to Friday and
1200–1400 Saturday.

ELECTRICITY: 110 V, 60 Hz

PUBLIC HOLIDAYS
1 January: New Year's Day
6 January: Epiphany
Monday and Tuesday before Lent
(Carnival)
Holy Thursday, Good Friday, Holy
Saturday

1 May
24 May: Battle of Pichincha
24 June: Birthday of Bolívar
10 August: Independence of Quito
Opening of Congress
9 October: Independence of Guayaquil
12 October: Discovery of America
1 November: All Saints' Day
2 November: All Souls' Day
3 November: Independence of Cuenca
6 December: Foundation of Quito
25 December: Christmas Day

COMMUNICATIONS
Long-distance telephone facilities are
available in all main towns. For the
international operator dial 116.
Collect calls can be made to the USA
and Canada, but not Europe or
Australasia.
The postal service is very unreliable.
There are international flights from
Quito to American and some West
European

capitals. There are also some
international flights from Guayaquil,
which has several flights to Quito every
day and one daily flight to the
Galapagos Islands.

DIPLOMATIC MISSIONS
In Quito:
Canada: Edificio Josueth Gonzalez,
Avenida 6 de Diciembre 2816 and James
Orton. ☎ (2) 564-795.
United Kingdom: Calle Gonzales Suarez
111. ☎ (2) 560-669.
United States: 120 Avenida Patria.
☎ (2) 548-000.

In Guayaquil:
Canada: Edificio Torres de la Merced,
General Cordova 800 and Victor Manuel
Rendon. ☎ (4) 313-747.
United States: 9 de Octubre and Garcia
Moreno. ☎ (4) 511-570.

but then the 1960s and 70s saw the unstable pattern of alternating civilian and military governments again. Rivalry between the Sierra and the Costa regions, as well as Peru encroaching on the eastern border, were problems that successive governments had to contend with. After the 1978 constitution ended military rule, a more stable period has ensued.

In the early 1970s the Ecuadorean economy was transformed from an agricultural to an oil economy. However, exports of bananas, coffee and cocoa are still important and fishing is a growing industry.

The 9.1 million inhabitants are mostly Quechua Indian or mestizo, while a small proportion of the population is of European, African and Asian origin. Spanish and Quechua are the main languages spoken and most people are Roman Catholic.

Although lying on the equator, the climate of Ecuador is very pleasant, temperatures along the coast showing little difference between seasons. The winds are mostly light southerlies. The climate in the interior is more varied and temperatures vary greatly with altitude.

Entry Regulations

Ports of entry
Manta 0°56′S 80°43′W, Esmeraldas 0°58′N, 79°41′W, Guayaquil 2°17′S 79°55′W, Salinas (La Libertad) 2°13′S 80°55′W, Puerto Bolívar 3°16′S 80°01′W.

Procedure on arrival
On arrival, the port captain should be contacted on VHF Channels 6 or 12, as Channel 16 is rarely used except as a general calling channel. The port captain will advise on where to berth the yacht for clearance. Yachts cruising the Ecuadorean coast must obtain a clearance (*zarpe*) before sailing to another port. The name of the next port of call is mentioned on the clearance and this must be adhered to.

The port captains require that an agent is used for typing the *zarpe* and the latter may attempt to charge large amounts ($30 to $100 reported in Esmeraldas). An agent must be used to check in and out of every port. It is advisable to enter at the ports where there are yacht clubs, such as Salinas or Guayaquil, as these ports are more used to foreign visitors and there are less problems with officials.

Guayaquil: This is the main port of Ecuador, and lies on the west bank of Guayas river, about 40 miles inland. There are two ports, the old port and the new Puerto Nuevo, on the Estero Salado, which is a saltwater estuary lying parallel to the freshwater Guayas river. Both are navigable although currents are strong. For a fee, the artificial canal, which has a depth of 9 feet at high water in parts of the entrance, can be used. The Guayaquil Yacht Club is in the old port in the centre of Guayaquil. The club can be contacted on VHF Channel 71 and it is possible to use their facilities and complete clearance formalities from there.

Esmeraldas: Yachts should anchor in the fishing boat section of the artificial harbour, opposite the port captain's office.

Salinas: The Salinas Yacht Club can be contacted on VHF Channel 18. There are some mooring buoys inside the new breakwater. The port captain should be contacted first for clearance formalities. Immigration is in the next town, Libertad, to which there is a regular bus service.

Manta: Yachts should moor in the area reserved for the local yacht club before contacting the port captain for clearance.

Customs

Firearms and animals must be declared.

Immigration

Visas are granted on arrival for West European and US citizens. French, Australian and New Zealand nationals are among those who must obtain a visa in advance. Normally 90 days are given on arrival.

One's passport should always be carried, especially if travelling inland.

Cruising permit

Foreign yachts cannot cruise the Ecuadorean coast without a special permit from the Ministry of Defence in Quito, which must be applied for through one's embassy. A yacht arriving without this permit is normally only given clearance for a foreign port or the Galapagos Islands (if one has a permit to go there, if not, one cannot name Galapagos as one's next destination). In practice, visiting yachts have found that it was possible to obtain permission to sail to another Ecuadorean port from the port captain at the port of entry. Sometimes this permission has to be obtained from a higher authority in Guayaquil.

Health

Amoebic dysentery is endemic in some parts of the country. Vaccination against yellow fever and malarial prophylaxis is recommended.

Fees

A tax for light dues of US$3 per gross ton must be paid to the port captain on arrival. One should get a receipt for this payment or one will have to pay it again in the next port.

There are also immigration charges, a US$3 clearance fee and agent's fees. A charge is also made for the *zarpe*. Apparently some yachts have been over-

charged and others have had to pay overtime, because they were leaving the harbour outside office hours, even when the formalities had been completed during office hours. This seems to be less of a problem in the ports of Salinas and Guayaquil, where foreign yachts are more common. Yachts should also avoid mooring in commercial harbours as yachts are charged the same rates as large ships, which are very high. There are not usually fees for anchoring in fishing harbours.

Facilities

Provisioning is adequate along the coast, but a better selection is found in larger towns. Because of a favourable exchange rate, prices are very low for both provisions and fuel. Water is sometimes scarce along the coast.

Esmeraldas is a small town with only basic necessities such as fresh produce and some hardware available. Fuel is delivered to the main dock in drums.

Only basic provisioning is possible locally in Salinas, but there are regular buses to Guayaquil where supplies are much better. Water and fuel are available inside the breakwater at a dock where one can come stern-to at high tide. The club has a travelift for 25 tons and simple repairs can be made. The yacht club is very helpful and will assist in an emergency.

The Guayaquil Yacht Club has pontoons with electricity and water and welcomes visitors. The town is good for provisioning, although marine supplies are not available. Charts are available at Inocar, a naval establishment south of Guayaquil. Repairs and hauling out can be done at the naval dockyard Astinave (which can be contacted on VHF Channel 21). Although it deals mainly with fishing boats, work done on yachts in the past was satisfactory. There is a branch of the Guayaquil Yacht Club at Puerto Arul, 6 miles from Guayaquil, where there is a marina with 24-hour security guard. Smaller yachts can be hauled out and a limited range of repair is available. Boats can be left safely for longer periods either in the water or on the hard.

Further Reading

South American Handbook
South America on a Shoestring

FRENCH GUIANA

French Guiana is an overseas department of France, sandwiched between Brazil and Suriname. The atmosphere in the country is more Caribbean, akin to Martinique and Guadeloupe than to the rest of Latin America. The low coastal regions gradually climb to the hills and forests of the interior from where twenty rivers flow down to the Atlantic Ocean. Cayenne is the capital, on the island of the same name at the mouth of the Cayenne river.

The coast itself has few ports or anchorages worth exploring, but the offlying Iles du Salut are a popular stop for sailors. These islands can only be visited after having cleared into the country. The best anchorage is on Ile St Joseph, although there are no completely protected anchorages. Also interesting to visit is the Ariane Space Centre at Kourou, west of Cayenne, although an appointment has to be made in advance. River trips, usually by canoe, are another attraction of this small country, which is only visited by a small number of cruising yachts, mainly French.

Country Profile

Columbus visited this coast in 1498, to be followed by Amerigo Vespucci, Sir Walter Raleigh and many other explorers. French settlers arrived in the sixteenth century and began extracting dye stuffs from the trees. Dutch and English attempts to gain control of the land were unsuccessful and the Peace of Breda in 1667 awarded the region to France. During the French Revolution political prisoners were deported to Guyane, a punishment which was known as the 'dry guillotine'. In 1809 an Anglo-Portuguese naval force captured the territory and handed it over to the Brazilians, until it was eventually restored to France at the end of the Napoleonic Wars.

A penal colony was established in the mid-nineteenth century on the inaccessible Iles du Salut, which became notorious, especially Ile du Diable – Devil's Island – where political prisoners, including Alfred Dreyfus, were kept. After the Second World War the colony became part of France as the department of Guyane and the prison was finally closed, the last prisoners leaving in 1953. In 1983 the country was given greater internal autonomy and a regional council elected.

The country's main resources are timber forests and minerals. Most food and manufactured goods are imported, mainly from France. Exports are shrimps, rum, essence of rosewood, hardwoods and gold. In recent years efforts have been made to develop local food production and to improve tourist facilities.

The 92,000 inhabitants are of Creole, Indian, Asian and European origin (mainly French). French is the official language and most of the population are Roman Catholic.

The rainy season is from November to July, while August to December are the best months. Rainfall can be heavy in this tropical climate where temperatures average 27°C (80°F).

Practical Information

LOCAL TIME: GMT - 3

BUOYAGE: IALA B

CURRENCY: French franc. It is recommended to arrive with francs as it is difficult to change money.

BUSINESS HOURS
Bank de la Guyane, Place Schoelcher 0715–1130, 1445–1730, and Saturday mornings.

ELECTRICITY: 110/220 V, 50 Hz

PUBLIC HOLIDAYS
1 January: New Year's Day
Easter Monday
1 May
Ascension
Whit Monday
14 July: National Day
1 November: All Saints' Day
11 November: Armistice Day
25 December: Christmas Day

COMMUNICATIONS
International telephone calls can be made to Europe, the USA and the French Antilles.
Foreign telegrams via Paramaribo or Fort-de-France from TSF station in Cayenne.

Post office 0700–1200 Monday, Friday, Saturday. 0700–1230 Tuesday, Wednesday, Thursday. Also 1500–1700 Monday to Friday,
There are flights from Cayenne to Paris, Miami, Caribbean and South American destinations.

MEDICAL
There are hospitals in Cayenne and Kourou.

DIPLOMATIC MISSIONS
In Cayenne:
Brazil: 12 rue L. Helder, corner Place des Palmistes.
Suriname: 38 rue Christophe Colombe.
United Kingdom: 16 Av. Monnerville.

Entry Regulations

Ports of entry
Degrad des Cannes 4°51'N 52°16'W, Cayenne 4°56'N 52°20'W.

Procedure on arrival
Degrad des Cannes: This is the main port of French Guiana, located on the NW bank of the Mahury river. The entrance is lit and buoyed, and yachts usually anchor outside the main channel by the shore. Normally the gendarmes will come out to the yacht to check passports and ship's papers. The port captain's office should then be visited.

It has been reported that the port captain does not approve of yachts clearing in at Degrad des Cannes and insists that formalities are completed at Cayenne. The approaches to Cayenne are difficult and the buoyed channel not easy to find, but this is not accepted as an excuse to clear at Degrad des Cannes instead.
Cayenne: The capital is no longer used as a commercial port. The Cayenne Channel should only be navigated in daylight, preferably on a high tide. It is possible to come alongside the jetty two hours before and two hours after high tide.

There are also customs offices at Kourou and Saint-Laurent-du-Maroni.

Customs
Firearms and animals must be declared.

Yachts can be temporarily imported for up to six months without paying duty, on condition that one does not enter into commercial activity ashore. Chartering is not allowed.

It is illegal for foreign tourists or sailors to sell any of their possessions to local residents and the penalties are heavy fines. As any informers receive a large proportion of the fine, visitors have been set up by some of these local informers.

Immigration
Visas are not required for nationals of many countries, including all of Western Europe, Canada and the USA. If staying more than three months, one needs income tax clearance before departure. Visas are required by nationals of Guyana, some African, Asian (except Japan) and East European countries.

Visas can be obtained from a French embassy or consulate.

Restrictions
A permit is necessary for visiting some Amerindian villages.

Health
Vaccination against yellow fever is recommended if staying more than two weeks, as is malaria prophylaxis.

Facilities

Provisioning is good, but expensive. There is a fresh produce market at Cayenne, Place du Coq, Tuesdays, Wednesdays, Thursdays, and Fridays. There is only a limited range of repair facilities. Good provisioning is also available in Kourou, where emergency repairs may be possible if the help of technicians from the French space centre can be enlisted.

Further Reading

South American Handbook

GUYANA

Guyana means 'land of many waters' in Amerindian, which is an accurate description of this small country of many swamps and rivers on the north-east Atlantic coast of South America. Most of the population live along the narrow coastal belt, which is very low and subject to floods. A difficult coast to approach because of the shallow and muddy waters, combined with lengthy formalities, do not make Guyana a natural cruising destination. Visiting the interior is only possible with special permission. This also applies to trips up the river Berbice, which is navigable for 100 miles past the port of New Amsterdam.

The capital Georgetown has a certain charm and the few yachts which do visit Guyana rarely go anywhere else. On the right bank of the river Demerara, the town has nineteenth century houses on stilts and boulevards built along disused Dutch canals. Seawalls and dykes protect the town, which is built on an alluvial flat area below the highwater mark.

Country Profile

Although the Spanish were the first to explore this coast, they were not very interested in what they found and it was the English and Dutch who were the first to settle in the seventeenth century. They disputed the ownership of the land until 1814, when the three counties of Essequibo, Berbice and Demerara were merged to form British Guiana. Initially plantations were established in the hills using African slave labour,

Practical Information

LOCAL TIME: GMT - 4

BUOYAGE: IALA B

CURRENCY: Guyana dollar (G$). Only G$40 can be exported or imported. There are strict controls on changing money, so it is better to arrive with cash than travellers' cheques.

BUSINESS HOURS
Banks: 0800–1200 Monday to Friday, 0800–1100 Saturday.
Shops and offices: 0930–1800, some half day Wednesday. Some shops are open Saturday afternoon.
Government offices: 0800–1130, 1300–1600 Monday to Friday, 0800–1200 Saturday.

ELECTRICITY: 110/220 V, 50 Hz

PUBLIC HOLIDAYS
1 January: New Year's Day
23 February: Republic Day
March: Holi Phagwa
Good Friday, Easter Monday
1 May
Eid el-Fitr
July: Caribbean Day (1st Monday in July)
Eid el-Adha
2 August: Commonwealth Day
Divali
Youm um-Nabi
25, 26 December: Christmas

COMMUNICATIONS
Guyintel, Bank of Guyana building, Georgetown for overseas telegrams, telex, international calls. Collect calls cannot be made.
Main post office in North Road, Georgetown, open 0730–1600 weekdays.
Post office in Robb Street for fax.
Emergency: dial 999.

There are flights from Georgetown to Barbados, Trinidad, Brazil, Miami and New York.

MEDICAL
Georgetown Hospital: treatment is free but the hospital is poorly equipped. Also St Joseph and Davis Memorial Hospitals.

DIPLOMATIC MISSIONS
In Georgetown:
Brazil: Church St. ☎ (2) 56070.
Canada: High and Young Streets. ☎(2) 72081.
Colombia: 306 Church and Peter Rose Streets. ☎ (2) 71410.
Suriname: 304 Church St. ☎ (2) 67844.
Trinidad and Tobago: 91 Middle St. ☎ (2) 72061.
United Kingdom: 44 Main St. ☎ (2) 65881.
United States: 31 Main St. ☎ (2) 54900.
Venezuela: 296 Thomas St. ☎(2) 61543.

but the poor soil forced the settlers to move down to the coast in the mid-eighteenth century. Coffee and cotton were the main crops and later sugar. In 1834 slavery was abolished and indentured Chinese and Indians plus some Portuguese from the Azores and Madeira were brought in as labour. At the end of the nineteenth century a boundary dispute with Venezuela was settled in favour of Britain, but this area is still claimed by Venezuela. In 1953 a new constitution introduced universal suffrage. Cheddi Jagan, prime minister in 1961–4, relied on the support of the Asian population, opposed by both the whites and blacks. In 1966 British Guiana was granted independence and took the new name of Guyana. Later the black leader Ford Burnham became president to be succeeded in 1985 by Hugh Desmond Hoyle.

Guyana's main income comes from sugar and bauxite. There are sugar and rice plantations on the coast. The small country's main problem is its large foreign debt.

The population is almost 100,000, of which half are Asian. There are also indigenous Indians and people of African, British, Chinese, European and American origins. English is the official language. The main religions are Christian, Hindu and Muslim.

The climate is hot and humid, especially from August to October. The wet seasons are from April to August, and November to January. Guyana lies outside of the hurricane belt.

Entry Regulations

Port of entry
Georgetown 6°49′N 58°11′W.

Procedure on arrival
Yachts should contact the harbour master, who will advise the captain on the procedure to be followed.

Customs
Firearms and animals must be declared.

Immigration
All nationals require visas and a single entry up to 30 days is normally given. Visas can be obtained in Suriname or other neighbouring countries. Those who arrive without a visa must give up their passport and collect it the next day before 1030 from Immigration, Camp Street, Georgetown. An extension needs the approval of the Home Department, 6 Brickdam, and takes about two weeks to process.

Restrictions
Permission is needed from the Home Affairs Ministry to visit the interior.

Health
Yellow fever vaccination certificate is required. Malaria prophylaxis is recommended.

Fees
There is an exit tax of G$50 payable to immigration.

Facilities

Provisions are limited and expensive. There is a daily fresh produce market in Georgetown. Occasionally there are fuel and water shortages. Only simple repairs are possible and there are no marine supplies available. The NGEC shipyard in Georgetown operates a dry dock and slipway and may do work on a yacht in an emergency.

Further Reading

South American Handbook

PERU

With its Inca ruins, old Spanish colonial cities and the magnificent Andes dominating the centre of the country, Peru has always been one of the most fascinating countries to visit in South America. In the last few years the increasing activity of guerilla groups, whose attacks in various parts of the country have affected foreign tourists as well as Peruvians, has made Peru much less of an attractive destination. Even before the present troubles, Peru was a difficult cruising destination, as there are few ports along its arid coast on the Pacific Ocean. The few yachts that call normally make their base at Callao, whose welcoming yacht club used to be a good place to leave the boat while touring the interior of this intriguing country.

Country Profile

Several different cultures rose and fell in this region before the Incas came to dominate Peru and Ecuador. The Inca civilisation dates from the eleventh century AD and, expanding outwards from the Cuzco basin, by the mid-fifteenth century the Incas had conquered much of the surrounding region. A strong state was established based on a rigid ruling hierarchy, who forced the masses to build temples and cities and a priestly caste who made human sacrifices to the sun. Gold and silver were easily available in large amounts and the Incas were highly skilled in metalwork and architecture. However, the empire grew too unwieldy and was in the throes of civil war just before the Spanish arrived.

In 1532 a small Spanish force led by Francisco Pizarro routed the Incas and sacked Cuzco, founding Lima as the capital of the newly conquered territory. The Spanish had voyaged through all America searching for treasure, and in Peru reached the end of their quest. They looted the treasure of the Incas, and forced them to work in the silver mines. The Inca civilisation rapidly declined, its people decimated by disease, civil wars and slavery. From Peru, the Viceroyalty ruled over Spain's South American possessions.

The ideas of the French Revolution fired the Spanish colonies to declare independence and then fight Spain for it. In Peru independence was declared in 1821, after José de San Martín's army crossed from Chile to fight the Spanish forces. Simón Bolívar and Antonio José de Sucre, already having freed Venezuela and Colombia, completed the war of liberation and in 1826 Spain capitulated and new republics were born across the continent. Efforts by Peru and Bolivia to form a confederation in the 1830s eventually came to nothing. At the end of the century the War of the Pacific saw Peru and Bolivia defeated by Chile, and Peru lost its southernmost territory. Political instability in Peru continued into the twentieth century with strong military regimes alternating with weak civilian governments. In 1968 a reformist military junta introduced reforms to raise the living standards of the workers and rural Indians, but the country's economic problems continued. The guerilla activity of the Sendero Luminoso (Shining Path) movement has been the major problem for Peru in recent years. During the recent troubles a curfew has sometimes been imposed in the capital Lima between 0100 and 0500 because of guerilla activity.

In the economy, efforts have been made to improve agriculture, the main export crops being sugar, cotton and coffee. Mining is of some importance, while oil reserves are sufficient to provide half of the domestic consumption. Even so, industry is in a slump and the country is close to bankruptcy.

The population of 20 million are mainly Indian and mestizo, with some of African, Chinese, European and Japanese origins. The majority are Roman Catholic. There are two official languages, Spanish and Quechua. The latter is an Inca language, spoken by millions of Indians, many of whom speak no Spanish. The Indian community is still large, most living in poverty in isolated settlements in the mountains.

The climate of coastal Peru is greatly influenced by the cold Humboldt current, which keeps temperatures cool throughout the year and often produces coastal fog. There is very little rain along the coast which is arid and desert-like. The prevailing winds are south or south-easterly and usually light.

Practical Information

LOCAL TIME: GMT - 5

BUOYAGE: IALA B

CURRENCY: Inti is the new currency, of 100 centimos. The Inti is worth 1000 sol, the old currency. Outside Lima and Cuzco, changing travellers' cheques is difficult.

BUSINESS HOURS
Banks: winter 0915–1245, summer (January to March) 0845–1130 Monday to Friday; some open in the afternoon or on Saturdays.
Shops: 0900–1230, 1600–1900 Monday to Saturday (some close Saturdays), January to March. The rest of the year 0930–1230, 1530–1900.
Government offices: January to March 0930–1130 Monday to Saturday, rest of the year 0930–1100, 1500–1700 Monday to Friday, 0930–1130 Saturday.

ELECTRICITY: 220 V, 60 Hz

PUBLIC HOLIDAYS
1 January: New Year's Day
Maundy Thursday, Good Friday
1 May: Labour Day
29 June: Saints Peter and Paul
28–29 July: Independence Day
30 August: Santa Rosa de Lima
8 October: Battle of Angamos
1 November: All Saints' Day
8 December: Immaculate Conception
24, 25 December: Christmas
31 December: New Year's Eve
Most shops and businesses close during family holidays, especially July to August.

COMMUNICATIONS
ENTEL, off Plaza San Martin, Lima, for international calls.

The postal service is slow and erratic. There are regular flights from Lima to European, North and South American destinations.

DIPLOMATIC MISSIONS
In Lima or its suburbs of Miraflores and San Isidro:
Canada: 130 Frederico Gerdes, Miraflores. ☎ (14) 94-4015.
Chile: Javier Prado Oeste 790, San Isidro.
New Zealand: Av. Salaverry 3006, San Isidro. ☎ (14) 62-1890.
United Kingdom: Edificio Pacifico-Washington, Plaza Washington, Av. Arequipa, Lima 100, ☎ (14) 33-4738.
United States: Corner Avenidas Inca Garcilaso de la Vega and Espana, Miraflores. ☎ (14) 28-6000.

The ruined Inca city of Macchu Picchu, one of the reasons for visiting Peru.

Entry Regulations

Ports of entry
Paita 5°05'S 81°07'W, Chimbote 9°05'S 78°38'W, Callao 12°03'S 77°09'W, General San Martín 13°50'S 81°16'W, Matarani 16°59'S 72°07'W.

Procedure on arrival
Callao: Visiting yachts are normally directed by the yacht club launch to a club mooring. The launch attendant should be asked to inform the authorities of the yacht's arrival and request them to come to the yacht to complete clearance formalities. No one should leave the yacht until it has been boarded by the various officials, including port authority, customs, immigration and possibly security. More formalities have to be completed later at the immigration office near the commercial harbour. Shore passes will be issued, but these are not valid for travel outside Callao and Lima, so a proper visa should be requested if intending to travel inland.
Paita: On arrival contact the coastguard (costera) on VHF Channel 16.

Customs
Firearms and animals must be declared. The export of objects of archaeological interest is prohibited.

Immigration
No visas are needed in advance by nationals of EC countries, Argentina, Austria, Bolivia, Brazil, Canada, Colombia, Ecuador, Finland, Honduras, Liechtenstein, Norway, South Korea, Sweden, Switzerland, Uruguay, the USA and Venezuela. All other countries, including Australia and New Zealand, need to obtain visas in advance.

The crew of foreign yachts who wish to visit the interior should insist on being given a tourist visa on arrival, particularly if intending to leave Peru for one of the neighbouring countries before returning to the yacht.

Visas can be renewed at Ministerio del Interior, Paseo de la Republica, Av. 28 de Julio, Lima.

Some identification should always be carried.

Health
If visiting the interior, yellow fever inoculation and malaria prophylaxis are recommended.

Security
A high number of robberies have been reported. The use or purchase of drugs is severely punished and can lead to 15 years imprisonment. There have been reports of the planting of drugs on foreigners by police followed by demands for high sums of money for the charges to be dropped. Guerilla activities of Sendero Luminoso and Tupac Amam are spreading, and police and army searches have increased.

United States citizens can obtain more information from the Country Officer for Peru, Office of Andean Affairs, Department of State, Washington DC.

Facilities

Callao is the port of the capital Lima, which is only a short distance inland. There is a good yacht club in Callao, which can advise on repair facilities. There are a number of workshops in the surrounding area, including a boatyard with a slipway. Fuel and water is available from the club dock. Provisioning is good from local supermarkets and an excellent fresh produce market. Marine equipment is in very short supply. Visitors are also welcome to use the facilities of the yacht club at La Punta, close to Callao. There is also a yacht club at Ancon, a town not far from Lima, which welcomes visitors and has some facilities.

There are chandleries at Paita, and the Port Authority sells Peruvian charts, almanacs and tide tables.

Further Reading

South American Handbook
South America on a Shoestring

SURINAME

Suriname before independence was known as Dutch Guiana, and lies on the north-east coast of South America between Guyana and French Guiana. There are ongoing border disputes with both its neighbours. Although discovered by Spain, the Guyanas have always been considered more Caribbean than Latin American, as Spain showed little interest and the area was colonised by the other European powers active in the Caribbean area.

Suriname has a flat, marshy coast, where most of the population live, although parts of the coast remain unexplored. Uplands rise up from the coastal plain and contain mineral reserves, while the coast is indented with rivers, which makes the sea muddy and navigation more difficult. Some of the wide rivers are navigable for a considerable distance inland, but to do this requires special permission from the authorities in Paramaribo, who treat all foreigners, including those arriving on yachts, with suspicion.

Practical Information

LOCAL TIME: GMT - 3

BUOYAGE: IALA B

CURRENCY: Suriname guilder (Sf) of 100 cents. Foreign visitors may have to change US$30 per day.

BUSINESS HOURS
Banks: 0700–1400 or 0800–1230 Monday to Friday, 0800–1200 Saturday.
Business: 0730–1700 Monday to Friday.
Shops: 0700–1300, 1600–1800 Monday to Thursday and Saturday (to 1900 Saturday). Friday 0730–1300, 1700–2000. Government offices: 0700–1400 Monday to Friday, 0700–1130 Saturday.

ELECTRICITY: 220 V, 60 Hz

PUBLIC HOLIDAYS
1 January: New Year's Day
25 February: Day of the Revolution
March: Holi Phagwa
Good Friday, Easter Sunday and Monday
1 May
1 July: National Unity
Eid el-Fitr
25 November: Independence Day
25, 26 December: Christmas

COMMUNICATIONS
Vaillantplein: telephone and telegraph office. Satellite calls to the USA and UK. Open 0700–2000.
Post office, Kerkelein.

There are international flights from Zanderji airport, 30 miles from Paramaribo to Amsterdam, Miami, Caribbean and Latin American destinations.

MEDICAL
There is a good hospital in Paramaribo.

DIPLOMATIC MISSIONS
In Paramaribo:
United Kingdom: the office in Guyana deals with Suriname.
United States: Dr Sophie Redmondstraat 129. ☎ 76459.

Country Profile

The coast was first sighted by Columbus in 1498. It was in the early seventeenth century that Dutch merchants began trading along what became known as the 'Wild Coast'. English settlers also came and planted tobacco. In the mid-seventeenth century the Governor of Barbados sent an expedition and an agricultural colony was founded with sugar plantations worked by African slaves. The colony grew in numbers with the immigration of Jews from the Netherlands and Italy, as well as Dutch Jews ejected from Brazil. In 1667 Suriname was conquered by the Dutch, a situation confirmed by the Peace of Breda with Britain. At the end of the eighteenth century a brief conquest was made by Britain, but Suriname was returned to the Netherlands in 1814. Soon afterwards slavery was forbidden, and instead labour was brought in from China and the East Indies.

In 1975 Suriname became an independent republic, but five years later a military coup overthrew the elected government, and a state of emergency was declared. Pressure from the Netherlands, who ceased all aid, and also from the United States, has helped a gradual move back towards democracy. There has been a new constitution and elections in recent years, and Dutch aid has been restored. Problems, however, continue; since 1986 there has been guerilla warfare in the interior, which is closed to travellers.

Agriculture is centred on the coast, the main exports being rice, sugar and citrus fruit, but food imports are high. Fishing and timber are other contributions to the national economy. Suriname is an important producer of bauxite and there are also some oil reserves.

The population numbers 400,000, over half of whom are Creole. There are also Asians, Indonesians, Chinese, Amerindians, Europeans and Bush Blacks, who are descendants of slaves who escaped to the interior in the seventeenth century. Dutch is the official language, but English and a local dialect called Negro English are widely spoken. Some Asian languages are also spoken. The main religion is Christian, also the Hindu, Muslim and Jewish religions. Paramaribo is the capital, on the banks of the wide Suriname river eight miles from the sea.

The climate is tropical and humid, but not too hot due to the NE trade winds. Coastal temperatures are around 23–31°C (75–88°F). The rainy seasons are November to February and April to August.

Entry Regulations

Port of entry
Paramaribo 5°50'N 55°10'W.

Procedure on arrival
Paramaribo: The harbour office keep a 24-hour watch on VHF Channels 12 and 16. A new harbour has been built one mile upstream and the old main wharf is now used by fishing vessels, so if there is space it may be possible to come alongside to complete clearance formalities.

Customs
Firearms and animals must be declared.

Immigration

Most countries need to obtain a visa in advance, which may take time as all applications have to be authorised in Paramaribo. Suriname has consular offices in French Guiana at 38 rue Christophe Colombe, Cayenne, and in Venezuela, 4a Avenida between 7a and 8a Transversal, Urb. Altmira, Caracas, which may be the most convenient places to obtain a visa. There is also the Consulate General of the Republic of Suriname, 7235 NW 19th Street, Suite A, Miami, FL 33126, USA.

Normally a visa is given for 30 days. Extensions can be obtained from the immigration office, Paramaribo, on arrival.

Health

Yellow fever vaccination is recommended as is malaria prophylaxis.

Facilities

Provisioning in Paramaribo is reasonable and there is a good supply of local produce. Only simple repairs can be effected. A shipyard operates in Paramaribo harbour and they have a dry dock and lift, where yachts can be hauled out if necessary.

Further Reading

South American Handbook

URUGUAY

One of the smaller South American countries, Uruguay has little coastline on the Atlantic. Lying on the northern bank of the Rio de la Plata, the name Uruguay means 'river of birds'. Uruguay enters the centre of the sailing world every four years, when the Whitbread maxis stop in Punta del Este twice in their race around the world. Besides Punta del Este and a few resorts in the vicinity, Uruguay holds little attraction for cruising yachts. There are more interesting things to see in the interior of this low, undulating country, which is the land of the gaucho.

Country Profile

Before the Europeans arrived, the semi-nomadic, warlike Charrúa lived here. In 1516 the Spaniard Juan Diaz de Solis landed near the site of present-day Montevideo. As there was no gold or silver to be found, the Spanish lost all interest until the end of the sixteenth century. In the following century Jesuit and Franciscan missionaries founded a settlement on Vizcairio Island. Cattle were introduced into the country and thrived so well they later became Uruguay's main commodity.

In 1680 Portugal founded a town to rival Buenos Aires on the opposite bank of the Rio de la Plata but it was Spain who founded the city of Montevideo several decades later. Montevideo changed hands several times and early in the nineteenth century declared its independence from Buenos Aires. In 1811 José Artigas led the fight for independence against both Brazilian and Argentinian claims. Then a Brazilian force occupied Uruguay and Artigas fled to Paraguay, but in 1825 thirty-three Uruguayan exiles, the '33 Orientales', returned to lead a successful revolt against the Brazilian occupation. Uruguayan independence was declared, and eventually with British intervention peace was established and the new republic recognised by its neighbours.

Civil war followed between the Liberals and Conservatives and only in 1872 was agreement reached between the two sides, dividing the country into spheres of influence. Gradually political stability was achieved, and from the early twentieth century, a welfare state with a mixed economy was established. The 1960s saw political turmoil, and guerilla activities, which were defeated by the military in 1972. The following year a military coup occurred, but the government lost a plebiscite held in 1980, and the country has since returned to democracy.

Much of Uruguay's former prosperity has gone, and the model welfare state declined. Agriculture, mainly livestock, dominates the economy, Uruguay being famous for its cattle-raising cowboys called gauchos. Other products are cereals, oilseeds, citrus fruits, and fishing. Manufacturing is mainly linked to agriculture.

The population is just over 3.5 million, the majority living in and around the only large city, Montevideo. Founded in 1726, the centre of the capital on the original site still has a colonial atmosphere. Most of the population are of Spanish or Italian origin, plus a few other European immigrants. There are no native Indians left. Spanish is the official language and Roman Catholicism the religion of the majority.

The climate is temperate but somewhat damp and windy. Winter lasts from June to September,

Practical Information

LOCAL TIME: GMT - 3

BUOYAGE: IALA B

CURRENCY: New peso (N$) of 100 centesimos

BUSINESS HOURS
Banks: 1300–1700 Monday to Friday.
Summer 1330–1730 (Montevideo),
1600–2000 (Punta del Este).
Business: 0830–1200, 1430–1630/1900
Monday to Friday.
Shops: 0900–1200, 1400–1900 Monday to
Friday, 0900–1230 Saturday.
Government offices: mid–March to
mid–April 1300–1630 Monday to Friday.
Rest of year 0700–1230 Monday to
Friday.

ELECTRICITY: 220 V, 50 Hz

PUBLIC HOLIDAYS
1 January: New Year's Day
6 January: Three Kings Day

Easter Week: Easter Monday is not a
holiday. Banks close all week, shops
close from Good Friday.
19 April: Landing of the 33 Orientales
1 May: Labour Day
18 May: Battle of Las Piedras
19 June: Artigas' Birthday
18 July: Constitution Day
25 August: Independence Day
12 October: Columbus Day
2 November: All Souls' Day
8 December
25 December: Christmas Day

EVENTS
Carnival: Monday and Tuesday before
Ash Wednesday
Easter Week: La Semana Criolla with
rodeos and music. Few shops and
offices are open.

COMMUNICATIONS
Antel (government run) office, Calle
Sarandi 478: open 24 hours for
international calls and telex.

Also All America Cables & Radio Inc.,
Plaza Independencia.
Post office: Calle Misiones 1328, open
0800–1845 Monday to Friday, 0800–1245
Saturday (0730 summer).
Post is unreliable and mail should be
sent registered.
Emergency: dial 999.
There are international flights from
Montevideo to Europe, North America
and all South American capitals.

MEDICAL
British hospital, Avenida Italia 2440,
Montevideo.

DIPLOMATIC MISSIONS
In Montevideo:
Brazil: Blvd Artigas 1257.
Canada: Juan Carlos Gomez 1348.
☎ (2) 958234.
United Kingdom: Calle Marco Bruto
1073. ☎ (2) 723533.
United States: Calle Lauro Müller 1776.
☎ (2) 409051.

averaging 10–16°C (50–60°F), but temperatures can drop below freezing. Summer is from December to March, when average temperatures are 21–27°C (70–80°F). The winds in the Rio de la Plata estuary are easterly in summer months. Strong SW winds called pamperos occur between June and October, occasionally reaching hurricane force.

Entry Regulations

Ports of entry
Punta del Este 34°58'S 54°57'W, Montevideo 34°54'S 56°16'W.

Procedure on arrival
Punta del Este: One should tie up to one of the municipal moorings. Officials do not normally board yachts for clearance. The marina office can be contacted on VHF Channel 71, but the captain has to go ashore and visit the offices. Immigration is in town, open 1300–1900; in the summer season the officials are in the harbour office.

Customs
Firearms must be declared to customs. Animals must be declared and may be confined on board.

Immigration
Nationals of other American countries need only an identity card, not a passport.

Visas are not required for nationals of West European countries, Israel, Japan and the USA.

Tourist cards, valid for three months, can be extended at Migraciones office, Calle Misiones, for a small fee.

One should carry one's passport, or a certified photocopy, at all times.

Health
If coming from Brazil a yellow fever vaccination certificate is required.

Facilities

The best facilities are at Punta del Este, which has a marina and yacht club, although the latter is not open to visiting cruising yachts. There are plenty of mooring buoys in the municipal marina, which can be hired for a daily fee which includes a launch service. There is good provisioning in town and fuel and water are available. There are adequate repair facilities locally and a travelift. Having had to deal with the Whitbread fleet, the local workshops have attained a certain degree of experience and most repairs can be carried out locally. However, nautical items are hard to get both in Punta del Este and Montevideo. There is a better selection in Buenos Aires, on the Argentine side of the river.

Further Reading

South American Handbook
Fodor's South America
South America on a Shoestring

VENEZUELA

Venezuela has over 1500 miles of Caribbean coastline, off which lie 72 islands including the popular yachting destination, Isla de Margarita. Venezuela was given its name, 'little Venice', by the Spanish after seeing the Indian pile dwellings on Lake Maracaibo. A poor country throughout its history, this changed dramatically with the discovery of oil in 1914, and since then Venezuela has enjoyed a greater measure of prosperity than most Latin American countries or her Caribbean neighbours.

Lying on the direct route to Panama and also being rarely affected by hurricanes, the Venezuelan coast and particularly the offlying islands have become a very popular cruising destination in recent years. This popularity has been matched by a rapid improvement in yachting facilities and services, with new marinas springing up all the time. Although visiting sailors will undoubtedly appreciate the wider availability of such services, the islands' main attraction, their simplicity, tranquillity and natural beauty, could be destroyed in the process. The islands abound in picturesque anchorages and diving is excellent almost everywhere, particularly among the scores of islets and cays of Los Roques.

Country Profile

The Carib and Arawak tribes who lived along the coast put up little resistance to the Spanish settlers who arrived at the start of the eighteenth century. Not finding any gold, the Spanish turned to agriculture, and gradually spread through the country, mixing with the Indians and later introducing African slaves to work on the sugar plantations. After several uprisings against Spain's colonial rule in the eighteenth century, early in the nineteenth century Francisco Miranda tried twice to gain independence for the region. Simón Bolívar who followed him was more successful, cross-ing the Andes with his men in 1819 and capturing Bogotá. The short lived independent Gran Colombia was created, a union of present day Ecuador, Colombia, Venezuela and Panama, but in 1830 Venezuela declared itself an independent republic. A succession of dictators ruled the country into the early twentieth century. After the Second World War a more democratic regime was followed by the dictatorship of General Marco Perez Jimenez, who was eventually overthrown giving way to the more stable democracy of today.

The Venezuelan economy is dominated by petroleum, although during the 1980s the role of oil has diminished, and efforts have been made to diversify. Venezuela has vast natural resources and is rich in energy sources. Mining and agriculture are increasingly important. Problems that remain are a large foreign debt, high food imports, as well as unemployment, illiteracy and an exodus from rural areas. In recent years there has been high inflation, which has led to shortages, especially of food, as supplies are withdrawn from the market when further cost increases are anticipated.

The population is over 18 million, mostly of mixed Spanish and Indian ancestry, with pure Indians living in the remoter parts, also some of African and European origins. The main language spoken is Spanish, and Roman Catholicism is the leading religion. Caracas is the capital, in the central highlands, at an altitude of 3148 ft (960 m).

Venezuela has a tropical climate and there is little change between the seasons, although it is drier from December to April. The northern coast and offlying islands are under the influence of the NE trade winds, which blow strongly between December and April. Summer winds are lighter and Venezuela is very rarely affected by tropical storms.

Entry Regulations

Ports of entry

Carúpano 10°41'N 63°15'W, Puerto Sucre (Cumaná) 10°28'N 64°11'W, Puerto La Cruz 10°13'N 64°38'W, Carenero 10°32'N 66°07'W, La Guaira 10°36'N 66°56'W, Puerto Cabello 10°29'N 68°00'W, Maracaibo 10°39'N 71°36'W, Pampatar (Isla de Margarita) 11°00'N 63°47'W.

Procedure on arrival

On entry into Venezuela, one must first clear with customs, then National Guard, immigration and port captain, in that order. In every major port after that, yachts must clear in and out with customs, National

Practical Information

LOCAL TIME: GMT - 4

BUOYAGE: IALA B

CURRENCY: Bolivar (Bs) of 100 centimos

BUSINESS HOURS
Banks: 0830–1130, 1400–1630 Monday to Friday.
Government offices: 0830–1200, 1400–1800; these hours vary and officials have special hours for receiving the public, usually 0900–1000, 1500–1600.
Shops: 0900–1300, 1500–1900 Monday to Saturday.

ELECTRICITY: 110/240 V, 60 Hz

PUBLIC HOLIDAYS
1 January: New Year's Day
Carnival: Monday, Tuesday before Ash Wednesday
Thursday, Friday, Saturday of Holy Week
19 April: Proclamation of Independence
1 May
24 June: Battle of Carabobo
5 July: Independence Day
24 July: Bolívar's birthday
12 October: Columbus Day
25 December: Christmas Day
31 December: New Year's Eve

Extra government and bank holidays (nearest Monday to the date):
19 March: St Joseph
6 January
Ascension Day
Corpus Christi
29 June
15 August: Assumption
1 November: All Saints' Day
8 December: Immaculate Conception
17 December: Bolívar's death

COMMUNICATIONS
CANTV for international and long-distance calls, 24 hours. No collect calls can be made. Post offices are open 0800–1800. Post is slow and unreliable.
The post offices on Isla Margarita (Pampatar and Porlamar) are open 0900–1130, 1400–1630.
There are regular flights from Caracas to Europe, USA, Caribbean and South American destinations.

MEDICAL
Health care in state hospitals is free, but the standards vary and foreign visitors are advised to have medical insurance.
For serious medical emergencies it may be worth contacting Hospital de Clínicas in Caracas (☎ (2) 572-2011), which

provides a full range of hospital and out-patients services. Many of the staff speak English. Cash payment is expected at the time of service, but fees are reported to be reasonable and the care excellent.

DIPLOMATIC MISSIONS
In Caracas:
Brazil: Edificio Central, Gerencial Mohedano, Av. Mohedano. Visas can be granted the same day if requested at 0900, returned at 1800.
Canada: Edificio Torre Europa, Av. Francisco de Miranda, Chacaito. ☎ (2) 951-6166.
Colombia: Av. E, Campo Alegre, Monday to Friday 0800–1730 for visas.
Guyana: Roraima, Av. El Paseo, Prados del Este.
Suriname: 4a Avenida between 7a and 8a Transversal, Urb. Altmira.
United Kingdom: Torre Las Mercedes, Avenida La Estancia, Chuao. ☎ (2) 751-1022.
United States: Av. Francisco Miranda and Av. Principal de la Floresta. ☎ (2) 284-7111.

In Maracaibo:
United States: Edificio Sofimara, Calle 77 and Av. 13. ☎ (61) 84-254.

Guard and port captain. Immigration clearance is only required when entering and leaving the country. As clearance is done from port to port, no cruising permit is necessary. It may be necessary to have an official pilot for entry into Maracaibo, La Guaira and Ciudad Bolívar.

Puerto Sucre: Formalities are reasonable as the officials are used to yachts. Cumaná town is a mile away.

Carenero: One can anchor off the yacht club and there is also a marina. The port captain's office is about a mile away.

La Guaira: This a big commercial port and yachts cannot clear in without using an agent. For a fee of about US$40, the agent does all paperwork and brings all the officials to the dock together. For outward clearance the agent delivers stamped passports and clearance papers to the fuel dock. Immigration is on the NW of the passenger terminal by the dock.

Pampatar: Customs, in the north-east corner of square, should be visited first, then police, immigration and lastly the port captain, whose office is in a

building along the coast past the Flamingo Beach Hotel. This can be time-consuming, and Shore Base Yacht Service, who monitor VHF Channel 68, will do all these formalities for a reasonable fee. One must check out at Pampatar not Porlamar.

Los Testigos: This is not a port of entry, so theoretically one should clear into Venezuela somewhere else before coming here. However, officials may come out by boat to check and clear yachts. Alternatively, one can check in at the army post on Isla Iguana.

If one wishes to stop at any of the Venezuelan islands between Isla de Margarita and Bonaire, this should be stated when clearing out of Pampatar. A mention will be made on the clearance paper that permission had been granted to stop at 'puntos intermedios'. This may not always be acceptable to other officials and some yachts trying to stop in La Blanquilla have had difficulties with officials. To avoid this it is advisable to call the coastguard (Guarda Costa) on VHF Channel 16 while approaching the island and state one's intention.

Customs

Firearms must be declared on arrival. They will be sealed on board by the National Guard. Should the seal be broken in an emergency, it must be reported immediately to the nearest National Guard station.

Animals are not restricted but should have a valid health certificate and anti-rabies vaccination. There is rabies in Venezuela.

Foreign yachts may remain in Venezuela for a 6 month period, after which they must not return for a further 3 months. Yachts that have left the country and returned before this 3 months is up have either been fined or asked to leave the country.

Immigration

All nationalities require a visa in advance. There are convenient Venezuelan consulates in Bonaire, Martinique, Barbados, Trinidad and Grenada. Both fees and the validity of the visa given may vary between embassies, from two to six months. A passport or certified copy of the passport should be carried at all times when travelling inland, as the police do spot checks.

Health

Malaria prophylaxis recommended. There is bilharzia in some rivers, so swimming in fresh water should be avoided.

Fees

Visa fee. There is an entry tax of Bs100. There is overtime for clearance outside of working hours. Agent's fee where applicable.

Charter

Chartering is illegal in Venezuela, especially to Venezuelan citizens, and can lead to heavy fines or confiscation of the boat. An exception to this rule is when a foreign flag vessel arrives to pick up charter guests from an international flight to cruise in Venezuelan waters, these being considered as crew.

Restrictions

Isla Orchilla is a military base and can only be visited with special permission from Caracas.

Security

The number of thefts, muggings and even knife attacks reported by visiting sailors has increased in recent years. They seem to occur both on the mainland and in the islands. Margarita, Cumaná and Puerto la Cruz seem to be particularly bad areas.

Facilities

Venezuela is a good place to provision, especially if continuing on to the Pacific. Prices are lower than most of the Caribbean. The selection is generally good, although shortages can occur lasting several months. Fuel is widely available and very cheap. Repair facilities are generally good and the prices competitive because labour costs are low; however, a written estimate should be obtained before embarking on any major work.

In Isla de Margarita six new marinas were under construction at the time of writing. The best facilities are at Pampatar, where Shore Base offers a full range of services, including chandlery, Imray charts, cruising publications, fuel, LPG, telephone, fax and mail. They also act as agents and can handle all entry and exit formalities. Various other facilities are available locally such as electronic and engine repair, fibreglass, carpentry, metalwork, rigging and upholstery. There are good supermarkets and fresh produce is abundant. There is no haul-out facility on the island and the nearest yard is at Cumaná.

There are good repair facilities and several boatyards in Cumaná. Among those who have been dealing with yachts, Astilleros Oriente does not have a good reputation and Varadero Caribe has been recommended by cruising sailors. It may be possible to leave the yacht at the Marina Publica Cumangoto for longer than the normal six-month period if wishing to leave the country by other means. Permission must be obtained from port captain and marina manager. Cumaná is one of the few places where this is possible. The marina has water, electricity and good security.

The Amerigo Vespucci marina in Puerto la Cruz operates a boatyard, where yachts can be slipped and hull repair can be undertaken. It is good for repairs and provisioning before sailing to the Pacific.

La Guaira is a large commercial port with no facilities for yachts, only worth visiting for clearance or visiting Caracas. Fuel is available on the dock and water at the military dock. At Carabelleda one can anchor off or use the public marina. Various repair facilities are available and there is a boatyard. Fuel is available at the dock. Puerto Cabello is a large commercial port with good repair facilities and provisioning, but apparently doubtful security.

Further Reading

A Cruising Guide to the Caribbean and the Bahamas
South American Handbook
Cruising Guide to the Eastern Caribbean, Vol. 4

8 North Pacific Islands

No other region described in this book presents such a marked contrast as that between the highly developed and fast pace of Hawaii and the tranquil traditional lifestyle of some of the Micronesian islands. For anyone cruising the North Pacific this way of life is the most interesting feature of these widely scattered islands, some of which are hardly ever visited by yachts or any other outsiders. Most yacht movement is centred on Hawaii, which serves as a convenient turning-point for the large number of yachts sailing over from mainland North America. Hawaii is also a good platform for starting a longer cruise, whether it be to Alaska, Micronesia or the South Pacific. The latter is still the favourite and Tahiti the usual destination after Hawaii.

Most of the former UN Trust Territories of the North Pacific have chosen some degree of autonomy, although they continue to maintain strong links with the United States, who had administered them since the Second World War. The USA maintains a military presence in some places, access to which is usually prohibited to yachts. In an attempt to protect their traditional lifestyle, most Micronesian nations do not actively encourage tourism and there are certain restrictions imposed on yachts wishing to visit some of the remote islands. Many of them insist on a cruising permit to be obtained in advance, but in some places this permit is issued on arrival.

Most of the area is under the influence of the NE trade winds which are most consistent during winter, from November to March. Their strength and consistency diminishes as one moves south towards the equator. Typhoons affect the area between the Carolines and Japan, most typhoons occurring between May and December, September being the most dangerous month. Typhoons do not reach the islands east of Guam.

Facilities are situated at the two extremes, in Hawaii and Guam, with very little in between. Anyone sailing west of Hawaii must be prepared to be able to cope with any emergency as the few facilities that are available are usually located in each territory's capital.

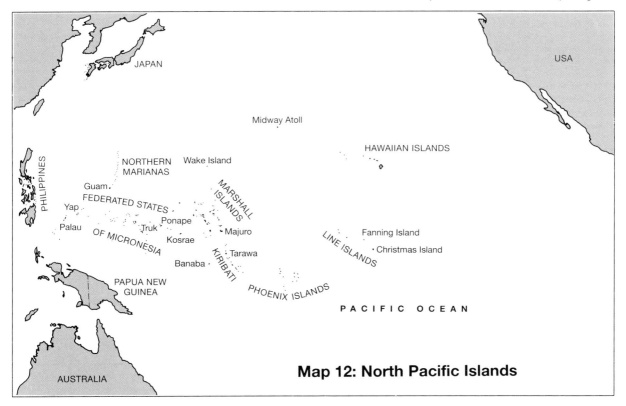

Map 12: North Pacific Islands

As can be expected, facilities in Hawaii itself are of the highest order, which means that the boat can be well prepared for the projected voyage. Facilities are also good in Guam, where most of what might be needed is available.

FEDERATED STATES OF MICRONESIA

The Federated States of Micronesia (FSM) are Kosrae, Pohnpei, Truk and Yap, stretching over a vast expanse of Pacific Ocean just north of the equator. Geographically, these four small states are part of the Caroline Islands, consisting between them of over 600 islands, of which only 65 are inhabited.

For the cruising sailor the Federated States of Micronesia offer a chance to come in contact with a Micronesian society which has managed to preserve most of its traditions despite successive waves of foreign domination. Close links with the United States have brought a higher living standard, but also the social problems of modern life, which the islanders are making an effort to overcome. Visiting sailors, coming by sea, with which the islanders have a deep affinity, can be sure of a warm and sincere welcome.

The four individual states each have their own distinct character, which adds to the attraction of sailing there. Pohnpei, formerly known as Ponape, is a lush island with eight outlying atolls. The ruins of Nan Madol, a city of nearly one hundred man-made islets dating back to AD 1200, are worth a visit. Another attraction of Pohnpei is the excellent diving, reputedly best at Ant Atoll, 10 miles SW of Pohnpei, although the atoll is privately owned and permission must be obtained from the authorities in the capital Kolonia before a visit.

Kosrae is a mountainous volcanic island, with a quiet atmosphere, especially since the Congregationalist church is very strong, and on Sundays even leisure activities are disapproved of.

The State of Truk has 192 small islands spread over nearly 1000 square miles of ocean, many of them uninhabited. The main centre is Truk Lagoon, where 15 islands and 80 islets surround the huge lagoon, where an entire Japanese fleet was trapped and sunk by a surprise US air attack in 1944, and is now Truk's main tourist attraction. Also part of Truk state are the isolated Mortlocks, Hall Islands and Western Islands, where a more traditional atmosphere may be experienced.

The islands of Yap are the most isolated and traditional in their ways and the Yapese are determined to

Tribal elder from Yap.

keep it that way. Yap Proper, consisting of 14 islands within a reef, is the centre of the state, while eastwards lie the 134 other islands. Yap is famous for its huge stone money, which was once transported from island to island in canoes.

Country Profile

Before the arrival of Europeans all the islands had developed civilisations based on highly stratified clan societies. These social divisions remain strong today. Pohnpei was inhabited as early as AD 200, and ruled in the thirteenth century by a royal dynasty from Nan Madol city. On Kosrae by the fifteenth century a highly developed society existed with its capital on the fortressed Leluh island. Only sighted in the nineteenth century by Europeans, it was named Strong's Island and was rarely visited. On Yap remains have been found dating back to AD 200, and Yap once reigned over a considerable island empire, built on the power of sorcerers.

Out of the way of the main trade routes, little

Practical Information

LOCAL TIME: Yap, Truk, GMT + 10.
Pohnpei, Kosrae, GMT + 11.

BUOYAGE: IALA A

CURRENCY: United States dollar (US$)

BUSINESS HOURS
Banks: 1000–1500 Monday to Thursday,
to 1700/1800 Friday.
Shops: 0800–1630 weekdays.
Government offices: 0800–1700 Monday
to Friday.

ELECTRICITY: 110/120 V, 60 Hz

PUBLIC HOLIDAYS
Mainly US holidays are observed:
1 January: New Year's Day
Third Monday in January: Martin Luther
King's Birthday
Third Monday in February: President's
Day

Good Friday
Last Monday in May: Memorial Day
4 July: US Independence Day
First Monday in September: Labor Day
First Monday in October: Columbus Day
24 October: United Nations Day
11 November: Veterans Day
Fourth Thursday in
November: Thanksgiving Day
25 December
Also:
10 May: FSM Constitution Day
12 July: Micronesian Day
Kosrae: 11 January: Constitution Day; 6
September: Liberation Day
Pohnpei: 24 February: Sokehs Rebellion
Day; 31 March: Traditional Culture Day;
17 May: Kolonia Independence Day; 11
September: Liberation Day (a week of
festivities); 8 November: State
Constitution Day, also Constitution Days
for each municipality.
Yap: 1 March: Yap Day

COMMUNICATIONS
International calls via the COMSAT
stations, normally open 24 hours.
The US postal system is used.
Zip codes: Pohnpei 96941; Truk 96942;
Yap 96943; Kosrae 96944;
Mail can be sent c/o General Delivery
with island zip code.
Moen, Truk: the post office is open
0900–1530 Monday, 0800–1530
Tuesday–Friday, 1000–1200 Saturday.
International onward connections are
best made via flights to Guam, Majuro
(Marshalls) or Nadi (Fiji). There are
flights between the islands.

MEDICAL
Facilities are available in all the states.

---

attention was paid to any of the islands until the nineteenth century, when traders, whalers and missionaries arrived. New diseases wiped out many of the islanders. The surviving inhabitants saw first the Spanish, then the Germans impose colonial rule, solely interested in exploiting the economic value of the islands' resources, and using the islanders as forced labour. The Germans fled at the start of the First World War, and the Japanese ruled the islands as League of Nation mandates. The Japanese embarked on an intensive cultivation of the islands, while the Micronesians, often outnumbered on their own islands, had little say in what went on. Then came the Second World War and the Americans gradually pushed out the Japanese, although the worst of the fighting took place elsewhere.

After the war the United States administered the islands as part of the UN Trust Territory. In 1979 the Trust Territory voted on a common constitution, which was rejected by the Marshalls and Palau, who went their own way. The remainder formed the Federated States of Micronesia. Each state has signed a separate Compact of Free Association with the USA, which means the US retains military freedom and the islands receive aid. Each state has its own constitution.

Millions of dollars in aid come into the FSM from the USA, aimed at building the economy towards self-sufficiency. Many projects are under way, but most islanders remain subsistence farmers and fishermen. There is little paid employment except in the government sector. Fishing rights fees are an important source of income, but otherwise there are few natural resources. Kosrae is known for its citrus fruits, and Pohnpei exports black pepper.

The populations of the states are as follows: Kosrae, 7000; Pohnpei, 30,000; Truk, over 46,000; Yap, over 10,000. All are Micronesians, except for the Nukuro and Kapingamarangi islanders in Pohnpei state who are Polynesian. English is the language spoken by all, as well as Kosraen, Pohnpeian, Trukese and Yapese. Some outer islands have their own languages. Most islanders are Protestants.

Each state has its own centre, but the FSM capital is Kolonia on Pohnpei. Colonia (the town is locally known as Donguch) is the capital of Yap, Tofol of Kosrae, and Moen of Truk.

The islands are under the influence of the NE trade winds, which blow between October and May. January to March is the dry season, while rainfall can be heavy in the summer months. The SW monsoon lasts from June to September, when there are frequent periods of calm. Strong SW gales can occur during August and September. They appear to be caused by the typhoons which are bred in this region but usually move away from the islands. Occasionally the islands are affected by typhoons.

Entry Regulations

Ports of entry
Pohnpei: Kolonia 6°59′N 158°13′E.
Truk: Moen (Truk Lagoon) 7°20′N 151°50′E, Lukunor Atoll (Mortlocks) 5°30′N 153°48′E, Satawan Atoll (Mortlocks) 5°25′N 153°35′E.
Yap: Colonia (Yap Proper) 9°30′N 138°08′E, Ulithi Atoll 9°55′N 139°30′E, Wolaei Atoll 7°21′N 143°53′E.
Kosrae: Lele/Leluh Harbour 5°20′N 163°02′E, Okat Harbour 5°21′N 162°57′E.

Procedure on arrival
Kolonia: For clearing in it is best to come alongside the commercial wharf as customs and immigration may wish to board the boat. Agriculture, police and health officials may also visit. If there is no space at the wharf, one can anchor and go ashore. The customs and immigration offices are in separate buildings in town.

On departure, it is possible to clear customs in town, but immigration may insist on clearing the yacht at the commercial wharf.
Moen: The government offices are on the NW side of the island near the airport.
Kosrae: Lele Harbour, protected by the reef and Leluh Island, is the harbour of the capital Tofol, on the eastern side of the island. Customs and immigration officials will come out to the yacht at anchor in a launch. After clearance, one should visit the Port Director at the Public Works Office in town. Clearance is also possible at Okat Harbour on the western coast.
Colonia: The town is on Yap Island inside the reef, by Tamil Harbour, and government offices are nearby.

Customs
Firearms must be declared to the police on arrival and may have to be surrendered until departure.

Animals require a veterinary certificate and must remain on board at all times. Birds such as parrots and parakeets cannot be imported without special permission from the Director of Health Services. Birds not having this permission may have to be destroyed or exported.

Immigration
Entry permits are granted for up to 30 days, with proof of adequate funds. One must clear in and out of each state, and a new entry permit of 30 days is given each time. Extensions for over 30 days in one state must be obtained in advance from Chief of Immigration, Dept of Resources & Development, FSM National Government, Pohnpei 96941. For stays over 90 days a visa will be needed.

Cruising permit
This must be obtained in advance of arrival. One should apply in writing to the Immigration Division, PO Box 490, Kolonia, Pohnpei 96941. The permit is issued for one year. Any yacht arriving without the permit may be asked to leave after three days. If the application has been made and the permit not yet received, one should make one's entry at the port of entry for a state capital.

Health
Truk has been cholera free only since 1984.

Fees
Yap: Overtime is charged after 1630 on weekdays, and at weekends: customs, immigration and health all charge $6 per hour.

Harbour fees are $0.06 times GRT divided by 24 hours.

Light dues are $0.06 times GRT. There are charges for fresh water.
Pohnpei: Overtime is charged outside of 0800–1700 Monday to Friday, and at weekends.

Harbour fee $15 entry, $5 per day for using the dock.
Truk and Kosrae: Overtime is charged outside of 0800–1700 weekdays, and all day Saturdays, Sundays and holidays.

Restrictions
When visiting outer islands of each state, not the main centres, permission must be asked for beforehand from the owner of the land. Even uninhabited islands and islets do have an owner. Permission is normally granted.

Facilities

Facilities vary widely across the Federation, with adequate repair facilities in the main centres and very little in the outer islands. A marina has been developed in Sokehs Bay, Kolonia, with berths for local boats as well as visiting yachts. There are fisheries plants in several islands and wherever there is a base for fishing boats, one can expect to find at least a modicum of repair facilities. One of the best is Yap Fisheries who maintain a 70-ton railway where boats can be hauled out and some repairs carried out.

Provisioning is good in all main centres where there is a selection of imported goods, mainly from the USA, although they tend to be on the expensive side. There are also fresh produce markets and some fresh produce can be found practically everywhere even if the selection is not always great. Water sources must be chosen carefully as often the public supply is not drinkable and should be treated. Generally, rain water is more reliable if one has access to a catchment tank, or provision should be made to collect one's own. Fuel can be bought in all centres, usually by jerrycan, although some fisheries have pumps or can arrange to have it delivered to the dock by tanker.

As in other remote cruising areas, one should carry a good supply of essential spares as the only parts that may be available locally are those used in trucks or heavy plant in use on the islands.

Further Reading

Micronesia – a travel survival kit
Landfalls of Paradise

GUAM

Guam is the largest and most populous island of Micronesia, a modern, Americanised metropolis and an important US military base. It is geographically the southernmost of the Mariana Islands, but forms a separate unit from the Commonwealth of the Northern Marianas. Guam is an Unincorporated Territory of the United States. Guam's close relations with the USA, and its role as a crossroads and distribution centre for the rest of Micronesia because of its air links, makes it rather different from the rest of the Pacific.

Cruising yachts will indeed find in Guam a contrasting atmosphere to the one they have experienced in other islands. The pace is faster, the buildings taller and everything can be fixed if one is prepared to pay the price. Guam is used by many American sailors as a long-term base, especially as US citizens can work in Guam without a permit.

Country Profile

The Chamorros inhabited the Marianas as early as 1500 BC, migrating east from South East Asia. A complex matrilineal hierarchical society developed and stone remains of this early civilisation are still visible on the island. Magellan's visit in 1521 marked the arrival of the Western world. In the sixteenth century Spain claimed the Marianas, which were valuable as a stopping point on the trade route between Mexico and the Philippines. In the next century Catholic missionaries

arrived, but their efforts to suppress old traditions led to rebellions by the Chamorros. By the end of the seventeenth century there were no Chamorro men left, either being killed in the fighting or by European diseases. Things improved as Spaniards and Filipinos settled and cultivated the island. At the end of the 1898 Spanish–American war, Guam was ceded to the United States. During the Second World War the Japanese occupied Guam, until the USA retook the island in 1944 after some fierce fighting. In 1950 a civilian government took over, Guam's population gaining US citizenship, although no vote in US elections. The close relationship between Guam and the USA is unlikely to change in view of Guam's strategic importance to the USA.

Since the 1960s Guam has seen considerable economic growth and a rise in the standard of living. The military bases are the largest employer and dominate the economy. Both the Air Force and Navy have a considerable presence here and there are bases for nuclear submarines and facilities for the storage of nuclear warheads. In the 1960s travel restrictions were lifted and tourism opened up, especially from Japan.

The population is 106,000. Half are Chamorro, the rest Asian and American. English is the main language and, to a lesser extent, Chamorro which has a Spanish influence, as does the main religion, Roman Catholicism. Agana has been the main centre on Guam since the Spanish period.

The climate is warm and humid. From January to April the NE trades blow, while from July to November it is rainy and stormy. Typhoons can occur between July and November.

Entry Regulations

Port of entry
Apra Harbour 13°27′N 144°37′E.

Procedure on arrival
One should contact harbour control on VHF Channels 16, 13 or 12 (call sign KUF 810) for instructions on where to berth for clearance. Usually visiting yachts are directed to the commercial pier near the two large cranes. If one has to anchor in Apra Harbour, the best dinghy landing area is the public launching ramp, west of the Mobil tanks.

Customs
Firearms must be declared on arrival and will be sealed on board. Permits may have to be shown.

Animals must be declared and should have up-to-date health certificates. They are not allowed to land.

Practical Information

LOCAL TIME: GMT + 10

BUOYAGE: IALA A

CURRENCY: United States dollar (US$)

BUSINESS HOURS
Banks: 1000–1500 Monday to Thursday, 1000–1800 Friday.
Shops: 0800–1630 weekdays.
Government offices: 0800–1700 weekdays.

ELECTRICITY: 110 V, 60 Hz

PUBLIC HOLIDAYS
US holidays:
1 January: New Year's Day
Third Monday in January: Martin Luther King's Birthday

Third Monday in February: President's Day
Good Friday
Last Monday in May: Memorial Day
4 July: US Independence Day
First Monday in September: Labor Day
First Monday in October: Columbus Day
24 October: United Nations Day
11 November: Veterans Day
Fourth Thursday in November: Thanksgiving Day
25 December
Plus:
First Monday in March: Guam Discovery Day
21 July: Liberation Day
8 December: Immaculate Conception

COMMUNICATIONS
Mail can be sent to c/o General Delivery, Agana 96910, open 0830–1700 Monday to Friday, 1200–1600 Saturday.
There are flights from Guam to the Philippines, Japan, Indonesia, Hong Kong and to the USA via Majuro and Honolulu.

DIPLOMATIC MISSIONS
In Agana:
Japan: ITC Building, Tamuning.
☎ 646-5220.
Philippines: ITC Building, Tamuning.
☎ 646-4620.
There is an office of the Commonwealth of the Northern Mariana Islands where one can get an entry permit for the Northern Marianas.

Immigration

US visa regulations are in force, and all nationals except US citizens are required to have a visa in advance. However, visa requirements are often waived for those arriving by yacht.

Fees

Overtime is charged for clearance outside of normal office hours.

Facilities

Because of the high frequency of typhoons, arrangements have been made in Apra Harbour for small boats seeking shelter during a typhoon. The refuge area is located in Piti Channel, which can be reached by boats with a maximum draft of 8 feet. The area is reputed to be well sheltered in any kind of winds.

The Marianas Yacht Club, located on Dry Dock Point opposite the commercial port, can be used by visitors who are required to pay a fee. This gives access to the club facilities, including showers and laundry. Some of the privately owned moorings managed by the club are occasionally made available to visitors. There are additional moorings in Piti Channel and also at Agana Boat Basin, a small boat harbour in East Agana.

Fuel and water can be obtained at the fishermen's wharf in Apra Harbour or at Agana Marina, which is located approximately eight miles up the coast.

Although an increasingly important cruising destination, yachting facilities are rather limited with only basic spares being available locally. However, as there are regular air links with mainland USA, most parts can be air freighted to Guam in a reasonable time. There are several supermarkets which have a good selection of food as well as a fresh produce market. Guam is one of the best places to reprovision in Micronesia.

Further Reading

Micronesia – a travel survival kit
Landfalls of Paradise

HAWAII

Hawaii, the 50th state of the USA, is in fact an archipelago stretching across the North Pacific from the remote Kure and Midway atolls to the more developed and heavily populated islands in the east. The islands are summits of an ancient volcanic mountain range, and have stunning scenery to match. On the largest, Hawaii Island, also known as Big Island, there is Mauna Loa, over 13,000 ft (4000 m) high, an active volcano, which erupted in 1959 destroying a village and thousands of acres of crops. The other major islands are Maui, Oahu, Kauai, Molokai, Lanai, Nihau and Kahoolawe. Hawaii is very different to the rest of the Pacific, mainly due to the strong American influence, also being very developed and commercial, such as the world-famous Waikiki Beach, although the old ways do survive in some places.

The ideal landfall and start of a cruise in Hawaiian waters is the small port of Hilo on Big Island as it is upwind of the entire archipelago. Hilo is a very pleasant place to unwind after the long passage from mainland USA and also to visit the interior of the spectacular Big Island. In most places in Hawaii only part of the sightseeing can be done from the cockpit, as many of the interesting places are either inland or difficult to reach by boat. The Big Island is an excellent introduction to Hawaii with its magnificent Kilauea Volcano, orchid gardens, cane fields and scenic coastline. A definite stop on the lee side of the island is at Kealakekua Bay, where Captain Cook lost his life in 1778.

The former whaling capital of the Pacific, Lahaina on Maui island is another popular cruising stop, as is the marine park at Hulopoe Bay on Lanai with its superb underwater scenery. Busy Honolulu with its excellent facilities has many tempting sights which should include a visit to the Bishop Museum, especially for those planning to continue their cruise to other Pacific islands, as many of the art treasures from these islands have been collected there. A good place to take one's leave from Hawaii is the northernmost island of Kauai and its spectacular Hanalei Bay, the set for many a South Seas movie.

Country Profile

Hawaii is said to have been discovered three times, the Polynesians claiming that Hawaii Loa was the first to land there over 1000 years ago. Some say that the Spanish were the first Europeans to discover the islands, but it was more likely Captain Cook in 1778, who named them the Sandwich Islands. This great navigator lost his life in a dispute between his crew and the islanders of Kealakekua (Hawaii Island).

At the end of the eighteenth century Kamehameha the Great united all the islands under his rule, and until 1882 his family reigned, later taken over by the Kalahaua dynasty. Missionaries and traders arrived during the nineteenth century. In 1893 Queen Lili'uokalani was dethroned and a republic proclaimed. Soon afterwards the US Congress passed a resolution annexing the islands. Many attempts were made by Hawaii to be recognised as a state, a status finally achieved in 1959.

The economy mainly relies on sugar, pineapples and tourism. Handicrafts, Hawaiian-style clothes, orchids and macadamia nuts are also exported. The scarcity of land is a problem and over a million people inhabit Hawaii. Following the immigration of Chinese and Japanese in the nineteenth century, Portuguese, Spanish and Russian in the early twentieth century, Hawaii's population is very mixed. Those of Polynesian origin form only a small minority. English is the main language. All Christian denominations can be found as well as Buddhism, Shintoism and Judaism. The capital is Honolulu on Oahu Island where most of the population lives.

The climate is subtropical in the low coastal areas and temperate in the mountains. There is no rainy season but showers, sometimes downpours, occur in winter. The islands are under the influence of the NE trade winds and are only rarely affected by tropical cyclones.

Entry Regulations

Hawaiian entry regulations are basically the same as the rest of the United States, but there are slight differences and regulations are usually applied in a more detailed manner. This is partly due to the fact that to arrive in Hawaii from the US mainland, yachts must leave US territorial waters.

Ports of entry
Honolulu (Oahu) 21°18'N 157°52'W, Hilo (Hawaii) 19°44'N 155°04'W, Kahului (Maui) 20°54'N 156°28'W, Nawiliwili (Kauai) 21°57'N 159°21'W, Port Allen (Kauai) 21°54'N 158°36'W.

Procedure on arrival
Customs telephone numbers: Hilo: 935-6976, Honolulu: 546-5168. The 24-hour number for both of these two is 836-3613. Kauai: 833-5521 (24 hours). Maui: 877-6013 (24 hours).

Yachts must report immediately on arrival to customs and formal clearance must be made within 48 hours of arrival. Working hours are 0800–1700 Monday to Saturday. After hours, one should telephone customs. Customs will inform immigration, agriculture and health officials who will board the yacht. A Ships Stores Declaration and Crew's Effects Declaration must be made as well as showing the clearance from the previous port. Customs may handle immigration and health formalities in some places. Sometimes one can first contact the harbour master who will inform customs. Quarantine will also have to be notified if there are animals on board.

On arrival no one must go ashore except for the person reporting the arrival to customs, who must

Practical Information

LOCAL TIME: GMT - 10

BUOYAGE: IALA B

CURRENCY: United States dollar (US$)

BUSINESS HOURS
Banks: 0830–1500 Monday to Thursday,
0830–1800 Friday.
Business and government
offices: 0800–1700 Monday to Friday.
Shops: 0930–1730 Monday to Saturday,
some stay open until 2100, some open
Sundays.

ELECTRICITY: 110 V, 60 Hz

PUBLIC HOLIDAYS
1 January: New Year's Day
22 February: President's Day
1 May: Lei Day (floral displays)
30 May: Memorial Day
11 June: Kamehameha Day
4 July: Independence Day
7 September: Labor Day
September/October: Aloha Week, on
Oahu
Last Thursday in
November: Thanksgiving Day
25 December: Christmas Day

COMMUNICATIONS
Public telephones can be credit card or
coin operated.
Stamps are available at post offices,
hotels and shops.
Emergency: Dial operator 0.
There are frequent flights from Honolulu
to mainland USA, the Far East, Europe,
Tahiti, Fiji, New Zealand and Australia.

MEDICAL
There are good medical facilities in all
islands, but as the costs tend to be high,
visitors are advised to have a
comprehensive health insurance.

afterwards return to the yacht, until formalities are completed. Violations of this rule can result in heavy penalties, even forfeiture of the boat.

Yachts must enter at an official port of entry. Yachts stopping elsewhere may be liable for heavy fines. This rule also applies to US registered vessels coming from foreign ports; they must call at an official port of entry before proceeding elsewhere. American captains have been fined for making landfall at other Hawaiian ports and attempting to clear customs by telephone.

US vessels arriving from a US port on the mainland who have not stopped at a foreign port en route or have had no contact with any other vessel at sea, and who have only US citizens on board, do not need to clear customs, but must be inspected on arrival by an agricultural inspector of the State of Hawaii. They must inform the agricultural department of their arrival.

After having cleared into Hawaii, US vessels are free to go anywhere they wish without any other formalities. Foreign vessels are given a cruising permit, if eligible, after clearance is complete. Foreign vessels must check in with customs at other ports of entry when they visit other islands. Precise instructions of the procedure will be given at the first port of entry.

Procedure on departure
All yachts, including US registered vessels, must obtain a customs clearance, both for foreign destinations and the US mainland.

Customs
Firearms must be declared to customs. The police may issue permits.

Hawaii is rabies-free, so regulations regarding animals on board yachts are more strict than on the US mainland. Animals must be declared on arrival, and will have to be sent to the Quarantine Centre in Honolulu within 72 hours, where they must remain for 120 days or until the yacht leaves Hawaii. This includes animals arriving from the US mainland. As air transport costs from other islands are paid by the animal's owner, it is better to make Honolulu the port of entry if one has an animal on board. There is a daily fee for quarantine, which must be paid in advance; unused days will be refunded. The quarantine station should be given 24 to 48 hours notice of departure and they will deliver the animal to the yacht. Penalties are very heavy for violation of this regulation.

Any dutiable items such as navigation equipment bought recently in the USA should be listed and certified by US customs before leaving the USA, or receipts kept showing the place of purchase, to avoid being liable for duty.

There are restrictions on importing plants and fresh produce. Fruit and vegetables may be confiscated on arrival when the yacht is inspected by the agriculture official.

Cruising permit
US regulations state that foreign yachts from certain countries can obtain a cruising licence on arrival, which exempts them from having to clear in and out in each port once the first entry clearance is completed. The countries which are eligible for this licence are Argentina, Austria, Australia, Bahamas, Belgium, Bermuda, Canada, Denmark, France, Germany, Greece, Honduras, Ireland, Jamaica, Liberia, the Netherlands, New Zealand, Norway, Sweden, the United Kingdom (including Turks and Caicos, St Vincent, Cayman Islands, British Virgin Islands, St Kitts and Anguilla). This list, which includes countries

that grant similar privileges to US yachts, is subject to change. The licence is issued on entry by customs. It is valid for up to one year. Successive licences are not usually granted. US mainland cruising permits are not valid in Hawaii and a separate permit must be obtained on arrival.

Foreign yachts, whether or not holding a cruising permit, are still supposed to notify customs by telephone on arrival in major ports.

Yachts not entitled to a cruising licence must obtain a permit before proceeding to each subsequent port. They must also contact customs at all major ports while cruising Hawaii.

Immigration

US citizens need proof of citizenship only.

Canadians need proof of citizenship only, unless they are arriving from outside of North America, when they must present a valid Canadian passport.

All other nationalities need a visa, which must be obtained in advance from US embassies and consulates. The passport must be valid at least six months beyond the period of stay.

Fees

Overtime is charged outside of working hours, and on Sundays and public holidays. Service will be provided at pro-rata overtime rates, not to exceed US$25 per boat.

Customs charges are: a user fee of US$25 (an annual processing fee), entry US$9, clearance US$9, cruising permit US$18.

Restrictions

The following are prohibited or restricted areas:
Hulopoe Bay on Lanai, is a marine conservation area.
Nihau Island is reserved for native Hawaiians. It can only be visited with official permission.
Military areas: Kahoolawe Island, just south of Maui, is under US Navy jurisdiction and access is forbidden, as it is used as a firing range; it should be given a wide berth.
The Midway Islands, 28°13'N 177°24'W, at the western extremity of the Hawaiian group, are not part of the state of Hawaii, and are administered by the US Navy. Johnston Atoll 16°45'N 169°31'W is administered by the US Air Force and is used for dumping all the chemical weapons removed from Europe in 1990 as well as other military purposes. The waters within a three-mile radius of both Midway and Johnston are off-limits to yachts unless they have special permission. In case of a real emergency, permission to enter would probably be given. In such a case one should contact the US Coast Guard

or the Rescue Coordination Centre in Honolulu.
Remote Island Wildlife Refuges: These are administered by the US Fish and Wildlife Service in Honolulu. Permission to land will only be given for legitimate reasons. These areas include:
The NW part of the Hawaiian archipelago, including Nihoa Island, but not Midway, from 161°W to 176°W.
Howland, Baker and Jarvis Islands, on the equator SSW of Hawaii.
Kure Island, west of Midway. Access is restricted to this island, which is administered by the state of Hawaii.
Palmyra Atoll 5°53'N 162°05'W is privately owned and permission to stop here should be obtained from the owners.
Wake Island 19°18'N 166°38'E is administered by the US Air Force but yachts can stop. The pass into the lagoon is not deep enough to enter so one has to anchor off the reef, making it only a temporary stop. Only military and contract workers live there.

Facilities

The number of marinas in Hawaii is less than one would expect in such a developed place and on the whole, yachting facilities are below US standards. The number of cruising yachts is not very large, except in the summer when many yachts make their way across from the mainland and facilities are stretched to the full.

With a few exceptions, all marinas are state-owned and operated. This means that they are subject to standard regulations and also that docking fees are lower than in private marinas. The basic rules are as follows: berths are assigned on a first come first served basis, but one may reserve a place either by writing a letter or telephoning in advance. The first three days are free, but those who stay longer have to pay for the entire period, including the first three days. The maximum stay in one year at any state marina or harbour is 30 days. The average cost is under $10 per day, water and electricity being included where available. Some yacht clubs also have docking facilities for visitors. The Hawaii Yacht Club in Honolulu will allow visitors to use its facilities for a fee, but this is usually limited to a maximum period of two weeks.

Major repair work and services, such as hauling out and hull, engine and sail repair, are available only at Honokohau Harbour on Hawaii (Big Island), at Kewalo Basin, Keehi Lagoon and at Ala Wai Boat Harbour in Honolulu on Oahu Island. Smaller repairs can be made at Hilo, Lahaina and Nawiliwili. Fuel and water are available on the dock in most harbours, otherwise it has to be carried in jerrycans. Marine supplies in the main yachting centres are good and there are several chandleries with a wide selection, including charts. One of the best is Ala Wai Marine Stores in Honolulu. Whatever is not available locally will be ordered from the mainland and air freighted to Hawaii in 48 to 72 hours.

Provisioning is good everywhere and Hawaii is a good place to victual the boat, especially if planning to cruise the outer islands of Micronesia or the South Pacific. However, the prices are 25 per cent higher than on the mainland so all non-perishable stores should be bought before leaving the USA. LPG bottles can be filled in most places, but non-US standard bottles must be fitted with an adaptor.

Further Reading

Landfalls of Paradise
Charlie's Charts of the Hawaiian Islands
Weather in Hawaiian Waters

KIRIBATI

The Republic of Kiribati (pronounced 'kiribass'), formerly the Gilbert Islands, is a group of more than 30 islands situated in the centre of the Pacific Ocean around the point where the international date line and the equator cross. Besides the 16 original Gilbert Islands, Kiribati also includes Banaba (Ocean Island), the eight Phoenix Islands, and eight of the eleven Line Islands. All of the islands are low atolls enclosing lagoons, rarely more than 12 ft (4 m) above sea level. The notable exception is Banaba, which is volcanic. Little grows on these islands except coconut palms and not all of them are inhabited. Kiribati is very isolated, its small islands spread out over more than one million square miles of ocean.

Visiting this sprawling archipelago needs careful planning, a task not made easier by the insistence of the authorities that one must clear in first at the capital Tarawa before going anywhere else. While this is relatively easy if one only intends to visit the northern group of the original Gilberts, where Tarawa occupies a central position, a visit to the outer islands such as Christmas, Canton or Fanning presents almost insurmountable logistical problems because of the prevailing winds and currents. Fortunately local officials often take a rather detached view of Tarawa's instructions, as everyone on these remote islands, officials included, are usually delighted to welcome visitors to their lonely outposts. This remoteness is one of the things which makes these islands so intriguing and any amount of officialdom cannot spoil the pleasure of visiting them.

Country Profile

The first inhabitants of these islands probably came from Australasia with migrations from Samoa in the thirteenth century AD. Although sighted by Spanish expeditions, the first real contact with Europeans came only in the mid-nineteenth century with the arrival of missionaries, whalers and blackbirders (slave traders). The islanders suffered greatly from new diseases brought by these visitors, especially measles. At the end of the century the Gilbert Islands, together with the Ellice Islands (now Tuvalu), willingly became a British Protectorate, hoping to end tribal conflicts and raiding of the population by blackbirders.

In 1900 phosphate was discovered on Ocean Island. The mining of this became an important industry and the administrative centre shifted there from Tarawa. In 1919 Christmas Island was annexed by the British, and later the other islands. During the Second World War the Gilberts were occupied by Japan and as the Americans advanced the islands were the arena for fierce fighting, especially at Betio on Tarawa. Relics of that battle still litter the shores of the lagoon today. Independence came to the Gilberts in July 1979, under their new name Kiribati.

The islanders live off fish, coconut, taro, bananas and breadfruit – everything else must be imported. The lack of resources is a problem, especially since the phosphates, once a vital source of income, have been exhausted. Some offshore mineral deposits have been found, but are not yet commercially exploited. The main exports are copra and fish, and foreign currency is earned by selling fishing rights to foreign countries in the 200 nautical mile exclusive economic zone. The sale of stamps and handicrafts also contributes some income, but considerable aid comes from Britain, Australia and New Zealand. Many work on Nauru in its phosphate industry, or as merchant seamen, sending home money. Tourism is fairly important in the northern Line Islands, due to their proximity to Hawaii.

There were 64,000 inhabitants in 1985, mostly Micronesian with some Polynesian, especially in the southern islands. English is spoken as well as I-Kiribati, a Micronesian language. The capital is Bairiki, one of the islands of Tarawa, a densely populated atoll, where about one third of the population live. The main port is on the neighbouring Betio islet in the same lagoon. Protestantism and Roman Catholicism are the main religious denominations.

Practical Information

LOCAL TIME: GMT + 12, Christmas Island GMT - 10

BUOYAGE: IALA A. Navigational aids are not very reliable and it is reported that most atolls are without lights after midnight.

CURRENCY: Australian dollar (Aus$)

BUSINESS HOURS
Business: 0800–1200/1300–1700 Monday to Friday, 0700–1200 Saturday.
Bank of Kiribati : 0900–1200/1400–1500 Monday to Friday.
Shops: 0800–1900 Monday to Friday, half day Saturdays and Sundays.

ELECTRICITY: 240 V, 50 Hz

PUBLIC HOLIDAYS
1 and 2 January: New Year
Easter Monday
12, 13, 14 July: Independence Day celebrations
August: Youth Day
10 December: Human Rights Day
25, 26 December: Christmas

COMMUNICATIONS
International telephone calls have to be made through an operator.
Post office, Betio 0900–1200/1400–1500 Monday to Friday.
Telegrams through the Telecommunications Dept. All the outer islands are in radio contact with Tarawa.

Emergency: dial 999.
There are flights from Tarawa to Funafuti (Tuvalu), Majuro (Marshalls) and Nadi (Fiji) for international flight connections. There are internal flights to most of the other islands and Christmas Island has a weekly flight to Honolulu.

MEDICAL
Tungaru Central Hospital, Bikenibeu, South Tarawa.

DIPLOMATIC MISSIONS
In Bairiki:
Australia: PO Box 77. ☎ 21184.
New Zealand: PO Box 53. ☎ 21400.
United Kingdom: PO Box 61. ☎ 21327.

Most islands have an equatorial climate, while the islands to the extreme north and south of the group are tropical. November to April is the rainy season, with high humidity and stronger winds. Rainfall is not reliable and drought can be a problem for all the islands. The prevailing easterlies keep the climate pleasant, although temperatures can be high, 27–29°C (80–85°F) on average.

Entry Regulations

Port of entry
Betio Islet on Tarawa 1°21′N, 172°55′E, Christmas Island, Fanning Island, Ocean (Banaba) Island.

Procedure on arrival
One should call Tarawa Radio on VHF Channel 16 when approaching the island and give one's ETA. The Marine Guard keeps 24-hour watch on 500, 2182 and 6215 MHz. Channel 16 is monitored only during office hours (0800–1230, 1330–1615 Monday to Friday). Having been advised beforehand, officials will be waiting in Betio when the yacht arrives. All formalities are supposed to be completed alongside in the small boat harbour in Betio, but this can only take yachts under 6 ft draft. Because of silting, the depths in the harbour are unreliable, so it may be safer for larger draft vessels to tie up to the commercial wharf on the way into Betio or anchor just outside the harbour entrance. The customs office is at Betio and immigration officials will come over from Bairiki, where the government offices are based. The captain must

show last port clearance and registry certificate.

A cruising permit should be obtained when clearing in. The authorities stipulate that in order to visit any of the other islands, one must clear in first at Tarawa and also clear out there at the end of the visit. They are strict about clearance, and Tarawa must be visited first, even if coming from the south. However, on departure it may be possible to get permission to call at an island and continue on from there out of the archipelago.
Canton: This atoll in the Phoenix Islands is a former US satellite tracking station. Only a handful of people live there and only three supply ships call a year. If one arrives with a Kiribati visa and emergency repairs have to be done, one probably can get permission to stay. The officials will request this by radio from Tarawa. The dredged ship pass should be entered near slack water and one can anchor inside the dredged turning basin. The natural pass is not recommended. The village is three miles away; officials will visit the yacht.
Tabuaeran (formerly Fanning Island): There is a wide pass on the west side but there is always a strong outflowing current. The anchorage is near the village. No one must be allowed to come on board until the officials have inspected the yacht. There is a Aus$20 harbour fee and also an Aus$5 fee for the boatman who brings out the officials.

Customs
Firearms and animals must be declared on arrival. Firearms will be taken into custody by customs until departure. Animals and agricultural produce must remain on board.

Prohibited exports are artefacts over 30 years old, traditional swords, tools and dancing ornaments.

Immigration

A visa must be obtained in advance from British consulates or from the Principal Immigration Office, Ministry of Foreign Affairs, PO Box 68, Bairiki, Tarawa. Visas are not required by nationals of Commonwealth countries, Denmark, Guam, FSM, Palau, Marshalls, Iceland, South Korea, Norway, the Philippines, Spain, Sweden and American Samoa.

A visitor's permit is normally issued on arrival. Yachts may remain up to 4 months.

Facilities

Tarawa: Most facilities available in Kiribati are concentrated on this atoll which comprises several islands around a lagoon. Basic services are available at Betio, including the government shipyard which has mechanical, electrical and engineering workshops capable of small repairs. They also have a slipway which can haul yachts with a maximum draft of 7 ft. Provisions are available in Betio, but a better supermarket is located at Bairiki. Gas bottles can be filled at Betio where reasonable amounts of diesel fuel and water are also available.

Facilities in all other islands are basic with few imported goods and a limited selection of locally produced fruit and vegetables, but there is plenty of fish everywhere. Water is often scarce and can be a problem in the southern and central parts of the group.

Further Reading

Landfalls of Paradise
South Pacific Handbook
Pacific Islands Yearbook
Pacific Odyssey

MARSHALL ISLANDS

In the central Pacific north of the Equator, the Republic of the Marshall Islands is part of Micronesia along with Kiribati and the Mariana and Caroline archipelagos. The Marshalls comprise over a thousand small low islands, forming two chains, the eastern Ratak (towards dawn) and the western Ralik (towards sunset). Their total land surface is only 70 square miles yet they are scattered over half a million square miles of ocean. Used as a site for nuclear tests by the USA, radiation effects are still a problem in some islands.

It was the nuclear tests which put the Marshalls on the world map in the early 1950s as they were little known before and are not much better known now. Not surprisingly, tourists have preferred to look elsewhere for their Pacific paradise and many cruising sailors also bypass the islands. The majority of yachts, which call at the Marshalls, are on their way from Hawaii to the rest of Micronesia, whose islands have escaped the nuclear pollution, which continues to blight some Marshall Islands to this day.

Country Profile

Little grows on these low coral islands, so the sea has always been the main resource for their inhabitants and the Marshallese were renowned as sailors and navigators. They navigated partly by observing the stars and patterns made by waves, but also using charts constructed of strips of wood tied together, which showed such patterns and the various islands. Visits from early European sailors were rare as the islands did not seem to have much to offer. It was an English captain, who sighted many of the islands at the end of the eighteenth century, whose name they have taken. Traders and missionaries avoided the Marshall Islands because they had acquired a reputation for violence after several traders had been attacked, some of whom had tried to abduct Marshallese women. From the mid-nineteenth century many islanders were converted by Protestant missionaries and the violence lessened.

Germany annexed the islands at the end of the century and developed the copra industry. Economic exploitation and development continued after the First World War when the islands were taken over and administered by Japan. In 1944 US forces captured the Marshalls from the Japanese after heavy fighting. Immediately after the war the Americans began nuclear testing on Bikini and Enewetok atolls, which took a terrible toll on the islanders and their way of life. Bikini, which was the site of the earliest known habitation in Micronesia, became uninhabitable after 23 tests. The islanders tried unsuccessfully to resettle there in the 1970s, but radiation was still too high. Enewetok, Rongelap and Utirik suffered similar fates. The USA had administered the Marshalls as part of the UN Trust Territory since 1947. The Marshalls rejected the common constitution which all members of the Trust Territory voted on in 1979, becoming a republic with its own constitution. In 1982, however, the Marshalls signed a Compact of Free Association with the USA, giving the US military rights in return for aid.

Practical Information

LOCAL TIME: GMT + 12

BUOYAGE: IALA A

CURRENCY: United States dollar (US$)

BUSINESS HOURS
Banks: 1000–1500 Monday to Thursday, 1000–1700 Friday.
Business: 0800–1630 weekdays.

ELECTRICITY: 110/120 V, 60 Hz

PUBLIC HOLIDAYS
US holidays are observed:
1 January: New Year's Day
Third Monday in January: Martin Luther King's Birthday
Third Monday in February: President's Day
Good Friday
Last Monday in May: Memorial Day
4 July: US Independence Day
First Monday in September: Labor Day
First Monday in October: Columbus Day
24 October: United Nations Day
11 November: Veterans Day

Fourth Thursday in November: Thanksgiving Day
25 December: Christmas Day
1 May: Constitution Day

COMMUNICATIONS
COMSAT on Delap for international calls; also at some hotels.
The Marshalls are part of the US domestic mail service so mail-order items from US mainland or Hawaii can be obtained quite quickly and cheaply. Zip code: 96960 except Ebeye, which is 96970.

The United States pays millions of dollars in rent for its base on Kwajalein. Income also comes from copra, tourism and handicrafts. The population numbers 37,000 and are mostly Protestant. Marshallese is the official language, but English is widely spoken. Majuro Atoll is the political and economic centre. It comprises 57 islets, the larger ones joined together by a road, around an oval lagoon. The most developed of the Marshalls, the atoll's main islands Delap, Uliga and Darrit, form the DUD municipality.

The climate is tropical and temperatures show little variation throughout the year. December to April is the NE trade wind season and even in the remaining months prevailing winds tend to be easterly. Occasionally the easterly flow is interrupted by strong SW winds. No tropical storms have been recorded and the only violent winds are those from the SW.

Entry Regulations

Ports of entry

Majuro 7°08'N 171°22'E, Ebeye Island (Kwajalein Atoll) 8°46'N 167°44'E.

Procedure on arrival

Majuro: Arriving yachts should call customs on Channel 16 and request clearance. A customs official will visit the yacht before one is allowed to go ashore. Those arriving at weekends can wait until Monday for immigration clearance. Customs and immigration are at the government offices in Delap. After clearing customs and immigration, one must visit the port director's office near the head of the pier in Uliga.

When clearing out, the offices have to be visited in reverse order, first the port director, then immigration and customs.

Ebeye (Kwajalein Atoll): One should contact officials on Channel 16 for instructions where to come alongside for clearance. If there is no space, one might have to anchor. Most yachts anchor on the east side of the T-pier, between the Mobil tanks and the old dock. Formalities are similar to those in Majuro.

Customs

Firearms must be declared on arrival. Animals must also be declared on arrival.

Immigration

It is an official requirement that entry permits must be obtained in advance for longer stays, but for short stays yachts which have arrived without a permit have been allowed to enter. One should apply for an entry permit from Chief of Immigration, Marshall Islands Government, Majuro, Marshall Islands 96960.

Cruising permit

To visit the other islands, special permission must be obtained in Majuro. A permit, one for each island, has to be applied for at the Department of Interior and Outer Islands Affairs. There is no charge, but each permit takes about a week to obtain. Each atoll is governed by a mayor and a chief from whom approval must be obtained by the Department before issuing a permit. Apparently obtaining the necessary permits is a lengthy procedure which can take several weeks in all.

Restrictions

Kwajalein Atoll is used by the USA as a missile testing area and the waters within a 200 mile radius may be affected. One should contact Kwajalein Atoll Control by radio beforehand if one is sailing in this area. Restricted islands are those used by the US army: Kwajalein Island is a closed military base, and the missile range includes Kwajalein and the islands up to Roi-Namur Island.

The following islands are under the Marshall Islands jurisdiction, but similar permission is needed to visit any of them: Bikini Atoll 11°30′N 165°34′E and Enewetok Atoll 11°30′N 162°24′E – these were sites of nuclear testing and are still contaminated; Rongelap Atoll 11°09′N 166°54′E is also polluted with fall-out from Bikini.

Facilities

The best facilities are in Majuro where provisioning is good with a wide selection, mostly imported from the USA. There is a good fresh produce market for locally grown fruit and vegetables. As the selection is much better than in the rest of Micronesia, long-term provisioning should be done in Majuro.

Only rain water should be used in Majuro as the water on the island is contaminated. Fuel can be ordered in bulk from Mobil or in smaller quantities from filling stations. Propane is available, but it is necessary to have the right adaptors as empty containers are gravity filled. Repair facilities are limited and only minor repairs can be undertaken. There are no marine supplies except for a limited selection of spares for diesel and outboard engines. Facilities in the other islands are even more limited.

Further Reading

Micronesia – a travel survival kit
Landfalls of Paradise

NORTHERN MARIANAS

The Commonwealth of the Northern Marianas in the Western Pacific has the special status of a US Commonwealth. The American influence is strong, although the legacy of Spanish colonial rule can also be seen. Of the 14 volcanic islands that stretch north to south in almost a straight line, the southernmost three, Saipan, Rota and Tinian, are the main islands. The Marianas may be regarded as the world's highest mountains, for their bases lie in the Mariana Trench, seven miles below the ocean surface, in the deepest part of the Pacific. Guam is geographically part of the Marianas, but politically separate.

These military-dominated islands, to which access

was forbidden for a long time, are now attracting a few cruising yachts every year. Most of these come from Guam, where there is a Northern Marianas representative who can issue the necessary permit to visit the islands. The southern islands are the more developed, while some of the northern islands are wildlife reserves and cannot be visited. The entire group is subject to typhoons for most of the year, another reason why cruising boats rarely sail there.

Country Profile

The original inhabitants of the islands were Chamorros, of Indo-Filipino origin, who developed a matrilineal society of nobles and commoners. Magellan was the first European to visit the islands in 1521, but the group only got its name in the seventeenth century when a Spanish priest named them Las Marianas. They came under Spanish rule as a useful stopover for ships on the Philippines to Mexico route. At the end of the nineteenth century the Germans bought the Marianas and developed the copra trade, followed by Japanese rule after the First World War when Germany lost all her Pacific colonies. The Japanese introduced sugar plantations and many Japanese settled on the islands, further eroding the indigenous way of life. The Second World War saw 'Operation Forager', the costly capture of the Marianas by US forces in June and July 1944. After the war all of Micronesia was administered by the USA as a UN Trust Territory. In recent years this entity has broken up. In 1975 the Marianas voted to become a US Commonwealth, which means that although US citizens, the islanders have no vote, a similar status to Puerto Rico in the Caribbean. The Marianas are of strategic importance to the USA, from whom they receive considerable aid every year. Another source of income is from tourism, most of the tourists coming from Japan.

The population is about 20,500, of whom 75 per cent are Chamorro, the rest Carolinian. English is the main language. Also spoken are Chamorro, Carolinian, and Japanese in the tourist areas. Most islanders are Roman Catholic. Saipan is the capital, and Susupe is the government centre.

The islands lie in the typhoon zone and typhoons can occur all year round, but are more frequent between June and November. It is always warm and humid. The NE trade winds blow from January to April. As the Marianas appear to be hit by typhoons every year, extreme caution must be exercised when cruising this area. One of the safest months is February, which has the lowest incidence of typhoons. A recommended hurricane hole is in Tanapag's inner

Practical Information

LOCAL TIME: GMT + 10

BUOYAGE: IALA A

CURRENCY: United States dollar (US$)

BUSINESS HOURS
Banks: 0900–1500 Monday to Thursday,
1000–1800 Friday.
Government offices: 0730–1130/
1230–1630 Monday to Friday.
Shops: 0800–2100 Monday to Saturday,
0800–1800 Sunday.

ELECTRICITY: 110/120 V, 60 Hz

PUBLIC HOLIDAYS
Mainly US holidays are observed:
1 January: New Year's Day
9 January: Commonwealth Day
Third Monday in January: Martin Luther
King's Birthday
Third Monday in February: President's
Day
24 March: Marianas Covenant Day
Good Friday
Last Monday in May: Memorial Day
4 July: US Independence Day
First Monday in September: Labor Day
First Monday in October: Columbus Day
24 October: United Nations Day
4 November: Citizenship Day
11 November: Veterans Day
Fourth Thursday in
November: Thanksgiving Day

8 December: Constitution Day
25 December: Christmas Day

COMMUNICATIONS
Telecommunications Office, Middle
Road, south of Garapan centre in Saipan
for international phone calls.
International calls can also be made
from hotels and phone booths.
The islands are part of the US mailing
system, so they have their own zip
codes. Mail can be sent c/o General
Delivery at either Saipan 96950, Rota
96951 or Tinian 96952.
Post office, Chalan Kanoa, SW end,
Saipan.
International flight connections are best
made via Japan or Guam to both of
which there are flights from Saipan.

harbour, also called Smiley's lagoon, where shelter is reputed to be good from every direction.

Entry Regulations

Ports of entry
Tanapag Harbour (Saipan) 15°12′N 145°43′E. Rota 14°08′N 145°08′E and Tinian 14°58′N 145°37′E can only be used as ports of entry by yachts who have these ports specified on their cruising permit.

Procedure on arrival
The Port Superintendent must be notified of the ETA of arriving yachts.
Tanapag Harbour: The approaches to the harbour are well marked. Visiting boats may anchor in the commercial harbour and on rare occasions can come alongside Charlie Pier. Baker's Pier is usually less crowded and one can anchor close to it and take a line ashore. The port captain will give directions where to moor when contacted on VHF Channel 16. Clearance is done by quarantine, customs and immigration officials.

Customs
Firearms should have valid licences from the owner's own country. Only .22 and .410 rifles are allowed to be kept and licensed in the Northern Marianas. On entry other licensed firearms will be confiscated by customs and held until departure. All non-licensed firearms will be confiscated and destroyed.

There is a four-month quarantine for dogs and cats. The cost is approximately US$2–3 per day.

Immigration
US citizens need only proof of citizenship.
Visas are not required for stays of up to 30 days and an entry permit of up to 30 days stay is given provided the onward passage of the yacht is assured and the crew are in possession of visas for the next destination if required. Extensions of up to 30 days can be applied for from the Immigration Office, Northern Marianas Government, Saipan.

Cruising permit
All yachts wishing to cruise in the Northern Marianas must be in possession of a permit, which must be obtained beforehand. A letter requesting the cruising permit should be written several months before the intended visit to: Chief of Immigration, Saipan, Mariana Islands, Commonwealth of the Northern Marianas 96950. A similar letter should also be sent to the Port Captain, at the same address. Alternatively, a cruising permit can be obtained from the Northern Marianas representative in Guam, which will allow a yacht to call at the islands of Tinian, Rota and Saipan. Proper clearing- in procedures must be completed on arrival in these places.
Yachts wishing to visit some of the outer islands must obtain special permission from the authorities in Saipan. It is advisable also to contact the Fish and Wildlife Office in Saipan, who are extremely concerned that certain plant diseases may be introduced acciden-

tally into the outer islands. The only inhabited islands are Alamagan, Agrihan and Pagan, the latter having been abandoned temporarily after a recent volcanic eruption. To visit Aguijan Island, south of Tinian, one must obtain a permit from Tinian's mayor.

Fees
Entry fee: US$25.
Dockage fee: under 100 feet, US$18 per day.
Immigration clearance fee: US$10.

Restrictions
Guguan, Asuncion and Maug islands are wildlife reserves and access to them is prohibited.

Facilities

Most facilities are in Saipan, which is the most developed island and attracts most tourists. Provisioning is good and there is a reasonable selection of imported goods, although they tend to be expensive. Locally grown fresh produce can be bought daily at the Farmers Market, opposite the post office, open 0800–1800 Monday to Saturday, 1000–1200 Sunday. Fuel must be bought in jerrycans from the filling station just north of the airport. Repair facilities are modest and only simple repairs can be done locally.

Tinian is less developed, but as it has a large farming community, fresh produce is easily available and of good quality. Rota is even less developed. There are a few shops in Songsong, the main settlement. Provisions in the outer islands are scarce and one should not expect to be able to buy more than the absolute minimum.

Further Reading

Landfalls of Paradise
Micronesia Handbook
Micronesia – a travel survival kit

PALAU

The Republic of Palau, now known as Belau, is part of the Western Caroline Islands. The richest flora and fauna in Micronesia are found here, both on land and underwater. Closely grouped together inside a barrier reef are the high islands of Babeldaob, the main island of Koror, Peleliu, and the many Rock Islands. Just

outside the reef are Anguaur and the atoll Kayangel, while to the south are a group of five small volcanic islands, stretching down towards Indonesia.

Conveniently situated on the route from the South Pacific to the Philippines, Palau lagoon and its many picturesque islands provide one of the most beautiful cruising grounds in the Pacific in one small area. This is slightly marred by the strict entry regulations, but this can be overcome by sorting out the necessary paperwork before one's arrival and, once there, by observing the rules. The effort is entirely justified as the scenery, both above and under the surface of the sea, is rarely matched elsewhere in the Pacific. The most fascinating place to visit are the Rock Islands, which are over two hundred limestone islets covered in jungle growth. Three major ocean currents meet in this area bringing food to nourish the rich marine life. The sea is teeming with turtles, manta rays, moray eels, fish of all descriptions, giant clams and even dugong. Occasionally one is brought back to earth by the sight of a wrecked ship from the bloody battles which were fought in and over these waters during the Second World War.

Country Profile

The Rock Islands were settled around 1000 BC and a complex matriarchal society developed. The first contact with Europeans was in the fifteenth century, when they were sighted by the Spanish, who called them the Arrecifos. At the end of the seventeenth century Spain claimed the islands, but only in the following century was real contact made when the *Antelope* was wrecked there and the islanders helped to rebuild the ship. Britain traded with the Palauans until the nineteenth century, when Spain pushed out the English. The local population was badly depleted by European-introduced diseases. After Spain's defeat in the Spanish–American War the islands were sold to Germany, which was interested in developing the islands' economy. The First World War saw the arrival of the Japanese, who had similar interests and Japanese culture and foreign immigrants overwhelmed Palauan traditional life. In the 1930s the islands were closed to the outside world while military fortifications were built. During the Second World War Palau suffered greatly from bombing and fighting.

After the war the USA administered Palau as part of the UN Trust Territory. In 1978 Palau voted against inclusion in the Federated States of Micronesia with the other states of the Caroline Islands and two years later formed a separate republic with its own constitution. However, a nuclear-free clause in the constitution was incompatible with the Compact of Free

Practical Information

LOCAL TIME: GMT + 12

BUOYAGE: IALA A

CURRENCY: United States dollar (US$)

BUSINESS HOURS
Government offices: 0730–1130,
1230–1630 Monday to Friday.

ELECTRICITY: 110 V, 60 Hz

PUBLIC HOLIDAYS
1 January: New Year's Day
14 March: Youth Day
15 May: Senior Citizens Day
9 July: Constitution Day
First Monday in September: Labor Day
24 October: UN Day
4th Thursday in
November: Thanksgiving
25 December: Christmas Day

COMMUNICATIONS
COMSAT station, Arakabesang Island,
for international calls.
Post office, central Koror.
There are flights to Guam or Manila,
from where international connections
can be made.

MEDICAL
Belau Clinic, Lebuu St, Koror has good
facilities.
There is also a government hospital.

Association signed by all the former Trust Territories, which gives the USA military rights in the area in return for financial aid. An amendment was made to the constitution, but while this issue remains unresolved, the Trust Territory remains formally in existence.

Palau depends very much on US aid, although relations between the two countries remain slightly strained as the nuclear issue has not been resolved. A huge power plant built on Aimeliik has proved a drain on the economy, needing US dollars to repay large debts. Exports are mainly fish and handicrafts, plus some income from tourism. Imports of fuel and food are high.

The 14,000 inhabitants are Micronesian, speaking English and Palauan. Sonsorolese is spoken in the south-west islands. There are various Christian denominations, Catholic, Protestant and Adventist. Many of the islanders still hold traditional beliefs.

Koror is the capital.

Palau lies on the edge of the typhoon belt and is only rarely affected by tropical storms. The typhoon season is from May to November. The wet season is June to September, which is the SW monsoon. The best weather is during the NE monsoon from December to March.

Entry Regulations

Port of entry
Malakal Harbour (Koror) 7°20′N 134°29′E.

Procedure on arrival
A yacht may not stop at any other place before clearing in at Malakal, unless the Chief of Immigration and Customs grants permission, if it is in the public interest of that place or an emergency situation. A yacht in distress may anchor or land at any port in Palau but must immediately notify the nearest government official to contact the Chief of Immigration and Customs. Yachts stopping anywhere else other than Malakal will be instructed to proceed to Malakal immediately.

Malakal: The port authorities should be notified in advance of a yacht's ETA. On entry and departure, inspections will be carried out by immigration, customs, agricultural and quarantine officials.

Customs
Firearms must be declared on entry and will be removed and held by the Bureau of Public Safety until departure. Animals must be declared.

Immigration
There are no visa requirements. Visitors are initially granted up to 30 days stay. Extensions require the approval of the Chief of Immigration. A 30-day extension may be given at a fee of US$50 per person.

Cruising permit
Yachts must obtain an entry permit in advance, otherwise they may be asked to leave after three days. The application should be sent well in advance to: Chief of Immigration, Division of Immigration & Customs, Bureau of Legal Affairs, PO Box 100, Koror, Republic of Palau 96940.

Applications should be received at least two weeks in advance of a yacht's expected arrival to allow sufficient time for processing the application. The application must be accompanied by a fee of US$75 (as a cashier's cheque, money order or cheque drawn on local bank made payable to National Treasury of the Republic of Palau).

The fee is doubled to US$150 if the permit is obtained on arrival. The permit is valid for 30 days and can be extended by another 30 days on payment of an additional US$100.

Fees
Overtime charges outside of official working hours Monday to Friday and on weekends are customs US$50 and immigration US$75.

Facilities

Most facilities are in Koror where the majority of the population live. There is a fishery cooperative in Malakal Harbour with workshops and a slipway. Nearby is a small chandlery with a limited selection. Provisioning is good with a reasonable selection of both imported goods and locally grown produce.

Further Reading

Landfalls of Paradise
Micronesia – a travel survival kit

9 Australia and South Pacific Islands

A voyage to the South Sea islands figures in most sailors' long-term plans, but their remoteness from the major yachting centres keeps them beyond the scope of the average cruise. This is the reason why in spite of the proliferation of yachts worldwide, the number of boats cruising the South Pacific is still relatively small and is not likely to increase much in the foreseeable future. The vastness of the Pacific Ocean and the great distances which separate most island groups make long passages a common feature of a cruise in this part of the world. The islands' isolation and general lack of facilities require the yacht to be well prepared and self-sufficient.

The region is under the influence of the SE trade winds, which are stronger and more consistent during the winter months, from May to October, with the best sailing weather between June and August. The trade winds are less reliable at other times. The western part of the ocean comes under the influence of the NE monsoon from December until March, which is also the season of tropical cyclones which affect the area south of latitude 10°S.

Most of the South Pacific is affected by tropical cyclones and the season lasts from December until the end of March. Although most cruising yachts leave the critical area by sailing either south to New Zealand or north to Papua New Guinea, some trust their luck and decide to stay in the hope of finding shelter should a cyclone come their way. The number of absolutely safe harbours is relatively small, which considerably restricts the freedom of movement during the cyclone season. Although there are reputedly good hurricane holes at Tahiti, Vava'u, Pago Pago and Suva, the risk still exists and in some countries, such as French Polynesia, Vanuatu and the Cook Islands, the authori-

ties now insist that cruising yachts leave the country before the onset of the cyclone season.

One of the advantages of spending the summer season outside of the tropics is that of being able to go to a place with good repair and service facilities. The most popular destination is New Zealand, where the Bay of Islands and Whangarei area have a complete range of facilities. Similar facilities are also available in some of the ports along Australia's east coast, although the more northern ones are themselves subject to cyclones. In the islands, the best repair centres are those which support their own boating community, such as Tahiti, Suva, Nouméa and Port Moresby. The establishment of charter operations in Raiatea and Vava'u has also brought about an improvement in the standard of facilities there. Adequate repair facilities are also available in Tongatapu, Port Vila and Rabaul.

AMERICAN SAMOA

The two neighbouring Samoas are very different from each other, American Samoa being a US Territory, while Western Samoa is an independent state. American Samoa comprises all the Samoan islands east of the 171° parallel, that is the main island of Tutuila, as well as Aunuu, the Manua Group, Rose Island, and Swains Island.

This US outpost in the South Seas has been best described as the place sailors love to hate. The features that attract most cruising boats to American Samoa, such as US goods, excellent provisioning and good communications, are those which have contributed to its seamier side. The Samoans have embraced the American way of life wholeheartedly, which has led to a high standard of living compared to their neighbours, but also to high criminality especially in the capital Pago Pago.

It is Pago Pago which attracts most cruising sailors, either to reprovision in its well-stocked supermarkets, or to spend the cyclone season in this scenically beautiful and well protected harbour, which unfortunately has been virtually destroyed by the local fish cannery, which fills the water with effluent and the air with revolting odours. Until there is a marked improvement in yachting facilities, Pago Pago is best regarded as a convenient reprovisioning stop and nothing more.

Outside of Pago Pago life has been affected less by this kind of progress and the other islands are not so hectic. It was on the island of Tau in the less developed Manua Group that Margaret Mead made her famous study, now somewhat discredited, *Coming of Age in Samoa*.

Country Profile

It is debated whether Manua in American Samoa or Savai'i in Western Samoa is the true ancient Samoa, cradle of Polynesia, from where intrepid navigators spread out eastwards across the South Pacific. Archaeologists have ascertained that Polynesians lived on Tutuila around 600 BC. They remained undisturbed until 1722 when the first European, a Dutchman named Jacob Roggeveen, visited the island. Few Europeans came to the islands, especially after the eleven

members of a French scientific expedition led by La Pérouse were killed here in 1787. Only in 1831 did the arrival of missionary John Williams mark a more permanent European interest and the Samoans proved enthusiastic converts, going forth as missionaries themselves to convert other nations of the Pacific.

In 1900 the United States established control of Tutuila as they wanted a coaling port in the South Pacific, and later they acquired the Manua group. Tutuila was an important base for the US Navy in the Second World War and the Navy administered

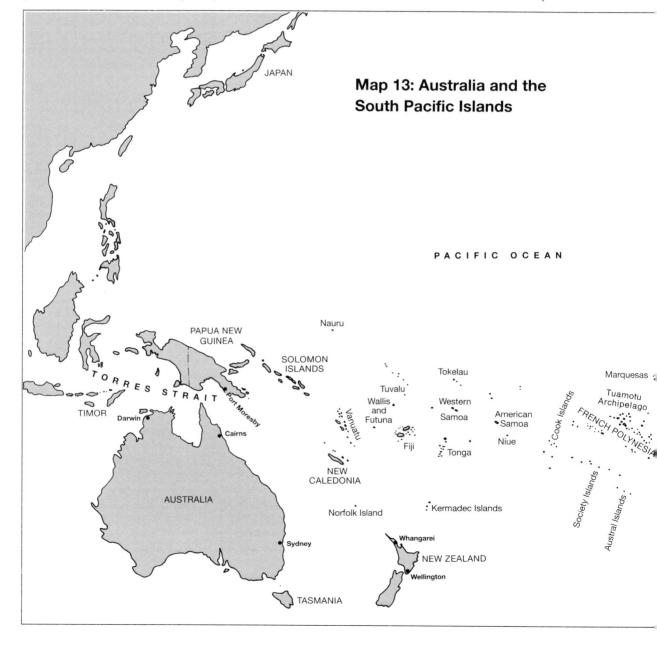

Map 13: Australia and the South Pacific Islands

American Samoa until 1951, when it was taken over by the Department of the Interior. American Samoans are US citizens.

The main economic activities are tuna fishing and canning. The USA has put a lot of money into the islands. Many Samoans work temporarily overseas, especially in the United States.

The mainly Polynesian population is 35,600. Samoan and English are spoken. The main Christian denominations are Protestant, Catholic, Mormon and Methodist. Pago Pago is the capital and its harbour is

the crater of an extinct volcano. It is a deep water duty-free port with three fish canneries for US, Korean and Japanese fishing fleets. Fagatogo is the business and administrative centre.

There is very heavy rainfall all year, especially from December to April, which is the cyclone season. The average temperatures are 24–31°C (75–87°F). May to November are the trade wind months and are less humid.

Entry Regulations

Port of entry
Pago Pago 14°17′S 170°41′W.

Procedure on arrival
Arriving yachts must tie up at the customs dock, which is on the port side on entering the harbour. They will be boarded here by customs, immigration and agriculture officials. It is also necessary to clear in and out with the harbour master's office which will assign an anchoring place. A yacht must not be moved without prior permission from the harbour master or one is liable to pay a large fine. When clearing out, one must come alongside the customs dock again.

If arriving at the weekend, one can anchor in the harbour and stay on board until Monday. In this case one should not anchor in the working area which leads out from the ramp, but one can anchor off the customs dock or in the north-west part of the harbour.

Yachts coming from Hawaii must clear customs in the same way as all foreign yachts.

Customs
A customs entry clearance permit is required for firearms. A Department of Agriculture entry clearance permit is needed for any animals, plants or vegetables.

Immigration
American Samoa is considered part of the United States, and US citizens can live and work there, but they should have valid passports for entry.

On arrival other nationalities are granted a 30-day stay. After this period a visa is required. Entry permits are granted to all those who can provide proof of their onward passage and have adequate funds for their stay. For extensions up to a maximum of 90 days, one should apply to the Immigration Office next to Court House, Fagatogo. An exit permit is needed from immigration.

The Passport & Visa Office in the Administration building is open 0830–1200 Monday to Friday and can issue US visas.

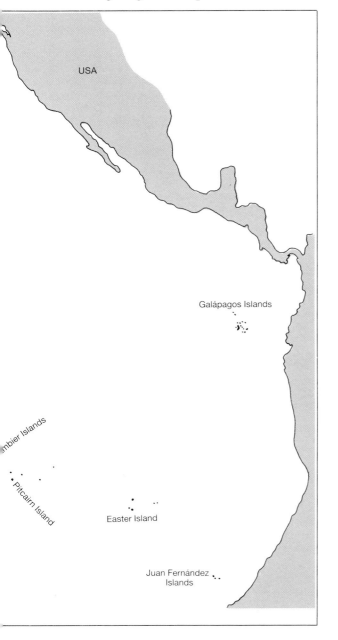

Practical Information

LOCAL TIME: GMT - 11

BUOYAGE: IALA A

CURRENCY: United States dollar (US$)

BUSINESS HOURS
Banks: 0900–1500 Monday to Friday.
Shops: 0800–1700 Monday to Friday,
0800–1300 Saturday.
Business and government
offices: 0800–1700 Monday to Friday,
0800–1200 Saturday.

ELECTRICITY: 110 V, 50 Hz

PUBLIC HOLIDAYS
1 January: New Year's Day
Third Monday in February: President's
Day
17 April: Flag Day
Last Monday in May: Memorial Day
4 July: Independence Day
First Monday in September: Labor Day
Second Sunday in October: White
Sunday
Second Monday in October: Columbus
Day
11 November: Veterans Day
Last Thursday in
November: Thanksgiving
25 December: Christmas Day

COMMUNICATIONS
Communications office, Fagatogo, open
24 hours, seven days a week has
facilities for international direct dialling,
telex, fax and telegrams.
American Samoa is tied into the US
postal system. Zip code 96799.
Main post office: Lumana'i Building,
Fagatogo, open 0800–1600
Monday to Friday, 0830–1200 Saturday.
Emergency: dial 000.
There are flights to Honolulu, Auckland,
Apia and Nadi (Fiji).

MEDICAL
LBJ Tropical Medical Center in Faga'alu
Village, west of Pago Pago, has 24-hour
services.

Fees

US$25 for clearing in and US$25 for clearing out is payable by visiting yachts as well as monthly harbour fees of approximately US$12 to US$15. These must be paid before departure as otherwise customs will not issue an outward clearance.

Restrictions

Rose Island, the easternmost island of the Samoan archipelago, is a National Wildlife Refuge administered by the US Fish and Wildlife Service in Honolulu. Permission from this service is needed to visit the island.

Facilities

Apart from the fact that most things American are available and therefore provisioning is better than in neighbouring countries, facilities for yachts in Pago Pago are very basic. There are plans to install some docks for visiting cruising boats to the west of Malaoa Marina. The holding in the harbour is also poor and it is advisable to anchor with two anchors and not leave the yacht unattended for long periods. To avoid the noise and smell of the cannery and generating plant it is best to anchor as far as possible from them.

There is no haul-out facility for yachts. There is a shipyard dealing mainly with repairs on fishing boats, but it sometimes accepts work on yachts. There are some small workshops in town for engine and electrical work. Stainless steel welding and general steel work is undertaken by Mr Wu, who has a workshop in

Lauli village. Best provisions can be bought at Arvenas and Tom Ho Chings, who give discounts on larger quantities, as does Burns Philp. Water can be obtained from the customs dock.

Further Reading

Landfalls of Paradise
Pacific Islands Yearbook
South Pacific Handbook

AUSTRALIA

Australia is the only nation which is also a continent: a land of few rivers, a vast desert plateau in the centre, with a chain of mountains, the Great Dividing Range, to the east and narrow coastal plains to the south-east. The island of Tasmania and the Torres Strait Islands are also part of Australia and there are the overseas territories of Norfolk Island, Cocos Keeling and Christmas Island.

In spite of the large number of yachts in Australia, the number of Australian yachts cruising overseas is surprisingly small and the only explanation for this is that Australia has been blessed by nature with such beautiful and varied cruising grounds that they do not need to go and look for variety elsewhere. From the wind-swept coasts of Victoria and Tasmania to the picturesque harbours of New South Wales, the tropical islands and Great Barrier Reef of Queensland to the huge shallow bays of the Northern Territory, Australia has it all. This vast country is a world in itself and even a short cruise through some of its waters will pay unexpected rewards.

Country Profile

The Aboriginal peoples of Australia probably arrived from Asia 60,000 years ago. Isolated for so long from the rest of the world, they developed a unique culture intrinsically bound up with the land. Up to the eighteenth century, Europeans believed that a great southern continent, Terra Australis Incognita, must exist to balance the land masses of the northern hemisphere. Australia was first sighted in the sixteenth century by the Portuguese and in the early seventeenth century the Spaniard Torres sailed through the Strait that came to bear his name. Dutch sailors charted the north and west and for a while Australia was called Van Dieman's land. In 1770 Captain Cook landed on the east coast at Botany Bay. Soon afterwards Captain Phillip officially took possession of the land for Britain, on the site of present-day Sydney. Britain used it as a penal colony and many convicts were deported there, often for relatively minor crimes.

The interior of the continent was opened up only

Cairns, Queensland.

gradually, not many people settling until the discovery of gold brought a rush of fortune hunters. The Aborigines suffered from this influx – their land and often their sacred sites were taken over and many perished, hunted by the new settlers or succumbing to European-brought diseases.

Farming, particularly sheep and other livestock, was developed and railways penetrated into the interior. At the end of the nineteenth century, the six colonies which had established themselves independently formed a Federation of States within the Commonwealth. Today each state has its own capital, parliament and laws. Australia's sovereignty was formally recognised in 1931 by the British Parliament. Australian forces played an important role in both world wars and after the Second World War, the country emerged as a modern industrial nation and power. ANZUS was formed in 1951 as a defence agreement between Australia, New Zealand and the USA. Australia maintains close links with the United States.

The rural sector produces important exports such as wool, although this has declined. Agriculture remains important, and the country being relatively free of pests and disease, Australia's quarantine laws are strict for visitors. Many unique animals can be found on this ancient continent, such as platypus, kangaroos and koalas. Australia's rich mineral resources are crucial to the economy and industry is expanding.

The population is 16.5 million, living mostly on the

Practical Information

LOCAL TIME: Western Australia GMT + 8. South Australia, Northern Territory GMT + 9½. Eastern Australia GMT + 10. Summer time + 1 from late October to late March in South Australia, NSW, Tasmania and Victoria.

BUOYAGE: IALA A

CURRENCY: Australian dollar (Aus$)

BUSINESS HOURS
Banks: 0900/1000 to 1600 Monday to Thursday, to 1700 Friday.
Shops: 0900–1730 Monday to Friday, 0900–1200 Saturday.
Thursday and Friday late night shopping until 2100.
Government offices: 0900–1700 Monday to Friday.

ELECTRICITY: 240 V, 50 Hz

PUBLIC HOLIDAYS
1 January: New Year's Day
26 January: Australia Day
Good Friday, Easter Monday
25 April: ANZAC Day
June: Queen's Birthday
First Monday in October: Labour Day
25, 26 December: Christmas

Also: State bank holidays and State Labour days

EVENTS
July: Darwin to Ambon Yacht Race

COMMUNICATIONS
Telecommunications Commission: 24-hour public telephone and telex services (Sydney, Melbourne, Brisbane, Canberra).
Telegrams through operator and at post offices.
Emergencies: dial 000.
There are flights worldwide from all major cities and a comprehensive internal network.

MEDICAL
Costs can be high for visitors, so medical insurance is recommended.

DIPLOMATIC MISSIONS
In Canberra:
Canada: Commonwealth Ave.
☎ (62) 73-3844.
Indonesia: 8 Darwin Ave, Yarralumla.
☎ (62) 73-3222.

New Zealand: Commonwealth Ave, Yarralumla. ☎ (62) 73-3611.
Papua New Guinea: Foster Crescent, Yarralumla. ☎ (62) 73-3322.
United Kingdom: Commonwealth Ave, Yarralumla. ☎ (62) 70-6666.
United States: Moonah Place.
☎ (62) 73-3711.

In Brisbane:
New Zealand: Watkins Place Bldg, 288 Edward St. ☎ (7) 221-9932.
Papua New Guinea: Estate Houses, 127 Creek St. ☎ (7) 221-7915.
United Kingdom: BP House, 193 North Quay. ☎ (7) 221-4933.
United States: 383 Wickham Terr.
☎ (7) 229-8955.

In Darwin:
Indonesia: Stuart Park. ☎ (89) 81-9352.

In Perth:
Canada: St Martin's Tower, 44 St George's Terr. ☎ (9) 221-1770.
New Zealand: 16 St George's Terr.
☎ (9) 325-7877.
United Kingdom: Prudential Bldg, 95 St George's Terr. ☎ (9) 322-3200.
United States: 246 St George's Terr.
☎ (9) 322-4466.

---

coasts and in the south-east. The majority are immigrants, mainly English, Irish, Italian, Greek, German, Yugoslav and more recently Asian. Aborigines form only 1 per cent of the population. Also indigenous to the area are the Torres Strait islanders. English is the main language. At one time there was thought to be 500 aboriginal languages, but today there are only about four main groups still spoken. The majority of the population are Christian, mainly Protestant and Catholic. Among other religions practised are Islam, Judaism and aboriginal traditional beliefs. Canberra is the Australian Federal Capital, and each state has its own capital.

The climate varies from one end of the country to the other. It is mainly temperate except for the tropical north and central desert. The north has two seasons, wet from November to March, with the heaviest rainfall after January. The winter months of April to October are drier and more pleasant. The cyclone season is from December to March on both the Pacific and Indian Ocean coasts.

Entry Regulations

Ports of entry

Queensland: Thursday Island 10°35'S 142°13'E, Weipa 12°40'S 141°55'E, Cairns 16°56'S 145°47'E, Townsville 19°15'S 146° 50'E, Bowen 20° 01'S 148°15'E, Mackay 21°06'S 149°13'E, Gladstone 23°50'S 151°15'E, Bundaberg 24°46'S 152°23'E, Brisbane 27°19'S 153°10'E, Rockhampton (Port Alma) 23°35'S 150°52'E, Maryborough (Urangan) 25°17'S 152°55'E.
Northern Territory: Gove 12°10'S 136°40'E, Darwin 12°30'S 130°52'E, Groote Eylandt (Milner Bay) 13°52'S 136°28'E.
Victoria: Melbourne 37°50'S 145°55'E, Westernport 38°20'S 145°15'E, Geelong 38°07'S 144°23'E, Portland 38°21'S 141°37'E.
South Australia: Cape Thevenard 32°09'S 133°39'E, Port Lincoln 34°45'S 135° 53'E, Whyalla 33°02'S 137°37'E, Port Pirie 33°11'S 138°01'E, Wallaroo 33°56'S 137°37'E, Port Adelaide 34°47'S 138°30'E,

Port Stanvac 35°07'S 138°28'E.
New South Wales: Coffs Harbour 30°18'S 153°09'E, Newcastle 32°56'S 151°47'E, Sydney 35°50'S 151°15'E, Port Botany and Kurnell 34°00'S 151°14'E, Port Kembla 34°28'S 150°54'E, Eden 37°04'S 149°55'E, Lord Howe Island 30°30'S 159°50'E.
Tasmania: Burnie 41°03'S 145°55'E, Devonport 41°11'S 146°22'E, Launceston 41°26'S 147°08'E, Hobart 42°52'S 147°20'E.
Western Australia: Broome 18°21'S 122°15'E, Port Hedland 20°20'S 118°37'E, Port Walcott 20°40'S 117°13'E, Dampier 20°39'S 116°43'E, Exmouth 21°54'S 114°11'E, Carnarvon 24°53'S 113°40'E, Geraldton 28°47'S 114°36'E, Fremantle 32°00'S 115°45'E, Bunbury 33°19'S 115°38'E, Albany 35°02'S 117°55'E, Esperance 33°52'S 121°53'E.

Procedure on arrival

The ports of entry all have 24-hour service. There are severe penalties for stopping anywhere else before clearing in, up to an Aus$50,000 fine. One should fly the Q flag as soon as one enters Australian territorial waters.

By law the captain must give a minimum of three hours' notice of arrival. One should contact any OTC (Overseas Telecommunications Commission) coastal radio station (2182 KHz or VHF Channel 16), requesting that they notify customs and quarantine of the boat name, ETA and number of people on board. If a boat has no radio, one is supposed to write to the Collector of Customs at the planned port of entry before leaving for Australia.

At the port of entry, clearance is done by customs, immigration and quarantine. They require a list of ship's stores, dutiable items, crew, and any animals on board as well as the previous port clearance. Everyone must remain on board until clearance is completed.

Procedure on departure

Clearing out can only be done at one of the ports of entry. The documents needed to get customs clearance are passports, crew list, list of ship's stores and registration certificate. Australian yachts must be registered before leaving Australia.

After clearing out, one is not allowed to stop at any other places, but anchoring for the night or in bad weather is permitted, provided one does not go ashore.

Customs

Firearms must be declared on entry. All military-type firearms (greater than .22), machine guns, pistols, revolvers, ammunition, as well as flick knives and knuckledusters are prohibited imports, and will be taken into custody at the first port of entry. Arrangements can be made to transport them to the port of departure if sufficient notice is given of that port and the date of departure. Sporting rifles and shotguns may be kept on board if a permit is obtained from the police.

Foreign yachts may enter Australia for up to 12 months without paying duty or sales tax, although they may be asked to give customs a bank or cash security to the value of the duty that would be paid if the yacht were imported. If paying cash, advance notice of departure and the port of exit must be given to customs in order to get a refund.

Customs require the itinerary that the yacht proposes to follow while in Australia. Yachts are supposed to keep customs informed of their whereabouts and to notify the nearest customs office if they change their itinerary.

Prescription drugs must be declared on arrival and their consumption recorded in the log book, which customs may check on departure.

Anyone over 18 years of age is entitled to bring in 1 litre of alcohol and 250 g tobacco or 250 cigarettes. All quantities in excess of this will be sealed on board.

A refund of sales tax paid on goods bought while in Australia can be obtained. On arrival one should ask customs for the special vendors form, and an Australian Tax Office refund of sales tax form. Then when buying any goods, one should ask for an itemised receipt, which shows the sales tax as a separate item. After leaving Australia, mail the tax form with the receipts for the goods bought and the sales tax will be refunded.

Quarantine

Yachts with animals on board may only anchor, and the animal must be kept on board and confined (in a cage or below decks) at all times. Quarantine must be notified of any intention to change mooring, as well as the proposed itinerary in Australian waters. The authority requires a bond of Aus$500 to be placed to ensure compliance with their requirements. Failure to comply can lead to destruction of the animal, loss of the bond, and heavy fines. If embarking animals in Australia, they must have a health certificate issued by a veterinarian.

Australia is free from many human, animal and plant diseases including rabies. All foodstuffs and plants, regardless of their origin, packaging or nature, are subject to a quarantine examination on arrival. All fresh produce as well as frozen and canned meat will be removed. The quarantine laws are strict and the penalties for breaking them severe.

Immigration

All nationalities, with the sole exception of New Zealanders, must obtain a visa in advance. Until recently the captain of a yacht was exempt, but the law has been changed and he or she must also have a visa. There are Australian diplomatic missions in American Samoa, Fiji, Indonesia, Kiribati, Nauru, New Caledonia, New Zealand, Papua New Guinea, the Solomon Islands, Tonga, Vanuatu and Western Samoa, where visas can be obtained. There is no charge for a tourist visa and a multiple entry visa valid for the length of the passport's validity can be obtained.

Cruising permit

This is obtained from customs on arrival, being granted when the officials are satisfied that the applicant is a genuine tourist, and has proof of sufficient funds for the maintenance of the vessel and the crew without work visas. Extensions are available from customs, upon application and assessment of the reasons. An initial six-month period is given, with provisions for extensions totalling a further six months. The permit enables foreign yachts to cruise freely between their port of entry and exit, and allows them to visit ports and places besides the official ports of entry. This permit is not for the use of anyone with the intention of using the vessel for commercial gain while in Australia.

Fees

No overtime fees are charged on entry, but can be charged on departure, if departure formalities are requested outside of office hours.

There is nothing to pay for pratique inspection if a yacht is under 25 metres; over 25 metres AUS$135 is charged. There is a departure tax of AUS$10 per person over 12 years old. This is payable whether one leaves by yacht or by air.

Restrictions

Some restricted areas are marked on the charts.
Aboriginal Reserves and National Parks: Entry to these may be restricted and special permission is required to visit them. The Northern Territory has several of these areas on its coast. For more details, write to the Department of Aboriginal Affairs in Darwin or enquire at the port of entry.

The coast and islands west of Gove are part of the Arnhem Land Aboriginal Reserve and one needs a permit for entry, obtainable from the Lands Office in Gove.

Cotton Island is off-limits as it has sacred burial sites.

Coburg Peninsula is a National Park and permission to enter can be obtained from the Ranger Station.

Ashmore Reef is a National Park, no spearfishing is allowed.
Note: In the Northern Territory, one must remember that salt-water crocodiles can be found in the sea and estuaries. Their numbers are growing as they are a protected animal.

In New South Wales living aboard a yacht permanently is illegal, although foreign yachts that are cruising are considered more leniently. The Maritime Services Board in Pittwater are more lenient than those in Sydney Harbour.

Artefacts and protected wildlife products cannot be exported unless special permission is obtained.

Facilities

Facilities in Australia are generally good and anywhere near a yachting centre are excellent. For yachts arriving from the Pacific it is a great relief to find a country where everything is available and virtually anything can be fixed. If in need of a major overhaul or repairs, it is advisable to head for a main centre, such as Sydney, Brisbane, Cairns or Darwin, where repair facilities are of a high standard and spares readily available.

The number of marinas is not as great as one would expect so in many places visitors have to anchor. Yacht clubs everywhere are welcoming and are also a valuable source of advice concerning repairs or provisioning. Australian charts are excellent and are continually kept up to date. They are available in any port of significant size. Fuel and water are easily available and gas bottles can be filled in most places. As can be expected in such a rich and varied country, provisioning is excellent everywhere and Australia is a good place to stock up the boat for the continuation of a voyage.

Visiting yachts are welcome at the Cairns Yacht Club in central Cairns, which gives temporary membership to visitors. There are a limited number of visiting berths at the Port Authority marina and most visitors have to anchor or moor across the river from the town. Most of the companies specialising in marine repair, whether electrical, engine, electronic, fibreglass, welding or sailmaking are concentrated in the Portsmouth area about two miles upstream from the city centre. The Cairns Cruising Yacht Squadron is based there, welcomes visitors and has a travelift and slipway. Larger boats can be slipped at the nearby Norship boatyard, which has a 120-tonne travelift.

In Darwin most visiting yachts anchor off the Darwin Sailing Club in Fannie Bay, which welcomes temporary members to use their facilities. A well stocked chandlery is on the premises. In Francis Bay there are several boatyards with haul-out facilities, both slipways and travelifts, near to the Mooring Basin, the cyclone refuge harbour where there may be some berths available when the prawnfishing boats are out. Due to the large fishing fleet based in Darwin, there are excellent repair facilities of all types and chandlers in the area around the Mooring Basin.

Further Reading

The Queensland Official Tide Tables and Boating Guide
Cruising Guide to the Northern Territory Coast
Cruising the Coral Coast

COOK ISLANDS

The Cook Islands are made up of 15 islands, spread over an area of over half a million square miles of ocean. The Southern Group, of which Rarotonga is the main island, also comprises Aitutaki, Atiu, Mitiaro, Mauke and Mangaia. These are high and fertile and most of the 18,000 inhabitants live there. The Northern Group are the low coral atolls of Penrhyn, Manihiki, Rakahanga, Pukapuka, Nassau and Suwarrow, which is a national park. Also part of the Cooks are the atolls of Manuae, Takutea and Palmerston Island.

The affection that most cruising sailors have for the Cooks is mainly due to two legendary figures who spent a great deal of their lives on these islands. Tom Neale, a modern day Robinson Crusoe, chose to maroon himself on Suwarrow atoll, the kind of tropical retreat of which dreams are made, and welcomed any yachtsmen that called. Father George Kester also ran away to the Cooks, but not in search of solitude, for his motives were altruistic. As a missionary he dedicated his life to the spiritual well-being of the islanders as well as the material well-being of all cruising sailors who happened to call at his island, first Rarotonga and then Aitutaki.

As most yachts sail to the Cook Islands from the east, a good time to plan one's passage is after the 14 July celebrations in French Polynesia are over, as the first week of August is the time when the Cooks put on their own festivities around Independence Day. Most of the action is in Rarotonga, but the other islands can be visited afterwards. Aitutaki is a popular stop and yachts are always assured of a warm welcome there. This is the case in all of the Cook Islands and as elsewhere in the Pacific, the more remote the island the more enthusiastic the welcome.

Country Profile

Folklore holds that in the early 1300s two chiefs, from Tahiti and Samoa, arrived on Rarotonga at the same time, and divided the island peacefully between them. From here it is believed that the Polynesians, forefathers of the Maori race, sailed down to New Zealand.

The first European to lay eyes on the Cooks was the Spanish explorer Mendana at the end of the sixteenth century. Others soon followed, and in the 1770s Captain Cook put many of the islands on the map. Traders and missionaries were the next to arrive, and eventually the Cooks became a British colony. The islands were handed over to New Zealand in 1901 and became independent in 1965. The Cooks today have internal self-government, with free association with New Zealand. There are very close ties to New Zealand and many Cook Islanders live there, perhaps as many as on the islands.

The economy is based on tourism and agriculture, citrus fruit, bananas and pineapples being the main exports. The northern islands mainly produce copra for export. Since the 1970s tourism has boomed, encouraged by the government trying to end dependence on foreign aid. However, imports are still well above exports and aid from New Zealand keeps the economy afloat.

The capital is Avarua on Rarotonga, the most developed island, which has beautiful mountainous scenery. The languages spoken are Cook Islands Maori and English. Christianity is important to the islanders and Sunday is a quiet day. The main faiths are Protestant, Catholic, Seventh Day Adventist, and Latter Day Saints.

December to March is rainy and also the cyclone season. Generally the climate is warm and sunny, but not too hot. During the winter, April to November, the islands are under the influence of the SE trade winds. However, sudden squalls can occur from other directions with little warning.

Entry Regulations

Ports of entry
Rarotonga: Avatiu and Avarua 21°12′S 159°47′W.
Aitutaki: Aitutaki 18°52′S 159°48′W.
Penrhyn: Omaka 9°00′S 157°56′W.
Sub-ports of entry are Pukapuka 10°53′S 165°49′W and Atiu (Avamutu) 19°59′S 158°08′W.

Procedure on arrival
For clearance, the captain must present the passports,

Practical Information

LOCAL TIME: GMT - 10. Summer time GMT - 9½ from the last Sunday in October to the first Sunday in March.

BUOYAGE: IALA A

CURRENCY: New Zealand dollar (NZ$), with local coinage.

BUSINESS HOURS
Banks: 0900–1500 Monday to Friday.
Business: 0730–1530 Monday to Friday, 0730–1130 Saturday.
Shops: 0800–1600 Monday to Friday, 0800–1200 Saturday.
Government offices: 0800–1600 Monday to Friday.

ELECTRICITY: 230 V, 50 Hz

PUBLIC HOLIDAYS
1 January: New Year's Day
25 April: ANZAC Day
Good Friday
Easter Monday
June: Queen's Birthday
4 August: Constitution Day
26 October: Gospel Day
25, 26 December: Christmas

COMMUNICATIONS
Cable & Wireless, open 24 hours, for overseas telephone calls, and telegrams.
Post office in Rarotonga 0800–1600 Monday to Friday for telephones, telegrams, fax and telex.

Emergencies: police 999, fire 996, ambulance 998.
There are flights from Rarotonga to Apia, Auckland, Honolulu, Nadi, Papeete and Sydney.

MEDICAL
Medical and dental facilities available 24 hours a day. There are modern hospitals in Rarotonga, Aitutaki and in some of the other islands.

DIPLOMATIC MISSIONS
New Zealand: Philatelic Bureau Bldg, Takuvaine Rd., Avarua, Rarotonga.
☎ 22-201.

clearance from the last port, stores list, four crew lists, health certificate of pratique as well as a general declaration and details of the yacht.

Rarotonga: One may clear at Avatiu, the commercial harbour or at Avarua, half a mile east along the coast. The harbour master can be contacted on VHF Channel 16 between 0800–1600 for berthing instructions. The working channel is 12. Radio Rarotonga (ZKR) monitors 2182 KHz and 4125 MHz as well as Channel 16.

Aitutaki: After entering the lagoon through the long channel one should anchor off Aratunga village, at the entrance to the small boat harbour. Customs will come out to the boat. Boats too large should anchor outside the reef to the north of the channel and the captain should come ashore to clear. The channel has a depth of only six feet and outflowing tidal currents can reach three to four knots. There is slightly more water on the port side, which should be favoured. If in any doubt, one should ask a local person to guide one in.

Penrhyn: One should anchor off Omaka village on the south side of the Taruia Pass. There is also a wharf where one can come alongside if there is no surge. After clearance one must get permission before moving elsewhere in the lagoon.

One may clear at Pukapuka and Atiu, but must pay for transporting the customs officer by air or sea.

Atiu Island: There is no harbour, so one has to anchor off the reef.

Customs

A list of firearms must be produced on arrival and these will be impounded until departure.

Animals have to be confined on board.

Agriculture

Animals, plants and fruit will be inspected, as the Cooks are free of serious diseases and pests, and their economy depends very much on agriculture. Fruit and meat cannot be imported, so it is advisable not to arrive with a lot of fresh supplies. Fortunately good local fruit is available. If coming from Tahiti, Fiji or areas considered infected by the rhinocerous beetle, the yacht will be searched and may be fumigated.

Immigration

If entering in Rarotonga a permit for up to 31 days will be given on arrival. This can be extended, on a monthly basis, up to three months maximum. Fourteen days before the permit expires one should apply for the extension. Proof of adequate funds may be requested for extensions. For longer visits a visa must be obtained from a New Zealand or British consulate before arrival in the Cooks.

In Aitutaki and other ports of entry, a 31-day permit will be given on arrival. Extensions have to be obtained in Rarotonga. If crew disembarks from the yacht, they must notify immigration and provide a baggage declaration.

Fees

Harbour fees in Rarotonga: There is a berthage charge of NZ$2 for yachts owned by non-Cook Islands residents. Harbour fees in Rarotonga must be paid before outward clearance is given.

Avatiu Harbour: Yachts must pay a daily fee depending

on length of between NZ$3 (yachts up to 8 metres) and NZ$6 (over 15 metres), with a minimum charge of between NZ$15 and NZ$30.

Avarua: The daily fee is NZ$1.50 (up to 8 metres) to NZ$2.50 (over 15 metres) with minimum charge of NZ$7.50–12.50.

There is also a small mooring fee at Aitutaki.

Visa extension fee amounts to NZ$20 per person. There is an exit fee of NZ$20 per person.

Overtime is charged before 0800 and after 1600 on weekdays, and all day at weekends and public holidays.

Restrictions

Yachts may not visit any other islands in the Cooks than those mentioned as ports of entry without permission from customs and immigration. To visit Suwarrow atoll national park, one should obtain permission from the resident park administrator.

Cruising yachts are not allowed to remain in the islands during the cyclone season, which is from December to March. Harbour masters in Rarotonga and Aitutaki will not even let transiting yachts stay overnight in port during the cyclone season.

Facilities

Avatiu Harbour is the commercial port of Rarotonga and should only be used for clearing in, getting fuel and provisions. The harbour is undergoing extensive construction to enlarge the existing port as well as to create a yacht harbour and workshop area. Avarua harbour has a new breakwater and has been dredged to form a small boat harbour for fishing boats and yachts.

There is a good selection of fruit and vegetables on this fertile island. Locally produced canned fruit juices are a good buy. Repair facilities are basic, although in Avatiu harbour there are fisheries workshops and a slipway which yachts may be able to use. There are no marine supplies or chandlery and any essential spares must be ordered from New Zealand, from where there are frequent flights. Gas bottles can be filled at an office near the harbour.

There is limited provisioning and facilities in Aitutaki, although one can enter the small boat harbour to take on fuel and provisions. At Penrhyn basic provisions are available as well as some fresh fruit and vegetables. A limited amount of water can be obtained from the islanders, but as this is often in short supply it is better to try and arrive with full tanks. As the supply ship is sometimes late, the islanders prefer trading in scarce items rather than money. Items in demand are fishing gear, dry cell batteries, rope and small anchors.

Further Reading

Landfalls of Paradise
Charlie's Charts of Polynesia
An Island to Oneself
Rarotonga and the Cook Islands – a travel survival kit

EASTER ISLAND

Mystery surrounds this remote South Pacific island, the people who once lived here and the origins of the giant statues that are scattered all over this small island. Lying at the south-eastern point of the Polynesian triangle, yachts rarely call at this lonely outpost of Chile to whom it belongs and from whom it is separated by over 2000 miles of ocean. Isla de Pascua, also known by its Polynesian name Rapa Nui, is totally isolated and its nearest neighbour is tiny Pitcairn, 1200 miles to the west.

There is no all-round protected anchorage on Easter Island and as the winds can be changeable, one has to be prepared to move at short notice. The anchorage off the main settlement of Hanga Roa is open but sheltered from the prevailing south-easterly winds. If the wind turns, one can move to Anakena Bay, site of some of the most interesting excavations and statues on the island, or to Huituiti in the east. Swell is a problem in all these anchorages.

For those who make the long passage, there are many rewards ashore: the crater of the Rano Kau volcano and above it the sacred site of Orongo where the birdman cult was practised. At the other end of the island is the volcano Rano Raraku, where the giant statues were carved out of lava and where many still lie abandoned and unfinished.

Country Profile

Debate has raged over the history of Rapa Nui before the outside world made contact with it. Some 600 huge abandoned lava statues, up to 9 metres (30 feet) high lie scattered around the island; who carved them and why remains a mystery. Easter Islanders were the only Pacific people to develop a form of writing, although no one survived who could read it.

The first European to visit the island in 1722 was a Dutchman, Jacob Roggeveen, at a time when the inhabitants had just finished a series of civil wars. The population remained stable at around 4000 until the 1850s, when Peruvian slave traders, smallpox and emigration to Tahiti saw the number of inhabitants fall considerably. At the end of the nineteenth century

Practical Information

LOCAL TIME: GMT - 8

BUOYAGE: IALA B

CURRENCY: Chilean peso, of
100 centesimos

BUSINESS HOURS
Banco del Estado de Chile: 0900–1400
Monday to Friday.

ELECTRICITY: 220 V, 50 Hz; 110 V at
Hotel Hanga Roa.

PUBLIC HOLIDAYS
1 January: New Year's Day
Holy Week (two days)
1 May
21 May: Navy Day
15 August: Assumption
9 September: Rapa Nui/Policarpo Day
10 and 18 September: Independence
Days
12 October: Discovery of America
1 November: All Saints' Day
8 December: Immaculate Conception
25 December: Christmas Day

COMMUNICATIONS
International telephone calls are made
by satellite. There is daily radio contact
with Valparaiso.
There is a twice-weekly flight from
Santiago (Chile) that goes on to Papeete
(Tahiti) and vice versa.

MEDICAL
There is a small hospital on the island.

Chile annexed the island. Mounting an expedition to the island in 1955 the Norwegian Thor Heyerdahl tried to unravel the mystery of the statues and proposed a theory that the islanders had originated in South America. This theory is not accepted today, but nevertheless it caught the imagination of countless people around the world, making Easter Island one of the most enticing tourist destinations. Today Easter Island is a dependency of Chile, with a military governor and a local mayor. It is part of the Fifth Region of Chile, with the capital at Valparaiso.

Mainland Chileans occupy most of the government posts, while the majority of the islanders live off subsistence farming, although unemployment is high. About half the island is turned over to sheep and cattle grazing and a third of the island is a national park. There is some tourism.

There are around 2000 islanders of Polynesian origin and a few hundred Chileans. Spanish is the official language, but Polynesian, closely akin to Tahitian, is spoken by the islanders. Almost all the islanders are Catholic. Hanga Roa is the only settlement and there is a large military garrison.

From October to April the SE trades prevail. The summer, mid-November to mid-February, is when winds tend to be lighter and the seas calmer. May to

Fishing boats on the beach at Hanga Roa.

September are the rainier months, when westerlies predominate. The island falls outside the cyclone belt.

Entry Regulations

Port of entry
Hanga Roa 27°09′S 109°26′W.

Procedure on arrival
On arrival the captain should proceed ashore. Landing the dinghy in Hanga Roa can be difficult if there is a big swell, although there is a beach protected by rocks which is used by the fishing boats. If Hanga Roa is untenable, one can land at Hanga Piko a mile from the main settlement around Point Roa. There is a pier there, but there is always swell, so it is not advisable to try and come alongside in a yacht.

Entry formalities are not complicated and are done ashore, although sometimes customs and immigration come out to the yacht.

On leaving, one must clear with customs and immigration again.

Customs
Firearms must be declared on arrival. Animals are not allowed to land.

Immigration
A visa is not usually required. Visitors are given tourist cards on arrival.

Facilities

All supplies are brought in from Chile by ship or air and goods in the supermarkets are quite expensive. Some locally produced fruit and vegetables are available. There is a water tap by the dinghy landing in Hanga Roa from where water can be taken in jerrycans. Fuel is also available. Although there are no repair facilities as such, the government has a workshop for maintenance purposes and in an emergency they would undoubtedly help.

Further Reading

Charlie's Charts of Polynesia
Pacific Islands Yearbook
Aku-Aku
Chile and Easter Island – a travel survival kit
Landfalls of Paradise
Pacific Odyssey

FIJI

Fiji is an archipelago of over 300 islands, from coral atolls to large volcanic islands. About 100 are inhabited, while many of the rest are used as fishing bases and planting grounds. The International Dateline runs through Fiji, although most of the islands are just west of 180°.

For the cruising sailor, Fiji has all the ingredients of a perfect destination – beautiful islands, secluded anchorages and welcoming people. This picture of perfection is somewhat marred by a menacing array of coral reefs that almost encircle the entire archipelago. The proliferation of radar and satellite navigation, particularly GPS, has significantly reduced the danger, but many a world cruise has come to a premature end on one of Fiji's reefs.

The majority of visiting yachts arrive from the east, which is where the reefs have claimed most victims. Part of the problem is that it is forbidden to stop at any of the eastern islands before clearing in and a careful watch is kept on yacht movement by the Fijian authorities. The location of the few ports of entry complicates the task of cruise planning, especially for those hoping to visit the eastern Lau group to windward of all ports of entry. The most convenient port for those intending to cruise eastern Fiji is Levuka on the island of Ovalau.

At the crossroads of Melanesia and Polynesia, the traditional way of life is still thriving in the islands and the unthinking attitude in the past of a few visiting sailors has caused offence and animosity, which led to a strict control of cruising permits. Local etiquette should be observed and one is expected to pay a courtesy visit to the chief or headman of the island or village bearing a gift of yagona (kava). A good supply should be taken on board from Suva market. The effort that the Fijians make to preserve their traditions is exactly what makes them so interesting and visitors who observe these simple rules can be assured of a genuine welcome.

Traditions are not so strong in the western islands, some of which have been developed as tourist resorts, such as the charming Mamanuca islands, which are a short hop from Nadi airport, convenient for crew changes. Further west is the Yasawa Group, one of the most popular cruising grounds due to scenic anchorages and clear waters.

Rotuma and several smaller islands lying approximately 200 miles NNW of Fiji, form a distinctive group and although administratively linked to Fiji, ethnologically they are very different as Rotumans are Polynesians. The administrative centre is at Ahau, but as Rotuma is not an official port of entry, access to it is only allowed with prior permission from the authorities in Suva.

Country Profile

The islands were first settled by Melanesians from South East Asia around 7000–5000 BC, while the Polynesians arrived in the fifteenth century AD. European discovery spread over two to three hundred years, after being first sighted in the mid-seventeenth century by Abel Tasman. Captain Cook visited several islands in the 1770s, and Captain Bligh sailed through on his epic voyage after being cast off from the *Bounty*.

During the nineteenth century traders arrived in search of sandalwood, as well as missionaries and land speculators. The introduction of firearms saw terrible tribal wars fought by a people renowned for their savagery and cannibalism. Gradually, however, Christianity spread its influence and the chiefs requested that the islands be taken under the protection of Great Britain to put an end to their exploitation by traders and freebooters.

Labour shortages in the nineteenth and early twenti-

eth centuries led to large numbers of Indian labourers being brought in by the British to work on the sugar plantations. Independence came to Fiji in 1970 and for some years the country enjoyed some stability and prosperity. Racial tension, however, remained close to the surface, as the Indian population grew to outnumber the native Fijians. After the socialist party, which is mainly Indian-supported, won the 1987 elections, Col. Sitiveni Rabuka staged a military coup to keep control in Fijian hands. Fiji declared itself a Republic and was expelled from the Commonwealth. The recent political upheavals have not affected visiting sailors greatly, although entry formalities have been further complicated by a compulsory security check.

The capital of Fiji is Suva, on the main island of Viti Levu. It is a large cosmopolitan city, with a good harbour and duty-free port. Sugar and tourism are the main Fijian industries, the latter starting to recover after the slump which affected both industries after the coup. Other industries are copra and gold mining, but unemployment is high. Fiji is an important communications centre for the South Pacific, and the main campus of the University of the South Pacific is located in Suva.

Tradewinds anchorage at Suva.

Practical Information

LOCAL TIME: GMT + 12 (the date line has been adjusted to fall east of the whole group).

BUOYAGE: IALA A

CURRENCY: Fijian dollar (FID, FI$). A maximum of FI$100 can be exported in local currency, and FI$500 in foreign currency.

BUSINESS HOURS
Banks: 1000–1500 Monday to Thursday, 1000–1600 Friday.
Shops: 0830–1700 Monday to Thursday, 0830–1300 Saturday. On Friday some stay open until 2000.
Business and government offices: 0800–1300, 1400–1630 Monday–Friday.
Recent laws call for strict enforcement of Sunday observance, when all commercial activities are banned, sporting games prohibited and even restaurants are closed. Public transport is limited on Sundays.

ELECTRICITY: 240 V, 50 Hz

PUBLIC HOLIDAYS
1 January: New Year's Day
Good Friday, Easter Saturday and Monday
June: Queen's Official Birthday (second Saturday)
August Bank holiday (start of the month)
October/November: Divali Day (Hindu festival of lights)
October: Fiji Day
October: Prophet Mohammed's birthday
16 November: Prince Charles' Birthday
25, 26 December: Christmas

EVENTS
July: Bula Festival in Nadi
August: Hibiscus Festival in Suva
September: Musket Cove to Vila Yacht Race
September: Sugar Festival in Lautoka

COMMUNICATIONS
Fintel (Fiji International Telecommunications Ltd) 158 Victoria Parade, Suva: international phones, telex and fax, open 24 hours, seven days a week.
Suva post office is open 0730–1630 Monday to Thursday, and to 1600 Fridays, Saturdays 0730–1300.

Post offices outside Suva open 0800–1600 Monday to Friday.
Emergency: Dial 000.
Nadi in the west of Viti Levu is the main international airport with flights to many Pacific destinations as well as Australia, New Zealand, US, European and Asian destinations. There are a few international flights from Suva airport, which connects with several daily flights to Nadi.

MEDICAL
There is a minimal charge in hospitals for non-Fijians. There are also private clinics.

DIPLOMATIC MISSIONS
In Suva:
Australia: Dominion House, Thomson St. ☎ 312844.
France: Dominion House, Thomson St. ☎ 312925.
New Zealand: Reserve Bank Building, Pratt St. ☎ 311422.
Papua New Guinea: Ratu Sukuna House, McArthur St. ☎ 25420.
United Kingdom: Victoria House, 47 Gladstone Rd. ☎ 311033.
United States: 31 Loftus St. ☎ 314466.

In 1986, the population was 714,550, 46 per cent Fijian, 48 per cent Indian and 5 per cent of other origins. Fijian, Hindustani and English are spoken, the latter being widely used by all sections of the population. The majority of Fijians are Methodists, some Roman Catholic, while the Indian population are mainly Hindu with some Muslims and Sikhs.

Fiji has a mild tropical climate. From May to November the SE trades blow, making it cooler and drier, while the summer months from November to April are wet and humid. Viti Levu and Vanua Levu can have a lot of rain and Suva is renowned for sudden but short torrential downpours. Cyclones occur during the period January to March. There are very few hurricane holes in Fiji and these quickly fill up with local boats.

Entry Regulations

Ports of entry
Suva (Viti Levu island) 18°09′S 178°26′E, Levuka (Ovalau island) 17°41′S 178°51′E, Lautoka (Viti Levu island) 17°36′S 177°26′E, Savusavu (Vanua Levu island) 16°47′S 179°21′E.
Savusavu has been declared a port of entry but is not fully established yet as there are, as yet, no officials stationed there.

Procedure on arrival
One should fly the Q flag and tie to the quarantine buoy or anchor in the quarantine area, which is marked on the charts. Quarantine, health and security will visit first, then a yacht can come to the wharf, if in Suva, for customs, immigration and agriculture. If arriving at night or weekends and not wanting to pay overtime charges, one is allowed to wait, but one must not move from the quarantine area until cleared. No one must go ashore until clearance is complete.

Security
Since the coup, all yachts must obtain a security clearance on arrival, for which there is a minimum charge of FI$20.

Customs

Firearms must be declared and handed over to the police to be kept in bond until departure (48 hours notice of departure must be given). If one enters at one port and exits at another, the guns may have to be transferred to the port of departure by the police.

A bond declaration must be signed for any animals on board and they must not be allowed to land on any of the islands.

An itinerary of places and dates where one is planning to cruise until departure from Fiji is required for customs clearance.

Yachts may remain one year without paying any duty.

Any amount over 1 litre of spirits and 2 litres of wine must be sealed on board or taken ashore and bonded. Customs often check the seal before departure.

No fruit or plants may be landed. All such produce on board must be declared and will be inspected on arrival. Garbage should be put in sealed plastic bags and handed over to be disposed into the port incinerator.

Immigration

Passports must be valid for at least six months from the date of entry.

A visa-free stay for up to 30 days (provided one has enough funds or an onward ticket) is allowed for United Kingdom, United States, Canada and most European nationals. Visas are required by only a few nationalities. After 30 days, an extension may be obtained for up to six months.

Cruising permit

After clearance is completed, a cruising permit can be obtained from the Department of Fijian Affairs (at 61 Carnavon Street in Suva) to visit other islands. The permit is written in Fijian and English, and must be presented at the islands visited when requested. Fijian customs and laws are strong and have to be respected. These will be explained by the Department when the permit is given or can be found in detail in *A Yachtsman's Fiji*.

Visits to the Lau Group and Kandavu need approval from the Prime Minister's office, which is more difficult, but not impossible, to obtain.

Fees

Customs: Weekdays after 1630, FI$10 per hour; after 2000 and on Saturdays, there is a 3 hour minimum charge. The charge is FI$15 per hour on Sundays (3 hour minimum).

Agriculture: After 1630 weekdays FI$18 per hour, weekends FI$24 per hour.

Facilities

Provisioning is good in Suva with several supermarkets and an excellent fresh produce market. Gas bottles can be filled in town and fuel is available at the yacht club. Suva is one of the few places in the Pacific where liferafts can be serviced. Suva has a reasonable range of repair facilities and a recently formed company, Yacht Help, has been specifically set up to assist the cruising sailor. The frequency of flights to Auckland means that whatever cannot be obtained or repaired in Suva can be quickly dealt with in New Zealand.

The Royal Suva Yacht Club is welcoming and is in the process of expanding its docking facilities to cater for the increasing number of visitors. An alternate anchorage with limited docking is off the nearby Tradewinds Hotel which is also used as a refuge during cyclones. There is a slipway at the government shipyard in Suva.

Provisioning is adequate in the other islands and some fresh produce is always available. Otherwise, facilities outside of Suva are basic with some workshops in Lautoka. A marina with its own travelift became operational in Lautoka in 1990. Work has also started on a marina at Malololailai island and one is also planned in Savusavu. Pickmere's Yasawa chartlets are essential for cruising the Yasawa group and are available in Lautoka.

Further Reading

Yacht Help leaflet
Fiji Marine Department Nautical Almanac
A Yachtsman's Fiji
Landfalls of Paradise
South Pacific Handbook
Pacific Islands Yearbook
Fiji – a travel survival kit

FRENCH POLYNESIA

French Polynesia covers an area of the South Pacific Ocean about the size of Europe. It is made up of 130 islands in five archipelagos: the Society Islands, the Marquesas, Tuamotus, Gambiers and Australs, as well as Clipperton atoll, a small French possession off Mexico. These coral and volcanic islands, some with spectacular scenery, are all very different from each other. Tahiti is the largest island and Papeete, the capital of the Territory.

So many superlatives have been bestowed on these islands in the days since Captains Cook, Wallis and

Bligh, the *Bounty* mutineers, Robert Louis Stevenson, Paul Gauguin and many others visited them, that one can only repeat some of these well-worn adjectives. As symbols of the South Seas, the islands of French Polynesia are indeed unbeatable and there are few sailors who do not dream of cruising one day among these enchanted isles.

From the rugged beauty of the Marquesas to the crystal clear waters of the Tuamotu atolls and the lofty peaks of the Society Islands, the variety in scenery and sailing conditions is unsurpassed anywhere in the South Pacific. Most yachts make their landfall in the Marquesas, which is a perfect introduction to this vast cruising ground. There are no man-made ports here and the swell can tuck into the anchorages, but this is more than made up for by the beauty of these high islands.

In complete contrast are the Tuamotus, once called the Dangerous Archipelago on account of its treacherous currents and lurking reefs. Yachts used to avoid

Cook's Bay on Moorea, a favourite anchorage for all boats that pass through the Society Islands.

this area, but now often stop and visit the low atolls, as the hazards have diminished considerably with the advent of radar and satellite navigation.

Papeete is enjoyed by many cruisers, able to berth Mediterranean-style in the centre of the town, which is the most chic, lively and cosmopolitan in the Pacific. Development, which has not affected the outer islands, has quickened the pace in Tahiti, but in the rest of the Society Islands life is as relaxed as ever. From Moorea to Bora Bora, the Societies are still some of the most beautiful islands in the world with the contrast of their towering volcanic peaks over lagoons set with low sandy atolls.

Entirely off the usual cruising routes are French Polynesia's other two groups, the Austral and Gambier islands. The latter is best visited if coming from Easter Island or Pitcairn, while the former are only a few days sail away from Tahiti or make a convenient landfall for yachts heading towards Tahiti from New Zealand.

Even more remote and only administratively linked to French Polynesia is the uninhabited Clipperton atoll, some 700 miles off the Mexican coast. The lagoon of this atoll has no pass, but the few yachts

Practical Information

LOCAL TIME: GMT - 10

BUOYAGE: IALA A. The Department of Fishing has laid out buoys which are often 2–3 miles off the islands. They have radar reflectors and are lit, but have been reported as being difficult to spot.

CURRENCY: Pacific franc (PFR/CFP)

BUSINESS HOURS
Banks: 0745–1530 Monday to Friday, some 0800–1100 Saturday.
Shops: 0730–1130, 1400–1730/1800 Monday to Friday, Saturday mornings.
Government offices: 0730–1200/1330–1700 Monday to Friday.

ELECTRICITY: 110/220 V, 50 Hz

PUBLIC HOLIDAYS
1 January: New Year's Day
5 March: Commemoration Day
Good Friday, Easter Monday
1 May: Labour Day
Ascension
Whit Monday
29 June: Tahitian National Holiday
14 July: Bastille Day
15 August: Assumption
1 November: All Saints' Day
11 November: Armistice Day
December: Tiare Tahiti Day
25 December: Christmas Day

EVENTS
Festival, three weeks around Bastille Day when there are song, dance and sport competitions including canoe racing.

COMMUNICATIONS
For international calls, dial 19 and wait for the different dialling tone.
Cables through Telefrance.
Post office: Papeete Waterfront, open 0700–1500 Monday to Friday, 0700–1000 Saturday.
Emergency: Police 17, Fire 18, Mamao Hospital 420101.
There are regular flights from Tahiti to the USA, Europe, Japan, New Zealand and Australia. There are frequent flights to all the Society Islands, but less frequently to the other island groups.

MEDICAL
Territorial Hospital Centre at Mamao. Medical facilities are of a high standard. There are dispensaries in all populated centres.

DIPLOMATIC MISSIONS
New Zealand: c/o Air New Zealand, Vaina Centre, Papeete. ☎ 430170.

which stop there can shelter in the lee of the reef. Landing through the surf is sometimes difficult but the diving on the surrounding reef makes up for it.

The grafting of French culture on to the Polynesian lifestyle has resulted in some strange phenomena, but on the whole the mix has worked to good effect. At no time is this more obvious than during the annual Bastille Day celebrations, the political significance of which few Polynesians care about, but every island puts on a breathtaking show of song and dance of unmatched colour and vivacity.

Country Profile

Tahiti and the surrounding islands were populated from around AD 850, but little is known of the origins of the original population. A system of chiefdoms developed, which later became a kingdom. Remains of the past are still to be found, especially the old marae temples.

Point Venus on Tahiti marks the first European visit in 1767 by Captain Wallis of the Royal Navy, searching for the great Southern Continent. He and his sailors found a welcoming people on a lush fertile island and he claimed it for Britain. Nine months later, the French explorer Bougainville claimed Tahiti for France. Next to visit was James Cook, on an expedi-

tion to observe the sun's eclipse by Venus. He made astute observations of the Tahitians and their lifestyle, including the name they gave to the island, Otaheite ('this is Tahiti'). In honour of the Royal Geographical Society, Cook named the islands Society Islands, and returned to them several times. Captain Bligh visited the islands in 1788 with the *Bounty* and the charms of Tahiti were one of the causes of the famous mutiny. The mutineers' efforts to settle on the unfriendly Australs failed. Some remained on Tahiti, while others sailed with their Tahitian wives to Pitcairn Island. The friendly islanders, who had few sexual constraints, suffered for all their contacts with European sailors, as diseases hitherto unknown to them decimated the population.

Next to arrive on the scene were missionaries, first Protestants, then Catholics. Despite requests from the Tahitians, the British refused to make the islands a Protectorate, so the islands were finally put under French protection. The Pomaré dynasty, in power since the eighteenth century, ruled until 1880, when Tahiti became a full French colony. After the Second World War the newly-named French Polynesia became a French Overseas Territory. An increase in internal autonomy was allowed in 1984, although foreign affairs, police, finance and justice are still in the hands of the French-appointed High Commissioner. The French maintain a military presence in the islands, particularly at Mururoa, an atoll in the Southern Tuamotus which is the centre of nuclear testing. Insistent protests from all neighbouring countries have resulted in a marked reduction in the number of tests being carried out.

Important products are mother-of-pearl, cultured black pearls, copra, vanilla and coffee. The tourist industry also contributes to the economy. Imports, however, are high, as is the cost of living. The Society Islands are more developed than the other groups, while on the more remote islands people live more of a subsistence existence.

The population is 175,000. Polynesians form the majority, although there are also quite a few Europeans and Chinese. There is a very mixed population in Tahiti itself, while the population of the outer islands is pure Polynesian. Tahitian and French are the main languages, although each island group has its own distinct Polynesian language. English is also quite widely spoken, especially in the tourist centres. Most are Christian of many different denominations, with a small percentage of Buddhists among the Chinese population.

The islands have a tropical climate. November to April is warm and rainy, while May to October is cooler and drier, when the islands are under the influence of the SE trade winds. The cyclone season is November to March and every year at least one cyclone affects one or more of the islands. Full cyclones rarely hit the Marquesas, but they can be affected by bad storms during the cyclone season.

Entry Regulations

Ports of entry

Society Islands: Papeete (Tahiti) 17°32′S 149°35′W, Afareaitu (Moorea) 17°32′S 149°46′W, Uturoa (Raiatea) 16°44′S 151°26′W, Fare (Huahine) 16°43′S 151°02′W, Vaitape (Bora Bora) 16°30′S 151°45′W.
Marquesas: Taiohae (Nuku Hiva) 8°56′S 140°06′W, Hakahau (Ua Pou) 9°21′S 140°03′W, Atuona (Hiva Oa) 9°51′S 139°02′W.
Austral Islands: Mataura (Tubuai) 23°22′S 149°28′W, Moerai (Rurutu) 22°27′S 151°20′W, Raima (Raivavae) 23°52′S 147°40′W.
Tuamotus: Tiputa (Rangiroa) 15°10′S 147°35′W.
Gambier Islands: Rikitea (Mangareva) 23°07′S 134°58′W.

Procedure on arrival

Papeete is the main port of entry and all yachts have to finalise their clearance here. However, because of the distances and sailing conditions, the outer islands have been made informal ports of entry, where yachts may initially clear in.

On arrival in one of the other islands, yachts should report to the local police (Gendarmerie). Failure to report may lead to a fine.

On arrival in Papeete one must report first to customs then immigration, both of which are in the Bureau des Yachts, Quai des Paquebots, close to OPATI, the tourist office on the waterfront in Papeete.

Permission should be obtained for any cruise which takes a yacht more than 50 miles from Tahiti. On departure yachts must clear with customs and immigration and apply for a permit to leave from the harbour master.

Customs

Firearms and ammunition must be declared. If staying less than three days they can be kept on board, otherwise must be bonded by the authorities in each island until departure.

Animals need health certificates. They must remain on board unless permission to land is given by customs. Yachts may remain for up to six months in a 12-month consecutive period without paying duty.

The import of plants and grains is forbidden.

Yachts coming from the western Pacific, such as Fiji or the Cooks, may have to be fumigated. On arrival they should anchor off and clear formalities before tying to the quay.

Immigration

Residents of France and citizens of Francophone Africa do not need visas, only a valid passport.

All visitors need a passport valid beyond their proposed stay in French Polynesia.

A visa-free stay is permitted for no more than three months for nationals of the EC countries, Monaco, Andorra, Switzerland and Liechtenstein. If these nationals plan to stay longer, a visa must be obtained in advance.

Citizens of the USA, Canada and Japan can get a visa on arrival. All other nationalities need a visa in advance, which can be obtained from French diplomatic missions, for example in Panama City.

Visas are normally valid for three months. Extensions of another three months are possible, but one should apply well in advance (one month) in writing to the High Commissioner in Papeete, although local immigration offices may be able to extend visas. Extensions can take up to a month to come through. Even for nationals who can get a visa on arrival, formalities are much simplified if the visa is obtained in advance.

Proof may be demanded of sufficient funds for one's

stay in French Polynesia, up to US$350 per month, especially for those arriving without a visa.

Crew arriving by air to join a boat should make this clear on their visa application, also to immigration on arrival at the airport, who should give them both an entrance and an exit stamp in their passport. The exit stamp is needed to clear out by boat.

Cruising permit

A special cruising permit is necessary for yachts spending longer in French Polynesia. This can be obtained on arrival from customs in Papeete or the Gendarmerie in other ports. The permit is valid for six months. Extensions are only granted in Papeete, but most non-French yachts are not allowed to stay longer than six months. All yachts are required to leave French Polynesia before the start of the cyclone season in November, but preferably earlier.

Bond

Each person on board the yacht must deposit in a French Polynesian bank a sum of money equivalent to a one-way air ticket back to their home country. This will be more expensive for Europeans than Americans and Canadians. The bond, called a *caution* in French, must be posted in order to obtain a visa. The French consulate abroad will need a receipt to show the bond has been sent before issuing a visa. The consulate can advise on the correct procedure for posting a bond. If a visa is obtained before arriving, the money can be telexed to a bank in Papeete. On arrival, if one has not posted the bond, arrangements have to be made immediately to have money telexed or to pay money into a bank. There are banks in the Marquesas (Nuku Hiva and Hiva Oa). If arriving there as one's first landfall in French Polynesia, the bond must be arranged on arrival. If one is planning to stay longer, it may be possible to pay the funds into an interest earning deposit account.

This money is normally refunded on the day before departure from French Polynesia. If the bond is posted in Papeete, and one leaves from Bora Bora, one must obtain a letter from the Papeete immigration officer confirming the bond. The letter and the receipt must be presented for the refund. Refunds can be in cash, or travellers' cheques, although the latter must be ordered in advance.

Yachts staying only a very short period (up to one week) may be able to have the bond requirement waived. The bond can be avoided by buying tickets for flights back to one's own country. The unused tickets can be refunded, although one may have to pay a handling charge of approximately 5 per cent. If resorting to this solution, one should make sure that the tickets are refundable and also that the issuing agency will actually authorise a refund.

Fees

There is a charge for visas granted on arrival. There are port charges.

Restricted areas

The approaches to the atolls of Mururoa, Hao and Fangataufa and the area around them are prohibited areas, classed as military zones.

Visitors are also discouraged from going to the Gambiers, because of the islands' proximity to Mururoa. However, yachts arriving from Pitcairn or Easter Island may be allowed to stay and the local gendarme will radio Papeete for approval.

Charter

Visiting yachts may not charter in French Polynesia.

People arriving by air to charter a boat need only a valid passport, return air ticket and a visa where applicable.

Facilities

The best facilities are to be found in Papeete which has several workshops in Fare Ute, on the east side of the harbour, specialising in yacht repair and maintenance. There is also a slipway and a small boatyard doing hull repairs. Nearby is a chandlery with a good selection of equipment, spares and also charts, both French and British Admiralty. Any spares or equipment that is not available can be ordered from France. There are no marina facilities in Tahiti, but the Tahiti Yacht Club in Arue has several docks where visitors may be able to berth if there is space available.

The only other centre with extensive repair facilities is on Raiatea, where two charter companies have their base. A small boatyard has a travelift and they also specialise in electrical, engine and sail repair, as well as rigging work. This is also a good place to leave the boat between seasons, either on the hard or in the small boat harbour of Apooiti.

In Bora Bora, both Hotel Oa Oa and Club Nautique have moorings for yachts and provide showers, laundry, water and other services for sailors.

Provisioning is best in Tahiti and adequate in the other Society Islands. There are fresh produce markets on most islands, the most colourful being the one in Papeete. Provisions in the Marquesas are limited, although there is plenty of local fruit and vegetables. There is usually a better selection when the supply ship arrives. In the more remote areas, it is sometimes possible to barter for fresh provisions. Fuel is available in the main settlements, although it is more difficult to find in the Tuamotus. Propane bottles can be refilled in Papeete, Bora Bora and Nuku Hiva.

Further Reading

Charlie's Charts of Polynesia
Cruising Guide to Tahiti and the Society Islands
Cruising Guide to Tahiti and French Polynesia
Landfalls of Paradise
Pacific Odyssey
South Pacific Handbook
Tahiti and French Polynesia – a travel survival kit

GALAPAGOS ISLANDS

The Galapagos Archipelago forms a group of volcanic islands on the equator about 600 miles west of Ecuador. There are 13 main islands and most have both English and official Spanish names. The Galapagos are known the world over for their tame and unique wildlife, sea lions, birds and iguanas, living amidst a barren volcanic scenery. Isolated from the rest of the world, evolution took a different course in these islands and the authorities want to preserve them for posterity. This is the reason for the difficulty, if not almost impossibility, for yachts to get permission to cruise these islands. In the past some yachtsmen have abused the privilege, by stealing eggs, shooting birds and causing destruction of the environment. The Galapagos are one of the 20 provinces of Ecuador and the Ecuadorian authorities take their custody of this unique wildlife sanctuary seriously.

Country Profile

The islands were found by accident early in the sixteenth century when a ship carrying the Bishop of Panama to Peru drifted off course. However, it is possible that South American Indians had visited the islands earlier. Named Islas Encantadas – the Enchanted Islands – for three centuries the Galapagos were used as a base by pirates, sealers and whalers. Famous sailors such as Drake, Raleigh, Cook and Hawkins stopped there for refuge and provisions. The giant tortoises, called 'galapagos' in Spanish, which could be kept alive in ships' holds for months on end, provided a source of fresh meat, and thousands were

captured or killed. In 1835 the islands received their most famous visit, from HMS *Beagle* and Charles Darwin. The expedition stayed five weeks, and Darwin's observations of how the wildlife there had developed into unique species in response to their surroundings were central to his theory of evolution. Eventually the islands were settled by Ecuador and used for some time as a penal colony.

In 1959 the Galapagos were declared a national park, and organised tourism since the 1960s brings thousands to the islands every year. The islands depend very much on tourism for their income.

In 1985 there were 4410 humans and 10,165 tortoises inhabiting the group. Spanish is the main language, although English is widely spoken. The administrative centre is Puerto Baquerizo Moreno or Wreck Bay on San Cristobal Island, while Puerto Ayora in Academy Bay, on Santa Cruz Island, is the main settlement.

The climate is equatorial, cooled by the Humboldt current. December to May is the better season when the weather is pleasantly warm and the winds are light. From June to November the weather is overcast and cool. The water around the islands is surprisingly cold and the meeting of the Humboldt current and the warm air sometimes causes mist over the islands. Occasionally the Humboldt current is replaced by the warm El Niño current, a phenomenon which can affect weather conditions throughout the South Pacific.

Entry Regulations

Ports of entry
Puerto Baquerizo Moreno, Wreck Bay (San Cristobal) 0°54'S 89°37'W, Puerto Ayora, Academy Bay (Santa Cruz) 0°46'S 90°18'W.

Procedure on arrival
Yachts should not stop anywhere but at a port of entry nor must anyone go ashore without an official guide. Yachts may be boarded at any time to check if one has a guide. The penalty is a fine and possible imprisonment for stopping at outer islands without permission. All the local boats have guides on board who are in radio contact with the port authority and will immediately report any yacht breaking the regulations.

On arrival the captain must go to the port captain's office, which is close to the dock in both Puerto Ayora and Puerto Baquerizo Moreno. If a yacht has no permit, it will be given 72 hours to stay, provided the yacht remains in the port of entry. Only the port captain has the authority to extend this period. He

Practical Information

LOCAL TIME: GMT - 6

BUOYAGE: IALA B

CURRENCY: Sucre (S) of 100 centavos. US$ are accepted.

BUSINESS HOURS
Banks: 0800–1230 Monday to Friday, at Puerto Ayora. Money changing facilities are not very good and occasionally one can get a better rate at shops or hotels than at the bank.
Shops: 0800–1200, 1400–2000 Monday to Saturday. Most food and tourist shops open Sunday morning.

ELECTRICITY: 120 V, 50 Hz

PUBLIC HOLIDAYS
Ecuadorean holidays:
1 January: New Year's Day
6 January
Monday and Tuesday before Lent (Carnival)
Holy Thursday
Good Friday, Holy Saturday
1 May
24 May: Battle of Pichincha
24 June: Birthday of Bolivar
10 August: Independence of Quito
Opening of Congress
9 October: Independence of Guayaquil
12 October: Discovery of America
1 November: All Saints' Day

2 November: All Souls' Day
3 November: Independence of Cuenca
6 December: Foundation of Quito
25 December: Christmas Day

COMMUNICATIONS
Long-distance telephone calls and cables from both Academy and Wreck Bay.
INGALA: emergency radio messages. Post office at Puerto Ayora. Mail is reported to be not very reliable. There are daily flights to Guayaquil and Quito from Puerto Ayora and Puerto Basquerizo Moreno.

MEDICAL
Hospital consultations at Ayora, 0800–1200, 1500–1800 Monday to Friday.

cannot grant cruising permits, only issue them on authorisation from Quito. He will keep the ship's papers until departure.

Extensions may be obtained on a day-by-day basis and depend on the port captain's discretion. Yachts who have had *genuine* reasons to stay a little longer have obtained extensions, for repairs or reprovisioning, but note that the port captain may send along a mechanic to verify that the alleged repairs are genuine. The feeling among the local population is that yachts should not be granted cruising permits at all, but should use local charter boats to visit the islands. If one arrives without a permit, but makes immediate arrangements to go on a charter boat, one may be allowed to stay longer than the usual 72 hours. If yachts have already spent 72 hours at Wreck Bay and then go to Academy Bay, they may not be allowed to stop, as they are deemed to have already made the one emergency stop allowed in the Galapagos. If one does not have a permit, it is not advisable to list the Galapagos as one's destination when clearing out from Panama. It is better to list the Marquesas or another destination, so as to be able to state that the Galapagos stop is indeed for emergency reasons and was not premeditated.

Customs
Firearms must be declared and will be sealed on board. Animals must be confined on board.

Immigration
Tourists are allowed to stay 90 days a year with no visa; extensions can be obtained from the Chief of Police, Puerto Baquerizo Moreno, San Cristobal.

Cruising permit
Yachts are only supposed to stop and visit the Galapagos Islands with an official permit, which is granted by the Ecuadorean Ministry of Defence in Quito. The procedure for obtaining a cruising permit is lengthy and carries no guarantee of success. The authorities have a quota for yachts, of between four and six per month, although these quotas change from year to year. Apparently large crews of more than four or five are not desired, as they are suspected of being on an unofficial charter. Any type of chartering by foreign yachts is resisted by the local boats which have to pay a fee to charter.

Two different permits must be obtained, one from the Ministry of Agriculture for entry to the park, and one from the Navy for permission to cruise in Galapagos waters. All applications for the permit must be in Spanish. The application should be made through the Ecuadorean embassy or consulate in the country of one's origin and addressed to: Armada del Ecuador, Dirección General de Intereses Marítimos. One should also write direct to: The Director, Nacional Forestal Ministerio de Agricultura y Ganderia, Quito, Ecuador. Telex: 2291 MAG-ED.

The letters should contain details of the vessel, the names and nationalities of the captain and crew, their permanent addresses, the vessel's port of registry, the date and port of departure, the estimated duration of the journey and date of arrival in the Galapagos and the planned itinerary. Photocopies of the first two pages of the passports of captain and crew, a photocopy of the vessel's registration certificate and a photocopy of the captain's certificate of competence should be included.

Photographs of the yacht and her crew could be a help.

The Navy should also be sent a Letter of Agreement in Spanish allowing representatives of the Navy and Board of Tourism to board the vessel if required, taking responsibility for any expenses incurred in their transport, and also undertaking to respect the plant and animal life of the park. The Spanish text of this letter is given below, as any application must mention the various stipulations listed above.

Señor Director General de Intereses Marítimos
Señor Director:

Dando cumplimiento a lo dispuesto en los literales i), j), y k) del Artículo 3, Capitulo II, 'Visitas turisticas y culturales' del Decreto No. 812, Registro Oficial 346 de Diciembre 29, 1980, por la presente me comprometo a embarcar en mi nave a los representantes de la Armada Nacional, Dirección Nacional de Turísmo o otras organismos nacionales cuando así lo requieran, haciéndome responsable por los gastos de movilización y estadía a bordo. Me comprometo también a entregar los resultados de la gira a la Dirección Nacional de Turísmo y a acatar las normas de preservación de Parques Nacionales y especies naturales, como también a resarcir los perjuicios que llegare a causar.

De usted, muy atentamente,
.... (signed)

The first application should be made a year in advance. This should be followed up every three months with copies of the original letters. If a permit is granted, the Ministry of Defence will telex the approval to the port captain, who will issue a cruising permit, which also includes the official guide's name. The permit allows a yacht to visit the islands, but only with an official guide on board. All visits to the islands must be accompanied by a guide, and this includes the local charter boats. There are about 40 places around the islands where tourists with guides may go ashore.

Fees

The entrance and clearance fee is approximately US$35. Overtime must be paid outside office hours, 0800–1700 Monday to Friday. The overtime fees are almost double the normal fee. Port fees are approximately US$27.

Everyone must pay an admission fee to the Galapagos National Park of approximately US$40, valid for one calendar year. The cost is the same whether staying three days or six months.

On yachts with a permit, an official guide must stay on board while visiting the islands; Spanish-speaking guides are about US$30 a day, and English-speaking guides about US$40 a day.

Facilities

Supplies at both Academy and Wreck Bays are in short supply, particularly fresh produce, which can cause a problem for those intending to provision their boats in the Galapagos for the long haul to the Marquesas. Fresh bread and some basic staples are available at both places. Vegetables and fruit can be scarce unless in season. Prices are expensive by South American standards. The best time to buy food is in the evening from Monday to Saturday, as the plane from the mainland lands at lunch time and supplies arrive in town from 1600 onwards.

There are very few parts available locally but essential spares can be obtained from the mainland, if one is prepared and able to wait. There are no haul-out facilities except for a drying grid in the inner harbour in Puerto Ayora. This can be used depending on the state of the tides. One must get permission from the port captain to use it.

Diesel fuel and water are also difficult to obtain, so it is advisable to arrive with full tanks and not expect to find too much in the islands. The islanders are not allowed to sell fuel to yachts, although one may be able to buy directly from a cargo ship if there is one in port, or get permission from the port captain to go to the military base at Baltra, where one can also get water. Water is not very good quality, but is more plentiful in the first four months of the year when enough rainwater can be collected.

Both the anchorage and supplies are better at Academy Bay and yachts arriving without a cruising permit might be better off going directly there and bypassing Wreck Bay altogether. Propane bottles cannot be filled locally and have to be sent to the mainland and as this may take some time, it is better not to resort to this solution unless in dire need.

Further Reading

Ecuador and the Galapagos Islands – a travel survival kit
Floreana
Landfalls of Paradise

JUAN FERNANDEZ ISLANDS

Some 400 miles off the coast of Chile lies a group of islands rarely visited by anyone, including yachts. The three islands, Robinson Crusoe, Alejandro Selkirk and Santa Clara, are a dependency of Chile. Discovered by

Practical Information (Juan Fernandez Islands)

LOCAL TIME: GMT - 6	*CURRENCY:* Chilean peso	*COMMUNICATIONS*
		The village has a post office, wireless
BUOYAGE: IALA B	*ELECTRICITY:* 220 V, 50 Hz	station, and there is an airstrip on the
		west end.

Juan Fernández in 1574, one island was the home of Alexander Selkirk, a seaman who was left on the island at his own request from 1704 to 1709. It is this willingly marooned sailor whom Daniel Defoe used as the inspiration for his character Robinson Crusoe. This island now bears the fictional character's name. Alejandro Selkirk Island is 80 miles further west. Only Robinson Crusoe Island (33°38′S, 78°50′W) is inhabited, by a population of around 500, most based in the San Juan Bautista village in Cumberland Bay. The names were given to the islands in 1935 when the group was made a national park.

The islands are visited very rarely by yachts as they are off the cruising routes. The occasional yacht that stops here is usually en route to Easter Island, Chile's other outpost in the South Pacific.

Procedure on arrival

Anchor off the village and small jetty in Cumberland Bay. If there is not too much swell, one can tie up alongside. Officials will come out to clear the yacht.

Facilities

Very few provisions can be obtained here, fuel could perhaps be bought from a local fisherman, and there is enough water, especially between May and November, the rainy months.

NAURU

The Republic of Nauru is one of the smallest countries in the world, an eight square mile coral island, lying just south of the equator, west of Kiribati. A stark island with little vegetation, but very wealthy due to its phosphate resources, Nauru is hardly an enticing destination for anyone cruising the South Pacific. Nevertheless, the island can be a useful stop, especially in an emergency, for boats bound for the Solomons or Papua New Guinea. There is only an open roadstead in the lee of the island, very deep for anchoring, where some mooring buoys have been laid for ships loading phosphate. If there is not too much surge and there is space available, it may be preferable, if draft permits, to try and enter the small boat basin.

Country Profile

Before the arrival of the Europeans, this isolated island had developed its own culture, a matrilineal society which traced descent through the female line. In the late nineteenth century Nauru was proclaimed a German territory and after the First World War it was administered as a League of Nations mandate. Occupied by the Japanese during the Second World War, after the war it was administered by Australia under a UN mandate until 1968.

Phosphate was discovered in 1900, but most of the money earned from its exploitation went abroad. With Nauru's independence in 1968, the Nauruans finally gained control of the phosphate industry and a determined effort has been made to ensure the country's self-sufficiency before the phosphate is totally exhausted.

Besides its dwindling phosphate deposits, the island has no natural resources. There is a shortage of drinking water, which sometimes has to be shipped in. Phosphate is Nauru's sole asset, but this is predicted to be exhausted by 1995. As a result of the phosphate, native Nauruans are prosperous, living in a perfect welfare state. Their hope for the future lies in shipping, their airline Air Nauru and a role as an international tax haven.

The 1983 census showed 8042 inhabitants. Many are immigrant workers (I-Kiribati, Chinese, Europeans and Indians). Nauruans, who form just over 60 per cent of the population, are a mixture of Micronesian, Melanesian and Polynesian. English is spoken as well as Nauruan, which is dissimilar to other Pacific languages, being a mixture of Kiribati, Carolines, Marshalls and Solomons' influences. Yaren District is the administrative centre. Most Nauruans are Protestant.

The climate is equatorial, 27°C (81°F) being the average temperature. The island is not affected by tropical cyclones.

Entry Regulations

Port of entry

Aiwo 0°31′S 166°56′E.

Practical Information (Nauru)

LOCAL TIME: GMT + 12

BUOYAGE: IALA A

CURRENCY: Australian dollars (Aus$)

BUSINESS HOURS
Banks: 1000–1500 Monday to Thursday, 1000–1700 Friday.
Business: 0800–1200, 1330–1645 Monday to Friday.

ELECTRICITY: 240 V, 50 Hz

PUBLIC HOLIDAYS
1 January: New Year's Day
31 January: Independence Day
Good Friday, Easter Monday
17 May
26 October: Angam Day
25, 26 December: Christmas

COMMUNICATIONS
There are good telephone links with the outside world.
Air Nauru has flights to various Pacific islands as well as to Australia, New Zealand and Hong Kong.

MEDICAL
There is a good hospital on the island.

Procedure on arrival

The port captain monitors VHF Channel 16 and will advise on the best procedure. If a large ship's mooring is available, he may advise a yacht to tie up to it. Entry formalities are completed ashore.

Customs

Firearms must be declared. Animals must remain on board.

Immigration

Visas are required by all visitors, but yachts on a short visit are normally exempt.

Facilities

Diesel fuel is usually available, but a drum may have to be sent out by lighter. Water is difficult to obtain as there is not much to spare on the island. There is a well stocked supermarket, where fresh provisions are usually available. Emergency repairs can be carried out at one of the workshops.

Further Reading

Pacific Islands Yearbook
Landfalls of paradise

NEW CALEDONIA

In the Western Pacific, bordering on the Coral Sea, New Caledonia is the French Overseas Territory of Nouvelle Calédonie, named by Captain Cook after the Roman name for Scotland. The main island is the mountainous Grande Terre, 250 miles long and 30 miles wide. The once stunning scenery now alternates between thick forest and bare slopes mined for miner-als, for the mountains of Grande Terre are almost solid mineral deposits. Grande Terre also boasts one of the largest insular coral reefs in the world, and one can sail around much of the island inside the reef. Also part of the territory are the offlying islands, the Loyalty Group to the east (Maré, Lifou and Ouvéa), the Ile des Pines, the Chesterfield Islands, and Belep Island.

New Caledonia is an interesting mixture of French and Pacific cultures. However, in recent years troubles have flared up as the indigenous Melanesians saw neighbouring countries becoming independent while they were increasingly outnumbered by immigrants, especially from France and ex-French colonies in North Africa. A separatist movement grew up demanding independence from France. Conflict was often violent, and visiting sailors reported that it was wise to avoid the eastern coast where most of the Melanesian population lives. More recently the situation appears to have calmed down and the violence has subsided.

Even at the height of the troubles foreign yachts were not greatly affected, as the conflict is an internal affair. New Caledonia, particularly the picturesque outer islands, has a lot to offer the cruising sailor. Nouméa itself is a cosmopolitan city and an excellent place to reprovision the boat, as virtually everything is available and repair facilities are very good.

Country Profile

For centuries this land was home to a Melanesian stone-age people and culture. When the first Europeans arrived towards the end of the eighteenth century, Grande Terre had a population of 50,000, speaking 32 languages, and numerous tribes who practised ritualised cannibalism and headhunting. Captain Cook found them quite friendly when he landed on the eastern coast, but when the French explorer Entrecasteaux visited a few years later, on his

Practical Information

LOCAL TIME: GMT + 11

BUOYAGE: IALA A

CURRENCY: French Pacific Franc (CFP)

BUSINESS HOURS
Banks: 0730–1030/1330–1530 Monday to Friday.
Shops: 0730–1100/1400–1800 Monday to Friday, half day Saturday.
Tahitian, Chinese and Indonesian shops round the central square in Nouméa are open seven days a week
Government offices: 0700–1100/1300–1700 Monday to Friday.

ELECTRICITY: 220 V, 50 Hz

PUBLIC HOLIDAYS
1 January: New Year's Day
Easter
1 May: Labour Day
Ascension
Whit Monday
14 July: Bastille Day
15 August: Assumption
24 September: National Day
1 November: All Saints' Day
11 November: Armistice Day
25 December: Christmas Day

COMMUNICATIONS
International dialling access code 19.
PTT (general post office), rue Eugène Porcheron, open 0715–1115/1330–1730 Monday to Friday.
Emergency: Police dial 17.
From Nouméa there are flights to several Pacific destinations, Australia, New Zealand, Jakarta, Singapore, Tokyo and Paris.

DIPLOMATIC MISSIONS
In Nouméa:
Australia: 18 rue du Maréchal Foch.
☎ 272414.
New Zealand: 4 Boulevard Vauban.
☎ 272543.

search for the missing La Pérouse expedition, he found a warlike people, their character changed by famine, drought and tribal wars. Entrecasteaux also discovered the Loyalty Islands and explored the west coast of Grande Terre.

In the nineteenth century French missionaries, traders and English settlers came to the islands. The Melanesians resisted this invasion violently and there were several revolts. Britain was not particularly interested in colonising the place, but the French were and in 1853 they claimed New Caledonia as a colony. They ran the island as a penal colony and brought thousands of convicts to the islands, putting them to work mining the nickel discovered on the island. Later Indonesians, Japanese and Indo-Chinese labourers were brought in to work the mines.

During the Second World War the colony declared itself on the side of de Gaulle and the Free French and it became an important American base. Today New Caledonia is part of France as an Overseas Territory. In recent years there have been troubles because of the separatist movement, but the Melanesians are outnumbered by those of European and other origins, who wish to stay part of France. The French government is striving to find a solution acceptable to the Melanesian minority, but as any move towards independence is fiercely resisted by the white New Caledonians, a division of the island along ethnic lines is a distinct possibility at some stage in the future.

Mining dominates the economy, with fishing, forestry and agriculture also important. There is a wealth of minerals on Grande Terre, nickel being the most important. Tourism has also developed considerably.

The cosmopolitan population is about 145,000.

Melanesians number over 60,000, living mainly on the east coast and the outer islands. There are more than 50,000 Europeans, and also immigrants from Wallis, Tahiti, Indonesia, Vietnam and Vanuatu. French is the official language and there are many indigenous languages. Bislama is the lingua franca, a dialect akin to Pidgin English, spoken in neighbouring Vanuatu. Beliefs vary from Catholicism and Protestantism to the traditional animism of the Melanesians. Nouméa on Grande Terre is the capital.

The cyclone season is November to March, when it is more humid and warm. It is cool and dry from April to November, when the prevailing SE trades are stronger.

Entry Regulations

Port of entry
Nouméa 22°16′S 166°27′E.

Procedure on arrival
Enter through Boulari Pass and, flying the Q flag, proceed to Quai des Scientifiques, Baie de la Moselle, which is the main wharf in the centre of Nouméa. Customs and immigration will come to the yacht and formalities are completed here. Yachts are also known to have cleared at the yacht club, Cercle Nautique Calédonien, in Baie de Pêcheurs, but the authorities prefer yachts to come to the above location.

Yachts must not stop anywhere else before clearing at Nouméa. Permission to visit the outer islands must be obtained in Nouméa. Yachts are no longer allowed to stop on their way out of the territory after clearance and so should return to Nouméa for final outward clearance.

Customs

Firearms are bonded by customs until departure.

Prohibited imports are birds, cats, dogs and plants. Animals must stay on board.

The maximum period a yacht may stay before becoming eligible for import duty is six months or one year in certain cases allowed by customs.

Immigration

No visa is required for up to three months for the nationals of EC countries, Austria, Finland, Iceland, Liechtenstein, Monaco, Norway, San Marino, Sweden and Switzerland.

No visa is required for stays of up to one month by nationals of Bahamas, Canada, Djibouti, Fiji, Guyana, Hong Kong, Japan, Solomons, Western Samoa, Senegal, Tonga and the USA. Nationals of New Zealand, Australia and other countries not mentioned above need to obtain a visa in advance.

Fees

Overtime is not usually charged. Port fees of CFP3125.

Facilities

Facilities in Nouméa are extensive as there is a fairly large local yacht population. There are several chandleries, with a good supply of French charts as well as a reasonable selection of both French and New Zealand yachting equipment. There are various specialised workshops concentrated around the yacht harbour offering a wide range of services, such as engine, electrical, electronic, refrigeration, rigging and sail repair. There are two travelifts, the one at the Cercle Nautique Calédonien has a capacity of 40 tons. Although there are several marinas, the number of available berths for visitors is limited, but a new marina at Port Moselle will considerably ease the situation. There are two fuel stations in the yacht harbour. Gas bottles can be filled at all service stations. There are several large supermarkets and a fresh produce market open from 0500 to 1100.

Further Reading

Pacific Islands Yearbook
Cruising New Caledonia and Vanuatu
Landfalls of Paradise

NEW ZEALAND

The most southerly of the Pacific countries, New Zealand lies over 1200 miles east of Australia and forms the south-western point of the Polynesian triangle. It is made up of two large islands, North Island and South Island, plus a number of smaller offlying islands. New Zealand has many attractions, not least as a cruising ground outside of the cyclone zone. It is a scenic land of mountains, glaciers, bubbling hot pools, giant ferns and a unique wildlife. The North Island is rolling, green and temperate, while the South Island is more mountainous and cooler.

There are reputedly more sailing yachts per head of population in New Zealand than in any other country. The beauty and variety of the coast, as well as the challenging sailing conditions that they grow up with, is almost certainly the explanation why there are so many good sailors in New Zealand, a country that can be best appreciated by those who visit it by boat. From the Bay of Islands in the north to wind-swept Stewart Island in the south, cruising in New Zealand can fulfil the requirements of even the most fastidious. The east coast of both islands has many harbours and anchorages, and in the summer the climate is gentle and the weather seldom threatening.

The Bay of Islands is the favourite place of entry and the cruising here is so pleasant that some visiting yachts never leave this large protected bay dotted with the many islands which gave its name. Sailing south from the Bay of Islands or Whangarei, it is worth taking an offshore tack to call at the Barrier Islands before heading for Hauraki Gulf and busy Auckland. Other highlights of a southbound trip are the capital Wellington and, across Cook Strait, picturesque Picton and the Marlborough Sound.

Sailing conditions around South Island are more challenging than in the benign north and those who are short of time can enjoy its majestic scenery by cruising on four wheels. This option is often taken by cruisers who leave their yachts in the protected Bay of Islands. It is particularly difficult to cruise in Fijordland with its deep windy anchorages and the awe-inspiring Milford Haven is best savoured from the deck of a locally skippered boat. Nevertheless, the east coast of South Island has several attractive harbours such as Dunedin, Timaru and Lyttleton, but not one of them matches the beauty of Marlborough Sound, which also has the advantage of being more accessible. Whether cruising New Zealand by yacht or car, one will soon understand why the locals call the islands God's Own country.

Country Profile

The first settlers in these islands were the Maoris, a Polynesian race, who called it Aotearoa, 'Land of the long white cloud'. Probably sailing down from the Cook Islands, the first came around the tenth century AD, although the main settlement, known simply as the 'Migration', occurred in the fourteenth century AD. A warlike people, the Maoris were also fine artists, decorating their canoes and meeting houses with wooden carvings, their faces with elaborate tattoos and making jade ornaments. The first European to visit was Abel Tasman in 1642. The islands were then left alone until 1769 when Captain Cook claimed them for Britain. The first European settlers were whalers and sealers, who brought diseases and firearms, both of which caused a rapid decline in the Maori population. The arrival of missionaries in the early nineteenth century saw a decline in violence, but in stamping out

cannibalism and warfare, the missionaries weakened the traditional Maori culture. The Treaty of Waitangi in 1840 between Maori chiefs and Britain made New Zealand into a British possession. Fierce conflict over the ownership of land continued between Maoris and Europeans. Gradually the situation calmed down and New Zealand became a prosperous agricultural country. Social reforms at the end of the nineteenth century introduced, among other things, pensions and the vote for women, making New Zealand one of the first countries in the world to do so.

In the early twentieth century New Zealand became a Dominion, and then slowly evolved into an independent nation. In more recent years New Zealand's non-nuclear policy has led to friction with the USA and the break up of ANZUS, the 1951 defence agreement with Australia and the United States. New Zealand's concern over French nuclear policy in the Pacific and the sinking of the Greenpeace vessel,

Kerikeri in the Bay of Islands.

Practical Information

LOCAL TIME: GMT + 12. Summer time
GMT + 13 October to early March.

BUOYAGE: IALA A

CURRENCY: New Zealand dollar
(NZD/NZ$) of 100 cents

BUSINESS HOURS
Banks: 0930–1600 Monday to Friday.
Business: 0900–1700 Monday to Friday.
Shops: 0900–1730 Monday to Thursday,
to 2100 Friday (sometimes Thursday
also).
Government offices: 0800–1600 Monday
to Friday.

ELECTRICITY: 230 V, 50 Hz

PUBLIC HOLIDAYS
1 January: New Year's Day
6 February: Waitangi Day
Good Friday, Easter Monday
25 April: ANZAC Day
June: Queen's Birthday
Fourth Monday in October: Labour Day
25, 26 December: Christmas Day

EVENTS
January: Auckland Yacht Regatta
February: Waitangi Day, Bay of Islands

COMMUNICATIONS
Telecom offices for cables and
telephone calls.
International calls have to be made
through the operator at phone booths.
Direct dialling is only available from
private phones.
Post office: 0900–1700 Monday to
Thursday, to 2000 Friday.
Post office, Rathbone St, Whangarei. In
Opua the post office is near the wharf
where the yachts clear in.
Emergency: dial 111.
It is illegal to use marine VHF handheld
radios ashore.
Auckland airport has excellent links with
all parts of the world, including most
Pacific nations.

MEDICAL
There are good hospitals in all towns
and medical care is of a high standard.

DIPLOMATIC MISSIONS
In Wellington:
Australia: 72–78 Hobson Street,
Thorndon. ☎ (4) 736-411.
Canada: ICI Building, Molesworth
Street. ☎ (4) 739-577 .
Papua New Guinea: Princess Tower,
180 Molesworth St, Thorndon.
☎ (4) 851-247.
United Kingdom: Reserve Bank of NZ
Building, 2 The Terrace. ☎ (4) 726-049.
United States: 29 Fitzherbert Terrace,
Thorndon. ☎ (4) 722-068.

In Auckland:
Australia: Union House, 32–38 Quay
Street. ☎ (9) 32-429.
Canada: Princes Court, 2 Princes Street.
☎ (9) 393-516.
United Kingdom: Faye Richwhite Bldg,
151 Queens Street. ☎ (9) 303-2973.
United States: Yorkshire General Bldg,
Shortland and O'Connel Streets.
☎ (9) 32-724.

Rainbow Warrior, in Auckland harbour by French saboteurs has also seen relations cool between France and New Zealand.

New Zealand is one of the world leaders in the export of wool, lamb, beef and dairy products. A lack of mineral resources is a problem, but in general it is a prosperous country.

The population is about 3.3 million, mostly of British descent, known as Pakehas by the Maoris who number about 400,000. In Auckland there is a considerable community of other Pacific Islanders, such as Tongans, Samoans and Cook Islanders. English and Maori are the main languages and various Christian denominations are practised as well as some traditional Maori beliefs. Wellington, on the southern tip of North Island, is the capital, although Auckland is the largest city and commercial centre.

The climate is varied from the subtropical in the north to snowy mountains and glaciers in the south. The summer from November to March is the more pleasant season, while the winter is wetter and windier. South Island is generally cooler in both summer and winter. Although out of the tropical cyclone area, occasionally in February or March the tail of a cyclone reaches North Island. Lying in the westerly wind belt, the east coast is more sheltered and the main yachting centres are along that coast.

Entry Regulations

Ports of entry
North Island: Opua 35°18′S 174°08′E, Whangarei 35°44′S 174°21′E, Auckland 36°51′S 174°48′E, Tauranga 37°39′S 176°10′E, Napier 39°29′S 176°55′E, New Plymouth 39°04′S 174°05′E, Wellington 41°17′S 174°46′E.
South Island: Nelson 42°16′S 173°19′E, Picton 41°16′S 174°00′E, Blenheim 41°30′S 174°00′E, Christchurch (Lyttelton) 43°37′S 172°43′E, Timaru 44°25′S 171°19′E, Dunedin 45°53′S 170°31′E, Invercargill (Bluff) 46°36′S 168°26′E.
Chatham Islands: Waitangi 43°57′S 176°34′E.
Arrival at any other port requires the written permission of a Collector of Customs.

Procedure on arrival
One is required to inform customs and agricultural quarantine officers by radio of the ETA and details of the yacht not later than 12 hours before arrival and 24

hours is preferred. Marine radio stations will pass messages to customs:

Auckland Radio (ZLD) – provides continuous listening watches on: 2182, 4125, 6215.5 KHz and VHF Channel 16.

Wellington Radio (ZLW) – provides continuous listening watches on: 2182, 4125 KHz and VHF Channel 16.

Awarua Radio (ZLB) – provides continuous listening watches on: 2182 and 4125 KHz.

Kerikeri Radio, located in the Bay of Islands, provides weather information for the Western Pacific and runs a maritime net on 4419.4 KHz at 0815 and 1900 (NZ Time). They will inform customs and immigration of a yacht's ETA if contacted on VHF Channel 16.

Whangarei harbour control can be contacted on VHF Channel 16 to notify customs to be ready to clear a yacht on arrival in the town basin.

If a yacht is not able to radio and arrives unannounced, the captain must immediately contact customs or police by telephone (toll free). No one else may go ashore until clearance is complete.

A customs officer is stationed in Opua in the Bay of Islands during the high season from November to March. At other times it may be necessary to contact Whangarei customs by telephone and request clearance (Whangarei Collector of Customs, ☎ 482 400).

Every yacht arriving from abroad has to clear customs and immigration, and undergo an inspection by an agricultural official before clearance is complete.

Procedure on departure

Confirmation of departure must be given at least 24 hours prior to leaving. Once issued with a clearance certificate, yachts are required to go to sea immediately.

The same entry and departure formalities apply to New Zealand yachts as to foreign vessels.

Customs

Firearms must be declared to customs, who will refer the declaration to the police. A permit can be obtained from the police on arrival if the firearms are on the approved list, such as sporting guns and shotguns. Handguns and pistols are not approved and will be kept in custody until departure. All firearms should have a licence from the country of origin.

All foreign yachts entering New Zealand on a temporary basis fill in a Temporary Import form. The duty payable is assessed, and the amount secured by declaration on entry. Departure must be within 12 months of entry. If not, this duty must be paid on the yacht and its equipment. Extensions are normally not given beyond the 12 month limit unless the yacht is unseaworthy.

All equipment other than fixtures must be declared, although these will not be subject to duty if remaining on board and re-exported on departure. Some may have to be sealed by customs. Items to be landed must be declared to customs on arrival. Goods imported into New Zealand such as radios and navigation equipment require a Temporary Import form and a deposit to cover duty and sales tax, which will be refunded on re-export. If imported permanently, they will be subject to duty.

Purchases made in New Zealand have duty paid on them, but if they are exported a refund of duty can be obtained from customs on proof of purchase and export.

Duty-free supplies vary from port to port. Purchases may be made from a Licensed Export Warehouse before departure, to be delivered just before departure and checked by customs.

Quarantine

New Zealand has very strict regulations on the importation of animals, animal and plant products, as it is a country so dependent on agriculture and relatively free from pests and diseases. On arrival, inspection is carried out by an agriculture quarantine officer from the Ministry of Agriculture and Fisheries (MAF), who should be contacted before arrival. If that cannot be done, one should telephone MAF on arrival – they accept collect calls – or contact them through the local police. Until clearance is completed, nothing must be landed and the crew must remain on board. After clearance is completed, if it has been necessary to place any provisions under seal or if there are animals on board, regular inspections by an agriculture officer may be carried out. It may be more convenient to destroy on arrival any provisions that have to be sealed or stores that cannot be landed. Obviously it is advisable to arrive with a minimum of fresh stores.

Items that must not be landed are fruit, vegetables, plant products, foodstuffs, eggs and waste from these items, pot plants, meat and animal products. All waste must be disposed of through the proper garbage disposal system including egg containers. The agriculture quarantine officer will explain this on arrival. Until such stores are consumed or destroyed the yacht will be under surveillance and restricted to berthing at a wharf where these garbage facilities are available. Organic garbage should be disposed of before entering New Zealand territorial waters (12 mile limit).

Bicycles, motorcycles and sporting equipment must be washed or cleaned before landing, for which a written authority is required.

Animals: New Zealand is a rabies-free country. The New Zealand authorities actively discourage animals arriving on yachts and the restrictions placed on those with animals on board are considerable. The master must place a bond of NZ$1000 for the secure custody of any pets aboard, and this will be forfeited if conditions are not met. Animals must be securely confined and not landed. The master is required by the bond to notify the MAF 48 hours before departure from a port, indicating the next port of call in New Zealand, and notification must be given even if only moving moorings. After six months the animals must be reshipped from New Zealand or destroyed; if not the yacht must leave the country. In the event of an animal becoming ill the MAF must be contacted immediately and private vets cannot be consulted without MAF approval. If a pet dies, its body must be given to the agriculture quarantine officer for disposal. The officer usually makes regular visits two to three times a week to check the animals and must see them immediately before departure. A charge is levied for the visits, based on time and mileage, approximately $40 per week. It is more expensive at outlying ports such as Opua, more reasonable in Whangarei. Any pets obtained in New Zealand must be added to the bond.

Immigration

Passports must be valid for at least three months beyond departure date. Australian citizens do not need visas.

A three month visitor's permit is granted on arrival to nationals of Austria, Belgium, Canada, Denmark, Finland, France (French citizens resident in France only), Germany, Greece, Iceland, Indonesia, Ireland, Italy, Japan, Kiribati, Liechtenstein, Luxembourg, Malaysia, Malta, Monaco, Nauru, the Netherlands, Norway, Portugal, Singapore, Spain, Sweden, Switzerland, Thailand, Tuvalu and the United States (US citizens not resident in the USA such as American Samoans need a visa).

British citizens may stay for up to six months on a visitor's permit.

Citizens of France living in French Polynesia or New Caledonia are allowed a visa-free visit of up to 30 days.

The visitor's permit is only granted on arrival if proof of sufficient funds can be given (cash, travellers' cheques, bank draft, letters of credit, major credit cards), which is set at NZ$400 per person per month if living on a yacht, NZ$1000 if living ashore, as well as evidence of the arrangements for one's onward travel. This can be either an air ticket or sufficient funds to purchase one, or for a yacht owner and his or her dependants' proof of ownership of the yacht plus

insurance for the yacht valid for the South Pacific. Proof of ownership alone is not sufficient as the yacht could be damaged beyond repair while in New Zealand. For crew members, either sufficient funds for the purchase of an onward ticket or a letter from the owner or captain guaranteeing their departure on board the yacht will be sufficient. With a visitor's permit, one may not work, study or undertake medical treatment in New Zealand. Extensions to the visitor's permit are possible for a small fee, and the application must be made while the current permit is valid; extensions are normally for a three-month period up to a maximum of one year.

All other nationalities have to obtain visas before arrival at a port from a New Zealand embassy or high commission.

Fees

There are no overtime charges for clearance. Quarantine and customs are on call 24 hours a day, seven days a week.

There are fees for visas and extensions to the visitor's permit. There are also fees for quarantine inspections.

Facilities

As the favourite place to spend the cyclone season in the South Pacific, New Zealand has built up a good reputation among cruising sailors as the place where everything can be fixed. The fact that hundreds of foreign yachts flock to New Zealand every year attests to this. Marine facilities are indeed of a high standard in the North Island, particularly around such yachting centres as Auckland, Whangarei and the Bay of Islands. There are haul-out and good repair facilities in all these areas. With several marinas for the considerable local yacht population in the Auckland area and also the experience of dealing with the Whitbread fleet every four years, facilities there are of the highest standard. In the Bay of Islands, Kerikeri Radio has come to the aid of visiting sailors by compiling a grid chart showing all anchorages as well as marine facilities available. This useful publication can be obtained from local shops and chandleries. Marine supplies are generally good and in Auckland excellent. With a very developed yachting industry of her own, New Zealand marine products are of good quality, particularly deck hardware, windlasses, paints and sails, as well as fibreglass or aluminium tenders. LPG refills are widely available, but one may need to obtain an adaptor for the local system. One must also check if the gas is compatible with the regulator if one switches from propane to butane or vice versa.

There are workshops specialising in marine services in most places and the quality of workmanship is usually high. However, one should always insist on being given a written estimate of the cost of the proposed work, as visiting sailors have encountered problems in the past when faced with bills much higher than the verbal estimate they had been first given. Facilities in South Island are less extensive, although even there one finds adequate services wherever there is a local yachting centre. Facilities are good in Marlborough Sound where there are several small boatyards.

As can be expected from a mainly agricultural country, provisioning is very good and New Zealand is an excellent place to stock up the boat for a voyage. As many non-food items are subject to tax, temporary visitors to New Zealand can claim a refund on all the tax and duty paid on such items which are going to be taken out of the country.

Kermadec Islands

These islands may only be visited with a permit from the Department of Conservation, Private Bag 8, Newton, Auckland. The cost of a permit is NZ$26 plus tax. There is a meteorological station on Raoul Island, the most northerly group, and yachts sailing there will find they are made most welcome if they take mail for the staff. Contact Wellington ☎ (4) 729379, ext. 8803.

Further Reading

Coastal Cruising Handbook of New Zealand
New Zealand's Bay of Islands
Pickmere's Atlas of Northland's East Coast
A Cruising Guide to the Marlborough Sound
Kerikeri Radio's Grid Chart of the Bay of Islands
New Zealand – a travel survival kit
Landfalls of Paradise

NIUE

The island of Niue is one of the world's smallest states, but the largest block of coral. Niue boasts amazing caves both under the ground and the sea and the diving here is excellent. Lying on the direct route from French Polynesia to Vava'u in Tonga, Niue is a favourite stop for westbound yachts. The anchorage is off the island's west coast, close to the main settlement at Alofi. Although the anchorage offers good protection from the prevailing SE winds, in westerly winds the island is a deadly lee shore and one must always keep an eye on the weather, particularly when visiting ashore.

Country Profile

Archaeological remains show that the island was inhabited by the Polynesians at least 1800 years ago. Captain Cook charted the island in 1774, and named it the Savage Island when the islanders resisted his landing. There was little contact with the outside world until the nineteenth century when Samoan missionaries settled on the island. The London Missionary Society followed and they administered Niue until 1900 when it became a British Protectorate, later under New Zealand administration. The Niueans, not wanting total independence, chose a free association with New Zealand, which means they have New Zealand citizenship and internal self-government. Since the 1960s Niue has developed considerably in such areas as health and education. An airport was built, but tourism remains carefully controlled.

The island's economy is heavily dependent on foreign aid, and many goods have to be imported. There are some exports to New Zealand, such as passionfruit juice, lime juice, coconut products, handicrafts and honey. The sale of stamps and remittances from Niueans working overseas are important income earners.

Over 2500 people live on Niue, and many more have settled in New Zealand. Niuean, a Polynesian language, is spoken and also English. Alofi on the western coast is the main town. The islanders are mainly Protestant.

Niue has a tropical climate being in the SE trade wind belt. December to March are the wetter, more humid months, which is also the cyclone season. The island was badly mauled by Cyclone Ofa in February 1990 which caused widespread destruction.

Entry Regulations

Port of entry
Alofi 19°03′S 169°55′W.

Procedure on arrival
There is an anchorage off the settlement of Alofi, but it offers no protection from westerly winds. There is a private mooring near the main dock, which can be used if the owner is not there. The dinghy can be left at the concrete pier under a green and red range marker.

Practical Information

LOCAL TIME: GMT - 11

BUOYAGE: IALA A

CURRENCY: New Zealand dollar (NZ$)

BUSINESS HOURS
Bank: 0900–1400 Monday to Thursday, 0830–1400 Friday.
Shops and businesses: 0730–1500 Monday to Thursday, to 1600 Friday.

ELECTRICITY: 240 V, 50 Hz

PUBLIC HOLIDAYS
1 January: New Year's Day
2 January : Commission Holiday
Easter Monday
25 April: ANZAC Day
June: Queen's Birthday
19 October: Constitution Celebrations
26 October: Peniaminas Day
25, 26 December: Christmas

COMMUNICATIONS
Telecommunications office for overseas calls.
Post office 0800–1500 Monday to Friday.
Emergency: Fire 133, Police 29, Hospital 98-101.

The Administration building at Alofi contains the post office, the Treasury (open 0800–1200, 1230–1430 Monday to Friday for changing money), the Telecommunications office, and the police station.
There are flights to Auckland and Samoa.

MEDICAL
Lord Liverpool Hospital and three health clinics around the island provide a 24-hour service.

DIPLOMATIC MISSIONS
New Zealand: Tapeu, Alofi. ☎ 4022.

Formalities are usually completed ashore in Alofi. For a small place, formalities are rather complicated and the captain must clear with customs, immigration, agriculture and health.

Customs
Firearms must be declared on arrival. Animals must stay on board.

Immigration
Australian and New Zealand citizens do not need an entry permit and all other nationalities are granted a 30-day entry permit on arrival. Extensions can be obtained from the Police in Alofi.

Fees
There is a daily port fee.

Facilities

There is a reasonable selection of provisions and a weekly fresh produce market on Fridays. Water is available by jerrycan. Only basic repairs can be carried out on the island and there is only a limited supply of hardware. Essential spares can be ordered from New Zealand.

Further Reading

Landfalls of Paradise
Pacific Islands Yearbook

NORFOLK ISLAND

Norfolk Island is a small volcanic island midway between Australia and New Zealand. Its fertile soil is the original home of the Norfolk pine, an excellent wood used for spars on sailing ships. The island is visited mainly by Australian boats on their way to the South Pacific islands or by those sailing from New Zealand to New Caledonia and beyond. There are anchorages at Sydney Bay near the main settlement of Kingston, Ball Bay, Cascade Bay and Headstone. However, none can be regarded as all-weather anchorages, therefore the boat should never be left unattended and one should go ashore only in settled weather. Yachts have been lost at Norfolk Island through ignoring this warning. There are landing jetties at both Kingston and Cascade Bay, but landing the dinghy can sometimes be very difficult.

Country Profile

Norfolk is one of the oldest British settlements in the Pacific. There is no evidence of Polynesian or Melanesian habitation on the island before Captain Cook discovered and named it in 1774. A few years later an attempt was made to establish a colony, now known as the First Settlement. Timber was made from the pines and flax gathered, but life was difficult on the isolated island with no natural harbour. In the early nineteenth century Norfolk was left uninhabited for some years, then a penal colony was set up for the worst of the Australian convicts. This period of the Second Settlement was brutal and stone buildings built by the

Practical Information

LOCAL TIME: GMT + 11½

BUOYAGE: IALA A

CURRENCY: Australian dollar (Aus$)

BUSINESS HOURS
Government offices: 0845–1700 Monday
to Friday.

ELECTRICITY: 240 V, 50 Hz

PUBLIC HOLIDAYS
Australian:
1 January: New Year's Day
26 January: Australia Day
Good Friday, Easter Monday
25 April: ANZAC Day
June: Queen's Birthday
First Monday in October: Labour Day
12 October: Show Day
25, 26 December: Christmas
Plus:
8 June: Bounty Anniversary Day

Last Thursday in November:
Thanksgiving Day

COMMUNICATIONS
International direct dialling available for
telephone calls.
There are flights to Auckland, Brisbane,
Sydney and Lord Howe Island.

MEDICAL
Norfolk Island Hospital

---

prisoners can still be seen. Finally the prison was closed in the middle of the last century.

Next to arrive were Pitcairn Islanders, brought there by Britain who decided to resettle them as their tiny island home had become overcrowded. Homesick and unhappy, some returned to Pitcairn, although many remained, forming the base of the present population. Norfolk is administered by Australia; since 1985 the island has had considerable internal autonomy.

Tourists from Australia and New Zealand are a major source of income. Agriculture is only for domestic consumption and food imports are high.

The population was 2367 in 1986. Most are descendants of the original Pitcairn Islanders and settlers from Australia. The Norfolk Islanders are Australian citizens. English and a Norfolkese dialect are spoken. Church of England, Catholic, Methodist and Seventh Day Adventist are the main religious denominations. Kingston is the main town.

The climate is mild and subtropical, with a well distributed rainfall. Summer winds are S to SE and winter winds W to SW. The cyclone season is December to March.

Entry Regulations

Port of entry
Kingston 29°01′S 167°59′E.

Procedure on arrival
One can either land at Cascade Jetty, on the north side, or at Kingston Jetty, on the south side. One should notify customs and quarantine as soon as possible after one's arrival if no prior contact has been made. Customs monitor VHF Channel 16 during working hours only, 0845–1700.

Customs
Firearms must be declared on arrival and be kept on board during the yacht's stay. Animals must be declared on arrival and remain on board. Landing of fruit and vegetables is prohibited.

Immigration
Visa requirements are the same as for Australia. All nationals, with the exception of Australians and New Zealanders, need to obtain a tourist visa in advance. These can be obtained free of charge from Australian high commissions or embassies. A multiple entry visa should be requested if a yacht is en route for Australia.

Fees
Overtime is charged for clearance outside of working hours or on public holidays. Customs charge Aus$45 for under six crew and Aus$60 for six crew and over.

Restrictions
Anchorage is prohibited in Anson Bay on the NW corner of the island.

Facilities

Provisioning is reasonable, but as yachts come to Norfolk from either Australia or New Zealand, one should only plan on buying the absolute minimum on the island. There is a good selection of locally grown produce. There is no public water supply, although one may be able to load a limited amount. Repair facilities are basic and should not be relied upon. Small quantities of fuel are available, but as this is brought to the island by ship and then transferred ashore by lighter, visitors should try not to put an unnecessary strain on the island's meagre resources.

Further Reading

Pacific Islands Yearbook

PAPUA NEW GUINEA

Papua New Guinea consists of the eastern half of the large island of New Guinea (the western half being the Indonesian territory of Irian Jaya), and hundreds of islands of all shapes and sizes, from towering active volcanoes to idyllic coral atolls.

One of the most fascinating countries in the world, Papua New Guinea is definitely best visited by cruising boat. This not only gives one the opportunity to catch a glimpse of life in a society still following ancient ways, but also avoids the lawlessness that increasingly affects the large towns of this rich, but poorly managed, country. Most cruising sailors will only come in passing contact with the less attractive features of a country that has tried to leap into the modern age from stone age in half a century. Outside of the main centres life is little changed and by using common sense one should be able to avoid the few hot spots of trouble. One place to avoid is Bougainville Island, where at the time of writing the vast copper mine has been shut down and the island is under the control of local rebels, the Papua New Guinea security forces and police having withdrawn from the island. Following this revolt there are likely to be similar claims to tribal lands in other parts of the country especially where there has been exploitation of mineral resources. The best way to find out about changing conditions is to listen to the news, both Radio Australia and Radio New Zealand having good Overseas Services for the Pacific area or by contacting one's high commission or embassy in Port Moresby, who are usually well informed. Port Moresby and Lae are particularly affected by the surge in criminality. The area around the yacht club in Port Moresby is relatively trouble-free.

There is a vast difference between these urban areas and other parts of the country, particularly the small islands. Rabaul, on New Britain Island, is a popular spot among cruising yachts, many of whom spend the cyclone season in its landlocked harbour, which is the crater of a volcano. The attractive town has been obliterated once by a volcanic eruption and a regular check is kept on the volcanoes in the area, but Rabaul is still considered to be living on borrowed time.

Madang on the northern coast of New Guinea also has a well-protected harbour in an area scattered with islands, reefs and lagoons. It has always been a popular stop, especially for those yachts taking the route north of New Guinea towards Indonesia, but it is now reported to have increasing problems similar to those afflicting Lae and Port Moresby.

The best cruising in Papua New Guinea is found among the many islands to the east of the main island, where islanders still live a peaceful life and sail large traditional canoes for fishing and trading voyages. A cruise in Papua New Guinean waters has been for many people the highlight of their world cruise, and if one chooses one's itinerary carefully it is a country well worth visiting.

Country Profile

Until the 1930s much of the highlands of Papua New Guinea and the stone age tribes who lived there were unknown to the rest of the outside world. Through the centuries, hundreds of tribes had lived apart, often two neighbouring tribes separated by a hillside of impenetrable vegetation, never knowing of each other's existence. Each had its own character and its own language, there being today several hundred different languages in PNG. It is an anthropologists' paradise. In the coastal areas and islands, however, contact with Europeans was established much earlier.

The original inhabitants probably came from South East Asia about 20,000 to 25,000 years ago. Later there were migrations from Micronesia and Polynesia, which forced the original population into the mountains or out to populate the other islands of present day Melanesia. Cultures developed with no larger a political unit than the tribe.

In the early sixteenth century the Portuguese sighted the main island, naming it 'Ilhas dos Papuas' – island of the fuzzy haired – later called 'New Guinea' by the Dutch. Traders and missionaries arrived in the nineteenth century. The Dutch claimed the western half of the main island, the Germans the north-east, and the British the south-east. At the start of the twentieth century the latter area was transferred to Australian control as Papua and joined with the German part after the First World War.

The Japanese occupied Papua New Guinea in the Second World War. After the war it became the UN Territory of Papua New Guinea and was administered by Australia. Self-government was gained in 1973 and full independence two years later.

The economy is based on mining plus timber and some food crops, particularly coffee. The country has rich deposits of minerals, gold, copper and oil. Most of the country's problems stem from the potential of this richness in an economy where the majority of the population are still subsistence farmers and much of the income has been earned by large foreign companies. There is high unemployment and a large drift to the towns by young men in search of jobs which do not exist.

Practical Information

LOCAL TIME: GMT + 10

BUOYAGE: IALA A

CURRENCY: Kina (K/NGK) of 100 toea

BUSINESS HOURS
Banks: 0900–1400 Monday to Thursday, 0900–1700 Friday.
Business: 0800–1630 Monday to Friday.
Government offices: 0745–1200/ 1300–1600 Monday to Friday.
Shops: 0800–1700 Monday to Friday, half day Saturday.

ELECTRICITY: 240 V, 50 Hz

PUBLIC HOLIDAYS
1 January: New Year's Day
January/February: Chinese New Year
Easter

June: Queen's Birthday
July: Remembrance Day
16 September: Independence Day
25, 26 December: Christmas

EVENTS
May: Frangipani Festival, Rabaul
July/August: Yam festival in Trobriand Islands
June: Port Moresby Show
August: Highlands Show, Mount Hagen
September: Eastern Highlands Show, Goroka
} alternate years

COMMUNICATIONS
Telephone, telex and fax facilities are available at telephone offices, post offices and hotels.

Papua New Guinea has a very developed internal air network. From Port Moresby there are international flights to other Pacific Islands, Australia, Singapore and Manila.

MEDICAL
Government hospitals in all major centres. Several private hospitals in the Port Moresby area.

DIPLOMATIC MISSIONS
Australia: Independence Drive, Waigani. ☎ 25 9333.
France: PO Box 1155. ☎ 25 1323.
Indonesia: Sir John Guisa Drive, Waigani. ☎ 25 3455.
New Zealand: Waigani (PO Box 1144 Boroko). ☎ 25 9444.
United Kingdom: Kiroki St, Waigani. ☎ 25 1677.
United States: Armit St. ☎ 21 1455.

The population is almost 3.5 million, mostly Melanesian, with some of the more eastern islands populated by Polynesians. The national languages are Motu and Pidgin (Tok Pisin), evolved to let a country of over 700 native languages understand each other. English is also widely spoken.

The main Christian denominations are Protestant and Catholic, but there are very many others, as well as local spirit and animist religions. The discovery of so many stone age tribes brought many enthusiastic missionaries and sects to the highlands, where in some towns there are more churches than any other buildings.

Port Moresby on the southern coast of Papua is the capital, with the seat of government in Boroko, which is spread out over a large area and modelled on Canberra.

The climate is tropical. From December to March is the north-west monsoon, while the south-east monsoon is from May to December. Only the south-east of the country is affected by tropical cyclones, whose season is from December until March.

Entry Regulations

Ports of entry
Port Moresby 9°26′S 147°06′E, Vanimo 2°41′S 141°18′E, Wewak 3°35′S 143°40′E, Samarai 10°36′S 150°39′E, Oro Bay 8°50′S 148°30′E, Rabaul 4°12′S 152°11′E, Lae 6°44′S 146°59′E, Kavieng 2°34′S 150°48′E, Daru 9°04′S 143°12′E, Alotau 10°19′S 150°27′E, Kieta 6°13′S 155°38′E, Madang 5°15′S 145°50′E, Kimbe 5°32′S 150°09′E, Lorengau 2°00′S 147°15′E, Misima Island 10°40′S 152°45′E.

Procedure on arrival
The captain should proceed ashore with all papers and go to the customs and immigration offices.

In Port Moresby the customs office is in the commercial harbour south of the yacht club.

One must clear in and out of every port and failure to do so can create serious problems.

On Misima Island if requested customs may issue a clearance for Australia with permission to cruise for a reasonable period of time in the Calvados Islands en route.

Customs
Firearms, including flareguns, are either detained until departure, or sealed on board.

Animals must remain on board at all times.

Prescribed medicines containing narcotics must be declared. One must have a prescription stating that these are necessary and being used under a doctor's direction. The medicines should be kept in the original containers.

Yachts staying longer than two months are required

to lodge a security on their yacht, equal to the duty on the yacht's value.

Prohibited exports are: bird of paradise plumes, artefacts dated pre-1960 and stone objects, except stone axes.

Immigration

Tourist visas for up to 30 days can be issued on arrival for nationals of Australia, Austria, Belgium, Canada, Cook Islands, Cyprus, Denmark, Fiji, France, Germany, Japan, the Netherlands, New Zealand, Norway, Portugal, Sweden, Switzerland, Thailand, Tonga, Tuvalu, the United Kingdom and the United States. For longer visits, visas must be obtained in advance. It is recommended that visas are obtained before arriving in the country even for those nationals listed above. These can be obtained from one of the PNG embassies or high commissions. There are PNG diplomatic missions in Canberra, Brisbane, Suva, Jakarta, Kuala Lumpur, Wellington and Manila. Usually visas are valid for 60 days, after which the passports have to be sent to Port Moresby for an extension. Occasionally passports have been reported lost, but they have invariably turned up later. Even if an extension has not been granted, people have been allowed to stay while the search for the missing passports is in progress. Proof of sufficient funds to support one's stay in PNG is necessary, otherwise one has to place an immigration landing bond of about US$1000, which is refundable. Passports must have a minimum one year validity from proposed date of entry.

South African nationals, including those with dual citizenship, are not permitted entry.

Health

This is a high-risk malaria area, where the disease has become resistant to many of the anti-malarial drugs in use. Advice should be taken as to the most suitable anti-malarial prevention to be followed. There is also a dengue fever risk.

Fees

Overtime is payable for clearance after 1600 Monday to Friday, and all day Saturday, Sunday and public holidays.

Facilities

There is a large number of locally owned yachts in the capital Port Moresby, where facilities are generally good. The Royal Papua Yacht Club has its own small marina with 24-hour security, but most spaces are occupied by members' boats so there is only a slim chance of mooring there. However, visitors can anchor close by and use the club facilities. Temporary membership is granted to members of other yacht clubs. Most repair facilities are concentrated around the yacht club, which is immediately north of the container terminal. There is a chandlery with a good selection in the yacht club building and the director is a radio expert. What is not available can be ordered from Australia and usually obtained within 72 hours. Lohberger is a very good engineering shop nearby, which can deal with diesel and outboard engines as well as electrical repair and rigging. They also have a good supply of spares and are the agents for various electronic products. With the assistance of the yacht club, a crane can be hired to lift smaller yachts, while larger ones can use the Steamship slipway in Port Moresby harbour. Provisioning is good with several supermarkets and fresh produce markets.

In Rabaul the local yacht club is very welcoming and helpful and will advise on where to find various repair facilities. These are satisfactory and, as in Port Moresby, what cannot be obtained locally can be ordered from Australia, although it may take a week or longer. Provisioning is good and Rabaul has one of the best fresh produce markets in the Pacific. There are fuel docks at Rabaul and Hadang.

Facilities in the commercial centres of Madang and Lae are adequate, while those in the smaller towns and outer islands are often basic. There are small boatyards with their own slipways dotted about the country, so one is never too far away should the need arise for some emergency repair. However, all essential spares should be carried on board and one should also provision the boat in one of the major centres before sailing to the islands, where little except a few locally grown vegetables is available.

Further Reading

Pacific Islands Yearbook
Cruising to Papua New Guinea
Papua New Guinea – a travel survival kit
Landfalls of Paradise

PITCAIRN ISLAND

Pitcairn Island is a small isolated volcanic island in the South Pacific, its closest neighbours the Gambier Islands to the west and Easter Island to the east. Only three square miles of land, with steep cliffs all around, the sole anchorage is at Bounty Bay which is tenable only in settled weather. Pitcairn is a dependency of Britain, together with the uninhabited Henderson, Ducie and Oeno islands. It is governed by the British High Commissioner in Wellington, New Zealand, but day-to-day affairs are run by an island council. Supply ships are supposed to call three or four times a year but there is no regular service. Other ships used to call regularly to buy fresh produce and handicrafts from the islanders, but this has declined with the cessation of passenger liners and the increase of container ships on tight schedules. For this reason a warm welcome awaits the cruising sailor who calls at this remote community, whose entire history has been intrinsically bound up with the sea. Although the anchorage in Bounty Bay is an open roadstead, by keeping an eye on the weather, one is usually able to spend some time on the island. Everyone leaves Pitcairn with unforgettable memories of having been hosted by one of the most isolated communities in the world.

Aventura *leaving Pitcairn Island.*

Country Profile

Pitcairn was named after the midshipman who spotted it in 1767 on board HMS *Swallow*. Some human remains have been discovered on the island, but who these original inhabitants were remains a mystery. When the island's most famous settlers, the *Bounty* mutineers, came to the island they found no one. After a long search for a hideaway, Fletcher Christian and his fellow mutineers arrived here in 1790 with their Tahitian wives and six Tahitian men on board the *Bounty*. The *Bounty* was burnt and scuttled by the new settlers in the bay which bears its name in order to avoid detection. Problems arose in the small community that dared not risk contact with the outside world and there was much violence. When the community was discovered in 1808 only one mutineer had survived with 10 women and many children. In the nineteenth century efforts to resettle the Pitcairn islanders on Tahiti and Norfolk Island were not successful, although some remained on the latter.

Practical Information

LOCAL TIME: GMT - 9

BUOYAGE: IALA A

CURRENCY: New Zealand dollar (NZ$).
Personal cheques and travellers'
cheques can be cashed at the Island
Secretary's office.

ELECTRICITY: This is provided by a
diesel generator for a few hours daily.

PUBLIC HOLIDAYS
January 1: New Year's Day
Good Friday, Easter Monday
25, 26 December: Christmas

COMMUNICATIONS
SSB and amateur radio only. There is a
daily radio link with Fiji.
There is a simple telephone system

connecting all houses on the island, but
this is not linked to the outside world.
There is no airport.

MEDICAL
There is no doctor permanently on the
island, but one is employed from time to
time for a few months. The rest of the
time there is a registered nurse at the
small dispensary.

Income is raised from the sale of stamps and handicrafts are sold to the infrequent ships that visit. Britain gives some aid. The land is fertile, and the islanders farm, fish and raise livestock for their own consumption. The only paid jobs are government-funded, such as for the upkeep of the generator, roads and longboats.

Just under 60 people live on the island, the population having dwindled as many have left for New Zealand. All the population are descendants of the *Bounty* mutineers and their wives, infused with some other blood from sailors and missionaries who settled on the island in the nineteenth century. None of the other islands in the dependency are inhabited, although the Pitcairners sometimes visit Oeno for a holiday and to collect shells, coral and pandanus. Henderson is a bird sanctuary, where the islanders sometimes call to collect wood for their carvings. The islanders have their own dialect, a blend of Tahitian and eighteenth century sailors' English, although standard English is spoken by all. Adamstown is the only settlement.

The public square houses the courthouse, post office, Adventist church, and the *Bounty*'s anchor. The islanders are all Seventh Day Adventists and Saturday is the day of rest. They are teetotal, eat no pork, and do not smoke.

The climate is subtropical in the SE trade wind belt, with the most pleasant weather from November to March, when the winds are also lighter and the seas smoother. Pitcairn is very rarely affected by tropical storms.

Entry Regulations

Port of entry
Bounty Bay 25°04′S 130°06′W.

Procedure on arrival
The islanders prefer to be informed by radio of a yacht's arrival. Yachts should anchor or heave-to off Bounty Bay. The dinghy can be landed at the slip, where the islanders launch their longboats to meet ships, but usually the islanders send out their inflatable rescue craft to advise where to anchor and also to take the crew ashore. Landing in one's own dinghy, especially if there is a big swell, is often impossible.

Once ashore, one should pay a call to the Island Magistrate to obtain permission to land and to have one's passport stamped and signed with the impressive Pitcairn stamp. Yachts may stay as long as this permission is in force.

Customs
Firearms and animals must not be taken ashore.

Health
A declaration may be requested stating that none of the crew have been in contact with anyone suffering from a contagious disease within three weeks prior to arrival. Only visitors in good health will be permitted ashore.

Fees
If local boats are used for commuting between the yacht and shore a fee may be charged.

Before leaving some service might be rendered or a useful supply of items not available on the island could be left as a token of appreciation.

Restricted areas
Henderson, Ducie and Oeno: Landing on these islands is forbidden without the prior consent of the Governor, British High Commission, Wellington, New Zealand, or the permission of the Island Magistrate, in which case the landing party must be accompanied by a resident of Pitcairn.

Facilities

The cooperative store is open three times a week, but only basic foodstuffs are available depending on supplies. Fresh produce is always available and also water. If any emergency repair needs to be made, the islanders will undoubtedly help, as they have to do all the maintenance on their own boats, generator and engines, both inboard and outboard, and are practised at coping without outside help.

Further Reading

Pacific Islands Yearbook
Pacific Odyssey
Landfalls of Paradise

SOLOMON ISLANDS

The Solomon Islands are a string of islands in the Western Pacific stretching from Vanuatu to Bougainville. Some of the fiercest battles of the Second World War occurred here particularly on Guadalcanal. There are over 900 islands, the main ones being Guadalcanal, Choiseul, Malaita, New Georgia and Santa Isabel. The Solomons' culture, or 'custom', is rich and varied, from wood-carving to beliefs such as shark-worshipping. Many islanders still live in the traditional way.

The authorities are making a determined effort to preserve this way of life and they enjoy the full support of the customary chiefs in their endeavours. This has put some restrictions on the movement of cruising yachts and permission to visit some of the more remote islands may take some time. Fortunately there is still a lot to see along the usual cruising route, for which special permission is not needed. Visiting yachts are welcomed in most villages, particularly by children who like to trade fruit or shells for ball-point pens, felt-tips or balloons.

One of the most interesting islands to visit is Malaita, particularly the Langa Langa lagoon, to savour village life virtually unaffected by the outside world. Another lagoon often visited by yachts for the excellent wood carvings of the villagers is Morovo lagoon in the New Georgia group.

Apart from traditional village life, when cruising through the Solomons one constantly comes across remains of the Second World War and to this day a lot of discarded military hardware is still put to good use, such as fuel tanks to catch rainwater or aircraft wings for pig enclosures. Some also find it interesting to sail through the same waters where the young Lt John F. Kennedy made his daring escape during the Second World War after his patrol boat was sunk in the Blackett Strait. Plum Pudding or Kasolo Island where he was rescued from has been aptly renamed Kennedy Island.

Country Profile

The first inhabitants probably came to these islands about four to five thousand years ago. The first European visitor was Alvaro de Mendana in 1568, who named the islands the Solomons, hoping it would hint back home of the famed King Solomon's treasure. Only at the end of the nineteenth century did Europeans such as traders and missionaries come on a more permanent basis. Many of the islanders were recruited to work on Fijian and Australian plantations and were often treated as slaves. Because of this, many Europeans were killed in retaliation and Britain made the Solomons a Protectorate in 1893 to maintain some law and order.

The Solomons' strategic position in the Pacific meant that the islands were crucial in the Pacific War. Much of the fighting was on Guadalcanal, until the Japanese were pushed out in 1943 and the island became a US base. When the war was over, many islands were left with new airstrips and roads built by both sides and the islanders were left with a new sense of national unity. The Solomon Islands became an independent nation in 1978.

The economy is basically agricultural with very little industry. Tourism is not very developed. The islands receive considerable foreign aid.

Of the 220,000 inhabitants most are Melanesian, with a few Polynesians on the south-eastern islands, plus some I-Kiribati, Chinese, and Europeans. At least 87 local dialects and languages exist and Solomon Island pidgin is used as a lingua franca. English is used in schools and businesses and is widely spoken by the younger generation especially. There are many Christian denominations. Tulagi on Florida Island was the original capital until it was flattened in the Second World War, after which Honiara, the US base on Guadalcanal, became the new capital.

The Solomons experience high temperatures and January to March are the months of heaviest rainfall. April to November is the season of the SE trades, while the rest of the year is the NW monsoon, which is also the cyclone season. Long periods of calm weather are not uncommon among the islands.

Practical Information

LOCAL TIME: GMT + 11

BUOYAGE: IALA A

CURRENCY: Solomon Island dollar
(SBD)

BUSINESS HOURS
Banks: 0900–1500 Monday to Friday.
Business and government
offices: 0800–1200/1300–1630 Monday to
Friday.
Shops: 0800–1200/1330–1700 weekdays
and half day Saturday.

ELECTRICITY: 240 V, 50 Hz

PUBLIC HOLIDAYS
1 January: New Year's Day
Good Friday, Saturday, Easter Monday

Whit Monday
June: Queen's Birthday
7 July: Independence Day
25 December: Christmas Day
26 December: National Day of
Thanksgiving
The provinces have their own holidays:
7 December: Western Solomons
8 July: Isabel
29 June: Central Solomons
31 July: Guadalcanal
14 August: Malaita
3 August: Makira
8 June: Temotu

COMMUNICATIONS
SOLTEL: international telephone calls,
fax, telex, telegrams, 0745–2200 Monday
to Friday, until noon on Saturday.

Post office, Main Street, Honiara
(phones, telegrams, telex, fax)
0700–1000 Monday to Friday, 0800–1200
Saturday.
Emergency: dial 11.
There are flights from Honiara to Papua
New Guinea, Fiji and Vanuatu with
onward international connections.

MEDICAL
Honiara General Hospital.

DIPLOMATIC MISSIONS
In Honiara:
Australia: Hong Kong & Shanghai Bank
Building, Mendana Avenue, ☎ 21561.
United Kingdom: Soltel House, Mendana
Avenue ☎ 21705.

Entry Regulations

Ports of entry
Honiara (Guadalcanal) 9°25'S 159°58'E, Gizo 8°05'S 156°52'E, Noro (New Georgia) 8°13'S 157°12'E, Yandina (Russell) 9°04'N 159°13'E, Lofung (Shortland) 7°04'S 155°52'E, Graciosa Bay (Ndende Island, Santa Cruz) 10°44'S 165°49'E.

Procedure on arrival
One should report one's arrival to the authorities and request clearance.
Honiara: Honiara Radio can be contacted on VHF Channel 16 or on 2182 and 6213 MHz to advise authorities of a vessel's arrival. This is not compulsory but is recommended. One should anchor and go ashore to contact the relevant officials. Customs is at the end of the commercial wharf area. Customs will call the other officials, who may come to the yacht club to be taken out to the boat, or if not one has to go to immigration oneself.
Graciosa Bay: Yachts sailing up from Vanuatu or points east can clear into the Solomons at Ndende Island. Usually the resident customs officer will give a two-week cruising permit so the yacht can sail to Honiara and complete formalities there. Some dues have to be paid on the spot, so one should try and arrive with at least 150 Solomon Island dollars.

Customs
Firearms must be declared, otherwise they may be forfeited.

Animals are not to be landed. If for any reason they are landed, they will be subject to quarantine.
Exports of genuine artefacts, not replicas, require permission.
A yacht may stay in the country up to four months.

Immigration
The time given on a visa was recently extended from two to three months in a 12 month period. Extensions of the visa for one month can be obtained for a fee.

Cruising permit
Each province requires notification of yachts that wish to cruise in their areas. All the land, including uninhabited areas, is someone's property, and in order to visit any uninhabited bays or islands, one must first obtain permission from the relevant chief. It can take time to find out which chief is responsible for which place. Fishing and collecting shells are not normally allowed unless one has been given permission, nor are coconuts and produce to be taken.
The authorities in Honiara will advise where a yacht can or cannot go. There are usually no problems in calling at the main centres or at islands used to cruising yachts.

Health
Malaria is endemic in the Solomons and malarial prophylaxis is essential.

Fees
Attendance and overtime fees are as follows: SBD18

on weekdays, SBD22 on Saturdays, SBD24 per hour on Sundays.

One should attempt to arrive during normal working hours. In most places one can wait at anchor until the offices open, but no one should go ashore before clearance is completed.

There is a clearance fee of SBD60 per visit, and light dues of SBD100 plus 5c per ton. There are also port and immigration charges.

It helps to have obtained Solomons' currency before arrival in order to pay these fees.

Social customs

The wearing of shorts or other scanty clothing by women is not allowed.

Morovo Lagoon: Most islanders are Seventh Day Adventists so their Sabbath is from sunset on Friday to sunset on Saturday, and visitors are not supposed to go ashore here during the Sabbath.

Facilities

In Honiara there are two supermarkets with a good selection and also a fresh produce market, which is best on Saturday morning. Government charts can be bought from the Hydrographic Office, near the immigration office. These are detailed, but apparently not completely reliable, so care must be taken. Diesel can be jerrycanned from the service station on the main street near the Point Cruz Yacht Club. One should ask for distillate, not diesel. Larger quantities can be ordered by tanker. Propane bottles can only be refilled in Honiara.

Repair facilities in Honiara are adequate and there are a few workshops capable of tackling simple engine or electrical repair. For larger jobs there is a good shipyard, Taroaniara Shipyard, which is an Anglican Training centre, at Taroaniara on Florida Island, which is close to Honiara across Iron Bottom Sound. The yard specialises in boat building, metal and electrical work, and also has a slipway.

Repair facilities in the other islands are limited. Diesel in larger quantities can only be obtained in Honiara and Gizo. Water should be treated everywhere including Honiara and Gizo. It is preferable and safer to try and catch rainwater. In many isolated villages, where money has little value, the age old barter system is still in use and one can trade with the locals to obtain fresh produce, fish, carvings and shells. One should take along a supply of useful objects such as fishhooks, fishing line, matches, sugar, rice, tobacco, clothing and shoes, coffee, soap, needles, cotton and rope.

Further Reading

Cruising the Solomons
Pacific Islands Yearbook
Landfalls of Paradise

TOKELAU

Tokelau lies just north of Samoa in the central South Pacific and consists of three small low coral atolls: Atafu, Nukunono, and Fakaofo. As a dependency of New Zealand, the islanders are New Zealand citizens.

One of the least visited countries in the South Pacific, only a few yachts make their way to this isolated group of atolls, which lack natural harbours and for most of the year are completely cut off from the outside world. Some formalities have to be complied with before sailing for the islands, but any difficulties are justified, as they give an opportunity to visit one of the most isolated communities in the Pacific.

Country Profile

Legend says that the Maui brothers pulled the three islands out of the sea while fishing. The original population probably came from Samoa, Rarotonga and Tuvalu. Tokelau was one of the last island groups found by the Europeans, not being discovered until the nineteenth century. The islands were rarely visited until the 1840s, when missionaries, beachcombers and slavers came, the latter taking many Tokelauans to Peru. In 1889 Britain claimed jurisdiction over the islands. For some time Tokelau was administered with the Gilbert and Ellice Islands, but in 1925 administration was transferred to New Zealand, an arrangement which continues today.

Copra is the only cash crop and the islanders lead a subsistence lifestyle. Some income comes from stamps, coins, handicrafts and remittances from workers overseas, mainly in New Zealand and Samoa. Licence fees are charged for foreign ships fishing in the 200 mile exclusive economic zone. New Zealand gives some aid, largely for public works, government services and salaries. The islands can only support a certain number of inhabitants.

About 1600 people live in Tokelau, while there are around 3000 Tokelauans in New Zealand. The islanders are Polynesian, close to Tuvaluans. Tokelauan, akin to Samoan, and also English are spoken. The islanders are Congregationalist or Roman Catholic. There is no administrative centre, each island having a

Practical Information

LOCAL TIME: GMT - 11

BUOYAGE: IALA A

CURRENCY: New Zealand dollar (NZ$) and Western Samoan tala. One can change money at the main administration centres.

BUSINESS HOURS
Official working hours: 0800–1630 Monday to Friday.

ELECTRICITY: There are generators on each atoll.

PUBLIC HOLIDAYS
New Zealand holidays:
1 January: New Year's Day
6 February: Waitangi Day
Good Friday, Easter Monday
25 April: ANZAC Day
June: Queen's Birthday
Fourth Monday in October: Labour Day
25, 26 December: Christmas

COMMUNICATIONS
There are radio stations on each of the atolls.
There are no airports on the islands.

MEDICAL
There are dispensaries on all three islands.

separate local government. The central administration's office is in Apia, Western Samoa.

From May to September the islands are under the influence of the SE trade winds. The weather is cooler than in the rest of the year when it is hot, particularly from December to March, which is the cyclone season. Tokelau is on the edge of the cyclone belt, but is only rarely affected by tropical storms.

Entry Regulations

Ports of entry
Fakaofo 9°23′S 171°15′W, Nukunonu 8°34′S 171°49′W, Atafu 8°34′S 172°30′W.

Procedure on arrival
Yachts have to be cleared in by the police, health and the Administration Officer.

Customs
Any firearms which are landed on any Tokelau island must be handed to the police to be kept until departure. Animals must remain on board.

Immigration
Visas are required by all nationalities before arrival.
A cruising permit is required in advance. This must be authorised by the Council of Elders (taupulega) of each island that the yacht wishes to visit. In view of the difficulty of communicating with Tokelau, the Official Secretary at the Office for Tokelau Affairs in Apia, Western Samoa, can contact the Council of Elders concerned, on behalf of those seeking permits. He will radio the islands for permission. Every visitor must pass a simple physical examination to ascertain that he or she has no obvious illness.

There is no limit on how long a yacht may spend in Tokelau; however, the Council has the right to ask a yacht to leave if the island's culture, customs, rules or regulations are violated.
Office of Tokelau Affairs: PO Box 865, Apia, Western Samoa. ☎ 20-822. Telex: 281 SX. Telegram: TOKALANI APIA.

Fees
No fees are charged. However, a donation should be made to the village, as appreciation of the assistance given by the villagers.

Social customs
Visitors should be very conscious of the island's customs, such as paying due respect to all older persons.

Facilities

There are no harbour facilities whatsoever, only passes for small boats through the reefs, but these are too shallow for most yachts. Normally a yacht must anchor on a shelf outside the reef, in the lee of the atoll. Fairly often conditions are not suitable for yachts to anchor.

There is one cooperative store on each island selling some staple foodstuffs, mostly imported. It is possible to buy some locally grown produce. Water is scarce everywhere.

Further Reading

Landfalls of Paradise

TONGA

This Polynesian kingdom, situated in the heart of the South Pacific, consists of over 160 coral and volcanic islands, of which only 36 are inhabited. Best known among sailors is the northern group of Vava'u, whose maze of islets and reefs provides one of the best cruising grounds in the South Pacific.

The capital Nuku'alofa on the main island of Tongatapu is slightly more advanced than the outer islands, but even there the pace of life is unhurried and peaceful. A spacious new harbour allows visiting sailors to leave their yachts in safety while visiting this interesting island to see the mysterious trilithon at Ha'amanga, the blowholes at Houma, the flocks of flying foxes at Kolovai, the tombs of the Tu'i Tonga in the ancient capital of Mu'a or the more recently built Victorian residence of the present King.

Country Profile

Tonga was probably inhabited over 2000 years ago by migrants from Samoa. The Tu'i Tonga chiefs reigned over Tonga, and by the thirteenth century had created a Pacific empire stretching from Fiji to Niue. The first contact with Europeans was in 1616, with the Dutchmen Schouten and Lemaire. Tasman, Wallis and Cook were subsequent visitors, the latter naming them the Friendly Islands.

In the 1820s missionaries arrived and their influence helped to end the fierce tribal wars which had been raging for thirty years. In 1845 King George Tupou I founded the present royal dynasty, which can trace its origins back to the Tu'i Tonga. To avoid German colonisation Tonga put itself under British protection at the end of the nineteenth century. In 1958 full sovereignty was restored. The present king is Taufa'a-hau Tupou IV.

The economy is agricultural, based on the export of copra, bananas and coconut products. Tongan women are skilled in mat weaving, basket work and the making of tapa cloth, and there is a small handicrafts industry. There is some effort being made to start small industries relying on skilled handwork. Young Tongans are very tempted to leave for New Zealand, although strict immigration laws have made this much more difficult.

Tourism is being developed as a source of foreign revenue, but considerable aid is given to the kingdom by New Zealand, Australia and West Germany.

The Polynesian inhabitants number around 100,000. Most people speak English as well as Tongan. Christianity plays a leading role in the community. Until recently even swimming and dancing were banned on Sundays, which remains a day where all of Tonga is supposed to shut down, including the airport. The official church is Wesleyan, but there are lots of other denominations, particularly the Church of Latter Day Saints (Mormons). Modesty in dress is essential in Tonga – in fact it is against the law to appear in public not wearing a shirt.

Nuku'alofa is the capital on the main island of Tongatapu. It is a flat coral island and heavily populated.

Tonga's climate is warm and humid, although less so than other tropical islands. December to March, which is also the hurricane season, has more rain. From April to November the SE trade winds predominate, although quick sudden squalls can occur from other directions.

Entry Regulations

Ports of entry
Nuku'alofa (Tongatapu) 21°08'S 175°12'W, Lifuka (Ha'apai) 19°48'S 174°21'W, Neiafu (Vava'u) 18°39'S 173°59'W, Niuatoputapu Island 15°58'S 173°45'W.

Procedure on arrival
The Q flag must be flown. The captain should contact the harbour master or customs, who may or may not board the yacht. One must present the outward clearance from the last port.

Nuku'alofa: Proceed into the Faua harbour basin, which has a narrow entrance west of the main cargo wharf. There is a minimum depth of 2.5 m (8.2 ft) in the centre of the access channel. Yachts drawing more than this can anchor in the yacht anchorage to the east of the main wharf. Certain areas in the approaches to Nuku'alofa are prohibited for anchoring and these are marked on the chart. The customs offices are in a building near the cargo wharf, north of the harbour basin. Immigration is in town.

Vava'u: On entering the harbour, one should go alongside the main wharf on the port side. Customs and immigration offices are situated by this wharf.

Lifuka: Anchor in front of Pangai village. The customs office is by the small dock.

Niuatoputapu: This small island lying some 175 miles north of the main Tongan island group is a convenient port of entry into the Kingdom of Tonga for yachts arriving from the north. A small pass on the NW side of the island with a minimum depth of 3.66 m (12 ft) leads into the anchorage off the main village where entry formalities can be completed.

Practical Information

LOCAL TIME: GMT + 13. Tonga is situated east of 180° but the International Dateline makes a detour to include Tonga west of the line. Take account of this in navigational calculations.

BUOYAGE: IALA A

CURRENCY: The Tongan dollar (T$) called Pa'anga has 100 seniti.

BUSINESS HOURS
Bank of Tonga (branches in Tongatapu, Vava'u and Ha'apai): 0930–1530 Monday to Friday and 0930–1200 Saturday. Business and government offices: 0830–1630 Monday to Friday.

ELECTRICITY: 240 V, 50 Hz

PUBLIC HOLIDAYS
1 January: New Year's Day
Good Friday, Easter Monday
April: ANZAC Day
4 May: HRH Crown Prince Tupouto'a's birthday
4 July: King Taufa'ahau Tupou IV's birthday
4 November: Constitution Day
5 December: King George Tupou I Day
25, 26 December: Christmas

EVENTS
Vava'u Festival, first week in May
Heilala Festival, June 29 to July 6

COMMUNICATIONS
Cable & Wireless, open 24 hours, international phone calls, can send and receive faxes on 22 970, telex on 66222. Post offices at Nuku'alofa, Ha'apai, Vava'u: 0830–1630 Monday to Friday. Emergency: dial 933.
The main gateway to international destinations is via Auckland although there are also flights to Fiji.

DIPLOMATIC MISSIONS
In Nuku'alofa:
Australia: Salote Rd. ☎ 23244.
New Zealand: Corner Taufa'ahau and Salote Rds. ☎ 23122.
United Kingdom: Vuna Rd. ☎ 21020.

Customs

Firearms must be declared on arrival and will be sealed on board. If this is not possible they will be held in custody ashore until departure.

Dogs and parrots are destroyed. Other pets will be quarantined. Animals, birds and plants need a quarantine certificate. Fresh produce may be confiscated. Garbage must be disposed of officially on arrival.

Yachts may stay in the country for four months. Tonga is duty-free for yachts in transit.

Immigration

For most nationals including Commonwealth countries, West European countries, the USA and Canada, a visa-free entry permit is issued for up to 30 days provided one has an assured onward passage and proof of sufficient funds. Extensions may be obtained from the principal immigration officer (six months maximum). Some nationals, such as those from East European countries, need to notify the authorities before arrival and request permission for a visa.

Fees

Overtime is payable outside of working hours: on weekdays, overtime clearance is T$40; on Sundays and public holidays: T$50. This is only if clearance is requested. One does not have to clear straight away and can wait on board until working hours.
Light dues: T$0.20 per GRT/month or part month.
Tonnage dues: T$4 per 15 GRT/month or part month.
Harbour fees: T$0.30 per GRT/month or part.
On payment of these, a yacht will receive inward clearance for the rest of the islands, which must be shown when visiting elsewhere.

Facilities

In spite of Tonga's remoteness, facilities are surprisingly good and the setting up of a small industrial centre near the capital Nuku'alofa has encouraged several boating-related foreign companies to start operations in Tonga. There is now a boat builder in fibreglass, sail loft and metalwork machine shop, all of which will undertake repair work on visiting yachts. In the harbour is a small shipyard with a 100-ton slipway, which also undertakes metal and electrical work and there is a diesel engineer nearby. There are no chandlery or marine supplies as such, although essential spares can be ordered from New Zealand from which there are several flights a week.

Fuel can be delivered by Shell tanker to the dockside but smaller quantities must be bought in jerrycans. Large amounts of water are delivered by tanker, although there is a water point in Faua harbour. Gas bottles can be filled at the Tonga Commodities Board. There are several supermarkets with a reasonable selection in Nuku'alofa and a good daily fresh produce market. Freshly caught fish is sold on the waterfront.

The existence of a Moorings charter operation in Vava'u means that facilities are also improving there. The Moorings maintain a small workshop, while the adjacent Coleman Marine Services also has a slipway, repair facilities as well as fuel and water on its dock. Paradise Hotel also has docking space for visitors, water, showers and a mail service. There are two good supermarkets in Neiafu and a fresh produce market every day except Sundays. As in Nuku'alofa, gas bottles can be refilled at the Commodities Board.

Further Reading

Landfalls of Paradise
South Pacific Handbook
Cruising Guide to the Kingdom of Tonga in Vava'u

TUVALU

Formerly the Ellice Islands, the name Tuvalu means 'cluster of eight' although the group in fact consists of nine low-lying coral atolls. Only eight of them were inhabited when the name was chosen, but a small community now lives on previously uninhabited Niurakita, the southernmost island of the archipelago. The islands lie just below the equator and west of the Dateline, their nearest neighbours being Kiribati, 200 miles to the north, and Fiji, 600 miles south. With a total land area of only 11 square miles (26 square kilometres), Tuvalu is one of the smallest countries in the world, spread out in half a million square miles of ocean.

The small island communities still lead a very traditional lifestyle. With the exception of the main island of Funafuti, yachts rarely visit the islands. Although some only have precarious anchorages in the lee of a fringing reef, the lagoon is accessible in at least two islands, at Nukufetau and Nanumea, and there are plans to open passes into some of the other lagoons. Particularly if sailing towards neighbouring Kiribati, one should try and obtain permission from the authorities in Funafuti to stop at some of the outer islands.

Country Profile

The first inhabitants probably arrived about 2000 years ago, mostly from Samoa, but also Tonga and Uvea (Wallis). The northern islands, especially Nui, were populated from Micronesia. A society under the leadership of chiefs developed and customs and traditions akin to Samoa remain today. The first European sighting of the islands was in 1765 and there was little other contact until the nineteenth century when traders, missionaries, and whalers came to the islands. The islands were named after the nineteenth-century politician Edward Ellice, owner of the ship *Rebecca*, which came to Funafuti in 1819. The blackbirders, who were slave traders, took hundreds of islanders to work in Peru, Fiji, Tahiti, Hawaii and Australia. The group became a British Protectorate and then part of the Gilbert and Ellice Islands colony.

During the Second World War the remoteness of the Ellice Islands spared them occupation by the Japanese. In 1943 Funafuti, the main atoll, was used by US forces as an advance base for the push to capture the Gilbert Islands. After a referendum in 1975 the Ellice Islands separated from the Gilberts and became Tuvalu, reaching full independence in 1978.

Most of the population work in subsistence agriculture. Foreign revenue comes from postage stamps and copra, as well as the sale of fishing rights. Remittances from Tuvaluans working overseas as merchant seamen and in Nauru's phosphate industry are also important. Overseas aid remains vital to the economy.

The population was 8229 in 1985. Tuvaluans are Polynesians and both Tuvaluan and English are spoken. Most are Protestant with small groups of other Christian denominations. The Church is very important in the community. Funafuti is the main island, capital and only port.

Tuvalu lies on the northern edge of the hurricane belt, and occasionally severe cyclones strike the islands, as did cyclone Ofa in February 1990. There is little seasonal change in the climate, although in October to March strong westerly winds and heavy rainfall can occur. The average temperature is 30°C (86°F).

Entry Regulations

Port of entry
Funafuti 8°31'S 179°12'E.

Procedure on arrival
Yachts should not stop at any of the other islands before clearing in at Funafuti.

Flying the Q flag, one should anchor for clearance near the wharf, where customs are located, the customs officials will come out to the yacht.

Permission must be requested to visit any of the other islands. It is sometimes possible, but not guaranteed, to get outward clearance which allows stops at the northern islands if heading towards Kiribati.

Customs
Firearms, animals and plants must be declared and kept on board.

Immigration
Entry visas are granted on arrival for one month, renewable for a maximum of another three months, if proof of sufficient funds can be shown.

Fees
Overtime is charged if a yacht clears in at a weekend.

Practical Information

LOCAL TIME: GMT + 12

BUOYAGE: IALA A

CURRENCY: Australian dollar (Aus$)
with Tuvaluan coins.

BUSINESS HOURS
Banks: National Bank of Tuvalu,
0930–1300 Monday to Thursday,
0830–1200 Friday.
Government offices: 0730–1600 Monday
to Thursday, 0730–1300 Friday.
Shops: 0630–1730 Monday to Friday.

ELECTRICITY: 240 V, 50 Hz

PUBLIC HOLIDAYS
1 January: New Year's Day
7 March: Commonwealth Day
Good Friday, Easter Monday
June: Queen's Birthday
1 August: National Children's Day
1 or 2 October: Tuvalu National Day
21 October: Hurricane Day
7 November: Prince Charles' Birthday
25, 26 December: Christmas

COMMUNICATIONS
On Funafuti the Telecommunications
Centre provides long-distance telephone
calls, telex and telegrams.
The grass airstrip on Funafuti built by
US forces during the war is still in
operation and there are regular flights to
Fiji, Kiribati and Majuro (Marshalls).
The outer islands only have links by a
supply ship, which makes the rounds
roughly every six weeks.

MEDICAL
There is a good small hospital on
Funafuti.

There is no charge during working hours. There is a visa charge of Aus$10 per person.

Social customs
One should remove shoes before entering church, the maneapa (meeting house) or private homes. The drinking of alcohol in public is not permitted.

Facilities

There is a cooperative store selling mostly imported food on all the islands. Local produce is available on all islands, but the selection is limited – taro, coconuts, papaya and bananas.

Limited amounts of fuel can be obtained in Funafuti from the BP office next to the large fuel tanks north of the ship dock. LPG is not available and empty bottles would have to be sent to Fiji by ship. Water is scarce, as the islands rely on rainfall. In the rainy season, rain can be heavy and one can easily collect enough. There are only simple repair facilities available in Funafuti and nothing in the other islands.

Further Reading

Pacific Odyssey
Pacific Islands Yearbook
Landfalls of Paradise

VANUATU

Vanuatu, formerly called the New Hebrides, is a group of over 80 volcanic islands in the Western Pacific. Espiritu Santo, Malekula, Efate, Erromango, Ambrym and Tanna are the main islands. Left alone by the Europeans for longer than other parts of the Pacific, Vanuatu leapt into the modern age quickly, while remaining a place where the rich Melanesian culture is kept very much alive.

It is the chance to experience a little of this fascinating culture that brings most sailors to this country which has been endowed with less cruising attractions than its neighbours. Nevertheless their beauty inspired James Michener to write his *Tales of the South Pacific* in which the island of Aoba, 25 miles west of Santo, was probably his Bali Hai. With the exception of the northern islands, the number of natural harbours is rather limited, with the notable exception of the main island Efate which has several attractive bays. One of the greatest attractions of the islands is a visit to the live volcano on Tanna, where one can ascend into the crater, the closest one can get to an active volcano safely anywhere in the world. Even sailing by the island one can be treated to a spectacular firework display, especially at night.

Unfortunately the land-divers of Pentecost Island, which used to be another attraction in the past, now only perform at the traditional time between April and early June, which is too early in the season for most yachts, with the exception of those sailing from New Zealand. The majority of yachts usually reach Vanuatu later in the year, many of them as part of the annual Musket Cove to Vila Race in September.

Practical Information

LOCAL TIME: GMT + 11. Summer time GMT + 12 end of September to end of March.

BUOYAGE: IALA A

CURRENCY: Vatu (VUV/VT). Aus$ are widely accepted and credit card transactions are done in Aus$.

BUSINESS HOURS
Banks: 0800–1100/1330–1500 Monday to Friday, some 0800–1100 Saturday.
Shops: 0800–1130/1400–1700 Monday to Friday, half day Saturday.
The lunch break is strictly observed.
Government offices: 0730–1130/1315–1630 Monday to Friday.

ELECTRICITY: 220/240 V, 50 Hz

PUBLIC HOLIDAYS
1 January: New Year's Day
Holy Thursday, Good Friday, Easter Monday
5 March: National Custom Chiefs Day
1 May: Labour Day
Ascension
30 July: Independence Day
15 August: Assumption
5 October: Constitution Day
29 November: National Unity Day
25, 26 December: Christmas

EVENTS
April/May: Land Divers of Pentecost Island
End of August: Toka Dance, Tanna Island

COMMUNICATIONS
VANITEL in Independence Park for international telephone calls, telex and fax. Open daily 0645–2200.

Post office, Kumul Highway 0730–1130/1330–1530 Monday to Friday, 0730–1100 Saturday.
Emergencies: Police ☎ 2222, Fire ☎ 2333, Ambulance ☎ 2100.
Air/Sea Rescue 2371.
There are flights from Vila to Australia, New Zealand, Nouméa, Papua New Guinea and Fiji.

MEDICAL
Central Hospital, Vila: 24 hours. ☎ 2100.

DIPLOMATIC MISSIONS
In Port Vila:
Australia: Melitco House, Pasteur St. ☎ 2777.
France: Kumul Highway. ☎ 2353.
New Zealand: Prouds Bldg, Kumul Highway. ☎ 2393.
United Kingdom: Melitco House, Pasteur St. ☎ 3100.

Country Profile

The exact origins of the indigenous population are not known and it has been suggested that the Melanesians probably came from Africa thousands of years ago. They spread across the part of the South West Pacific which is now called Melanesia, and developed different cultures from Papua to New Caledonia. Isolation was broken when in 1606 the explorer Fernandez de Quiros, looking for land and gold for Philip III of Spain, came across Espiritu Santo, and believed it to be the mythical southern continent, which Ptolemy and Marco Polo had claimed existed. The islanders' first contact with Europeans was not propitious, as although they made efforts to be friendly, the sailors were very hostile. Quiros' findings were ignored when he returned to Spain. Over 150 years later Bougainville was the next to visit Espiritu Santo and establish that it was not a continent after all. Soon afterwards Captain Cook charted the islands, naming them the New Hebrides, although they bore little resemblance to the original Hebrides. Missionaries, whalers, sandalwood traders and blackbirders followed as they did in so many parts of the Pacific. Violence was common as the islanders tried to resist these intrusions.

By the end of the nineteenth century both French and English settlers had arrived, so the governments of both countries decided to set up a joint Naval Commission to keep law and order. German efforts to gain influence there prompted the creation of a Franco-British Condominium in 1906. It was popularly known as the Pandemonium, as it brought to the islands two sets of laws, education systems, two languages, and so on. However, it helped to keep the peace, and brought some development to the islands. Until independence, yachts could choose whether to clear in with a French gendarme or a British bobby.

During the Second World War the New Hebrides were in the forefront of the fight for the Pacific. Espiritu Santo boomed from a quiet backwater to a US base with ships, equipment and servicemen.

Independence was achieved in July 1980 and the islands became the Republic of Vanuatu. Its government is noted for the independent line they take in Pacific politics.

Vanuatu is a rural country and very fertile. Copra, cocoa and beef are the main produce. There is a large fishery on Santo. Tourism is increasingly an important source of revenue and the capital Port Vila is being developed as a tax haven and offshore financial centre.

The 140,000 inhabitants are mainly Melanesians, calling themselves Ni-Vanuatu. There are also some Chinese, Vietnamese, Europeans, Australians, New Zealanders and small communities of other Pacific islanders. The national language is Bislama, which is a pidgin English. French and English are both widely spoken, and there are 115 local languages. There are a large number of Christian denominations and also animist beliefs. Tanna is the centre of the Jon Frum cargo cult. Port Vila, on Efate, is the capital.

The climate is semi-tropical. There are two distinct seasons. May to October is relatively cool and dry, while November to April is hot and humid. January to March are the rainy months. The cyclone season lasts from December until the end of March.

Entry Regulations

Ports of entry
Port Vila (Efate) 17°44′S 168°18′E, Luganville (Espiritu Santo) 15°31′S 167°10′E.

Procedure on arrival
Port Vila: Entering the harbour one should fly the Q flag and tie up to the yellow quarantine buoy, until customs and immigration authorities arrive to clear one in. The port authority can be contacted on VHF Channel 16, but this is monitored only during office hours.
Espiritu Santo: One can tie up to or anchor off the commercial dock at Luganville, or alternatively one can anchor in Palikoulo Bay and go overland to clear in at Luganville.

If visiting any other islands, one must request permission from the authorities, especially if wishing to stop at Tanna.

Yachts may be able to obtain permission to clear outwards for foreign ports via other islands within Vanuatu.

Customs
Firearms and ammunition must be declared on arrival and surrendered to customs, to be returned at departure, of which 48 hours notice should be given. If there is a satisfactory locker on board, the arms can be sealed on board.

Private yachts are considered to be temporarily imported into Vanuatu and do not have to pay duty provided the yacht is owned by the importer and a stay of six months in a two-year period is not exceeded. Yachts must not be used commercially if temporarily imported, or they will become liable for duty.

Duty-free goods may be taken on board after clearance or when about to clear out in Port Vila, but not Luganville. One can take on duty-free in Port Vila, have it sealed until clearance outwards in Luganville. Customs may check it before clearance and the penalty for breaking the seal is a fine.

Quarantine
Strict quarantine regulations are in force in Vanuatu and no animals, birds, reptiles, fresh meat, fruit or vegetables may be taken ashore. Also some of these goods may not be allowed to remain on board; the agricultural officer will decide this at the port of entry. If animals are landed, the owner will have to pay a substantial fine and the animal will be destroyed.

On arrival, the agriculture quarantine service's permission must be obtained to land garbage.

Immigration
On arrival immigration will issue an entry permit for one month. Extensions must be applied for to the immigration authorities, the maximum permitted stay being four months.

Anyone who leaves the yacht must obtain an air ticket out of the country immediately. The captain is responsible for notifying immigration when a crew member wishes to leave a yacht, and he will be liable for their repatriation unless released from this obligation.

No visas are required for nationals of Commonwealth countries, EC countries, Austria, Bermuda, Cameroon, People's Republic of China, Cuba, Cyprus, French overseas territories and departments, Fiji, Finland, Japan, South Korea, Maldives, Marshalls, FSM, Niue, Norway, Palau, Pakistan, Philippines, Singapore, Sweden, Switzerland, Taiwan, Thailand and the USA. All others must obtain a visa in advance, valid up to three months, either from a British high commission or embassy, or direct from the Immigration Office in Vila, Private Bag, 014, Vila. The fee is VT2500 which is approximately US$25.

Health
Malaria prophylaxis is essential as malaria is endemic in Vanuatu.

Fees
Overtime is charged outside of working hours on weekdays, all day Saturdays and Sundays.

Harbour fees are 4500 vatu for a 30 day period or any part thereof. After 30 days, there is an additional charge of 60 vatu per day. Port dues are to be paid to customs at the port of departure.

Vila Harbour regulations
There is an overhead power cable between the eastern side of Iririki Island and Vila, and no vessel whose height from waterline exceeds 62 ft (19 m) should try to pass under it except by passing close to the westward of the red buoy on the east (the Vila side of the cable), where the maximum clearance is 75 ft (23 m). It is an offence to contravene this rule and yachts not observing it will be fined and will also have to bear the costs of any damage. Yachts with taller masts can tie stern to the quay or anchor in the quarantine buoy area.

All vessels in Vila Harbour must show a riding light if at anchor, between the hours of sunset and sunrise.

Anchoring near Efila Island is prohibited due to a land dispute between the islanders and the authorities, so this area should be avoided.

Facilities

In Port Vila provisioning is good with some duty-free shops for visitors. There is a good market on the waterfront, opposite the Government building, Wednesday, Friday and Saturday mornings 0600–1300. Most shops are on Kumul Highway, the main street, and there are three supermarkets in town. Gas bottles can be filled at the local filling station located by the large LPG tanks on the south side of the harbour.

A local company offering services to visiting yachts, Yachting World, has a few moorings behind Iririki Island. They have published an excellent Cruising Guide to Vanuatu. Water and fuel can be obtained at the company's dock. Larger amounts of fuel can be delivered by road tanker to the commercial wharf.

Repair facilities in Port Vila are adequate and either the staff at Yachting World or one of the members of the Vanuatu Cruising Club, who share the same premises, will advise visitors on where to have things fixed locally. There is a small chandlery, Pentecost Motors, with a limited selection of goods and also some charts. They also deal with engine repair, both diesel and outboard. Radio repair can be undertaken at the Sound Centre who also stock duty-free equipment. A small company building aluminium boats undertakes metal work. Simple sail repairs can also be arranged locally.

In Santo provisioning is good from the local supermarkets and a daily fresh produce market. Water can be taken on at the commercial wharf and fuel bought from the Shell depot. There is a slip for vessels up to 400 tons at South Pacific Fishing company in Luganville who also do metal and general repair work. There are a few smaller workshops in town for electrical or engine repair.

If planning to cruise the outer islands, one should have a good supply of staples, although local fresh produce is always available in these fertile islands, payment for which the islanders often prefer in goods rather than money.

Further Reading

Vanuatu Cruising Guide
Cruising New Caledonia and Vanuatu
Landfalls of Paradise

WALLIS AND FUTUNA

Wallis and Futuna are two island groups separated by 150 miles of ocean in the central South Pacific. Since 1959 they have been joined together as a French overseas territory. Lying west of Samoa and slightly off the route to Fiji, Wallis and Futuna are not often visited by cruising yachts. The pass into the lagoon at Wallis is relatively easy to negotiate and there are several anchorages, the most popular and best protected being at Gahi Bay. There are also several small islets in the lagoon which can be used as day anchorages. Ashore one can come in contact with a relatively unspoilt Polynesian society where the rule of the traditional Polynesian chieftain, the Lavelua, still commands more respect than the French administration. The singing and dancing of the Wallisians is vigorous and one of the few places where traditional songs have not been changed by missionary influences.

A similar atmosphere survives on the smaller Futuna, which does not have a protected lagoon, but only an anchorage at Sigave Bay on the west coast.

Country Profile

The island of Uvea, as the islanders still call it, was first sighted by Captain Wallis, who renamed it after himself, while on an expedition to find the mythical southern continent. The mountainous Futuna's first contact with Europeans was with the Dutch explorer Schouten in 1616. At the end of the nineteenth century the islands became a French Protectorate. United States forces built a runway on Wallis during the Second World War, which is now the civil Hihifo airport.

Yam, taro, bananas and pineapple are the main produce of the economy. Remittances from islanders working overseas, especially in New Caledonia, and grants from France, provide important sources of income.

The Polynesian population numbers over 8000 on Wallis, and about 4000 on Futuna. Many islanders live in New Caledonia and Vanuatu. Wallisian, which is similar to Tongan, and French are spoken. Most people are Roman Catholic and an interesting feature of Wallis are the massive churches built in the style of those in Normandy, rather incongruous on a tropical island. Mata Utu on Wallis is the main town.

The SE trade winds blow over the islands during the winter months from April to November. Winds are variable during summer when the weather is sometimes sultry. Westerly gales occur in summer and the islands are rarely affected by tropical storms.

Practical Information

LOCAL TIME: GMT + 12

BUOYAGE: IALA A

CURRENCY: French Pacific franc (CFP)

BUSINESS HOURS
Government offices: 0700–1200 Monday to Friday.
Banque Indosuez, Mata Utu: weekdays except Tuesday 0900–1200, 1300–1500.
Gendarmerie: 0700–1130, 1500–1700 Monday to Friday.

ELECTRICITY: 220 V, 50 Hz

PUBLIC HOLIDAYS
1 January: New Year's Day
Easter Monday
1 May
8 May: Liberation Day
Ascension
Monday after Pentecost
14 July: Bastille Day
15 August: Assumption

1 November: All Saints' Day
11 November: Armistice Day
25 December: Christmas Day

COMMUNICATIONS
Long-distance calls can be made at the post office in Mata Utu. There are twice weekly flights from Mata Utu to Nouméa (New Caledonia) and Nadi (Fiji) connecting with the international network. There are also flights from Mata Utu to Futuna.

Entry Regulations

Ports of entry
Mata Utu (Wallis) 13°17'S 176°08'W, Anse de Sigave (Futuna) 14°18'S 178°10'W.

Procedure on arrival
Wallis: One should anchor behind the small reef in front of Mata Utu. The captain should then proceed ashore and check in with customs and police (Gendarmerie).
Futuna: One should anchor off Sigave and the captain should go ashore. One can land by dinghy at the dock and check in with customs and police in town.

Customs
Firearms must be sealed on board.
   Animals must have a rabies vaccination certificate.
   Yachts may stay a maximum of six months in a 12 month period without paying duty.

Immigration
Nationals of the European Community, Andorra, Austria, Canada, Cyprus, Finland, Iceland, Liechtenstein, Monaco, Norway, Sweden, Switzerland and the United States do not need visas. All other nationalities need visas which must be obtained in advance from a French diplomatic mission. Yachts on a short visit are usually exempt from visa requirements.

Facilities
The lagoon at Wallis is entered through the Honikulu Pass, which is easiest at slack low water. Diesel is available from the service station near the Gendarm-erie. There is good provisioning in Mata Utu, where there are a few shops with a relatively good selection. Fresh produce is available on both islands.

   Only simple repairs can be carried out, but in an emergency one may be able to enlist the help of the military. Essential spares can be ordered from Nouméa.

Further Reading

Pacific Odyssey
Pacific Islands Yearbook
Landfalls of Paradise

WESTERN SAMOA

Western Samoa comprises the two islands of Upolu and Savai'i, as well as several smaller islands. Savai'i is the largest, but Upolu is the most developed and centre of government and commerce. Robert Louis Stevenson was the first in a long line of famous travellers to be seduced by the Samoan way of life, and today's sailors can still find a Samoa whose ways have changed very little during the century since Stevenson lived here. Tusitala, meaning teller of tales, as he was affectionately called by the Samoans, is buried on top of Mount Vaea. The view from his tomb over the whole island and Apia harbour is well worth the stiff climb. Cruising along the sheltered northern coast of the two main islands, one can anchor off villages such as Asau on Savai'i, from where one can explore the interior of these verdant islands with their gushing waterfalls and lush rain forests.

Practical Information

LOCAL TIME: GMT - 11

BUOYAGE: IALA A

CURRENCY: Tala (SAT/WS$) of 100 sene

BUSINESS HOURS
Banks: 0930–1500 Monday to Friday.
Shops: 0800–1200/1330–1630 Monday to Friday, 0800–1200 Saturday.
Business and government offices: 0800–1200/1330–1630 Monday to Friday.

ELECTRICITY: 240 V, 50 Hz

PUBLIC HOLIDAYS
1 January: New Year's Day
Good Friday, Easter Monday
25 April: ANZAC Day
1–3 June: Independence Celebrations
12 October: Arbour Day
25, 26 December: Christmas
31 December: New Year's Eve

COMMUNICATIONS
Telegraph office, above main post office, open 24 hours daily.
Post office: letters, telegrams, telephones, cable, radio.
Open 0900–1200/1300–1600 Monday to Friday.

Emergency numbers: 22222 police, ambulance 21212, fire 20404.
There are flights from Apia to Fiji, Auckland and Sydney from where further connections can be made.

MEDICAL
The Apia government hospital in Motootua has small charges for non-residents. ☎ 21212. There are also private clinics.

DIPLOMATIC MISSIONS
In Apia:
Australia: Fei Gai ma Leala Bldg, Beach Rd. ☎ 23411.
New Zealand: Beach Rd. ☎ 21711.
United States: PO Box 3430. ☎ 22474.

Country Profile

It is said that Savai'i is the legendary Hawaiki from which the first Polynesians spread out across the Pacific. The American Samoans may dispute this, saying it was Manua, but today Western Samoa seems much more the Polynesian of the two, not having experienced the cultural invasion of America as has its neighbour. Traditions have remained strong, despite absorbing some Western influence and *fa'a Samoa*, 'the way of the ancestors', rules the lives of Samoans, centred around the extended family, with its etiquette and rituals.

Jacob Roggeveen first sighted the Samoas in 1722, and they were named the Navigator Islands 64 years later by Bougainville. The arrival of the missionary John Williams in the 1830s marks the beginning of modern Samoan history. A German trading firm was established to trade in copra and the islands which make up present-day Western Samoa were administered by Germany from 1900 until the First World War when they were taken over by New Zealand. This was not a popular rule and in 1962 Western Samoa was the first Polynesian nation to regain its independence.

The economy is mainly agricultural, producing coconuts, copra and bananas. Efforts have been made to diversify, and to expand both tourism and other new industries. The population is 160,000, the great majority being pure Polynesians. Samoan and English are spoken and most islanders are practising Christians. Apia, on Upolu's north coast, is the capital. It is a waterfront town, a mixture of the old and the new.

Apia harbour is worth entering, for the simple reason that to get into the harbour, yachts must go around a headland called Cape Horn.

Samoa has a tropical climate with the more pleasant season being the south-east trade wind season from April to November. During the cyclone season, from December to March, the weather is hotter and wetter. As the Samoan islands are quite high, local weather conditions can be quite varied.

Entry Regulations

Port of entry
Apia (Upolu) 13°48'S 171°46'W.

Procedure on arrival
Yachts are requested to radio their ETA to the harbour master via Apia Radio 24 hours before arrival. When a yacht is within 40 miles they should confirm their arrival to Harbour Control, VHF Channel 16. Health, customs, immigration and quarantine officers will come aboard on arrival. Do not come alongside the main wharf until permission and directions are given by harbour control.

The anchorage is south of a line extending 097°T from Cape Horn.

Customs
Firearms must be declared and will be sealed on board by customs or kept ashore until departure.

Animals are not permitted ashore.

Yachts are normally granted a 14-day permit.

Immigration

No permit or visa is necessary if staying less than three days. A visitor's permit is given on arrival for up to 30 days. Extensions are possible from immigration for a fee of WS$20 per person.

A visa or entry permit is required if staying longer and should be obtained prior to arrival from Samoan, New Zealand or British consulates or from the immigration office in Apia.

Cruising permit

This is required if wishing to visit other harbours besides Apia. An application may be made in writing on arrival, but it is better to do so in advance. Write to the Secretary for Foreign Affairs, PO Box L 861, Apia and send a copy to the Secretary for Transport, PO Box 1607, Apia. The letter should state the yacht's name, port of registry, the names and nationalities of the master and crew, ETA Apia, and a list of places one intends to visit, plus planned duration of stay.

On outward clearance it is possible to get permission to stop in Asau on Savai'i, before continuing on to other destinations.

Prohibited areas

It is prohibited to enter the ferry terminal ports of Mulifanua and Salelologa, except with special permission from the Ministry of Transport.

Fees

Overtime is charged outside of working hours for clearing services at a rate of WS$6 per official. There is WS$10 customs clearance fee.

Facilities

There are no facilities for visiting yachts to come alongside, only the protected anchorage off the capital Apia. Provisioning in Apia is good and there are various stores to choose from. The fresh produce market is excellent. Diesel fuel is available from the fuel station north of the river. For larger quantities it is possible to order a tanker from Mobil who will send it down to the dock.

Engine repair is undertaken by Ken-Do Engineering. Stainless steel welding and metal work can be done at Brueger Industries. There are no haul-out facilities.

All garbage must be put into sealed plastic bags and given to the quarantine office at the wharf gate for disposal. There is a charge of WS$1 per bag.

Asau on Savai'i is a well-protected anchorage, but only limited supplies are available, so it is better to provision in Apia.

Further Reading

Landfalls of Paradise
Pacific Islands Yearbook
South Pacific Handbook

10 South East Asia and Far East

Typhoons in the Far East, boat people in the China Sea, rumours of pirates in the Southern Philippines, restrictions on cruising in Indonesia – no other region in the world presents so many different problems to anyone planning to cruise there and all of them have combined to discourage many people from sailing to South East Asia and the Far East.

The need for a cruising permit in Indonesia and the difficulty of obtaining it in the past has raised an artificial barrier in the path of yachts sailing to this area from the South Pacific. The threat of typhoons is very real in Japan and the surrounding area, although with proper planning it is possible to make the best of the safe season. The other risks are largely exaggerated and although some parts of the Philippines are considered dangerous, there have been no reports of violent attacks on yachts in recent years although robberies are on the increase. Certain areas are best avoided and visiting sailors should also avoid getting caught up in the internal conflicts which affect the Philippines. Also to be avoided are the waters surrounding Cambodia, Vietnam and North Korea where the authorities do not welcome visitors of any sort. Although the People's Republic of China has now reluctantly opened its frontiers to visitors, those arriving by yacht still have to go through a maze of formalities. The situation is not much better in South Korea, whose military has yet to accept the end of the Cold War.

Facilities for cruising yachts vary considerably, and the countries which have their own boating communities, such as Hong Kong, Singapore and Japan, are also those where the best repair facilities are available. The one exception is Taiwan, which has a large yacht-building industry and therefore better than average facilities, but no resident sailing community as such. In all other countries facilities are very limited and even in popular cruising destinations, such as the west coast of Malaysia or Phuket, facilities are barely adequate.

BRUNEI

The full name of Brunei is Negara Brunei Darussalam. This small state, situated on the north-west side of Borneo, is made up of two separate areas divided by the Malaysian state of Sarawak. The 100 miles of coast are cultivated plain, while inland the highlands are covered by tropical rainforest. The western part is made up of Brunei-Muara, Belait and Tutong, and the eastern part is Temburong. Although small, the country is extremely rich because of its oil and gas reserves and the Sultan of Brunei is reputed to be one of the richest men in the world.

There are few anchorages on the coast and the many oil rigs make navigation difficult, especially at night. Muara at the mouth of the Brunei River has a deepwater port and from there it is 16 miles to the capital.

Country Profile

Negara Brunei Darussalam is Sanskrit for 'seaform'. Recent discoveries confirm that Brunei had links with countries on the Asian continent as early as the sixth to seventh centuries AD. During the fourteenth to sixteenth centuries Brunei became the centre of an empire, mainly due to the efforts of the seafaring Sultan Bolkiah, who extended his rule over much of Borneo, the Sulu Islands, and the Philippines. Islam came to Brunei in the fifteenth century. The first European to visit was Magellan in 1521, and thereafter others followed on their search for trade and territories and Brunei's empire soon disappeared.

At the end of the nineteenth century a treaty between the Sultan and Britain saw Brunei become a British Protected State. Although never a colony, Britain advised the Sultanate on all matters except those relating to custom and religion. Until the 1920s, Brunei was not seen as a very important part of the British Empire, but then oil was discovered and a new era of prosperity began. Negotiations with Britain led to a written constitution in 1959, introducing full internal self-government. Full independence was finally granted in 1984.

The oil and gas industries dominate the economy, but efforts are being made to diversify, particularly to develop the agricultural sector to reduce dependence on food imports, which currently run at about 80 per cent. Because of the oil revenues, the people of Brunei enjoy very high living standards.

The population is about 230,000, mainly Malay and Chinese, some Europeans, Indians and Filipinos, also the indigenous Iban and Dusun. Malay is the official

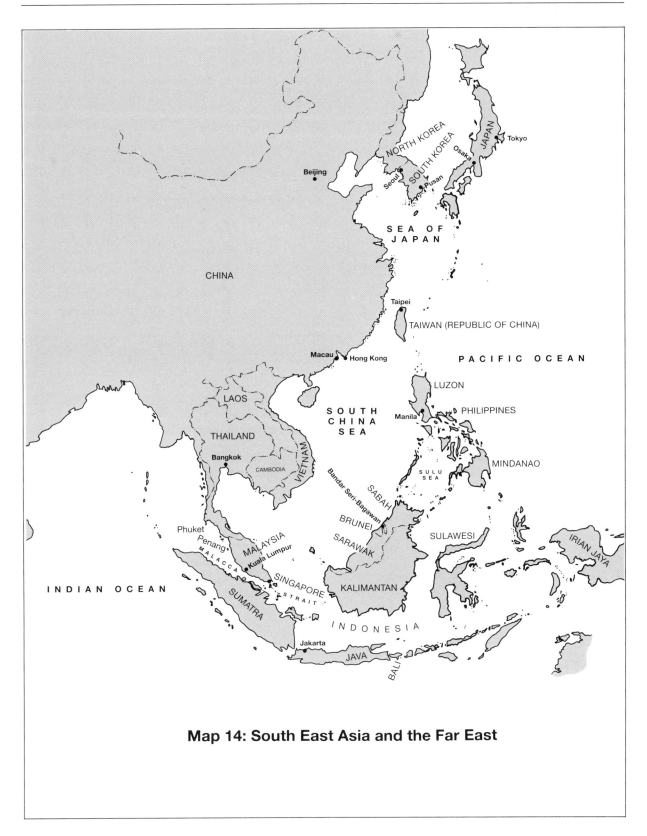

Map 14: South East Asia and the Far East

Practical Information

LOCAL TIME: GMT + 8

BUOYAGE: IALA A

CURRENCY: Brunei dollar (B$) of 100 cents/sen. On a par with the Singapore dollar, the two currencies are interchangeable in both states.

BUSINESS HOURS
Banks: 0900–1500 Monday to Thursday, 0900–1100 Saturday.
Shops: 0730–1900/2200 Monday to Thursday, Saturday.
Government offices: 0745–1215, 1330–1630 Monday to Thursday, Saturday.

ELECTRICITY: 220 V, 50 Hz

PUBLIC HOLIDAYS
Muslim holidays are variable in date
1 January: New Year's Day
Chinese New Year
23 February: National Day
Israk Mekraj
First Day of Ramadan
Anniversary of the Revelation of the Koran
Hari Raya Puasa (Idul Fitri)
31 May: Anniversary of the Royal Brunei Armed Forces
15 July: Sultan's birthday
Hari Raya Haji (Idul Adha)
Hijrah (Muslim New Year)
Moulud (Prophet Mohammed's Birthday)
25 December: Christmas Day

COMMUNICATIONS
International telephones, telex and fax available at telecommunication offices.
Main post office, corner of Jln Elizabeth

Dua and Jln Sultan in BSB, open 0730–1600 Monday to Thursday and Saturday, 0830–0930 Fridays and holidays.
Brunei international airport has flights to most Asian capitals, Singapore being the most useful for connecting to European and North American destinations.

MEDICAL
The health service is good. A flying doctor service is operated.
In BSB, RIPAS General Hospital, ☎ 42424.

DIPLOMATIC MISSIONS
Australia: Teck Guan Plaza, Corner Jln Sultan and Jln MacArthur. ☎ 29435.
United Kingdom: Hong Kong Chambers, Jln Pemancha ☎ 22231.
United States: PO Box 2991. ☎ 29670.

language, but English is widely spoken as well as Chinese, Iban and other native dialects. Islam is the official religion and is strictly observed by the majority. However, other religions are freely allowed, 30 per cent being Buddhist and 5 per cent Christian. The capital is Bandar Seri Bagawan (BSB), called Brunei Town until 1970, when it was renamed after the 28th Sultan. Half the population lives in Kampong Ayer, a 400-year-old village built on stilts, which is the largest of its kind in the world.

The climate is tropical and very humid, averaging 25 to 35°C (77–95°F). There are heavy and sudden rains all year round, especially November to February during the NW monsoon.

Entry Regulations

Ports of entry
Muara 4°53′N 114°56′E, Kuala Belait 4°35′N 114°11′E, Bandar Seri Bagawan 4°52′N 114°55′E.

Procedure on arrival
Muara: Port control should be contacted on VHF Channel 16. Yachts can anchor past the pier. One has to clear with customs, immigration and health.
Bandar Seri Bagawan: The port is up the river and is no longer used as a commercial port, but local boats use it and yachts can clear there.

Customs
Firearms should be declared to customs or police. There are no restrictions on animals.

Immigration
A visa-free stay is granted for up to 14 days for the nationals of Belgium, Canada, France, Germany, Japan, South Korea, Luxembourg, Maldives, Malaysia, the Netherlands, Singapore, Sweden, Switzerland and the United Kingdom. Nationals of these countries will require a visa if they plan to stay longer.

All other nationalities, including British Overseas citizens and British dependent territories citizens, require a visa in advance, which can be obtained from Brunei or British consulates.

Fees
A visa fee of B$15 is charged if these are issued on arrival.

Restrictions
Muslim religious laws should be respected and no alcohol consumed in public.

Facilities

Provisioning is good, as Brunei has a high standard of living and imported goods are widely available. The best shopping is in the capital BSB, where in the area bounded by Jln Sultan, Jln Pretty, Jln Pemancha and Jln MacArthur, one can find lots of shops. A good open-air market is held each day along the Kianggeh river, in front of a Chinese temple.

Repair facilities for yachts are limited and only simple repairs can be carried out.

Further Reading

Malaysia, Singapore and Brunei – a travel survival kit

CHINA

China is the third largest country in the world, a country of extremes from the harsh north to the tropical south. Since 1949 it had been a closed communist state, but the opening up of China in the early 1980s brought many tourists to the country. Cruising yachts have also been able to take advantage of the more tolerant attitude of the authorities but the number of yachts who sail to China is still very small. In most places, foreign yachts are treated with suspicion and their freedom of movement is limited. The recent reversing of many liberal reforms does not bode well and although China has not reverted to the xenophobia of Mao's time, the Beijing Spring may be short lived.

The main fascination that China holds for visitors, including those on yachts, is the fact that most of the country has been forbidden territory for so long. Although there are countless interesting sites worth visiting in the interior, from the cruising point of view, China's coasts do not have much to offer. Most of the ports open to yachts are busy commercial harbours, facilities are virtually non-existent and the scenery only rarely matches that of neighbouring countries. As a cruising destination, China's attractions are rather limited.

Country Profile

An organised state existed in China in the twenty-first century BC, ruled by a succession of imperial dynasties, first based on slavery then on a feudal system. The Chinese elite were far ahead of the rest of the world in their culture and thinking, but then an isolationist attitude developed, which lasted until the nineteenth century when the European powers, on their imperialist drive, sought to open China in order to exploit its vast markets. There were several wars, which resulted in Europeans securing trading concessions.

In 1912 the Imperial Regime, seen as hindering China's development into a modern state, was toppled in a republican uprising. The new republic, under Sun Yat Sen, was beset by problems and faced the opposition of the Chinese Communist Party, created in 1921, which temporarily allied with the new republican nationalist party, Kuomintang, under Chiang Kai Shek. The latter turned on the Communists and, led by Mao Tse Tung, the Communists fled to the remote north-west. After the Second World War the civil war was renewed.

In 1949 the nationalists were defeated and fled to Taiwan, where they declared a separate state as the Republic of China. On the mainland, the People's Republic of China was proclaimed under Mao's leadership. Initially popular, the regime became too hardline for many, and the Cultural Revolution 1966–76 saw extensive purges. After Mao's death, there was a move towards flexibility, and a more pragmatic path was taken. The limits of this new spirit of reform were demonstrated by the massacre of students in Tian'anmen square in 1988. Relations with Taiwan have remained strained and the rulers in Beijing still refuse to have diplomatic relations with anyone who recognises the regime in Taipei.

China is mainly an agricultural country and there is little industry. Beijing (Peking) is the capital. At 1.06 billion people, China has the highest population in the world. The majority are Han, but there are also a multitude of national minorities such as Mongols, Tibetans, and Manchus. Mandarin is the main spoken language, there being many minority languages and dialects. Written Chinese, made up of ideograms, is standard. Although officially an atheist state, many still follow traditional Chinese beliefs and Muslims, Buddhists, Lamaists and Christians also exist.

The climate along the coast is mostly temperate, although there are pronounced variations between the south and the far north. The tropical areas in the south are affected by typhoons, which are most frequent between May and October. The weather in winter is cool and the coast is under the influence of the NE monsoon. The summers are hot, humid and rainy.

Entry Regulations

Ports of entry
The following ports are those open to foreign vessels. Foreign vessels may not enter anywhere else.
Basuo (Hainan Island) 19°06′N 108°37′E (also known as Dongfang), Beihai 21°27′N 109°03′E,

Practical Information

LOCAL TIME: GMT + 8

BUOYAGE: IALA A

CURRENCY: Renminbi (RMB) or yuan = 10 jiao = 100 fen. All records of exchange should be kept. One cannot import or export local currency. There are two kinds of currency in China, RMB which is the local currency, and 'foreign exchange' currency, which has the same face, but the back is printed with the words *foreign exchange.* Only the latter can be used to pay in hotels and the state-owned stores, and, more important, is the only currency that can be changed back into foreign currency on departure. Too much ordinary RMB should not be acquired as it cannot be changed back.

BUSINESS HOURS
Business and government offices: 0800–1230, 1400–1700 Monday to Friday, 0800–1200 Saturday.
Banks: 0900–1200, 1345–1630 Monday to Saturday.

Shops: 0800–1200, 1400–1800 Monday to Saturday (or 0900–2100).

ELECTRICITY
220/380 V, 50 Hz, 110/220 V, 60 Hz and 220/240 V, 50 Hz.

PUBLIC HOLIDAYS
1 January: New Year's Day
Chinese New Year (Spring festival), three days
1 May: Labour Day
1, 2 October: National Day

MEDICAL
Hospitals are good and inexpensive.

COMMUNICATIONS
International phone calls have to be made through the international operator, who speaks English and French. Calls may have to be booked in advance. This can be done at hotels and post offices. The main airport for international flights is at Beijing.

DIPLOMATIC MISSIONS
In Beijing:
Australia: 15 Donzhimenwai St, San Li Tun. ☎ (1) 532-2331.
Canada: 10 San Li Tun Rd, Chao Yang district. ☎ (1) 532-3536.
New Zealand: Ritan Dongerjie 1, Chao Yang district. ☎ (1) 532-2731.
United Kingdom: 11 Guang Hua Lu, Jian Goo Men Wai. ☎ (1) 532-1961.
United States: Guang Hua Lu 17.
☎ (1) 522-033.

In Shanghai:
Australia: 17 Fixing Road West.
☎ (21) 33-4604.
Canada: Union Building, 100 Yan'an Road. ☎ (21) 20-2822.
United Kingdom: 244 Yong Fu Lu.
☎ (21) 33-0508.
United States: 1469 Huai Hai Middle Road. ☎ (21) 37-9880.

Chiwan 22°28'N 113°53'E, Dalian 19°06'N 108°37'E, Dandong 40°08'N 124°24'E, Fuzhou 26°03'N 119°18'E, Guangzhou (Canton) 23°06'N 113°14'E, Haikou (Hainan Island) 20°01'N 110°16'E, Haimen 28°41'N 121°26'E, Huangpu 23°05'N 113°25'E, Jinshan 30°43'N 121°19'E, Jinshou 40°45'N 121°06'E, Lanshantou 35°06'N 119°22'E, Lianyungang 34°44'N 119°27'E, Longkou 37°41'N 120°18'E, Ningbo 29°52'N 121°33'E, Qingdao 36°05'N 120°18'E, Qinhuangdao 39°54'N 119°36'E, Quanzhou 24°54'N 118°35'E, Sanya (Hainan Island) 18°25'N 109°27'E, Shanghai 31°15'N 121°30'E, Shantou 23°20'N 116°45'E, Tianjin 39°06'N 117°10'E, Weihai 37°30'N 122°09'E, Wenzhou 28°02'N 120°39'E, Xiamen 24°27'N 118°04'E, Xingang (the foreign trade port of Beijing) 38°59'N 117°45'E, Yangpu (Hainan Island) 19°42'N 109°20'E, Yantai 37°34'N 121°26'E, Yantian 22°36'N 114°16'E, Yingkou 40°41'N 122°14'E, Zhanjiang 21°12'N 110°25'E, Zhongshan 23°03'N 113°31'E, Zhuhai 22°17'N 113°35'E (also known as Jiushou).

Yangtze River Ports: The river has a total length of nearly 4000 miles (6300 km), of which more than 1600 miles (2600 km) are navigable. During the past few years certain ports have been opened to foreign vessels but access to them is strictly controlled. There are 28 ports along the river, of which the most important are Nanjing, Nantong and Zhangjiagang.

Procedure on arrival

Intended ports must be notified one week in advance of ETA and again 24 hours before ETA.

Foreign vessels may not enter or leave ports, or shift berths within a port, without permission from the port authority and without a pilot being sent on board.

Vessels entering or leaving any port may be submitted to a quarantine examination and an inspection by the port authorities and other relevant organisations.

After having berthed in the place assigned by the port authority, the captain must present the ship's papers and crew's passports and also prepare the following documents: foreign vessel's entry report, crew list, import manifest and a customs declaration. Other documents that may be required are a valid survey certificate of vessel or builder's certificate, and the captain's certificate of competence.

Before departure, the captain must submit a foreign vessel departure report, an export manifest and a list of crew replacements, if any have occurred.

In the recent past, some yachts which have visited China have not been obliged to engage the services of a pilot, although the regulations stipulate that this is compulsory. The same applies to the services of an agent, but as there is only one official organisation allowed to act as agents on behalf of foreign vessels, its services, or at least advice, should be sought by anyone planning to sail to China. China Ocean Shipping Agency (Penavico) is a state-owned company under the Ministry of Communications and is the sole organisation offering services to foreign vessels calling at Chinese ports. The company has offices located in many coastal cities. The Lloyd's Agents in China are the People's Insurance Company of China, 22 Xi Jiao Min Xiang, Beijing, ☎ 654231/654310, Cables 42001, Beijing, Telex 22102 PICC CN.

Customs
Prohibited imports are firearms, pornographic material and any material considered politically offensive.

Immigration
A visa is required by all visitors, obtainable in advance from Chinese embassies or consulates. Travel permits may also be required for visits to certain areas. Passports must be valid for at least two months after the date of the intended visit. After the vessel has been inspected by the authorities, in some ports crew members may have to apply to the Frontier Inspection office for landing permits.

Health
On arrival, a complete health declaration must be made. Malaria prophylaxis is recommended.

Restrictions
Vessels are prohibited from entering or passing through forbidden areas unless specially authorised by the relevant authorities. There are strict regulations concerning the access and movement of foreign vessels in Chinese territorial waters and ports. The most important regulations have been outlined, and although they may not be applied as strictly to yachts as to cargo ships or passenger vessels, anyone sailing to China should be aware of them.

No passenger or crew member of foreign vessels is allowed to photograph or make sketches of harbours.

While entering or leaving port, or shifting berths within a port, foreign vessels are not allowed to take any soundings other than those taken by means of a hand lead line and only under the supervision of an official pilot.

Radios, radio telephones, radar, RDF, echo sounders, sextants, signal rockets, signal flares or signal guns shall not be used while in port. In case of an emergency or for dispatching urgent messages, one of the above may be used, but a report must be submitted immediately after usage.

Facilities

Yachting facilities and services are practically non-existent. The best repair facilities are those of the China State Shipbuilding Corporation POB 2123 Beijing, ☎ 891953, Telex 22335 and 22029 CSSC CN. They control 17 yards situated in major ports along the coast. All types of repair can be carried out at these yards. Some of the ports where facilities are located are Dalian, Guangzhou (Canton), Quingdao, Shanghai and Tianjin. Although small local boatyards or workshops may be able to help in emergencies, the State Corporation should be contacted for more complex work.

Provisioning is also limited, particularly in rural areas, so one should arrive with a well-stocked boat and only rely on buying fresh produce, which is usually available. Foreign visitors can use Friendship stores and international trade centres, where they can make purchases with the foreign exchange version of the RMB, although things are often a lot cheaper outside of these stores. Change may be given in ordinary RMB, which has to be spent in local markets and independent restaurants. Fuel in small quantities is available in most ports; for larger amounts one may require special permission.

HONG KONG

The British Crown Colony of Hong Kong is made up of the small Hong Kong Island, the commercial centre, and the Kowloon Peninsula, the main district for shopping and entertainment. Between the two lies the well-protected Victoria Harbour. Also part of Hong Kong are the New Territories, a large area on the mainland, as well as some 235 islands, many uninhabited, in the South China Sea.

Although not offering a cruising ground in itself, Hong Kong is rarely bypassed by yachts cruising in the Far East, who are attracted by the excellent service and repair facilities available. There are several yacht clubs and a thriving sailing community, visiting yachts being always warmly received in this dynamic metropolis.

Practical Information

LOCAL TIME: GMT + 8

BUOYAGE: IALA A

CURRENCY: Hong Kong dollar (HK$)

BUSINESS HOURS
Banks: 1000–1500/1600 Monday to
Friday, 0930–1200 Saturday.
Offices: 0900–1300, 1400–1700 Monday to
Friday, 0900–1300 Saturday.
Shops: Hong Kong Island, 1000–1800
Monday to Friday; Kowloon and
Causeway Bay, 1000–2100/2130 Monday
to Friday.
Government offices: 0830–1245,
1400–1700 Monday to Friday and
0900–1200 Saturdays.

ELECTRICITY: 220 V, 50 Hz

PUBLIC HOLIDAYS
Many holidays vary with the lunar
calendar.
1 January: New Year's Day
Chinese New Year, three days
5 April: Ching Ming Festival
Easter

12 May: Buddha's birthday
June: Queen's Birthday (two days)
August Holiday
Last Monday in August: Liberation Day
26 September: Birthday of Confucius
September: Mid-Autumn Festival
October: Cheung Yeung Festival
25, 26 December: Christmas

COMMUNICATIONS
Area codes: Hong Kong Is. 5, Kowloon
3, New Territories 0.
Overseas calls can be made from public
phones and also from Cable & Wireless
offices (Connaught Road, Central, near
Star Ferry and Gloucester Rd, Wanchai).
Collect calls to nine countries are
available on a push button basis.
Dial 013 for information.
Emergency: dial 999.
Main post offices: Connaught Pl., Hong
Kong Star Ferry and
10 Middle Road, Tsim Sha Tsui,
Kowloon. Open 0800–1800 Monday to
Saturday.
Hong Kong has excellent flight
connections with all major centres of the
world.

MEDICAL
There are good hospitals, doctors and
dentists. There is both private and
national health care.
Queen Elizabeth Hospital, Wylie Rd,
☎ (3) 7102111. Main emergency hospital
for Kowloon and New Territories.
Queen Mary Hospital, Pokfulam Rd,
☎ (5) 8192111. For Hong Kong Island.
St John's Ambulance: Hong Kong (5)
766555; Kowloon (3) 7135555; New
Territories (0) 4937543.

DIPLOMATIC MISSIONS
Australia: 25 Harbour Road, Wanchai.
☎ (5) 731881.
Canada: One Exchange Square, 8
Connaught Place. ☎ (5) 8104321.
New Zealand: 3414 Jardine House,
Connaught Rd. ☎ (5) 255044.
Taiwan: Chung Hua Travel Service, East
Tower, Bond Centre, 89 Queensway.
☎ (5) 258315.
United Kingdom: Government House,
Central. ☎ (5) 232031.
United States: 26 Garden Road.
☎ (5) 239011.

Country Profile

Hong Kong was ceded to Britain in 1842 after the First Opium War, when Chinese efforts to expel the European opium traders failed. When first colonised, there were few inhabitants, but archaeological discoveries have shown the area to have been populated thousands of years ago. Hong Kong became an important trade centre and gateway to China and after the Second Opium War the Kowloon peninsula was added. In 1898 a 99-year lease was granted to Britain for the New Territories. Hong Kong was occupied by the Japanese during the Second World War. At present Hong Kong is a British Dependent territory, but in 1997 the sovereignty reverts to China and therefore Hong Kong's future remains uncertain. In an agreement signed in 1984 China promised to respect Hong Kong's freedom, but many are unconvinced that the communist state will leave this capitalist enclave alone.

Hong Kong is a leading producer of textiles and electrical goods as well as being a shipping, banking and insurance centre. Until recently, the New Territories were mainly agricultural, but now these are also becoming industrialised.

The population is 5.5 million, mostly of Chinese origin from the southern provinces of China. There is a small European community, mostly English. Cantonese is the most widely spoken Chinese language. English is also widely spoken. Victoria on Hong Kong island is the capital. A mixture of local beliefs are practised – Confucianism, Buddhism, Taoism – and a small percentage are Christian.

The climate is subtropical. June to September is hot, humid and rainy. October to January is cooler and less humid. The typhoon season is from May to December with the highest frequency between June and September.

Entry Regulations

Port of entry
Victoria Harbour 22°18′N 114°10′E.

Procedure on arrival
The Hong Kong Port Operations Service operates on VHF Channel 12, call sign 'MARDEP' 24 hours a day. Yachts may be boarded and searched in Hong

Kong territorial waters, as illegal immigration and smuggling are major problems. It is recommended to time one's arrival in daylight hours.

On arrival, one should proceed to the Western Quarantine & Immigration anchorage. After clearance one may go to a designated anchorage or yacht club. Within 24 hours of arrival one should report to the Port Formalities Office with the ship's papers and crew lists (Port Formalities Office, Marine Department, 3rd floor, Room 318 Harbour Building, 38 Pier Rd, Central). A General Declaration form must be completed and port and light fees paid.

Procedure on departure

It is necessary also to report to the Port Formalities Office again 17 hours before departure with the necessary papers, that is the Pleasure Vessel Licence or registration certificate. A Port Clearance Permit must be obtained before departure, which is valid for 48 hours.

Customs

Firearms must be declared and handed into custody until departure.

All animals require a special permit, to be obtained in advance from the Senior Veterinary Officer, Agriculture and Fisheries Department, 393 Canton Road Government Offices, 12F, Kowloon, Hong Kong.

Yachts may remain up to six months, after which a Pleasure Vessel Licence must be obtained, and the yacht must have third party insurance.

Immigration

British citizens can stay for up to six months without a visa.

Nationals of the USA, West European, South American, most Asian, Commonwealth and non-communist countries are granted one to three months visa-free stay. Those allowed visa-free stays may be required to show proof of adequate funds for their stay. Other nationals require a visa to be obtained in advance from a British diplomatic mission.

Some form of photo identification such as a passport should always be carried while in Hong Kong.

Fees

Harbour fees are HK$45/100 tons per day. Light dues are HK$37 per 100 NRT per entry. Outward port clearance is HK$50 per vessel.

Restrictions

Prohibited areas are Kai Tak Airport Area No. 1 and 100 metres from both Green Island and Stonecutters Island.

Typhoon procedures

Typhoons are most likely in September, but can occur all year round. When a typhoon is expected, information and warnings are broadcast at 15 minute intervals day and night.

Visiting yachts may seek refuge in an approved typhoon shelter, of which there are 14 in Hong Kong for small craft, some for less than 50 metres LOA, others for less than 30 metres LOA. Alternatively one can secure to a government B class mooring, for which advance booking is necessary. Yachts too large for the shelters can either find a mooring or a sheltered anchorage, notifying the port authority of their position.

The Marine Guide published by the Marine Department for visiting yachtsmen details very thoroughly the procedures to be followed during a typhoon.

Facilities

There are various anchorages used by visitors, the most popular being the typhoon shelter in Causeway Bay, the small boat harbour in Aberdeen and Hebe Haven. There are several yacht clubs, which usually offer temporary membership to visitors if they are members of an overseas club or are introduced by a local member. Most clubs have some moorings and also repair facilities.

Repair facilities in Hong Kong are extensive, with several boatyards undertaking work on yachts. Hebe Haven Yacht Club has a whole range of services and repair facilities. Emergency repairs can also be carried out at the Royal Hong Kong Yacht Club in Causeway Bay on the north side of Hong Kong Island. This area has many stores, open air markets and restaurants as well as various workshops.

Provisioning in Hong Kong is generally good and there is always a selection of fresh produce. Fuel is widely available. LPG bottles can be filled at Hong Kong Gas Co. Ltd. As Hong Kong is a duty-free port, prices of electrical or electronic goods are mostly very reasonable.

Further Reading

The Marine Guide
Guide to Hong Kong Waters

INDONESIA

The Indonesian archipelago of 13,677 islands stretches from Australia to Asia, the largest island group in the world. The main islands are Java, Sumatra, Irian Jaya (the western part of Papua New Guinea), and Kalimantan (formerly Borneo). Indonesia is a place of tropical forests, neat terraced rice fields and active volcanoes, the most famous being Krakatoa. The culture is rich with traditions and relics from past civilisations as well as modern day arts and crafts.

For many cruising sailors Indonesia is the temptation of forbidden fruit. Access to this fascinating country has been denied to most cruising yachts by the need for a cruising permit and although the formalities are being eased slightly, obtaining the necessary permit is still a lengthy and costly procedure. The number of yachts which manage to obtain this valuable piece of paper is small, although every year some yachts manage to enter Indonesia by the back door by taking part in the annual Darwin to Ambon Race. This event organised by the Darwin Sailing Club has the blessing of the Indonesian authorities and participants in the race are granted a cruising permit.

Whether taking part in this event or being fortunate in having obtained a permit through the approved channels, most yachts cruise the islands from east to west. Such a cruise along the island chain offers a panoramic view, each island different from its neighbour. Just as different are the myriad sailing craft one encounters along the route – single, double and treble hulled, from fragile one-man fishing boats to heavy inter-island schooners laden to the gunwhales with salt, turtles, copra or rice. Much of the inter-island traffic is done under sail and some of these craft cover thousand of miles.

On the more remote islands, rarely visited by foreign yachts, one may be greeted by a crowd of curious people. Elsewhere one can discover the mysterious dragons of Komodo, explore the wild interior of Kalimantan, follow a funeral procession on Bali or visit the ancient ruins of Borobodur.

Benoa Harbour in Bali is the most popular port of call for cruising yachts. Bali is more on the beaten track, but the Balinese have retained a distinctive and rich culture as well as being renowned for their artistic talents.

Benoa Harbour in Bali.

Practical Information

LOCAL TIME:
GMT + 7 in the West Zone (Java, Sumatra, Bali); GMT + 8 in Central Zone (Kalimantan, Sulawesi); GMT + 9 in East Zone (Maluku, Irian Jaya).

CURRENCY: Indonesian rupiah (Rs) of 100 sene.

BUSINESS HOURS
Banks: 0800–1400 Monday to Friday, 0800–1300 Saturday.
Shops: 0800/0900–2000 Monday to Saturday, half day on Sunday; some close 1300–1700.
Government offices: 0800–1500 Monday to Thursday, 0800–1130 Friday, 0800–1400 Saturday (this may vary between islands).
Business: 0800/0900–1600/1700 weekdays, half day Saturday. Sunday is the day of rest, but government offices close at 1130 on Friday.

ELECTRICITY: 220 V, 50 Hz. Some areas 110 V.

PUBLIC HOLIDAYS
Muslim, Christian, Hindu and Buddhist holidays are respected.
1 January: New Year's Day
21 April: Kartini Day
Idul Fitri, end of Ramadan

Good Friday
Ascension Day
Idul Adha, Muslim day of sacrifice
17 August: Independence Day
Muslim New Year
Moulud Nabi, birthday of Mohammed
25 December: Christmas Day
31 December: New Year's Eve
There are many festivals on Bali, which are public holidays, the most important being Nyepi Day in March, which is a day of curfew.

COMMUNICATIONS
International telephone calls, telex and fax from telecommunications offices and hotels.
There are international flights from Jakarta to destinations worldwide. There are also flights from Bali to Europe, Australia, the USA and Singapore. There is an extensive network of internal flights between the islands.

DIPLOMATIC MISSIONS
In Jakarta:
Australia: 15 Jl. M.H. Thamrin. ☎ (21) 323109.
Belgium: 4 Jl. Cicurug. ☎ (21) 348719.
Brunei: Central Plaza, Jl. Jenderal Sudirman Kapling 48. ☎(21) 510576.
Canada: Wisma Metropolitan 1, Jl. Jenderal Sudirman Kav. 29. ☎ (21) 510709.

Denmark: Bina Mulia Bldg, Jl. H.R. Rasuna Said Kav. 10. ☎ (21) 518350.
France: 20 Jl. M.H. Thamrin. ☎ (21) 332807.
Finland: Bina Mulia Bldg, Jl. Rasuna Said Kav. 10. ☎ (21) 516980.
Germany: 1 Jl. M.H.Thamrin. ☎ (21) 323908.
Italy: 45 Jl. Diponegoro. ☎ (21) 348339.
Japan: 24 Jl. M.H.Thamrin. ☎ (21) 324308.
Malaysia: 17 Jl. Imam Bonjol. ☎ (21) 332170.
Netherlands: Jl. H.R. Rasuna Said Kav. S-3. ☎ (21) 511515.
New Zealand: 41 Jl. Diponegoro. ☎ (21) 330552.
Norway: Bina Mulia Bldg, Jl. H.R. Rasuna Said Kav. 10. ☎ (21) 517140.
Papua New Guinea: Panin Bank Centre, Jl. Jenderal Sudirman. ☎ (21) 711218.
Singapore: 23 Jl. Proklamasi. ☎ (21) 348761.
Sweden: 12 Jl. Taman Cut Mutiah. ☎ (21) 333061.
Switzerland: Jl. Rasuna Said Blok X/3/2, Kuningan. ☎ (21) 516061.
Taiwan: Chinese Chamber of Commerce to Jakarta, 4 Jl. Banyumas. ☎ (21) 351212.
United Kingdom: 75 Jl. M.H. Thamrin. ☎ (21) 330904.
United States: 5 Jl. Merdeka Selatan. ☎ (21) 340001.

Country Profile

Some of the Indonesian islands were populated half a million years ago, as proved by the Java man remains discovered in 1890. Gradually people migrated to Indonesia from Asia, and by the first century AD the Indian influence predominated with the growth of the Hindu and Buddhist Empires, which at the height of their power dominated the whole region. Empires based first in Sumatra then in Java followed, the latter surviving until the sixteenth century, marking the start of this island's dominance over the rest of the archipelago. During the fourteenth century the expansion of Islam through Arab traders marked a new era, and only on Bali does the Hindu legacy survive.

Marco Polo was the first European to arrive, landing on Sumatra in 1292, followed by the Portuguese in 1509, in search of the Spice Islands. At the end of the sixteenth century the Dutch arrived and for 300 years controlled the archipelago, which was known as the Dutch East Indies. In the early twentieth century the movement for independence gathered momentum. The Japanese occupation during the Second World War was a stimulus and in 1945 the Republic of Indonesia was declared. War with the Dutch followed until the UN intervened and in 1949 the independent state of Indonesia was recognised. Sukarno, leader of the national movement, became president, although his corrupt rule and attempts to draw closer to China were not popular. An attempted coup in 1965 by the Communist party failed. General Suharto became president in 1968, and the country moved closer to the West.

Oil and rubber are important exports, also palm oil, coffee, tin and tobacco. Indonesia is rich in agricultural and mineral resources. Agriculture predominates, although efforts have been made to develop some industry. Tourism is expanding and is particularly important on Bali.

With 170 million inhabitants, Indonesia is the fifth most populous country in the world. The Indonesians are a Malay race, but there are also Chinese and European minorities, and some aboriginal tribes in Kalimantan and Irian Jaya. Bahasa Indonesia, related to Malay, is the national language. There are 250 local languages and dialects. Often older people speak Dutch, and many speak English. Indonesians are predominantly Muslim, but Christian areas remain from colonial days, and the Balinese are Hindu. Jakarta on Java is the capital.

The climate is hot and humid. July to September is the dry season, December to January the rainiest period. Temperatures range from 24–33°C (75–90°F). The islands are under the influence of the SE monsoon from April to October and the NW monsoon from November to March, although land and sea breezes predominate close to the islands. The islands are not affected by tropical cyclones

Entry Regulations

Ports of entry
Visa-free entry is permitted at the following ports:
Java: Tanjung Priok (Jakarta) 6°06′S 106°52′E, Tanjung Perak (Surabaya) 7°12′S 112°44′E, Tanjung Emas (Semarang) 6°58′S 110°25′E.
Bali: Benoa 8°45′S 115°15′E, Padang Bai 8°31′S 115°35′E
Sulawesi: Bitung 1°26′N 125°11′E, Manado 1°30′N 124°50′E.
Sumatra: Belawan (Medan) 3°48′N 98°43′E, Batu Ampar (Batam) 1°10′N 104°00′E.
South Maluku: Yos Sudarso (Ambon) 3°42′S 128°10′E.
If one has a cruising permit, security clearance and also a visa obtained in advance, it is possible to enter at the first port marked on the cruising permit, even if it is not one of the above.

Although not listed as a visa-free port of entry, yachts on passage to or from Sri Lanka have been able to stop at Sabang, on Pulau Wé (5°53′N, 95°19′E), a small island off the north end of Sumatra.

Procedure on arrival
Fly the Q flag, anchor and wait for customs, immigration and port officials to come to the vessel, during office hours. No one must go ashore or make contact with other vessels until clearance is complete. For clearance outside of working hours, a small charge is made.

In remoter islands, however, the captain may have to go ashore to find and report to the officials.

Customs
Firearms may be left on board if they can be locked and sealed. If not, they will be taken ashore and bonded until the yacht leaves.

Animals must remain on board on most islands. There are severe penalties on Bali for landing animals.

In principle a yacht can stay indefinitely in Indonesia, provided the security clearance is extended.

Immigration
Passports must be valid for more than six months after date of entry.

Visas are not required for nationals of Australia, Austria, Belgium, Brunei, Canada, Denmark, Finland, France, Germany, Greece, Iceland, Ireland, Italy, Japan, Liechtenstein, Luxembourg, Malaysia, Malta, the Netherlands, New Zealand, Norway, Philippines, Singapore, South Korea, Spain, Sweden, Switzerland, Taiwan, Thailand, the United Kingdom or the United States. All other nationalities require a visa, which must be obtained in advance.

Those not requiring visas are given a tourist pass on arrival, which is valid for a maximum of two months, not extendable, and can only be issued at certain ports of entry (see above list). If entry is made elsewhere a visa is required for all nationalities. It is, however, strongly recommended that all those arriving on yachts obtain a visitor's visa in advance from an Indonesian embassy or consulate.

Visas obtained in advance are valid for one month, extendable for up to six months. The extensions can cost up to US$75 for six months.

One should carry a large quantity of photocopies of documents, especially the cruising permit and yacht registration document, enough to be given to officials at all ports of call.

Crew wishing to join a boat or to leave Indonesia by air may find that immigration officials may want them to leave by the same means that they arrived. Their intentions should be made clear on the visa application and again on entry into the country.

Cruising permit
Yachts without a cruising permit may stop in Indonesia, for 48 hours only, in a serious emergency and only at one of the ports of entry specified above. This may be extended in case of a genuine emergency.

Otherwise, all yachts must obtain a cruising permit and security clearance in advance. The formalities for this must be done through an approved agent. Agents should be chosen with care as yachts have sometimes not been dealt with fairly. The Bali International Yacht Club can help to arrange permits and have experience in this matter. They are also on the spot in Bali to deal with any complications. They can be contacted at PO Box 155, Denpasar 80001, Bali. Fax. (361) 88391. The following details and items are required and should be sent with an application:

1. Details of the yacht (including photocopies of ship's papers).
2. The planned itinerary including last port of call before entering Indonesia, ports of call and approximate dates in Indonesia and destination after leaving Indonesia. It is wise to put down all the islands on the intended route as it is very difficult to make any changes later. Restricted areas are East Timor and Irian Jaya. Modifications may be made to the itinerary by the authorities in Jakarta.
3. Copies of the first few pages of all the crew's passports, which must be valid for six months at the time of applying for a visa.
4. A copy of a letter of acknowledgement, from the respective embassy in Jakarta or place where the cruising permit is being initiated, as an indication that they are aware that one of their citizens is sailing with his or her yacht in Indonesian waters. The wording of the letter should be approximately the following and addressed to:
    i) Department of Foreign Affairs
    ii) Department of Tourism
    iii) Department of Defence and Security
    iv) Department of Sea Communications

To Whom It May Concern

The .... Embassy, Jakarta, certifies that .... holder of .... passport number 000000 is a citizen of .... and his/her passport is valid for travel to that country. Mr/Ms .... states he/she is the captain of his/her yacht .... registered number 000000 and he/she is requesting a sailing permit to enter Indonesian waters.

signed (Consul)

If all these papers are sent to the Bali Yacht Club, they will then write back and ask for a transfer of money of US$250 for processing the cruising permit.

One can also obtain a cruising permit directly through the Indonesian Yachting Sports Union PORLASI (Persatuan Olah Raga Layar Seluruh Indonesia), Sutimah Building, Jl. Kemang Raya 2, Jakarta 12730. ☎ (21) 799-3764. Fax (21) 799-3530. At the time of writing, PORLASI is the officially recognised body for arranging permits, which involves dealing with several government departments in Jakarta. If obtaining the permit through PORLASI, the same details should be sent as mentioned above. For yachts intending to call in Bali, it is best to arrange the cruising permit through the Bali International Yacht Club.

The cruising permit (or Clearance Approval) for Indonesian waters is valid for three months from the date of entry specified. It is important to specify this date of arrival in Indonesian waters fairly accurately on one's application, as the three months begins from this date, not the date the yacht actually arrives. If wishing to stay longer, one must have visas obtained in advance. Once in Indonesia, it may be possible to obtain a three-month extension to the original permit, by applying for a new clearance permit before arrival. Once all details have been sent, it is difficult to modify them, whether dates, itinerary or ports. For any substantial changes the initial fee may be charged again.

Health
Malaria prophylaxis is recommended.

Fees
Overtime is charged outside of working hours. There is a harbour departure charge in Bali of 5000 Rs, which is not included in the cost of the cruising permit.

Facilities

With only a handful of cruising boats calling at Indonesian ports and hardly any locally owned yachts at all, it is not surprising that yachting facilities are virtually non-existent. For any kind of repair in the islands one has to rely on workshops that repair cars or trucks. Where there are larger diesel powered fishing boats, there might be a boatyard capable of carrying out simple repairs. The situation is slightly better in Bali, where the yacht club in Benoa Harbour can advise on what is available locally. The yacht club is not a club with members but is run as a commercial enterprise, providing a bar, restaurant and showers for visitors as well as being able to arrange the cruising permit.

Spare parts and marine supplies are also virtually non-existent and essential spares have to be ordered from Australia, another area in which one can use the services of the Bali Yacht Club. They can arrange the duty-free importation of items needed by yachts in transit. The only spares available locally are those for some diesel engines, particularly if they are also used in trucks or heavy plant. Outboard engines are also becoming more popular and some makes are now represented in the more developed centres.

Provisioning in most islands is fairly basic, although there is a good supply of locally grown fruit and vegetables everywhere. Water is available, but should be treated. Fuel is also widely available and relatively cheap as Indonesia is an oil-producing country. In some places the fuel will be delivered in drums and as it tends to be either dirty, or deliberately laced with water, filtering it properly is essential.

Further Reading

Indonesian Handbook
Indonesia – a travel survival kit

JAPAN

Japan is made up of four main islands that stretch about 1600 miles in a NE to SW direction off the Chinese mainland. Honshu is the largest, most heavily populated and industrialised; Hokkaido in the north is forested and mountainous; Kyushu and Shikoku to the south are smaller. There are also some 3000 smaller islands. Most of Japan is mountainous and volcanic, with frequent earthquakes. Mount Fujiyama, an almost perfectly symmetrical cone, is the highest point at 12,400 ft (3776 m).

Being distant from the popular cruising routes, not many cruising yachts visit Japan, but those who do find the Japanese very welcoming, often going out of their way to help visiting sailors. Until not so long ago even local yachts were a rarity as the Japanese have no tradition as a sailing nation. However, recently the government has decided to actively develop the yachting industry, many more marinas are to be built, various international regattas are being organised and Japan is also preparing a challenge for the America's Cup. However, the one aspect that even the ingenious Japanese cannot do much about is their weather, which does not encourage cruising, for a cruise often turns into a battle against wind and current.

Fortunately this one major disadvantage is made up for by the many attractions that Japan offers the visiting sailor. One major attraction is the Inland Sea (Seto Naikai), a large body of water, connected by three passes to the surrounding ocean, which allows a yacht access into the very heart of the country. The place abounds with pretty anchorages or small fishing harbours, but there are also many marinas as well as yacht clubs, which usually offer hospitality to visitors. Those in the smaller places have only basic facilities, while in the larger towns clubs are on a par with the best yacht clubs in Europe or America.

Country Profile

The earliest inhabitants of these islands probably came from Korea and China, although links with South East Asia are also a possibility. By the fourth century AD the country was already developing into a united state and a distinctive national culture emerged with Chinese, Korean and Buddhist influences. The latter mixed with Shinto became the state religion. In the eighth century in the capital Kyoto both arts and industry flourished, although the provinces remained poor and were infested with bandits, which prompted the rise of the class of 'samurai' warriors. At the end of the twelfth century civil wars between leading clans disrupted the country and a system of military governments was created led by the 'shogun' chiefs with a puppet emperor. This form of government lasted into the nineteenth century. A period followed which rejected all foreign influences and contact with the outside world until 1853 when the American Commodore Perry's visit began the opening up of Japan. At the end of the nineteenth and in the early twentieth century, a new spirit arose, introducing industry and modernity into the country. An expansionist policy abroad led to wars with Russia and China, military rule in the 1930s and the Pacific War from 1941. The crushing defeat in 1945 and nuclear bombing of some cities led to a rejection of the traditional warlike spirit. Today Japan is one of the world leaders in economic affairs.

The economy has a high sustained rate of growth. Expanding industries are petrochemicals, electronics, optics and motor vehicles. However, Japan has few natural resources and all raw materials must be imported. External markets are essential to the economy.

The population numbers 123 million. The Japanese are descended from a mixture of peoples from the East Asian region, although some people in the north are possibly indigenous. Tokyo, Osaka and Yokohama are the main cities. Tokyo, the capital, is one of the world's most populous cities. Japanese is the main language and English is the second language spoken. Shintoism, which is native to Japan and a development of early shamanism and animism, is the main religion. Buddhism is also widespread and many Japanese observe the ceremonies of both religions. There is a small percentage of Christians.

The north is cold, while the south is in the monsoon belt. Most of the country is in a temperate four seasonal zone. Summer sees SE winds and a rainy season in June and July. Typhoons are most frequent mid-July to October, but can occur at any time; five to ten days warning are usually given.

Practical Information

LOCAL TIME: GMT + 9

BUOYAGE: IALA B

CURRENCY: Yen ¥ (JYE)

BUSINESS HOURS
Banks: 0900–1500 Monday to Friday,
0900–1200 Saturday.
Government offices: 1000–1700 Monday
to Friday, 1000–1200 Saturday.
Business: 0900–1700 Monday to Friday,
0900–1200 Saturday.
Shops: 1000–1800 Monday to Friday,
0900–1200 Saturday.

ELECTRICITY: 100 V, 50 Hz (east), 60 Hz
(west), the dividing line being
approximately half way between Tokyo
and Nagoya.

PUBLIC HOLIDAYS
Japan uses the western calendar, but
some official publications such as tide
tables use the Showa calendar. This has
the same days, but the Showa year is 25
years behind the western year. 1990
would be 1965 in the Showa calendar.
1–3 January: New Year
15 January: Coming of Age
11 February: National Foundation

20/21 March: Vernal Equinox
19 April: Greenery Day
3 May: Constitution Day
4/5 May: Children's Day
15 September: Respect for the Aged
23/24 September: Autumnal Equinox
10 October: Physical Education Day
3 November: Culture Day
23/24 November: Labour Day
23 December: Emperor's birthday
When a national holiday falls on a
Sunday, the following Monday is a
holiday.
During Golden Week (April 29–May 5)
and Obon festival (late July to the third
week in August) most people are on
holiday.

COMMUNICATIONS
Telephone directories in English are
available in some places.
International calls can be made from
hotels or post offices. Only a few public
phone booths allow direct international
dialling.
Blue phone booths are for emergencies,
operator and information.
Emergency: dial 110 police (Koban), 119
fire/ambulance (push the red button
first).
Telex and telegrams can be sent from
KDD (Kokusai Denshin Denwa Co. Ltd).
Post offices for stamps and telegrams:

open 0900–1600 Monday to Friday.
Travel Phone: for English language
assistance and travel information: Tokyo
(3) 502-1461, Kyoto (75) 371-5649,
Eastern region 0120-222800, Western
region 0120-4448000.
There are international flights from all
Japan's main cities, particularly Tokyo,
Nagoya, Okinawa and Osaka, which
have regular flights to Europe, America
and Asia. There is also a good network
of internal flights.

MEDICAL
Medical facilities are of a high standard
and there are many English-speaking
staff.

DIPLOMATIC MISSIONS
In Tokyo:
Australia: 1-12 Shiba Koen, 1-Chome,
105. ☎ (3) 435-0971.
Canada: 3-38 Asasaka, 7-Chome,
Minato-ku, 107. ☎ (3) 408-2101.
New Zealand: 20-40 Kamiyama-cho,
Shibuya-ku, 150. ☎ (3) 467-2271.
Taiwan: Association of East Asian
Relations, 8-7 Higashi-Azabu, 1-Chome,
Minato-ku, 106. ☎ (3) 583-2171.
United Kingdom: 1 Ichiban-cho,
Chiyoda-ku, 102. ☎ (3) 265-5511.
United States: 10-1 Akasaka 1-Chome,
Minato-ku, 107. ☎ (3) 583-7141.

Entry Regulations

Ports of entry
Aioi 34°46′N 134°28′E, Fukuyama 34°26′N
133°27′E, Kobe 34°40′N 135°13′E, Nagasaki
32°43′N 129°50′E, Nagoya 35°03′N 136°51′E, Naha
(Okinawa Island) 26°13′N 127°40′E, Osaka 34°39′N
135°24′E, Shimonoseki 33°56′N 130°56′E, Tokyo
35°41′N 139°44′E, Yokohama 35°27′N 139°40′E.

Procedure on arrival
The formalities are time-consuming as there are lots of
forms to fill in, but this is mostly routine and officials
are always very friendly and courteous. On entry,
inspections will be carried out by quarantine, customs
and immigration, and maybe also the Maritime Safety
Agency (coastguard). A de-ratting certificate is sometimes required, but this seems to depend on the
discretion of the local quarantine officer. The customs,

immigration and quarantine offices are normally in the
same building in the main harbour – sometimes one
can tie up to their jetty to complete the formalities.
They will advise on the best berth or anchorage.
Sometimes they will come to the yacht, if not the
captain should go to their offices.

Clearance with customs and immigration must be
carried out at every port, although this is routine and a
question of filling out a lot of forms. The last port may
telephone ahead to the next port to notify them of a
yacht's arrival. Alternatively the number can be
obtained from the last customs office and one can
telephone oneself on arrival. If arriving at a weekend
officials may decide only to come on Monday, but it is
possible to go ashore. If a place does not have a
customs office, one should check in and out at the local
police station (Koban); in these places the Maritime
Safety Agency may check the yacht themselves. The
Maritime Safety Agency office can often be a useful
source of local information.

Customs

Firearms must be declared on arrival and the penalty for non-declaration is imprisonment.

If wishing to import animals, one should have all the necessary certificates and undergo quarantine inspection. Dogs require a rabies inoculation certificate and will be quarantined. Otherwise animals must be confined on board.

Immigration

In principle, all visitors must obtain visas before arriving in Japan, but for many nationalities on a visit solely for tourist purposes, the visa requirement is waived, and one is accorded the 4-1-4 status. Should one wish to enter into any other sort of activity, the regulations become very much more complicated.

No visa is required for stays of not more than six months for tourists from Austria, Germany, Ireland, Liechtenstein, Mexico, Switzerland and the United Kingdom (except for UK colonial territories).

No visa is required if staying up to three months for nationals of Argentina, Bahamas, Barbados, Bangladesh, Belgium, Canada, Chile, Colombia, Costa Rica, Cyprus, Dominica, Dominican Republic, Denmark, El Salvador, Finland, France, Greece, Guatemala, Honduras, Iceland, Iran, Israel, Italy, Lesotho, Luxembourg, Malaysia, Malta, Mauritius, the Netherlands, New Zealand, Norway, Pakistan, Peru, Portugal (except for present or former Portuguese colonial territories), San Marino, Singapore, Spain, Suriname, Sweden, Tunisia, Turkey, Uruguay, the USA and Yugoslavia.

All other nationalities must obtain a visa in advance. For citizens of a country without a visa-waiving agreement (including Australia and South Africa) on entry into Japan usually 60 days is granted, normally extendable for two further 60-day periods, after which one must leave Japan, and re-enter having obtained another visa elsewhere.

It is possible to obtain a multiple entry visa.

One may be able to leave the boat in Japan and re-enter for another period.

Fees

There are no charges for clearance or overtime.

Cruising permit

To cruise the Inland Sea (Seto Naikai) a cruising permit must be obtained from the Department of Transportation in Hiroshima. One must present a planned itinerary, first checking which ports are off limits.

The local tourist office can provide a map of the area which shows all the attractions.

Restrictions

A number of ports are closed to yachts, such as Urakawa (in the SE of Hokkaido), and these can only be entered in an emergency.

VHF Channel 16 is primarily a shipping communications channel and should only be used in an emergency. Japanese yachts are not allowed to use it.

Navigation

Day-sailing is recommended along the Japanese coastlines due to the very high concentration of shipping and the innumerable fishing boats, nets and aquaculture projects. Along the Hokkaido coast a hazard are the salmon nets, up to 1000 metres long and lying very close to the surface.

Currents can be very strong in the Inland Sea, especially at the entrances, where they may reach 6–8 knots.

Facilities

Most things are available in Japan, but are extremely expensive in comparison to Europe or America. Chandleries are well-stocked, but expensive. Ironically, even Japanese electronic equipment costs more in Japan than abroad, particularly compared to the USA. Locally produced sails and nautical charts also cost much more than their equivalent elsewhere and the same applies to provisions, so it is best to arrive with all necessary supplies and a well-stocked boat. Local fresh produce is more reasonable. Fuel, water and LPG are available everywhere.

Repair facilities are generally good and there are boatyards in most ports. Prices for haul-outs vary greatly, but appear to be more reasonable away from the large cities.

Marinas in the Inland Sea are generally expensive, but some of them offer free berthing to foreign visitors for a few days. There are no charges for tying up to a dock in a commercial or fishing harbour. There are many yacht clubs, most of whom give free membership to visiting foreign sailors. It is best to approach them for advice if in need of a repair job or if one cannot find something such as fuel or gas. Naha Harbour in Okinawa has an American Seaman's Club, near the small boat harbour, which is very helpful. They offer temporary membership and can help find workshops for repairs.

Further Reading

Japan Handbook

The Japan Hydrographic Department publishes harbour guide books for all of Japan, including the small harbours. Although written in Japanese, these are basically a collection of very detailed charts. They are essential for cruising in Japan, and can be ordered from the department's Service Centre, No. 3-1 5-Chome Chuo-ku, Tokyo 104.

Also recommended if sailing the Inland Sea is the Tide Table published by the Maritime Safety Agency (Publ. No. 781, Vol. I).

MACAO

On the south-eastern coast of China, Macao consists of the peninsula on which the city of Macao is built, and the islands of Taipa and Coloane in the Pearl River delta. Macao is under Portuguese administration, but enjoys considerable internal autonomy. The governor is appointed by Portugal, but members of the legislative assembly are locally elected. Sometimes known as the Las Vegas of the East, Macao has six casinos, a Grand Prix in November as well as regular greyhound racing. These are probably also the attractions that bring most yachts to Macao, the majority of whom sail over from neighbouring Hong Kong. One can also use Macao as a base for visiting China overland, obtaining visas from the China Travel Service.

Country Profile

Before the Portuguese arrived in the sixteenth century, there was only a Chinese village and when the Portuguese sailors asked the name, the locals replied 'A-Ma-Gao', Bay of A-Ma, who was a Chinese goddess popular with seafarers and fishermen. A-Ma-Gao became corrupted into the name Macao. Macao prospered as China and Japan began trading with the European powers. This Portuguese territory also became a base for the introduction of Christianity into China and Japan. The Dutch tried to invade Macao several times in the seventeenth century without success. This privileged trading position ended with the establishment of Hong Kong by the British in the mid-nineteenth century, only 40 miles north-east of Macao and with a better deepwater port. Nevertheless Macao does retain a trading role today.

Tourism is an important source of revenue, especially due to the government-owned casinos, as gambling is forbidden in Hong Kong. The textile industry and a growing financial sector are other contributors to the economy.

The population of around 435,300 are mostly Chinese with about 3 per cent Portuguese and other Europeans. Portuguese and Cantonese are the official languages, but English is widely spoken. The main religions are Buddhism, Catholicism and Protestantism.

Temperatures average 14°C (57°F) in January and 28°C (82°F) in July and there is high humidity. The best period is the autumn, October to December. May to September is hot and humid, with occasional typhoons.

Entry Regulations

Port of entry
Macao 22°12′N 113°33′E.

Procedure on arrival
Macao Radio can be contacted on VHF Channel 16 between 0700–0300. One should enter the inner harbour which has a depth of approximately 9 feet. The outer harbour is used mainly for ferries and hydrofoils going to Hong Kong. The harbour office will give berthing instructions. If the yacht is not

Practical Information

LOCAL TIME: GMT + 8

BUOYAGE: IALA A

CURRENCY: Pataca of 100 avos. Hong Kong $ accepted at par value.

BUSINESS HOURS
Banks: 0930–1630 Monday to Friday, 0930–1300 Saturday.

ELECTRICITY: 110/220 V, 50 Hz

PUBLIC HOLIDAYS
1 January: New Year's Day
25 April: Anniversary of Portuguese Revolution
1 May: Labour Day
10 June: Camoes Day and Portuguese Communities Day
24 June: Feast of St John the Baptist (Patron Saint)
1 October: Chinese National Day

5 October: Republic Day
1 December: Restoration of Independence
8 December: Immaculate Conception
24, 25 December: Christmas

COMMUNICATIONS
International calls can be made from the post office, Leal Senado Square.
There are regular flights to Europe and neighbouring Asian countries. There is a hydrofoil service to Hong Kong.

visited by officials within 24 hours, the captain should go to the harbour master's office with the ship's papers.

On departure, the harbour master should be notified not later than six hours before departure.

Customs
Animals and firearms should be declared to customs.

Immigration
Visas are not required for up to a 90-day stay for the nationals of EC countries (except Luxembourg and Ireland who must get tourist visas, which can be obtained on arrival), Australia, Canada, Japan, Malaysia, New Zealand, Norway, Philippines, Sweden, Thailand and the USA.

Nationals of Brazil do not require a visa if staying less than six months. Hong Kong residents do not require visas. Commonwealth nationals not mentioned above do not need visas for up to 20 days. Other nationalities can only stay up to three days without a visa.

For any stays longer than those specified above, a visa is required. Nationals of countries which do not maintain diplomatic relations with Portugal must obtain a visa before arrival from a Portuguese embassy or consulate.

Facilities

Repair facilities are available at a government workshop in the port area, which also has a slipway. However, because of the proximity of Hong Kong, it is preferable to use the better facilities available there. Provisioning is good, although the selection is not as wide as in Hong Kong.

MALAYSIA

The Federation of Malaysia consists of thirteen states, eleven stretched out on the long peninsula between Thailand and Singapore plus the states of Sabah and Sarawak on the north west coast of Kalimantan. Malaysia is a constitutional monarchy, in which the throne is occupied in rotation by the various Sultans of the principal states. It is a country of tropical rainforests and temperate highlands, which is fast modernising yet retains many traditional ways.

The west coast attracts most cruising yachts and there is plenty to see, from the attractive old city of Malacca and the fishing port of Lumut to the islands of Penang and Langkawi. The latter are close to the border with Thailand and possess the finest scenery anywhere in Malaysian waters. The east coast is less visited as it is not on a cruising route and its harbours are better protected during the SW monsoon, when few cruising yachts linger in SE Asia. The best weather is during the NE monsoon when the west coast provides an excellent lee and most yachts cruise up the coast from Singapore to Thailand.

Sabah and Sarawak along the northern coast of Kalimantan are visited by yachts en route to or from the Philippines and Hong Kong. Although slightly out of the way, a cruise to these two small states provides a unique opportunity to visit part of the interior of Kalimantan, such as a river trip into the jungle or a climb up Mount Kinabalu, which is the highest peak south of the Himalayas.

Country Profile

From ancient times the Malay peninsula has played a role in the trade routes from central Asia to the Pacific, and the influences of Indian, Chinese, Thai, Arab and European traders may be seen everywhere. The first civilisation in Malaysia was around AD 400. From the eighth to the fourteenth centuries the peninsular kingdoms were dominated by neighbouring empires. In 1511 the Portuguese conquered Malacca, which they held until 1641 when their Dutch rivals seized it. By a treaty in 1824 the British gained possession of the city, and linking up with Penang and Singapore, gradually the entire peninsula came under British rule. The nineteenth century saw the country open up, with railways and roads built to develop the tin, rubber and timber industries. Labourers were brought in from India and China.

In the 1930s an independence movement developed, which was halted by the Japanese occupation during the Second World War, but fulfilled in 1957 when the Malay states gained independence. In 1963 Malaysia came into being as the federation of the peninsular states, Sabah, Sarawak and Singapore, the latter leaving the Federation in 1965.

Malaysia is a leading exporter of rubber, tin, timber, palm oil and pepper. Agriculture remains an important sector of the economy, as is fishing. The country has mineral reserves, oil and natural gas deposits.

The 16.5 million inhabitants are Malay, Chinese and Indian, plus the indigenous peoples of Sabah and Sarawak. Bahasa Malaysia (Malay) is the official language, but English is widely used. Also spoken are the various Chinese languages, Tamil and Arabic. Islam is the religion of the Malay majority. Buddhism, Hinduism, Christianity and Taoism are also practised.

Practical Information

LOCAL TIME: GMT + 8

BUOYAGE: IALA A

CURRENCY: Malaysian dollar or ringgit (RGT) divided into 100 cents or sen.

BUSINESS HOURS
Shops: 0930–1900 Monday to Friday.
Supermarkets: 1000–2200 Monday to Friday.
(Some Muslim businesses close on Friday.)
Banks: 1000–1500 Monday to Friday, 0930–1130 Saturday (in some regions these close on Fridays).
Government offices: 0800–1245, 1400–1615 Monday to Thursday, 0800–1215, 1445–1615 Friday, 0800–1245 Saturday.

ELECTRICITY: 220 V, 50 Hz

PUBLIC HOLIDAYS
1 January: New Year's Day
1 February: Kuala Lumpur City Day
Chinese New Year
Easter Monday
Wesak Day
1 May: Labour Day
Hari Raya Puasa
June: King's Birthday
31 August: National Day
Moulud, Prophet Mohammed's Birthday
Divali, Hindu Festival of Lights
Hari Raya Haji
25 December: Christmas Day

COMMUNICATIONS
Telephone calls from public booths and post offices.
Telegrams and telexes may be sent from main telegraph offices.
Main post office in Kuala Lumpur: Kompleks Dayabumi.

There are regular flights from Kuala Lumpur airport to Europe, America, Australia and the Far East, also to Sabah and Sarawak.
There are flights from Penang to Bangkok, Phuket, Singapore and Hong Kong.

DIPLOMATIC MISSIONS
In Kuala Lumpur:
Australia: 6 Jalan Yap Kwan Seng. ☎ (3) 242-3122.
Canada: Plaza MBF, 172 Jalan Ampang. ☎ (3) 261-2000.
New Zealand: 193 Jalan Tun Rasak. ☎ (3) 248-6422.
Taiwan: Far East Trading & Tourism Centre, SDN.BHD. Lot 202, Wisma Equity 150, Jalan Ampang. ☎ (3) 243-5337.
United Kingdom: Wisma Damansara, Jalan Semantan. ☎ (3) 254133/2487122.
United States: 376 Jalan Tun Razak. ☎ (3) 489011.

Kuala Lumpur is the capital in the west of the Malay peninsula with nearby Port Kelang on the coast serving it.

On the coast the temperatures do not rise too high in this tropical climate, averaging 21–32°C (70–90°F). November to February is the rainy season when sudden downpours are frequent, especially on the west coast. The NE monsoon is from November to March, but on the west Malaysian coast local land breezes have a major effect on sailing conditions.

Entry Regulations

Ports of entry
Malay Peninsula: Kuala Perlis 6°24′N 100°07′E, Teluk Ewa 6°26′N 99°46′E, Kuah 6°19′N 99°51′E, Kuala Kedah 6°07′N 100°17′E, Penang 5°25′N 100°20′E, Lumut 4°16′N 100°39′E, Telek Intan 4°01′N 101°01′E, Port Kelang 3°00′N 101°24′E, Port Dickson 2°31′N 101°47′E, Melaka/Malacca 2°15′N 102°35′E, Muar 2°02′N 102°34′E, Johore Bahru 1°28′N 103°50′E, Pasir Gudang/Johore Port 1°26′N 103°54′E, Pulau Langkawi 6°18′N 99°50′E, Mersing 2°26′N 103°51′E, Kuantan 3°58′N 103°26′E, Kemaman/Tanjong Berhala 4°15′N 103°28′E, Kerteh 4°28′N 103°24′E, Kuala Trengganu 5°20′N 103°09′E, Tumpat 6°13′N 102°11′E.
Sarawak: Kuching 1°34′N 110°24′E, Sibu 2°17′N 111°49′E, Bintulu 3°10′N 113°02′E, Miri 4°23′N 113°59′E.
Sabah: Labuan 5°16′N 115°09′E, Kota Kinabalu 6°00′N 116°04′E, Lahad Datu 5°02′N 118°20′E, Sandakan 5°50′N 188°08′E, Tawau 4°15′N 117°53′E.

Procedure on arrival
Yachts are only allowed to enter at one of the official ports of entry; preferably giving 24 hours notice.

One must clear in with the Marine Department, also called harbour master's department (arrival report and ship's papers), immigration (crew list and passports), customs (list of ship's stores and last port clearance) and health (crew list, animals and health certificates). The health department may also require a de-ratting certificate or a de-ratting exemption certificate.

Procedure on departure
Yachts must clear in and out of each port visited. When clearing out, all the above offices must be visited and a port clearance must be obtained from customs. Yachts are only allowed to leave from official ports of entry, but if one wants to sail on to a place, which does not have facilities for clearance, permission may be obtained when the port clearance is requested.

Customs
The Malaysian authorities make it very clear that

trafficking in illegal drugs carries the death penalty, and that this applies also to foreign nationals. This death penalty has been carried out.

Firearms must be declared and then sealed by the customs officer. A permit for firearms is required.

Animals will not be allowed ashore unless cleared by the health department. An import permit must be obtained from the Ministry of Agriculture, Veterinary Services Dept.

Immigration

All visitors must have a passport valid six months beyond the planned stay in Malaysia.

Visas are not required for Commonwealth citizens (except India), British Protected persons whose return to their country of origin is assured, nationals of Ireland, Switzerland, the Netherlands, San Marino, Liechtenstein and Pakistan.

No visa is required for a stay of less than three months for nationals of Austria, Belgium, Denmark, Finland, France, Germany, Iceland, Japan, South Korea, Luxembourg, Norway, Sweden, Tunisia, Italy and the USA.

No visa is required for a stay of less than one month for ASEAN countries.

All other nationalities are allowed a 14-day stay in transit without a visa, except nationals of Albania, Bulgaria, China, Cuba, Czechoslovakia, Hungary, India, Israel, Kampuchea, Laos, North Korea, Poland, Romania, the USSR, South Africa, Taiwan, Vietnam and Yugoslavia, who must obtain a visa in advance. These transit stays with no visa are allowed only if the person is in possession of a visa for the next country.

All other nationalities or those planning to stay longer than the specified time must obtain visas in advance.

Citizens of Israel and South Africa may not be allowed entry.

A visitor's pass is issued on arrival at the port of entry. Its period of validity is at the discretion of the local immigration officer. Extensions are difficult to obtain. In principle, yachts may remain indefinitely, but this depends on getting extensions of the visitor's pass. All visitors, whether with or without visas, must possess adequate funds for their stay.

Sabah and Sarawak: People who have entered at one of the ports on the Malay peninsula must obtain new visitor's passes to visit Sabah and Sarawak.

Fees

Overtime fees are charged for clearance after working hours, at weekends and on public holidays. Penang has a 24-hour clearance service, but overtime is payable 1800–0700. Light dues are payable at 20 cents per NRT. Harbour fees are payable according to tonnage and length.

Restrictions

The Security area Pulau Song Song and firing ranges as notified in Notices to Mariners are prohibited areas.

Facilities

The best facilities are in the Port Kelang area, where the Port Kelang Yacht Club may be used by visiting yachts and will normally advise where to find the necessary repair facilities. There is a slipway in Port Kelang and a boatyard working on yachts. There are several small boatyards, often with their own slips, on both coasts of the peninsula but as they are used to working on local craft, standards are not high. Simple repair facilities are also available at Malacca, Lumut and Penang. Engine and electrical repair can be undertaken in most centres. Marine supplies are in short supply even in Port Kelang and essential spares may have to be flown in.

A limited selection of provisions is available in all ports and fresh produce is available everywhere. Diesel fuel is widely available although it is normally delivered by drum.

As facilities in Malaysia are generally poorer than those in Singapore, yachts coming from that direction should try and have all work done beforehand.

Limited repair facilities are available in Kuching, the river capital of Sarawak, at the Industrial and Scientific Company, who also have a supply of local charts.

Further Reading

Malaysia, Singapore and Brunei – a travel survival kit

PHILIPPINES

The Philippines are an archipelago of over 7000 islands lying between the Pacific Ocean and the South China Sea. They are divided into three regions: Luzon to the north, the Visayas in the centre, and Mindanao in the south. The islands are mountainous and volcanic with fertile plains and tropical rainforests.

The Philippines have been a popular cruising destination for many years. Day-sailing through the archipelago is undoubtedly the best way to visit this vast area and one can find a good anchorage every night. This also avoids the danger of running into one of the many unlit fishing boats, as well as their nets or traps.

Practical Information

LOCAL TIME: GMT + 8

BUOYAGE: IALA B

CURRENCY: Philippine peso (PHP) of 100 centavos

BUSINESS HOURS
Banks: 0900–1600 Monday to Friday.
Government offices: 0800–1200, 1300–1700 Monday to Friday, some half days on Saturday.
Shops: 1000–2000 Monday to Friday.

ELECTRICITY: 220 V, 60 Hz, except Baguio 110 V.

PUBLIC HOLIDAYS
1 January: New Year's Day
25 February: People Power Anniversary Day

Easter Week (Holy Thursday, Good Friday)
1 May: Labour Day
6 May: Araw ng Kagitingan (Heroes Day)
12 June: Independence Day
1 November: All Saints' Day
30 November: Bonifacio Day
25 December: Christmas Day
30 December: Dr José Rizal Day
31 December: New Year's Eve

COMMUNICATIONS
Public telephones for international calls can be found in main centres.
Tourist Information Hotline: 24-hour assistance for emergencies and language problems 50-16-60 or 50-17-28.
Civil Defence Operation Centre: extreme emergencies such as typhoons, 77-49-71, 77-49-72.
There are flights from Manila to worldwide destinations. There is also a network of internal flights.

DIPLOMATIC MISSIONS
In Manila:
Australia: Bank of the Philippine Islands Building, Ayala Avenue, Corner Paseo de Roxas, Makati. ☎ (2) 817-7911.
Canada: Allied Bank Centre, 6754 Ayala Avenue, Makati. ☎ (2) 815-9536.
Indonesia: Salcedo St, Lagaspi Village 185/187. ☎ (2) 855061.
New Zealand: Gammon Center, 126 Alfaro St, Salcedo Village, Makati. ☎ (2) 818-0916.
Taiwan: Pacific Economic and Cultural Center, BF Homes Condominium Bldg, Advana St, Intramuros. ☎ (2) 472261.
United Kingdom: Electra House, 115–117 Esteban Street, Legaspi Village, Makati. ☎ (2) 853-002.
United States: 1201 Roxas Boulevard. ☎ (2) 521-7116.

Cebu and the surrounding islands have some of the most attractive anchorages and places such as Romblon, Puerto Galera and the South Gigantic Islands should not be missed.

People are extremely friendly everywhere and in spite of persistent rumours about the danger of pirates in the south of Mindanao and the Sulu Sea, no cases involving yachts have been reported for a long time, although this could well be because yachts avoid these areas. However, the uncertain political situation in some parts of the country affects security generally and yachts should try and avoid any troubled areas. Another problem that affects sailors to a greater or lesser degree is the level of corruption among local officials. Although the government is trying to stamp out corruption and also to standardise the entry and exit charges applied to yachts, the situation is confused. On the positive side, however, the Philippines have a lot to offer the cruising sailor and in spite of such inherent difficulties, it remains a country well worth visiting.

Country Profile

The islands were always a commercial centre for Chinese, Arab and Indian traders, who regularly visited them over the centuries. The indigenous population came originally from the Asian mainland and developed a distinctive culture and system of government. Ferdinand Magellan's arrival on the island of Cebu in 1521 marked the first European contact of the modern era. It was here that he lost his life at the hands of Lapulapu, a local chief. The islands were named after King Philip II of Spain, and soon afterwards the Spaniards asserted their rule, which continued until 1898. The Spanish spread Christianity in the Luzon and Visayan regions, but had less impact in Mindanao, which still shows its Islamic heritage. Manila became an important centre for the trade in silk and spices between China, the East Indies and Spanish America.

At the end of the nineteenth century, the writer Dr José Rizal came to the fore to lead a national movement. His execution by the Spanish and Spain's defeat in the war with the United States provoked a revolution, but independence was brief and the United States ruled the islands until the Second World War. Due to their strategic importance the islands saw heavy fighting during the Pacific War. Peace and the end of Japanese occupation led to independence in 1946. Democracy was shortlived and ended with President Marcos' imposition of martial law in 1972 and a personal dictatorship. His downfall came rapidly in the 1986 revolution, when Corazon Aquino, widow of Marcos' main opponent who had been assassinated in 1983, took over as President. A new constitution has been introduced, although the country is still troubled as democracy is only slowly being established.

The economy is agricultural, producing rice, maize, sugar, copra, tobacco and coffee. Fishing is also important. Rich natural mineral resources include gold, silver, oil and iron. Light industries are also being developed and tourism encouraged.

Most of the 58 million Filipinos are of Malay origin, with some inhabitants of Chinese, Spanish, Indian and American origins. Filipino or Tagalog is the national language. There are 111 dialects and 87 languages spoken in total. English and Spanish are also widely used. The Philippine islands are the only Christian nation in Asia, 80 per cent of the population being Roman Catholic, a legacy from their Spanish past, while the rest are Protestant, Muslim or Buddhist. Manila is the capital on the island of Luzon and metropolitan Manila is made up of four cities.

The Philippines have a tropical climate. The rainy, SW monsoon season is from May to October, the dry season November to April. The average temperature is 27°C (81°F) and humidity is high. The Philippines have a high incidence of typhoons, which are most frequent between June and October. The best season for cruising is from early January to mid-May when the weather is pleasant and the danger of typhoons is minimal.

Entry Regulations

Ports of entry
Luzon: Manila 14°35'N 120°58'E, Aparri 18°21'N 121°38'E, San Fernando La Union 16°37'N 120°19'E, Subic Bay 14°48'N 120°16'E, Tabaco 13°22'N 123°44'E, Legaspi 13°09'N 123°45'E.
Cebu Island: Cebu City 10°18'N 123°54'E, Iloilo 10°41'N 122°35'E, Panay Island 10°42'N 122°34'E.
Mindanao: Davao 7°04'N 125°37'E, Zamboanga 6°54'N 122°04'E, Cagayan de Oro 8°29'N 124°39'E.

Procedure on arrival
The authorities do not seem concerned about yachts anchoring at islands en route although one must check in with customs and immigration when one arrives at the first convenient port of entry.

Yachts with animals must contact the quarantine medical officer 24 hours before arrival.

Customs
Firearms must be declared to customs on arrival. Animals must be cleared with an animal quarantine officer. They are not allowed to land.

Immigration
Any visitor, except nationals of certain restricted coun-
tries with which the Philippines have no diplomatic relations, may enter without a visa and stay for 21 days provided their onward passage is assured.

Citizens of India and France require a visa.

Hong Kong British citizens may only stay seven days without a visa.

For stays longer than 21 days, it is necessary to get a visa in advance. The validity of the visa starts from the date one checks in at the first port of entry. It is advised that anyone planning to cruise in the Philippines should obtain a 60-day visa in advance. Extensions of this visa for a further 60 days can only be done by the Manila Immigration Office.

Health
Malaria prophylaxis is recommended.

Fees
Overtime charges are payable for clearance outside of office hours, at weekends and on holidays. The health inspection fee is 300 pesos.

Facilities

There are small boatyards in various islands and the Filipinos are skilled workers, particularly in wood. Teak is still widely available, but while its price is steadily increasing, its quality is deteriorating. General repair facilities, such as engine or electrical repair, are also available in most centres, the widest range being concentrated in and around Manila. Most marine supplies have to be imported, but local nautical charts are available both in Manila and Cebu. Manila Yacht Club offers members of other clubs the use of its services. There are good repair facilities around the yacht club as well as skilled workers to call on. Fuel is available in most places, provisioning is reasonable and fresh produce widely available.

Further Reading

Philippines – a travel survival kit

SINGAPORE

Singapore is an island-state lying at the southern end of the Malay peninsula and linked to the Malaysian state of Johor by a long causeway.

This Asian metropolis might have everything for the duty-free shopper, but its yachting facilities are rather disappointing and the fast moving city and over-crowded harbour has little to recommend it as a cruising destination in itself. However, as many cruising sailors arrive in Singapore after a lengthy cruise, often in undeveloped areas, this clean, well organised city has its attractions and as a convenient stop for provisioning and essential services is difficult to beat. With the exception of its lack of docking facilities for visiting yachts, virtually everything is available in Singapore, although it can take time to find it. Occasionally this is frustrating, but chasing an elusive spare part in this cosmopolitan city is an experience in itself.

Visiting yachts usually anchor as close to the Changi Sailing Club as they can, either across the river or in the next bay, as the Club rarely has any spare moorings. A recent government statement encouraging development of the leisure boating industry bodes well for the future, for once the government approves, things happen fast in Singapore. There is already more than one marina in the pipeline. The new Raffles Marina will provide an attractive alternative for cruising boats, although it is far from downtown Singapore. Changi is

Singapore.

popular as it has a village atmosphere with a fresh produce market, good shopping and other facilities within walking distance.

Country Profile

By the seventh century AD Singapore was a trading centre of Sumatra's ancient Srivijaya empire, and by the thirteenth century had become one of its three kingdoms. Legend says that when a prince landed on the island he saw a strange animal, probably a native tiger, which he thought was a lion, hence the name 'Singa Pura' (Lion City in Sanskrit). During the fourteenth century the Javanese and Siam empires struggled with the Chinese for dominance and the city was destroyed and largely forgotten.

Only 500 years later did some Malays settle on the island and then in 1819 Sir Thomas Stamford Raffles chose the island as a British maritime base. From where there was nothing, he planned the development of a city as a free port and international market for South East Asia. By his death in 1827 the Sultan of Johore had ceded full sovereignty of the island to

Practical Information

LOCAL TIME: GMT + 8

BUOYAGE: IALA A

CURRENCY: Singapore dollar of 100 cents (SIN$). Brunei notes are interchangeable, but Malaysian dollars are not.

BUSINESS HOURS
Banks: 1000–1500 Monday to Friday, 0930–1130 Saturday.
Business: 0900–1300, 1400–1700 Monday to Friday, 0900–1200 Saturday.
Shops: many open seven days a week, approximately 1000–2100.
Government offices: 0800–1300, 1400–1700 Monday to Friday, 0800–1300 Saturday (some offices).

ELECTRICITY: 220/240 V, 50 Hz

PUBLIC HOLIDAYS
1 January: New Year's Day
Chinese New Year
Good Friday
1 May
May: Vesak Day
9 August: National Day
25 December: Christmas

EVENTS
There are many festivals of the different cultures and religions:
January: Thaipusam (Hindu), penitents' procession through the streets.
January: Chinese New Year.
May: Hari Raya Puasa (Muslim), end of Ramadan.
May: Vesak Day (Buddhist).
June: Dragon Boat Festival.
September/October: Mooncake Festival.
October: Divali (Hindu), festival of lights.

COMMUNICATIONS
Singapore is the telecommunications centre for South East Asia.
International direct dialling from public phones using Singapore Telecom cardphone service. Also Home Country Direct Service where calls are connected through own country operator, charged collect or against a telephone credit card.
International access code 104.
Emergency: dial 999.
Singapore has frequent air links with most parts of the world and all major international airlines have flights in and out.

MEDICAL
The medical standards are high. Many doctors and dentists speak English. Government Vaccination Centre, Institute of Health, 226 Outram Road.

DIPLOMATIC MISSIONS
Australia: 25, Napier Road. ☎ 737-9311.
Brunei: 7A Tanglin Hill. ☎ 466-4806.
Canada: 80 Anson Road, IBM Towers. ☎ 225-6363.
Indonesia: 7 Chatsworth Road. ☎ 737-7422.
Malaysia: 301 Jervois Road. ☎ 235-0111.
New Zealand: 13 Nassim Road. ☎ 235-9966.
Philippines: 20 Nassim Road. ☎ 737-3977.
Taiwan: Trade Mission of the Republic of China, 460 Alexandra Road, PSA Building. ☎ 278-6511.
United Kingdom: Tanglin Road. ☎ 473-9333.
United States: 30 Hill Street ☎ 338-0251.

Britain. Trade grew as tea, china, ivory and spices from China and Indonesia were shipped to London on the East Indiamen. Later rubber and tin contributed to the economic prosperity of Singapore. During the Second World War the Japanese occupied Singapore from 1942 to 1945. With peace came demands for self-determination and in 1959 Singapore became a self-governing state. For two years Singapore was one of the 14 States of the Malaysian Federation, but in 1965 Singapore left to become an independent republic.

As one of Asia's wealthiest nations, prosperity is very much due to its free port status. Singapore is an important transit port, the third busiest in the world, as well as a financial and industrial centre.

The population of 2.65 million are mostly Chinese, also Malay, Indian, Eurasian (mainly of Portuguese origins), European, with small Jewish and Armenian minorities. Mandarin Chinese, English, Malay and Tamil are the main languages spoken in this diverse cosmopolitan community. Most major religions are practised, particularly Buddhism, Taoism, Islam, Hinduism and Christianity.

The climate is hot and humid all year round with heavy rainfall especially November to January. Singapore is not affected by tropical storms and the only violent winds are the sumatras, which are strong, short-lived squalls that occur between April and November. Throughout the year the winds are light and there are frequent calms.

Entry Regulations

Port of entry
Port of Singapore 1°16′N 103°50′E.

Procedure on arrival
Yachts may anchor in a convenient place, such as close to the Changi Sailing Club, on the NE side of the island, or from 1992 at the new Raffles Marina in Tuas, on the west side of Singapore. Visiting yachts may also anchor in Sembewang, on the north side, or near West Park Road, close to the Republic of Singapore Yacht Club. In the past, immigration have some-

times insisted that yachts come to Finger Pier to clear, but as this is not only difficult but also dangerous because of the heavy traffic, one should berth somewhere else and visit the relevant offices by bus or taxi.

Within 24 hours of arrival the captain must report to Finger Pier to clear immigration and customs. The customs office is in the Port of Singapore Authority (PSA) Building a few blocks west of Finger Pier. After immigration and customs one must check in with the Port Master, whose office is on the 3rd floor in the PSA building.

On departure the harbour fees will have to be paid at the Port Master's office in the PSA building.

Customs do not usually visit yachts, but random spot checks are made from time to time.

Customs

Firearms, including spear guns, need an import permit from the Marine Police. The permit must be obtained in advance – two weeks is the minimum period necessary for obtaining a permit. Firearms will then be sealed on board. Yachts arriving without a permit will, after declaring their firearms to customs, have to return to the boat with the Marine Police who will escort them to the armoury by taxi to deposit the firearms. On departure, they will be escorted back to the yacht with the firearms, for which a fee will be charged.

Animals must remain on board.

The relevant prescriptions for any prescribed medicines held on board may have to be shown to customs. The Singapore authorities have a very strict policy regarding illegal drugs and there is a death penalty for drug trafficking.

Yachts can remain indefinitely, but the captain must report to the authorities every two months.

Immigration

No visa is required for citizens of Australia, Bangladesh, Brunei, Canada, Hong Kong, Malaysia, the Netherlands, New Zealand, Sri Lanka, Switzerland, the United Kingdom and the United States.

No visa is required for up to a stay of 90 days for citizens of Austria, Belgium, Denmark, France, Germany, Italy, Japan, South Korea, Norway, Pakistan, Spain and Sweden.

No visa is required for a stay of up to 14 days for citizens of Bahrain, Brazil, Burma, Egypt, Greece, Indonesia, Israel, Kuwait, Mexico, the Philippines, Saudi Arabia, South Africa, Taiwan, Thailand and United Arab Emirates.

Visas are required for all other nationalities or for longer stays.

Immigration may want to see proof of sufficient funds.

Fees

The officials do not work outside working hours, so there is no overtime. Nominal harbour and light dues are calculated per GRT.

Restrictions

Some areas of the harbour, which are marked on the charts, are prohibited either for anchoring or for passing through – for example there is a height restriction of 15 m (45 ft) in the area close to the airport.
City laws: Pedestrians crossing the road within 50 metres of a pedestrian crossing, an overhead pedestrian bridge or underpass, risk a SIN$50 fine. There is a fine of up to SIN$1000 for littering. Smoking is illegal in all public places, subject to a SIN$500 fine.

Facilities

Repair facilities are not as comprehensive as one would expect in a developed place such as Singapore. The situation should improve with the new government policy, meanwhile finding the relevant part or workshop takes time and patience.

A boatyard operates at Changi next to the Sailing Club, which undertakes hull and general repairs, and has its own slipway. Another small boatyard with slipping facilities is Precision Craft, off Tangong Rhy Road. Hull, engine and electrical repair are also undertaken by Keppel Marina Services, who also have a travelift as well as a small chandlery. For any metal work, electrical or engine repair a highly recommended company is Juat Lip Engineering.

Although there is not one chandlery with a wide selection of goods, most items are available somewhere in Singapore and many shops dealing in marine equipment, such as outboard engines or inflatable tenders, often also stock spares. Some hardware stores and commercial ships chandlers stock stainless steel nuts, bolts and rigging. Radio equipment is also available and the prices are very competitive. For any duty-free shopping one should look out for the Good Retailer Scheme emblem (red decal with white lion).

Provisioning is excellent with many well-stocked supermarkets. Singapore is an excellent place to stock up the boat as both the selection and costs are good compared to the places one will visit next, whether west or eastbound.

Further Reading

Singapore Street Guide and Bus Guide
Malaysia, Singapore and Brunei – a travel survival kit

SOUTH KOREA

The Korean peninsula is one of rugged mountains and dramatic scenery, bordered by China to the north, with Japan to the east. The peninsula is divided at the 38th parallel into the Democratic People's Republic of Korea to the north and the Republic of Korea in the south.

Neither country is particularly welcoming to cruising yachts, but while in the North the discouragement of foreign visitors is undisguised, in the South, cumbersome and time-consuming formalities convey the same message. Although officially most of South Korea is open to cruising, the constant harassment from army, navy and police spoils the pleasure of visiting this otherwise beautiful and interesting country.

The most attractive cruising to be found is along the south coast, roughly between the ports of Kunsan and Pusan, where the coast is indented with countless coves, anchorages and hundreds of small islands. Pusan gained temporary fame as the world's sailing centre during the Seoul Olympics and the marina built for that occasion can now be used by cruising yachts. Pusan is Korea's principal port and second largest city. It is the gateway to the Hallyo Sudo Waterway, a national sea park comprising hundreds of picturesque islands along the coast west of Pusan. Cheju Island, off the southern tip of the peninsula, is a useful stop for southbound yachts or those who wish to make a stop while on passage from Japan towards the Asian mainland.

Country Profile

The peninsula was settled over 2000 years ago by tribes of Mongol origin. From the first century BC to the seventh AD three kingdoms ruled, until they were united by the strong Silla tribe. With their capital at Kyongju, the Silla era marked a flourishing of Korean culture. However, over the centuries Korea suffered repeated invasions by Mongols, Manchus and Japanese. The Yi dynasty ruled until 1910, when Japan annexed the peninsula.

The Japanese defeat in 1945 saw Korea divided between Soviet and American occupying forces. Victims of the Cold War, in 1948 two republics were proclaimed. North Korean efforts to overrun the south led to war in 1950–1 and the separation continues today. An authoritarian regime lasted until 1987 when elections and a new constitution, then the Olympic Games of 1988, raised hopes of more prosperity and freedom. In recent years the country has seen widespread disturbances.

The plains and mild climate has meant the predominance of rice cultivation. Industry, such as textiles, shipbuilding and electrical, has grown especially in Seoul and Pusan. Most exports go to the USA and Japan.

The 42 million inhabitants are Koreans of Mongol origin. There is a small Chinese minority. Korean is an Ural-Altaic language akin to Hungarian and Finnish. It is not related to Chinese, although many Chinese words have been absorbed. The main religion is Buddhism. Shamanism, Confucianism and Christianity are also practised. Seoul is the capital of South Korea.

The country has a temperate, seasonal climate, with rainy, hot summers and dry, cold winters. Typhoons can affect the coastal areas at any time, particularly from May to October.

Entry Regulations

Ports of entry

Cheju 33°31′N 126°33′E, Inchon 38°28′N 126°36′E, Kunsan (Gunsan) 36°00′N 126°43′E, Pusan (Busan) 35°06′N 129°04′E, Uban 35°29′N 129°24′E, Yosu 34°45′N 127°47′E.

Procedure on arrival

Pusan: It is compulsory to call port control on VHF Channel 16 or 12 and request permission to enter the harbour. If the call is not acknowledged, the vessel should be brought alongside the Navy barge moored close to the harbour entrance. The yacht may be searched here and firearms must be declared. Although foreign yachts are supposed to employ the services of a local agent to deal with all formalities, this rule is not strictly applied and one can carry out the clearing formalities oneself. This entails visits to customs, immigration and the port authority, all of which are located within the port compound. When leaving the harbour, it is necessary to stop again at the Navy barge and hand in the clearance papers. A copy will be retained, but the originals should be kept, as they will have to be shown at the next port of call.

Cheju: There is an Army check point just inside the harbour entrance, where one should stop for inspection. Formalities are completed inside the main harbour where yachts sometimes tie up to one of the coastguard boats. Arriving yachts are visited by quarantine, customs and immigration.

Kunsan: This is an estuarine harbour affected by strong currents. Although a port of entry, it is not recommended for yachts.

Inchon: This is the port of the capital Seoul. The port

Practical Information

LOCAL TIME: GMT + 9

BUOYAGE: IALA B (IALA A in North Korea)

CURRENCY: Won of 100 chun. Import or export of local currency is illegal. Exchange receipts should be kept.

BUSINESS HOURS
Banks: 0930–1630 Monday to Friday, Saturdays 0930–1330.
Government offices: 0900–1800 Mondays to Fridays, March to October; 0900–1700 November to February; Saturdays 0900–1300.
Business: 0900–1800 Monday to Friday.
Department stores: 1030–1930 Monday to Friday.
Smaller shops: 0800–2200 Monday to Friday; Saturdays half day.

ELECTRICITY: 220 V, 60Hz. 100 V in some urban areas.

PUBLIC HOLIDAYS
1–3 January: New Year
February Folklore Day
1 March: Samiljol/Independence Movement Day

5 April: Arbour Day
5 May: Children's Day
May: Buddha's Birthday
6 June: Memorial Day
17 July: Constitution Day
15 August: Liberation Day
September: Ch'usok/Thanksgiving
1 October: Armed Forces Day
3 October: Kaech'onjul/National Foundation Day
9 October: Han-gul Day/Korean Alphabet Day
25 December: Christmas Day

COMMUNICATIONS
International calls can be made from cardphones in hotels and airports; 5000 and 10,000 won card values.
Telegrams can be sent from post offices open 0900–1730 or by dialling 115.
Telexes 24-hour service KTI (Korean National Telegram).
Emergency: dial police 112, fire 119.
Overseas mail may be opened and censored.
There are regular flights from Seoul to all major destinations in America, Europe and Asia. There are flights from Pusan to Japan and Taiwan.

MEDICAL
There are good hospitals, many with English speaking doctors.
Imported medicines are expensive.

DIPLOMATIC MISSIONS
In Seoul:
Australia: 58-1, Shinmunno 1-ga, Chongno-gu. ☎ (2) 730-6490.
Brunei: 1-94, Tongbinggodong, Yongsan-gu. ☎ (2) 796-8643.
Canada: Kolon Bldg, 45 Mugyo-dong, Chung-gu. ☎ (2) 753-2605.
Indonesia: 55 Youido-dong, Yongdungp'o-gu. ☎ (2) 793-0491.
Japan: 18-11, Chunghak-dong, Chongno-gu. ☎ (2) 733-6704.
New Zealand: Kyobo Bldg, 1 Chongno 1-GA, Chongno-gu. ☎ (2) 730-7794.
Taiwan: 83 Myong-dong 2-ga, Chung-gu. ☎ (2) 776-2721.
United Kingdom: 4 Chong-dong, Chung-gu. ☎ (2) 735-7341.
United States: 82 Sejongno, Chongno-gu. ☎ (2) 722-2601.

is very busy and port control should be contacted on VHF Channel 16 for instructions where to berth for clearance.

Customs
Firearms must be declared.
An up-to-date health certificate for all animals must be shown. Cats and dogs need a rabies vaccination certificate from one's country of origin and must spend 10 days in quarantine.

Everything brought into the country must be exported. Special approval is needed from the Art & Antiques Assessment Office to export antiques and valuable cultural items.

Immigration
No visa is required for stays of less than 90 days for nationals of Austria, Bangladesh, Barbados, Chile, Colombia, Costa Rica, Dominican Republic, Greece, Liberia, Malaysia, Mexico, Pakistan, Peru, Singapore, Switzerland and Thailand.

No visa is required for stays of less than 60 days for nationals of Belgium, Denmark, Finland, Germany, Iceland, Italy, Lesotho, Luxembourg, the Netherlands, Norway, Portugal, Spain, Suriname, Sweden, Turkey and the United Kingdom.

No visa is required for stays of less than 30 days for French and Tunisian citizens.

All others must obtain visas.

Tourist visas for 30 days may be renewed for another 30 days. If longer than a 90-day stay is planned, a special long-term visa must be obtained in advance and one will have to apply for a residence certificate at the local immigration office.

Visa regulations change frequently and it is recommended that anyone planning to visit South Korea should obtain a visa in advance. There are South Korean embassies in most capitals and also consulates in neighbouring countries, such as Japan, where there are consulates in Kobe, Shimonoseki and Fukuoka, the latter being reported as the most efficient in granting a visa.

Restrictions

Entry formalities and dealings with officials are generally difficult and time-consuming, the matters being further complicated by the fact that very few officials speak English or any other foreign language. Because of the delicate nature of South Korea's relations with North Korea, the military authorities are extremely suspicious of any foreign vessel. Also, as it is forbidden to sail in South Korean waters at night, one should time one's arrival in daylight. It is compulsory to clear in and out at every place and one is also likely to be stopped by various patrol boats belonging to the Navy, coastguard, marines or customs. One must also avoid the various firing ranges, which are not always clearly marked.

Facilities

Provisioning is good everywhere, which includes the electronic products that are manufactured in increasing quantities in South Korea. Excellent fresh produce can be bought on Cheju Island which has a large farming community. Diesel fuel can be bought in most places, sometimes being delivered by fuel barges which supply the harbour launches. LPG is widely available, as most taxis run on propane. The best repair facilities are in the Pusan area, which also has marina type docking in the Olympic Basin. Electrical, electronic and engine repair is available locally. There is also a small boatyard at Cheju where boats can be hauled out. Generally there are adequate repair facilities in all ports which have a fishing fleet.

NORTH KOREA

Communist North Korea occupies the northern half of the Korean peninsula and its capital is Pyongyang. All foreign visitors require visas, which must be applied for well in advance.

Visiting yachts are not welcome and the country is best avoided.

Further Reading

Northeast Asia on a Shoestring
Korea and Taiwan – a travel survival kit

TAIWAN

Taiwan, officially called the Republic of China, is a large island straddling the Tropic of Cancer, about 120 miles off the Chinese mainland. Taiwan is a prosperous country, largely due to its exporting industry, and it is also one of unspoilt natural beauty.

Known all over the world for its yacht-building industry, Taiwan was the first Asian country to mass produce fibreglass boats and its leading position is still unassailed in the Far East. Very few of those yachts return to Taiwan, although every year a number of owners come to take possession of their craft and sail them away. Unfortunately this beautiful island is not geared up for cruising so these new owners have to savour other cruising grounds.

Country Profile

From the twelfth century AD the island was frequented by merchants and pirates. Portuguese sailors named the island Ilha Formosa, meaning 'beautiful island', at the end of the sixteenth century. The name Taiwan means terraced bay. Claimed by China, during the seventeenth century it was settled by Chinese immigrants, mainly Ming loyalists fleeing from the Manchus. Also at this time the Dutch and Spanish established themselves in the south and north respectively. At the end of the century the island was incorporated into the Chinese Empire. The Treaty of Shimonoseki in 1895, at the end of the Sino-Japanese war, saw Taiwan handed over to Japan. Japanese rule lasted until the end of the Second World War, when the island reverted to China. In 1949 Taiwan served as a refuge for Chinese nationalists led by Chiang Kai-shek, who established the Republic of China with its capital in Taipei. Until 1971 this government represented China at the United Nations. Elected in 1988, Lee Teng-huei is the first native-born president.

Agriculture is the main industry and the land is intensely cultivated, the main crops being sugar cane, rice, fruit and vegetables. Other industries are textiles, electrical goods and yachts, both sail and motor. Nearly everything the economy produces is exported.

The majority of the 19.5 million inhabitants are of Chinese origin, although some indigenous peoples live in the mountains. Mandarin Chinese is the official language, Taiwanese and Hakka are also spoken and many people speak some English. Confucianism, Buddhism, Taoism and Christianity are the main religions. Taipei is the capital.

The climate is subtropical with average temperatures from 21–24°C (70–75°F) and high humidity.

Practical Information

LOCAL TIME: GMT + 8

BUOYAGE: IALA A

CURRENCY: New Taiwan dollar (NT$).
All conversion receipts should be kept,
so as to be able to change back any NT$
when leaving.

BUSINESS HOURS
Banks: 0900–1530 Monday to Friday,
Saturday 0900–1200.
Shops: 0900–1200, 1330–1730 Monday to
Friday.
Government offices: 0800–1200,
1300–1700 Monday to Friday .

ELECTRICITY: 110 V, 60 Hz

PUBLIC HOLIDAYS
1 January: New Year & Founding Day
2 January: Public Holiday
29 March: Youth Day
5 April: Tomb Sweeping Day
1 May: Labour Day
10 October: Confucius' Birthday and
Double Tenth National Day
25 October: National Day
31 October: Taiwan Restoration Day and
Chiang Kai-shek's birthday
12 November: Dr Sun Yat Sen's birthday
25 December: Constitution Day

COMMUNICATIONS
Direct dialling to most countries.
General post office, Chung Hsiao Road,
Taipei.
Tourist Information Hotline: ☎ (02)
717-3737.
There are international flights to most
Asian capitals.

DIPLOMATIC MISSIONS
In Taipei:
American Institute: 1 Lane 134, Hsin Yi
Road, Section 3. ☎ (2) 709-2000. (Also 88
Wu Fu 3d Road, Kaohsiung,
☎ (7) 221-2444.)
Anglo-Taiwan Trade Committee: West
Wing 11/F, China Bldg, 36 Nanking E.
Rd, Section 2. ☎ (2) 521-4116.
Australian Commerce and Industry
Office: 4/F, 148 Singchiang Rd, Shen
Hsiang Tang Bldg. ☎ (2) 542-7950.
Canada Trade Office: Bank Tower, 205
Tunhra N. Rd. ☎ (2) 713-7268.
Japan Interchange Association: 43
Chinan Rd, Section 2. ☎ (2) 351-7250.

There are mild winters from December to February. The summer from May to September is hotter and also the rainy season. Typhoons are most frequent from June to September.

Entry Regulations

Ports of entry
Kaohsiung 22°37′N 120°15′E, Keelung 25°09′N 121°44′E, Taichung 24°15′N 120°30′E, Hualien 23°59′N 121°38′E, Suao 24°36′N 121°52′E.

Procedure on arrival
No other harbour apart from the above ports can be visited. At all ports of entry the port authority should be contacted on VHF Channel 16 before entering the harbour. Each vessel is obliged to contact the port authority so as to be issued with entry and exit permits, and also for the assignment of a berth. One may be required to use a shipping agent for one's application to the port authority for an entry permit.

One should call the joint inspection centre giving one's ETA and to arrange for a security inspection.

One is boarded by customs officers when clearing in.

Customs
A written declaration of firearms carried must be submitted to the customs boarding officer and firearms will be sealed on board.

Animals are not allowed ashore, unless possessing quarantine certificates from both one's home country and the Republic of China.

All electrical goods, such as stereos, televisions or video-recorders must be declared.

Immigration
Passports must be valid for more than six months.

All nationalities must obtain a visa before arrival from a Republic of China embassy, consulate or trade mission abroad. The most convenient offices will probably be in Hong Kong, Indonesia, Japan, Malaysia, the Philippines, Singapore or Thailand. From these offices one may obtain a visa or letter of recommendation exchangeable for a visa. The letters may be exchanged at a Republic of China diplomatic or consular office en route, or on arrival at Keelung or Kaohsuing ports, these two being the only ports where these letters may be exchanged.

A visitors' visa is valid for three months from the date of issue and is good for a single visit for a 60-day period. Provided one can give grounds, one may apply for a maximum of two extensions, each for 60 days.

Yachts from the Soviet Union, North Korea, Albania and Cuba are not allowed entry.

Cruising permit
One must apply to the Ministry of Communications for a cruising permit if intending to visit more than one port.

Fees

Harbour fees are NT$ 207 per day. There is a health inspection fee of NT$ 600. Agent's fee is about NT$ 5000.

Facilities

Having a well developed indigenous yacht and ship-building industry, repair facilities are widely available in Taiwan. There are slipways in all ports and local boatyards offer a whole range of services. Provisioning is good, both for long-term stores and fresh produce.

Further Reading

Korea and Taiwan – a travel survival kit
Northeast Asia on a Shoestring

THAILAND

The kingdom of Thailand, previously known as Siam, lies between Burma, Laos and Kampuchea on the Asian mainland jutting south into the Malay peninsula. It has two coasts, on the west bordered by the Andaman Sea and on the east around the Gulf of Thailand.

A relatively late addition to the international cruising circuit, Thailand is now visited every year by an increasing number of yachts and a charter fleet is also established in the area around Phuket. This large island off Thailand's west coast has jumped in less than a decade from a sleepy backwater to an international tourist resort with high-rise hotels, bars, night clubs and crowded beaches. Much of the charm of Phuket has been lost in the process and it now is an over-crowded and increasingly polluted island. Fortunately cruising yachts have the ability to seek out the less crowded places, which still abound around Phuket Island and its many offshore islets. The spectacular Ko Phi Phi is one such destination, a weathered pinnacle rising like a gigantic stalagmite out of the sea.

There are also many secluded anchorages along the stretch of coast as one sails north from Malaysia. While Burma remains closed to cruising, Thailand's northernmost islands and anchorages are rarely visited.

Country Profile

Thailand is one of the few Far Eastern countries never to have been under colonial rule. Recent findings suggest it has been inhabited since the earliest Bronze Age. The Thai tribe was pushed out of southeast China and slowly populated the land in the seventh to eighth centuries AD, establishing small independent states in the north of present Thailand. After being dominated by the Khmer Empire, in the thirteenth century, the Thais fought for independence and established their own royal capital at Sukhothi, from where Thai civilisation flowered. Later the centre of power moved to Ayatthaya where Thai culture and the Buddhist religion flourished until 1767, when the city was sacked by the Burmese. Eventually Bangkok became the new capital, under King Rama I, founder of the present Chakri dynasty.

The first Europeans to visit the country made little progress against Thai hostility, although under pressure from the West in the nineteenth and early twentieth century Kings Rama IV and Rama V introduced a series of reforms. An army coup in 1932 ended the absolute power of the monarchy, and the army continues to play an important role in Thai politics.

The country is more economically stable than many of its neighbours, although sometimes there are problems on the north and east borders. Thailand has an agricultural economy, and around 80 per cent of the population are employed in agriculture, forestry and fishing. Recently efforts have been made to diversify and develop a manufacturing industry. The main exports are rice, teak, rubber and minerals, especially tin and tungsten. Thailand is probably the most popular tourist destination in South East Asia, and tourism is an important source of foreign revenue.

The population is 55 million, of whom more than 5 million live in Bangkok. As well as Thais there are also some hill tribes in the north-east and Malays in the south. Thai is the national language and has its own alphabet. Many in the north east speak a dialect akin to Lao. English is also widely understood. Most Thais are Buddhists, although some are Muslim, Confucian or Christian. All young men are expected to spend a minimum of three months in a Buddhist monastery. Bangkok, the capital, is a crowded metropolis, with many interesting places, from over 400 temples to floating markets and royal palaces.

The tropical climate is very humid. March to May are the hottest months and it is cooler from November to February. June to October is the rainy season and the SW monsoon, while November to May is the period of the NE monsoon. The latter is the more pleasant season on account of its weather, but also because it affords better sailing conditions along the sheltered west coast, most of whose ports are untenable during the SW monsoon.

Practical Information

LOCAL TIME: GMT + 7

BUOYAGE: IALA A

CURRENCY: Baht (BHT) of 100 satang

BUSINESS HOURS
Banks: 0830–1530 Monday to Friday.
Shops: 0800–2000/2100 Monday to
Saturday.
Government offices: 0830–1630 Monday
to Friday.

ELECTRICITY: 220 V, 50 Hz

PUBLIC HOLIDAYS
1 January: New Year's Day
9 February: Makha Bucha Day
6 April: Chakri Day
13 April: Songkran Festival (Thai New
Year's Day)

1 May: Labour Day
5 May: Coronation Day
May: Wisakha Bucha
July: Asalaha Bucha
July: Khow Phansa (Buddhist Lent)
August: Queen's Birthday
23 October: Chulalongkorn Memorial
Day
5 December: King's Birthday
10 December: Constitution Day
25 December: Christmas Day
31 December: New Year's Eve

EVENTS
Early December, King's Cup Regatta
week in Phuket.

COMMUNICATIONS
There are public telephone offices in the
main centres for international calls.
Bangkok airport is connected to all
major cities of the world. There are also

international flights out of Phuket, both
regular and charter, to Europe as well as
to Singapore and Kuala Lumpur. There
is a good network of internal flights.

DIPLOMATIC MISSIONS
In Bangkok:
Australia: 37 South Sathorn Road.
☎ (2) 287-2680.
Canada: Boonmitr Building, 138 Silom
Road. ☎ (2) 234-1561.
Indonesia: 600–602 Petchburi Road.
☎ (2) 252-3125.
New Zealand: 93 Wireless Road.
☎ (2) 251-8165.
Taiwan: The Far East Trade Office, Kian
Gwan Bldg, 140 Wit Thayu Road.
☎ (2) 251-9274.
United Kingdom: Wireless Road.
☎ (2) 253-0191.
United States: 95 Wireless Road.
☎(2) 252-5040.

Entry Regulations

Ports of entry
Bangkok 13°26′N 100°36′E, Phuket 7°55′N
98°24′E, Krabi 8°04′N 98°44′E, Turong.

Procedure on arrival
One should anchor flying the Q flag. Customs very
rarely visit yachts. Within 24 hours of arrival, except at
weekends, the captain must go to immigration, then
customs, during working hours (0830–1200, 1300–
1630 Monday to Friday).
Phuket: Although there is a customs office in the
Deep Sea Port, yachts are supposed to clear in at the
office in Phuket Town. It is best to anchor near the
port and the captain should go into town. However,
this regulation may change in the future as the
authorities intend to set up a one-stop clearing facility
in the port itself. At present the customs and immigration offices are in Phuket Town, about three miles
inland from the port.
Krabi: Formalities are apparently simpler in this
mainland port. After anchoring in the harbour, the
captain should go ashore to customs and immigration
whose offices are in the port.

Customs
Firearms should be declared. They will be removed
and held until departure, unless there is a secure locker

on board, where they can be sealed under the supervision of customs officials.
There are no restrictions on animals.

Immigration
No visa is required for nationals of most countries for a
stay of up to 15 days.
For a stay of over 15 days a visa should be obtained
in advance from a Thai embassy or consulate, for
example in Singapore or Penang. A transit visa is
issued for 30 days, a tourist visa for 60 days, a
non-immigrant visa for 90 days.
Conditions vary and frequently change and the time
a person on a yacht may be allowed to stay seems to
depend occasionally on the whim of the individual
immigration officer. Some yachts have reported that it
is better to clear in at Krabi than Phuket, as the
immigration officers are more cooperative.
There appears to be some confusion because yachts
are treated in the same way as commercial ships, and
crew are not regarded as tourists. On arrival, almost
everyone is given a visa for 14 days and extensions to
this appear to be hard to come by, another 14 days at
the most. One solution to these restrictions imposed
on those arriving by yacht is for the captain to declare
everyone on board as passengers and not as crew. In
this case they are treated as ordinary tourists and it will
be easier for them to obtain visa extensions. It is highly
recommended that all nationalities obtain a visa

Nai Harn Bay on Phuket Island.

beforehand, as then one month or even three month extensions can be asked for.

Crew members are supposed to leave by the same means as they arrived, which can cause problems if crew members try and leave Thailand by air. This is also solved by declaring anyone planning to leave the yacht as a passenger. If the captain wishes to leave the country, he will have to post a bond of 20,000 baht. This can only be done via a local agent and in Phuket a company willing to do this is the Phuket Shipping Company which charges a fee of 1500 baht for this service. However, if a captain knows in advance that he will be leaving the country, he should perhaps declare one of the crew members staying on the boat as captain and himself as a passenger. There must always be someone who is designated to be in charge of the boat; and it is not possible for everyone to be declared as passengers.

Fees

600 baht is charged for each visa extension. There is a departure tax of 600 baht per yacht.

Health

Malaria prophylaxis is recommended as there is some risk existing all year in all areas.

Facilities

In spite of Phuket's popularity as a cruising desti-nation, yachting facilities are still very limited although specialised companies are slowly being set up. Elec-trical, engine and sail repair can be undertaken locally. There is also a small boatyard with a drying out grid, but there are no reliable hauling out facilities available. A local company specialises in fibreglass work and inflatable dinghies, which they repair and also manu-facture. Fuel is available by jerrycan. Provisioning in Phuket Town is good with several grocery stores and a daily fresh produce market.

Facilities in the other ports are even more limited. More repair facilities are obviously available in the capital Bangkok, but it is a busy polluted city, totally unsuitable for yachts. The Royal Varuna Yacht Club has its base in Pattaya, the resort on the Gulf of Thailand which serves Bangkok. They organise the King's Cup Regatta, one of South East Asia's prime yachting events every year in Phuket.

Further Reading

Southeast Asia on a Shoestring
Thailand – a travel survival kit

11 North Indian Ocean and Red Sea

Very few yachts make this area their cruising destination and usually visit when on their way from South East Asia to the Mediterranean. The only place where yachts spend longer is the Red Sea, not only those sailing north and taking their time to reach the Mediterranean, but also an increasing number who come south to spend the winter in the Red Sea and return to the Mediterranean in the spring. For the time being, only the western shore of the Red Sea north of Port Sudan is accessible to yachts, as both Ethiopia in the south and Yemen and Saudi Arabia in the east do not allow cruising in their waters.

At the southern entrance to the Red Sea, Djibouti and Aden provide convenient stops, facilities being somewhat better in Djibouti. At the northern end, the Suez Canal gives access to the Mediterranean and formalities for transiting the Canal are not complicated, particularly if one employs the services of an agent. Complicated and time-consuming formalities are the bane of those cruising the rest of the countries of this region and probably also the reason why more people are not tempted to visit it. Only in places used to yachts, such as Sri Lanka, Djibouti and Aden, are formalities becoming easier, whereas in India, Sudan and Somalia formalities are so complicated that they tend to spoil any pleasure of visiting those countries.

Limited or non-existent facilities are another reason why few cruising yachts are seen in the area. Having any repairs done in most places is difficult and as there are virtually no locally owned yachts, the existing workshops are not used to dealing with yachts. Marine equipment and spares are also non-existent and as even ordinary provisioning is often difficult, yachts planning to sail in this region should be as self-sufficient as possible.

Sailing in the north Indian Ocean has always been dictated by the monsoons and as Arab traders in their dhows discovered hundreds of years ago, only fools try to sail against them. The NE monsoon lasts from November to March favouring westbound passages, while the strong SW monsoon is from June to September. Tropical cyclones can occur in the Arabian Sea and Bay of Bengal particularly at the changeover of monsoons, May to June and October to November.

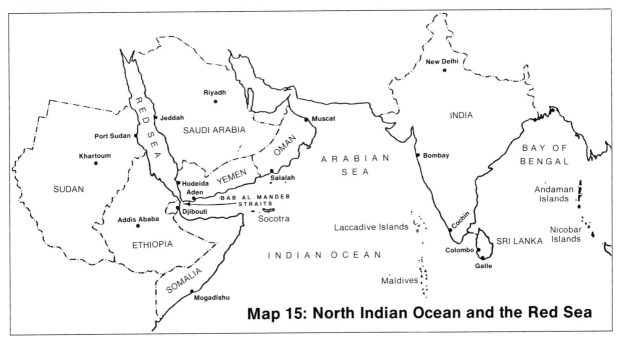

Map 15: North Indian Ocean and the Red Sea

DJIBOUTI

The Republic of Djibouti was previously the French Territory of the Afars and Issas. It is a small country, little more than the port of Djibouti and the surrounding semi-desert hinterland, lying around the Gulf of Tadjoura in the westernmost corner of the Gulf of Aden. Djibouti's position between the Red Sea and Indian Ocean makes it a convenient port of call for both east or westbound yachts. The great majority are bound for the Mediterranean and arrive in Djibouti during the NE monsoon, mainly between January and March.

Country Profile

Before the French arrived the land was used for grazing by nomadic tribes. France occupied the area in the mid-nineteenth century to counter the British presence in Aden, making agreements with the Sultans of Obock and Tadjouran. In 1888 the construction of Djibouti was begun. At the end of the century, following a treaty with the Ethiopian Emperor, the Addis Ababa–Djibouti railway was built. As Djibouti's borders do not tally with ethnic or linguistic lines, these issues have dominated its history.

In 1949 anti-colonial demonstrations were staged by Somalis and Issas in support of Britain's attempts to unite the Italian, French and British Somalias. The French supported the Afars, who voted in the 1967 referendum to continue under French rule. Issa opposition grew and during the 1970s the Somali Coast Liberation Front carried out various terrorist acts. International pressure on France and continuing internal unrest led France in 1977 to give independence to the last French colony on the African mainland. Unfortunately tribal harmony did not come with independence. Trade agreements have been signed with both Somalia and Ethiopia, and Djibouti would like to see a truce between these two countries.

Revenue comes mostly from port dues and the Addis Ababa–Djibouti railway, which is Ethiopia's main outlet to the sea. French aid is important and France maintains a naval base in the port. Djibouti is poor in natural resources and many still live a traditional subsistence life.

The population of over 300,000 are mainly Afars, who are ethnically part of Ethiopia, and Issas, who are closer to Somalia, both being Muslim peoples. There are also minorities of Somalis, French, Yemenis and refugees from the Ogaden war. Arabic is the official language, but French is widely used. Afar and Somali are also spoken. Djibouti is the capital.

It can be very hot in Djibouti, especially from June to August, when temperatures can reach 45°C (112°F). The *khamsin* wind blows from the desert bringing dust. October to April is a little cooler and the winds are mostly easterly.

Entry Regulations

Port of entry
Djibouti 11°36′N 43°09′E.

Procedure on arrival
One should call the port on VHF Channel 12 or 16. On arrival the port captain (Capitainerie) should be visited. A permit to cruise Djibouti waters is obtained on arrival.

Customs
Firearms are prohibited and must be declared to customs on arrival.

There are no restrictions on animals, if their vaccination certificates are valid.

Immigration
French nationals do not need visas and can stay up to three months. All other nationalities need to have a visa, which should be obtained in advance, unless planning to spend less than ten days, when it is usually possible to get a transit visa on arrival. There are few Djibouti embassies abroad, but visas can be obtained from French embassies. The usual validity is ten days.

Israelis and South Africans are prohibited entry.

Yachts may only remain in Djibouti for the duration of the owner's visa.

Health
Malaria prophylaxis is recommended.

Fees
Port charges are around US$80 per month. Health dues are US$10. Light dues are US$5. There are overtime charges outside of working hours.

Restrictions
Travelling on the Addis Ababa–Djibouti railway is not allowed.

Facilities

Repair facilities for yachts are rather limited, although there are a few workshops capable of carrying out

Practical Information

LOCAL TIME: GMT + 3

BUOYAGE: IALA A

CURRENCY: Djibouti franc

BUSINESS HOURS
The normal working week is Sunday to Thursday.
Banks: 0700–1200 Monday to Saturday.
Government offices: 0630–1300 Saturday to Thursday.

ELECTRICITY: 220 V, 50 Hz

PUBLIC HOLIDAYS
1 January: New Year's Day
Lailat al-Miraji
1 May: Labour Day
Eid al-Fitr
27 June: National Day
Eid al-Adha
15 August: Assumption
Muslim New Year
Al-Ashura
1 November: All Saints' Day
Prophet's Birthday
25 December: Christmas Day

COMMUNICATIONS
There are daily flights to Paris and regular flights to other cities in France, Africa, Mauritius and the Middle East.

DIPLOMATIC MISSIONS
Ethiopia: ☎ 35 07 18.
France: ☎ 35 25 03.
Somalia: ☎ 35 35 21.
Sudan: ☎ 35 14 83.
Yemen: ☎ 35 37 04.
United States: Villa Plateau du Serpent, Boulevard Maréchal Joffre. ☎ 35 39 95.

simple repairs. The Djibouti Yacht Club allows visitors to use its services and will advise on the repair facilities available.

Provisioning is expensive, mainly due to the presence of the French Navy. However, the French influence means food and wine are of good quality compared to Djibouti's neighbours. There is a lively market in the town centre. Although expensive, provisioning is generally better than in Aden. Fuel and water are available in the port area.

Further Reading

Africa on a Shoestring
Traveller's Guide to East Africa and the Indian Ocean

ETHIOPIA

Ethiopia, formerly called Abyssinia, lies in the northeast of Africa, between Sudan and Somalia, and has a coast on the Red Sea. Ruled by a Marxist regime, Ethiopia was often in the news in the 1980s because of both the famine that ravaged the country and the destructive civil war in Eritrea.

Ethiopia is visited only by yachts which stray into Ethiopian waters involuntarily, usually as a result of a navigational error. The border area between Sudan and Ethiopia is rather confusing, landmarks are difficult to identify and there is also an onshore setting current, all of which makes navigation difficult. Yachts are advised to stay well offshore, as gunboats patrol 12 miles and more offshore and have been known to intercept and apprehend yachts that have strayed into Ethiopian territorial waters.

Country Profile

In 1952 the province of Eritrea, which had been colonised by the Italians in 1889, was joined to Ethiopia in a federation. Then in 1962 the Ethiopian Emperor Haile Selassie annexed Eritrea, sparking off guerilla warfare. Dissatisfaction over the ongoing war was one of the main reasons which provoked the Marxist revolution in 1974, when a military regime took power and overthrew Haile Selassie. The Eritrean conflict is still raging and the guerillas control nearly all of Eritrea, having intensified their activity in 1988. There is also fighting in the Ogaden region on the border with Somalia.

As well as war, the country has been weakened by drastic droughts, famine spreading across the northern provinces in 1984–5 and 1989.

The majority of Ethiopians belong to one of the two main religions, either Islam or the Ethiopian Orthodox Church, which is one of the oldest Christian churches.

The official language is Amharic, which is spoken throughout the country. English is the second official language. Addis Ababa is the capital.

Diplomatic missions
In Addis Ababa:
Canada: Churchill Ave. ☎ 511100.
United Kingdom: Fikre Mariam Abatechan St. ☎ 182354.
United States: Entoto Street. ☎ 110666.

INDIA

Known as Bharat in Hindi, the Republic of India covers a subcontinent bordered to the north by the Himalayas, and in the south projecting into the Indian Ocean between the Arabian Sea and the Bay of Bengal. Although a country of infinite variety, India is avoided by most yachts cruising the Indian Ocean and for good reason. Entry formalities are more complex, cumbersome and time-consuming than in almost any other country and the attitude to yachts is often outrageous. This may not be a policy dictated by the authorities in New Delhi, but local officials in some ports do make life impossible by taking the law into their own hands and interpreting it to suit their own, often corrupt, purposes. Several visiting yachts, and apparently cargo ships as well, have had items or foreign currency confiscated, because they had not been listed on the declaration filled in on arrival. This declaration stipulates that every removable item must be itemised and can be interpreted literally down to the last pencil, spoon or fork. Unless the present situation shows a marked improvement, it might be advisable to avoid India altogether.

Once things improve there is much to see, particularly along the western coast, which provides better sailing conditions during the winter months and NE monsoon. Most yachts which are prepared to brave the bureaucracy make a quick call at Cochin, conveniently placed close to the Red Sea route. Further up the coast, the old Portuguese trading port of Goa (Mormugao), can provide an interesting and colourful interlude. However, if wishing to visit India, Bombay is the best place to head for, especially as some of the customs officials are keen and experienced sailors. Bombay's yacht club is particularly welcoming and visiting sailors are spared some of the frustrations experienced elsewhere. Bombay is a good place from which to travel inland to experience India's rich and ancient culture.

Yachts do not normally visit the east coast, although Madras is a port of entry. India's coastal waters are teeming with small craft and especially when sailing at night one must be extremely careful, as most of them do not carry lights and collisions are a frequent occurrence.

Country Profile

India has been inhabited from prehistoric times, and Neolithic man originated from the Indus basin. Around 2000 BC the Aryans from Central Asia colonised north India, bringing with them the basis of Indian culture: the Sanskrit language, the religion which developed into Hinduism, and the caste system. Many empires rose and fell and in the fifteenth century contacts with Europe developed, first with the Portuguese, then the British, French and Dutch.

By the early nineteenth century Britain controlled most of India, developing the tea and cotton industries. The Indian mutiny of 1857 was only a temporary setback to British colonial power and India lay at the centre of Britain's empire. Early in the twentieth century, however, moves for independence began, and in the 1920s Mahatma Gandhi led a civil disobedience campaign. Full independence came only in 1947. The 1950 constitution created a federal state of 24 states and seven territories. India has followed a policy of non-alignment under Prime Ministers Nehru and Indira Gandhi. The latter was assassinated in 1984 by Sikh extremists, whose activities continue to trouble the country.

India has the second highest population in the world and is a generally poor country. Agriculture employs half the population, and rice, cotton, tea and sugar are the main crops. India has substantial natural resources, both minerals and energy sources. There is some industry. The pressure of the high population sends many into the towns, even if they can find no employment.

The population numbers 762 million of many ethnic strains, from the Mongoloid-Tibetan peoples of the north to the Tamils of the south. New Delhi is the capital. Hindi is the official and most widespread language and English is spoken by many. There are also 14 official regional languages and 250 dialects. India is the birthplace of both Hinduism and Buddhism, the majority of the population now being Hindu. About 10 per cent of the population are Muslim, mainly in the north, and there are also Sikhs, Jains, Pharsees, Christians and Jews.

The coastal regions can be very hot and humid and the best time to visit is during the NE monsoon from November to April, when it is dry and sunny, and if cruising the SW coast one has the benefit of more protected harbours. In the SW monsoon period the west coast is mostly unprotected, there being rain and heavy swell from June to October.

Entry Regulations

Ports of entry

Bombay 18°54′N 72°49′E, Mormugao (Goa) 15°25′N 73°48′E, Cochin 9°58′N 76°14′E, Madras 13°05′N 80°17′E. These are the only recommended ports for visiting yachts.

Practical Information

LOCAL TIME: GMT + $5\frac{1}{2}$

BUOYAGE: IALA A

CURRENCY: Rupee (RP) of 100 paise. No Indian currency may be imported or exported, except rupee travellers' cheques, so exchange receipts should be kept for reconversion on departure. Foreign currency must be declared to customs on arrival or it could be confiscated.

BUSINESS HOURS
These vary between regions.
Banks: 1000–1400 Monday to Friday, 1000–1230 Saturday.
Offices: 0930–1700 Monday to Friday, 0930–1300 Saturday (some open alternate Saturdays).
Shops: 0930–1800 Monday to Saturday.
Government offices: 0930–1730 Monday to Friday.

ELECTRICITY: 220 V, 50 Hz

PUBLIC HOLIDAYS
Public and religious holidays vary in different regions.
26 January: Republic Day
15 August: Independence Day
2 October: Mahatma Gandhi's birthday
25 December: Christmas Day

COMMUNICATIONS
Telexes and telegrams can be sent from telegraphic offices in main cities.
Post offices: 1000–1700 Monday to Friday, Saturday mornings.
There are international flights from Bombay both to Europe and the rest of Asia. There are also internal flights connecting the more important centres around the country.

MEDICAL
There are state operated health facilities in all towns and private consultants in urban areas. Most doctors speak English.

DIPLOMATIC MISSIONS
In Bombay:
Australian: E Block, Maker Towers, Cuffe Parade, Colaba. ☎ (22) 211071.
Canada: Hotel Oberoi Towers, Nariman Point. ☎ (22) 202-4343.
United Kingdom: Hong Kong Bank Bldg, Mahatma Gandhi Rd. ☎ (22) 274874.
United States: Lincoln House, 78 Bhulabhai Desai Rd. ☎ (22) 823611.
In New Delhi:
New Zealand: 25 Golf Links.
☎ (11) 697318.

Procedure on arrival

One must notify customs and immigration authorities on entry and arrival at every port.

Cochin: Yachts must anchor for clearance off the steamer point on the north tip of Willingdon Island, opposite the two jetties of the port office and the Malabar Hotel. One must not land before clearing customs, who will come out in a launch. A list must be made of *all* movable items on board, including foreign currency. This list should be specific, not general, as yachts have had items not mentioned on the list, such as binoculars, confiscated by customs. Customs will check the list, then the captain can go ashore and clear at the port office (open 1000–1700), where port dues must be paid. The port office may keep ship's papers until departure. The customs and immigration offices must be visited next. The immigration office is near the railway terminus and landing passes will be issued by them. After clearance, one may then go to the yacht anchorage south of Bolghatty Island, off the Bolghatty Hotel.

Mormugao: Port control should be contacted on VHF Channels 16 or 12. After anchoring in the inner harbour, the yacht is inspected by customs and possibly health. Other formalities are completed ashore.

Bombay: The Bombay port control operates 24 hours on VHF Channels 16 and 12, and should be contacted on arrival. Inside the harbour, one should anchor off the Royal Bombay Yacht Club by the Gateway of India. The captain should go ashore to clear customs and immigration, whose offices are in the vicinity of the anchorage.

Customs

Certain firearms and weapons are prohibited, and those permitted require a Possession Licence.

There are no restrictions on animals.

Live plants cannot be imported. Skins of all animals, such as snakes, tigers, etc. and articles made of them cannot be exported. There are also restrictions on the export of antiquities.

Alcohol is prohibited in some states and a Liquor Permit must be obtained from government offices.

Yachts normally can remain six months, although this can be extended.

Immigration

A tourist visa must be obtained in advance, which is valid for a three month stay. Tourists must arrive within six months of the date of issue of the visa. Requests for extension for another three months by bona fide tourists are considered on merit. Applications for extensions should be addressed to Foreigners' Regional Registration Offices in New Delhi, Bombay, Calcutta, Madras or the local Superintendent of Police.

Apply in advance with form and three passport size photographs.

Visas can be obtained in Colombo, Sri Lanka.

South African and Israeli nationals may be refused entry.

On arrival, yachtsmen are granted a landing pass which restricts them to a certain area, so permission must be obtained to travel inland.

Health

Cholera vaccination and malaria prophylaxis is necessary. Water must be treated everywhere.

Fees

Overtime fees are charged for clearance on Saturdays and Sundays.

Restrictions

There are many restricted areas in India. The island groups of Amindivi and Laccadive (Lakshadweep) in the Arabian Sea and Nicobar and Andaman in the Bay of Bengal should be avoided.

Facilities

Locally produced items and fresh produce are very cheap, as the cost and standard of living are very low. Fuel in Cochin is available 24 hours at the fuel dock to starboard on entering the port. In Bombay fuel can be obtained from the Bombay ferry dock fuel station, and there is water nearby for which there is a charge. In Bombay, one must call first port control on Channel 12 for permission to change anchorage as the movement of yachts within the harbour is strictly controlled.

The Royal Bombay Yacht Club gives honorary membership to visiting sailors and allows them to use its facilities. Its members can also give advice if any repairs need to be done. In Bombay limited fibreglass repairs are possible and there is a workshop near the anchorage, where boats under 6 tons can be lifted. The yacht club anchorage is a good place to leave a yacht if wishing to travel inland. Spare parts can be air freighted from abroad without the recipient paying customs duty.

In most places along the coast there are small workshops capable of simple repairs, such as on diesel engines, electrical repair or metal work, but as spare parts are almost unobtainable, one should have all essentials on board. There are several boatyards with slipways, but as they are not used to dealing with keeled yachts one should only use their services if absolutely necessary.

Further Reading

Red Sea and Indian Ocean Cruising Guide
India – a travel survival kit

MALDIVES

The Maldives consist of an archipelago of 1190 islands in the Indian Ocean south west of Sri Lanka, of which some 200 are inhabited. All are low-lying coral islands, grouped naturally into 20 atolls protected by surrounding reefs. The word 'atoll' is in fact derived from the Maldivian language. Administratively the Maldives are divided into 19 atoll groups. Gan Island lies south of the other islands and was a British base until 1976.

Cruising yachts are increasingly welcome in the Maldives, the government regarding yachting as a valuable contribution to their tourist industry. From the cruising sailor's point of view, the Maldives have many attractions, but one major disadvantage is the lack of all-weather anchorages. Although there are plenty of islands to visit, in most lagoons the anchorages are very deep and exposed. This is the reason for the popularity of islands such as Furana and Thulusidhoo, which have shallow well-protected anchorages. Apart from this shortcoming, the Maldives are an interesting cruising ground and the diving in some atolls is excellent.

Country Profile

The origin of the Maldive islanders is not known, although it is thought that they probably came from India and Sri Lanka. Until 1153 AD the Maldivians were ruled by Buddhist kings, then an Islamic sultanate was established. The islands remained independent except for a brief rule by the Portuguese during the sixteenth century. Attacks by India in the seventeenth century were held off with the help of France. In 1887 the Maldives by agreement became a British protectorate. Since 1965 a non-aligned position has been maintained, and the Maldivians have refused to allow any foreign powers to establish military bases within the island group. The present Republic was founded by referendum in 1968.

The island groups are basically self-contained, relying on fishing for subsistence. Fishing has always been the major source of income, and the traditional dhoni boats can still be seen, although many are now being converted from sail to motor. Tourism has become increasingly important since its introduction in the early 1970s, helped by good airlinks via Malé

Practical Information

LOCAL TIME: GMT + 5

BUOYAGE: IALA A

CURRENCY: Rufiya (Rf) of 100 lari. US$ accepted on the tourist islands.

BUSINESS HOURS
Friday is the day of rest.
Banks: 0900–1300 Sunday to Thursday.
Government offices: 0730–1330 Saturday to Thursday.
Shops: 0730–2200 (some do not open Friday morning).

ELECTRICITY: 220/240 V, 50 Hz

PUBLIC HOLIDAYS
1 January: New Year's Day
2 February: Huravee Day
31 March: Martyrs' Day

Start of Ramadan
Eid el-Fitr
Eid el-Adha
26 July: Independence Day
Islamic New Year
Moulud, Prophet Mohammed's Birthday
24, 25 October: National Day
11 November: Republic Day

COMMUNICATIONS
International calls are handled by operator: dial 190.
International calls, fax, telex and cables: Dhiraagu, on Chandhani Magu, off Marine Drive 0700–2000 weekdays and 0800–1800 holidays.
Post office (corner of Marine Drive and Chandhani Magu): 0730–1330, 1600–1750 Saturday to Thursday.
There are international flights from Malé to Singapore, Amsterdam and Colombo.

MEDICAL
Central Hospital, Sosun Magu, Henveiru, Malé. ☎ 322400.
Flying Swiss Ambulance Clinic, Huvadhoo, Marine Drive, Malé, 24-hour emergency service. ☎ 324500.
There are health centres on all the inhabited atolls.

DIPLOMATIC MISSIONS
In Malé:
France: 1/27 Chandhani Magu.
☎ 323760 (for visas for Réunion, Mayotte and Comoros).
India: Orchid Magu. ☎ 323015.
Sri Lanka: Orchid Magu. ☎ 322845.
United States: Mandhu-edhuruge, Violet Magu. ☎ 322581.

International Airport. Tourist resorts have been set up on uninhabited islands, while in other islands efforts are made to preserve the purity of local culture and religion.

Malé, the capital, is the sole urban settlement, the centre of government and economic life. Of the 200,000 inhabitants, over a quarter live in Malé. The population is a mixture of Sri Lankan, Indian, Indonesian, Malay, Arab, African and European origins. Dhivehi is the main language, which is strongly influenced by Arabic, although English is widely understood. The Maldives are an Islamic country, which means certain customs must be respected. Pork and alcohol are only available on the tourist islands. A certain modesty in dress is expected.

Lying close to the equator, the monsoons are mild and calms common. The SW monsoon blows from May to October, bringing more rain and stronger winds especially in June and July. The NE monsoon lasts from November to April. Temperatures average between 25°C and 31°C (77–88°F).

Entry Regulations

Port of entry
Malé 4°10′N 73°30′E.

Procedure on arrival
Yachts can only clear in and out at Malé and should not stop anywhere else without written permission.

On arrival, the port should be contacted on VHF Channel 16. One may first be boarded by security, especially if arriving at night. Customs, immigration and health will board during office hours to carry out clearance. On departure, one should first clear immigration, then the port authority and finally customs. This can take some time.

Customs
Firearms must be declared on arrival and will be confiscated until departure. One must make sure one gets a receipt. One should have a firearms permit, otherwise on departure one has to go to the Ministry of Defence with the receipt to get approval for the return of the firearms.

Being a Muslim society, dogs are considered unclean and are required to be kept on board.

Prohibited imports are alcohol, pork products, and pornographic material. The export of tortoiseshell, turtleshell and whole black coral is forbidden.

As Malé is a free port, no duties are levied, but goods must be declared.

Immigration
All tourists except Sri Lankans are given a 30-day visitor's permit on arrival. Indians, Pakistanis, Bangladeshis and Italians are given a 90-day permit. For a nominal fee the permit may be extended. Sri Lankans must obtain a visa in advance.

Cruising permit

A special permit must be obtained if wishing to sail to any other atolls besides Malé Atoll. Application should be made to the Ministry of Atolls Administration, Faashanaa Building, Marine Drive, Malé 20-05.

Health

Malaria prophylaxis is recommended.

Fees

Port charges are Rf50.

Anchorage charges: the first two weeks are free, after that there is a fee according to the length of stay:

Rf 50 per day 15 to 45 days
Rf 80 per day 46 to 90 days
Rf 150 per day over 91 days.

Facilities

The few available facilities are all on Malé which has some small workshops capable of simple repairs. As most food has to be imported, mainly from Sri Lanka, provisions are expensive. There is a good fresh produce market on Marine Drive on the waterfront and also a fish market nearby. Fuel and even water are only available in Malé, the latter being scarce in the outer islands. There are weekly flights to Singapore so emergency spares could be flown in.

OMAN

Oman is a sultanate on the eastern end of the Arabian peninsula. Tourism is not encouraged and virtually all the foreigners allowed into the country come on business. Recently there has been a change of heart concerning yachts, some being allowed to stop for a few days at Mina Raysut, near the town of Salalah. However, cruising the coast is still forbidden and occasionally in some parts there has been guerilla activity. Practically all yachts which call in Oman are bound for the Red Sea and although a detour is necessary if coming from Sri Lanka, the route from India, particularly Bombay, passes very close to Raysut, the only place where yachts appear to be tolerated at the moment.

Country Profile

During the first centuries AD the Persians dominated the northern coastal districts. By the seventh century Sohar, the Omani capital, had become one of the most important of the Indian Ocean sea ports, and gradually Omani maritime power came to dominate the Persian Gulf and Indian Ocean, controlling the main trade routes to the Far East and Africa. In the early sixteenth century the first Portuguese visited the Omani coast, establishing trading posts, and until 1650 they controlled Muscat and several other coastal settlements. From the seventeenth century the Omanis grew in power, resisting Persian invasions, and conquering Portuguese settlements in the Indian Ocean including Mogadishu, Mombasa, and the islands of Zanzibar and Mafia. The present dynasty began with Ahmad ibn Said, elected Imam in 1749. The maritime empire reached its height under Sultan Seyyid Said (1807–56) who moved the centre of his empire to Zanzibar. Omani power was eroded by European expansion and especially the growth of British influence in the Indian Ocean.

Since the decline of its trading empire Omani economy remained largely at subsistence level, based on agriculture, fishing and herding. Then in the 1960s oil was discovered, and the revenues from this soon brought the country prosperity. From 1970 Sultan Qaboos ibn Said undertook to modernise the country. In 1982 the first refinery for the domestic market was opened, and reserves of natural gas are starting to be exploited. However, a large percentage of the population remain in the agricultural sector, being nomads raising livestock. Apart from oil, the main exports are dates, limes and dried fish.

The population of 1,130,000, consists of two main tribes, the Yemeni, and the Nizanis who came originally from north-west Arabia. In the urban areas there are minorities of Indians, Pakistanis, Baluchis and East Africans. Arabic is the official language, but there are also many dialects, and English is spoken by businessmen. Oman is a Muslim country, but Omanis appear to be more tolerant in their views and attitudes than some of the more fundamentalist Muslim nations. The capital is Muscat.

April to October is very hot with high humidity along the coasts – it can reach up to 50°C (122°F) in the shade. During November to March, the period of the NE monsoon, the climate is more pleasant, with occasional rains.

Entry Regulations

Ports of entry

Mina Raysut 16°56′N 54°00′E, Mina al Fahal 23°39′N 58°32′E, Mina Qaboos (Muscat) 23°38′N 58°34′E.

Practical Information

LOCAL TIME: GMT + 4

BUOYAGE: IALA A

CURRENCY: Omani rial of 1000 biaza

BUSINESS HOURS
Friday is the day of rest.
Banks: 0800–1200 Saturday to
Wednesday, 0800–1130 Thursday (opens
1 hour later during Ramadan).
Shops: 0900–1300, 1600–1930 Saturday
to Thursday.

ELECTRICITY: 220 V, 50 Hz

PUBLIC HOLIDAYS
Muslim New Year
Prophet's Birthday
Prophet's Proclamation
Eid el-Fitr (five days)
Eid el-Adha (five days)
National Day (five days)

COMMUNICATIONS
There are good international
telecommunications.

There are regular flights to Europe and
South East Asia from Seeb international
airport. Salalah airport is used only for
domestic flights.

MEDICAL
Good medical care and hospitals in all
towns.

DIPLOMATIC MISSIONS
In Muscat:
Canada: PO Box 443. ☎ 601680.
New Zealand: PO Box 520. ☎ 794932.
United Kingdom: ☎ 738501.
United States: PO Box 966. ☎ 745006.

Procedure on arrival

Mina Raysut: The port authority should be contacted on VHF Channels 12 or 16. The ship's papers and passports should be taken to the port authority, where they will be retained until departure. Yachts are normally advised to anchor inside the protected naval base. Shore passes must be obtained to leave the port for visits to Salalah.

Limited travel inland may be allowed with special permission. Pleasure yachts do not appear to be welcome at Mina al Fahal and Mina Qaboos.

Customs

Firearms must be declared. Dogs are not allowed to land.

Immigration

Visas are not normally issued to tourists; however, people arriving on yachts without a visa have been allowed to stay a few days.

Israeli passport holders or those with an Israeli visa in their passport are forbidden entry.

Visas are required by all except countries of the Arabian peninsula. The normal procedure for obtaining a visa entails obtaining a NOC (No Objection Certificate) from the Directorate General of Immigration (the Royal Oman Police) by contacting the Oman Chamber of Commerce (businessmen) or hotels and tour operators (tourists). The NOC authorises the Directorate General to issue a visa, which will be deposited by the sponsor at the point of entry (normally Seeb International Airport) to be stamped in the passport on arrival.

Health

Malaria prophylaxis is recommended.

Warning

It has been reported that satellite fixes cannot be obtained from approximately 40 miles offshore and when approaching Mina Raysut. The authorities in Oman are aware of this phenomenon, but have not been able to offer an explanation.

Facilities

There is a supermarket and fresh produce market in Salalah, which is seven miles from the port. Some repair facilities are available in the port area as well as fuel and water. For emergency repair, one should contact the naval base.

SAUDI ARABIA

Saudi Arabia is a vast desert country on the Arabian peninsula between the Persian Gulf and the Red Sea. Mecca, the holiest place of Islam, is sited here and Saudi Arabia is a very conservative Muslim country, difficult to visit by foreigners, except Muslims on a pilgrimage to Mecca. In order to preserve religious purity, tourism is actively discouraged. This also includes cruising yachts. A few yachts which have been forced to call at a Saudi port have been treated courteously, once the authorities have ascertained that the stop has been caused by a genuine emergency. Yachts that have either strayed into Saudi waters or have been apprehended cruising the offlying Farasan Islands without permission, have been escorted into port and detained for a few days before being allowed to go on their way. Anyone intending to sail to Saudi Arabia must approach the authorities in advance to

Practical Information

LOCAL TIME: GMT + 3

BUOYAGE: IALA A

CURRENCY: Saudi riyal (SR) of 100 halalah

BUSINESS HOURS
Banks: 0830–1200 Saturday to Thursday and 1600/1700 to 1800/1900 Saturday to Wednesday.
Business: 0800–1300, 1700–2000, closing 1300 on Thursday for weekend (Thursday/Friday).

Government offices: 0730–1430 Saturday to Wednesday. Smoking is forbidden in government buildings.

ELECTRICITY: 110/120 V, 60 Hz

PUBLIC HOLIDAYS
There are no official public holidays, but businesses close a few days before the end of Ramadan and reopen after the end of Eid el-Fitr. They close one week before 10th Dhu el-Hijja until the end of Eid el-Adhar.

COMMUNICATIONS
There are regular international flights from both Jeddah and Riyadh.

DIPLOMATIC MISSIONS
In Jeddah:
Australia: 59 Al Amir Abdullah, Al-Faisal Street, Al Hamra District 5. ☎ (2) 665-1303.
Canada: Headquarters Building, Zahid Corporate Group. ☎ (2) 667-1156.
New Zealand: c/o Associated Agencies, Sindus Bldg, Al Madian St. ☎ (2) 651-2109.
United Kingdom: Jeddah Towers, City Bank Building. ☎ (2) 691-5852.
United States: Palestine Road, Ruwais. ☎ (2) 667-0080.

obtain the necessary permission. Otherwise it is better to avoid its waters, unless one is forced to make an emergency stop there.

Country Profile

As the site of Mecca and Medina this area has always been of prime importance to the Islamic religion. From these holy cities the Arabs disseminated Islam to the world and spread Arab power west throughout North Africa to Spain, and east to India and Indonesia. For centuries most of the Arab peninsula was under Ottoman rule, and its peoples were largely nomadic tribes. The nineteenth century saw the rise of the fervent Wahabis, who wanted to restore Islam to its original purity, coming into conflict with the Turks. After the collapse of the Ottoman empire at the end of the First World War, Saudi Arabia came into being.

King Ibn Saud, ruling from 1932 to 1953, modernised the country and succeeding members of his family have ruled since. The stability of the country grew under King Faisal, who was assassinated in 1975, to be succeeded by his brother Khaled and then in 1982 by another brother King Fahd.

Most of the land is desert, and only a small area is cultivable. The vast oil reserves around the Gulf provide a huge income, which Saudi Arabia is investing in various projects in order to end its dependence on oil revenue. A labour shortage means that a lot of Egyptian and Palestinian workers have been brought in, but also many European and American specialists. Although tourism is officially frowned upon, a considerable income is generated by the many

pilgrims visiting the holy site of Mecca.

Of the more than 10 million inhabitants, many are nomadic peoples and about 2.5 million are foreign workers. Arabic is the official language, while some government officials and businessmen speak English. Riyadh is the capital.

Islam is very strictly observed in Saudi Arabia, which is the main reason why non-Islamic tourists are not welcome. Alcohol is banned and photography frowned upon. Female visitors are only allowed into the country if they are chaperoned by a male. Mecca and Medina are off limits to non-believers.

The climate is very hot from April to September. Winters are cooler and the weather in coastal areas is very pleasant.

Entry Regulations

Ports of entry
Yanbu' al Bahr (Yenbo or Yambo) 24°06′N 38°03′E, Mira' al Jeddah 21°28′N 39°10′E.

Procedure on arrival
Yachts are allowed to enter the above ports, which are the main ports of Saudi Arabia, only in an emergency. Port control should be contacted on VHF Channel 16 before arrival. Only the captain is allowed ashore to complete formalities. Both the yacht and crew are normally restricted to the port area, but if allowed ashore everyone must return aboard before sundown. Travel inland is not permitted, nor may anywhere else but these two ports be visited. Cruising along the coast is strictly forbidden.

Customs

A licence is required for firearms. Dogs are banned. Alcohol and pork products are prohibited. All alcoholic drinks and products which contain pork will be sealed on board during the duration of the stay.

Immigration

Visas are difficult to obtain as tourism is not encouraged. A three-day transit/business visa is all that is normally issued. For a visa application submitted outside of one's country of residence, it may be necessary to produce a letter of reference from one's own embassy. Yachts arriving with no visas will probably be allowed a few days stay only. Entry visas are not normally issued to holders of Israeli passports, passports which have been stamped with Israeli visas, or if there is some proof that one has been or intends to go to Israel.

Restrictions

One should not take photographs of Saudi women, airports or government buildings.

Facilities

Both repair facilities and provisioning are better at Jeddah, which is Saudi Arabia's main port. Fuel is easily available. There are several workshops, as well as a ship repair yard with a slipway in Jeddah, which can also undertake electrical and electronic repair. Yanbu also has some local workshops well equipped to deal with emergency repairs.

SOMALIA

Somalia, or the Somali Democratic Republic as it has been called since the 1969 military coup, lies on the Arabian Sea at the mouth of the Red Sea. With nearly 2000 miles of coast around the Horn of Africa, Somalia has the second longest coastline in the continent. The interior is mostly desert where nomadic peoples roam, with mountains to the north and plains in the south.

With the exception of a few man-made ports, there are no natural harbours and there is little to attract cruising yachts to this country. For many years, foreign visitors were not welcome, although recently more travellers have been to the country, as visas have been easier to obtain. A few yachts have called in at one of the ports on the eastern coast, but most stops were dictated by emergency reasons. The total lack of facilities and the likelihood of having to deal with corrupt officials are sufficient reasons to avoid Somalia for the time being.

Country Profile

The Somalis have inhabited this area for many thousands of years. Greek and Arab writers of the ancient world used to call these handsome people the 'Black Berbers'. The Egyptians, who in 1500 BC knew of the port of Mogadishu, named it the Land of Punt. Mogadishu sent frankincense and myrrh to the Arabian peninsula, and traded as far as China. The whole Somali coast was part of the Arab trading routes around the Indian Ocean, a network extending down the East African coast as far as Mozambique. This prosperity faded when Portugal found the sea route to India via the Cape of Good Hope. Somalia, with no resources that Europeans could exploit, was largely ignored.

In the nineteenth century Somalia was divided up between its neighbours and the colonial powers. The Sultanate of Oman controlled southern Somalia, while Britain claimed northern Somalia, and the French took Djibouti. Italy bought Mogadishu and the surrounding area from the Omanis in 1889. Ethiopia meanwhile occupied much of the Ogaden Desert, an area ethnically part of Somalia, which remains a source of bitter conflict between the two countries up to the present day.

The British and Italian Somalias both became independent in 1960, and were united soon afterwards. In 1969 a radical socialist regime came to power after a military coup and the Somali Democratic Republic was formed. The United States withdrew its aid and this was replaced by economic and military aid from the USSR, until the latter decided to also support Ethiopia and was therefore ordered out of Somalia. During the 1970s Somali guerillas, supported by the government, tried to recover Ogaden, but failed due to Russian and Cuban aid given to Ethiopia. The guerilla warfare still continues in the north. There has been some rapprochement with the West in more recent years and diplomatic relations were reinstated with Ethiopia in 1988.

The lack of natural resources is a major problem and the majority of the population are nomadic herdsmen. Agricultural production is mainly for domestic consumption, although some export crops are being developed. The fishing industry is expanding, but there is little else. Frequent droughts and the influx of refugees from Ogaden are both burdens on the economy.

The population of 5 million is concentrated in the

Practical Information

LOCAL TIME: GMT + 3

BUOYAGE: IALA A

CURRENCY: Somali shilling (SSh) of 100 cents. The best currency to exchange is US dollars. Saudi riyals and pounds sterling are also accepted but nothing else. Foreign currency declaration forms must be filled in on arrival and one may have to show them when changing money.

BUSINESS HOURS
Banks: 0800–1130 Saturday to Thursday. Business and shops: 0900–1300, 1600–2000 Saturday to Thursday. Government offices: 0800–1400 Saturday to Thursday.

ELECTRICITY: 220 V, 50 Hz

PUBLIC HOLIDAYS
1 January: New Year's Day
1 May: Labour Day
Eid el-Adha
26 June: Independence of Somaliland
1 July: Independence of Somali Republic
Eid el-Arifa
Hijra
Ashoura
21, 22 October: Anniversary of the 1969 Revolution
Mouloud (Prophet's Birthday)

COMMUNICATIONS
The international telephone service is relatively good.
There are international flights from Mogadishu to Rome, Frankfurt, Nairobi, Cairo and other Middle Eastern cities for onward connections.

DIPLOMATIC MISSIONS
In Mogadishu:
Kenya: Km 4, Via Mecca. ☎ 80857.
Sudan: Via Hoddor.
United Kingdom: Waddada Xasan Geedd, Abtoow. ☎ 20288.
United States: Corso Primo Luglio. ☎ 28011.
Yemen: Via Berbera or Corso Republica.

---

coastal towns, near the Juba and Shebelle rivers in the south, while there are scattered nomadic peoples inland. Islam is the religion of the majority, although traditional rituals may still be found. Somali is the official language, although a written form was only developed in 1972. Educated Somalis speak Arabic, some English in the north and Italian in the south. Swahili is spoken widely in southern coastal towns. The capital is Mogadishu.

The climate is dictated by the two monsoons. It is hot all year round and also humid in the rainy seasons. The temperatures are very high in summer and can reach up to 42°C (108°F) from June to September in the northern coastal towns. At the height of the SW monsoon, May to October, winds often reach gale force. The current along the Somali coast can be very strong, particularly during the SW monsoon.

Entry Regulations

Ports of entry
Mogadishu 2°01′N 45°21′E, Kismayu/Chisimaio 0°23′S 42°33′E, Berbera 10°27′N 45°01′E, Merca/Marka 1°43′N 44°46′E.

Procedure on arrival
Mogadishu: Port control monitors VHF Channel 16 and should be contacted to announce the yacht's ETA and request clearance.
Berbera: Port Radio (call sign 60Y) monitors MF 500 KHz and should be contacted to advise a yacht on procedure.

Customs
Firearms will be retained. Animals should be declared.

Immigration
All nationalities must obtain visas before arrival. In the proximity of Somalia, visas can be obtained from Nairobi at International House, Marma Ngina St. A letter may be required from one's own embassy. The Italian embassy in Dar es Salaam also issues Somali visas and there is also a Somali embassy in Djibouti.

Restrictions
A permit is needed if a camera is taken ashore. Permits are issued by the National Censorship Office near the US embassy in Mogadishu.

Health
Yellow fever and cholera vaccination is essential. Malaria prophylaxis is also recommended. A yellow fever vaccination certificate must be shown on entry, otherwise the vaccination will be done on the spot and not under very hygienic conditions.

Fees
There are very high harbour charges.

Facilities

Provisioning is rather limited, although there is some fresh produce available depending on the season. Mogadishu is very rarely visited by yachts. The harbour is safe, but the area where small boats anchor is shallow due to silting. Some repairs are possible as there are various workshops in the port area in Mogadishu, but they may take time. There is a Swedish company building fibreglass boats, so they could be approached in an emergency. A good source of help or advice in Mogadishu is the Anglo-American Club, near the old port in Lido Road, where visiting sailors are welcome.

Further Reading

Traveller's Guide to East Africa and the Indian Ocean

SRI LANKA

This large island shaped like a teardrop lies to the south of the Indian subcontinent, from which it is separated by the Palk Strait. The island is one of coastal plains and central highlands covered in forests. Inland can be seen the ancient cities and palaces of one of the oldest civilisations in the world.

Sri Lanka is a popular stopping point for yachts on their way to the Red Sea. Most come from the Pacific, the Far East or South East Asia, and the traffic is mostly westbound as only a few sail to Sri Lanka from the west. Sri Lanka is also a good point of departure for cruising the Maldives, Chagos and Seychelles. As a cruising destination in itself, Sri Lanka has little attraction and the troubles that have befallen the island during the last decade, although not affecting cruising yachts greatly, have almost destroyed the tourist industry. The situation appears to be improving and it is hoped that before too long visiting sailors will once again be able to tour the interesting interior of this country.

Virtually all yachts that call at Sri Lanka do so at the old port of Galle, conveniently located on the island's southern tip. Very few yachts cruise outside of Galle and the beautiful natural harbour of Trincomalee on the east coast is for the time being out of bounds because of recurrent political troubles, while Colombo's large commercial harbour has no attractions as there are no provisions for yachts and formalities are even more complex than in Galle.

Fishermen mending nets at Galle, Sri Lanka.

Practical Information

LOCAL TIME: GMT + 5

BUOYAGE: IALA A

CURRENCY: Sri Lanka rupee (CER or Rs) of 100 cents. All foreign currency must be recorded on arrival on a currency declaration form, which is surrendered on departure. Unspent rupees can be reconverted.
In Galle only banknotes and travellers' cheques can be changed.
Obtaining cash on a credit card is possible only in Colombo.

BUSINESS HOURS
Banks: 0900–1330 Tuesday to Friday, 0900–1300 Monday.
Business and government offices: 0800/0830–1630 Monday to Friday.
Shops: 1000–1800 Monday to Friday, 1000–1400 Saturday.

ELECTRICITY: 230/240 V, 50 Hz

PUBLIC HOLIDAYS
Poya Day: the full moon day of each month is a public holiday and all offices are closed.
4 February: Independence Day
13 April: Sinhalese and Tamil New Year
Easter Monday
1 May: Labour Day
May: full moon, Vesak Festival
22 May: National Heroes Day
25 December: Christmas

COMMUNICATIONS
International telephone, telex and telegraph services are available.
In Galle international telephone calls can be made via Don Windsor.
General post office, in Galle, and small one in the suburb Magalle, opening hours: 0900–1630.
There are international flights from Colombo to European and Asian destinations.

MEDICAL
Colombo General Hospital.
Karapitiya General Hospital, Galle.
There are hospitals with casualty departments and private clinics in all major centres.

DIPLOMATIC MISSIONS
In Colombo:
Australia: 3 Cambridge Place.
☎ (1) 598767.
Canada: 6 Gregory's Rd, Cinnamon Gardens. ☎ (1) 595841.
India: 36–38 Galle Rd. ☎ (1) 421604.
New Zealand: c/o Aitken Spence & Co. Ltd, PO Box 5. ☎ (1) 27861.
United Kingdom: Galle Rd, Kollupitiya. ☎ (1) 27611.
United States: 201 Galle Rd. ☎ (1) 421604.

Country Profile

Sri Lanka's written history begins in 544 BC with the arrival of the Indian prince Vijaya, marking the start of the Mahavansa chronicles. The Sinhalese kings ruled for 21 centuries, despite regular invasions from southern India, developing an advanced civilisation, with the Buddhist religion at its core. The third century BC was a time of painting and literature, of building monasteries and cities with elaborate irrigation schemes, and remains of all this can still be seen.

In the sixteenth century the Portuguese were the first Europeans to visit and secured a monopoly over the spice and cinnamon trades. The Sinhalese resisted annexation and continued to rule from the capital Kandy in the central highlands. The Dutch expelled the Portuguese in the mid-seventeenth century, and suffered the same fate in their turn being ousted by the British at the end of the eighteenth century. Early in the nineteenth century the island became the Crown Colony of Ceylon, and the Sinhalese King was exiled. Coffee, tea and rubber plantations were developed, and railways and roads built. Tamils were brought in from southern India as labourers.

Independence was finally regained in 1948. The name Ceylon was later changed to Sri Lanka when the country's status was changed to that of a Democratic Socialist Republic. Since 1983 tensions often followed by violent clashes have existed between the Sinhalese and Tamils. Tamils make up 18 per cent of the population and are concentrated in the north of the island. Many of them have been there for over 2000 years, but the rest are descended from more recent immigrants from neighbouring Tamil Nadu state in southern India. Tamil separatists want an independent state in the northern part of Sri Lanka. In 1987, India intervened to re-establish order, but this brought renewed fighting between Indian forces and the Tamil rebels. India finally withdrew her forces in 1990 and peace negotiations between the Tamil rebels and the government began.

Sri Lanka is famous for its tea and is one of the top world suppliers. Also exported are rubber, coconut products, clothes, cinnamon, precious and semi-precious stones. Agriculture is an important part of the economy and much rice is grown for domestic needs.

The population numbers 16.4 million. As well as Sinhalese and Tamils, there are also Moors, Burghers (of Portuguese and Dutch origin), Eurasians and Malays. The majority of Sinhalese are Buddhist, most Tamils are Hindu, while some Sri Lankans are Christian and Muslim. Sinhala and Tamil are the official languages and English is also widely spoken. Colombo is the capital.

The climate is tropical, with two distinct monsoon seasons. Heavy rainfall along the western coast occurs during the SW monsoon, particularly between May and September. The temperatures on the coast are usually high, while in the hills it is pleasant all year round. The island is occasionally affected by tropical cyclones, which develop in the Bay of Bengal, the worst months being November and December.

Entry Regulations

Ports of entry
Galle 6°01′N 80°13′E, Colombo 6°57′N 79°51′E, Trincomalee 8°36′N 81°15′E, Jaffna 9°40′N 79°59′E, Kankesanthurai 9°49′N 80°03′E.

Procedure on arrival
On arrival in a Sri Lankan port, the captain should inform the harbour master, or report to the nearest customs officer or police station immediately. A health officer will board the yacht and inspect it before granting pratique. Then the yacht will be inspected by a customs officer, who will require the last port clearance. Crew lists and details of any passengers or crew who are leaving the vessel have to be given to the immigration office.

Colombo: Arriving yachts should contact the port authority on VHF Channel 16 before proceeding into the harbour. The instructions detailed above should then be followed.

Galle: Flying the Q flag, one should anchor in the inner harbour tying the stern to one of the buoys to prevent swinging. A port authority official will come out to the boat during office hours (0800–1200, 1300–1600 Monday to Friday) to fill in an arrival report (yacht details, crew list, etc.). All foreign yachts are supposed to appoint an agent and names of agents will be given by the port authority official. The agent appointed will come to the yacht after having been informed by the port authority. Usually the agent will bring the health officer for the quarantine inspection.

The captain can come ashore in an emergency and contact customs and immigration at the gate and inform the port authority of arrival. The captain can appoint an agent whilst ashore.

Clearance must be carried out through this agent, both on arrival and departure. The agent is supposed to ensure that the captain complies with port and immigration regulations, that he has sufficient funds in foreign exchange for the fees and that all port dues and customs duties are settled before departure. The ruling concerning agents has not been confirmed officially from Colombo, although this appears to be the current

procedure accepted by officials in Galle.

It has sometimes taken several days for yachts to complete all the clearance operations.

The port authority will indicate the area in each port where yachts may anchor. Yachts should not move from their original mooring without the harbour master's permission. Permission is also needed before hauling out a yacht. One should only land by dinghy at the appointed places in each port.

Procedure on departure
On departure a clearance certificate must be obtained from customs. If the yacht is sailing along the coast, a clearance certificate must be obtained for calling at other ports in Sri Lanka. Access is only permitted to official ports of entry.

Customs
Firearms must be declared on arrival and held in custody by customs until departure. One must ensure that a receipt is obtained for the firearms.

Animals should not be taken ashore. Rabies is widespread and in 1989 over one hundred people died of it in Sri Lanka.

All electrical and electronic goods such as cameras or radios must be re-exported.

Customs permission has to be obtained for any item that is taken off or put on board the yacht, including ship's stores and items being repaired. In Galle the customs at the harbour gate will often check the contents of any bags carried.

Yachts may stay up to two months.

Immigration
For all nationalities arriving on a yacht, a visa is granted on arrival for one month. This visa can be extended for up to two months.

Any crew or passengers leaving the yacht in Sri Lanka must get a landing endorsement from immigration or police before leaving the harbour. It is an offence for someone who is not a crew member or no longer a crew member to move ashore without a landing endorsement. Likewise, the master may not engage any crew while in Sri Lanka without permission from immigration or police. A new crew list should be given to the police if there are any crew changes.

Fees
Port dues: Rs 1000 (approximately US$66), for one month or part thereof, which must be paid on arrival. Payment made at one port is valid for other ports.

Agent fee: In Galle approximately US$40 for the first 30 days or part thereof.

Customs departure tax: Rs 500
No overtime fees apply as all formalities are completed within normal working hours.

Restrictions

Anchorage in any other area in Sri Lankan territorial waters except a port of entry is forbidden to yachts, unless in distress or an emergency situation.

Facilities

Facilities are generally poor and as there are very few local yachts, the only workshops that are used to dealing with yachts are those in Galle. The fishing cooperative has a slipway, but this is temporarily out of action. It is soon to be reopened under naval management. There is a fuel pump on the dock, where small amounts of diesel fuel can be bought. Larger amounts can be ordered by road tanker. Water can be obtained from a tank at the fisheries dock. There are various workshops in Galle capable of electrical or engine repair. There is also a small boatyard building fibreglass boats near the old harbour, which can deal with some repairs.

A local entrepreneur, Don Windsor, has set up a yacht service company, run from his home near Galle harbour. He is the best man to contact in an emergency. His office can also be used for overseas telephone calls, mailing address and to book excursions into the interior. He can arrange most repairs including electronic, engine, and sail repair as well as metal work and welding. He can also supply courtesy flags, fill LPG bottles and arrange for essential spares to be ordered from abroad and airfreighted by courier. More complex engine or electrical repairs may have to be made in Colombo.

There are no chandleries or marine supplies either in Colombo or Galle. Marine Overseas Agency in Colombo has a stock of nautical charts and publications. There are no supermarkets in Galle and most provisioning has to be done from small grocery shops, which have a rather limited selection. There is a very good daily fresh produce market in Galle, where provisions can be bought for the onward voyage.

Further Reading

Red Sea and Indian Ocean Cruising Guide
Sri Lanka – a travel survival kit

SUDAN

Sudan is the largest country in Africa, but only a small part is on the Red Sea coast. The north is desert, and the south tropical and it is the country where Arab and black African cultures meet. The River Nile runs through the country from Kenya down to Egypt past Khartoum, the capital, in the centre of the country.

Most sailors only come in contact with Port Sudan, the country's main port on the Red Sea. It is a convenient stop for yachts sailing up or down the Red Sea, although its facilities are poor and nothing has been done to improve them. A dirty and crowded harbour and town, Port Sudan is a poor introduction to this vast country and those who come from the south should try and stop at Port Suakin. In the fifteenth century it was the major port of the western Red Sea. Huge camel caravans brought copper, ivory, hides and slaves from the interior, returning with cotton, spices, silks and beads. By the sixteenth century the harbour could hold 600 ships, and during the nineteenth century Suakin became even more cosmopolitan, only to prove too small for large ocean steamers. Today it is deserted, a sad ghost town of ruined buildings, where Kitchener's old headquarters can still be seen overlooking the harbour.

Port Sudan's position at the halfway point of the Red Sea also marks the point where the winds change from prevailing southerlies to northerlies. Northbound yachts, as are the majority who call here, face an uphill beat all the way to the Suez Canal, while southbound boats usually have to fight contrary winds as far as Bab el Mandeb and even beyond. If not in a great hurry, the best tactic for northbound boats is to cover as much ground as possible inside the reefs, which extend parallel to the shore along most of Sudan's coastline. This not only makes life easier but also more pleasant as the reef anchorages offer perfect shelter and the diving and fishing are superb.

Country Profile

The Ancient Egyptians called the lands to their south 'bilad al sudan', 'lands of the blacks', and they made occasional forays into it for ivory, ebony and slaves. From the fourth century Christian kingdoms ruled over the area, but from the sixth century they were progressively taken over by the Arabs. In the north Sultans established their rule and Islam extended its influence. In 1821 the Egyptians, then under Ottoman rule, took control of north Sudan. Only the Fur Sultanate in the south-east remained independent. In

Practical Information

LOCAL TIME: GMT + 2

BUOYAGE: IALA A

CURRENCY: Sudanese pound (£S) of 100 piastres (PT). It is illegal to export any £S on leaving. Foreign currency must be declared on arrival and departure. Kenyan or Egyptian currency cannot be exchanged.

BUSINESS HOURS
Banks: 0830–1200 Saturday to Thursday.
Shops: 0800–1400, 1800–2000 Saturday to Thursday.
Government offices: 0800–1430 Saturday to Thursday.

ELECTRICITY: 240 V, 50 Hz

PUBLIC HOLIDAYS
1 January: Independence Day
3 March: Unity Day
Sham el Nassim (Spring Festival)
25 May: May Revolution day
Eid el-Fitr
Eid el-Adha
Islamic New Year
Mouloud (Prophet's birthday)

COMMUNICATIONS
Phone calls can be made at post offices and hotels.
Telegraph offices open 24 hours daily.
Post office open 0730–1300, 1730–1830 Saturday to Thursday.

Khartoum airport has international flights and can be reached from Port Sudan by air, train or bus. There are also flights from Port Sudan to Cairo and Jeddah, which both have good onward connections.

DIPLOMATIC MISSIONS
In Khartoum:
Egypt: Mogram Street.
United Kingdom: New Aboulela Building. ☎ 70767.
United States: Abdel Latif Avenue. ☎ 7470.
There is an Egyptian consulate in Port Sudan, where it is convenient to obtain an Egyptian visa.

1881 Mohammed Ahmed al-Mahdi led a successful uprising against the Ottomans and a puritanical Islamic state was established. Al-Mahdi's rule was short-lived and ended in 1898, when his forces were defeated by those led by Field Marshal Kitchener from British-occupied Egypt. The southern Sultanate was also overthrown by Anglo-Egyptian forces in 1916 and as a result Sudan was made an Anglo-Egyptian condominium.

From the 1930s onwards a movement for independence grew. Civil war between the north and south began in 1955, and a year later the independent Republic of Sudan was established. The continuing war caused great economic problems for the country and civil governments alternated with military regimes. The war finally ended in 1972 and the south gained some autonomy. A civil government was established in 1986. The antagonism of the southerners was exacerbated after the declaration of Islamic Law in 1984, as there are very few Muslims in the south. Problems continue in the south with the guerilla activities of the Sudanese People's Liberation Movement.

Sudan's history has been dominated by the division between north and south – the northerners have always tended to dominate the country's affairs, much to the southerners' resentment. Among the nearly 22 million Sudanese, there are 500 ethnic groups. Northerners are generally Muslim of Arab origin and language, while the Southerners are African, animist or Christian, with no common language, and closer in lifestyle to neighbouring countries. Although Arabic is the official language, only half the population speak it.

A hundred other languages are spoken, including English in the south.

Sudan is mainly an agricultural country. Cotton is the main export and the development of irrigation, especially along the Nile, is a top priority in this dry country. The foreign debt is large and in the past shortages have been a major problem.

The climate is tropical, hot and dry in the north, and rainier in the south. The Red Sea area is very hot in summer when the winds are mostly northerly. The winter months are very pleasant and the prevailing winds are from the south.

Entry Regulations

Port of entry
Port Sudan 19°37′N 37°14′E.

Procedure on arrival
One should remain on board until cleared by health, then the captain should go to the port office, which will hold the ship's papers until the port dues are paid on departure. The passports must then be left with immigration, which usually holds them until the following day. The immigration fee is then paid and another immigration office has to be visited in East Town to get shore passes.

Yachts have been allowed to anchor along the coast before clearing in, provided no one goes ashore. Yachts stopping in Suakin can check in with the police in New Town (El Geif), which is reached over the causeway.

Procedure on departure

On departure, one must clear with the port office, then pay the port dues at the Port Corporation in East Town. They insist the fee must be paid in convertible foreign currency, preferably US dollars. Next one has to clear customs, and return to the port office to get back the ship's papers.

Customs

Firearms must be declared. Animals are not allowed to land.

Immigration

Yachts in transit are normally allowed visa-free entry for a short period of stay. Visas must be obtained in advance by those who wish to spend longer in the country or who wish to visit the interior. A passport must be valid at least six months beyond the intended period of stay. Visas are valid for three months from the date of issue, for a one month stay. Extensions for two months are obtainable.

South Africans and Israelis are not allowed entry, nor is anyone with evidence of a visit to those countries in their passports.

Health

Cholera and yellow fever vaccinations recommended. An international certificate for yellow fever may be demanded even though it is not obligatory. Malarial prophylaxis is recommended if travelling inland, when one should also avoid swimming in fresh water, as the bilharzia parasite is endemic.

Fees

Port dues, payable in US dollars.

Restrictions

Travel permits are necessary when travelling anywhere in Sudan. These are obtained from the Foreigners Registration Office. The country south of Kosti is closed, due to the activities of the Sudanese People's Liberation Movement. Borders with Ethiopia and Libya are closed.

Facilities

Provisioning with fresh produce is very good in Port Sudan where there is a daily market. There are also various grocery shops, some of them selling in bulk. Fuel is available from the fuel dock in South Town. Water is also available, but must be treated. There is also a good market in Port Suakin (New Town) but one must go early in the morning. There are few other provisions and what is available is expensive. There is no bank in Suakin.

There are only limited repair facilities in Port Sudan, although there are some workshops around the harbour that can undertake simple repairs. No kind of spares are available and as flights to Khartoum are infrequent, one should not rely on being able to obtain essential spares from abroad.

Further Reading

Africa on a Shoestring
Traveller's Guide to East Africa and the Indian Ocean
Africa, The Nile Route
Red Sea and Indian Ocean Cruising Guide

YEMEN

Yemen lies on the south-western edge of the Arabian peninsula, with coasts on the Gulf of Aden and Red Sea. The reunification of the People's Democratic Republic (South Yemen) and the Yemen Arab Republic (North Yemen) occurred in May 1990 at the time of writing and so it is expected that some changes will take place. The information below is compiled from the previous procedures for entering the two separate Yemens.

Previously North Yemen had not encouraged visitors, although a few yachts had called at Hodeidah, the main port. Mainly to shelter from the weather, yachts have sometimes stopped at the Jabal Zugar and Hamish Islands. This practice seemed to be tolerated by the authorities, although one should refrain from going ashore.

Yachts more often call at Aden, the capital of South Yemen, which has been an important port since ancient times and is still a useful stop on the way to or from the Red Sea. It is a busy commercial port, which holds little attraction for cruising yachts. Formalities are complicated and the freedom of movement enjoyed by visiting sailors is full of constraints. The only other choice for a stop in this area is Djibouti, on the African coast, where facilities are better, but prices much higher, the latter being the main factor which has persuaded some cruising yachts to prefer Aden.

Country Profile

In ancient times various kingdoms ruled in Yemen, the most important being that of Saba (Sheba), the

Practical Information

LOCAL TIME: GMT + 3

BUOYAGE: IALA A

CURRENCY: North Yemen: rial; South Yemen: dina of 1000 fils. The dina is also divided into 20 shillings and prices in the market especially are often quoted in shillings.

BUSINESS HOURS
Banks: 0800–1200 Saturday to Thursday.
Business: 0800–1200, 1600–1900 Saturday to Thursday.
Government offices: 0800–1400 Saturday to Thursday.

ELECTRICITY: 220/240 V, 50 Hz

PUBLIC HOLIDAYS
1 January: New Year's Day
Birthday of the Prophet
8 March: International Woman's Day
1 May
22 June: Rectification Movement
Al Isra'a (Al Mi'raj)
Eid El-Fitr (two days)
26 September: Anniversary of the 1962 Revolution
14 October: Anniversary of the 1963 Revolution
30 November: Independence Day
Eid El-Adha (three days)
Islamic New Year

COMMUNICATIONS
Post office at Steamer Point in Aden 0800–1300, 1600–2000 Saturday to Thursday.

There are international flights from Sana'a to many European, Middle East and Asian destinations. Aden has flights to destinations in the Middle East and Eastern Europe, Djibouti and Cairo.

MEDICAL
Aden General Hospital

DIPLOMATIC MISSIONS
In Aden:
United Kingdom: 28 Shara Ho Chi Minh, Khormakasar. ☎ 32711.
In Sana'a:
United Kingdom: 129 Haddah Road. ☎ 215630/33.
United States: PO Box 1088. ☎ 271950/58.

Yemenis then being known as Sabeans. The famous Queen of Sheba travelled north, with many treasures, to visit King Solomon. Myrrh and frankincense, much-prized luxuries in the ancient world, grew naturally in Yemen, and the Sabeans prospered with trade. Also they had a monopoly on the trade of goods from India and Africa, while keeping the origin of the goods a secret, so that in Mediterranean countries Saba was believed to be a very rich place. From the sixth century AD the area lost its importance, being occupied by the Ethiopians and then the Persians. The arrival of Islam in the seventh century saw Yemen become a province on the southern edge of the Islamic Empire. In the ninth century the Zaydi dynasty was established which survived until 1962.

A sultanate independent of the Zaydis established itself in the south of the country. In 1839 the British conquered Aden and established a protectorate in southern Yemen. The Turks occupied the north in 1848, and the eventual border which was settled between Britain and Turkey remained the division between the two Yemeni countries. The south stayed under British rule, but from 1959 Aden and most of the sultanates of southern Yemen increasingly pushed for independence. There was fighting against the British forces from 1963 until independence was gained in 1967. In 1970 South Yemen became the People's Democratic Republic of Yemen with a Marxist-Leninist regime.

North Yemen was occupied by the Turks from 1848 and only after they withdrew at the end of the First World War was the independence of the Zaydi kingdom finally recognised. In 1962 a *coup d'état* saw the 1100 year old Zaydi dynasty overthrown and a republic proclaimed. Until 1970 civil war continued between the royalists supported by Saudi Arabia and the republicans supported by Egypt. The Yemen Arab Republic was proclaimed in 1970.

In May 1990 the two Yemens decided to unite and until elections decide otherwise the new government is drawn from both previous regimes and the capital will be in Sana'a, the previous capital of North Yemen. The decision to reunite the two countries was partly to redress the arbitrary division of the country by Britain and Turkey in the last century, but mainly it was prompted by economic reasons as oil has been discovered in the border area between them.

The population of around 9 million speak Arabic and are Muslim. English is spoken by many in the town of Aden.

Yemen has a subtropical climate. May to September is the period of the SW monsoon, when it is humid and rainy. October to February is drier and cooler, with easterly winds predominating.

Entry Regulations

Ports of entry
Aden 12°48′N 44°58′E, Hodeidah 14°47′N 42°57′E.

Procedure on arrival

Aden: Yachts are usually met by a port control launch on entering the harbour. The yacht anchorage is west of the customs wharf. Formalities are carried out on board. To go ashore, one must exchange one's passport for a shore pass at the immigration office. The pass must be shown at the customs gate at the entrance to the port area, whenever leaving or entering the port. On departure, a duty stamp of 100 fils must be bought from the post office. One must then go to port control to obtain a form for the passports to be returned from immigration.

Hodeidah: Port control in Hodeidah should be contacted in advance on VHF Channel 16 to advise ETA, name of vessel and other details, otherwise the yacht may not be allowed into the port. Hodeidah is approached through a 10 mile long channel. Pilotage is only compulsory for vessels over 150 GRT.

Customs

Firearms must be declared to customs. Animals must not be landed.

Immigration

No entry visa is required for crew members of foreign vessels. This ruling is limited to the Aden area only.

Visas are essential for all nationalities if intending to visit other parts of Yemen outside of the port of Aden. Yachts may be able to stop at Hodeidah in an emergency without the crew having visas, but the nature of this emergency should be made clear during the conversation with Hodeidah port radio.

Cruising permit

It may be possible to obtain a permit to cruise the South Yemen coast, obtainable from customs and immigration. A yacht should not stop in any coastal areas without written permission.

Restrictions

Cameras are not permitted ashore and no photographs should be taken in the port area. Visiting other yachts in the harbour needs permission from customs.

It is forbidden to stop at the islands of Socotra (off Somalia), Perim and Kamaran.

Facilities

Repair facilities in Aden are limited to those operated by the National Dockyard which has a slipway and undertakes general hull and engine repair, as well as electronic repairs on radios and radars. However, they are only supposed to work on commercial vessels, so one may need special approval for them to work on a yacht.

Provisioning is also limited, but there is a daily fresh produce market at Steamer Point. Cheap diesel fuel can be bought at the eastern end of the customs wharf, which also has a water outlet. There is a Sailors Club near the anchorage which has showers and can be used by visitors on yachts.

In Hodeidah a limited amount of provisions may be obtained in the port. There is a small shipyard, with its own slipway, which repairs port craft and navy boats, so they might be able to help out in an emergency.

Further Reading

Red Sea and Indian Ocean Cruising Guide

12 South Indian Ocean

Scattered along the trade wind route from the South Pacific to the Cape of Good Hope, the islands of the South Indian Ocean are visited by a relatively small number of yachts every year. The most popular destinations are the various islands on this route as well as the Seychelles where restrictions imposed on cruising yachts are gradually being eased. On mainland Africa cruising yachts are now welcome in both Tanzania and Kenya, while Mozambique also looks more positive as more yachts sail there.

The region is under the influence of the SE monsoon for most of the year, which provides good sailing conditions. The cyclone season lasts from December to the end of March, but only affects the area south of Mauritius and Madagascar, so that the more northerly islands, such as the Seychelles and Chagos, as well as most of the African coast can be cruised safely all year round. However, to cruise the African coast under the best conditions, it is advisable to do it during the SE monsoon and sail from south to north so as to take advantage of both favourable winds and current, by sailing first to Tanzania, stopping in Dar es Salaam, Zanzibar, Pemba and Mombasa.

Repair facilities for yachts are available in only the few places which have either a resident boating population, such as Kenya and Réunion, or a charter operation, such as the Seychelles. In all other places only basic repairs are possible. Provisioning follows the same pattern, with only basic supplies available in the smaller places and a somewhat better selection in the larger centres. Spares and marine supplies are not available throughout the region, so all essential spares should be carried on board.

CHAGOS

The Chagos archipelago is a collection of islands, reefs and shoals in the Indian Ocean, lying between the 5th and 8th parallel south of the equator. The group has been a British Indian Ocean Territory since 1965, and the largest island, Diego Garcia, is leased to the United States as a military base and is off limits to yachts. There are some 55 other islands, all uninhabited. The group is a British dependency and administered by the British Navy.

Yachts have stopped at some of the outer islands in the group, some people even having spent long periods on these uninhabited islands. This appears to be tolerated, although the islands are sometimes patrolled and one may be asked to show papers and passports. There are British police, customs and immigration officials on Diego Garcia. It is in the best

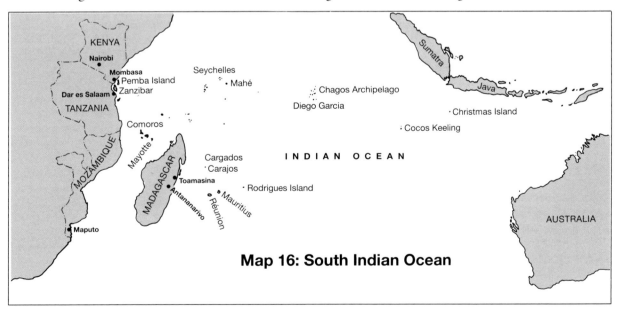

Map 16: South Indian Ocean

interests of all sailors not to upset the present status quo by abusing this tolerance. There are strict conservation rules, which must be observed in order to preserve this unique sanctuary in its present state.

Country Profile

Arab and Malay sailors probably stopped at the Chagos archipelago long before the Portuguese sighted it in 1743. Later that century a French colony was established and a copra industry developed on the larger islands with slaves brought across from Africa and Madagascar. Mauritius administered the group and established a leper settlement there. The inhabitants, a mixture of African and Tamil became known as Ilois and worked on the plantations as well as growing food for themselves. In 1965 the British Indian Ocean Territory was created, which also included several of the islands of the Seychelles. The British removed the entire population to Mauritius, because the United States were looking for an uninhabited group of islands to lease. Some compensation was paid to the Ilois, on condition that they renounce their rights to the islands. The Mauritian government does not recognise the detachment of Chagos from its territory.

Entry Regulations

Diego Garcia may only be entered in a serious emergency. Yachts trying to enter will be stopped outside the main pass and searched by the Navy. If an emergency stop is being made, it is best to contact the authorities on VHF Channel 16, while approaching the island, and advise them of the nature of the emergency. In the past the authorities have done their best to render assistance to yachts with genuine problems.

Restrictions
The islands are a conservation area and all flora and fauna, such as turtles, coconut crabs, live coral and shells, are protected. Spearfishing is not allowed, nor should the heart of palm be taken.

Anchorages
The Egmont Islands, 70 miles north-west of Diego Garcia, have a lagoon which can be entered on its north-west side. Care should be taken when navigating in the lagoon as there are many coral heads. There is an anchorage in the south-east corner by Sudest Islet, but it is not protected from the north-west.

In the north-west of the archipelago, the Peros Banhos atoll consists of about 30 islets and reefs. Most anchorages offer little protection, but there is a good anchorage in the lee of Ile du Coin in the south-east of the atoll.

The Salomon Islands, south-west of Blenheim Reef, are one of the most popular anchorages with yachts. The small lagoon can be entered in the north close to Ile de la Passe and the recommended anchorage is in the south-east.

CHRISTMAS ISLAND

Christmas Island is an Australian territory lying in the Indian Ocean 260 miles south of the Sunda Strait between Sumatra and Java. The island is the tip of an extinct volcano, about 300 metres above sea level, and the cliffs are almost continuous around its coast. The island is a favourite port of call for yachts on passage to the Cocos Keeling Islands, another Australian dependency in the Indian Ocean.

Country Profile

The island was sighted early in the seventeenth century and was only later named Christmas Island on Christmas Day 1643. Inaccurate charts showed several islands during the seventeenth century, but in fact there is only one. The first recorded landing was in 1688, although not until the 1820s did anyone stop for any length of time. In the first half of the nineteenth century, the island became a regular stop for vessels supplying the Cocos Islands. Phosphate was discovered by an expedition in the 1870s, which led to Britain taking control of the island. Soon the first settlers arrived at Flying Fish Cove and phosphate mining began, Chinese labour being imported to work the mines. Mining was disrupted during the Second World War, and most of the inhabitants evacuated to Australia. Bombed by the Japanese, the island surrendered following a mutiny by the Indian troops stationed there. After the war the New Zealand and Australian governments bought the mining company, changed the name to the Christmas Island Phosphate Commission, and set up an intensive mining operation.

The mining of the phosphate reserves dominates the island's economy, although reserves of the best quality phosphate are running out. In 1987 the mine was closed by the Australian government due to industrial unrest. Efforts have been made to develop tourism.

The 3000 inhabitants are Malay, Chinese, Indian

Practical Information

LOCAL TIME: GMT + 7

BUOYAGE: IALA A

CURRENCY: Australian dollar (Aus$).

BUSINESS HOURS
Banks: 1000–1500 Monday to Friday.
Post office: 0800–1200, 1300–1500
Monday to Friday.
Supermarket: 1000–1700 Monday to
Friday, 0830–1130 Saturday.

PUBLIC HOLIDAYS
1 January: New Year's Day
26 January: Australia Day
Chinese New Year
Good Friday, Easter Monday
25 April: ANZAC Day
June: Queen's Birthday
Hari Raya Puasa
Territory Day
Hari Raya Haji
25, 26 December: Christmas

COMMUNICATIONS
Radio telephone to Perth: one can book
a call from the radio shack or post office,
0700–1700 Monday to Friday, and limited
periods at weekends.
Mail can be sent to Poste Restante, Post
Office, Christmas Island, Indian Ocean. It
is recommended to write 'Via Australia'
on letters to ensure there is no confusion
with the Pacific Christmas Island.
There are air links to Perth and
Singapore.

MEDICAL
There is a good hospital.

and Australian. English is the main language and Islam the main religion. The best time to visit the island is during the SE trade wind season, from April to November, as the weather is more pleasant. There is no safe anchorage during the remaining months from December to March, which is the period of the NW monsoon. During this time the weather is wet, March being the wettest month.

Entry Regulations

Port of entry
Flying Fish Cove 10°25′S 105°43′E.

Procedure on arrival
The only anchorage is at Flying Fish Cove on the north-west tip of the island. Yachts should beware of the chains between the shore and the large mooring buoys. The anchorage can be badly affected by swell and yachts are sometimes advised to move either by the police or harbour master.

Arriving yachts should contact the harbour master on VHF Channel 16, who will inform customs and immigration, who are situated in the police station. Outward clearance is also required by the harbour master on leaving, when all bills must be settled. The immigration office is open 0800–1600 Monday to Friday.

Customs
Firearms must be declared to customs and must remain on board. Animals are not allowed to land, as there is a National Park and strict quarantine regulations are in force.

Immigration
No visas are required. Yachts are allowed six months stay, which can be extended if required.

Restrictions
Garbage must not be dumped in Flying Fish Cove, but put in receptacles near the Boat Club. Birds and turtles are protected species in the National Park.

Facilities

Because of the mining operations, facilities are relatively good. Diesel can be bought alongside the barge jetty, where it is delivered by tanker. This must be arranged with the Transport Pool. They can also arrange the filling of LPG bottles and some repairs as they have good engineering facilities. Some spare parts for engines are also available from the same source.

Provisioning is good and there is a supermarket opposite the service station, which will deliver large orders. It has been reported that the surcharge which was applied to yachts making purchases and reprovisioning in the island is no longer in force. In spite of the distance and difficulty of shipping fresh produce from Australia, the availability and prices are quite reasonable.

The Boat Club, located south of the dinghy landing, welcomes visitors. The bar operates an honour system and all outstanding bills at the Club must be settled before outward clearance is given.

Further Reading

Red Sea and Indian Ocean Cruising Guide

COCOS KEELING

The Cocos Keeling Islands lie about 500 miles west of Christmas Island in the South Indian Ocean. They consist of two atolls, North Keeling and South Keeling, comprising 27 low coral islands, most of them clustered around South Keeling's lagoon. Most of the smaller islands are uninhabited. Cocos Keeling is an Australian territory.

The islands are a convenient stop for westbound yachts in the South Indian Ocean. The anchorage in the lee of Direction Island has been described as being particularly beautiful. This is perhaps the reason why some yachts which call for only a few days stay longer than intended.

Country Profile

North Keeling was probably first sighted by Captain William Keeling in 1609, and gradually the rest of the group was charted. In 1826 two Englishmen settled on South Keeling. There was some disagreement and after a few years one of the men left, leaving John Clunies-Ross, who brought labourers from Malaya and established a copra plantation. In 1857 the islands were considered as belonging to Britain and were administered first from Ceylon and then Singapore. In 1886 George Clunies-Ross was granted all the land by Queen Victoria. During the First World War Direction Island was used as a cable station, and was raided by the German cruiser *Emden* in 1914. In 1955 the islands became a dependency of Australia and the Clunies-Ross family were left with only a plantation on one of the islands. A High Security Animal Quarantine Station was opened on West Island in 1981. It is used for cattle being imported into Australia.

Meteorology and communications are important activities. The group is not self-sufficient, although some local produce is grown. Foods, fuel and all consumer items are imported from Australia. Coconuts are the sole cash crop, as well as the sale of postage stamps. The population is about 550, being Malays and Australians. English and Malay are spoken.

The islands are under the influence of the SE trade winds for most of the year. The winds are strongest in August. During the cyclone season, from December to March, the winds are lighter. The islands are rarely affected by tropical storms.

Entry Regulations

Port of entry
Direction Island, South Keeling 12°05'S 96°53'E.

Procedure on arrival
Entrance to the lagoon of South Keeling is between Horsburgh Island and Direction Island. The best anchorage is in the lee of the latter. A set of mooring buoys have been laid down for the use of visiting yachts but as they are not checked regularly, these moorings should not be trusted completely.

Customs, immigration and quarantine are on West Island, but the officers prefer to board yachts at Direction Island. Customs and quarantine officers normally visit Direction Island every day, so after anchoring one should fly the Q flag and wait for clearance. Everyone must remain on board until the yacht has been cleared.

If arriving at the weekend, the officials should be contacted on VHF radio. It may be possible to get a temporary pratique until Monday, so as to be able to go ashore.

Customs
Firearms must be declared on arrival.

Quarantine
West Island has an animal quarantine station and there

Practical Information

LOCAL TIME: GMT + 6	*PUBLIC HOLIDAYS* 1 January: New Year's Day	*COMMUNICATIONS* Radio, telephone, telegram and
BUOYAGE: IALA A	26 January: Australia Day Good Friday, Easter Monday	international telephone links via Perth. Mail comes fortnightly.
CURRENCY: Australian dollar (Aus$)	25 April: ANZAC Day June: Queen's Birthday First Monday in October: Labour Day 25, 26 December: Christmas	Poste Restante, Post Office, Cocos (Keeling) Islands, Indian Ocean 6799. There is a weekly air service to Perth. *MEDICAL* There is a small hospital at West Island.

are very strict quarantine regulations. If a yacht has animals on board, it must anchor outside the quarantine buoy at Direction Island. Animals must not be taken ashore. All animal and food waste must be taken to Direction Island for proper disposal where it is burnt in pits.

Immigration

Visas are not required and permission to land is granted on arrival.

Restrictions

In order to visit Home Island, which is where the Malay population lives, one must get permission from the local council, through the customs officer on West Island.

Spear fishing is not permitted on the south-east corner of Direction Island.

Facilities

Provisions are available, but fresh food is expensive as most of it has to be flown in from Perth. Basic supplies are available from West Island. There is no duty on alcoholic drinks. One can order fresh vegetables, which will be brought in by plane the following week. Similarly, essential spares can also be ordered from Australia. Gas bottles can be filled on West Island, where the Australian community lives. Fuel can be bought through the local agent, but it is expensive. Water is available from a tank on Direction Island. Simple repairs can be carried out at a small workshop run by a Malay on Home Island.

Further Reading

Red Sea and Indian Ocean Cruising Guide

COMOROS

This small archipelago lying in the Indian Ocean between the northern tip of Madagascar and the African mainland consists of four main islands: Grande Comore (Ngazidja), Moheli (Mwali), Anjouan (Ndzuani) and Mayotte (Maore). Formerly a French colony, the islands are now independent, except for Mayotte which is an overseas territory of France and a naval base. Mayotte is dealt with separately on page 416.

The islands are volcanic and Mount Kartala on Grande Comore is still active. They are mostly pro-

tected by coral reefs and the surrounding seas are rich in marine life. The coelacanth, a 350 million year old species of fish believed to be extinct, was rediscovered in Comoron waters.

Most yachts who visit the Comoros are sailing between Mauritius and East Africa, the islands being very conveniently located on that route. The underwater scenery is their prime attraction and the south side of the island of Moheli is particularly beautiful, with good snorkelling, although the anchorage at the main town Fomboni is only an open roadstead. The anchorage is not good either at Moroni, the capital, on Grande Comore. The main port of Mutsamudu has the best protection. More sheltered anchorages are to be found in neighbouring Mayotte.

Country Profile

The islands were originally settled by Malays, Africans and Arabs. Refugees from Persia, prosperous from the slave and spice trades, established a number of rival sultanates. During the seventeenth century Portuguese pirates used the islands as a base from which to attack ships returning from the East laden with goods. In the nineteenth century the Sultan of Mayotte sold his island to the French, and the rest followed suit after being subjected to French naval bombardment. France maintained strict control over the islands, and no one was allowed in or out of the islands without permission from the colonial authorities.

In 1912 Comoros was declared a colony and was under the administration of Madagascar until 1946. Some internal autonomy was granted in 1961, and after mass demonstrations in 1968, the French were forced to allow the formation of political parties. Tension grew between those for and against independence, and after a referendum, independence was declared in 1975. Mayotte meanwhile asked France for protection and became a 'territorial community' within the French Republic. In independent Comoros, political unrest followed, radical policies were taken and relations worsened with France. The economy also deteriorated. In 1978 a coup carried out by mercenaries saw the creation of the Federal Islamic Republic of the Comoros, and a return to a more conservative line. The mercenaries remain quite powerful, and neighbouring Madagascar, the Seychelles and Tanzania are suspicious of the regime. However, relations with France improved after the coup.

Many Comorons work abroad in France or Africa as land shortage is a problem, most land being cultivated by foreign companies and a few Comoron families.

Practical Information

LOCAL TIME: GMT + 3

BUOYAGE: IALA A

CURRENCY: Comoron franc. All foreign currency must be declared on arrival.

BUSINESS HOURS
Banks: 0700–1200 Monday to Thursday and 0700–1130 Friday.
Business: 0800–1200/1400–1600 Monday to Thursday, 0900–1200 Friday. Offices and shops close for lunch.
Government offices: 0630–1400 Monday to Thursday, 0630–1200 Friday.

ELECTRICITY: 220 V, 50 Hz

PUBLIC HOLIDAYS
1 January: New Year's Day
Easter Monday
1 May
13 May: Second Coup d'Etat
Ascension
Whit Sunday and Monday
6 July: Comoron National Day
14 July: National Holiday
Assumption
1 November: All Saints' Day
11 November: Armistice Day

12 November: Recognition of Comoron State by the UN
25 December: Christmas
The variable Muslim holidays, start of Ramadan, Eid el-Fitr,
Eid el-Kebir, Eid el-Adha, Hijra, Ashoura and Mouloud are also public holidays.

COMMUNICATIONS
Grande Comore has an international airport with flights to East Africa, Mauritius and Madagascar.

MEDICAL
Only Moroni has a good hospital.

The export of perfume from ylang-ylang, jasmine and orange trees is important. Other exports are vanilla, cloves and pepper.

The population numbers about 500,000 and are a mixture of Arab, African, Malay, Malagasy and French origins. Most of the population are Muslim. French and Arabic are the official languages, but people also speak Comoron, a variant of Swahili. Moroni on Grande Comore is the capital.

The dry season, from May to October, is the best time to visit when the average temperature is 24°C (75°F). November to April is the rainy season, when temperatures range from 27° to 35°C (81–95°F), although the coast is cooled by sea breezes. The NW monsoon season from December to March can have high winds and cyclones.

Entry Regulations

Ports of entry
Mutsamudu (Anjouan) 12°10′S 44°24′E, Moroni (Grande Comore) 11°42′S 43°15′E.

Procedure on arrival
The port captain should be contacted on VHF Channel 16 and asked for instructions.

Customs
Firearms must be declared to customs. Animals need a rabies vaccination and health certificate.

Immigration
Visas are required by all nationalities, but can be obtained on arrival from immigration in either Moroni (Grande Comore) or Mutsamudu (Anjouan). The visas are valid for three months.

Health
Malarial prophylaxis is essential.

Facilities

There are only limited facilities available, although at Mutsamundu, which is the main commercial port, there is a small boatyard and some workshops. Provisioning is basic, although some produce is available. Supplies are better in neighbouring Mayotte.

Further Reading

Africa on a Shoestring
Traveller's Guide to East Africa and the Indian Ocean

KENYA

Kenya has 300 miles of coastline made up of beaches, mangrove swamps and creeks. Much of the coast is protected by coral reefs, which provide excellent diving, while the beaches are reputed to be the best in Africa. This scenic country is the most popular tourist destination in Africa with its beaches, savannah grasslands, safari parks, Lake Victoria and spectacular mountains.

Kenya is also visited by an increasing number of sailors who seek a taste of Africa, especially if they visit the interior during their stay. The coastal towns have a different character, having been subjected to the Arab influence for many centuries. Trading dhows from the Persian Gulf still ply these waters, arriving with the

Practical Information

LOCAL TIME: GMT + 3

BUOYAGE: IALA A. The lights and buoys on the coast cannot be relied upon and entry anywhere is not advisable at night.

CURRENCY: Kenyan shilling (Ksh) of 100 cents. All foreign currency must be declared on arrival and exchange transactions recorded on the declaration form. Ksh cannot be exported and must be changed back before departure.

BUSINESS HOURS
Banks: 0900–1400 Monday to Friday, Saturday 0900–1100.
Business and shops: 0830–1230, 1400–1730 Monday to Friday, 0830–1200 Saturday.
Government offices: 0800–1200, 1400–1600 Monday to Friday.

ELECTRICITY: 240 V, 50 Hz

PUBLIC HOLIDAYS
1 January: New Year's Day
Good Friday, Easter Monday
1 May
1 June: Madaraka Day
20 October: Kenyatta Day
12 December: Independence Day
25 December: Christmas Day
Also Eid el-Fitr and Eid el-Adha

COMMUNICATIONS
Kenya Post and Telecommunications Corporation provides telephones, fax, telegraph and telex.
There are frequent flights from Nairobi to Europe and other African cities. There are less frequent regular flights from Mombasa as well as many charter flights. There is also a good network of internal flights.

DIPLOMATIC MISSIONS
In Nairobi:
Australia: Development House, Moi Avenue. ☎ (2) 334-666/7.
Canada: Comcroft House, Haile Selassie Ave. ☎ (2) 334-033/4.
Egypt: Total House, Koinage St.
New Zealand: Nanak House, Kimathi St. ☎ (2) 331-244.
Sudan: Shankdass House, Government Rd.
United Kingdom: Bruce House, Standard St. ☎ (2) 335-944.
United States: Moi/Haile Selassie Avenue. ☎ (2) 334-141.

In Mombasa:
United States: Palli House, Nyerere Ave. ☎ (11) 315101.

NW monsoon at the end of the year and leaving with the SE monsoon. They can be seen at Mombasa and also at Lamu, a small island and northernmost port of entry, whose fourteenth-century Arab town is a centre of Islamic learning. Lamu is the island of the legendary Sinbad the Sailor and the surrounding area, a small archipelago of coral-fringed islands, bears witness to the convoluted history of this part of the world. The most interesting sites are the ruined Swahili cities on Manda and Pate islands. Mombasa, also built on an island, is Kenya's chief port, its cosmopolitan atmosphere reflecting the port's history as an important Persian, Arab and Portuguese trading centre. The most popular base for visiting yachts is Kilifi, north of Mombasa, where good repair facilities are available and a yacht can be left in reliable hands, while touring the interior.

Country Profile

In Kenya remains of man have been found that are between 2.5 to 3 million years old. Later the country was gradually populated by migrations of Cushites, Bantu and Nilotes. Trade came to dominate eastern Africa, ivory being the main export, as Arab traders settled along the coast. The Bantus occupied the interior, and the mixture of these two peoples led to the Swahili culture and language. When the Portuguese arrived at the end of the fifteenth century

Mombasa was a powerful merchant city. The Portuguese established themselves on the coast, but were later driven out by the Arabs. In 1837 the Sultanate of Oman and Zanzibar took over. The people of the interior were always suspicious of the coastal traders, and thus avoided becoming victims of the slave trade, unlike the peoples of West Africa.

Britain became interested in the area at the end of the nineteenth century and took over Kenya as a British protectorate. Thousands of Indian labourers were brought over by the British, some of whom settled permanently as well as the Europeans, gradually pushing out the Africans. The 1920s saw the rise of Kikuyu nationalism, the Kikuyu being the largest tribe in Kenya, culminating in the Mau Mau revolt in 1952–6. Kenya became independent in 1963. The majority of the Asians chose not to take up citizenship of the new state and were forced to leave the country.

The Kenyan economy is based on the production and processing of agricultural produce. Tea and coffee are major exports. The country has the largest tourist industry in Africa.

The 21 million inhabitants are mainly African, with a minority of Asian, European and Arab origins. Most speak Swahili, but English is also widely spoken. Christianity is the main religion, Islam predominates on the coast, Hinduism in the Asian community and traditional beliefs are still prevalent. Nairobi in the interior is the capital.

The climate on the coast is tropical and hot. April to

June is called the season of long rains, October to November the season of short rains. The weather is under the influence of the monsoons, which also dictate the direction of the currents. This must be borne in mind when planning a cruise along this coast as the best period for southbound voyages is during the NW monsoon and for northbound voyages during the SE monsoon.

Entry Regulations

Ports of entry
Mombasa 4°04′S 39°41′E, Lamu 2°18′S 40°55′E, Malindi 3°13′S 40°07′E.

Procedure on arrival
In all ports one should report first to customs.
Mombasa: One can proceed into the harbour, or call port control on VHF Channel 12 or 16 beforehand. Sometimes one is asked to wait at the first buoy for a pilot boat, although the entrance is simple and a pilot is hardly necessary.

There are two places in Mombasa where clearance is possible. Formalities appear to be simpler at the Old Port, on the northern side of Mombasa Island, where officials are more efficient than those at Kilindini Harbour, which is the main commercial port. While clearing, one can anchor beyond the port building among the dhows. At the Old Port a launch may come out with the officials. If no one comes, the captain should go ashore and report first to customs and then immigration. Customs and immigration offices are by the jetties, which are used by small local freighters and dhows. The officials at the Old Port do not work at weekends or on holidays when it is necessary to go to Kilindini Harbour. Here it is best to proceed to the police pontoon, where one can be cleared by customs, health and immigration.

Those who need a visa will have to go to the immigration office in town, where a three-month visa is easily obtained, renewable for another three months. The cost of a visa is US$10 payable in US dollars.

Yachts can also clear at Kilifi and Shimoni, where there is customs, but immigration formalities still have to be completed in an official port of entry.
Kilifi: One can check in with customs, although immigration formalities have to be completed in Mombasa. Apparently the immigration authorities do not approve of this, although they raise no objections if a captain drives immediately from Kilifi to Mombasa with the passports in order to complete immigration formalities.

Customs
Firearms must be declared on arrival. These will be impounded and released only on departure.

There are no restrictions on animals, although they should have up-to-date rabies vaccinations, as rabies is endemic on the East African coast. Inoculations can be done in Mombasa if required.

There is no specified limit on the period a yacht may remain in Kenya and some have remained for several years while the owners were absent.

Visiting sailors can buy or have sent out capital equipment such as engines, instruments and sails. By using a clearing agent, who will provide a bond, it is possible to avoid paying local importation taxes.

Immigration
Visas are not required for nationals of Commonwealth countries (except Australia, Nigeria, Sri Lanka and India), Denmark, Ethiopia, Finland, Germany, Ireland, Norway, San Marino, Spain, Sweden, Turkey and Uruguay. Normally visitor's permits are issued free for three months.

Britons of Asian origin require a visa.

All other countries require visas, but these are normally issued on arrival for three months. An extension of three months can be obtained with proof of sufficient funds.

Visas must be obtained in advance by South African residents, and those who have spent more than three months in South Africa during the last 12 months, regardless of their nationality.

Visas and entry permits can be extended if they are applied for in person before the date of expiry.

Health
Malaria prophylaxis is recommended, as malaria is prevalent on the coast. Do not swim in fresh water, as this may be infected with bilharzia parasites. AIDS is endemic in East Africa.

Fees
Overtime is charged on weekends and holidays.

There are light dues, government charges for which change frequently.

Foreign yachts have to pay harbour charges, which may work out cheaper if bought for one year in advance, unless one intends to spend only a short time in Kenya.

A navigation fee of approximately US$10 is payable when clearing out.

Restrictions
The authorities are trying hard to protect wildlife, and

it is a serious offence to buy and attempt to export ivory, animal skins and stuffed animals.

It is forbidden to photograph ports, police, naval buildings, vessels or personnel.

Cruising permit

A transit log is necessary for any movement in Kenyan waters. The log is obtained from customs on arrival and must be presented to customs when calling at the following ports: Shimoni, Mombasa, Kilifi, Malindi and Lamu. One should inform customs of the intended itinerary, time of departure and ETA in the next port.

Facilities

Although slowly improving, yachting facilities are still limited. However, provisioning is generally good and less expensive than the Indian Ocean islands. Diesel and LPG are also reasonably priced. There is a problem of theft in some places and outboard engines, dinghies and any loose equipment should be put away or watched carefully, except in the few places where security is provided. In some places for a minimal charge one can employ a guard for the night.

The best facilities are those at Kilifi, a well protected port on a creek spanned by a bridge to be completed in 1991. The bridge has a projected clearance of 24 m (80 ft), although the actual height might be less than that. One must also be careful not to touch the telephone and power lines. Swynford Boatyard, based on the southern shore beyond the bridge, operates a full service yard with hauling out facilities for boats up to 12 tons or 40 ft LOA, drying out grid for larger boats, mechanical, electrical and carpentry workshops as well as information on local marine services. The boatyard has moorings and fees include a night watchman for the boat if the crew make trips inland. The Kilifi Yacht Club is very welcoming and provides a mail service (PO Box 153, Kilifi), showers, bar and water. Provisioning in Kilifi is good with a supermarket, fresh produce market, bank and frequent buses to Mombasa 35 miles away.

Facilities in Mombasa itself are more limited. The Mombasa Yacht Club welcomes visiting yachts and offers its facilities for a daily fee. The anchorage there is very deep, but the club has some moorings. There are several good supermarkets in Mombasa as well as a daily market. Although there are some local workshops in Mombasa, because of the proximity of Kilifi, it is better to use the boatyard there as they are used to dealing with yachts.

Limited supplies are available in Malindi, which is a tourist resort with banks and several shops. Facilities in Lamu are poor. Fuel and water have to be taken in jerrycans and there are only limited food supplies with the exception of fresh produce. The situation is similar in Shimoni, the southernmost port in Kenya.

Further Reading

Africa on a Shoestring
Traveller's Guide to East Africa and the Indian Ocean
Africa, The Nile Route

MADAGASCAR

This large island off the east coast of Africa is very different from its continental neighbours, since the majority of its inhabitants are descended from Malay and Asian migrants, mixed with Africans and Europeans. Centuries of relative isolation have produced an interesting culture and unique wildlife. A rugged mountain chain runs down the centre of the island, dividing the narrow tropical eastern coast from the savannah and forests of the west. The southern part is very arid.

For many years ruled by a Marxist government, the officials have not especially welcomed visiting sailors, who were invariably treated with suspicion. As a result very few yachts stopped in Madagascar. The situation is gradually changing and as the island is attracting an increasing number of tourists to its resorts, it is expected that the attitude to visiting yachts will also change.

The most attractive ports and anchorages are on the north-west coast where Antseranana, formerly known as Diego Suarez, has a beautiful natural harbour. The old town has a cosmopolitan atmosphere with its mixed population of Malagasy, Arabs, Indians, Africans and Réunionnais. Further along the coast is Madagascar's prime attraction, the picturesque island of Nossi-Be, now a thriving tourist resort. Another island worth visiting is Nossi Boraha (Ile Sainte Marie), close to Toamasina, the country's chief commercial harbour and main port of entry. The latter is a good place to stop for yachts on passage to the Cape of Good Hope. Another interesting stop for southbound yachts is at Taolanaro, formerly Port Dauphin, the site of the first French settlement in the seventeenth century.

Practical Information

LOCAL TIME: GMT + 3

BUOYAGE: IALA A

CURRENCY: Malagasy franc (MFr) of 100 centimes. There is strict currency control on arrival and departure. Prices may also be quoted in piastres or ariary (1 ariary = 5MFr).

BUSINESS HOURS
Banks: 0800–1100, 1400–1600 Monday to Friday.
Business and government offices: 0800–1130, 1400–1730 Monday to Friday, 0800–1200 Saturday.
Shops: 0800–1200, 1400–1800 Monday to Friday (some open Sunday morning).

ELECTRICITY: 220 V, 50 Hz

PUBLIC HOLIDAYS
1 January: New Year's Day
29 March: Memorial Day
Good Friday, Easter Monday
1 May
Ascension
Whit Monday
26 June: Independence Day
15 August: Assumption
1 November: All Saints' Day
25 December: Christmas Day
30 December: Anniversary of the Republic

COMMUNICATIONS
There are regular flights to Europe and Africa, and internal flights around the country.

MEDICAL
There are hospitals in the main centres, but the standards of medical care are not very high.

DIPLOMATIC MISSIONS
In Antananarivo:
France: 3 rue Jean Jaures.
United Kingdom: Immeuble Ny Havana, Cite de 67 Ha. ☎ (2) 27749.
United States: 14 Lalana Rainitovo, Antsahavola. ☎ (2) 21257.

Country Profile

The earliest inhabitants are thought to have arrived by sea from Indonesia around 220 BC to AD 800. In this latter period the Sumatran Srivijaya empire controlled much of the Indian Ocean's maritime trade. The migrants brought crops from South East Asia, an influence which can still be seen in Malagasy agriculture. Arabs and Swahilis established towns on the coast, and from the sixteenth century the Europeans used the island as a stopping point for ships on the Cape of Good Hope route. In the eighteenth century the Merina Kingdom united the island and set about creating a modern state. France became interested in the island and invaded it in 1895, the Merina Queen was deposed and a republic declared. Madagascar became a colony and foreigners expropriated the land, developing an import-export economy with coffee as the main crop.

Having been independent for so long previously, the Malagasy grew more and more dissatisfied. In 1947–8 a violent insurrection occurred, in which several thousand Malagasy died. In 1960 independence was granted although France retained a hold on trade and military bases. Initially links were kept with France, but aspirations were not met by economic growth and in 1972 a military regime took power. The government cultivated relations with socialist countries and drew away from France. A political crisis in 1975 led to a radical socialist government coming to power. Recently relations with France have improved, although there are still disputes over the sovereignty of some small islands to the north, Iles Glorieuses, Juan de Nova and Europa, which are administered by France.

The economy is predominantly agricultural, with coffee, vanilla, spices, perfume and sugar the main exports. Rice is cultivated all over the island mainly for domestic consumption. Since independence the economy has suffered the loss of the French farming community and French aid. Efforts are being made towards greater self-sufficiency. Tourism is also beginning to expand.

The 10 million inhabitants are a mixture of Malay and African. Malagasy and French are the main languages. The main religions are Christianity, Islam, and some traditional beliefs. The capital is Antananarivo in the centre of the island.

The climate is tropical. November to March is the rainy season. The SE trade wind season lasts until the end of October and the trades can be very strong at times, occasionally being accompanied by violent thunderstorms. From December to March cyclones are common on the east coast.

Entry Regulations

Ports of entry
Toamasina 18°09′S 49°25′E, Antseranana 12°16′S 49°18′E, Mahajanga 15°43′S 46°19′E, Toleara 23°22′S 43°40′E, Nossi-Be 13°24′S 48°17′E.

Procedure on arrival
One should try and contact the harbour master on VHF Channel 16. If one's call is not acknowledged, tie

up to the dock and await to be contacted by the officials.

Customs
Firearms may be removed for the duration of the stay. Animals are not allowed to land.

Immigration
Visas are required by all nationalities. Usually a visa is granted for one month. There are very few Malagasy embassies in the world, although there are diplomatic offices in some capitals, such as London, Washington, Bonn, Paris, Rome, Brussels and Tokyo, as well as in some African capitals. For those sailing to Madagascar from neighbouring countries the most convenient places to obtain a visa from a Malagasy consulate are Mauritius, Réunion or Tanzania.

Visa extensions up to two months are available from the Ministry of Interior. A charge of 1500 MFr per month is made and one may have to submit a short letter in French explaining why the extension is wanted.

Health
If coming from continental Africa, yellow fever and cholera vaccination certificates will be required. Drinking water should be treated everywhere. Malaria prophylaxis is recommended.

Facilities

The cost of living is quite high and many basics are only available on the black market at very high prices. Locally grown fruit and vegetables are readily available and there are good markets in most places.

Repair facilities are limited. The best facilities can be found at Mahajanga, on the west coast, which is used by many foreign shrimping boats as a base of operations. There is a ship repair yard with a slipway. They can undertake hull and engine repair. Similar facilities are also available in Toamasina, where a repair yard with a slipway and workshops is operated by the port authority.

Further Reading

Traveller's Guide to East Africa and the Indian Ocean

MAURITIUS

Joseph Conrad called Mauritius 'sugary pearl of the Indian Ocean' to describe the sweet beauty of this island situated in the centre of that sea. A volcanic outcrop of the land bridge that once connected Africa and Asia, Mauritius lies about 500 miles east of Madagascar. Part of the Mascarene archipelago, Mauritius also includes the islands of Rodriguez, Agalega, and the Cargados Carajos archipelago.

Yachts calling in Mauritius are usually on passage westwards across the Indian Ocean and in a hurry to leave before mid-November due to the number of early cyclones that have hit the island in the past. Yet a few who have spent time cruising the Indian Ocean have dallied and enjoyed the beauty of this high island and the exotic mixture of its culture and peoples. Grand Baie on the north-west coast is the favourite anchorage with a friendly yacht club and good basic facilities.

Some cruisers also break their passage at the smaller island of Rodriguez, which is a pleasant stop due to easier formalities and friendly islanders.

The inner harbour in Mathurin Bay is very well protected and the yacht can be left there while exploring the interior, particularly the caves on the windward side of the island.

Occasionally yachts stop at the Cargados Carajos Shoals, a large reef area lying some 200 miles northeast of Mauritius. Although one is supposed to obtain prior permission to stop, this rule does not seem to be strictly enforced. However, one should ask permission from local fishermen to anchor off one of the four islands they occasionally inhabit. Over fifty islets and cays make up this small archipelago which abounds in marine life. The chart of this area is badly out of date and it is reported that the lighthouse, which is marked as being on Ile du Sud, is in fact on Ile Coco. Eyeball navigation is essential throughout this reef-infested area.

Country Profile

Mauritius was uninhabited until the end of the sixteenth century, although often visited by Arab and Malay sailors. The Portuguese were the first Europeans to visit 'Ilha do Cirne' (Isle of the Swan) at the start of the sixteenth century. That famous bird the dodo once lived here before sailors killed it off for food. In 1598 the Dutch took possession of the island, naming it after Prince Maurice of Nassau. Rivalry was considerable between the Dutch, French and English for the island, both for the valuable ebony found there and, as trade opened up with the East, for its important strategic position on the Cape of Good Hope route. In 1715 the French gained control, renaming it Ile de France, and their influence is clearly visible today. Rapid strides were made under Governor Mahé de Labourdonnais: Port Louis became the capital, the sugar industry was developed, fortifications were built and the French used their naval base for harassing ships of the East India Company.

A century later the Treaty of Paris ceded Mauritius, as well as the Seychelles and Rodriguez, to Britain, resuscitating the previous name. Emancipation of the slaves in 1833 led to labour shortages on the sugar plantations, and a large influx of labour from India occurred. With the opening of the Suez Canal, Mauritius lost some of its importance to world trade. Independence from Britain came in 1968.

The sugar industry is still the backbone of the economy, although efforts are being made to diversify away from dependence on a single crop. Tea and tobacco are now significant exports, tourism has expanded and the island is opening up to becoming an offshore financial centre.

The history of the island is reflected in its 1 million inhabitants, who are a mixture of Indian, French, English, African and Chinese origins. English is the official language, but Creole, French, Hindi and Bhojpuri are also widely spoken and Hinduism, Islam, Christianity and Buddhism make up the island's religions.

Mauritius has a tropical climate with a high humidity and temperatures of up to 35°C (95°F). January to May has heavier rainfall, while September, October and November are the most pleasant months. The cyclone season is from mid-November to April.

Port Louis (Mauritius Government Tourist Office).

Practical Information

LOCAL TIME: GMT + 4

BUOYAGE: IALA A

CURRENCY: Mauritian rupee (MRS) of 100 cents. Only MRS 350 may be exported.

BUSINESS HOURS
Banks: 1000–1400 Monday to Friday, 0930–1130 Saturday.
Business: 0845–1630 Monday to Friday, 0900–1200 Saturday.
Shops: 0900–1700 Monday to Friday, 0900–1200 Saturday.
Government offices: 0900–1600 Monday to Friday, 0900–1200 Saturday.
Port offices: Monday to Friday 0700–1500, Saturday 0700–1300.

ELECTRICITY: 220 V, 50 Hz

PUBLIC HOLIDAYS
1, 2 January: New Year
12 March: Independence Day
1 May: Labour Day
15 August: Assumption
24 October: UN Day
1 November: All Saints' Day
25 December: Christmas Day
Variable religious holidays:
Yaum-un-Nabi
Cavadee (Tamil)
Chinese Spring Festival
Maha Shivaratree (Hindu)
Ougadi
Easter
Varusha Piruppu
Eid El-Fitr
Ganesh Chaturthi
Chinese Autumn Festival
Divali, Hindu Festival of Lights
Eid El-Adha
Ganga Asnan

COMMUNICATIONS
International calls, telex and telegrams from the Overseas Telecommunications Service offices, Rogers House, and PCL Building, both in Port Louis, while in Cassis, OTC has a 24 hour service. Main post office, Quay Street, Port Louis, 0800–1100, 1200–1600. There are flights to many destinations in Europe, Asia, Africa and Australia.

MEDICAL
Medical care is free in hospitals.

DIPLOMATIC MISSIONS
In Port Louis:
Australia: Rogers Building. ☎ 08170.
Madagascar: 6 Sir William Newton St.
New Zealand: Edgar Aubert St.
☎ 24920.
United Kingdom: King George V Avenue, Floreal. ☎ 865795.
United States: Rogers Bldg, 5 President John Kennedy St. ☎ 23218/9.

Entry Regulations

Port of entry
Port Louis 20°09′S 57°29′E.

Procedure on arrival
Port Louis is the main harbour and the only official port of entry and exit for Mauritius. One must clear in here before visiting any other anchorage.

One should radio one's ETA to the port authority in Port Louis, who keep 24-hour watch on VHF Channel 16. On arrival, contact Port Louis Harbour Radio and request permission to enter. Authorities expect yachts to come alongside, but the jetty has been damaged by larger vessels and yachts may find it difficult to lie alongside the rough dock. The radio station will usually advise arriving yachts where to dock and will also call customs and immigration.

Clearance can be obtained in Port Mathurin on Rodriguez island. This clearance is only valid during the stay in Rodriguez and one must clear in again on arrival in Mauritius.

St Brandon (Cargados Carajos Shoals) and Agalega should not be visited without prior permission in writing from the Ministry of External Affairs & Emigration in Port Louis, except in an emergency.

Procedure on departure
Although not an official port of entry, yachts have been allowed to stay in Grand Baie and leave from there after clearing out in Port Louis. There does not seem to be a strict rule about this and a yacht wishing to clear out may be required to return to Port Louis.

Customs
Firearms must be declared on arrival.

All animals need (a) Import Permit from Ministry of Agriculture & Natural Resources & the Environment, obtained in advance; (b) health certificate from country of origin. They must be declared to customs on arrival and landing is allowed if (a) and (b) agree, otherwise animals must remain on board. Quarantine for dogs and cats is six months, for birds it is three weeks. Dogs and cats from areas where rabies has occurred in the last 12 months are prohibited.

It is prohibited to import fresh fruits from Asia east of 60°E (including India and Pakistan), plants, fresh vegetables and sugar cane.

Immigration
A three-month stay is normally granted. Visitors in transit, who arrive and depart with the same yacht, do not require a visa. If a visa is required it may be obtained abroad from Mauritius high commissions or embassies and where these do not exist from British embassies. In Mauritius one should contact the Passport & Immigration Officer, Line Barracks, Port

Louis. To extend a stay beyond three months one must apply for a visa, provided the reasons given are considered justifiable.

Health

A yellow fever inoculation is required if coming from an infected area. Malaria prophylaxis is recommended.

Restrictions

The use of harpoons for fishing is forbidden.

Facilities

Port Louis is being expanded and developed, there being a possibility of a new marina. There is a dry dock in Port Louis, Taylor-Smith General Engineering, which undertakes some general repair work. Other repair facilities are available including sail repair. Fuel is available and gas bottles can be filled at the Shell depot in St Louis.

The Grand Baie Yacht Club offers temporary membership to visiting sailors at a reasonable cost. Water and fuel can be obtained from the jetty.

In Rodriguez water and fresh provisions are available, but little in the way of repairs, although long-distance telephone communications are excellent thanks to a new satellite link. The water available in the harbour may be poor quality and should be treated. The meteorological office is extremely helpful and forecasts are made available free of charge to departing yachts.

Further Reading

Traveller's Guide to East Africa and the Indian Ocean
Africa on a Shoestring

MAYOTTE

Mayotte Island is part of the Comoros archipelago, a small group of islands lying between the northern tip of Madagascar and East Africa in the Indian Ocean. Mayotte is an overseas territory of France and the French Navy maintain a naval base on the island. The island is surrounded by reefs and the main harbour at Dzaoudzi is very well-protected. There are many anchorages inside the reef and diving is excellent.

The other three islands in the group, Grande Comore, Moheli and Anjouan, now form an independent republic.

Country Profile

The early history of Mayotte is described in the section dealing with the Comoros, with whom Mayotte was united until 1975, when the Comoros became independent while Mayotte remained French. The economy of Mayotte is totally dependent on France, whose military base provides the main source of revenue.

The local name for Mayotte is Maore and the capital is Dzaoudzi. The population of 52,000 are a mixture of African, Arab, Malagasy and French origins. French and Arabic are the main languages, while the main religions are Islam and Catholicism.

The climate is tropical, with two seasons, the dry season lasting from May to October, with an average temperature of 24°C (75°F), and the rainy season from November to April, when both temperature and humidity are higher. The cyclone season is from December to March.

Entry Regulations

Port of entry

Dzaoudzi 12°47'S 45°15'E.

Procedure on arrival

One should contact harbour control (Commandant du Port) on VHF Channel 16, who will give directions about clearance procedure.

Customs

Firearms must be declared to customs and the gendarmerie for authorisation to be held on board during stay in port.

Animals need a rabies vaccination and health certificate.

Yachts can stay up to six months in Mayotte.

Immigration

French visa regulations apply. Nationals of the European Community, Andorra, Austria, Canada, Cyprus, Finland, Iceland, Liechtenstein, Monaco, Norway, Sweden, Switzerland and the United States do not need visas. All other nationalities need visas which must be obtained in advance.

People who come from the Comoros and already have a Comoron visa are allowed to stop without a French visa.

Health

Malaria prophylaxis is recommended.

Practical Information

LOCAL TIME: GMT + 3

BUOYAGE: IALA A

CURRENCY: French franc (FF)

BUSINESS HOURS
Banks: 0700–1200 Monday to Thursday
and 0700–1130 Friday.
Business: 0800–1200/1400–1600 Monday
to Thursday, 0900–1200 Friday.

Offices and shops close 1200–1500 daily.
Government offices: 0630–1400 Monday
to Thursday, 0630–1200 Friday.

ELECTRICITY: 220 V, 50 Hz

PUBLIC HOLIDAYS
1 January: New Year's Day
Easter Monday
1 May
Ascension
Whit Sunday and Monday

14 July: Bastille Day
15 August: Assumption
1 November: All Saints' Day
11 November: Armistice Day
25 December: Christmas Day
Some Muslim holidays are also
observed.

COMMUNICATIONS
A flight has to be taken to Grande
Comore for onward connections to
international destinations.

Fees

Overtime is charged 1700–0630 Monday to Friday and after 1200 on Saturday, also on Sundays and holidays. Customs fees are payable.

Facilities

Some repair facilities are available in Dzaoudzi. Supplies are better than in the neighbouring Comoros and most imported goods are French. There is a good market for local produce every morning.

Further Reading

Africa on a Shoestring

MOZAMBIQUE

The People's Republic of Mozambique has some 1400 miles of coastline on the Indian Ocean. The country stretches along the eastern coast of Africa, being mostly a coastal plain rising inland to mountainous borders with Zimbabwe, Zambia and Malawi. The island area of Bazaruto and the area around Maputo provide some of the best cruising. Although not particularly welcoming cruising yachts in the past, those yachts which have stopped in one of Mozambique's ports have been treated courteously by the officials. Stopping at other places between major ports is not allowed, although in the case of those who have arrived with visas obtained beforehand, some freedom of movement was allowed. Recently the country does appear to be opening up to yachts and South African yachts have cruised there.

Country Profile

There were several independent kingdoms thriving on trade in this region before the Europeans came to Africa. Then in the late fifteenth century the Portuguese established trading posts along the coast, trading for gold, slaves and ivory from the interior. It was only at the end of the seventeenth century that colonisation began, when the Portuguese settled and established a plantation economy using slave labour, and after slavery was abolished, forced labour. Large estates were owned by these settlers and in the nineteenth century foreign companies were also given concessions. When Salazar's regime came to power in Portugal in the 1920s, protectionist measures were brought in and attempts were made to bring the colony more closely under Portuguese control. The country was not prosperous and the Africans had no say in the country's affairs.

In 1962 Frelimo was formed and mounted campaigns against the Portuguese. Frelimo gained control of several areas, where it established a socialist and more egalitarian economy. In 1975 after the revolution in Portugal, the new regime in Lisbon decided to put an end to the wasteful war and Frelimo came to power under the presidency of Samora Machel. Efforts were made to raise living standards, increase literacy, and there was extensive nationalisation. The country's resources were drained by attacks from Rhodesia, as Frelimo supported Robert Mugabe's forces. There were also attacks from the Mozambique National Resistance rebels (MNR), who were supported by South Africa. Therefore the government was forced to change its policy in order to save the economy. The Nkomati Accord was signed with South Africa and efforts made to attract foreign capital. Until recently the MNR rebels were still supported by South Africa, although operating on a more limited scale.

The economy is mainly agricultural, with some

Practical Information

LOCAL TIME: GMT + 2

BUOYAGE: IALA A

CURRENCY: Metical (meticais) of 100 cents. The import and export of local currency is forbidden. Foreign currency must be declared on arrival. Visitors must change some foreign currency on arrival.

BUSINESS HOURS
Banks: 0730–1130 Monday, Tuesday, Thursday, Friday, and 0800–0915 Wednesday, Saturday.

Shops: 0730–1130, 1330–1730 Monday to Friday.

ELECTRICITY: 220 V, 50 Hz

PUBLIC HOLIDAYS
1 January: New Year's Day
3 February: Heroes Day
7 April: Mozambican Women's Day
1 May: Labour Day
25 June: Independence Day
7 September: Victory Day
25 September: Revolution Day
25 December: National Family Day

COMMUNICATIONS
There are flights from Maputo to Zimbabwe, South Africa, Lisbon, Madrid and Copenhagen.

DIPLOMATIC MISSIONS
In Maputo:
United Kingdom: Av. Vladimir Lenin 310. ☎ 321404.
United States: 35 Rua da Mesquita. ☎ 26051.

limited industry. The main exports are cotton, sugar, copra, sisal and tea. Previously considerable income had come from Mozambiqueans working in the mines in South Africa, but these were expelled following the application of sanctions. Recently efforts have been made to strengthen links with the west and restrictions on tourists have been reduced. However, shortages are still a major problem and both fuel and food are rationed.

The population numbers 14.5 million, made up of various tribes, the most numerous being the Makua-Lomwe. Portuguese is the official language, but many African languages are spoken. In remoter areas Portuguese is less widely spoken. Most people hold traditional animist beliefs, although there are about 2 million Christians, mostly Catholic, and 2 million Muslim. The capital is Maputo, formerly called Lourenço Marques under the Portuguese.

The climate is tropical and mostly hot and humid. The country is plagued by irregular rainfall, the rainy season being from November to March. The prevailing winds are SE to SW. Much of the coast is under the influence of sea breezes with stronger onshore winds in the afternoons. In the northern part of the coast, the SE trade winds blow during the winter months, February to June, while NE winds prevail in summer, from July to January.

Entry Regulations

Ports of entry
Maputo 25°59′S 32°36′E, Beira 19°50′S 34°50′E, Nacala 14°32′S 40°40′E.

Procedure on arrival
Maputo: The harbour is approached through two main channels, the south channel being recommended only for small vessels and those with local knowledge. Port control maintain continuous watch on VHF Channel 16. It is possible to come alongside one of the wharfs for clearance formalities.
Beira: The port is located in the estuary of the River Pungue and access to it is through the Maputi Channel, which is approximately 10 miles long. Small vessels can anchor inside the inner harbour.
Nacala: Port control maintains watch on HF 8.499 KHz.

Customs
Firearms must be declared and may be detained.

Immigration
All nationalities require visas. Visas can be obtained in Dar es Salaam (Tanzania) and Johannesburg (South Africa). Special permission may be necessary to travel inland outside the Maputo province if the security situation is bad. A permit is needed from Ministerio de Cultura e Educação to take anything out of the country that has been bought there, so all receipts should be kept.

Health
Malaria prophylaxis is recommended.

Restrictions
It is prohibited to take photographs of public buildings, military installations or soldiers.

Facilities

Provisioning is very difficult because of frequent shortages. Fuel and food can only be bought with ration cards. It is sometimes possible to obtain some fresh produce. Repair facilities are available in Beira and Maputo, where there are dockyards dealing with repairs on fishing vessels.

Further Reading

Africa on a Shoestring

REUNION ISLAND

La Réunion Island is a small French territory in the South Indian Ocean lying south-west of Mauritius. It is a useful stop for yachts sailing from the latter to South Africa. The lush interior of this volcanic island has some stunning mountain scenery, such as the Cirque de Cilaos, a crater 1220 metres high, once a refuge for runaway slaves, and the spa town of Cilaos with its hot springs. Piton des Neiges is the highest summit at over 3000 metres. In the south-east of the island is Piton de la Fournaise, an active volcano, with a black lava landscape. Many people go walking through the mountains and there are lodges where overnight stops can be made. It is a last opportunity to stretch one's legs before the long and possibly rough passage to South Africa.

Country Profile

Réunion was discovered by the Portuguese Pedro de Mascarenhas in 1513. The island was uninhabited, although visited occasionally by Malay, Arab and European sailors. In the second half of the seventeenth century French settlers and their Malagasy slaves came to the island. The island was then called Isle Bourbon, and the French East India Company administered it. Britain began to take an interest in the island, so the French government took over the administration.

In the late eighteenth century slave revolts broke out and some escaped to the interior, where they lived in communities with elected chiefs. The name of the island was changed to La Réunion after the French Revolution. Réunion was part of the French Mascarene Islands along with Mauritius and Rodriguez, and was occupied by Britain during the Napoleonic Wars. Sugar was introduced to Réunion when the French re-established their rule, and soon came to dominate the economy. With the abolition of slavery, contract labourers from India were brought in to fill the labour shortage. Later the economy suffered from competition by sugar-producing countries in other parts of the world. After the Second World War Réunion became an overseas department of France. In recent years efforts have been made to gain more independence from France, but with little success.

Sugar still dominates the agricultural economy. Other exports are vanilla essence and tobacco. The fishing industry is also being developed. Industry is expanding as well as banking. Trade is predominantly with France. Réunion imports almost all of its food and consumer goods from France and the cost of living is high. Unemployment is a problem and many young people have emigrated to France.

The population is around 600,000. Most Réunionnais are of French, African and Indian origins. Also there are Asian and European communities and a Chinese minority. The majority are Roman Catholics, but there are also Hindus, Muslims and some Buddhists. French and Créole are the main languages. Saint Dénis on the north coast is the capital.

The average temperature on the coast is 18–31°C (66–88°F), although it is cooler in the hilly interior. The island is divided by its mountain range into the lusher, rainier windward side and the drier leeward side to the south and west. Réunion lies in the E to SE trade wind area, and the cyclone season is from December to March. The island is occasionally affected by cyclones.

Entry Regulations

Ports of entry
Pointe des Galets 20°55'S 55°18'E, Saint-Pierre 21°20'S 55°29'E.

Procedure on arrival
Pointe des Galets: One should tie up alongside the fisherman's wharf. Yachts should contact the Capitainerie du Port on VHF Channel 16 and they will advise on the correct procedure. Yachts which arrive outside working hours usually have to wait until offices open.

Customs
Firearms must be declared on arrival.

Animals need rabies vaccination and health certificates.

There are restrictions on the importation of plants.

Yachts can stay up to six months in one or several visits during a 12-month period, without paying duty, as long as the crew do not enter into employment ashore or charter the vessel. If the owner wants to leave

Practical Information

LOCAL TIME: GMT + 4

BUOYAGE: IALA A

CURRENCY: French franc (FF)

BUSINESS HOURS
0800–1200, 1400–1800 Monday to
Saturday.

ELECTRICITY: 220 V, 50 Hz

PUBLIC HOLIDAYS
1 January: New Year's Day
Easter Monday
1 May: Labour Day
Ascension
Whit Monday
14 July: Bastille Day
14 August: National Day
15 August: Assumption
1 November: All Saints' Day
11 November: Armistice Day
25 December: Christmas Day

COMMUNICATIONS
International direct dialling from

telephone offices.
There are daily flights to Mauritius,
which connect with flights to Europe,
Africa and Australia.

MEDICAL
There are good facilities on the island.

DIPLOMATIC MISSIONS
In Saint Dénis:
United Kingdom: rue de Paris.
☎ 210619.
There are Madagascan and South
African consulates in Saint Dénis.

Réunion by other means, the vessel has to be put in the custody of customs until the owner's return. The ship's papers must be left with customs. This period will be deducted from the time spent in Réunion.

Immigration

French immigration regulations apply. Nationals of the European Community, Andorra, Austria, Canada, Cyprus, Finland, Iceland, Liechtenstein, Monaco, Norway, Sweden, Switzerland, the United States and some African countries do not need visas for up to a three-month stay.

All other nationalities require visas, which should be obtained from a French embassy or consulate in advance. One should ensure that the visa given is valid for Réunion.

Facilities

Pointe des Galets is an artificial harbour about 12 miles west of the capital Saint Dénis. Visiting yachts are given free berthing for the first week. There are only limited facilities for yachts and the nearest stores are about two miles away. Provisioning is very expensive as the bulk of food is imported. Fuel and water can be taken on at the fisherman's wharf. There is a good morning market for local produce in the capital Saint Dénis.

Saint Pierre on the south-west coast also welcomes yachts and there is a marina at Saint Paul, further west from Pointe des Galets. Saint Paul is the old capital of the French East India Company. Repair facilities at all these places are limited and only some simple repairs can be undertaken locally. Essential spares can be flown in from France, but this can take at least one week.

Further Reading

Traveller's Guide to East Africa and the Indian Ocean
Africa on a Shoestring

SEYCHELLES

The Seychelles lie in the south Indian Ocean and number over 100 islands, some granite, others coral atolls including one of the world's largest atolls, Aldabra. Having been uninhabited by man until 200 years ago, the islands are rich in unique wildlife, such as the giant land tortoise, many species of birds, strange plants such as the giant Coco de Mer, and untouched forests. Mahé, La Digue and Praslin have all been developed for foreign visitors to enjoy these natural advantages, but the number of tourists is kept controlled.

With the reputation of being the site of the Garden of Eden, it is not surprising that the Seychelles have had such a fascination for sailors, who are forever searching for paradise on earth. The anchorages at La Digue and Praslin Islands are particularly striking and one of the chief attractions on the latter is Baie St Anne, with its thousands of Coco de Mer palms, some of them reputedly 800 years old. The gigantic nuts of these palm trees have a suggestive female shape and when they were first discovered washed up on distant shores, mystical qualities were attributed to them. As their origins remained a mystery for many hundreds of years, they were believed to grow under the sea.

Scenically the Seychelles may come close to being heavenly, but the formalities and bureaucracy that visiting yachts are subjected to may seem more like hell to some. Fortunately the rigid restrictions are being

Practical Information

LOCAL TIME: GMT + 4

BUOYAGE: IALA A

CURRENCY: Seychelles rupee (SR) of 100 cents. One cannot export more than SR100.

BUSINESS HOURS
Banks: 0830–1300 Monday to Friday. Banque Française Commerciale: 0830–1500 Monday to Friday, 0900–1130 Saturday.
Business and government offices: 0800–1200, 1300–1600 Monday to Friday.
Shops: 0800–1200, 1330–1700 Monday to Friday.

ELECTRICITY: 240 V, 50 Hz

PUBLIC HOLIDAYS
1, 2 January: New Year's Day
Good Friday, Easter Monday
1 May: Labour Day
5 June: Liberation Day
29 June: Independence Day
Corpus Christi
15 August: Assumption Day
1 November: All Saints' Day
8 December: Immaculate Conception
25 December: Christmas Day

COMMUNICATIONS
Cable & Wireless Ltd for telephone calls, telex, telegraph and radio (24 hours). Main post office in Victoria: airmail collections at 1500 weekdays, noon on

Saturdays, open 0800–1200, 1300–1600 Monday to Friday, 0800–1200 Saturday. Emergency: dial 999.
Seychelles International Airport on Mahé has regular flights to Europe, Africa, Asia and the Middle East.

MEDICAL
One can obtain emergency treatment under the National Medical Service for a basic fee. Main hospital, out-patients clinic; dental clinic at Mont Fleuri.

DIPLOMATIC MISSIONS
In Victoria:
France: Arpent Vert, Mont Fleuri.
United Kingdom: Victoria House.
☎ 23055.
United States: Victoria House ☎ 23921.

gradually eased and the previous ruling that allowed overnight anchoring only in Victoria has been lifted. Several places can now be used as overnight anchorages. In spite of all difficulties, cruising yachts still call at the Seychelles and sample the beauty of the islands.

Country Profile

Vasco da Gama sighted the Seychelles in the sixteenth century, but they were only occasionally visited until the French settled with their African slaves in the mid-eighteenth century. During the Napoleonic Wars the control of the islands became unsure, until they came under British control in 1814. However, French culture remains predominant, despite the lengthy British rule. In the nineteenth century the group was administered by Mauritius and the population expanded as slaves freed by the British Navy settled there, as well as Mauritians, Indians and Chinese. The Seychelles have been independent since 1976, in recent years following a moderate socialist path. With the example of the Comoros close by, the government is concerned about a group of mercenaries attempting to take control, and so has built up a regular army and militia. An attempt was made in 1981 by some notorious mercenaries and was only just foiled.

Efforts are being made to raise living standards and tackle the economic problems of unemployment and a trade deficit. The traditional exports of cinnamon and copra have declined in importance in recent years. Since the opening of the international aiport on Mahé

in 1971, tourism has become a major factor in the economy. The fishing industry is also expanding.

The 70,000 Seychellois are a mixture of African, Asian and European origin. There are also Indians, Chinese and Europeans. The majority of the population are Roman Catholic. French and English are the official languages, but Créole is spoken by most people. Victoria, on Mahé is the capital. Mahé is the economic and political centre of the Seychelles, and most of the population live there.

The climate is tropical, but outside of the cyclone belt. Temperatures average 24–30°C (75–86°F). The NW monsoon lasts from November to April, while from March it is hotter and the winds are lighter until the SE monsoon sets in from May to October.

Entry Regulations

Port of entry
Port Victoria (Mahé) 4°37′S 55°27′E.

Procedure on arrival
The port control keeps a 24-hour watch on VHF Channel 16. On arrival, one should fly the Q flag and anchor about 3.3 cables north of the Victoria Lighthouse, bearing 274°T. Do not go directly to the yacht club. The health, customs, immigration and security officials usually board the yacht for clearance. The Entomological Department requires yachts to be sprayed on arrival.

Once cleared, yachts may proceed into the inner

harbour to anchor as directed by the port authority. Within 24 hours, weekends and public holidays excluded, the captain must report to the Port Office, Mahé Quay, through the Port Security Gate on Latanier Road. An arrival form must be completed and the boarding fee paid. Three crew lists and the ship's papers should be taken, and the latter will be held until departure. The captain must also report to the Immigration office, Independence House, Victoria, with crew lists and passports.

The authorities recommend having at least ten copies of crew lists, as other departments will also ask for them.

Procedure on departure

On departure from the Seychelles, one must first visit the immigration office 12 hours prior to departure with all passports and permits, then obtain port and customs clearance, the latter from the customs office, Latanier Road.

Port clearance must be obtained to visit any of the other islands. Clearance must be made within working hours (0800–1200, 1300–1600 Monday to Friday). Before leaving Victoria to visit other islands, port control must be advised on VHF Channel 16. Usually one is asked to come to the commercial wharf for a security check before being allowed to leave. The same operation must be followed on one's return, when a yacht is subjected to an incoming security check before being allowed to anchor.

On the other islands, one must check in with local police or the Island Manager, who will sign the clearance form which must be returned to the port office within 24 hours of one's return to Victoria. On holidays the form can be left at Mahé Quay police station.

Customs

All arms and ammunition, including spearguns, must be handed to the police or customs on arrival and a receipt obtained. The bonded firearms will be returned on departure.

The Seychelles are rabies-free so regulations regarding animals are strict. Yachts with animals on board will only be allowed to visit other islands if pets are not let ashore. They must be kept confined on board in port. Only with special written permission from the Veterinary Section may animals be taken ashore. Illegal landing of animals can lead to a heavy fine, imprisonment and confiscation of the animal.

Stores under bond will be sealed and are not to be used while in the Seychelles without payment of duty. Customs officers may ask for a declaration of all food and provisions on board, but dutiable goods will not be charged duty, provided they are declared properly and are obviously for personal consumption.

Immigration

Normally a visitor's permit for two weeks is given on arrival. This is extendable up to three months. One should apply for the renewal at least one week before expiry of the existing permit. Crew leaving the yacht in the Seychelles must first obtain an authority from immigration. If crew are arriving by air to join a yacht, the captain must give immigration written confirmation prior to their arrival.

Health

Cholera vaccination certificate is required if coming from Africa.

Fees

Harbour dues (port and light dues): under 20 GRT, SR50 per day; 20–300 GRT, SR100 per day. The charges are levied for every day spent by the yacht in the Seychelles. There is a fee of SR100 for pratique. There is a charge of SR200 for fumigation of the yacht on arrival. SR50 is charged for each port clearance.

Restrictions

Anchoring in North West Bay, Mahé (Beau Vallon Bay) is strictly prohibited.

It is forbidden to spend the night in any anchorage except for the following designated anchorages:
Schedule A (islands within 60 miles of Mahé): Yacht Basin, Port Victoria; Baie-Ste-Anne, Praslin; La Passe (within one mile offshore), La Digue; Bird Island/Ile aux Vaches, Denis and Fregate, all within three miles from the shore.
Schedule B (islands 60 to 240 miles from Mahé): within three miles from the shore.
Schedule C (over 240 miles from Mahé): within three miles from the shore.

The authorities should be consulted concerning islands in schedules B and C.
National Park: Shell collecting and spearfishing in protected areas is forbidden. The environment should not be disturbed in these areas. Penalties can be a large fine and imprisonment. The protected areas, including the sea up to 400 m offshore, are as follows:

1. Mahé from Rat Island south to Pointe au Sel, also from North East Point north to the Carana Beach Hotel.
2. The Sainte Anne Marine National Park (the islands of Ste Anne, Cerf, Long, Moyenne, Round).
3. The islands of Cousin, Curieuse and Cachée.

4. Praslin from Anse Boudin east to Pointe Zanguilles.
5. La Digue: La Passe lighthouse north to Gross Roche.

Chartering is not allowed unless a licence has been obtained.

Facilities

With the increase in the number of cruising yachts visiting the Seychelles and also because some charter boats are based there, facilities are steadily improving. All repair services are concentrated in Victoria, where there are several boatyards with slipways. The largest is Naval Services, which undertakes electrical, engine and transmission repair as well as metal work. There are other companies dealing with electronics, sails, rigging, fibreglass and refrigeration work. Only a limited amount of marine supplies is available locally. Fuel can be taken on at the commercial wharf in Port Victoria, but the cost is very high. LPG bottles can also be filled and there are several supermarkets with a good selection as well as a daily fresh produce market. There is no marina at the moment, although there are plans to build one in the future. For the time being yachts use the facilities of the Seychelles Yacht Club in Port Victoria's inner harbour, where visitors are welcome.

Further Reading

Traveller's Guide to East Africa and the Indian Ocean
Africa on a Shoestring

TANZANIA

The United Republic of Tanzania came into existence as the result of political union between mainland Tanganyika and the offshore islands of Zanzibar and Pemba. The largest country in East Africa, the mainland boasts some fine scenery, the volcanic Rift Valley with its many lakes, the high steppes and savannahs rising from the coast up to Mount Kilimanjaro, which at 19,335 ft (5895 m) is Africa's highest mountain. A concerted effort is being made to protect the environment, and a large part of the country has been declared national parks and reserves.

In line with a general opening up of the country to tourism, cruising yachts are now welcome to all parts of the country and even areas which were closed in the past, such as Pemba Island, are now accessible by sea.

The underwater scenery and marine life are of comparable beauty to the spectacular interior of the country. The main attractions inland are the game parks, such as the Serengeti or Ngorongoro, which can be visited by leaving the yacht in the care of one of the yacht clubs. The spice island of Zanzibar is worth a visit to see the relics of its colourful trading history, although security is a problem and one should employ a guard if leaving the boat unattended.

Country Profile

In the Rift Valley ancient remains of Stone Age man have been discovered. Around 100 BC Bantu-speaking peoples came from the west and mixed with the original inhabitants and other peoples from the north. Along the coast, Arabic and Bantu merged into the Swahili language, named Swahili from the Arabic word for coast. Towns were established, which thrived on trade from the interior, especially slaves, gold and ivory. In the tenth century Persians came, bringing Islam to the region. From the fifteenth century the Portuguese became rivals in trade, but the Arab and Swahili traders still dominated the area. The interior remained much less developed and the Europeans did not explore there until the nineteenth century, when such famous explorers as Livingstone and Stanley went deep inland.

The island of Zanzibar was ruled by Oman and became so prosperous from trade in slaves and spices, especially cloves, that in 1840 the Sultan Seyyid Said moved his capital there from Muscat. Zanzibar became a British protectorate in 1890.

In 1885 the German East Africa Company took over the mainland, which was administered by Germany until the First World War. After the war, Britain took over Tanganyika under a League of Nations mandate to be followed by a United Nations mandate.

In 1954 the Tanganyika Africa National Union (TANU), led by Julius Nyerere, began its campaign for independence, and this was achieved in 1961. Two years later Zanzibar followed suit, and in 1964 a violent revolution ousted the Sultan. The same year Zanzibar united with Tanzania, although Zanzibar retains some autonomy.

After independence, efforts were made to establish a socialist state based on collective agriculture, the village economy and traditional way of life. Tanzania's support for refugees from Uganda led to an invasion by Idi Amin's forces in 1978. Tanganyika responded and helped topple Amin, at huge expense to the country.

The economy was weakened by the break-up in

Practical Information

LOCAL TIME: GMT + 3

BUOYAGE: IALA A

CURRENCY: Tanzanian shilling of 100 senti. The import or export of shillings is prohibited. Some services, such as entry to the national parks, must be paid in convertible foreign currency.

BUSINESS HOURS
Banks: 0830–1230 Monday to Friday, 0830–1130 Saturday.
Business: 0730–1430 Monday to Friday.
Shops: 0800–1200, 1400–1715 Monday to Saturday.
Government offices: 0830–1430 Monday to Friday, 0830–1230 Saturday.

ELECTRICITY: 220 V, 50 Hz

PUBLIC HOLIDAYS
12 January: Zanzibar Revolution Day
5 February: CCM Day
Good Friday, Easter Monday
26 April: Union Day
1 May: Labour Day
Eid el-Fitr
7 July: Peasants Day
Eid el-Hadj
Moulud
9 December: Independence Day
25 December: Christmas Day

COMMUNICATIONS
International calls can be made from Extelcom's office, Samora Avenue, Dar es Salaam, but as there are not sufficient lines, it is difficult to get through.
International calls can also be made from large hotels.
Air Tanzania operates internal flights to all major towns. There are international flights from Dar es Salaam and Kilimanjaro. Foreigners must pay for international air tickets in convertible foreign currency.

DIPLOMATIC MISSIONS
In Dar es Salaam:
Canada: Pan Africa Insurance Bldg, Samora Machel Avenue, ☎ (51) 20651.
Kenya: NIC Investment House, Samora Machel Avenue, junction with Mirambo Street.
Madagascar: Magoret Street.
☎ (51) 68229.
Mozambique: 25 Garden Avenue.
☎ (51) 33062.
France: Bagamoyo Road (visas for Francophone countries can be obtained here). ☎ (51) 68601.
Somalia: 31 Upanga Road.
☎ (51) 32104.
Sudan: 64 Upanga Road. ☎ (51) 32022.
United Kingdom: Hifadhi House, Samora Machel Avenue. ☎ (51) 29601.
United States: 36 Laibon Road (off Bagamoyo Road) ☎ (51) 68894.

1977 of the East African Economic Union (Tanzania, Kenya and Uganda), which had been in place since independence. In 1985 Nyerere, president since independence, resigned and was succeeded by Ali Hassan Mwinyi, although Nyerere still remains chairman of the ruling party.

The economy is mainly agricultural depending on coffee, cotton, sisal, tea and cloves. A large trade deficit, population growth, foreign debt, poverty and droughts have put a considerable burden on the economy. The aim of achieving self-reliance and a radical socialist state has not worked and recently the government has opened up the economy to foreign capital. Tourism has been encouraged, although it suffered from the closure of the border with Kenya after the Economic Union broke up. This border has recently been reopened.

The population is 22.6 million, made up of over 100 tribal groups, mainly Bantu-speaking. The people of Zanzibar and Pemba are a mixture of Arab, Comoron and Shirazi (Persian) origins. Ki-Swahili is the official language, although English is widely spoken. There are also many local African languages, including Sandawe the 'click' language. In Zanzibar most of the population is Muslim. On the mainland Christianity, traditional beliefs and Islam all have their followers. Dar es Salaam has been the capital since 1891.

The climate depends on the altitude, being temperate in the mountains and tropical along the coast. The rainy months are April, May, November and December. The coast is very hot and humid especially during the NW monsoon which lasts from December to April. The SE monsoon is from May to October.

Entry Regulations

Ports of entry
Dar es Salaam 6°49′S 39°19′E, Tanga 5°04′S 39°06′E, Mtwara 10°15′S 40°12′E, Zanzibar 6°10′S 39°11′E.

Procedure on arrival
Tanga: This is usually the first port of entry into Tanzania if coming from the north, and a popular place to obtain clearance. Smaller than Dar es Salaam, the offices are closer together and the officials less busy. Tanga Signal Station maintains 24-hour watch on VHF Channel 12. Captain C.J.E. Pearson, Harbour Master, Harbour Pilot and Commodore of Tanga Yacht Club will advise yachts on procedure during office hours. Customs formalities are completed at the office on Dhow Wharf, beyond the commercial wharf,

then immigration clearance is obtained from the town office, close to the post office.

Dar es Salaam: Yachts should anchor in the inner harbour flying the Q flag and await customs, immigration and port health officials. Port officials usually work 0700–1700.

Afterwards it is possible to anchor off the Dar es Salaam Yacht Club.

Customs

Firearms must be declared to customs who will seal them on board in a secure locker.

There are no restrictions on animals as long as they have a health certificate, although they should have had a rabies vaccination for their own protection.

Immigration

Visas are not required for nationals of Commonwealth countries, Ireland and Scandinavian countries. Other nationalities may obtain visas from immigration on arrival. South Africans and South Koreans are not admitted. One may have difficulties if there is evidence of a previous visit to South Africa.

Cruising permit

There are no restrictions for yachts on coastal cruising, although a transit log must be obtained from customs on arrival for cruising inside Tanzania. The transit log may be inspected if stopping at Pemba Island.

Health

Yellow fever and cholera vaccination certificates must be shown. Malaria prophylaxis is recommended. One should not swim in fresh water, because of the danger of the bilharzia parasite. AIDS is endemic in East Africa.

Restrictions

Photographs must not be taken of police stations, prisons, party offices, military areas, bridges or dams.

As a Muslim island, Zanzibar has strict rules regarding dress – shorts are forbidden, women should not expose their knees and men with longer hair should keep it tied up or wear a hat.

Facilities

Provisions are sometimes in short supply and there are both fuel and water shortages. Even when water is available, it must be treated and possibly filtered as well. Both the Dar es Salaam and Tanga Yacht Clubs are particularly welcoming to visiting yachts. Most visitors try and leave their yachts in the care of a yacht club to travel inland. Theft is a problem and a yacht should be properly watched at all times. In Dar es Salaam this applies during the day as well as at night and it is not recommended to stay in the inner harbour longer than it takes to complete clearance. Some simple repairs are possible in the bigger ports, but any spares must be flown in from abroad.

Further Reading

Traveller's Guide to East Africa and the Indian Ocean
Africa on a Shoestring

SECTION III

1 IALA Maritime Buoyage System

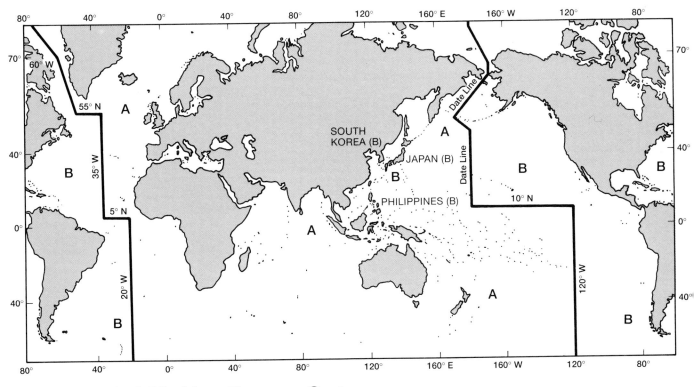

Map 17: IALA Maritime Buoyage System
BUOYAGE REGIONS A AND B

2 International Direct Dialling Codes

Region 1 Mediterranean and Black Sea

Albania	n/a	Malta	356
Algeria	213	Monaco	3393
Bulgaria	359	Morocco	212
Cyprus	357	Romania	40
Egypt	20	Spain	34
Gibraltar	350	Syria	963
Greece	30	Tunisia	216
Israel	972	Turkey	90
Italy	39	USSR	7
Lebanon	961	Yugoslavia	38
Libya	218		

Region 2 Northern Europe

Belgium	32	Netherlands	31
Denmark	45	Norway	47
Finland	358	Poland	48
Germany	49	Sweden	46

Region 3 Western Europe and North Atlantic Islands

Azores	351	Greenland	299
Bermuda	1809	Iceland	354
Canary Islands	34	Ireland	353
Cape Verde Islands	238	Madeira	35191
Channel Islands	44	Portugal	351
Faeroes	298	United Kingdom	44
France	33		

Region 4 West Africa and South Atlantic Islands

Ascension Island	247	Namibia	264
Falkland Islands	500	St Helena	n/a
Gambia	220	Senegal	221
Ivory Coast	225	South Africa	27
Mauritania	596	Tristan da Cunha	n/a

Region 5 Caribbean

Anguilla	1 809 497	Jamaica	1 809
Antigua and		Martinique	596
Barbuda	1 809 46	Montserrat	1 809 491
Aruba	297 8	Puerto Rico	1 809
Bahamas	1 809	Saba	599 4
Barbados	1 809	St Barts	590
Bonaire	599 7	St Eustatius	599 3
British Virgin Islands	1 809 49	St Kitts and Nevis	1 809 465
Cayman Islands	1 809 94	St Lucia	1 809 45
Cuba	53	St Martin	590
Curaçao	599 9	St Vincent and the	
Dominica	1 809 44	Grenadines	1809 45
Dominican Republic	1 809	Sint Maarten	599 5
Grenada	1 809 440/3/6	Trinidad and Tobago	1 809
Guadeloupe	590	Turks and Caicos	1 809 964
Haiti	509	US Virgin Islands	1 809

Region 6 Central and North America

Belize	501	Honduras	504
Canada	1	Mexico	52
Costa Rica	506	Nicaragua	505
El Salvador	503	Panama	507
Guatemala	502	USA	1

Region 7 South America

Argentina	54	Guyana	592
Brazil	55	Peru	51
Chile	56	Suriname	597
Colombia	57	Uruguay	598
Ecuador	593	Venezuela	58
French Guiana	594		

Region 8 North Pacific Islands

Federated States of		Kiribati	686
Micronesia	n/a*	Marshall Islands	n/a
Guam	671	Northern Marianas	670
Hawaii	1 808	Palau	507

* not applicable as direct dialling not available.

Region 9 Australia and South Pacific Islands

American Samoa	684	Niue	n/a
Australia	61	Norfolk Island	6723
Cook Islands	682	Papua New Guinea	675
Easter Island	n/a	Pitcairn	n/a
Fiji	674	Solomon Islands	677
French Polynesia	689	Tokelau	n/a
Galapagos Islands	n/a	Tonga	676
Juan Fernandez Islands	n/a	Tuvalu	n/a
Nauru	674	Vanuatu	678
New Caledonia	687	Wallis and Futuna	n/a
New Zealand	64	Western Samoa	685

Region 10 South East Asia and Far East

Brunei	673	Malaysia	60
China	86	Philippines	63
Hong Kong	852	Singapore	65
Indonesia	62	South Korea	82
Japan	81	Taiwan	886
Macao	853	Thailand	66

Region 11 North Indian Ocean and Red Sea

Djibouti	253	Saudi Arabia	966
Ethiopia	251	Somalia	252
India	91	Sri Lanka	94
Maldives	960	Sudan	249
Oman	968	Yemen	967

Region 12 South Indian Ocean

Chagos	n/a	Mauritius	230
Christmas Island	6724	Mayotte	n/a
Cocos Keeling	6722	Mozambique	258
Comoros	n/a	Réunion	262
Kenya	254	Seychelles	248
Madagascar	261	Tanzania	255

3 Chart Agents and National Hydrographic Offices

British Admiralty Chart Agents

ANTIGUA
The Map Shop
St Mary's Street, ST JOHN'S
☎ 809 462 3993

ARGENTINA
N H Neilson & Co Ltd
Australia 1770, 1296 BUENOS AIRES
☎ 210501

AUSTRALIA
Boat Books (Brisbane) Pty Ltd
109 Albert Street, BRISBANE,
Queensland 4000
☎ 07 2296427

Department of Marine & Harbours
Marine House, 1 Essex Street,
FREMANTLE, Western Australia 6160
☎ 09 3350888

J Donne & Son
372 Little Bourke Street, MELBOURNE,
Victoria 3000

RAN Chart Distribution
161 Walker Street, NORTH SYDNEY,
NSW 2060
☎ 02 9254800

S G Kennon & Co Pty Ltd
Winnellie Road, PORT DARWIN, NT 5789
☎ 089 843088

Ivimey & Associates Pty Ltd (Boat Books)
31 Albany Street, Crows Nest, SYDNEY,
NSW 2065
☎ 02 4391133

BELGIUM
Martin & Co
37 Oude Leeuwenrui, ANTWERPEN B 2000
☎ 03 225 0383

BERMUDA
Pearman, Watlington & Co Ltd
Front Street, HAMILTON
☎ 809 29 53232

BRUNEI
David Y Seheult & Associates
B-2 Dayang Besar Flat, Jalan Sumbiling,
BANDAR SERI BEGAWAN 2084
☎ 0802 25313

BULGARIA
Inflot State Shipping Agency
Blvd 'Chervenoarmeiski' 1, VARNA 9000
☎ 230243

CANADA
Bovey Marine Ltd
375 Water Street, VANCOUVER,
BC V6B 5C6
☎ 604 683 7475

Maritime Services Ltd
3440 Bridgeway Street, VANCOUVER BC
V5K 1B6
☎ 604 294 4444

CHILE
Ian Taylor y Cia Ltda
Prat 827 Oficina 301, Casilla 752
VALPARAISO
☎ 259096

COLOMBIA
Sistemas Tecnicos Maritimos Ltda
Carrera 55 No. 72–35,
BARRANQUILLA
☎ 341645

CYPRUS
Theseas Savva
118 Franklin Roosevelt Ave
LIMASSOL
☎ 051 55899

DENMARK
Iver Weilbach & Co A/S
Toldbodgade 35, KOBENHAVN DK 1253
☎ 01 13 5927

EGYPT
Marinkart
29 Ramses Street, BOR SA'ÎD FREEZONE
☎ 220148

Marinkart
14 Gohar Alkaid Street, Port Tewfik, SUEZ
☎ 29045

FALKLAND ISLANDS
Customs & Harbour Department, STANLEY

FIJI
Carpenter's Shipping
Tofua Street, Walu Bay, SUVA ☎ 312 244

FINLAND
Oy Maritim AB
Veneentekijantie 1, SF 00210 HELSINKI 21
☎ 673 331

FRANCE
The Riviera Chart Agent (Lt Cdr Michael Healy)
Le Silmar, 10 Rue Jean-Bracco, 06310
BEAULIEU SUR MER
☎ 93 01 15 72

2K
4 Rue Amiral Troude, 29200 BREST
☎ 98 44 84 69

Docks et Entrepots Maritimes de Keroman
12 Blvd Abbe Le Cam, 56103 LORIENT
☎ 97 37 17 99

Librairie Nautique et des Voyages
6 Rue de Mezieres, 75006 PARIS
☎ 42 22 21 38

GERMANY
Seekarte (Kapt A. Dammeyer)
Korffsdeich 3, Vd Europahafen
2800 BREMEN 1

Nautischer Dienst (Kapt Stegmann & Co)
Maklerstrasse 8, 2300 KIEL 17
☎ 0431 33 1772

GIBRALTAR
Gibraltar Chart Agency Ltd
4 Bayside, GIBRALTAR ☎ 76293

GREECE
John S. Lazopoulos & Co
85 Akti Miaouli, GR-185 38 PIRAIEVS
☎ 41 31 902

GRENADINES
Bo'sun's Locker
Port Elizabeth
BEQUIA, St Vincent
☎ 809 45 83246

HONG KONG
Geo Falconer (Nautical) Ltd
Room 806-7 The Hong Kong Chinese Bank
Building,
61–65 Des Voeux Road, Central
☎ 5 226741

Walter Dunn & Co
Room 502 Man Yee Building,
60–70 Des Voeux Road,
Central ☎ 1 610230

ICELAND
Sjomaelingar Islands
Seljavegur 32, 127 REYKJAVIK
☎ 91 10230

INDIA
C & C Marine Combine
25 Bank Street, 1st Floor, BOMBAY 400023
☎ 28 60 525

IRELAND
Union Chandlery Ltd
Andersons Quay, CORK
☎ 271643

Windmill Leisure & Marine Ltd
3 Windmill Lane, Sir John Rogerson's
Quay, DUBLIN 2 ☎ 772008

ISRAEL
IM Techno-Marine Equipment Co Ltd
Room 731 Haifa Levant Bldg, Palmer's Gate
No. 1, HAIFA
☎ 04 645622

ITALY
Cooperativa per Azioni Armamento
Imprese
Marittime ARL
Piazza S Sabina 2, 16124 GENOVA
☎ 10 200930

JAPAN
Cornes & Co Ltd
Towa Bldg, 2-3 Kaigan Dori, Chuo-Ku KOBE
☎ 078 332 3361

Cornes & Co Ltd
Yokohama Daiei Building 6th floor,
2-10 Hon Cho, Naka-Ku, YOKOHAMA 231
☎ 045 664 6512

KOREA
Korea Ocean Development Co Ltd
1 GA71-1 Nampo-Dong, Jung-ku, BUSAN
☎ 22 3869

MALAYSIA
Motion Smith
49 Lorong Ewan, 88000 KOTA KINABALU
Sabah ☎ 088 52044

The Industrial & Scientific Co Ltd
12 Gartak Street, KUCHING, Sarawak
☎ 21404

MALTA
Thos C Smith & Co Ltd
12 St Christopher Street, VALLETTA
☎ 625071

NETHERLANDS
L J Harri BV
Prins Hendrikkade 94-95,
1012 AE AMSTERDAM
☎ 20 248035

Datema-Delfzijl BV
Oude Schans 11, 9934 CM DELFZIJL
☎ 05960 13810

NEW ZEALAND
Trans Pacific Marine Ltd
30 Quay Street, AUCKLAND 1
☎ 31459

RNZN Chart Agency
Burns Avenue, Takapuna, AUCKLAND 9
☎ 495063

NORWAY
Nautisk Forlag AS
Dokkvn 1, Akker Brygge, OSLO 2
☎ 02 413 690

PANAMA
Islamorada International SA
No. 7 Edificio Minerva El Cangrejo,
PANAMA
☎ 23 7279

PORTUGAL
J Garraio & Ca Lda
Avenida 24 de Julho 2-10 D, 1200 LISBOA
☎ 373081

SINGAPORE
Motion Smith
1st Floor Marina House, 70 Shenton Way,
Mistri Road, SINGAPORE 0207
☎ 2205098

SOUTH AFRICA
Chandling International Ltd
53 Carlisle Street, Paardeneiland,
CAPE TOWN 7405
☎ 021 512336

The Tyneside Shop No.5, John Ross
House, Victoria Embankment, DURBAN
4001
☎ 031 377005

SPAIN
Blanco Montejo SA (Premenaca SA)
Urb El Cebadal, Vial 1, Nro. 211, 35008,
LAS PALMAS DE GRAN CANARIA
☎ 224 504

SRI LANKA
Marine Overseas Agency
Paul VI Centre, 3rd floor, Room 8,
24 Malwatta Road, COLOMBO 11
☎ 26262

SWEDEN
Aktiebolaget Nautic
Skeppsbroplatsen 1, S411 21 GÖTEBORG
☎ 031 112421

Stavfeldts Nautiska A/B
Packhusplatsen 2, S411 13 GÖTEBORG
☎ 031 100885

Nautiska Forlaget A/B
Norrtullsgaten 4, S113 29 STOCKHOLM
☎ 08 345493

TRINIDAD
Marine Consultants (Trinidad) Ltd
43 Charles Street, PORT OF SPAIN
☎ 62 52270

TURKEY
Deniz Malzeme Ltd
Sirketi Tophane, Iskele Cad No. 17,
ISTANBUL
☎ 443197

UNITED STATES OF AMERICA

Tradewind Instruments Ltd
2540 Blanding Avenue, ALAMEDA
Nr San Francisco, California 94501
☎ 415 523 5726

Boxell's Chandlery
68 Long Wharf, BOSTON,
Massachusetts 02110
☎ 617 523 5678

Bahia Mar Marine Store
801 Seabreeze Boulevard,
FORT LAUDERDALE, Florida 33316
☎ 305 764 8831

Pacific Map Centre
647 Auahi Street, HONOLULU,
Hawaii 96813
☎ 808 531 3800

Safe Navigation Inc
107 East 8th Street,
LONG BEACH, California 90813
☎ 213 590 8744

New York Nautical Instrument and Service
Corporation
140 West Broadway, NEW YORK 10013
☎ 212 962 4523

Captain's Nautical Supplies
138 NW 10th Street, PORTLAND,
Oregon 97209
☎ 503 227 1648

Captain's Nautical Supplies
1914 4th Avenue, SEATTLE,
Washington 98101
☎ 206 448 2278

URUGUAY

Marine Technical Services
Florida 1562, MONTEVIDEO
☎ 985161

UNITED KINGDOM, CHANNEL ISLANDS

Aberdeen
Kelvin Hughes
21 Regents Quay, Aberdeen AB1 2AH
☎ 0224 580823

Thomas Gunn Navigational Services
62 Marischal Street, Aberdeen AB1 2AL
☎ 0224 595045

Avonmouth
W F Price & Co Ltd
24 Gloucester Road, Avonmouth, Bristol,
Avon BS 11 9AG
☎ 0272 823888

Belfast
James Tedford & Co Ltd
5 & 9 Donegall Quay, Belfast,
N. Ireland BT1 3EF
☎ 0232 226763

Brighton
Russell Simpson Marine Ltd
The Chandlery, Brighton Marina, Brighton,
E. Sussex BN2 5UF
☎ 0273 697161

Cowes
Pascall Atkey & Son Ltd
29–30 High Street, Cowes,
Isle of Wight PO31 7RX
☎ 0983 292381

Dover
Dover Marine Supplies
158–160 Snargate Street, Dover,
Kent CT17 9BZ
☎ 0304 201677

Falmouth
Marine Instruments of The Bo'sun's Locker
Upton Slip, Church Street, Falmouth,
Cornwall TR11 3PS
☎ 0326 312414

Glasgow
Kelvin Hughes
375 West George Street, Glasgow G2 4LR
☎ 041 221 5452

London
Brown & Perring Ltd
Redwing House, 36–44 Tabernacle Street,
London EC2A 4DT
☎ 071 253 4517

Kelvin Hughes
145 The Minories, London EC3N 1NH
☎ 071 709 9076

Lymington
Nick Cox Yacht Chandler Ltd
King's Saltern Road, Lymington,
Hampshire SO41 9QD
☎ 0590 73489

Plymouth
A E Monsen
Vauxhall Quay, Plymouth, Devon PL4 0DL
☎ 0752 665384

St Peter Port (Guernsey)
Boatworks Plus Ltd
Castle Emplacement, St Peter Port,
Guernsey, Channel Islands
☎ 0481 26071

Southampton
Kelvin Hughes
19–23 Canute Road, Eastern Docks,
Southampton SO1 1FJ
☎ 0703 631286

US Defence Mapping Agency Agents

ARGENTINA
Securnavi SA
Av Luis M Campos 653,
BUENOS AIRES 1426

AUSTRALIA
Victoria
Grigor & Associates Pty Ltd
268 St Kilda Rd,
ST KILDA 3182

New South Wales
Ivimey and Associates Pty Ltd
31 Albany St,
Crows Nest, SYDNEY 2065

Queensland
Boat Books
109 Albert St, BRISBANE 4000

The Navigation Center,
9C Palmer St,
SOUTH TOWNSVILLE 4810

BAHAMAS
John S George Co Ltd
Palmdale Shopping Center,
PO Box 6330-SS, NASSAU-New
Providence

Outboard Services Ltd
PO Box F-908, FREEPORT

BELGIUM
Bogerd NAVTEC NV
Brouwersvliet 36-38, ANTWERP B-2000

Martin & Co Ltd
28 Brouwersvliet, ANTWERP B-2000

BERMUDA
Pitt's Bay Boat Co Ltd
PO Box 840, HAMILTON 5

CANADA
British Columbia
Alexander Marine Ltd
570 Davie St, VANCOUVER V6B 2G4

Bovey Marine, 375 Water St,
VANCOUVER V6B 5C6

Maritime Services Ltd,
Division of Triton Holdings Inc,
3440 Bridgeway St, VANCOUVER V5K 1B6

Sailtrend Chandlers & Riggers, 1327 Beach
Drive (at Oak Bay Marina)
VANCOUVER V85 2NY

Bosun's Locker
580 Johnson St, VICTORIA V8W 1MA

Newfoundland
Campbell's Ships Supplies
PO Box 274, 689 Water St, West,
ST JOHN'S A1C 5J2

Nova Scotia
Gabriel Aero-Marine Instruments Ltd
1576 Hollis St, HALIFAX B3J 1V4

Quebec
Gabriel Aero-Marine Instruments Ltd,
351 St Paul St West, MONTREAL H2Y 2A7

McGill Maritime Services Inc
369 Place D' Youville, MONTREAL H2Y 2G2

COLOMBIA
Sistemas Tecnicos Maritimos Ltda
Apartado Aereo 50042
(PO Box), Carrera, 55. No 72–35
BARRANQUILLA

Sistemas Tecnicos Maritimos Ltda,
Apartado Aereo 2996 (PO Box)
CARTEGENA

DENMARK
Iver C. Weilbach & Co A/S
35 Toldbodgade, COPENHAGEN DK-1253

ECUADOR
Instituto Oceanografico de la Armada
Casilla de Correos, No 5940, GUAYAQUIL

EGYPT
Edwardo Marine Services
PO Box 179, 41 El Tour St, PORT SAID

International Shipping Enterprise
PO Box 252, 18 Safia Zaghloul St,
PORT SAID

ENGLAND
Brown & Perring Ltd
Redwing House, 36/44 Tabernacle St,
LONDON EC2A 4DT

Kelvin Hughes
145 The Minories, LONDON EC3N 1NH

FRANCE
Friebe France
B P 129 Aerodrome de Cannes,
CANNES-LA BOCCA Cedex 06322

Societe 2K
25 Rue d'Astorg, PARIS 75008

Librairie Arthaud
6 Rue de Mezieres, PARIS 75006

Outremer Librairie Maritime
17 Rue Jacob, PARIS 75006

GERMANY
Bade & Hornig
Stubbenhuk 10, D-2000
HAMBURG 11

Eckardt & Messtorff
Rodingsmarkt 16,
D-2000 HAMBURG 11

GREECE
J & D Athanassiadis S/A
Kastoros St,
No 78/A PIRAEUS

HONG KONG
Geo Falconer (Nautical) Ltd
806-7 Hong Kong Chinese Bank Bldg,
61–65 Des Vouex Rd, Central District

Hong Kong Ship Supplies Co
Room 1614, Melbourne Plaza, 33 Queen's
Rd, Central District

ICELAND
Iceland Hydrographic Service
PO Box 7120, 127 REYKJAVIK

ITALY
Cooperativa Armamento Imprese
Marittime
Piazza S, Sabina N 2, GENOA 16124

Societa Italiana Radio Marittima
Via San Benedetto 14, GENOA 16126

JAPAN
Japan Hydrographic Charts & Publications
Co Ltd
Kobe Branch, Shosen-Mitsui Bldg No 5,
Kaigan-Dori, Chuo-Ku, KOBE

Japan Hydrographic Charts & Publications
Co Ltd
Konwa Bldg, No 12-22, 1-Chome, Tsukiji,
Chuo-Ku, TOKYO

Nippon Oceanic Survey Co Ltd
Matsui Bldg, 1st Floor, 17–22 Shinkawa,
1-Chome, Chuo-Ku, TOKYO 104

KOREA
Korea Ocean Development Co Ltd
Sam Oh Bldg, Room 105,
5-20 Chung-Moo-Ro,Joong-Ku, SEOUL 100

MEXICO
Salvamentos y Servicios Navales de
Mazatlan,
SA Apartado Postal 1086, MAZATLAN

NETHERLANDS
L J Harri BV
'Schreerstoren', Prins Hendrikkade, 94–95,
AMSTERDAM 1012 AE

Observator BV, Charts & Marine Supplies
Vasteland 18–26,
ROTTERDAM-CENTRUM 3011 BL

NETHERLANDS ANTILLES
Island Water World Inc NV
PO Box 234, Philipsburg, SINT MAARTEN

NEW ZEALAND
Trans Pacific Marine Ltd
31 Fort St, AUCKLAND 1

NORWAY
Navicharts A/S
Nordensvei 15, PO Box 83, N-2013,
Skjetten, OSLO

PANAMA
Islamorada International SA
Apartado 9662, No 7 Edificio Minerva El
Cangrejo, PANAMA 4

PERU
Direccion de Hidrografia y Navegacion de
la Marina
Avda Gammara No 500, Chucuito,
CALLAO 1

PHILIPPINES
Morbai Enterprises
Insurance Ctr Bldg, Ground Floor, 633
General Luna St, Intramuros, MANILA

PORTUGAL
G Vieira Ltd
Travessa do Carvalho 15-1, LISBON 1200

SCOTLAND
Kelvin Hughes
Pegasus House, 375 W George St,
GLASGOW G2 4LR

SINGAPORE
Fathima News Enterprise
VM Haja Moideen, PO Box 3943, Maxwell
Rd Post Office, SINGAPORE 9050

Motion Smith
70 Shenton Way, 02-03 Marina House,
SINGAPORE 0207

SOUTH AFRICA
Time & Tide
31 Parry Rd, DURBAN 4001

SPAIN
Deposito Hidrografico SA
Avda Marques de L'Agentera, BARCELONA
5

Fernando Blanco Montejo
28009 Lope de Rueda 27, MADRID 9

SWEDEN
Aktiebolaget Nautic
Skeppsbroplatsen 1,
GÖTEBORG S-411 18

Nautiska Forlaget A/B
Norrtullsgatan 4, PO Box 6108,
STOCKHOLM S-102 32

TAIWAN
China Marine Institute
Room 208, 4 Kang Si St, KEELUNG

Agents in United States Possessions

GUAM
Coral Reef Marine Center
PO Box 2792, Marine Drive Asan,
AGANA 96910

PUERTO RICO
Miramar Marine
PO Box 1881,
SAN JUAN 00903

VIRGIN ISLANDS
Anchor Marine Supply
PO Box 8740, Red Hook, St Thomas,
CHARLOTTE AMALIE USVI 00802

Agents in the United States

HAWAII
Ala Wai Marine Ltd
1651 Ala Moana Blvd, HONOLULU 96815

Pacific Map Center
647 Auahi St, HONOLULU 96813

National Hydrographic Offices

ARGENTINA
Servicio de Hidrografia Naval
Avenida Montes de Oca 2124, 1271
BUENOS AIRES

AUSTRALIA
Royal Australian Navy Hydrographic
Service
PO Box 1332, NORTH SYDNEY, NSW 2059

BELGIUM
Dienst der Kust Hydrografie Administratief
Centrum
Vrijhavenstraat 3, B-8400 OOSTENDE

BRAZIL
Directoria de Hidrografia e Navegação
Rua Barão de Jaceguay S/No
Ponta da Armação, 24000 NITEROI-RJ

CANADA
Canadian Hydrographic Service
615 Booth St, OTTAWA Ontario KIA OE6

CHILE
Instituto Hidrografico de la Armada
Casilla 324, VALPARAISO

CUBA
Instituto Cubano de Hidrografia Apartado
606, Marianao 13, CIUDAD DE LA HABANA

DENMARK
Farvandsdirektoratet
Nautisk Afdeling, Esplanaden 19, DK-1263
KØBENHAVN K

ECUADOR
Instituto Oceanográfico de la Armada
Casilla de Correos 5940,GUAYAQUIL

EGYPT
Idaret Al Misaha Al Baharia
Ras el Tin, EL ISKANDARIYA

FIJI
Hydrographic Office, Fiji Navy
PO Box 2525, Government Buildings,SUVA

FINLAND
Merenkulkuhallitus
Merikarttaosasto
Vuorimiehenkatu 1, 00 141 HELSINKI 14

FRANCE
Etablissement Principal de Service
Hydrographique
et Océanographique de la Marine
13 rue du Chatellier BP 426, 29275 BREST
CEDEX

GERMANY
Deutsches Hydrographisches Institut
Bernhard-Nocht-Strasse 78, Postfach 200
D-2000 HAMBURG 4

GREECE
Hellenic Navy Hydrographic Service
TGN 1040 ATHÍNAI

ICELAND
Sjómaelingar Islands
Seljavegur 32,REYKJAVIK

INDONESIA
Dinas Hidro-Oseanografi
Jalan Pantai Kuta V No. 1, Ancol Timur,
JAKARTA

ITALY
Istituto Idrografico della Marina
Passo Osservatorio 4, 16134 GENOVA

JAPAN
Kaijohoan-Cho Suiro-Bu (Hydrographic
Department of Maritime Safety Agency)
No. 3-1 Tsukiji 5 Chome,Chuo-Ku,
TOKYO 104

MALAYSIA
Hydrographic Department, Department of
Navy
Ministry of Defence, Jalan Padang Tembal,
KUALA LUMPUR 50634

MEXICO
Direccion General de Oceanografia Naval
Secretario de Marina
Medellin No. 10 1 er Piso, Col Roma,
Delegacion Cuanhtemoc 10, 06700
MEXICO DF

NETHERLANDS
Dienst der Hydrografie van de Koninklijke
Marine 171, Badhuisweg, 2597 JN 's
GRAVENHAGE

NEW ZEALAND
Hydrographic Office, Royal New Zealand
Navy
PO Box 33341, Takapuna, AUCKLAND 9

NORWAY
Norges Sjøkartverk
Lervigsveien 36, PO Box 60, 4001
STAVANGER

PERU
Direccion de Hidrografia y Navegacion de
la Marina
Avda Gamarra No. 500, Chucuito
CALLAO 1

PHILIPPINES
The Surveys Department, National
Mapping & Resource Information Authority
(NAMRIA)
421 Barraca St, San Nicolas, MANILA

POLAND
Biuro Hydrograficzne Marynarki Wojennej
PRL 81-912 GDYNIA 12

PORTUGAL
Instituto Hidrograficio
Rua das Trinas 49, LISBOA

SINGAPORE
Hydrographic Department
Port of Singapore Authority
7 Keppel Rd, No. 2-28 Tanjong Pagar
Complex, SINGAPORE 0208

SOLOMON ISLANDS
Solomon Islands Hydrographic Unit
Survey & Cartographic Division
PO Box G13, HONIARA

SOUTH AFRICA
The Hydrographer SA Navy
Hydrographic Office
Private Bag XI, Tokai 7966, CAPE TOWN

SPAIN
Instituto Hidrográfico de la Marina
Tolosa Latour No. 1 CADIZ

SWEDEN
Sjökarteavdelningen
S-601 78, NORRKÖPING

THAILAND
Hydrographic Department, Royal Thai
Navy
BANGKOK 10600

TRINIDAD AND TOBAGO
Hydrographic Unit
PO Box 1104, PORT OF SPAIN

TURKEY
Seyir Hidrografi ve Osinografi Dairesi
Baskanligi
Çubuklu 81647, ISTANBUL

USA
National Oceanic & Atmospheric
Administration
(NOAA) National Ocean Service
ROCKVILLE, Maryland 20852
(Waters of USA, Great Lakes, Hawaii,
Puerto Rico)

Defence Mapping Agency Hydrographic
Topographic Centre (DMAHTC)
6500 Brookes Lane, WASHINGTON D.C.
20315
(Worldwide except tidal waters of USA and
its possessions)

URUGUAY
Servicio de Oceanografia Hidrografia y
Meteorologia de la Armada
Capurro 980, Casilla de Correo 1381
MONTEVIDEO

USSR
Glavnoe Oupravlenie Navigatsii I
Okeanografii
Ministetstva Oborony
8 11 liniya B-34, LENINGRAD

VENEZUELA
Comandancia General de la Marina
Direccion de Hidrografia y Navegación
Apartado Postal No. 6745, Carmelitas,
CARACAS

YUGOSLAVIA
Hidrografski Institut Jugoslavenske Ratne
Mornarice
Zrinsko-Frankopanska 66, 58000 SPLIT

4 Glossary of Useful Terms in French, Spanish and Portuguese

	Français	*Español*	*Portugues*
Clearance Formalities			
yacht harbour	port de plaisance	dársena de yates	doca de recreio
harbour master's office	capitainerie du port	comandancia de marina	capitania
customs office	bureau de douane	aduana	alfandega
pilot station	station de pilotage	caseta de prácticos	estaçao de pilôtos
prohibited area	zone interdite	zona prohibida	zona proibida
dock	bassin, dock	dique	doca
breakwater	brise-lames	rompeolas	quebra-mar
mole	môle	muelle	molhe
slipway	cale de halage	varadero	rampa
landing steps	escalier de débarquement	escala de desemarque	secada de desembarque
mooring	amarrage	amarradero	cabeço
dolphin	duc d'Albe	noray	duque de alba
skipper	capitaine	patrón	patrao
crew	équipage	tripulación	tripulaçao
Certificate of Registry	Certificat de Francisation	Patente de Navegación	Certificado de Registro
Ship's Articles	Rôle d'equipage	Rol	Rol de Equipagem
Ship's Log	Livre de bord	Bitácora	Diário de Bordo
Bill of Health	Patente de santé	Patente de Sanidad	Certificado de Saúde
pratique	libre-pratique	plática	livre prática
insurance certificate	certificat d'assurance	poliza de seguro	cetificado de seguro
charter party	charter-partie	contrato de flete	fretador
customs clearance	libre-sortie, congé de douane	despacho de aduana	despacho
bonded stores	sous douanes, en franchise	viveres precintados	mantimentos desalfandegados
passport	passeport	pasaporte	passaporte

	Français	*Español*	*Portugues*
Charts and Publications			
Pilot, Sailing Directions	Instructions Nautiques	Derrotero	Pilôto, Roteiro da costa
Nautical Almanac	Almanach Nautiques	Almanaque Náutico	Almanaque Náutico
Tide Tables	Annuaire des Marées	Tabla de Mareas	Tabela Marés
List of Lights	Livre des Phares	Cuaderno de Faros	Lista de Faróis
Notices to Mariners	Avis aux Navigateurs	Aviso a los Navegantes	Avisos aos Navegantes
North, South East, West	Nord, Sud Est, Ouest	Norte, Sur Este, Oeste	Norte, Sul Este, Oeste
scale	échelle	escala	escala
lighthouse	phare	faro	farol
fixed light(F)	feu fixe(F.f)	luz fija(f)	luz fixa(F)
flashing light (Fl)	feu à éclats (F.é)	luz de destellos(dest)	relampagos(Rl)
quick flashing light	feu scintillant	luz centelleante	relampagos rápidos
occulting light (Oc)	à occultations (F.o)	luz de ocultaciones	ocultaçoes (Oc.)
group occulting light(OC)	à occultations groupées(F.2.o)	luz de grupos ocultaciones	grupo n. ocultaçoes
alternating light	à changement de coloration	luz alternativa	alternada
intermittent	feu intermittent	luz intermitente	intermitente
interrupted	feu interrompu	luz de grupos de centelleos	interompida
quick flashing (IQ)			
fixed and flashing(F FL)	fixe blanc varié par un éclat (F.b.é.)	luz fija y destellos (f.dest.)	fixa e com relampagos(F.Rl)
light buoy	bouée lumineuse	boya luminosa	bóia luminosa
whistle buoy	bouée sonore à sifflet	boya de silbato	bóia de apito
bell buoy	bouée sonore à cloche	boya de campana	bóia de sino
can buoy	bouée plate, cylindrique	boya cilindrica	bóia cilindrica
conical buoy	bouée conique	boya cónica	bóia cónica
spar buoy	bouée à espar	boya de espeque	bóia de mastro
pillar buoy	bouée à fuseau	boya de huso	bóia de pilar
barrel buoy	bouée tonne	barril	bóia de barril
topmark	voyant	marca de tope	alvo
fixed beacon	balise fixe	baliza fija	baliza fixa
floating beacon	balise flottante	baliza flotante	baliza flutuante
chequered	à damiers(dam)	damero, a cuadros	aos quadrados(x)
horizontal stripes	à bandes horizontales	franjas horizontales	faixas horizontales
vertical stripes	à bandes verticales	franjas verticales	faixas verticais
black (B. blk.)	noir(n)	negro(n)	preto(pr)

	Français	*Español*	*Portugues*
red(R)	rouge(r)	rojo(r)	vermelho(vm)
green(G)	vert(v)	verde(v)	verde(vd)
blue(Bl)	bleu(bl)	azul(az)	azul
yellow(Y)	jaune(j)	amarillo(am)	amarelo(am)
white(W)	blanc(b)	blanco(b)	branco(b)
orange(Or)	orange(org)	naranjo	côr de laranja
violet(Vi)	violet(vio)	violeta	violeta
brown	brun	marrón	castanhao
grey	gris	gris	cinzento
high water	pleine mer	pleamar	preia-mar
low water	basse mer	bajamar	baixa-mar
flood	marée montante	entrante	enchente
ebb	marée descendante	vaciante	vasante
spring tide	eau vive	marea viva	águas-vivas
neap tide	eau morte	aguas muertas	águas-mortas
one	un	uno	um
two	deux	dos	dois
three	trois	tres	três
four	quatre	cuatro	quatro
five	cinq	cinco	cinco
six	six	seis	seis
seven	sept	siete	sete
eight	huit	ocho	oito
nine	neuf	nueve	nove
ten	dix	diez	dez
eleven	onze	once	onze
twelve	douze	doce	doze
thirteen	treize	trece	treze
fourteen	quatorze	catorce	catorze
fifteen	quinze	quince	quinze
sixteen	seize	diecisés	dezaseis
seventeen	dix-sept	diecisiete	dezasete
eighteen	dix-huit	dieciocho	dezoito
nineteen	dix-neuf	diecinueve	dezanove
twenty	vingt	veinte	vinte
thirty	trente	treinta	trinta
forty	quarante	cuarenta	quaranta
fifty	cinquante	cincuenta	cinquenta
sixty	soixante	sesenta	sessenta
seventy	soixante-dix	setenta	setenta
eighty	quatre-vingt	ochenta	oitenta
ninety	quatre-vingt-dix	noventa	noventa
one hundred	cent	cien	cem
thousand	mille	mil	mil

5 Bibliography

A Cruising Guide to the Caribbean and Bahamas; Hart & Stone; Putnam's, New York.

A Cruising Guide to the Chesapeake; Stone, Blanchard & Hays. Putnam's, New York.

A Cruising Guide to the Florida Keys; Papy, Frank; Cruising Guide Publications, Florida.

A Cruising Guide to the Maine Coast; Taft, Hank & Jan; International Marine.

A Cruising Guide to the Marlborough Sound.

A Cruising Guide to the New England Coast; Duncan & Ware; Putnam's, New York.

A Motoring Guide to St Kitts; Cotner, Janet.

A Pocket Guide to the South East Aegean; Heikell, Rod & Harper, Mike; Imray, Huntingdon.

A Yachtsman's Fiji; Calder, Michael; The Cruising Classroom, Forestville, Australia.

Adriatic Pilot; Thompson, T. & D.; Imray, Huntingdon.

Africa, Nile Route; Naylor; R. Lascelles.

Aku-Aku; Heyerdahl, Thor; Unwin Hyman, London.

An Island to Oneself; Neale, Tom; Collins, London.

Ardnamurchan to Cape Wrath; Clyde Cruising Club.

Atlantic Coast Spain and Portugal; RCC Pilotage Foundation; Imray, Huntingdon.

Atlantic Islands; RCC Pilotage Foundation; Imray, Huntingdon.

Bahamas: Insight Guide; APA Publications, Singapore.

Balearic Islands Yachtsman's Directory; Cindy Cody, Japon 8, 07016 Portals Nous, Mallorca, Spain.

Baltic Southwest Pilot; Brackenbury, Mark; Adlard Coles Nautical, London.

Barrier Reef Rendezvous; Lucas, Alan; Horwitz Grahame, Cammeray, Australia.

Belize Cruising Guide; Sorem, Bill; Treasure Island, Florida.

Blue Guide to Greece; A. & C. Black, London.

Blue Guide to Israel; A. & C. Black, London.

Bristol Channel and Severn Pilot; Cumberlidge, Peter; Adlard Coles Nautical, London.

Brittany and Channel Islands Cruising Guide; Jefferson, David; Adlard Coles Nautical.

Canary Islands Cruising Guide;World Cruising Publications, London

Caribbean Islands Handbook; Trade and Travel Publications, Bath.

Carte-Guide Navigation Fluviale; Editure Cartographique Maritime.

Centreport Gibraltar; Sloma, A. A. & D. M.; Gibraltar Books Ltd.

Channel Harbours and Anchorages; Coles, Adlard; Adlard Coles Nautical, London.

Channel Islands: Insight Guide; APA Publications, Singapore.

Channel Islands Pilot; Robson, Malcolm; Adlard Coles Nautical, London.

Charlie's Charts of Hawaii; Wood, Charles; Surrey, British Columbia.

Charlie's Charts of Polynesia; Wood Charles; Surrey, British Columbia.

Charlie's Charts, Western Coast of Mexico; Wood, Charles; Surrey, British Columbia.

Coastal Cruising Handbook of New Zealand; Royal Akarana Yacht Club.

Cruise Cape Breton; Cape Breton Development Corporation.

Cruising Association Handbook; Cruising Association, London.

Cruising French Waterways; McKnight, Hugh; Adlard Coles Nautical, London.

Cruising Guide to British Columbia; Wolferston, Bill; Whitecap Books, Vancouver.

Cruising Guide to Tahiti and French Polynesia; The Moorings; Clearwater, Florida.

Cruising Guide to Tahiti and the Society Islands; Davock, Marcia; Cruising Guide Publications, Florida.

Cruising Guide to the Abacos and the Northern Bahamas; Wilensky, Julius; Wescott Cove Publishing Co., Stamford, Connecticut.

Cruising Guide to the Bay Islands; Wilensky, Julius; Wescott Cove Publishing Co., Stamford, Connecticut.

Cruising Guide to the Eastern Caribbean (4 vols); Street, Donald; Norton, New York.

Cruising Guide to the Kingdom of Tonga in Vava'u; The Moorings; Cruising Guide Publications, Florida.

Cruising Guide to the Leeward Islands; Doyle, Chris; Cruising Guide Publications, Florida.

Cruising Guide to the Netherlands; Navin, Brian; Imray, Huntingdon.

Cruising Guide to the Nova Scotia Coast; McKelvy, John.

Cruising Guide to the Turquoise Coast of Turkey; Davock, Marcia.

Cruising Guide, Block Island to Nantucket; Better Boating Association.

Cruising Guide, Long Island Sound; Better Boating Association.

Cruising New Caledonia and Vanuatu; Lucas, Alan; Horwitz Grahame, Cammeray, Australia.

Cruising Ports, California to Florida via Panama; Rains, John.

Cruising the Coral Coast; Lucas, Alan; Horwitz Grahame, Cammeray, Australia.

Cruising the Pacific Coast; West, Carolyn & Jack; Pacific Search Press.

Cruising the San Juan Islands; Calhouan, Bruce; Norton, New York.

Cruising the Solomons; Lucas, Alan; Horwitz Grahame, Cammeray, Australia.

Cruising to New South Wales; Lucas, Alan; Horwitz Grahame, Cammeray, Australia.

Cruising to Papua New Guinea; Lucas, Alan; Horwitz Grahame, Cammeray, Australia.

East Coast Pilot Guide from Ramsgate to the Wash; Bowskill, Derek; Imray, Huntingdon.

East Spain Pilot; Brandon, Robin; Imray, Huntingdon.

Egypt for Yachtsmen; Luxor, Hassan; Egyptian Authority for the Promotion of Tourist & Egyptian Yachting and Water Ski Federation.

Embassy Complete Guide to Cape Cod and Rhode Island; Borton, Mark.

Embassy Complete Guide to Long Island; Borton & Grant.

Evergreen Cruising Atlas (Olympia to Skagway); Straub Printing and Publishing, Seattle.

Falkland Island Shores; Southby-Tailyour, Ewen; Adlard Coles Nautical, London.

Fiji Marine Department Nautical Almanac.

Firth of Clyde; Clyde Cruising Club.

Floreana; Wittmer, Margret; Anthony Nelson, Shropshire.

Fodor's Brazil; Fodor Publications Ltd.

Fodor's South America; Fodor Publications Ltd.

Foreign Cruising Notes, Vol. 1 Northern Europe, Vol. 2 Mediterranean; Cruising Association, London.

Foreign Port Forms; Imray, Huntingdon.

French Inland Waterways; Cruising Association, London.

French Pilot (Vols 1–4); Robson, Malcolm; Adlard Coles Nautical, London.

Frisian Pilot; Brackenbury, Mark; Adlard Coles Nautical, London.

Greek Waters Pilot; Heikell, Rod; Imray, Huntingdon.

Grid Chart of the Bay of Islands; Kerikeri Radio; PO Box 131 Kerikeri, New Zealand.

Guide to Hong Kong Waters; Hownan-Meek.

Harbour and Yacht Club Regulations and Facilities in the Cape Province; Cruising Association of South Africa, Cape Town.

How to Cruise to Alaska without Rocking the Boat too Much; Woodward, Walt; Norwesting Inc., Edmonds, WA 98020.

IJsselmeer Harbours; Keatinge, Hilary; Barnacle Marine.

Improbable Voyage; Jones, Tristan; Grafton Books, London.

Indonesia Handbook; Moon Publications.

Inland Waterways of Belgium; Benest, E. E.; Imray, Huntingdon.

Inland Waterways of France; Imray, Huntingdon.

Italian Waters Pilot; Heikell, Rod; Imray, Huntingdon.

Japan Handbook; Moon Publications.

Landfalls of Paradise; Hinz, Earl; Western Marine Enterprises, Marina del Rey, California.

Lundy, Fastnet & Irish Sea Pilot (3 vols); Taylor, David Imray, Huntingdon.

Mediterranean Cruising Handbook; Heikell, Rod; Imray, Huntingdon.

Micronesia Handbook; Stanley, David; Moon Publications.

Mull of Kintyre to Arnamurchan; Clyde Cruising Club.

New Zealand's Bay of Islands; Jones, Claire; Port of Opua Trading Co., Opua, New Zealand.

Normandy and Channel Islands Pilot; Brackenbury, Mark; Adlard Coles Nautical, London.

North and East Coast of Scotland; Clyde Cruising Club.

North and East Coasts of Ireland Sailing Directions; Irish Cruising Club.

North Biscay Pilot; RCC Pilotage Foundation; Adlard Coles Nautical, London.

North Brittany Pilot; Adlard Coles Nautical/RCC Pilotage Foundation; Adlard Coles Nautical, London.

North France Pilot; Thompson, T. & D.; Imray, Huntingdon.

North Sea Harbours and Pilotage; Coote, Jack; Adlard Coles, London.

North Sea Passage Pilot; Navin, Brian; Imray, Huntingdon.

Northern Territory Coast, A Cruising Guide; Knight, John; 81 Alawa Crescent, Casuarina, NT 5792 Australia.

Northwest Boat Travel; Anderson Publishing, Anacortes Washington.

Norwegian Cruising Guide; Brackenbury, Mark; Adlard Coles Nautical, London.

Orkney Islands; Clyde Cruising Club.

Outer Hebrides; Clyde Cruising Club.

Pacific Boating Almanac, Pacific Northwest & Alaska; Western Marine Enterprises, Marina del Rey, California.

Pacific Islands Yearbook; Angus & Robertson, New South Wales.

Pacific Odyssey; Cornell, Gwenda; Adlard Coles Nautical, London.

Pickmere's Atlas of Northland's East Coast; Transpacific Marine, Auckland.

Pickmere's Yasawa Chartlets; Transpacific Marine, Auckland.

Queensland Official Tide Tables and Boating Guide.

Red Sea and Indian Ocean Cruising Guide; Lucas, Alan; Imray, Huntingdon.

Sailors' Guide to the Windward Islands; Doyle, Chris; Cruising Guide Publications, Florida.

St Helena including Ascension Island and Tristan da Cunha; Cross, Tony; David & Charles, Newton Abbot.

St Vincent and the Grenadines; Jinkins, Dona & Brobrow, Jill; Concepts Publishing, Stockbridge, Mass.

Scottish West Coast Pilot; Brackenbury, Mark; Stanford Maritime, London.

Second Chance, Voyage to Patagonia; Bailey, Maurice & Marilyn; David McKay Company Inc., New York.

Shell Pilot to the English Channel, Volume 1: English Coast, Volume 2: French Coast; Coote, John; Faber & Faber, London.

Shetland Islands; Clyde Cruising Club.

Singapore Street Guide and Bus Guide.

Sint Maarten/St Martin Area & St Kitts & Nevis Cruising Guide; Virgin Island Plus Yacht Charters Inc., Philadelphia.

Solent (Selsey Bill to Needles); Bowskill, Derek; Imray, Huntingdon.

South American Handbook; Trade and Travel Publications.

South and West Coast of Ireland Sailing Directions; Irish Cruising Club.

South Biscay Pilot; Brandon, Robin; Adlard Coles Nautical, London.

South England Pilot (several vols); Brandon, Robin; Imray, Huntingdon.

South France Pilot (6 vols); Brandon, Robin; Imray, Huntingdon.

South Pacific Handbook; Stanley, David; Moon Publications.

Southern Turkey, the Levant and Cyprus; Denham, H. M.; John Murray, London.

The Adriatic; Denham, H. M.; John Murray, London.

The Aegean; Denham, H. M.; John Murray, London.

The Bridge and Galley Guide to Tunisia; Maurice, Ann & Lockyear, Brian; McMillan-Graham.

The Gentleman's Guide to Passages South; Sant, Bruce Van; Cruising Guide Publications, Clearwater, Florida.

The Greek Islands; Bradford, Ernie; Collins, London.

The Intracoastal Waterway; Moeller, Jan & Bill; International Marine.

The Ionian Islands to the Anatolian Coast; Denham, H. M.; John Murray, London.

The Tyrrhenian Sea; Denham, H. M.; John Murray, London.

The West: A Sailing Companion to the West Coast of Scotland; Faux, Ronald; Bartholomew, Edinburgh.

Traveller's Guide to East Africa and the Indian Ocean; IC Publications Ltd., London.

Traveller's Guide to North Africa; IC Publications Ltd, London.

Traveller's Guide to West Africa; IC Publications Ltd, London.

Turkey and the Dodecanese Cruising Pilot; Petherbridge, Robin; Adlard Coles Nautical, London.

Turkish Waters Pilot; Heikell, Rod; Imray, Huntingdon.

USA *Yachtsman's Guide to the Bahamas*; Tropic Isle Publishers Inc., Florida.

Vanuatu Cruising Guide; Colfelt, David; Yachting World Yacht Charters, Vanuatu.

Votre Livre de Bord (Mediterranne).

Votre Livre de Bord (Mer du Nord–Manche–Atlantique).

Weather in Hawaiian Waters; Haraguchi, Paul; Pacific Weather Inc., Honolulu.

Welcome to Durban; Watt, Tony; The Point Yacht Club, Durban 4000, South Africa.

West Country Cruising; Fishwick, Mark.

Yacht Scene Gibraltar; Sloma, D. M.; PO Box 555, Gibraltar.

Yachtsman's Guide to the Bermudan Islands; Voegli, Michael.

Yachtsman's Guide to the Virgin Islands; Tropic Isle Publishers Inc., Florida.

Yachtsman's Pilot to West Scotland (several volumes); Lawrence, Martin; Imray, Huntingdon.

LONELY PLANET PUBLICATIONS

These small paperback guides, which are aimed at the independent traveller who wants to visit out of the way places, and has a limited budget, are eminently suitable for cruising sailors. They cover many places off the mass tourism track.

Africa on a Shoestring
Australia – a travel survival kit
Chile and Easter Island – a travel survival kit
Ecuador and the Galapagos Islands – a travel survival kit
Fji – a travel survival kit
India – a travel survival kit
Indonesia – a travel survival kit
Korea and Taiwan – a travel survival kit
Malaysia, Singapore and Brunei – a travel survival kit
New Zealand – a travel survival kit
North East Asia on a Shoestring
Papua New Guinea – a travel survival kit
Philippines – a travel survival kit
Rarotonga and the Cook Islands – a travel survival kit
South America on a Shoestring
South East Asia on a Shoestring
Sri Lanka – a travel survival kit
Tahiti and French Polynesia – a travel survival kit
Thailand – a travel survival kit
West Africa – a travel survival kit
Yemen – a travel survival kit

BOOKLETS

Quite a few countries publish useful booklets, some of them specifically for sailors. Often these are only available in the country, but some may be ordered by mail and sometimes there is no charge for the booklet or leaflet.

'Afloat, The Mariner's Guide to Antigua and Barbuda'. Marine Marketing International Ltd, Antigua.

'Almanak voor Watertourisme', Parts 1 and 2. ANWB (Royal Netherlands Touring Club).

Baldwin, Larry. 'Crew List for Spanish Speaking Countries'.

Batsport-kort. Swedish charts reproduced on small scale.

'The Bonaire Marine Park Guide'. STINAPA.

'Handbook for Aaland and South coast'. Finnish Cruising Club.

'Guest Harbours in Norway' and 'Cruising in Norwegian Waters'. The Norwegian Tourist Board.

'Handbog for Tursejlere'. Danish Yachting Association.

'Information Sheet for Yachts'. Bermuda Department of Tourism. PO Box HM 465, Hamilton.

'Information for Visiting Yachtsmen'. Turks and Caicos.

Japan Hydrographic Department harbour guide books with detailed charts of small harbours, text in Japanese. Hydrographic Department Service Centre, No. 3-1 5-chome Chuo-ku, Tokyo 104.

Japan Inland Sea Tide Table, published by the Maritime Safety Agency (Publication No. 781, Vol I).

'The Marine Guide'. Hong Kong Marine Department.

'National Guide to the Adriatic'. Adriatic Club Yugoslavia.

'Panama Canal Guide for Yachts'. Panama Canal Commission.

'Seglarhamnar pa Ostkusten'. Swedish Cruising Club. Plans of ports and anchorages on the east and south coasts.

'Swedish Guest Harbours'. Swedish Tourist Board.

'Tunisie Plaisance'. The Tunisian National Tourist Office.

US Customs Service, Washington, DC 20229. Leaflets on the various import restrictions and import duty.

'With Pleasure Craft in Scandinavia'. Nordic Council of Ministers.

'Yacht Help'. PO Box 13107, Suva, Fiji.

'Yachting in Malta'. Anatlus Publications. PO Box Gzira 24 Malta.

Index

COURTESY FLAGS

NOTE: some of the colonies may have the same flag as the metropolitan power

continued from front endpaper

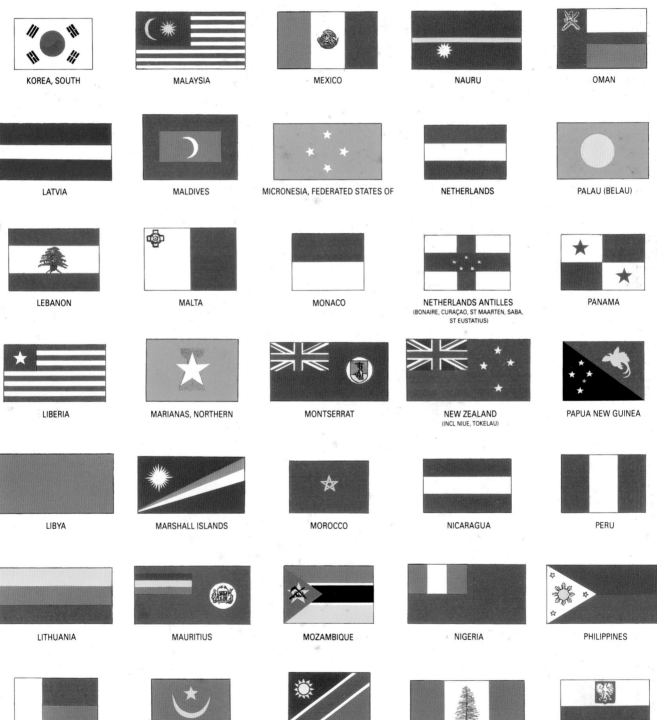

NORWAY

KOREA, SOUTH

MALAYSIA

MEXICO

NAURU

OMAN

LATVIA

MALDIVES

MICRONESIA, FEDERATED STATES OF

NETHERLANDS

PALAU (BELAU)

LEBANON

MALTA

MONACO

NETHERLANDS ANTILLES
(BONAIRE, CURAÇAO, ST MAARTEN, SABA, ST EUSTATIUS)

PANAMA

LIBERIA

MARIANAS, NORTHERN

MONTSERRAT

NEW ZEALAND
(INCL NIUE, TOKELAU)

PAPUA NEW GUINEA

LIBYA

MARSHALL ISLANDS

MOROCCO

NICARAGUA

PERU

LITHUANIA

MAURITIUS

MOZAMBIQUE

NIGERIA

PHILIPPINES

MADAGASCAR

MAURITANIA

NAMIBIA

NORFOLK ISLAND

POLAND